HANDBOOKS OF AMERICAN NATURAL HISTORY

ALBERT HAZEN WRIGHT, ADVISORY EDITOR

Handbook of Snakes

BY ALBERT HAZEN WRIGHT

AND ANNA ALLEN WRIGHT

HANDBOOK OF

SNAKES

OF THE UNITED STATES AND CANADA

BY ALBERT HAZEN WRIGHT

AND ANNA ALLEN WRIGHT

VOLUME I

Comstock Publishing Associates

A DIVISION OF CORNELL UNIVERSITY PRESS

ITHACA AND LONDON

First published 1957
Second printing 1965
Third printing 1967
Fourth printing 1970

International Standard Book Number 0-8014-0463-0
PRINTED IN THE UNITED STATES OF AMERICA
BY VALLEY OFFSET, INC.

TO *the herpetologists of four agencies:*

ZOOS, R. Conant, A. M. Greenhall, C. F. Kauffeld, M. J. R. Lentz, W. M. Mann, R. H. Mattlin, J. A. Oliver, C. B. Perkins, R. M. Perkins, J. E. Werler.

MUSEUMS, C. M. Bogert, D. M. Cochran, R. Kellogg, E. B. S. Logier, A. Loveridge, M. G. Netting, C. H. Pope, K. P. Schmidt.

ACADEMIES, E. R. Dunn, H. K. Gloyd, L. M. Klauber, J. R. Slevin.

SUPPLY HOUSES, E. R. Allen, D. L. Gamble, W. T. Neill, Jr., O. Sanders, P. Viosca.

Although these centers of natural history do not offer training leading to the degree of Doctor of Philosophy, they do, like some small colleges, often arouse the enthusiasm of our budding herpetologists and sometimes launch them on their careers.

Preface

IN RECENT years we have had several superb accounts of the snakes of one or two states or provinces, such as A. F. Carr's *A Contribution to the Herpetology of Florida* (1940), R. Conant's *The Reptiles of Ohio* (1938), R. H. McCauley, Jr.'s *The Reptiles of Maryland and the District of Columbia* (1945), J. M. Linsdale's "Amphibians and reptiles in Nevada," *Proc. Amer. Acad. Arts Sci.*, **73** (1938–1940): 197–257, E. B. S. Logier's *Reptiles of Ontario* (Handbook, no. 4; Ont., 1939), and W. J. Breckenridge's *Reptiles and Amphibians of Minnesota* (1944).

Of county lists, one which is replete with data is H. K. Gloyd's *The Amphibians and Reptiles of Franklin County, Kansas* (1928). Another fine and well-illustrated account worthy of attention is C. B. Perkins' "The snakes of San Diego County," *Bull. Zool. Soc. San Diego*, no. 13 (1938).

If one wishes an account of reptile life by districts instead of by states or counties, he may choose L. M. Klauber's summation, "Studies of the reptile life of the arid Southwest," *Bull. Zool. Soc. San Diego*, no. 14 (1939), or his "A statistical survey . . . ," *Trans. San Diego Soc. Nat. Hist.*, **6** (1931): 305–318; J. C. Marr's meaty "Notes on amphibians and reptiles from the central United States," *Amer. Midl. Naturalist*, **32** (1944): 478–490; or Conant's several publications on the northeast (e.g., Del-Mar-Va Peninsula). If the city is the focus of one's interest, he may choose the artistic *Amphibians and Reptiles of the Chicago Area* (1944) by C. H. Pope; there is no better author for marshaling material for popular consumption.

No other group of animals has been more ably described in recent books than the snakes. From C. H. Curran and C. F. Kauffeld's *Snakes and Their Ways* (1937), Pope's *Snakes Alive and How They Live* (1937), and R. Conant and W. Bridge's *What Snake Is That?* (1939) to K. P. Schmidt and D. D. Davis' *Field Book of Snakes* (1941), we have had a succession of books seldom equaled for any other group of animals.

It is unfortunately impossible to keep a work on a live and popular subject absolutely up to date. By the time a major work is finished, it is somewhat behind the times, and it becomes more so before the day of publication. Consequently, it will be no surprise to our readers to find that many fine articles that have appeared since January, 1955, have not been mentioned. Only a few significant papers of 1955 and 1956 could be noted in footnotes.

In all our portrayals, we have sought to emphasize the living animal by our photographs from life, by our color descriptions from life, by journal notes from the field, and particularly by excerpts from the work of others pertaining to live material. In many regions where we have been transitory visitors, the resident naturalists can tell a more complete story than we can. The photographs were taken by us. In the rare instances in which a snake was photographed by another person, that fact is stated. The names in the legends are those of friends and others who furnished us the live snakes. The numbers in the legends refer to the different sections in the figures beginning at the upper left.

We have the warmest feelings for the countless friends and strangers who have helped us at different times and in different places. We have seen most of the preserved materials of the important collections, and we thank their custodians. An especial effort has been made to secure live material, and many people have contributed it. Staff members at most of the large zoos in the country offered to loan and some of them gave us much-needed material. In a similar spirit, specialists and workers—one hundred or more—in many other places and institutions served us in countless fashions. The supply houses and biological bureaus were very eager and willing to help. The list of former students who have mailed or shipped live amphibians and reptiles to us would be hard to compile. Many have contributed to these almost weekly surprises through many years, and these live specimens have added sprightliness to our fortnightly seminars. Our helpers are legion.

Throughout many of the years of making this *Handbook,* our efficient and trustworthy secretary, Mrs. Kay Kapp, has helped us. For the final typing of the manuscript, for her patience and helpful comment, we are especially thankful to Mrs. Richard F. Darsie, Jr., of Newark, Delaware.

Four associates who have assisted particularly are Professors William J. Hamilton, Jr., Edward C. Raney, and W. R. Eadie and Dr. Ann L. Dunham.

ALBERT HAZEN WRIGHT
ANNA ALLEN WRIGHT

Ithaca, New York

Contents

VOLUME I

Page Number of

Account Fig. Map

Page Number of

	Account	Fig.	Map

VOLUME II

CONTENTS

Handbook of Snakes

Introduction

ACCOUNTS of species of snakes of the United States and Canada form the main body of this work. Under each account we have treated a number of topics; these are arranged in a pattern which is followed more or less closely throughout the book. Sometimes a topic is omitted from an account when data are not available, and sometimes a new topic is introduced for a particular snake, but in general the topics are arranged in the following order:

Names of snakes; Range, with state list and elevation; Size (of adults); Longevity (data are not available for many forms); Distinctive characteristics; Color; Habitat (and habits); Period of activity; Breeding, including mating, eggs, and young; Ecdysis; Food; Venom; Enemies; Field notes; Authorities.

The following pages explain our use of these topics and are intended to serve as a guide to this book.

Names of snakes: *Common names*—These come from widely different sources, such as the personal name of the collector or namer; the name of the country, state, or province where the snake is found; or perhaps the scientific name of the snake. The list below indicates how some snakes were given their common names.

Habitat—desert boa, pine snake, prairie rattler.

Genus—Arizona snake, Sonora ring snake, elegant Virginia.

Indian names (scarce)—Osceola, massasauga.

Botany—vine, white-oak, and poplar-leaf snakes.

Climate—summer snake, thunder snake.

Size—small brown snake, large ground snake, pigmy rattler.

Structural characters—flat-nosed snake, short-mouthed snake, blunt-tail moccasin.

Locomotion—banded burrowing snake, sidewinder.

Breathing or voice—bull snake, puffing adder.

Senses—blind worm, deaf adder.

Quality and appearance—gentle brown snake, glossy snake.

Folklore and legend—hoop, horn, milk, whip, chaser, and pilot snakes.

Food—gopher, rat, chicken, mouse, and fish snakes and mole catcher.

Color—blue runner, copperhead, coral king snake.

Pattern—annulated snake, spotted adder.

I

In the accounts, each snake is listed under its most common name or names, that is, the one most often used in the last hundred or more years. The number of times the name has been in the literature may appear in parentheses. Following the scientific name, other common names are given in a separate paragraph.

Scientific names—Snakes belong to a suborder (Serpentes or Ophidia) of the order Squamata of the class Reptilia. The five families with their 290 forms (species, subspecies, and phases) in the United States and Canada are:

Family name	Common name	Genera	Number of forms
Leptotyphlopidae	Blind snakes	1	6
Boidae	Boas	2	6
Colubridae	Harmless snakes	39	239
Elapidae	Coral snakes	2	4
Crotalidae	Pit vipers	3	35

In the last two years at least 18 new forms have been named, making a total of 308.[1]

We have attempted no departures in generic splitting or fragmentation. In general, this work agrees with the 1953 check list of K. P. Schmidt; in only a few instances do we depart from his names. Except in quotations, we drop the terminal reduplicated *i* of the species name.

In the five *Check List* editions before Schmidt's last list, the species and subspecies of Baja California were given. (Thanks to the California scholars from the time of Slevin and Van Denburgh onward, Baja California is the best canvassed state herpetologically of any in Mexico.) At present there are 69 species and subspecies recorded in this peninsula; 42 of these do not occur in the United States, and these are: *Arizona elegans pacata, Chilomeniscus punctatissimus, C. stramineus stramineus, C. esterensis, Crotalus enyo, C. exsul, C. mitchelli mitchelli, C. m. muertensis, C. molossus estebensis, C. ruber lucasensis, C. tortugensis, C. viridis caliginis, Diadophis amabilis anthonyi, Elaphe rosaliae, Hypsiglena torquata slevini, H. t. tortugaensis, H. t. venusta, Lampropeltis catalinensis, L. getulus conjuncta, L. g. nitida, L. zonata agalma, L. z. herrerae, Leptotyphlops humilis slevini, Lichanura trivirgata, Masticophis anthonyi, M. aurigulus, M. barbouri, Natrix valida, Pelamis platurus, Phyllorhynchus decurtatus arenicola, P. d. decurtatus, Pituophis catenifer bimaris, P. c. coronalis, P. c. fuliginatus, P. c. insulanus, P. c. vertebralis, Sonora bancrofti, S. mosaueri, Tantilla planiceps, Thamnophis digueti, T. elegans hueyi, Trimorphodon lyrophanes.*[2]

---

[1] By 1956, 313 species were recognized. With Baja California species included, the total becomes 357.

[2] By 1956 two more species had been added: *Hypsiglena torquata gularis* and *Masticophis bilineatus slevini.* Our distribution maps were made before K. F. Murray's article (*Herpetologica* [1955], 11:33–48), with its significant Baja California additions, appeared.

Of the 69 forms in Baja California, 27 extend from California and Arizona into Baja California or vice versa. These are: *Arizona elegans eburnata, A. e. occidentalis, Chilomeniscus cinctus, Crotalus atrox, C. cerastes laterorepens, C. ruber, C. viridis helleri, Diadophis amabilis similis, Hypsiglena torquata ochrorhyncha, Lampropeltis getulus californiae, L. g. yumensis, Leptotyphlops humilis cahuilae, L. h. humilis, Lichanura roseofusca gracia, L. r. roseofusca, Masticophis flagellum piceus, M. lateralis, Pituophis cateniter annectens, Rhinocheilus lecontei lecontei, Salvadora hexalepis hexalepis, S. h. klauberi, S. h. virgultea, Sonora semiannulata isozona, S. s. linearis, Tantilla eiseni transmontana* (?), *Thamnophis elegans hammondi, Trimorphodon vandenburghi* (?).

English equivalents of Latin names—Formidable as they sometimes look to an unfamiliar eye, the learned names of American snakes are not difficult to understand. If one learns a few stems such as *ophis* (snake), *peltis* (shield), *scutum* (scale, shield), *stomus* (mouth), *urus* (tail), *notus* (back), *gaster, venter* (belly), *ops* (eye), *fer* or *phor* (bearing), he is well launched in understanding the formation of the snake names of the United States and Canada. Several classical color names have been taken over into English, so that most of them should present no serious problem. Some of the more common ones are:

albus: white	*cinereus:* ashy	*niger:* black
ater: black	*cupreus:* coppery	*purpureus:* purple
aureus: golden	*cyaneus:* deep blue	*roseus:* rosy
azureus: sky blue	*flavus:* light yellow	*ruber:* red
brunneus: deep brown	*leucus:* white	*viridis:* green
caeruleus: blue	*luteus:* yellow	*xanthus:* orange, yellow

To the color names should be added a few common pattern names such as *annulatus* (ringed); *cinctus* (girdled); *fasciatus* (banded); *lineatus* (lined); *maculatus* (spotted); *punctatus* (dotted); *taeniatus* (thin-banded); and *vittatus* (filleted).

Present classification—This work has the primary purpose of presenting the living animal. For fully fifty years the emphasis of students and teachers has been almost solely taxonomic. Other phases have been studied more or less incidentally. For example, most of our life-history studies are of captive specimens in our zoos. Herpetology needs field studies of life histories, food, movements, habits, general ecology, associations, and color phases. External characters have been thoroughly described, but we still need more studies of distribution.

The first doctoral thesis revising a snake genus was published in 1908. Dr. A. G. Ruthven set the stage with his important *Thamnophis* study, and in the years since then almost every other genus of the United States has been revised by some student or master. These works have contributed greatly to our understanding of the descriptions, ranges, and variations of snakes.

It has been asserted that the reptilian orders are as well known as those of any other vertebrate group. But in our own time they have grown, in some classifications, from 12 or 15 orders to 25, thanks to the discoveries of paleontologists. Every time a new specimen appears with a more or less fragmentary description, a new order is established until the type becomes better known; often it is finally included in an already-established order.

To old timers who were entering college around 1900, just as Cope's work appeared, it is a welcome but amusing experience to return to old names. Cope used the species names *contortrix, platyrhinus, doliata,* and *elegans vagrans* for four of our most common snakes—the copperhead, spreading adder, milk snake, and wandering garter. When the first check list appeared (L. Stejneger and T. Barbour, *A Check List of North American Amphibians and Reptiles,* 1917), we who had seen garter snakes in the south and the north hated to see *ordinatus* disappear from the roster. The names toward which we inclined and which we are now using are in almost perfect accord with those employed in C. B. Perkins' *A Key to the Snakes of the United States* (2d ed., 1949). Both of us follow L. M. Klauber and H. S. Fitch. In 1948 the former brought out his epochal "Some misapplications of the Linnaean names applied to American snakes" in *Copeia,* and the latter, his "Further remarks concerning *Thamnophis ordinoides* and its relatives," also in *Copeia.* Another work that has proved useful is *An Annotated Check-List and Key to the Snakes of Mexico* (1945) by H. M. Smith and E. H. Taylor. It was fortunate that K. P. Schmidt's very careful and scholarly *A Check List of North American Reptiles* (6th ed., 1953) appeared before the last stages of work on the manuscript.

To those of other disciplines let us say that naturalists cannot always be consistent any more than can other specialists in fields that are rapidly expanding. Specialists change formulas and theories with great rapidity, but Nature can outdo any of us. Sometimes she plays with one character, then another. We might emphasize the external ear opening as a difference of suborders (*Lacertilia* usually with and *Ophidia* without), yet there are lizards like *Rhineura* (Florida blind worms) which have no ear openings. In the lizard group, *Holbrookia texana* of one genus may look like *Callisaurus ventralis* of another genus, but *Holbrookia* has no openings, and *Callisaurus* has ear openings. Or in subgenera we have the horned toad *Phrynosoma* with ear openings and *Anota* without. The character vacillates from subgenus to suborder. To take minor characters: the possession of one internasal plate does not always distinguish the snake genus *Haldea.* In the first and second Stejneger and Barbour *Check Lists,* the listing included *Amphiardis* (with two internasals), which is now reduced to an aberrant *Haldea.* In *Carphophis* there occur two internasals and two prefrontal plates, or the four may be united into two. We prefer to know where specimens come from before naming them. Just because it has four prefrontals, a snake is not necessarily *Pituophis deppei* if taken in the United States; for Nature at times does not respect our chosen cardinal characters.

Perfect standardization or stability cannot be obtained in a growing science because the number of workers is constantly increasing. The personal equation of the worker, whether young or old, radical or conservative, in the vicinity of a group or distant from it, and many other considerations enter. What are the emphases of the period? Are certain individuals or institutions dominant? Are certain types of problems being worked out to the very end and others rigorously excluded for the moment? What kind of a group is being studied, sea snakes or land snakes, subterranean or epigean, diurnal or nocturnal? Is the group very isolated or limited, perhaps very individualistic in some respects? Many factors enter the evaluation. At times a subspecies in one group may be considered equivalent in value to a species in another group. In the same way, a species in one group may seem equivalent in value to a genus in another. Any science is a composite of the work of many people; hence inconsistencies galore appear. Herpetological procedure may, we hope, become more consistent as knowledge becomes more complete and co-operation more widespread.

One of the most recent attempts at definition of a species by herpetologists is that of Smith and Taylor (Gen., 1945): "We take as a species any population isolated reproductively, geographically, morphologically (lacking other data) or (rare cases) by total ensemble of characters, that has attained an evolutionary state in which at least one recognizable character always distinguishes that population from all others. With one or two exceptions, a subspecies is the same as a species; the exception may be only that reproductive isolation is incomplete, or only that a lesser per cent (as little as 75) of its population is recognizably different; subspecies of the latter type may be either completely or incompletely isolated from the nearest related form."

Synonyms—We originally listed all the synonyms of each form. Space considerations later dictated that we omit them. Specialists can and will consult check lists, catalogues, or revisions of groups for such material. For two hundred years, since Linnaeus wrote in 1758, herpetologists have used many scientific names for snakes. *Lampropeltis* alone has had 180 names for 28 forms. There have been no less than three dozen names for *Lampropeltis doliata doliata* (*Lampropeltis elapsoides elapsoides*).

Synonyms for the generic names used for the species in the United States appear at the end of the descriptions of genera.

Problematical species—Several forms have been sent into synonymy (and rightly so), but we nevertheless place them in a separate section at the end of the proper genus. Present emphasis may seem important to the fast-publishing workers of today, but we wish stability also. Problems should be

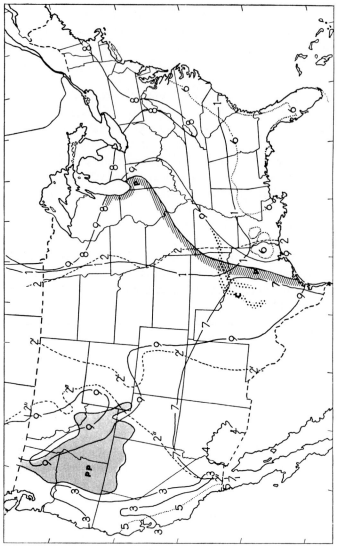

Map 1. Important plant ranges. *P*, Cross timbers. *P*, Eastern border of prairie (grassland, deciduous, forest transition). *PP*, Palouse prairie. 1, *Acer saccharum*, sugar maple (western line of deciduous forest). 2'-2, *Bulbilis dactyloides*, buffalo grass. 2-2'', Grassland. 3, *Castanopsis chrysophylla*, golden chinquapin. 4, *Carnegiae (Cereus)*. 5, *Cupressus macrocarpa*, Monterey cypress. 6, *Pinus palustris*, long-leaved pine. 7, *Prosopis juliflora*, mesquite. 8, *Thuya occidentalis*, white cedar. 9, *Solidago missouriensis*.

Ranges from Clements and Shelford, Ecol., 1939 (*PP*); Livingston and Shreve, Ecol., 1921 (*P*, 1, 2', 2, 4, 9); Sargent, Ecol., 1884 (3, 5, 7, 8).

re-examined from time to time even if positive evaluations have been made on valid grounds.

Mexican border species—At the ends of several genera are listed a few Mexican border species exclusive of species of Baja California, Mex., which are listed on pp. 2–3.

Range: This topic includes not only the geographical range [1] and a list of the states in which a species have been found, but the elevation.[2]

The range of an animal is the range of its food (Maps 1, 2). The types of rock masses together with the temperature and rainfall control the varied vegetative areas of the country and these in turn control the food and shelter on which the animal is dependent. We can to some extent associate certain species with distinctive soil and vegetative areas.

The structural map (Map 3) is conventionalized to make it easier to have straight bands across the country on parallels of latitude. The location of the rock structures is taken from the large colored geological map of the U.S. Geological Survey, Department of the Interior, with some structures from the Tectonic Map of the United States published by the American Association of Petroleum Geologists.

Size (of adults): Approximate sizes were determined from our examination of material, living and dead, and from the literature.

On the basis of size, snakes may be divided into the following seven categories:

Very small (16 or more forms) 4.5–15 inches, average 8–10 inches, such as *Carphophis, Chilomeniscus, Ficimia, Gyalopion, Haldea, Leptotyphlops.*

Small (64 or more forms) 6–21 inches, average 13–15.5 inches, such as *Chionactis, Contia, Diadophis* (exclusive of *regalis* group), *Hypsiglena, Phyllorhynchus, Rhadinaea, Seminatrix, Sonora, Storeria, Tantilla, Tropidoclonion.*

Small medium (about 20 forms) 8–28 inches, average 16–22 inches, such as *Cemophora, Charina, Coniophanes, Heterodon simus, Liodytes, Micruroides, Opheodrys vernalis, Stilosoma.*

Medium (about 100 forms) 12–50 inches, average 22–35 inches, such as *Heterodon nasicus, Lampropeltis d. syspila, Leptodeira a. septentrionalis, Lichanura, Micrurus f. tenere, Natrix clarki, Pelamis, Rhinocheilus, Salvadora g. lineata, Sistrurus m. miliarius,* most *Trimorphodons.*

Large medium (about 40 forms) 21–60 inches, average 27.5–48 inches, such as *Drymobius.*

Large (about 12 forms) 28–72 inches, average 44–53 inches, such as *Abastor, Coluber constrictor constrictor, Coluber constrictor flaviventris, Farancia.*

---

[1] See *Amer. Midl. Naturalist,* **48:** 574–603.
[2] See C. F. Kauffeld's chart, *Amer. Midl. Naturalist,* **29:** 342–359.

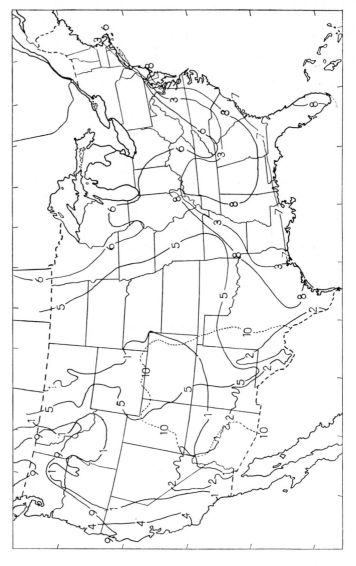

Map 2. Other important plant ranges. 1, *Artemesia tridentata*, big sagebrush. 2, Northern limit of *Covillea tridentata*, creosote bush. 3, *Ilex opaca*, holly. 4, *Quercus* (*Lithocarpus*) *densiflora*, chestnut oak. 5, *Opuntia polyacantha*, cactus and closely related varieties. 6, *Pinus strobus*, northern white pine. 7, *Serenoa serrulata*, saw palmetto. 8, *Taxodium distichum*, cypress. 9, *Thuya gigantea*, red cedar. 10, *Pinus edulis*, piñon pine.

Ranges from Livingston and Shreve, Ecol, 1921 (1, 2, 3, 5, 7, 10); Sargent, Ecol, 1884 (4, 6, 8, 9).

8

Very large (about 25 forms) 32–100 inches, average 62–69 inches, such as
4 *Crotalus, Drymarchon,* 5 *Elaphe,* 2 *Farancia,* 1 *Lampropeltis,* 3 *Masti-cophis,* 8 *Pituophis.*

Longevity: Many records of longevity have been assembled by Flower
(Gen., 1925 and 1937), Perkins (Gen., 1947, 1948, 1949, 1950, 1954), Conant
and Hudson (Gen., 1949), and Kauffeld (Gen., 1951).

Distinctive characteristics: Explanation of this topic does not seem necessary.

Color: Color descriptions were often written in the field and were factual
notes, unaffected by the literature of the species. If then we entirely omit
or seemingly forget the so-called recognition marks, it is not from design.
Our descriptions from 1916 onward were often written before the particular character of a new species or subspecies was erected. We used Robert
Ridgway's *Color Standards and Color Nomenclature* (1912), which through
the years has issued duplicate sheets. An elaborate Ridgway-color-from-life
description fits only one individual, but it is far better than color descriptions
of specimens preserved in alcohol. In some instances, structural characteristics of the specimen described are included under the "Color" heading.

As evidence for the unreliability of color descriptions from preserved specimens, the following table compiled from the literature is presented:

Colors Recorded of the Venters of Tantillas

Species	In alcoholic specimens	In live specimens
atriceps	White	Lighter than *eiseni*
coronata	White	Shell pink, pale vinaceous pink
eiseni	Grayish white	Coral red, rose doree
e. transmontana	Cream	Coral red or lighter
gracilis	Yellow, orange	English red, brazil red
nigriceps	White	Coral red
n. fumiceps	Dirty white	Etruscan red, dragon's blood red
planiceps	Soiled white	Coral red
utahensis	Gray, white	Coral red, pink
wagneri	White	Pale flesh color, pale grayish vinaceous
wilcoxi	Grayish white	Coral red

Tantilla snakes are ventrally coral red to pink in life, but the alcoholic
color descriptions would give little suggestion of that fact. The pink or
reddish venter is a good means of identifying a *Tantilla* specimen.

Variation in coloration—Several kinds of metachrosis or abnormal coloration occur frequently among snakes. Many deviations from the customary
patterns occur, and some of them are recorded; but yet no one in the

United States has attempted a serious study of the succession of color patterns. What are the relations of striped, cross-banded, blotched, spotted, and plain patterns to each other, and what is their order if there is one? Eimer in discussing orthogenesis claims that the order of variation is longitudinal stripes, longitudinal rows of spots, crossbands, self color (uniform). Does this succession obtain among the snakes? [1]

Habitat: In most instances, this topic is a condensed summary from the writings of workers in various portions of the ranges of the snakes. We hope thus to have provided a picture of the "homeland" of these lowly neighbors of ours and to have indicated likely places for successful searching.

Also under this topic occur statements regarding zonal and ecological associations (see Maps 4-6). Range terms have varied from period to period. The terms of 125 years ago, such as domaine and regnum, are now seldom heard. These were succeeded by areas, realms, forests, belts, districts, and many other terms of faunal or botanical distribution. We grew up under the dominance of the term zone, but when ecology became popular, zone became taboo and province and associations became the vogue. One of the best plans of recent times reminds us of Cooper's excellent plan and terms of 1859. All fields hark back to the background of their science.

Period of Activity: Under this heading will be found data from the literature on spring appearance, fall disappearance, hibernation, and so forth. These will aid those hunting snakes. We have included from Klauber's "Sixteen Year Census of San Diego County, 1923–1938" in his "Studies of reptile life in the arid Southwest" (Gen., 1939a), the distribution by months. For example, the commonest form, *Pituophis catenifer annectens,* has this record: Jan., 21, Feb., 50, Mar., 194, Apr., 484, May, 764, June, 602, July, 160, Aug., 63, Sept., 89, Oct., 103, Nov., 38, Dec., 23. Total 2,591 snakes. Rank 1. Per cent 20.01. "Rank 1" means most numerous in the catch and "Per cent 20.01" means this form was ⅕ of all snakes caught, which was the highest percentage of any species caught. "Rank 17" was assigned to the sidewinder, *Crotalus cerastes laterorepens,* because 151 of these snakes were caught, and this was 1.17 per cent of all snakes caught in the period reported, the low percentage making the rank low in the scale.

Breeding: In the early days of zoology two characterizing terms were used—oviparous and viviparous, i.e., egg laying and bringing forth the young alive. Oviparous was generally interpreted to mean not dependent on the parent or mother for nourishment before birth. In time, a new term arose—ovoviviparous—to mean hatching within the mother, but dependent on the egg or yolk mass, not on the mother, for nourishment. When some zoologists preferred to reserve the term viviparous for so-called warm-blooded

---

[1] In the Sept. 1955 issue of the *Quart. Jour. Fla. Acad. Science* (**18**:207–215), W. T. Neill and E. R. Allen discussed metachrosis in snakes, with particular attention to *Crotalus adamanteus, C. atrox,* and *C. cerastes laterorepens.*

mammals, implying umbilical or placental dependence on the mother, they ran into difficulties with the implacental mammals. The oviparous group, restricting themselves to independence of the parents after deposition, had trouble with characine and catfish species, in which the males carry eggs in their mouths; with sea horses and pipe fishes, which carry eggs in post or preanal pouches; or with pipe fishes, which carry eggs on the venter with no pouches. When a South American catfish carries the eggs on individual ventral vascularized pedicels and cups, we have, so to speak, an ectoplacenta. The term ovoviviparous encounters worse conditions when, in certain fish, some egg masses break down and the other egg embryos rely on them plus their own mass for development, or when small eggs are laid with a small yolk mass but a few large young are born alive. It was simple in the old days to say that oviparous meant laying eggs; that ovoviviparous meant bringing forth young alive in so-called cold-blooded fish, amphibia, and reptiles; and that viviparous meant bringing forth young in so-called warm-blooded mammals. In the light of the discoveries of Cowles, Bogart, and others, zoologists cannot so glibly or simply divide animals into cold-bloods and warm-bloods. Hence, inasmuch as all animals from fishes to mammals (with the single exception of birds) have some groups which extrude living young and some groups which lay eggs, this handbook will return to the simple terms oviparous and viviparous until more is known. At least 33 genera of American snakes are oviparous while only 13 are viviparous.

The sizes of males and females given under the heading Breeding are those of the snakes at the time of mating. Because data are often lacking, we have frequently had to omit the smallest size at which breeding occurs.

Courtship—The authors who have contributed most to our understanding of courtship and mating behavior in United States snakes are F. N. Blanchard, D. D. Davis, C. B. Perkins, R. M. Perkins, A. C. Weed and H. K. Gloyd, C. H. Lowe, Jr., and C. E. Shaw. The male crawls along the back of the female seeking to get the tail beneath the female for insertion of one of the hemipenes. At times a male may capture a female by seizing her neck with his jaws, but he does not hold it long. At first some of the elaborate dances were thought to be courtship dances of male and female, but, in general, opinion inclines to the view that they are combat dances between two males. For detailed discussions of some species, see accounts of the common garter snake, also of *Thamnophis radix radix* and of some rattlesnakes like *Crotalus atrox* and *C. ruber.*

The 1951 paper by C. E. Shaw, "Male combat in American colubrid snakes with remarks on combat in other colubrid and elapid snakes" (Gen.), is a summary of previous interpretations and extended observations on four more American colubrids, particularly *Pituophis m. melanoleucus,* of which he and Perkins have made many observations and photographs. He also

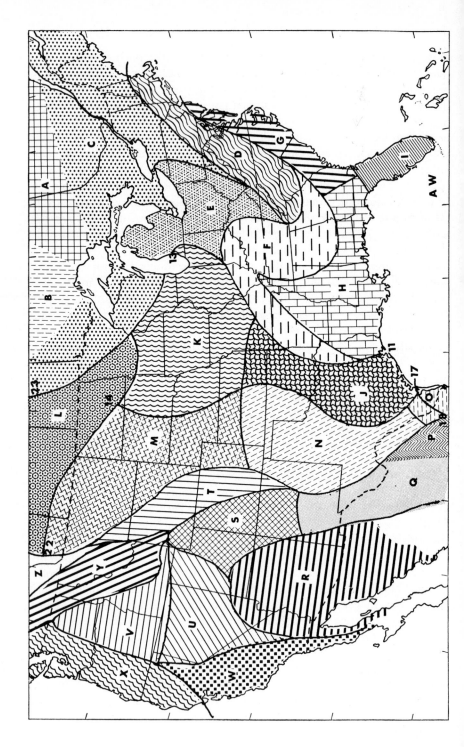

Map 4. Distribution of forests and trees in the United States (after Cooper, Ecol., 1859). *Lacustrian Province: A*, Algonquin region; *B*, Athabascan region; *C*, Canadian region. *Apalachian Province: D*, Alleghany region; *E*, Ohio region; *F*, Tennessee region; *G*, Carolinian region; *H*, Mississippian region. *West Indian Province: I*, Floridian region. *Campestrian Province: J*, Texan region; *K*, Illinois region; *L*, Saskatchewan region; *M*, Dakotah region; *N*, Comanche region. *Mexican Province: O*, Tamaulipan region; *P*, Choahuilan region; *Q*, Chihuahuan region. *Rocky Mountain Province: R*, Arizonian region; *S*, Wasatch region; *T*, Padoucan region; *U*, Utah region; *V*, Shoshonee region. *Nevadian Province: W*, Californian region. *Caurine Province: X*, Oregonian region; *Y*, Kootanic region; *Z*, Yukon region.

Lines: 11–13, Eastern border of prairies. 13–23, Northeastern border of prairies. 13–14–22, A good geographical boundary, which also nearly coincides with the isothermal of summer 70°, differing much at the two extremities. 14–18, Line of about 2,000 feet general elevation, west of which scarcely any of the eastern trees extend—in all not over six or eight species. 17–18, Boundary of the tropical group of animals and plants which are found on the lower Rio Grande.

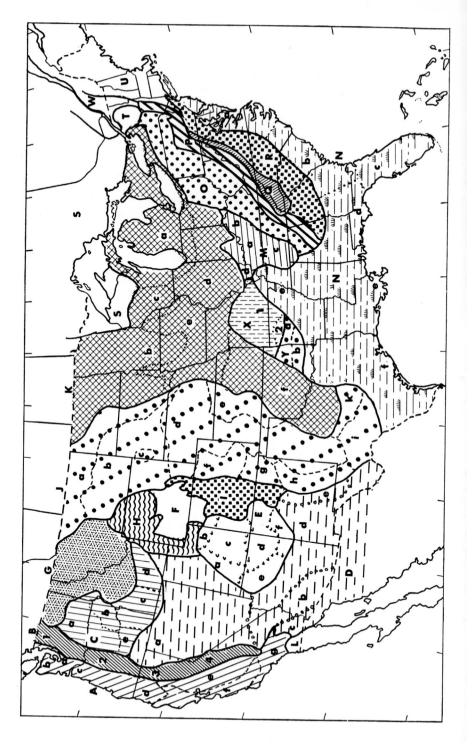

14

Map 5. Physical divisions of the United States (after Fenneman, Ecol, 1931). A, *Pacific Border Province: a,* Puget Trough; *b,* Olympic Mts.; *c,* Oregon Coast Range; *d,* Klamath Mts.; *e,* California Trough; *f,* California Coast Ranges; *g,* Los Angeles Ranges. B, *Sierra Cascade Mts.:* 1, Northern Cascade Mts.; 2, Middle Cascade Mts.; 3, Southern Cascade Mts.; 4, Sierra Nevada. C, *Columbia Plateaus: a,* Walla Walla Plateau; *b,* Blue Mt. section; *c,* Payette section; *d,* Snake River Plain; *e,* Harney section. D, *Basin and Range Province: a,* Great Basin; *b,* Sonoran Desert; *c,* Salton Trough; *d,* Mexican Highland; *e,* Sacramento section. E, *Colorado Plateaus: a,* High Plateaus of Utah; *b,* Uinta Basin; *c,* Canyon Lands; *d,* Navajo section; *e,* Grand Canyon section; *f,* Datil section—lava flows, etc. F, *Wyoming Basin.* G, *Northern Rocky Mts.* H, *Middle Rocky Mts.* I, *Southern Rocky Mts.* J, *Great Plains Province: a,* Missouri Plateau glaciated; *b,* Missouri Plateau unglaciated; *c,* Black Hills; *d,* High Plains; *e,* Plains Border; *f,* Colorado Piedmont; *g,* Trenched peneplain; *h,* Pecos Valley; *i,* Edwards Plateau; *k,* Central Texas section. K, *Central Lowland: a,* Eastern lake section; *b,* Western lake section; *c,* Wisconsin section; *d,* Till Plains; *e,* Dissected Till Plains; *f,* Osage Plains. L, *Baja California Province.* M, *Interior Low Plateaus: a,* Highland Rim section; *b,* Lexington Plain; *c,* Nashville Basin; *d,* Possible western section delimited. N, *Atlantic Coastal Plain: a,* Embayed section; *b,* Sea Island section; *c,* Floridian section; *d,* East Gulf Coastal Plain; *e,* Mississippi Alluvial Plain; *f,* West Gulf Coast Plain. O, *Appalachian Plateaus.* P, *Valley and Ridge Province.* Q, *Blue Ridge Province.* R, *Piedmont Province.* S, *Laurentian Superior Upland.* T, *Adirondack Province.* U, *New England Province.* W, *St. Lawrence Valley.* X, *Ozark Plateaus:* 1, Springfield-Salem plateaus; 2, Boston Mts. Y, *Ouachita Province: a,* Arkansas Valley; *b,* Ouachita Mts.

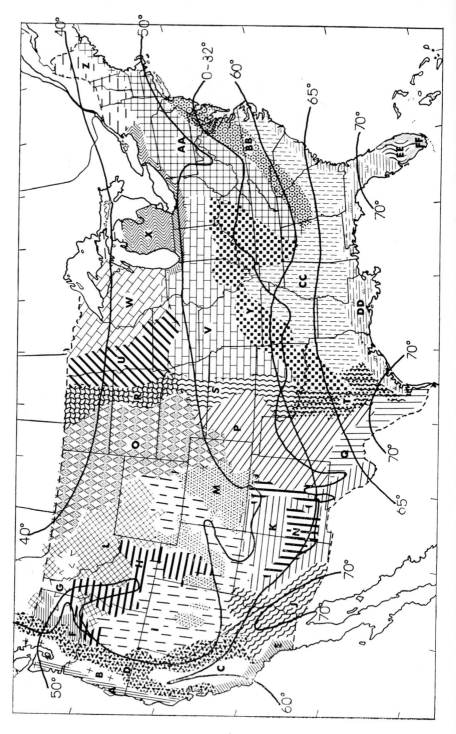

Map. 6. Plant-growth regions of the United States (after Mulford in Van Dersal, Ecol., 1937–38). A, North Pacific Coast, B, Willamette Valley-Puget Sound, C, Central California Valleys, D, Cascade-Sierra Nevada, E, Southern California, F, Columbia River Valley, G, Palouse-Bitterroot Valley, H, Snake River Plain, Utah Valley, I, Great Basin-Intermontane, J, Southwestern Desert, K, Southern Plateau, L, Northern Rocky Mountains, M, Central Rocky Mountains, N, Southern Rocky Mountains, O, Northern Great Plains, P, Central Great Plains, Q, Southern Plains, R, Northern Black Soils, S, Central Black Soils, T, Southern Black Soils, U, Northern Prairies, V, Central Prairies, W, Western Great Lakes, X, Central Great Lakes, Y, Ozark Ohio-Tennessee River Valleys, Z, Northern Great Lakes-St. Lawrence, AA, Appalachian, BB, Piedmont, CC, Upper Coastal Plain, DD, Swampy Coastal Plain, EE, South-central Florida, FF, Subtropical Florida.

The normal mean annual isotherms, 40, 50, 60, 65, 70°F, are also shown. Line 0–32° is the frost line, i.e., a line delimiting the area with no days of low normal daily mean temperature of 32°F or below.

records observations on *P. c. annectens, Elaphe g. guttata,* and *Lampropeltis d. annulata.* In American colubrids the horizontal position obtains in the combat or "dance," not the vertical as in the crotalids.

A topic which has come to recent notice is crossmating in species of the same genus, e.g., *Crotalus viridis helleri* x *C. ruber ruber, C. durissus unicolor* x *C. scutulatus scutulatus* (Perkins, Gen., 1951a), also *Heterodon platyrhinos* x *H. simus* (Neill, Gen., 1951). Reports of interspecific hybridization are rare, but may be expected more often in the future; they lend support to theories of intergeneric hybridization. Such evidence may lead some skeptics to believe that Bailey's (Ia., 1942) presumed hybrid between *Crotalus horridus horridus* and *Sistrurus catenatus catenatus* is a genuine hybrid, not an old aberrant *S. c. catenatus*.[1]

Hemipenis (Figs. 1, 2)—Inasmuch as Cope and others have used hemipenial characters in classifications, we shall give a short account of these structures here. Descriptions of type are given in generic descriptions. In snakes, the male possesses two intromittent organs or hemipenes. These are cylindric hollow bodies retracted into cavities on either side of the anus. This makes the base of the tail in males frequently larger than the end of the body. When in use, the hemipenis is protruded, the inner surface becoming the outer surface. Variations in this surface are frequently used to distinguish different genera of snakes, a common type being reticulate like tripe, the enclosed areas forming calyces which have suctorial function. Some are plicate or flounced, others calyculate or ruched in varying extents with spines below. Others are entirely spinous. In one the apex is furnished with a rigid papilla or awn, or may be smooth. The organ is marked by a longitudinal groove, the sulcus spermaticus, which may be simple or bifurcate. The organ itself as well as the sulcus is bifurcate in Crotalidae, with flounces in *Ancistrodon* and in Elapidae. The hemipenis is bifurcate in *Abastor, Farancia,* and *Heterodon* also, with a tendency to be bilobed in *Lampropeltis getulus* and slightly lobed in *Masticophis* and *Coluber.* Among snakes with hemipenis not deeply bifurcate, we find those with the sulcus forked and the surface flounced transversely in *Charina* and flounced pinnately in *Lichanura;* the sulcus forked, the crown calyculate and fringed in *Carphophis,* but not conspicuously so in *Diadophis, Coniophanes,* and *Rhadinaea.* We find in many the sulcus undivided, but only one with large apical papillae (*Tropidoclonion*). There are many types among the rest: spinous in *Natrix, Haldea, Virginia, Liodytes, Thamnophis, Storeria;* only the crown calyculate in *Lampropeltis, Rhinocheilus, Stilosoma, Tantilla;* abundant calyces and calyces fringed in *Coluber, Drymarchon, Pituophis, Contia, Chilomeniscus, Ficimia, Gyalopion, Drymobius,* and *Lampropeltis doliata;*

---

[1] In 1955 S. F. Cook, Jr. (*Copeia,* 139–141), reported intraspecific hybridization between a male *Crotalus v. oreganus* and a female *C. s. scutulatus,* with a resulting litter of 12 hybrids.

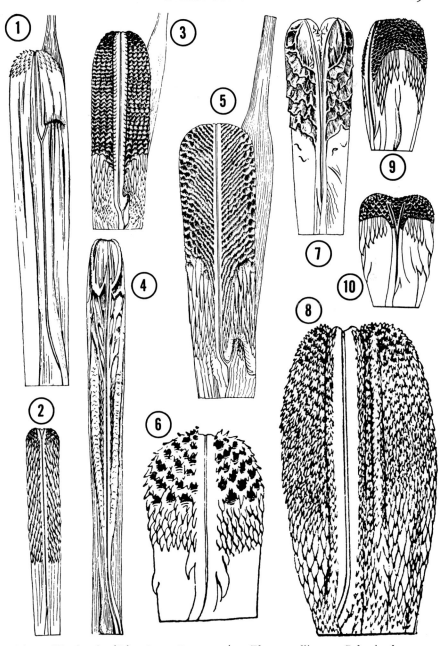

Fig. 1. Hemipenis. (After Cope, Gen., 1900.) 1, *Elaps corallinus*. 2, *Pelamis platurus*. 3, *Crotalus viridis*. 4, *Trimorphodon biscutatus*. 5, *Ancistrodon piscivorus*. 6, *Tantilla melanocephala*. 7, *Lichanura trivirgata*. 8, *Oxybelis acuminata*. 9, *Leptodeira septentrionalis*. 10, *Coniophanes fissidens*.

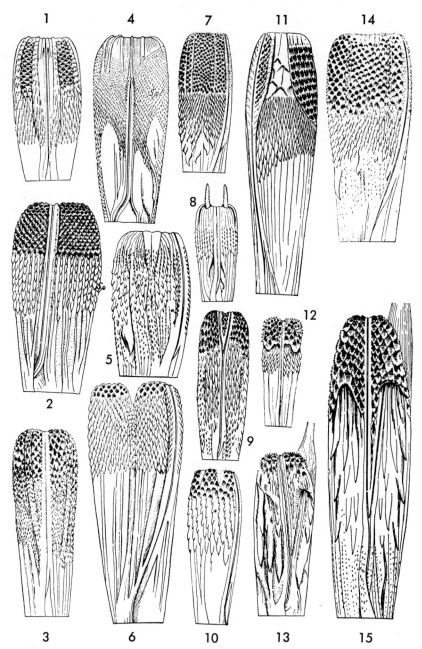

Fig. 2. Hemipenis. (After Cope, Gen., 1900.) 1. *Phyllorhynchus browni*. 2, *Coluber constrictor*. 3, *Lampropeltis triangulum*. 4, *Natrix sipedon*. 5, *Thamnophis sirtalis*. 6, *Lampropeltis getulus*. 7, *Opheodrys vernalis*. 8, *Tropidoclonion lineatum*. 9, *Diadophis regalis*. 10, *Cemophora coccinea*. 11, *Elaphe emoryi*. 12, *Hypsiglena ochrorhyncha*. 13, *Farancia abacura*. 14, *Masticophis flagellum*. 15, *Heterodon platyrhinos*.

abundant calyces but calyces not fringed in *Cemophora, Lampropeltis c. rhombomaculata, L. calligaster,* and *L. getulus.* When the area of the calyces presents a free margin to the upper part of the spinous region, the organ is called capitate as in *Leptodeira, Hypsiglena,* and *Coniophanes.*

Eggs (Figs. 3, 4)—The eggs are symmetrically elliptical (rarely pointed at one end), and leathery or membranous in their outer cover, never with hard calcareous shells. In general, their depth is ⅓ to ½ the length of the egg.

Site of eggs. In general, the eggs are not buried deep in the earth, yet we have instances like Woodbury's *Pituophis catenifer deserticola* buried in loose soil at a depth of several inches. The customary places are in rotten stumps, hollow logs, sawdust, and manure piles. Snakes often lay eggs in the sand on lake beaches and on the banks of streams, lakes, or canals. Often they lay under bark litter, the bark of fallen trees, the debris of city lots or lumber mills, or rubbish piles of various sorts. In Florida snakes lay eggs under heaps of dead water hyacinths.

Number of eggs. Few genera of the small snakes such as *Leptotyphlops, Cemophora, Chionactis, Hypsiglena, Phyllorhynchus, Sonora,* and *Tantilla* have as many as 6–8 eggs; some have only 1–4. A few smaller snakes such as *Diadophis, Carphophis,* and *Opheodrys* may have up to 12. Several of intermediate sizes such as *Arizona, Salvadora,* and some small species of *Coluber, Elaphe, Heterodon, Masticophis, Lampropeltis,* and *Pituophis* give complements of 3–24, but many of the last six genera range from 6 to 24 eggs or may attain 40 in *Coluber,* 42 in *Heterodon,* 50 in *Abastor,* or 104 in *Farancia.* Usually the very large complements are from very large females.

Time of deposition. The eggs may be laid from late May to Sept. 1. Most eggs are laid in June or early July. For example, Klauber found *Pituophis catenifer annectens* eggs from May 27 to Aug. 29 and recorded hatchings Aug. 8–21. So far as we know, there are no instances of eggs remaining in the ground over winter and hatching in the spring, as happens with some turtles; neither do the eggs hatch in the fall and the young remain in the nest. Most snake's eggs we have found in single complements, each complement laid in a separate place. Herpetologists know so little about the deposition in nature that they can formulate no rules. If one finds that *Diadophis punctatus edwardsi* lays a complement of eggs in a log or at the top of a high bank in debris, gravel, or ordinary dirt, one must also remember that Blanchard found a large number of complements in one spot in Michigan. If the fox snake lays a single complement in one place in Iowa, one must recall the 120 eggs that Max and Bessie M. Hecht extracted from one log. Maybe only one suitable place was available.

Surface. Eggs may be smooth as in *Salvadora* or rough (with tubercles or encrustations on the outside) as in some *Coluber* species. In captivity and in the field as well, we have found king snakes, pilot snakes, and others

Fig. 3. Eggs. 1, 2, *Drymarchon corais couperi*. 3, *Lampropeltis getulus splendida*. 4, *Abastor erythrogrammus*. 5, *Heterodon platyrhinos platyrhinos*. 6, *Farancia abacura abacura*. 7, *Masticophis flagellum testaceus* (A. J. Kirn, Somerset, Tex.). 8, *Elaphe vulpina gloydi* (Max and Bessie Hecht). 9, *Coluber constrictor constrictor*. 10, *Diadophis*, ovarian egg. 11, *Cemophora*, ovarian egg. 12, *Haldea striatula*, ovarian capsule with embryo.

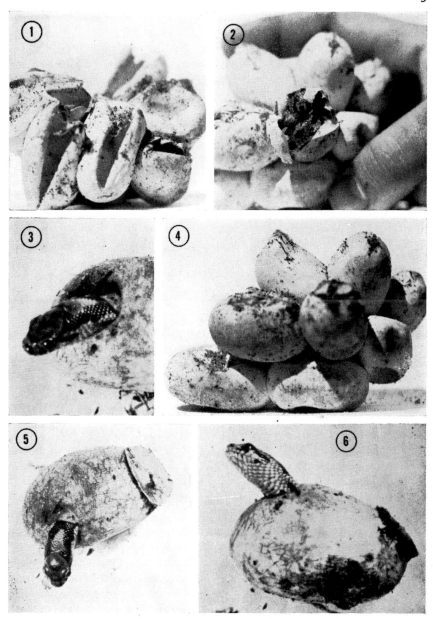

Fig. 4. Eggs hatching. *Elaphe vulpina:* 1,2,4, collected by Max and Bessie Hecht; 3,5,6, photos by W. J. Koster and Harold Trapido.

laying adherent complements; usually most of the eggs are attached slightly, with an occasional egg or two apart from the mass. When the eggs are laid, a fluid covers the exterior and in drying makes the eggs adhesive, much as frogs' eggs are often adhesive at first.

Size. Sometimes the eggs vary considerably in size; e.g., there are records of *Diadophis punctatus arnyi* eggs from 16 to 52 mm. long and from 5.5 to 7.6 mm. wide. A few genera have eggs only 4 to 6 mm. deep, such as *Leptotyphlops, Sonora,* and *Tantilla;* a few range from 5.5 to 6 to 10 mm., such as *Phyllorhynchus, Hypsiglena,* and *Diadophis;* several are from 13 to 16 or 18 mm., such as *Arizona, Carphophis, Drymobius, Opheodrys, Rhinocheilus,* and *Salvadora.* Some of the deepest eggs are *Abastor* (29 mm.), *Drymarchon* (32 mm.), *Elaphe* (31 mm.), *Farancia* (26 mm.), *Lampropeltis* (24 mm.), and *Pituophis* (45 mm.). Sometimes in a genus or even individual species a wide range may occur, such as *Opheodrys* 8–18 mm., *Pituophis* 25–45 mm., *Lampropeltis* 18–24 mm., *Heterodon* 13–20 mm., *Diadophis* 5.5–12 mm., or *Coluber* 13–23 mm.

In length, the shortest eggs are about 14–16 mm. (*Leptotyphlops*). The range in length in several genera is quite extensive, and an occasional egg may be large for its species.

Abastor 22–50 mm.	*Heterodon* 24–36 mm.
Coluber 26–50 mm.	*Lampropeltis* 30–55 mm.
Diadophis 16–27 mm.	*Masticophis* 36–50 mm.
Drymarchon 75–100 mm.	*Pituophis* 42–90 mm.
Drymobius 32–45 mm.	*Rhinocheilus* 30–41 mm.
Elaphe 29–60 mm.	*Salvadora* 24–34 mm.
Farancia 30–40 mm.	

In conclusion, the smallest eggs are 4 or 5 mm. by 15 mm. in *Leptotyphlops,* the largest 27 to 32 by 75 to 100 mm. in *Drymarchon,* 25 to 45 by 42 to 90 in *Pituophis,* or 14 to 31 by 29 to 60 mm. in *Elaphe.*

Young—The young are unknown or poorly known in 11 or 12 genera: In over half of the rat snakes, racers, and king and milk snakes, the sizes of hatchlings are unknown. For many forms one must take the smallest recorded specimen to estimate the size of the hatchling.

Time of birth. The young of most viviparous snakes are born in August. In some species there are records for June and July. Records derived from captive specimens showing births between November and May may be abnormal. In oviparous snakes the time of hatching seems to accord with the time of birth of viviparous snakes, mainly in August and September. When we began our herpetological studies a half-century ago, much was made of the date of deposition and date of hatching—the so-called gestation period. Many species seemingly required between 55 and 80 days for hatching, but periods of 40, 45, or 90–100 days were recorded. Now we suspect some eggs are advanced in development when laid. The gestation period may therefore have less significance than was once supposed. Even when fertilization takes place in the spring, development must begin soon after coitus. But with late-summer, fall, or delayed fertilizations, we have difficulty determining actual gestation periods. How many times does the female mate, when, and how long before actual recorded mating? Ruthven found great variation in one species of the garter snake, as much as 40 days from coitus to birth on one occasion, 104 on another, and 114 days on still another. Mrs. Wiley in her Huckleberry Finn rattlesnake observations gives 5½ months as the period of gestation. We fear it is yet a nebulous subject. In 1952 C. B. Perkins (Gen.) of the San Diego Zoo wrote an admirable article on the "Incubation period of snake eggs." From Perkins we learn that in 16 species the incubation period is from 51 to 101 days; in most species 60 or 70.

In the viviparous snakes we have 13 genera. These genera, with the number of their young, are: sea snakes, *Pelamis* (6 young); boas, *Charina* (2–6); *Lichanura* (6); 7 natricine genera—*Haldea* (4–13), *Liodytes* (6–34), *Natrix* (4–101), *Seminatrix* (3–13), *Storeria* (3–24), *Thamnophis* (10–80), *Tropidoclonion* (2–12)—and 3 crotaline genera. Our crotaline snakes are *Ancistrodon* (1–17 in number of young), *Sistrurus* (5–18), and *Crotalus* (4–25). Some of the largest, like *C. adamanteus, C. atrox, C. horridus,* or *C. viridis oreganus,* may have from 6–25; the records of *C. horridus* young are mainly 6–12. Most records of *C. atrox* are 10–20, yet there may be only 4. For the smaller rattlers like *C. willardi* and *C. pricei pricei* there are 4–6 and for *Sistrurus, C. cerastes,* and medium forms 4–10 young.

Size.   Some of the smallest young are (in mm.):

Oviparous	*Tantilla* (112–115)
Carphophis (87–105)	Viviparous
Chionactis (124)	*Haldea* (93–125)
Contia (103)	*Liodytes* (136)
Diadophis (100–125)	*Seminatrix* (95–116)
Hypsiglena (100–156)	*Storeria* (78–108)
Sonora (99–133)	*Tropidoclonion* (90–125)

The snakes of a small group are less than 200 mm. long when newborn, the smallest being 125 mm. They include *Opheodrys* (100–200 mm.), *Natrix* (Regina group 125–200 mm.), and *Natrix* (brackish water group 140–190 mm.). Another group begins at 150–225 mm. or more, such as *Farancia* (156–225 mm.), *Heterodon* (163–210 mm.), some larger *Natrix* (175–260 mm.), and *Micrurus* (175–225 mm.). Many larger *Natrix* begin free life at 200 mm. or more; *Ancistrodon* is 200–325; *Rhinocheilus* is 190–260; *Arizona* is 175–294; *Coluber* ranges from 225 or 350; *Masticophis* is 205–250; *Lampropeltis* is 200–270 and more. The largest newborn snakes are those of some *Coluber* species, which reach 300–350 mm., *Elaphe*, which may be 237–400, *Natrix*, which is 250–275, *Pituophis*, which is 310–440; and finally

Drymarchon, which sometimes attains 600–675 mm. In other words, the smallest snakes are only 3½ inches long when born; most are 7–9 inches, several 10–12, a few 13–15, one or two as much as 16, and one 24–27.

Ecdysis (Fig. 5): Not regularly treated under the accounts of species is this well-known practice of snakes.

The outer skin or coat of the snake, a wrapper somewhat resembling cellophane, is sloughed off as the snake grows larger and as a new surface forms on the scales below. As the time of shedding approaches, the snake becomes blind and the eye looks cloudy, sometimes being bluish opaque for 10 days or 2 weeks before the moult, as the scale over the eye loosens and the snake's colors become dull. Newborn snakes usually shed soon after birth, though sometimes not until 3 or 4 weeks thereafter, and often several times in the first year or in a few months. Of his brood of *Natrix kirtlandi,* Conant (Gen., 1943) says, "All shed their skins within 36 hours of birth." The number of segments in a perfect, complete rattle of a rattlesnake indicates not its age but the number of times it has shed. Most rattlesnakes have lost part of the tip of the rattle. If a snake grows fast from birth to adulthood, it sheds often, but during estivation or hibernation we presume it sheds seldom or not at all. Shedding is an accomplishment of growth and healthy activity. It is a very necessary and convenient process to make the skins of the snakes fit their growing bodies.

The snake sloughs his coat wrong side out, making it easy to see the tucks that permit the skin to expand and contract. The snake's prey is often larger around than the snake, and the snake's skin must be able to accommodate the bulge made by the ingested prey and to vary as the bulge moves backward in the snake's body. The slough may be longer than the snake itself, as when a common water snake 43.5 inches long crawled out of a 51-inch coat which was becoming too tight.

Food (Fig. 6): Our knowledge of the food of many snakes is very scanty. Much of our information comes from observing captive snakes. At least two of our snakes, *Tantilla wilcoxi* and *Storearia dekayi victa,* were first described as food of other snakes, *Diadophis regalis laetus* and a coral snake, respectively.

Studies of reptilian diets have been all too few since that made by Surface in 1906. The food of special species like *Natrix s. sipedon* have received attention (E. E. Brown, C. Lagler, J. C. Salyer, II) because of wildlife-management interests. When it was found that this snake fed considerably on the supposed trout-egg eaters called Miller's thumbs, there was rejoicing, and the snake was given a chance to live in the balance of nature. Several snakes are preferential in their diet: *Natrix septemvittata* likes crayfishes; *Carphophis amoenus amoenus* earthworms; *Farancia* congo eels. Some, like the common pine snakes, feed principally on warm-blooded prey; others, like *Heterodon platyrhinos,* prefer a cold-blooded diet, such as toads and frogs.

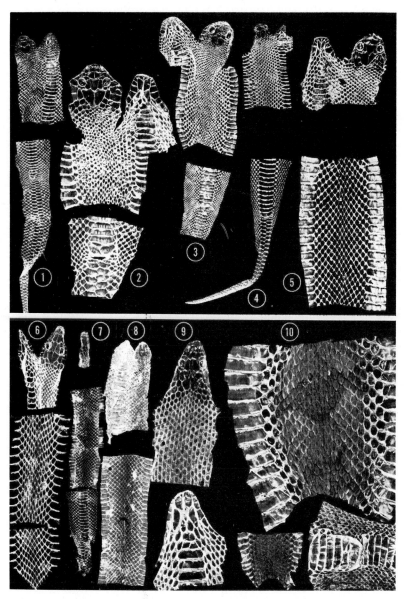

Fig. 5. Sloughs. 1, *Hypsiglena,* showing spines on scales of anal region. 2, *Leptodeira,* supraocular separated from prefrontal because preorbital reaches corner of frontal. 3, *Pituophis catenifer,* anal entire, scales partly keeled, temporals 3 + 5. 4, *Storeria occipitomaculata,* anal divided, scales keeled, 15 rows scales. 5, *Lampropeltis zonata zonata,* supraocular separates preocular and frontal, anterior of frontal truncate, 19 rows of scales. 6, *Oxybelis,* 17–13 rows of scales, prefrontals contact labials 2 + 3. 7, *Micruroides.* 8, *Ficimia,* large rostral, 1 pair chin shields. 9, *Natrix sipedon sipedon,* keels on scales, large interspace between scales, snake 43½ inches, slough 51 inches. 10, *Crotalus horridus,* anal entire, caudals undivided, keeled scales, middorsal line shorter than midventral.

Fig. 6. Food. 1, *Farancia abacura reinwardti* swallowing *Amphiuma* (photo by George Meade). 2, *Lampropeltis getulus californiae* (*boyli*) swallowing *Crotalus oreganus* (photo by C. S. Hazeltine). 3, *Lampropeltis getulus getulus* constricting *Natrix sipedon* (photo by F. Harper and A. H. Wright). 4, *Thamnophis sirtalis sirtalis* swallowing *Rana p. sphenocephala* (photo by F. Harper and A. H. Wright).

Environment obviously is one determinant of diet. It is natural to expect a water snake, such as *Natrix s. sipedon,* to feed on fish; subterranean species to eat earthworms, grubs, ants, and insect larvae; most epigean species to have quite diversified diets; and arboreal forms to eat birds, squirrels, and bats.

The size of a snake partly determines its diet. The young of almost all forms may feed on insects, while many of our smaller forms are forever restricted to insect larvae, ants, earthworms, lizards, and other small food.

In general, a snake's food is limited to what it can catch, master, and engulf. There are many remarkable stories of apparently impossible ingestions made possible by the stretchability of snakes' mouths and bodies. And many experimental attempts to swallow prey that is too large result in a snake's death. See the picture (Fig. 32, p. 102) of an adult *Arizona elegans philipi* and a Texas horned toad or Vorhies' account of a young *Crotalus atrox* killed by a horned toad (*Copeia,* 1948, 302–303).

Brown, Lagler, Salyer, Raney, Roecker, Uhler, Cottam, Clarke, and Barbour have given us fine studies of the food of snakes, but we seldom find herpetologists working on this time-consuming subject today. We know of one such study now in the making by a master in the field, W. J. Hamilton, Jr.

In the accounts of species we have restricted ourselves to a summation of the foods and a listing of the principal authors.

Venom and bite: We cannot discuss this topic at length. Numerous articles may be found in the Surgeon General's Library catalogue.

In 1908 Calmette (Gen.), 1909 Noguchi (Gen.), 1910 Aaron (Gen.), and 1910 Moody (Gen.) discussed serpent wounds and their treatment. In 1921 and 1922 the *Phisalix* volumes (Gen.) appeared. In 1925 Morgan (Gen.) and A. do Amaral (Gen.) began a very active period which bore fruit in the *Bulletin* of the Antivenin Institute. In the five years from 1925 to 1930 one of the most significant events was Dudley Jackson's *First Aid Treatment* in 1927. These five years probably contributed 25 papers, Amaral's, Hutchinson's, and Jackson's being outstanding.

In the last five or ten years Pope, Gloyd, Kauffeld, Schmidt, and Allen have published several articles of value to the general public. Allen writes on treatment by blood plasma. A recent and excellent article is James A. Oliver's "The Prevention and Treatment of Snakebite" (Gen., 1952). An equally good and generally available pamphlet is W. H. Stickel's *Venomous Snakes of the United States and Treatment of Their Bites,* published in 1952.

Enemies: Because of his fear, his agricultural practices, his livestock, and his vehicles, man is the worst enemy of snakes. From senseless fear man kills beautiful small ringnecks and useful large rodent eaters with a wantonness hardly believable. In earlier days in his clearing of land and in annual burnings of fields and forests he killed many snakes. Later his clean fences (not root or rail) reduced the cover for animals in general. When he brought his hens, ducks, turkeys, and geese into his yard, small snakes and the young of large kinds, such as garters, king snakes, and rat snakes, suffered. When he introduced swine, the hogs rooted out and ate snakes of all kinds and sizes. The railroads took their toll, but it was as nothing compared to the terrible slaughter of snakes by the automobile. Many large snakes, such as bull snakes, king snakes, and rat snakes, are frequently seen on our smooth roads where these snakes come to rest on the warm surfaces. In fact, herpetologists have often used records of these DOR (Dead on Road) snakes for population studies. Many small snakes are also killed by the automobile, though the public does not note them. A good summary of the road kill appears in Howard Campbell's "Observations on Snakes DOR in New Mexico" (N.M., 1953).

Mammals, such as skunks, raccoons, bears, coyotes, and even little *Blarina,* eat adult garters and racers and the young of several large species. The first three mammals named love reptilian eggs and hatchlings.

Herons, night herons, egrets, cranes, ibises, cormorants, and other aquatic birds prey on young cottonmouths, water snakes, some rat snakes, and the young of other forms. Nocturnally the small snakes, such as burrowers, ringnecks, and ground and blind snakes, suffer from small owls, and racers, king snakes, young cottonmouths, and young rat snakes are eaten by the great horned owl. Diurnally hawks and eagles catch young and adult aquatic snakes. Many hawks, such as red-tailed hawks, marsh hawks, and Swainson hawks, seize garters, racers, and other medium-to-large snakes, and they sometimes suffer for it. Even terrestrial birds like western thrashers and road runners try them as food.

Some aquatic reptiles other than snakes, e.g., alligators and turtles, eat young water snakes and cottonmouths. Do amphibians eat snakes? A bull-frog may swallow a ringneck, but imagine it swallowing a coral snake! Rarely do our common leopard frogs and other species of a similar size eat small snakes. The western amphibian with the largest appetite for snakes is *Dicamptodon ensatus,* a large aquatic salamander, a foot or more long. Predaceous fish like pike and pickerel eat snakes, and morays eat sea snakes.

The snake eaters par excellence are snakes themselves. The poisonous rattlers, pigmy rattlers, and copperheads generally do not prey on snakes, but cottonmouths may eat young *Natrix* and small water snakes like *Liodytes* or *Seminatrix.* The one poisonous snake that loves a snake diet is the coral snake. The small species (*Opheodrys, Diadophis, Haldea, Tantilla, Storeria, Tropidoclonion,* and others) which the coral snake eats make an imposing list. The first-discovered specimens of *Storeria dekayi victa* came from the stomach of a Florida coral snake. It also eats young garters, coachwhips, and water snakes. Even the little *Micruroides* coral snake feeds on snakes and lizards. But the title "king of snakes" belongs to indigo snakes, king snakes, milk snakes, and at times racers, which do not hesitate to seize and devour rattlers, pigmy rattlers, copperheads, rat snakes, corn snakes, and many more.

Small snakes prey on smaller ones. If the water snakes suffer from alligators, turtles, and cottonmouths, they in turn feed on young *Farancia, Abastor,* and others. If the ringnecks (*Diadophis*) are victims of several large foes, they in turn feed on worm snakes and other smaller ones. The first-discovered *Tantilla wilcoxi* came from the stomach of a *Diadophis.*

Some snakes, of course, do not eat other snakes, but those whose diet preferences are for other things may occasionally become ophiophagous.

Few visible invertebrates prey on snakes. Several cases of tarantulas' feeding on snakes are known. Spiders which catch small or young snakes in their webs have been many times reported. External parasites such as mites or at times insects may trouble snakes, or barnacles may attach themselves to sea snakes. Internally snakes are a great storehouse of parasites—nematodes, intestinal worms, and the like.

Consciously or unconsciously, however, man remains the greatest enemy, still following blindly the biblical injunction "to crush under the heel" the allegorical satanic serpents. The demand for large snakeskins is considerable.

Field notes: We urge young naturalists to keep journals. Some of the best naturalists have conscientiously kept to the habit. Voluminous writers, such as Ernest Thompson Seton, and reticent superb field men, such as W. DeWitt Miller, have religiously recorded their observations. These notes prove very useful, however good your memory may be.

Authorities: We have been privileged to know many of the principal authors of herpetologic and vertebrate literature. Like Franklin Sherman, Jr., we struggled with herpetological specimens supplied by C. S. and H. H. Brimley. The first fishes which we identified were collected by David Starr Jordan, Barton W. Evermann, Seth E. Meek, and Thomas L. Hankinson. Many of our college students remember the assistance and encouragement of the superb naturalists W. T. Davis and G. Engelhardt. Many a herpetologist holds the herpetologic patron, Thomas Barbour, in deep appreciation; many a west coast boy revered the memory of Joseph Grinnell; and many, such as E. D. McKee and R. Kellogg, respect the influence of the master field naturalist, V. Bailey. We enjoyed meeting O. P. Hay, R. W. Shufeldt, Gerrit S. Miller, Jr., and Leonhard Stejneger in our Washington visits. We did not know the young R. L. Ditmars, but he never forgot S. Weir Mitchell's surprise visit to him nor we the unsolicited interest of Theodore N. Gill, "the pope of the Cosmos Club." Many a worker mourns Frank Blanchard's early demise. Who can resort to the authorities on any Texan amphibian without scanning Strecker's records and publications?

Under "Authorities" will be found a list of the outstanding writers on the species in question. The articles they have written are listed in the bibliography, which will be the third volume of this work. The bibliography has three sections: a general list, an ecological list, and state lists, and each is arranged chronologically. The abbreviations and dates following the names of the authorities refer to these lists. For authors cited in the account of a given species but not listed in the "Authorities" section, the bibliographical data are usually given in parentheses after the authors' names. However, in some sections where numerous authors are cited, the bibliographical data have sometimes been omitted.

Accounts of Species

CLASS REPTILIA

ORDER SQUAMATA Oppel

Suborder SERPENTES Linné

KEY TO FAMILIES (Figs. 7, 8)

1. No elongate transverse ventral plates; scales uniform on back and belly; no loreal.
   a. Tail rounded, tip rounded or ending in small spine; body rounded; no chin shields; small burrowing snakes; eye covered by a shield; head plates with special nomenclature; no upper teeth; 14 scale rows around body; size 4–16 inches. **I. LEPTOTYPHLOPIDAE**
   aa. Tail strongly compressed, paddle-shaped; body compressed posteriorly, width ½–⅔ depth; chin shields (sublinguals) inconspicuous; if present, posterior pair usually separated; sea snakes; eye conspicuous; head plates more or less regular; teeth on both jaws; 17–93 scale rows; size 21–36 inches. **II. HYDROPHIDAE**
2. With elongate transverse ventral plates; teeth on both jaws.
   a. No pit near nostril.
   b. Ventrals short, much less than width of body; scales in rows 35–53 (29–91 in some forms outside U.S.); usually no chin shields and no mental groove; dorsal head plates more or less irregular (covered with small scales in *Lichanura*); rudimentary hind legs either side of anus; anal plate same size as adjacent ventrals. **III. BOIDAE**
   bb. Ventrals equal to or exceeding width of body; scale rows less than 35; normally 2 pairs of enlarged chin shields (geneials); dorsal head plates large, regular.
   c. Without pair of permanently erect fangs near front of upper jaw; solid teeth along full length of upper and lower jaws; color, if in rings, red and yellow separated by black. **IV. COLUBRIDAE**
   cc. Pair of permanently erect grooved fangs near front of upper jaw;

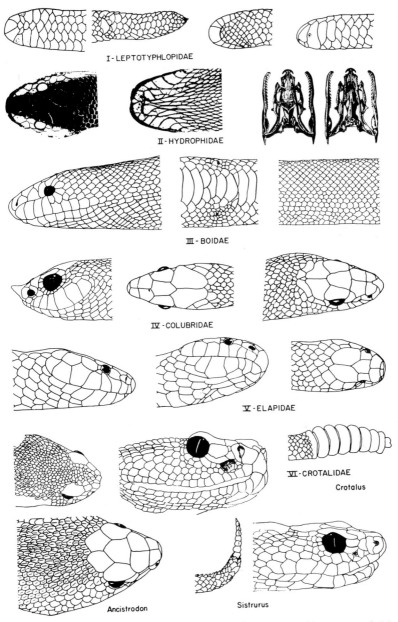

Fig. 7. Family characters. I, Leptotyphlopidae: *Leptotyphlops:* 1,2, *dulcis;* 3,4, *humilis.* II, Hydrophidae: *Pelamis platurus* snake sloughs. III, Boidae: *Charina bottae,* 2 spurs either side of anus. IV, Colubridae: 1, *Heterodon simus;* 2, *Opheodrys aestivus;* 3, *Pituophis.* V, Elapidae: 1,2,3, *Micrurus.* VI, Crotalidae: 1,2, *Crotalus atrox;* 3, *C. scutellatus;* 4, *Ancistrodon mokasen;* 5, *Sistrurus m. streckeri;* 6, *S. miliarius.* (Drawings by the authors except illustrations for II, *Pelamis platurus,* which are after Adrian Vanderhorst, *Herpetologica,* 2, no. 2; with skulls from Boulenger, Gen., 1893–96.)

color in U.S. forms in rings, red separated from black by yellow;
maxillary horizontal and immovable.   **V. ELAPIDAE**

aa. Pit on either side of head behind nostril; movable sheathed fangs;
head much broader than neck posteriorly; normally 1 pair of enlarged
chin shields; dorsal head plates (1) normal (*Ancistrodon, Sistrurus*),
(2) small, irregular, numerous (*Crotalus*); maxillary vertical and movable.   **VI. CROTALIDAE**

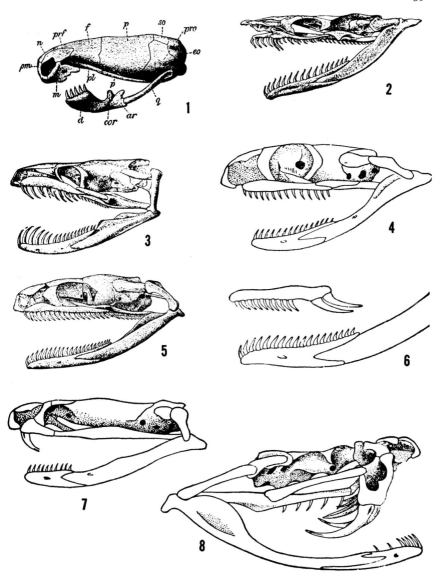

Fig. 8. Skulls. 1, *Leptotyphlops*. 2, *Pelamis*. 3, Boidae. 4–6, Colubridae: 4, *Lampropeltis;* 5, *Coluber;* 6, *Heterodon*. 7, Elapidae: *Micrurus,* maxillary horizontal and immovable. 8, Crotalidae: *Crotalus,* maxillary vertical and movable. (Nos. 1–3,5–6 are from Boulenger, Gen., 1893–96; 4,7–8 from Stejneger and Jan, Gen., 1895.)

THE BLIND SNAKES

FAMILY LEPTOTYPHLOPIDAE Stejneger

Total length 16–24 inches; tail rounded, with width and depth fairly equal; tail tip rounded or somewhat pointed, ending in a small spine; body rounded, diameters not disproportionate; head very small, continuous with neck, somewhat depressed; snout blunt, rostral large, rounded, overlapping considerably the lower jaw; nasal plate large (1–2), reaches margin of lip with nostril lateral between upper and lower parts; 1 ocular shield which extends to labial border with eye seen through the plate; supralabials 4–5 (nasal, anterior supralabial, ocular, posterior supralabial); no enlarged chin shields; 1 or 2 large plates precede anus (preanal); medial row of scales extends over head to rostral; pelvic girdle present but no external traces of limbs; lower jaw toothed; maxillary bordering the mouth forming suture with frontal, prefrontal, and premaxillary, toothless. "Pelvis present, consisting of ilium, pubis, and ischium; the latter forming a ventral symphysis; a rudimentary femur" (Boulenger, Gen., 1893). (One genus in U.S.— *Leptotyphlops*.)

BLIND SNAKES

Genus *LEPTOTYPHLOPS* Fitzinger (Fig. 9)

Size very small, 4–16 inches; slender, wormlike; tail and body rounded, a burrowing snake; scales smooth, uniform, in 14 rows around body; anal entire; no conspicuous head plates, dorsal or ventral; eye a darkened area in middle of large ocular plate; median dorsal scale row 200–330; color, in life, a silvery sheen with pinkish tones, and purplish vinaceous to lilac gray, drab gray, or brown dorsum.

Let Klauber (Gen., 1940a) speak on this point. "Live specimens are so transparent that they all have a pinkish or purplish cast, differences which are very apparent after preservation being hardly noticeable. So, in color studies, the worm snakes are better considered preserved than alive; while the contrary is true of most other families, since preservation quickly removes certain bright colors, particularly the reds and yellows. With worm snakes, although the preservative has a tendency to bring out important color differences which otherwise would not be apparent, it is desirable to

36

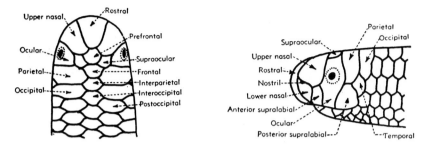

Fig. 1 Dorsal head scales.

Fig. 2 Lateral head scales

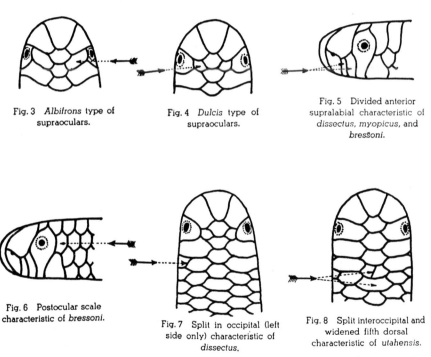

Fig. 3 *Albifrons* type of supraoculars.

Fig. 4 *Dulcis* type of supraoculars.

Fig. 5 Divided anterior supralabial characteristic of *dissectus, myopicus,* and *bressoni.*

Fig. 6 Postocular scale characteristic of *bressoni.*

Fig. 7 Split in occipital (left side only) characteristic of *dissectus.*

Fig. 8 Split interoccipital and widened fifth dorsal characteristic of *utahensis.*

Fig. 9. *Leptotyphlops* drawings showing scale nomenclature and specific characteristics. (From Klauber, Gen. 1940a.)

have a uniform method of preservation, so that comparisons can be fairly made. Also, it is necessary with these snakes, as with others, to store them in the dark to avoid fading." Synonyms: *Catodon, Glauconia, Rena, Siagonodon, Stenostoma.*

KEY TO THE GENUS *LEPTOTYPHLOPS*
(After Klauber, Gen., 1940a) [1]

a. With supraocular (supraorbital) (*dulcis* group); 7 median brown or light brown rows; head brown, but rostral, lips, underjaws light; 10 rows of scales around tail; rostral reaches back to a point even with anterior edge of eye or even to center; subcaudals 11–17.

 b. One undivided anterior supralabial; 206–255 dorsal scales in row; first 4 middorsal head scales (prefrontal, frontal, interparietal, interoccipital) increasing in size in order 2-4-1-3. (Cent. Oklahoma and the panhandle, s. through cent. Texas to n. Tamaulipas and cent. Nuevo León, Mex.)   *L. dulcis dulcis*

 bb. Anterior supralabial divided vertically into 2 plates.

  c. 224–246 dorsal scales in row; middorsal head formula 1-2-4-3. (Coahuila, trans-Pecos Texas, s. New Mexico, s.e. Arizona, s. Kansas, cent. and n.e. Oklahoma.)   *L. d. dissecta*

  cc. 199–222 dorsals; middorsal head formula 1-2-3-4. (N. Veracruz, San Luis Potosí, s. Tamaulipas, s. and cent. Nuevo León, and Pueblo, Mex.)   *L. d. myopicus*

aa. No supraocular (supraorbital) (*humilis* group); 5–9 median rows more deeply pigmented than venter; 10 or 12 rows of scales around tail; rostral never reaching back to point above center of eye, sometimes not even to line of anterior of eye; subcaudals 12–21.

 b. 10 scale rows around tail; 261–271 (more than 250) dorsal scales in row; 7 pigmented rows; middorsal head formula of increase in size 2-1-3-4. (S.e. Arizona through trans-Pecos and Big Bend, Tex., to cent. Coahuila.)   *L. h. segregus*

 bb. 12 scale rows around tail.

  c. 4th middorsal scale (interoccipital or interpostparietal) often divided longitudinally; 5th dorsal much wider than 6th; 289–308 dorsal scales in row; 7 pigmented rows; middorsal head formula of increase in size 1-2-3-4. (Extreme s.w. Utah.)   *L. h. utahensis*

  cc. 4th middorsal undivided; 5th dorsal not much if any wider than 6th; less than 288 dorsal scales in row (except *h. cahuilae*, 280–305).

   d. 244–269 dorsal scales in row; 5 pigmented dorsal rows (light brown); middorsal head formula 1-4, all about equal. (Cape region of Baja California.)   *L. h. slevini*

   dd. 257–305 dorsal scales in row; middorsal head formula of increase in size 1-2-4-3.

    e. 7–9 heavily pigmented dorsal rows; 257–283 dorsal scales in row. (Cent. Baja California, Mex., to Santa Barbara, Calif.; Mojave Desert; extreme s. Nevada s.e. to Tucson, Ariz., area;

---

[1] See Fig. 9 and Glossary for the terms peculiar to this species.

Cedros Is.) *L. humilis humilis*
ee. 5 lightly pigmented dorsal rows; 280–305 dorsal scales in row.
(Colorado Desert in s.e. California, Yuma Desert in s.w. Arizona, and Viscaíno Desert in cent. Baja California, Mex.)

L. h. cahuilae

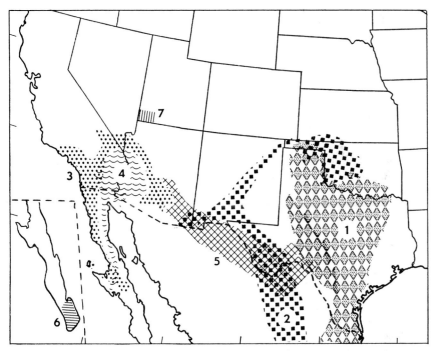

Map 7. *Leptotyphlops*—1, *d. dulcis*; 2, *d. dissecta*; 3, *h. humilis*; 4, *h. cahuilae*; 5, *h. segregus*; 6, *h. slevini*; 7, *h. utahensis*.

Texas blind snake (6—Ditmars 1907), **Blind snake**
(7—Ortenburger 1927)

Leptotyphlops dulcis dulcis (Baird and Girard) 1853. Fig. 10; Map 7

Other common names: Burrowing snake; eastern worm snake; Texas Rena; Texas worm snake; worm snake (6—Strecker 1908).

Range: From panhandle and Red River sections of Oklahoma, through cent. Texas, Tamaulipas, and Nuevo León to Hidalgo, Mex.—U.S.A.: Okla.; Tex. Mex.: Hidalgo; Nuevo León; Tamaulipas. *Elevation*—Mainly seacoast to 2,000 feet, sometimes to 4,000 feet.

Size: 4-13 inches. There are records of 3.6, 5, 7, 7.5, 8, 8.8, 9, and 13 inches. We are sure we have seen DOR specimens 10–15 inches, and Klauber records a 13-inch specimen (271 mm.). The largest series of adults taken at one

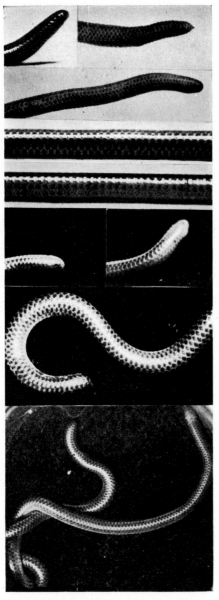

time by Taylor and Smith (reported by Taylor) numbered 8; the series ranged from 158 to 200 mm. (6.3–8 inches).

Distinctive characteristics: Scales equal on back and belly; 7 rows on mid-back drab or light brown, silvery; belly grayish pink; very small, blind, wormlike, glistening burrower; 10 scale rows around tail; single or undivided anterior supralabials.

Color: Snake received from B. C. Marshall, Apr. 8, 1929. The upper parts are cinnamon-drab with a silvery cast. Under the lens the scales look light drab or hair brown. The eye is black under a light drab scale. The undersurface of the snake is light vinaceous-fawn or pale grayish vinaceous.

A second snake is actually drab-gray, but in general appearance is hair brown with a silvery cast. Each upper scale is hair brown, but the rear margin is translucent and colorless. The snake is darker on the rear than on the cephalic half. The venter is pale grayish vinaceous.

Habitat: "The burrowing worm snake of Texas is *Leptotyphlops dulcis* (Baird and Girard). It is a characteristic inhabitant of moderately sandy, semi-arid prairies of the lower middle west, where it may be found either in the vicinity of trees or away from them. The present Texan series was secured between March 29 and April 24, 1931, from under flat rocks on hillsides where they were very frequently associated with the banded and unicolor phases of the prairie snake *Sonora semiannulata,* and with the collared lizard *Crotaphytus collaris"* (Burt, Tex., 1935a).

Fig. 10. *Leptotyphlops dulcis dulcis:* 1,4,5, San Antonio, Tex.; 2,3, Hebbronville, Tex.; 6–9, Imboden, Ark.

"A series of *Leptotyphlops dulcis* . . . was collected by Hobart M. Smith and myself near Brownsville, Texas, Sept. 8, 1932, during an overflow of the river. The specimens were found in a cornfield on floating debris. The water was from three to four feet deep" (Taylor). Ortenburger and Freeman found it in a rolling plain of red, sandy, very dry clay, grass-sodded, with clumps of mesquite.

Strecker published references to this form in 1908, 1909, 1915, 1922, 1926, 1928, and 1930. He found it dead in a path, under a log, under stones and rocks, on hills, and along stream beds. In 1950 Milstead, Mecham, and Mc-Clintock in Stockton Plateau secured it under a rock in the cedar-savannah association and from a road runner taken in the cedar-ocotillo association. It occurs also in the Osage-plains cent.-Texas section of Fenniman and Johnson (Ecol., 1931) and in the s. part of the cent. great plains plus s. black soil section of Mulford (Ecol., 1937).

Period of activity. *First appearance*—Mar. 11, May 7 (Strecker, Tex., 1927), Mar. 29, Mar. 30, Apr. 24 (Burt, Tex., 1935a). *Fall disappearance*—Sept. 8 (Taylor).

Breeding: Oviparous. *Young*—The smallest specimen Taylor had was 91 mm. (3.5 + inches) long.

Food: Ants. Strecker and Williams (Tex., 1927).

Field notes: Apr. 24, 1934. Went to Classon's Ranch with Roy and Ellen Quillin. Roy turned over a small stone and grabbed quickly as a small, pinkish snake drew back into a hole as an angleworm does. Sure enough it is *L. dulcis*. Do they go deeper in the daytime and approach the surface later toward evening?

Authorities:

Burt, C. E. (Gen., 1935; Tex., 1935a)
Dundee, H. A. (Okla., 1950)
Klauber, L. M. (Gen., 1940a)
Lane, H. H. (Gen., 1926)

Milstead, W. W., J. S. Mecham, H. Mc-Clintock (Tex., 1950)
Ortenburger, A. I., and B. Freeman (Okla., 1930)
Strecker, J. K., Jr. (seven references)
Taylor, E. H. (Gen., 1939)

New Mexican worm snake (Klauber 1938), **New Mexican blind snake**

Leptotyphlops dulcis dissecta (Cope) 1896. Fig. 11; Map 7

Range: S.w. Kansas, n.w. Oklahoma, diagonally across New Mexico to s.e. Arizona, e. to trans-Pecos Texas, and s. into Coahuila.—U.S.A.: Ariz.; Kan.; N.M.; Okla.; Tex. Mex.: Coahuila. *Elevation*—2,000 to 5,000 or more feet. 2,800–5,000 feet (Bailey, N.M., 1913).

Size: 5.3–11 inches.

Distinctive characteristics: Like *L. dulcis* except anterior supralabial divided vertically into 2 plates; back purplish brown; belly purplish pink; head drab; differs from *d. myopicus* in having usually more than 224 dorsal scales.

Color: Snake received from A. L. Hershey, Mesilla Park, N.M., Oct. 29, 1936. The whole snake glistens with a silvery sheen and in general appears brownish vinaceous. The mid-back for 4 or 5 rows of scales is vinaceous-brown or deep corinthian red. The sides and belly are corinthian pink. The head plates from the eye backward are buffy brown or drab. The iris is black.

Habitat and habits: "It was slow in movements, but the body muscles seemed very strong when it twisted about the finger. The specimens recorded were of a beautiful iridescent pinkish lavender color, with a silvery sheen" (Force, Okla., 1930).

The longest account is that of Smith: "It lives in rocky semiarid areas where moisture may locally be present. . . . Loose sandy soil is preferred. In captivity moist sand is preferred to dry. The snakes are nocturnal, emerging at about sunset, and actively moving about for 2 hours or more; they are most active from 8:00 to 8:30 P.M. They emerge only when the temperatures at night are 64°F. or higher; optimum temperatures are between 78° and 82°F. They are most easily obtained by driving slowly along paved highways and watching the lighted road."

This form occurs in what has been termed semidesert grassland by one writer or small-tree semidesert and succulent desert to moist grassland by another.

"The largest number of specimens, 27, collected in Tulsa County, were taken by Hamon May between April and October 1935; he found them under sandstone slabs and frequently under a limestone boulder which had to be broken before one person could move it" (Force, Okla., 1936a).

Period of activity: *First appearance*—Apr. 15 (A. E. Borell, Carlsbad, N.M.); May 27 (Burt). *Fall disappearance*—Aug. 2 (Burt); Sept. 15 (Borell); Oct. (Force, Okla., 1930).

Breeding: Oviparous. *Eggs*—"The largest specimen was a female collected June 6, 1935. It was 225 mm. in total length and 5.5 mm. in diameter. Upon dissection it disclosed 7 eggs measuring 7–8 mm. x 1.2 mm., besides others from microscopic size to 2.3 and 4 mm. in length. The largest eggs would doubtless have matured this season. Two other females collected at the same time measured 193 and 195 mm. in length and contained only eggs of the smaller sizes 2.3 and 4 mm. in length and 2.5 mm. in diameter" (Force, Okla., 1936a).

Smith in 1950 gave 7 for the complement, with eggs 15x4.5 mm. as in other species, and 7⅝ inches as a minimum for the adult female.

Food: Ants and their eggs. Force (Okla., 1936a).

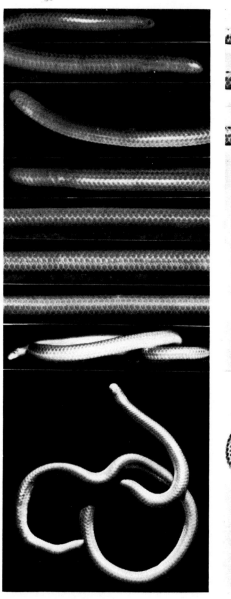

Fig. 11. *Leptotyphlops d. dissecta,* Mesilla Park, N.M., A. L. Hershey.

Fig. 12. *Leptotyphlops humilis humilis,* San Diego, Calif., L. M. Klauber.

Authorities:

Burt, C. E. (Gen., 1935; Tex., 1935a)   Klauber, L. M. (Gen., 1940a)
Dundee, H. A. (Okla., 1950)   Schmidt, K. P., and T. F. Smith (Tex.,
Force, E. R. (Okla., 1930; 1936a)   1944)
Hibbard, C. W. (Kan., 1937)   Smith, H. M. (Kan., 1950)

1901: A. E. Brown (Gen.) held that "*G. dissecta* Cope may prove to be distinct, but the inconstancy of the head shields in these low, burrowing forms is a strong presumptive against it."

Western worm snake (12—Van Denburgh 1922), Worm snake (4—Stejneger 1891)

Leptotyphlops humilis humilis (Baird and Girard) 1853. Fig. 12; Map 7

Other common names: Blind snake; brown blind snake; California blind snake (3); California Rena; California worm snake; Cedros Island worm snake; humble sheep snake (Cronise 1868); sheep-nosed snake.

Range: N. and cent. Baja California northward w. of the mountain crest to Santa Barbara and e. through Mojave Desert and s. tip of Nevada, thence s.e. to cent. Arizona.—U.S.A.: Ariz.; Calif.; Nev. Mex.: Baja Calif. *Elevation*—0 to 5,000 feet. From the coast line to edge of the desert basin (Klauber, Calif., 1931a); ocean to desert (Perkins); 1,600–3,000 feet (Stephens, Calif., 1918).

Size: 4–14 inches. Klauber had specimens from 103 to 315 mm. Perkins records one 13½ inches.

Distinctive characteristics: Scales of back and belly alike (no enlarged ventrals); 7–9 rows on mid-back Indian purple above, pale vinaceous-lilac below; very small, blind, cylindrical, polished, subterranean snake; 12 scale rows around the tail; dorsal scales usually less than 285 (265–280); no supraoculars.

Color: Snake received from Klauber, San Diego, Calif., May 25, 1928. This is a glistening silvery snake, each dorsal scale with a striking sheen and outlined with silver. Seven middorsal rows of scales are darker, being dark grayish brown, vinaceous-slate, or blackish plumbeous. Sometimes 1 or 2 of these darker rows are mouse-gray or deep grayish olive. The broad transparent or translucent margin of each dorsal scale gives an effect of lilac-gray or French gray because of the underlying dark plumbeous or blackish plumbeous center of the adjoining scale. The scales of the venter are translucent with broad distinct marginal bands, the general effect being deep olive-gray or tea green. Sometimes the under parts appear a glistening silvery white. This last is especially true in the animal preserved in formalin.

Habitat: They have been found in foothills, near water (Van Denburgh and Slevin, Ariz., 1913); in pile of manure on greasewood plains (Ruthven);

in gulch on chaparral-covered mountain (Stephens, Calif., 1918); in ditch diggings (Linsdale). Klauber's "Sixteen Year Census, San Diego County, 1923–1938" (Gen., 1939a) gives 38 coast, 15 inland valleys, 25 foothills, 2 mountains, 8 desert foothills.

Perkins and Klauber supply most of the known information: "It is subterranean, being found under rocks and among the roots of bushes from the coast to the edge of the desert. A large specimen was brought to the Reptile House a few years ago that had been found 10 feet above the ground in a date palm in the dirt and decayed wood between the sawed off leaf and the trunk. A great many are dug out in the process of constructing new roads" (Perkins).

"Daytime captures of *Leptotyphlops* are usually effected by overturning rocks or in the course of excavations. . . . Thus they are not often found when hunting for *Xantusia henshawi* under the higher flakes. One of the best places to search for them is to locate a flake leaning against a large boulder, near the ground line, and then to dig below the flake. They may also be under flakes or stones lying on the ground, particularly where some moisture is present. Specimens of *humilis humilis* have been found under stones in this manner in every month from March to July, inclusive. One was collected under a board lying on the ground. Worm snakes are often discovered in the course of excavations for foundations, pipe lines, post-holes, etc. Frequently several may be found together; for example, 3 specimens were disclosed in digging out the rotted butt of a fence post. If the soil be loose or rocky they are difficult to capture, since they are very active and burrow immediately. Major Chapman Grant, while supervising the work of a CCC camp at El Capitan, San Diego County, found one about 4 feet down and 2 feet in from the face of an earth bank. Another was located in loose soil only a few inches below the surface. On June 21st, 2 were found 4 feet below the surface on a side hill. A week later another was discovered at a depth of 2 feet, but escaped . . ." (Klauber, Gen., 1940a).

"This snake when above ground seems to progress with less lateral undulations than do other snakes. On smooth surfaces it attempts to employ the tail spine to aid in its motion. When placed in loose or sandy soil it burrows immediately. It is never peaceful or quiet when above ground, but continually searches for something in which to burrow; it is therefore difficult to photograph" (Klauber, Gen., 1931e).

Period of activity: *First appearance*—Mar. 20, Mar. 28, Apr. 20 (Klauber, Gen., 1931e; Calif., 1931a); Apr. 11, May 10 (Linsdale). *Monthly catch*— In his "Sixteen Year Census" (Gen., 1939a) Klauber reports snakes captured as follows: Jan., 4 snakes; Feb., 4; Mar., 4; Apr., 7; May, 17; June, 19; July, 13; Aug., 9; Sept., 5; Oct., 2; Nov., 2; Dec., 2.

Breeding: Oviparous. *Eggs*—"*Humilis* is a larger snake [than *dissecta*]. I have not observed a female less than 245 mm. long with eggs. . . . The eggs are long and thin, as might be expected in so attenuated a creature. Measurements were made on those contained in a *humilis* and were found to be about 15x4½ mm." (Klauber, Gen., 1940a). *Young*—"The smallest I ever saw was about 4 inches long and smaller than a safety match in diameter. It was coming into the old Reptile House under the back door" (Perkins). "The smallest specimen measured about 90 mm. long and 1.8 mm. in diameter, being as long and somewhat thicker than a large darning needle" (Klauber, Gen., 1931e). "The young at birth are about one third of maximum size" (Klauber, Gen., 1940a).

Food: Insects, salamanders, termites. Perkins, Klauber (Gen., 1940a).

Authorities:

Klauber, L. M. (Gen., 1931e, 1939a, 1940a; Calif., 1931a)

Linsdale, J. M. (Baja Calif., 1932)

Perkins, C. B. (Calif., 1938)

Ruthven, A. G. (Ariz., 1907)

Vorhies, C. T. (Ariz., 1929)

1954: D. A. Langebartel and H. M. Smith in their Sonora, Mex., paper (Gen.) discuss populations and characters of *L. humilis humilis* and *L. h. dugesi.*

Desert worm snake (8—Klauber 1931), Western worm snake (3—Klauber 1928)

Leptotyphlops humilis cahuilae Klauber 1931. Map 7

Other common names: California blind snake; worm snake.

Range: From Yuma Desert of s.w. Arizona to tip of Nevada through Colorado Desert in s.e. California into the e. side of Baja Calif., Mex.— U.S.A.: Ariz.; Calif. Mex.: Baja Calif.; Sonora. *Elevation*—Less than 500 to 1,000 feet. Desert foothills, desert (Klauber, Gen., 1939a).

Size: Adults, 4.6–16 inches.

Distinctive characteristics: Like *h. humilis* except that it has 5 dorsal rows of light brown instead of 7 of dark brown; usually 285 (280–305) or more dorsal scales. Like blind snakes in general it is transparent or translucent in life, actually light purplish vinaceous above and pale brownish vinaceous below. It is the longest form of our U.S. blind snakes, reaching 16 inches.

Color: Snake received from Lee W. Arnold, Wellton, Ariz., 35 miles e. of Yuma, caught March 9, 1941. In cephalic portion of body, dorsal and ventral surfaces are light purplish vinaceous becoming, caudad, pale purplish vinaceous. There is a silvery sheen to the whole snake, and it is semitransparent or translucent—hence the pinkish tone of the animal. The 5 dorsal scale rows are pigmented with quaker drab. The pupil is large and black, outlined with a narrow ring of purplish vinaceous.

Snake taken from Scissors Crossing, San Felipe wash, below Julian in the Borego stretch w. of Sentenac Canyon in San Diego Co., Calif. It was caught near a cattleguard in a pile of stones on May 8, 1942. The back is light brownish vinaceous, the underside pale grayish vinaceous with areas on the forward part rhodonite pink. The eye is black with a suffusion of daphne pink. There is a silvery sheen over the entire snake.

Habitat: In his "Sixteen Year Census" Klauber (Gen., 1939a) took 18 in desert foothills and only 2 on the desert.

When Klauber described this form, he assigned it to "Colorado and Yuma Deserts of California and Arizona along the lower desert fringes of the Peninsula range and along the banks of the Colorado River" (Gen., 1931e). The region of its range has been called by different authors desert, extreme desert, southwestern desert, Salton Trough and n. part of Sonoran desert, California microphyll desert, Arizona succulent desert, and so forth. Klauber named the snake after old Lake Cahuilla.

Mosauer (1936a) in Baja California recorded its habits and locomotion in considerable detail: "At San Angel in 3 evenings 5 specimens of *Leptotyphlops* were collected in the sand hills, 4 of them by following their typical tracks. These little burrowing snakes regularly emerge on the surface at or shortly after nightfall, and travel about for some time. They use the horizontal undulatory type of locomotion . . . and thus leave tracks somewhat similar to those of *Sonora* and *Chilomeniscus*. Because of its cylindrical body, however, which lacks the ventro-lateral edges of the other snakes, *Leptotyphlops* encounters more side slipping in its movement, which is therefore less efficient and shows typical signs of 'skidding' in the tracks. Moreover, the fine spur at the end of the worm snake's tail drags in the sand and leaves a sharp, sinuous line in the track, which identifies it at once. All the specimens were found on the surface of the sand, the first one when it was entering a crack in the woody trunk of a desert shrub, the second out in the open, and the 3 others within bushes. *Leptotyphlops* does not seem to travel parallel to and just below the surface of the sand, as does *Chilomeniscus*."

The author who has contributed the most information is the describer of this species, Klauber (Gen., 1931e). From his 1940 monograph we present several excerpts: "Aside from the presence of dampness, rocks and boulders seem essential to the worm snakes, at least to *humilis* and its subspecies. Throughout the Cahuilla Basin, and other desert areas of the southwest, we find that worm snakes are seldom or never found on the sandy flats, dry lakes, or alluvial fans, but are usually in the rocky canyons or on mountain slopes. . . . Many miles of night collecting, by driving on desert roads . . . , have taught us that *Leptotyphlops* does not follow *Sonora*, *Phyllorhynchus*, and *Crotalus cerastes* out onto the desert flats. . . . The finding of specimens run over on the road (DOR) suggested that these little snakes were not entirely subterranean, but must spend at least a part of their nocturnal activities on the surface. As the method of collecting by driving on desert roads at night became perfected, we found that such was indeed the case, and we began to pick up live specimens in some numbers. The technique does not differ from that involved in the collection of other small nocturnal desert snakes, except that *Leptotyphlops,* being both smaller and more translucent than any other genus, is naturally more difficult to see. Slow driving and a dark paved road are essential; and even then a good pair of eyes and a certain experience are required for success, since the quarry does not stand out in the headlights to the degree characteristic of *Phyllorhynchus* and *Sonora.* They have, in fact, a sort of ghostly appearance when the light strikes them."

Period of activity: *First appearance*—Feb. 20–26 (W. F. Wood); Apr. 22 (Slevin); May 22 (Hurter, Calif., 1912). *Monthly catch*—The "Sixteen Year Census" gives Apr., 2 snakes; May, 12; June, 1; July, 2; Aug., 1; Sept., 1; Dec., 1 (Klauber, Gen., 1939a).

Hibernation—We have visited the Potholes and will give some of the late Wallace F. Wood's account: "During the course of mammalogical work I spent a large portion of 5 months, October 1939 to March 1940, along the Colorado River in the vicinity of the Laguna Dam Potholes, Imperial County, California. . . . Fundamentally it is solid rock and massed boulders overlaid with a mixture of sand, gravel and smaller rocks. Aside from a little cottonwood grove at the lower end and an old alfalfa patch, the vegetation is largely cone willow (*Echinochloa*), arrowweed (*Pluchea sericea*), mesquite and catclaw. . . . Early in February I began to find the ground snakes in considerable abundance and on February 20, another *Leptotyphlops* was secured. In about 4 hours collecting, in the next few days, I took 17 worm snakes and approximately 70 *Sonora.* Both kinds of snakes were taken in the same situations, usually within 6 inches of the surface in a loose mixture of sand, gravel and small stones. In the early morning specimens were found close to the surface on exposed flats and small banks. Toward noon we had better collecting in damper ground under arrowweed and mesquite. Our procedure was to rake over the loose soil, turning the larger stones individually. *Leptotyphlops* was often found in groups of 3 individuals, usually 2 adults and a juvenile."

Breeding: Oviparous. *Eggs*—"The following are some records of the eggs in specimens of *humilis-cahuilae* intergrades from the Sentenac Canyon area, the first figure giving the length of the snake in mm., the next, in parentheses, the number of eggs: *248* (3), *250* (2), *267* (4), *281* (6), *290* (2), *294* (4), *321* (6), *340* (6). The average number of eggs is 4. . . . Thus, the larger specimens are likely to have more young, as was found to be the case with the rattlesnakes" (Klauber, Gen., 1940a). *Young*—"Young specimens are the size of a large darning needle" (Klauber, Calif., 1934a). Measurements on 44 little specimens, collected April 22, 1941, at the Potholes by Slevin and Wood, ranged from 102 to 130 mm.

Food: Ants. Perkins, Mosauer (Baja Calif., 1936a).

Authorities:

Brattstrom, B. H., and R. C. Schwenkmeyer (Calif., 1951)
Klauber, L. M. (Gen., 1931e, 1939a,
1940a; Calif., 1931a, 1934a)
Mosauer, W. (1936a)

Perkins, C. B. (Calif., 1938)
Slevin, J. R. (Calif., 1950)
Taylor, E. H. (Gen., 1939)
Wood, W. F. (Calif., 1945)

1950: J. R. Slevin extended Wood's account and gave 3 habitat pictures of the region. "In such a limited area it was not difficult to pick out the most likely spots for hunting, and after making camp and looking over the situation in general picked up 3 worm snakes and striped ground snake as a beginning. Next morning we started out early before the sun got too warm and by noon had 26 striped ground snakes, 99 worm snakes, and 4 milk snakes (*Lampropeltis getulus yumensis*). The following day, Apr. 23, netted 36 worm snakes and 27 striped ground snakes. On the 24th, 3 worm snakes were taken and on the 25th, 1, these days being given over to working on the mainland."

1951: B. H. Brattstrom and R. C. Schwenkmeyer found 7 with *Isoptera* (adults, workers, or eggs) and one with ants and eggs of ants. They found plenty of internal parasites, captured more on moonlight nights than moonless ones, and recorded a maximum of 93°F and a minimum of 68°F for activity records.

Trans-Pecos worm snake (Klauber 1940)

Leptotyphlops humilis segregus Klauber 1939. Map 7

Range: S.e. Arizona to Big Bend region of Texas and into Coahuila—U.S.A.: Ariz.; N.M.; Tex. Mex.: Coahuila, Chihuahua (?) *Elevation*—3,000 to 5,000 or more feet.

Size: 12.5 inches. Less than a dozen specimens mentioned in literature. We have seen specimens 5.7–11.2 inches long, and Klauber's longest one is 319 mm. Schmidt and Smith have three specimens, 267, 271, 275 mm., or 10.75–11 inches long.

Distinctive characteristics: Like *humilis* except 10, not 12, scale rows around tail. It has more than 250 dorsal scales (261–275). From preserved specimens, it seems brown above and cream or light buff below.

Habitat: We have seen all the localities for it except those in Coahuila. It is found in the grassland-desert transition and Texas succulent desert of Shreve (Ecol., 1921). In 1949 Jameson and Flury recorded that "two specimens were collected, active at about 10 P.M., one each from the stream bed and catclaw-grama associations. This species probably occurs throughout the Roughland belt and on the rocky areas of the Plains belt." In the Stockton Plateau, Milstead *et al.* took it in Terrell County from under a rock in the morning in the cedar-ocotillo association.

Enemies: A specimen of *segregus* (Cornell 1670), from 15 miles s.w. of Marathon, Brewster Co., Tex., was removed from the stomach of a curved-billed thrasher by Dr. George M. Sutton. Another of the same species (MZUM 65,381 from near Phantom Lake, Tex.) was found crushed in a cow tract.

Field notes: As yet we have not seen this form alive, although we have visited Marathon and the Phantom Lake region.

Authorities:

Jameson, D. L., and A. G. Flury (Tex., 1949)

Klauber, L. M. (Gen. 1940a; Ariz., 1939b)

Milstead, W. W., J. S. Mecham, and H. McClintock (Tex., 1950)

Schmidt, K. P., and T. F. Smith (Tex., 1944)

Utah worm snake (Klauber 1940), Tanner's blind snake

Leptotyphlops humilis utahensis Tanner 1938. Map 7

Range: S.w. Utah.

Elevation: 3,000 to 4,000 feet.

Size: 4.6–15 inches. Tanner's series ran from 114 to 284 mm. Klauber gives 324 mm. as the longest specimen.

Distinctive characteristics: Like *humilis* except high number of dorsals (289–308) and medium dark pigmentation of dorsals; "a proportion of transversely divided interoccipital (fourth dorsal) scales; or if the fourth dorsal is not divided, the fifth is very much wider than the sixth" (Klauber). Like *cahuilae* in high dorsal count.

Habitat: "All specimens were taken in the moist red sandy soil" (Tanner, Ut., 1938). We have seen the cemetery and the base of the Sugar Loaf near the edge of St. George, Ut., but all we succeeded in getting were shed skins.

Period of activity: *First appearance*—Apr. 1936, 1938 (D. E. Beck); Apr. 1938 (Tanner, A. Paxman). *Fall disappearance*—Dec. 5, 1937 (Cannon).

Breeding: Oviparous. *Young*—The smallest Tanner recorded were (in mm.) 114 (tail 6), diameter 2.5; 117 (tail 5.1), diameter 2.2; 118, diameter 2.5. The size of newborn young has not been recorded.

Field notes: June 3, 1942, St. George, Ut. Ralph Hofen took me to a lady who had a baby *Crotalus v. lutosus*. She gave it to me. Hofen was along when V. M. Tanner and Arthur Paxman collected *L. h. utahensis* on Red Hill beyond their cave. . . . She said one of the *L. h. utahensis* came from digging in a gravel pit.

Authorities:

Klauber, L. M. (Gen., 1940a)

Tanner, V. M. (Ut., 1935, 1938)

THE SEA SNAKES

Family HYDROPHIDAE Boie (Figs. 7, 8)

Tail strongly compressed, paddle-shaped, $\frac{1}{7}$–$\frac{1}{10}$ of total length; body short, more or less compressed posteriorly, width $\frac{1}{2}$–$\frac{2}{3}$ of depth; nostrils on the upper surface of the snout (except in *Laticauda*); chin shields inconspicuous, if present, posterior pair usually separated; eye with round pupil; tongue short, only the cleft portion protrusible; poison fangs present, and usually teeth on the maxillary bone behind them; neural spines and hypapophyses very strongly developed in the caudal region; hypapophyses more or less developed throughout the vertebral column. Hemipenis—"Throughout the family the organ is calyculate and spinous except at the base, although modifications in the size and shape of the calyces and in the length of the spines occur in different species. The *sulcus spermaticus* is divided, the bifurcation in the great majority of species taking place near the tip of the organ" (Smith, Gen., 1926). In general these are marine snakes. (One genus in Mexican waters, *Pelamis*.) Synonyms of *Pelamis: Anguis, Hydrophis, Hydrus, Pelamydrus.*

THE BOAS

FAMILY BOIDAE Gray

Scales smooth in rows 35–53 (29–91 in some forms outside U.S.); ventrals short; anal single, same size as adjacent ventrals; caudals single in U.S. forms and practically equal to ventrals and anal; tail short, blunt, and rounded; rudimentary hind legs showing as small spurs at either side of anus, more evident in males; dorsal head plates irregular; scales on chin between lower labials small; no mental groove; pupil vertical; labials frequently with pits (not present in *Charina* or *Lichanura*); maxillary and mandibular teeth in graduated series: Hemipenis—simple, apex and base smooth, surface with flounces. (Two genera in U.S.: *Charina, Lichanura*.)

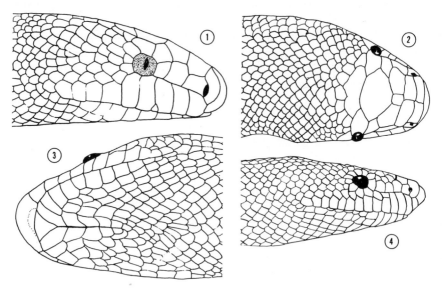

Fig. 13. 1–3, *Charina bottae bottae;* 4, *Lichanura roseofusca gracia.*

KEY TO THE GENERA (Fig. 13)

a. Large median shield on top of head; tail very blunt; snout short, broad; rostral large, broad; 1–2 loreals; eye rests on upper labials 4 and 5; dorsal color uniform.   *Charina* aa. With no large dorsal head plates; tail not very blunt; snout elongate; rostral moderate deeper than broad; 3-8 loreals (scales between preocular and nasal, 1-2 of which are cut off from upper labials 4 and 5); eye separated from labials; a complete sclerotic ring of 7-11 nearly uniform scales; dorsum with color pattern. *Lichanura*

RUBBER BOAS

Genus *CHARINA* Gray

Size small medium, 12-27 inches; slight or no neck; anal entire; ventrals short, caudals in single series; scales small with length and width about equal, smooth, in rows 35-45 or more; rudimentary hind legs present (more evident in males); tail very short, blunt, rounded, and ending in large rounded plate not prehensile; large median shield on top of head; scales on chin between lower labials small; snout short and broad; 1-2 loreals; eye small with vertical pupil; eye rests on upper labials; hemipenis simple; sulcus single (Klauber), forked (Cope); apex and basal portion smooth; transversely plicate, plicae distant toward apex.

"The average for the 47 California specimens is 44.38 rows while for the 26 Utah specimens it is 41.34 rows, a difference of about three rows" (Tanner, Ut., 1933). Synonyms: *Pseudoeryx, Tortrix, Wenona*.

KEY TO THE GENUS *CHARINA* (After Klauber, Calif., 1943d)

a. Scale rows 45 or more; parietal usually divided. *C. bottae bottae*
aa. Scale rows 44 or less; parietal usually entire.
   b. Ventrals more than 191; posterior edge of frontal sharply angular or semicircular; sharp point of supraocular penetrating to some depth between frontal and parietal. *C. b. utahensis*
   bb. Ventrals less than 192; posterior edge of frontal only slightly convex; supraocular with blunt end, penetrating little between frontal and parietal. *C. b. umbratica*

Pacific rubber snake (14—Van Denburgh 1922), **Rubber boa**
(10—Ditmars 1907)

Charina bottae bottae (Blainville) 1835. Figs. 13, 14; Map 8

Other common names: Boa; Botta's worm snake; Charina; Great Basin rubber boa; Great Basin rubber snake; lead-colored worm snake; rubber snake; silver snake; timber snake; two-headed snake; wood snake; worm snake.

Range: Coast range from Monterey Co., Calif., to Washington; Sierra

Nevada Mts. from Tulare Co., Calif., to Puget Sound and British Columbia.
—U.S.A.: Calif.; Ore.; Wash.   Can.: B.C. *Elevation*—Possibly 1,000 feet or
lower to 8,000 or 9,000 feet. 40–2,000 feet (Lewis, Wash., 1946); 5,500 feet
(Ross); 6,400–7,800 feet (Linsdale, Nev., 1938–40); 7,600–8,500 feet (Ruthven,
Ut., 1932).

Size: Adults, 15–24 inches.

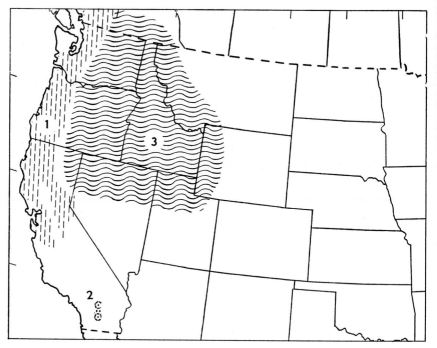

Map 8. *Charina*—1, *bottae;* 2, *b. umbratica;* 3, *b. utahensis.*

Distinctive characteristics and color: Small, thickset burrower with very
short, blunt tail. The fine scales have a sheen, the back uniform greenish
brown or drab, sides olive brown, and the belly some tone of yellow-orange
or orange-yellow. This slow gentle inhabitant of coniferous regions frequently rolls into a knot or ball upon capture.

Habitat: Similar in habitat to *C. b. utahensis,* which see under "Habitat."
"The one individual noted by us in the Yosemite region was found Oct. 7,
1914, in a road near Sentinel Ridge. It had been killed by some workmen
who had passed along just previously. .... . The Rubber Snake is not only
harmless, but, for a reptile, it makes an admirable pet. We have never known
of a snake of this species attempting to bite or resent handling in any way"
(Grinnell and Storer, Calif., 1924).

"It is slow of movement, and very gentle. When handled, it usually ties itself into a curious ball-like knot often with the head hidden and the tail held as though it were the head, which it much resembles. Like *Lichanura,* it never tries to defend itself by biting" (Van Denburgh).

"The region was in the Transition life-zone; the location was a silt filled canyon, called Sand Flat. Except for cloudy days it was usually 5 P.M. before the rubber snakes were abroad, along the moist forest bottoms, or river sands, or the small sandy islands; after dusk they could still be found. Mornings they seemed to disappear along about 8 A.M. The numerous individuals I kept in cages with 2 inches of sand seldom were out during the day. They showed greatest activity evenings from late afternoon up to 8 P.M., when they retired at temperatures varying from 52 to 50 F. I never saw one abroad in the cage when the atmospheric temperature was below 50°. . . . I surmised that its predilection for climbing brought it into more trouble than others more terrestrial in habits. It could not grip a smooth peeled trunk, but upon rough-scaled lodgepole bark the *Charina* had no difficulty clinging; it was not necessary for it to girdle the trunk, but only to zig-zag across one side or up. The snake was sure of itself, and composed upon rough trunks; it was uneasy upon smooth poles and showed no tendency to twine. Upon a trunk the snake gravitated to the slant side and progressed nicely upwards. When twigs were reached it readily used them, rather lumpily, but surely, and if touched twined readily about them. Another individual was found upon the ridgepole of a two story frame house under construction and unroofed" (Ross).

Period of activity: *First appearance*—Apr. 27-30, 1911, Mendocino Co., Calif. (J. Slevin); May 18, 1928, Wallala, Mendocino Co., Calif. (E. R. Leach). *Fall disappearance*—Oct. 7, 1914 (Grinnell and Storer, Calif., 1924). MVZ has dates from Feb. 2 to Oct. 2.

Breeding: Viviparous. *Sexual dimorphism*—"There seems little or no sexual dimorphism in the ventrals of *Charina*. It is easy to sex these little boas, the presence of anal spurs indicating the males, as was first pointed out by Dr. Frank N. Blanchard" (Klauber). *Young*—The evidence is scanty. "A female caught in June contained large eggs" (Van Denburgh). "One captive rubber snake gave birth prematurely to three young. Each was enclosed in an amniotic membrane along with a relatively large mass of yolk. The young made feeble movements; a few hours later they were killed by sunlight falling upon them. Their premature birth was probably a result of the abnormally high temperature at which the mother was kept" (Fitch). Some small sizes we have seen in MVZ and CAS collections are 185, 189, 194, 206, 219, 224 mm., some close to hatching.

Food: Insects, mammals, lizards. Cronise (Calif., 1868), Cope, Van Denburgh, Ross, Fitch, Hanley.

Authorities:

Baird, S. F., and C. Girard (*Proc. Acad. Nat. Sci. Phila.*, 1852: 176)
Blainville, H. D. (Baja Calif., 1835)
Cooper, J. G., and G. Suckley (Gen., 1860)
Cope, E. D. (Gen., 1910; Baja Calif., 1862, 1889)
Fitch, H. S. (Ore., 1936)
Gadow, H. (Gen., 1905)
Gray, J. E. (Gen., 1849)
Hanley, G. H. (Calif., 1943)
Keegan, H. L. (Gen., 1943)
Klauber, L. M. (Calif., 1943d)
Pickwell, G. B. (Gen., 1947)
Ross, R. C. (Calif., 1931)
Stejneger, L. (Calif., 1890, 1893)
Van Denburgh, J. (Gen., 1922)
Werner, F. (Gen., 1921)

Southern California rubber snake

Charina bottae umbratica Klauber 1943. Fig. 15; Map 8

Range: San Jacinto Mts., Riverside Co., Calif., and San Bernardino Mts., San Bernardino Co., Calif. *Elevation*—5,800 feet (Klauber, Calif., 1943d).

Size: Adults, 10.6–11.8 inches. In 1943 Klauber gave 264 mm. (immature) and 295 mm. for males. These were the only specimens then known to him.

Distinctive characteristics: A rare diminutive of the common small boa, *C. bottae bottae;* reduced or fewer scale rows (39–41), ventrals less than 192 (184–190); rear of frontal and front of parietal straight; rear point of supraocular blunt penetrating slightly between frontal and parietal. Buffy citrine or sayal brown above, colonial buff or straw yellow below.

Color: A snake from Idyllwild, Calif., loaned us by C. B. Perkins, of the San Diego Zoo, on Aug. 5, 1950. Dorsal color is buffy citrine or sayal brown, the top of head and face above upper labials is snuff brown. The belly plates and scale rows 1 and 2 are colonial buff or straw yellow, underside of head and of rostral the same. The stubby tail has a tip of tawny. The eye has a vertical pupil with a narrow rim of orange-cinnamon. *Structure*— The parietal is broken into 4 parts (2 interparietals). The supraocular on one side has a rounded tip and on the other side a slightly pointed one which does not, however, extend far between frontal and parietal. There is a straight suture from rostral to frontal and perhaps ⅓ into the frontal

Habitat: "The snake was found under a slab of fallen pine bark" (Klauber, Calif., 1943d).

Period of activity: The only records we have are May, 1925, and July 1, 1929, and the one mentioned under "Color" above.

Field notes: Imagine our delight on receipt of the following airmail letter of Aug. 1, 1950, from C. B. Perkins: "I am shipping you today, air express, a small *Charina b. umbratica,* collected at Idyllwild, California. Of all the snakes on your list this is the one I didn't expect to get hold of. We would like to have it back alive but if anything should happen to it, please pickle it for us as it is *worth its weight in gold* as you know."

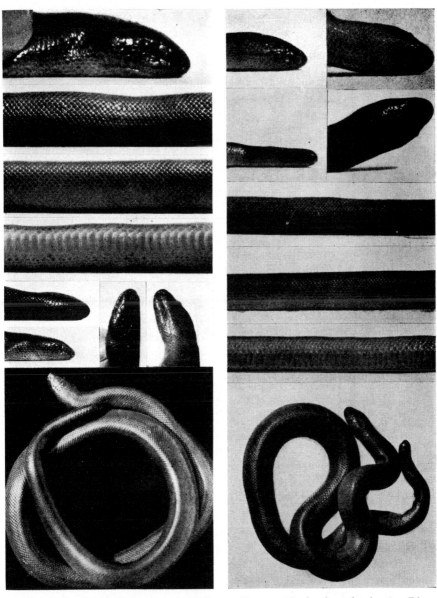

Fig. 14. *Charina bottae bottae:* 1–8, Mariposa Co., Calif., C. Hemphill; 9, Oregon State College, Corvallis, Ore., K. Gordon.

Fig. 15. *Charina b. umbratica,* San Diego, Calif., C. B. Perkins.

Authorities:

Bogert, C. M. (Calif., 1930)   Klauber, L. M. (Calif., 1929, 1943d)

Great Basin rubber snake (5—Van Denburgh 1922), Rubber snake (Bailey 1930)

Charina bottae utahensis Van Denburgh 1920. Fig. 16; Map 8

Other common names: Great Basin rubber boa; lead-colored worm snake; Pacific rubber snake; rubber boa; two-headed snake.

Range: Mountain districts of Snake River plain and Utah Valley, comprising w. Wyoming, n. Utah, n. Nevada, Idaho, e. Oregon; upper Columbia River basin, e. Washington into cent. British Columbia and w. Montana. Roughly, Palouse prairie. U.S.A.: Calif.; Ida.; Mont.; Nev.; Ore.; Ut.; Wash.; Wyo. Can.: B.C. *Elevation*—4,000 to 8,500 feet. 4,000 feet (Borell); 6,400, 6,800, 7,000, 7,800 feet (Linsdale, Nev., 1938, 1938–40); 7,600–8,500 feet (Ruthven). Below 5,000 feet (Ferguson, Ore., 1952).

Size: Adults, 18–27 inches.

Distinctive characteristics: Like *bottae* except that the scale rows are usually 44 or less while *bottae* has 45 or more; parietals usually divided in *bottae* but entire in *utahensis;* like *bottae* ventrals 192 plus and supraocular point sharp between frontal and parietal. A lustrous, small, brown, crepuscular snake with orange-yellow or yellow-orange belly.

Color: Snake from Pullman, Wash., Mar. 14, 1928. The dorsum is mummy brown, clove brown, or drab with an opalescent sheen. The sides are olive brown, olive, or dresden brown. All the dorsal scales are hexagonal. Of the eye, most of the exposed portion is the pupil. The area in front of the pupil next to the anterior rim and that above is light drab or the color of the dorsum. Back of the pupil is a light cinnamon drab ring with the rest ecru drab and light grayish olive. At times, all of the eye has an opalescent sheen. The throat region is grayish olive or citrine drab becoming buffy brown on the lower labial and underside of the upper labial rim. The venter is a clear ochraceous-buff, light ochraceous-buff, pale orange-yellow, or pale yellow-orange, with an occasional spot of the dorsal color.

Habitat: Several of these snakes have been taken in canyons, in the conifers and outside them, along roads, and in open spaces. They are essentially mountain dwellers in forested or wooded areas and in mountain meadows. Hardy (Utah, 1938) observed: "Due to the cool air of early morning the snake was very inactive when found on a bale of hay." According to Pack (Utah, 1930), "This harmless snake is found in the moist and shady parts of our mountains. It is slow, retiring, and gentle. Practically nothing is known of its habits." Logier wrote that "the specimen taken at Summerland was found sunning itself beside a creek in the early forenoon." An extended discussion was given by Linsdale in 1938: "Five rubber-snakes found in the Toyabe Mountains constitute all the records of this species in Central

Nevada." In 1888 Townsend (Calif.) wrote that at Berryvale, near the western base of Mt. Shasta, a boy killed a snake which he thought had "a head at each end," a notion not unlikely to be suggested by the appearance of this short-tailed snake.

Period of activity: *First appearance*—We have few early dates: Mar. 14, 1928, Leffingwell, Pullman, Wash.; May 18, 1938, Hardy, Ut.; May 14, 1942, Utah. *Fall disappearance*—Most of the records are of September up to the 15th, such as Sept. 15, 1941, Cle Elum, Wash. (S. Nichitami); Sept. 9, 1938 (Tanner and Tanner); Sept. 14, 1921, Bear Lake, Ida. (B. C. Cain).

Breeding: Viviparous. *Young*—number, 2–8, 170–175 mm. long. Fall or following spring.

"A large specimen, number 842, measuring 556 mm. in length, collected at Aspen Grove on July 30, 1926, contained 5 eggs. . . . Another specimen, number 676, collected in Rock Canyon east of Provo on August 17, 1938, contained only 2 eggs. . . . A specimen, number 1387, was collected at Aspen Grove on July 29, 1935, which measured 629 mm. This female contained 8 eggs, the greatest number found in any one specimen. . . . The largest specimen of this species in our collection, No. 174, was collected at Aspen Grove on August 4, 1938, and contained 3 eggs. A fifth specimen, number 690, taken on August 9 at Aspen Grove, was kept alive in a breeding cage for food study purposes. . . . On September 9, while removing the dry grass, 3 small snakes and an undeveloped egg were observed in the cage. The young snakes were dead. . . . The specimens were removed and preserved. The largest . . . measured 170 mm. long with a head diameter of 6.1 mm. and a dorsal count of 42 scales. . . . A young Rubber Snake [was captured] at Vivian Park in Provo Canyon on June 27, 1939. It is 175 mm. long with a head width of 6.2 mm. and a dorsal scale count of 41. The color is a reddish brown similar to the young snakes born in captivity to specimen Number 690. From our findings, it appears that *C. bottae* in Utah gives birth to her young in the fall of the year, or in some cases where development commences late in the year as in number 1387, in the early spring" (Tanner and Tanner).

In 1943 Svihla reported a female rubber boa that was taken Sept. 15, 1941, and gave birth to four young Sept. 20 or 21. On Sept. 24 they "measured 215, 220, and 225 mm. and weighed 7.2, 7.4, 7.6 and 7.2 grams respectively." One shed its skin on Sept. 30 and the other 3 on the following day. By the second week in March they had increased in length 50 to 100 mm.

Food: Lizards, mice, insects, small birds, cold-blooded vertebrates. Woodbury, Borell, Logier, Tanners.

Field notes: May 21, 1942, Wells, Nev. F. W. Jewkes reports that the power plant owner has at the power plant a curious snake no one ever saw before. Head and tail just alike. Has it preserved in alcohol. Is it a rubber boa? Went to power plant and lo and behold it is a rubber boa. H. H. Cazier, president of Wells Power Co. and owner of ranch on which snake was found, could find no one who had ever seen such except one person of Starr Valley. He and one of his helpers were up at the reservoir in Trout Creek to clean out the screens a week or so ago. There was snow all around. The helper saw this snake coiled up next to the snow. At first he jumped from it. Then he sought to catch it. It started burrowing in the snow. This is apparently the first record for the Ruby Mts.

Authorities:

Allen, A. R. (Ida., 1951)
Borell, A. E. (Ida., 1931)
Cope, E. D. (Ore., 1884)
Klauber, L. M. (Calif., 1943c, 1943d)
Linsdale, J. M. (Nev., 1938)
Logier, E. B. S. (B.C., 1932)
Ortenburger, A. I. (Wyo., 1921b)

Ruthven, A. G. (Ut., 1926)
Svihla, A. (Wash., 1943)
Tanner, V. M. (Ut., 1933)
Tanner, V. M., and W. W. Tanner (Ut., 1939)
Van Denburgh, J. (Ut., 1920)
Woodbury, A. M. (Ut., 1931)

ROSY BOAS

Genus *LICHANURA* Cope

Size medium, 17–44 inches; slight or no neck; anal entire; ventrals short, caudals in single series; scales small, smooth, in rows 35–45; rudimentary hind legs may be evident; tail not very blunt, slightly prehensile; no large dorsal head plates; scales between lower labials all small; snout elongate; 3–8 loreals (scales between preocular and nasal, 1–2 of which are cut off from upper labials 4 and 5); eye small with vertical pupil, surrounded by complete ring of 7–11 scales; hemipenis simple; sulcus forked; apex and basal portion smooth; lamina pinnate from the sulcus. Synonym: *Charina*.

KEY TO THE GENUS *LICHANURA*
(After Klauber, Calif., 1931d)

a. Longitudinal stripes, if present, have edges uneven (zigzag) and ill defined.   *L. roseofusca roseofusca*

aa. Longitudinal stripes are present and with even (but serrated) edges.

  b. Longitudinal stripes dark chocolate brown; ventrals average 222.
        L. trivirgata

  bb. Longitudinal stripes red brown; ventrals average 230.   *L. r. gracia*

Fig. 16. *Charina b. utahensis*, Pullman, Wash., D. G. Leffingwell.

Fig. 17. *Lichanura roseofusca roseofusca:* 1, Poway, Calif., L. M. Klauber; 2-9, San Diego Zoo, Calif.

California boa (18—Van Denburgh 1897), Rosy boa
(6—Yarrow 1882)

Lichanura roseofusca roseofusca Cope 1868. Fig. 17; Map 9

Other common names: California rosy boa; many-scaled boa; rubber boa; rubber snake; two-headed snake.

Range: In coast and desert foothills, Los Angeles and San Bernardino Cos., Calif., s. to n. Baja California, Mex. (lat. 31°). U.S.A.: Calif. Mex.: Baja Calif. *Elevation*—Sea coast to 4,500 feet. "From the coast line to the lower edges of desert foothills, excluding the mountains above 4500 feet" (Klauber, Calif., 1931a). Cabazon, San Jacinto region, 1,700 feet; Palm Canyon 3,000 feet (Atsatt); Ocean to desert (Perkins); 1,900, 2,500 feet (Van Denburgh, Gen., 1922).

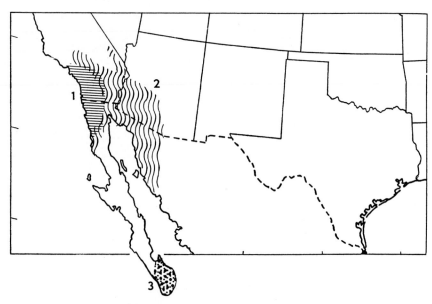

Map 9. *Lichanura*—1, *roseofusca;* 2, *r. gracia;* 3, *trivirgata.*

Size: Adults, 17–42 inches.

Longevity: 11 years 6 months (Perkins, Gen., 1948); 12 years (Perkins, Gen., 1953).

Distinctive characteristics: Unlike *Charina,* it has no large dorsal head plates; possesses a complete eye ring of small scales which thus separates the eye from the upper labials; has normally ill-defined, uneven, zigzag longitudinal stripes. A medium-sized (17–42 inches), attractive snake, pale olive-gray above, deep quaker drab (purplish) below. Middorsal stripe cinnamon brown, lateral bands vinaceous fawn.

Color: Snake from Poway, Calif., received from L. M. Klauber on April 6, 1928. Down the middle of the back is a broad irregular band, 4 or more scales in width, which is sudan brown or cinnamon-brown. There is another on each side. A space of 2 to 3 scales' width between the middorsal and lateral bands is pale olive-gray. Below the lateral band 1 of 2 rows of scales is marked with vinaceous-fawn or light grayish vinaceous. The centers of the first 5 to 7 rows of scales are pale campanula blue, pearl blue, or pallid quaker drab. The iris is black with a plum purple or nigrosin blue cast. The ventrals are deep quaker drab in front, with the rear edges campanula blue to pallid quaker drab. All the pale campanula blue areas of the ventrals have a sprinkling of vinaceous-fawn, especially on the underside of the tail.

Habitat: We quote the incomparable Grinnell and Grinnell: "During a camping trip the last week of March 1906, at the mouth of the San Gabriel, our field party secured no less than 4 boas along the rocky southern base of the hills and at the mouth of Fish Canyon, a tributary of San Gabriel River. One was discovered during a driving rain. It was crawling in the open canyon bed near the margin of a torrent. And this seems characteristic of this species, that it comes out in cloudy weather or else frequents shady places. Its movements are slow. When picked up, it winds tightly about one's arm or else coils up in an intricate knot. Hence one boy who had seen the species before called it the 'rubber snake.'"

From 1924 to 1939 Klauber published several notes. In 1924 (a, Calif.) he wrote: "The boas are tame and make good pets except that they do not feed well in captivity; they do not attempt to escape even when first captured, and none of our specimens ever tried to bite. One was found near Glen Lonely, April 15, 1923, braced in a vertical position between two granite boulders, immediately above and evidently watching a wood-rat's nest. A second was found coiled and wedged tightly in a fissure."

From Klauber's "Sixteen Year Census" (Gen., 1939a) we quote: "Forms largely diurnal on the coast . . . tend to become crepuscular or nocturnal on the desert either in the same form or as an analogue. . . . Live snakes found on road: California Boa *L. r. roseofusca* 9 daytime, 9 nighttime. . . . Times observed active on road: *L. r. roseofusca:* 8:10; 9:14; 10:43; 10:47 P.M. Temperatures at which snakes have been observed at night: *L. R. roseofusca* 73°F. . . . Ecological conditions of roadsides: 1 pond, creek, or river bank, 4 cultivated fields, 3 grass, 1 light brush, 11 heavy brush chaparral, 10 rocks, boulders, 1 brushy desert. Total 31. . . . Zones—*L. r. roseofusca*—coast 50; inland valleys 157; foothills 176; mountains 2; desert foothills 71; desert 2. Total 458."

In 1929 Burt and Burt found these boas in brush and rocks; in 1932 Linsdale took one "on open ground of a dry bog"; in 1942 Von Bloecker (Calif.) recorded one on the meadow side of a dune; and in 1938 Perkins said it was "common and found in the chaparral and among the boulders from ocean to the desert."

Period of activity: *First appearance*—Apr. 15 (Klauber, Calif., 1924a); May (Van Denburgh, Calif., 1912); May 1 (Von Bloecker, Calif., 1942). *Monthly catch*—Klauber's "Sixteen Year Census" recorded: Jan., 1 snake; Feb., 3; Mar., 32; Apr., 92; May, 109; June, 140; July, 31; Aug., 13; Sept., 10; Oct., 15; Nov., 8; Dec. 4. Total found, 458. Rank 9. Per cent 3.54. *Fall disappearance*—Nov. 25 (Linsdale, Baja Calif., 1932).

Breeding: Viviparous. Until Klauber's note of 1933 (Calif.), "A Brood of Boas," we knew next to nothing about this form. The young are 295 to 305 mm. in length. "The young, usually six to ten, are born alive" (Perkins).

Food: Mice. Atsatt, Wright, Klauber, Mosauer, Perkins.

Authorities:

Atsatt, S. R. (Calif., 1913)
Cope, E. D. (Calif., 1868; Baja Calif., 1862)
Grinnell, J. and H. W. (Calif., 1907)
Klauber, L. M. (Gen. 1939a; Calif., 1924a, 1930a, 1931a, 1933, 1934a)
Linsdale, J. M. (Baja Calif., 1932)
Mosauer, W. A. (Calif., 1935a)
Perkins, C. B. (Calif., 1938)
Stejneger, L. (Calif., 1889, 1890, 1891)
Van Denburgh, J. (Baja Calif., 1896a)
Wright, A. H. (Calif., 1921)

1890: L. Stejneger recognized three more forms, *L. myriolepis, L. orcutti,* and *L. simplex.* These three forms are now held to be within *L. roseofusca.*

"As a pet I consider it the finest native snake of the states. It is gentle, never bites, is clean and glossy of skin, coils into a ball or up the arm and is a beautifully patterned snake. This individual was befriended by the whole neighborhood of children" (Wright).

Desert boa (6—Klauber 1931), **California boa**
(5—Grinnell and Camp 1917)

Lichanura roseofusca gracia Klauber 1931. Figs. 13, 18; Map 9

Other common names (Desert) rosy boa; rubber boa; rubber snake.

Range: Desert regions of s.e. California, s.w. Arizona, n.e. Baja California, and n.w. Sonora, i.e., from Mojave Desert to Guaymas, Sonora, Mex.— U.S.A.: Ariz.; Calif. Mex.: Baja Calif.; Sonora. *Elevation*—Sea level or below to 2,000 or more feet.

Size: Adults, 17–44 inches.

Distinctive characteristics: Like *L. r. roseofusca* except that it is lighter, glaucous-gray, light-pinkish cinnamon, or even white above, pale green-blue gray on sides, and sky gray or pale pinkish buff below; middorsal (1) and lateral (2) stripes reddish brown (argus brown), distinct, and more or less even (some 3-striped almost white specimens from desert very striking).

Color: A snake from near Colton, Calif., received from A. J. Kirn of Somerset, Tex. The background of the back is court gray or glaucous-gray.

The lower sides are sky gray or pale green-blue gray. There is a middorsal band of argus brown or amber brown to cinnamon-brown, which averages at least 3 or 4 scales wide. At regular intervals there are triangular lateral expansions where this band is 6 to 7 scales wide. From the 8th to 12th rows of scales is a pronounced lateral band similar in color to the middorsal one. There are a few spots or collections of spots of the same color in the interval between the dorsal and lateral stripes. The light scales of 2 rows below the lateral brown band, namely the 7th and 8th, are clear or practically so of black or black edging, but on the 1st to 6th rows are many black edgings, some completely black scales and a few argus brown ones with black edges. Black is entirely absent from the dorsal stripe and very slightly edges the scales of the lateral band. On the forward half of the body in the light interval below the lateral band, an occasional scale bears a touch of orange-pink or capucine orange. In the rear half of the body a few whole scales of this light area may have this color. The head bears a combination of argus brown and sky gray. The brown dorsal band extends onto the head, expanding between the eyes to cover the width of the head, and continuing almost to the tip of the snout. The lateral band also extends onto the head. In the temporal region, the black edges become more prominent, and as it passes the eye, the band becomes a black stripe or mainly black to the nostril. An occasional scale is centered with argus brown. The iris of the eye is black flecked with olive-gray and argus

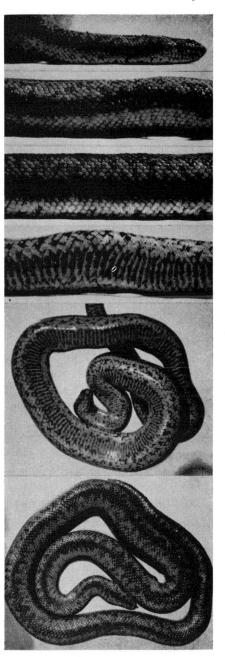

Fig. 18. *Lichanura r. gracia*, Colton, Calif., through A. J. Kirn.

brown. The rostral is cream-buff, and the scales of the throat are tinged with the same. The gulars and throat scales are more or less spotted with black, as the the temporal scales, suboculars and 4 or 5 upper labials below and back of the eye. The ventrals are sky gray, but each plate is dominantly marked for two-thirds of its front with a mingling of black and argus brown, the latter prevailing toward the ends of the plate. The caudal edge is sky gray. In the rear third of the body, the sky gray becomes more prominent.

Habitat: Desert, barren mountains. Doubtless much like the habitat of *L. r. roseofusca.* One of the most recent notices of it is the record from Providence Mts., Calif. "Only one boa was encountered, a large male found near Mitchells at about 6 A.M. on June 10, 1938. It was lying across a path on a steep rocky slope. This snake was extremely sluggish, and, when picked up, made no attempt to bite or escape" (Johnson, Bryant, and Miller).

Breeding: Viviparous. Klauber's 1933 specimen from Guaymas, Sonora, had 3 developing eggs. In 1936 Taylor wrote: "The specimen (No. 129) was captured June 29, 1934, just after daybreak in a mass of boulders 5 miles southwest of Hermosilla. It is a pregnant female with the embryos probably two thirds developed. No fear was shown at my approach, and when picked up the snake remained quite docile. The embryos were removed when it was preserved. These are Nos. 166–169. They show the typical striped color pattern of the mother. . . . The young measure 160 to 172 in total length, the tails measuring about 25 mm. Three of the young are males . . . ; one is a female; the latter has slightly shorter tail than the males."

Authorities:

Bogert, C. M. (Calif., 1930)
Johnson, D. H., M. D. Bryant, and
    A. H. Miller (Calif., 1948)
Klauber, L. M. (Calif., 1931d, 1933)

Taylor, E. H. (Gen., 1936a)
Van Denburgh, J., and J. R. Slevin
    (Gen., 1922; Ariz., 1913)

1933, L. M. Klauber: "I have lately seen two boas which might be considered *roseofusca-gracia* intergrades. The first was from Twenty-nine Palms, San Bernardino County, California; it had distinct dorsal stripes, but the edges were irregular, thus falling between the chaparral dwelling *roseofusca* and the even-striped snakes from such Mohave Desert localities as Victorville, Oro Grande, and Randsburg. This tendency toward intergradation is here more pronounced than in the desert-edge specimens from eastern San Diego County, which, for all their contrasting colors, remain essentially *roseofusca roseofusca.*"

COMMON HARMLESS SNAKES

FAMILY COLUBRIDAE Gray

Without a pair of permanently erect fangs near the front of the upper jaw (5 genera, *Coniophanes, Leptodeira, Oxybelis, Tantilla, Trimorphodon,* however have posterior grooved teeth—Opisthoglyphs, glyphodonts, or Boigidae, the rear-fanged group); maxillary horizontal, immovable, articulating with anterior frontal by a lateral process; maxillary and dentary bones armed with solid teeth along whole length; palatines and pterygoids usually toothed; scales usually imbricate; top of head with plates; pattern, if in rings the red one not separated from black by yellow (white). Hemipenis—various. On the variations of the hemipenis and on the nature of the vertebrae, this big family of 39 genera has been divided into 8 subfamilies, 3 of which are represented in the U.S.

KEY TO THE GENERA (Figs. 19–25)[1]

a. Anal entire.

  b. Most caudals single; scales smooth in 23 rows; rostral long, extended tapering upward; dorsal pattern alternating black and red (or orange) or black and white saddles, many lateral scales yellow or white spotted.   *Rhinocheilus* 1

  bb. Caudals paired.

    c. Rostral enlarged; scale rows 19; posterior chin shields separated by 1–3 gulars and 1 or 2 rows of gulars between their tips and the first ventral.

      d. Snout acute, projecting beyond lower jaw and red or pink.

                                              Cemophora 2(12)

      dd. Snout truncate, shovellike; rostral with free lateral edges; snout pale olive-buff or pale olive-gray.   *Phyllorhynchus* 3

    cc. Rostral normal.

      d. Parietals and prefrontals usually in contact with upper labials; no loreal; extremely slender; tail very short (1/10 or less of total length, caudals 33–46); upper labials 6, lower 5.   *Stilosoma* 4

      dd. Parietals and prefrontals not in contact with upper labials; loreal present; width to length normal.

        e. Scale rows 27–35; rostral penetrates internasals; several (3–4) rows of gulars between tips of chin shields and ventrals; caudals 43–84; upper labials normally 8, lower 10–15.

        f. Scales smooth, 29–31 rows, usually 29; 1–2 postoculars.

                                       Arizona 5

        ff. Scales partly keeled; 3 or more postoculars; vertical laminiform epiglottis enables snake to make a loud hiss or roar.

                                      Pituophis 6

      ee. Scale rows fewer than 27; rostral not or slightly penetrating between internasals.

        f. Scales mostly keeled, few (1–2) rows of gulars between the tips of chin shields and ventrals.

          g. Lower labials 5–7; head small; 1 nasal; temporals 2 + 2; posterior chin shields not separated by gulars; middle of venter with 2 close-set rows of prominent spots which become 1 row forward; size to 21 inches; caudals 32–45.

                                       Tropidoclonion 7

---

[1] Numbers following the generic names refer to separate drawings in Figs. 19–25. When a genus such as *Elaphe* appears more than once in the key, the drawings for each inclusion are indicated thus, 17 (47,48); 17 is the pertinent appearance, with other locations indicated for ready reference.

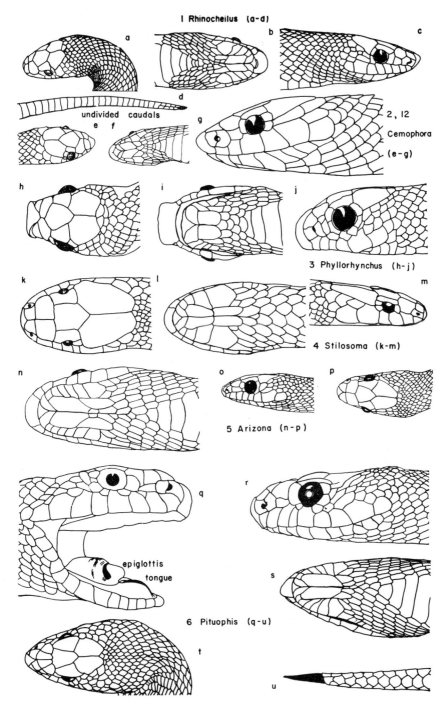

Fig. 19 (Key nos. 1–6). a–d, *Rhinocheilus;* e–g, *Cemophora;* h–j, *Phyllorhynchus;* k–m, *Stilosoma;* n–p, *Arizona;* q–u, *Pituophis.*

gg. Lower labials 8 or more; 2 nasals; single anterior temporal; gulars
separate posterior chin shields; caudals 49+.   *Thamnophis* 8

ff. Scales smooth.

  g. Head distinct from neck; eye large with pupil vertically elliptic;
scale rows 21–24; upper labials 9 (8), lower 11–13; preoculars 3
(2), postoculars 3 (2,4); loreals 2 with subloreal usually present;
temporals 2 + 3 to 4 + 5 (often irregular); light ⅄ mark on head,
stem forward; rear fangs present; dark dorsal saddles split transversely by a light line (*T. vandenburghi*).

                                    Trimorphodon (part) 9(46)

  gg. Head not distinct from neck; pupil round; scale rows 17–27; preocular 1, postoculars 2; loreal 1; temporals 2 + 3 (2) or 1 + 2;
no rear fangs.

    h. Dorsal color uniform bluish black.

      i. Scale rows 17; upper labials 8 (7), lower 8; temporals 2 + 2;
anterior of frontal angulate; few gulars between chin shields
and first ventral; form chunky; size very large, up to 8 feet;
caudals 55–88.   *Drymarchon* 10

      ii. Scale rows 21–27; upper labials 7 (8), lower 9 (8–10); tem-
porals 2 + 3; posterior chin shields separated by gulars, 3–4
rows gulars between chin shields and first ventral; anterior
of frontal truncate; form medium; size large medium, up to
4 1/2 feet; caudals 38–57 (*L. calligaster*, black phase and
L. g. niger).   *Lampropeltis* (part) 11(13)

   hh. Dorsal color not uniform bluish black; a pattern of transverse
bands, rings or unsplit saddles.

     i. Scale rows 19; belly glistening pearly white; snout pointed;
rostral projecting beyond lower jaw; upper labials normally
6, lower 8; temporals 1 + 2.   *Cemophora* 12(2)

     ii. Scale rows 17–27; belly in blocked pattern, checked or ringed
or ventrals dark edged; snout normal; upper labials 7 (8),
lower 9 (8–12); temporals 2 + 3; light Y mark on head, if
present, with stem backward.   *Lampropeltis* 13(11)

aa. Anal divided.

  b. Back and head light bright green (blue-gray in alcohol); loreal 1.

    c. Scale rows less than 20; ventrals 116–237.

      d. Venter of body orange with black spots; venter of tail red
(often held in a coil); scale rows 17, smooth; nasal plate divided; upper labials 7, lower 8; preoculars 2; temporals 1 + 1
(2); posterior chin shields short and broad, not separated, and
with 3–5 rows of gulars between tips and ventrals; young with
uniform dorsum; ventrals 204–236, caudals 53–79. (*D. regalis*).

                               Diadophis (part) 14 (35, 36)

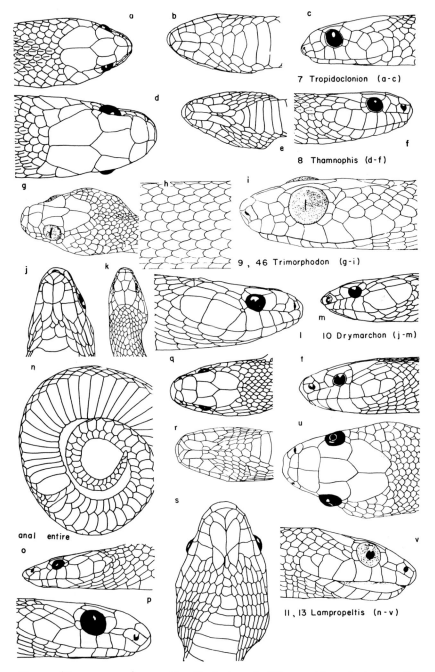

Fig. 20 (Key nos. 7–13). a–c, *Tropidoclonion;* d, *Thamnophis r. butleri;* e, *T. e. vagrans;* f, *T. e. atratus;* g,i, *Trimorphodon vandenburghi;* h, *T. lyrophanes;* j,k,m, *Drymarchon c. couperi;* l, *D. c. erebennus;* n,q,t, *Lampropeltis c. calligaster;* o, *L. d. doliata;* p, *L. pyromelana;* r, *L. g. yumensis;* s,u,v, *L. alterna.*

dd. Under parts unspotted, yellow to white; scale rows 15–17.

    e. Nasal plate not divided; frontal shield pointed in front, evenly tapering caudad; posterior chin shields long and slender, widely diverging for half their length with 1–2 rows of gulars between their tips and first ventral; preocular 1, postoculars 2; temporals 1 + 2; upper labials 7; scales smooth or keeled; young with uniform back; ventrals 116–156, caudals 60–148.   *Opheodrys* 15

    ee. Nasal plate divided; frontal shield rounded or straight in front, sides concave; posterior chin shields diverging only at tips with 2 rows gulars between tips and ventrals; preoculars 2, postoculars 2; temporals 2 + 2 (3); upper labials 8 (7), lower 8–9; scales smooth; young spotted; ventrals 151–184, caudals 72–108. (*C. stejnegerianus* and *C. c. mormon*).   *Coluber* (part) 16(34)

cc. Scale rows 25–33; ventrals 246–260; indistinct, faintly outlined dorsal saddles, lateral spots and head spots, one a **V** with apex caudad; labials upper 8–9, lower 10–11; 1 preocular, 2 postoculars, temporals 2 + 3; nasal plate divided; caudals 107–113; young spotted. (*E. t. intermedia*).   *Elaphe* (part) 17(47,48)

bb. Back and head not light bright green.

  c. Scale rows less than 20.

    d. Scale rows 13, smooth; size very small (6–16 inches); temporals 1 + 1 (2).

      e. Pattern in ringlike bars, red, black, and yellow, the black crossing or nearly crossing the venter; no sharp angle between belly and sides as in *Chionactis occipitalis* of the same region, which however has 15 scale rows; lower labials 8 or 9; 4–5 rows of gulars between tips of chin shields and ventrals.

                              Chilomeniscus 18

      ee. Pattern not in rings or bars, but uniform with uniform under parts; lower labials 6 (5).

        f. Upper labials 5, lower 6; caudals 23–28; large loreal and prefrontal enter orbit; none or one row gulars between tip of chin shields and ventrals; venter pink.   *Carphophis* 19

        ff. Upper labials 7; caudals 37–46; neither small loreal nor prefrontal enter orbit; 7 or 8 rows of gulars between tips of chin shields and ventrals; venter yellowish glaucous. (*S. e. taylori*).   *Sonora* (part) 20(30,41)

dd. Scale rows over 13 but less than 20.

  e. Rostral abnormal; scale rows 17, smooth.

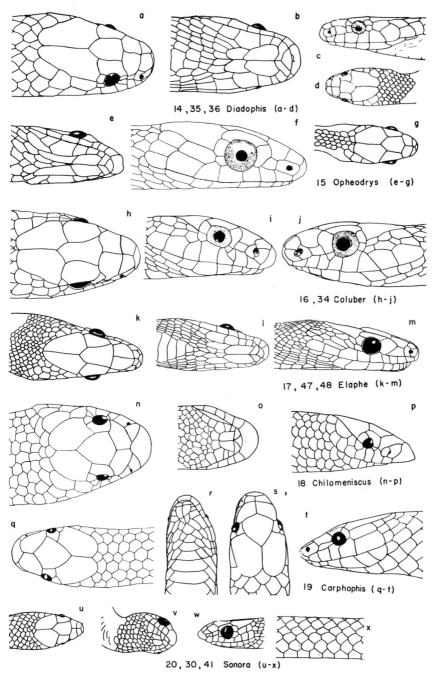

14, 35, 36 Diadophis (a-d)

15 Opheodrys (e-g)

16, 34 Coluber (h-j)

17, 47, 48 Elaphe (k-m)

18 Chilomeniscus (n-p)

19 Carphophis (q-t)

20, 30, 41 Sonora (u-x)

Fig. 21 (Key nos. 14–20). a, *Diadophis a. occidentalis;* b,c, *D. a. pulchellus;* d, *D. a. vandenburghi;* e,f, *Opheodrys aestivus;* g, *O. vernalis;* h,i, *Coluber c. mormon;* j, *C. c. stejnegerianus;* k–m, *Elaphe t. intermedia;* n–p, *Chilomeniscus cinctus;* q,r, *Carphophis a. helenae;* s, *C. a. vermis;* t, *C. a. amoenus;* u–x, *Sonora e. taylori.*

f. Snout very long and sharp, 3–4 times the eye, overhanging the lower jaw; rostral barely visible from above and far separated from frontal; form slender; long neck; tail 2/3 as long as body; scale rows 13 near vent; 2 pairs of very long chin shields in contact, with 3–4 rows of gulars from their tips to ventrals.   *Oxybelis* 21

ff. Snout not long and sharp, not 3–4 times the eye.

    g. Rostral flattened and recurved in a sharp point; size very small, 5.5–14 inches; posterior chin shields small, widely separated with 3–6 rows of gulars between tips and ventrals; ventrals 125–160, caudals 23–44; dorsal pattern of spots or crossbands.

       h. Rostral contacts frontal.   *Ficimia* 22

      hh. Rostral separated from frontal by prefrontals.   *Gyalopion* 23

   gg. Rostral thickened, widened, with projecting edges and extending backward over the snout; form long and slender; size medium, 20–46 inches; tail long; 2–3 rows of gulars between tips of separated, well-developed, posterior chin shields and ventrals; ventrals 177–212, caudals 66–152; dorsal pattern of dark longitudinal stripes.   *Salvadora* 24

ee. Rostral normal.

  f. Scale rows 19 at mid-body; temporals 1 + 2; mostly aquatic.

   g. Scales smooth, glossy, without pits.

    h. Size large to very large, to 72 and 84 inches; no preocular; nasal semidivided; back dark violet black with yellow to pale greenish yellow under head and pink to red blocked with black on belly.

      i. Internasal single; 8–10 lower labials; dorsum without longitudinal light stripes; rose of belly extends up sides in triangles.   *Farancia* 25

     ii. Internasals 2; 9–10 lower labials; dorsum with 3 longitudinal stripes of carmine.   *Abastor* 26

    hh. Size small medium, to 25 inches; 1 preocular; belly pink or salmon, but not blocked with black.

      i. Internasals 2; nasal divided; upper labials (7) 8 (9), lower 9; dorsum with middorsal stripe of purplish gray bordered on either side with buffy brown bands; pinkish buff eye stripe.   *Coniophanes* 27

     ii. Internasal single, small; nasal semidivided; upper labials 8 (7), lower 9–11; dorsum dark without stripes; no light eye stripe; zigzag dark lines along mid-sutures of caudals.   *Liodytes* 28

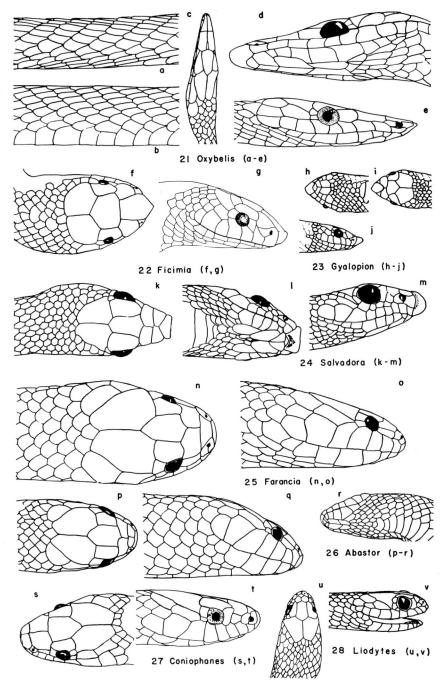

Fig. 22 (Key nos. 21–28). a–e, *Oxybelis a. auratus;* f,g, *Ficimia o. streckeri;* h–j, *Gyalopion canum;* k–m, *Salvadora hexalpis;* n,o, *Farancia a. reinwardti;* p–r, *Abastor erythrogrammus;* s,t, *Coniophanes imperialis;* u,v, *Liodytes alleni.*

gg. Scales keeled (1st row often smooth), with pits; nasal divided; lower
labials 9–11, except *kirtlandi* (7); 2 preoculars except *kirtlandi* (1);
1–2 rows dark spots on venter in middle or on ends of ventrals. (*Regina*
group: *grahami, kirtlandi, rigida, septemvittata*)   *Natrix* (part) 29(49)

ff. Scale rows 15–17, smooth or keeled; mainly terrestrial or arboreal except
Seminatrix.

  g. Dorsal body pattern a bright middorsal stripe or ringlike cross bars;
ventral color white or yellow, many with black bars; tail short;
scales smooth; posterior chin shields small; sand burrowers.

    h. Abdomen rounded; no nasal valve; snout rounded and rounded in
profile; 1, occasionally 2, maxillary foramina; posterior chin shields
separated and with 5–9 rows of gulars between their tips and first
ventral; scales with light edges. (Exceptions: the uniform colored
Sonora species, among them *S. e. taylori* with 13 scale rows).
Sonora (part) 30(20,41)

   hh. Abdomen angulate; nasal valve; snout flattened, very pointed in
profile; 3 maxillary foramina; posterior chin shields usually in
close contact with 3–5 rows of gulars between their tips and the
first ventral (*C. palarostris* 7); lacks the *Sonora* pattern of light
edges on scales.   *Chionactis* 31

  gg. Dorsal body pattern with neither bright middorsal stripe nor ringlike
cross bars; not primarily sand burrowers.

    h. Long and slender, 2–5 1/2 feet; tail long; head distinct.

      i. Upper labials 9; nasal single; preocular 1; 1 row gulars between
chin shields and ventrals; posterior chin shields widely separated caudad; some dorsal scales keeled though feebly; sides of
frontal evenly tapering; color green with each scale with central
spot of yellow, blue, or orange, a very regular pattern.
Drymobius 32

     ii. Upper labials 7 or 8; preoculars 2 (1); nasal divided; 3 rows of
gulars between chin shields and ventrals; scales smooth; sides of
frontal concave; color pattern, not uniform, not with single
central light spot on each green scale.

       j. Head narrow in proportion to length .41–.44; throat usually
spotted; upper labials 8; frontal not or but slightly wider
than supraocular; dorsal color, striped, banded, dotted, or,
in some, plain; venter usually with some pink to coral red
in life; scale rows at posterior end of body 13, 12, 11; ventrals
183–214, caudals 94–160.   *Masticophis* 33

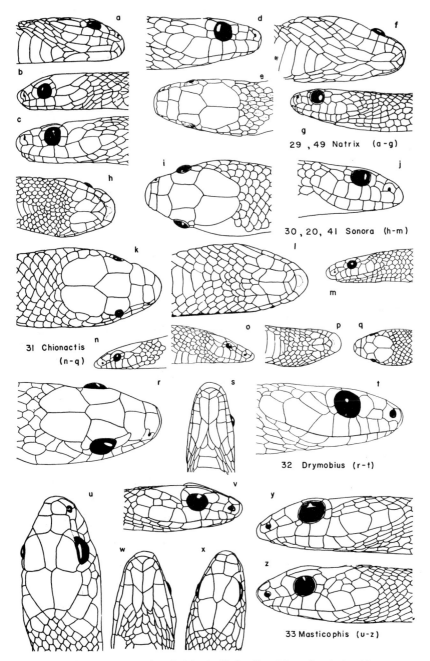

Fig. 23 (Key nos. 29-33). a,b, *Natrix kirtlandi;* c, *N. grahami;* d,e, *N. septem-vittata;* f,g, *N. rigida;* h, *Sonora s. semiannulata;* i,j, *S. s. linearis;* k,l, *S. s. isozona;* m, *S. s. blanchardi;* n-q, *Chionactis o. occipitalis;* r-t, *Drymobius margaritiferus;* u,w, *Masticophis f. piceus (frenatus);* v, *M. t. ruthveni;* x,z, *M. f. flagellum;* y, *M. b. bilineatus.*

jj. Head wider .44–.52 in length; underside of head and neck white; upper labials 7 (8 in *C. mormon* and *C. stejnegerianus*); frontal anteriorly wider than supraocular; dorsal color green, blue-gray or black without pattern (except aberrant form in Louisiana, *anthicus*, spotted); scale rows at posterior end of body 15; ventrals 151–192, caudals 72–120.   *Coluber* 34(16)

hh. Small, 12–20 inches; dorsum black, brown, green, or gray.

   i. Scales of body smooth; 2–5 rows of gulars between chin shields and ventrals.

     j. With an orange neck ring, dorsum brown or green; form slender; scale rows 15–17; temporals 1 + 1; ventrals 126–236.
                                   Diadophis (part) 35(14,36)

    jj. No neck ring.

      k. Rows 17.

        l. Temporals 1 + 1; preoculars 2; dorsum green or gray; belly orange; under tail red; form slender; ventrals 204–236; caudals 53–79.   *Diadophis regalis* 36(14,35)

       ll. Temporals 1 + 2; preocular single; dorsum not green.

         m. Dorsum black; venter red with dark spots on ends of ventrals and dark bars on same plates; scales of tail obtusely keeled; aquatic; upper labials 8 (6–9); caudals 35–56.   *Seminatrix* 37

        mm. Dorsum brown; yellow or white stripe on lip outlining dark band at eye level; under parts yellow; upper labials 7 (8); caudals 65–77.   *Rhadinaea flavilata* 38

   kk. Scale rows 15; dorsum brown, gray, grayish olive; body slender.

      l. Ventral plates pale glaucous green or smoke gray, each with a conspicuous black transverse bar; tail sharp-tipped, moderately short; loreal 1 or absent; nasal entire, divided, or semidivided; no to 3 rows of gulars between tips of posterior chin shields and ventrals.   *Contia* 39

      ll. Ventral plates uniform in color with no dark bars; tail normal.

        m. Venter coral red or pink; head low, flat, very dark in color; 1–5 rows of gulars between tips of chin shields and ventrals; no loreal; temporals 1 + 1; nasal divided; preoculars 1, postoculars 1 (2).   *Tantilla* 40

        mm. Venter light yellow to sulphur or greenish yellow; posterior chin shields small, separated, with 5–9 rows of gulars between their tips and the ventrals; 1 loreal; temporals 1 + 2; nasal entire; preoculars 1, postoculars 2 (unicolored ones).   *Sonora* (part) 41(20,30)

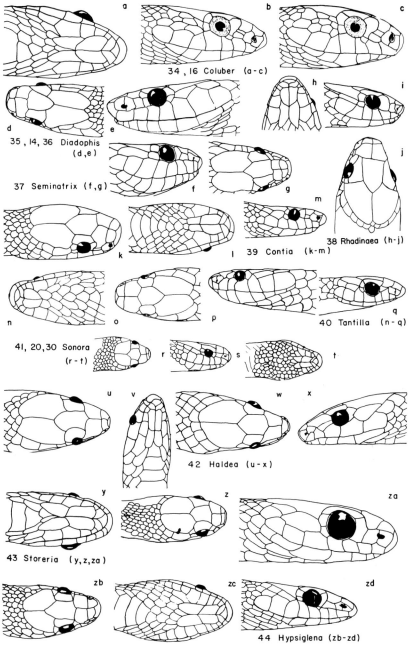

Fig. 24 (Key nos. 34–44). a, *Coluber c. constrictor;* b,c, *C. c. flaviventris;* d, *Diadophis a. pulchellus;* e, *D. p. edwardsi;* f,g, *Seminatrix pygaea;* h–j, *Rhadinea flavilata;* k–m, *Contia tenuis;* n–p, *Tantilla e. eiseni;* q, *T. n. nigriceps;* r–t, *Sonora e. episcopa;* u, *Haldea (Amphiardis) inornatus;* v–x, *H. striatula;* y,za, *Storeria d. dekayi;* z, *S. o. occipitomaculata;* zb–zd, *Hypsiglena t. ochrorhyncha.*

　　ii. Scales keeled; dorsum brown; no or few gulars between chin shields and ventrals. Ventrals 110–148.

　　　　j. No preocular; loreal, and prefrontal contacting eye; upper labials 5 or 6; few or many scales keeled; no spots on back or on ends of ventrals. *Haldea* 42

　　　　jj. Preoculars 1 or 2; with or without loreal; upper labials 6 or 7; neck spots often present; two rows of spots, often indistinct, on back; black spots on either end of ventrals. *Storeria* 43

cc. Scale rows 20 or over; nasal divided.

　　d. Scales smooth; no suboculars (except *Elaphe subocularis*).

　　　　e. 21–24 scale rows in mid-body; enlarged posterior fangs; pupil vertical and elliptical; preoculars 2–3; upper labials 7–10; 1–3 rows of gulars between points of chin shields and ventrals.

　　　　　　f. Postoculars (1) 2 (3); lower labials 9–10 (11); loreal 1; temporals 1 + 2 + 3.

　　　　　　　　g. Preoculars (1) 2 (3); preocular not in contact with frontal; chin shields contact 5–6 lower labials; tips of posterior chin shields separated with 2 rows gulars between tips and ventrals; 21 scale rows; snout projecting beyond mouth; 2 ungrooved, posterior, fanglike teeth in upper jaw; venter white or cream buff; size to 26 inches. *Hypsiglena* 44

　　　　　　　　gg. Preoculars 3; preocular contacts frontal separating supraocular and prefrontal; chin shields contact 6 labials; posterior chin shields well developed, tips separated, 2–3 rows of gulars between them and ventrals; 21–23 scale rows, first much wider than others; 2 enlarged grooved posterior fangs in upper jaw; venter orange with ends of plates heavily flecked; head distinct with a large bulge just back of eyes; crown flat; size to 32 inches. *Leptodeira* 45

　　　　　　ff. Postoculars 3 (4); preocular not in contact with frontal; loreals 2–5; lower labials 10–14; temporals various 2 + 3 or 3 + 4 (2 + 4 to 4 + 5); scale rows often 22 or 24, first row not enlarged; posterior grooved fangs inconspicuous; eye extremely large and protuberant; head distinct, bulging back of eyes; ventrals mostly deep olive buff. *Trimorphodon* (part) 46(9)

　　　　ee. Scale rows 25–33; no enlarged posterior fangs; venter angulate, ventrals extending up sides; preocular 1, postoculars 2; posterior chin shields widely separated by 1 or 2 rows of scales, with 1–3 rows gulars between their tips and the ventrals. *Elaphe* 47(17,48)

　　dd. Scales keeled; scales in 21–33 rows.

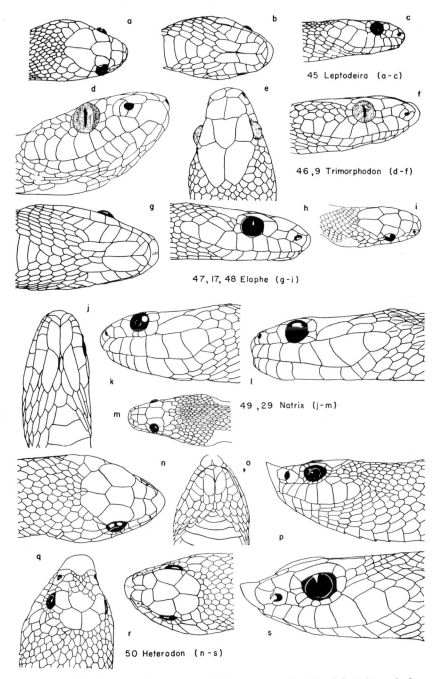

Fig. 25 (Key nos. 45–50). a–c, *Leptodeira a. septentrionalis;* d–f, *Trimorphodon lambda;* g,h, *Elaphe o. williamsi;* i, *E. o. spiloides;* j, *Natrix e. transversa;* k, *N. c. cyclopion;* l, *N. r. rhombifera;* m, *N. taxispilota;* n, *Heterodon p. browni;* o,r,s, *H. p. platyrhinos;* p, *H. simus;* q, *H. n. nasicus.*

e. Rostral normal; 2 pairs of chin shields well developed; suboculars absent (except *E. subocularis* and *N. cyclopion*); no azygous plate.
f. Weak keels on middorsals (5–17 rows); posterior dorsals sometimes all smooth (see above for other characters); a slender form; ventrals 197–246. *Elaphe* 48(17,47)
ff. Heavy keels on all dorsal scales, 21–33 rows, rarely 1st row smooth; posterior chin shields well developed, separated completely or incompletely, with 1–2 rows gulars between tips and venters; oculars 3–7; suboculars in *N. cyclopion;* last 2 or 2 1/2 upper labials turned upward; temporals normally 1 + 2 (3) –2 +3 (4,5); a stocky form with short tail; caudals 55–95. *Natrix* (part) 49(29)
ee. Rostral upturned, keeled above; suboculars present; ocular ring 8–12; 1–20 unpaired (azygous) scales between rostral and prefrontal separating internasals and sometimes prefrontals; anal plate double; posterior maxillary teeth much enlarged; posterior chin shields absent or very small in contact and with 4–5 rows of gulars between tips and ventrals; scale rows 23–25; a stocky form; caudals 27–60. *Heterodon* 50

RAINBOW SNAKES

Genus *ABASTOR* Gray (Fig. 22)

Size large, 20–60 inches; form cylindrical, heavy; head not distinct from neck; tail short, abruptly tapering with spine at tip; anal divided; scale rows 19 at mid-body, smooth, without pits, about square; labials 3 and 4 contact orbit; no preocular; loreal and prefrontal contacting orbit; postoculars 2; nasal single, semidivided; upper labials 6–8, lower 8–10; internasals 2 (except for this character, the above description might be of *Farancia,* from time to time collectors have thought there were hybrids between the two); several rows of gulars between chin shields and ventrals; ventrals 158–182; caudals 37–49; hemipenis—"bifurcate, each apex with a moderate number of slightly serrate calyces, spines numerous" (Cope, Gen., 1900). Synonyms: *Callopisma, Calopisma, Coluber, Helicops, Homalopsis, Hydrops, Natrix.*

Rainbow snake (20—Löding 1922),
Hoop snake (10—Yarrow 1882)
Abastor erythrogrammus (Latreille) 1802. Fig. 26; Map 10

Other common names: Horn snake (Yarrow 1882); mud snake; red-lined snake; red-lined horned snake; red-sided snake; sand hog; sand snake; striped wampum.
Range: Coastal plain from Charles Co., Md., to Florida, w. to Florida

parishes of Louisiana—Ala.; Fla.; Ga.; La.; Md.; N.C.; S.C.; Va. *Elevation*
—Mostly below 100 feet; a few possibly to 500 feet.

Size: 20–60 inches. The largest we have seen was more than 5 feet, taken
by C. C. Tyler, Eureka, Fla., August, 1928.

Distinctive characteristics: Back violet-black with 3 narrow carmine
stripes; lower lateral scales edged with yellow; underside of head yellow;

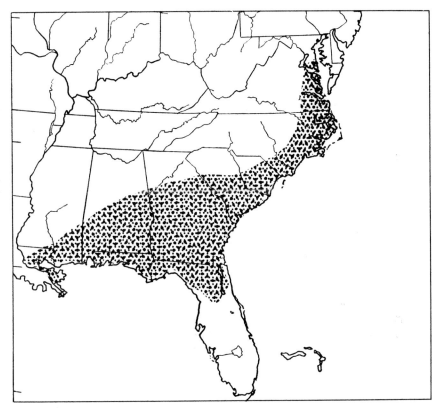

Map 10. *Abastor erythrogrammus.*

belly old rose with row of violet-black spots on either end of the ventrals; a
median row for the greater length of the body. A large, smooth, shiny,
striped, heavy-bodied burrower; tail short ending in a spine.

Color: "The rainbow snake is one of, if not the, most beautiful species
in America. This snake is a thing of beauty, with a most artistic color dec-
oration of red and black going the entire length of the body" (Haltom).

A snake from Salt Springs near Lake Kerr, Fla., caught June 9, 1928, and
bought from C. C. Tyler, Eureka, Fla. It had not shed recently. The back
is dusky slate violet or dusky violet blue or black, with 3 carmine stripes.

The middorsal stripe extends only to the tail; the lateral stripe, which is on the 6th row of scales, extends to the top of the tail. The sides below the carmine stripes are dull violet black (1) or dusky slate blue. The top of the head is as dark as the body with carmine or oxblood red edges to the plates and with some of this color on the parietals. The iris looks dusky slate blue or indigo blue, the pupil rim carmine or eugenia red. The underside of the head and upper and lower labials are lemon yellow or lemon chrome, the labials, chin shields, mental, and first 4 lower labials have centers of dusky slate violet. The yellow of the throat continues along the sides as edgings to the first 2 rows of scales and appears near the lower caudal edge of the 3rd row. In the middle half of the body this becomes martius yellow, next sulphur yellow, and then pale cinnamon pink or cartridge buff. The centers of the 1st and 2nd rows of scales are coral red, which becomes eugenia red on the rear half of the body, and the cephalic half of the center soon becomes dull violet black. The entire belly, except for the spots, is eugenia red, the plates with pale flesh-colored edges. On the forward part of the venter are 2 rows of dusky slate violet rectangular spots on the ends of the ventrals. Soon there appears in the central eugenia red area a median row of hemispherical dusky slate violet spots, which continues to the vent, the tail having only 2 rows of spots.

Habitat: 1885: "Though preferring damp and marshy ground it never voluntarily takes to water" (Kingsley and Bumpus, *Standard Natural History,* Gen., 1885, p. 372). What strange statements fine authorities sometimes make when they write textbooks, encyclopedias, etc., on some subjects about which they know nothing!! Rainbow snakes do not catch fish on dry land.

"This species is a burrower. . . . The Pemunky River specimens were dug up from a clay bank beneath ten feet of sand. Mr. Clarence B. Moore in his excavations of Indian mounds in Florida has dug it from nearly as great a depth beneath the surface, in sand" (Cope, Gen., 1900).

Frequents spring-fed rivers (Van Hyning).

"Local residents say that this is a common snake and that many are plowed up in a field of loose, sandy soil which is surrounded by marsh." (Richmond and Goin).

"All were dug up from the earth during the month of July 1937, by CCC workers engaged in road-building operations on Stump Neck. . . . The soil is very sandy throughout. Except for the open marsh and a cultivated field the land is densely overgrown with shrubs and trees. . . . The second two specimens were found beneath stumps along the marsh" (McCauley).

"Somewhat fossorial; aquatic. . . . Spring runs; calcareous springs; E. Ross Allen collected one in a sink hole pond near Ocala. . . . I saw a snake which I believe was this species on the bottom of a spring 15 feet deep" (Carr, Fla., 1940a).

Period of activity: Scanty records, such as April, 1878 (Goode, Fla.), April 14, 1909 (Mobile Co., Ala.), May, 1920 (Brimley, N.C., 1927).

"During late fall (October and November) and early spring (April and May), young specimens have been found under boards, logs, tar-paper, and other objects lying on the surface of the ground. The largest number of all sizes, however, were turned up by the plow in late March and April. The rainbow snake apparently has no definite period of hibernation, since active specimens have been recorded in every month of the year. Even during the colder months they venture above ground, for a hawk was observed eating one on the ice of the marsh in February" (Richmond, Va., 1945).

Breeding: Oviparous. *Sexual dimorphism*—Blanchard (Gen., 1931) reports keellike ridges on the dorsal scales of the anal region of males. *Mating* —No records.

Eggs—Number 22–50. "A large female . . . was killed July 15, 1928, and found to contain 22 well-developed eggs. These eggs which averaged 29 mm. by 37 mm. were covered with a cream-colored leathery integument" (Van Hyning). Fifty (Ditmars, Gen., 1936). Four-foot specimen laid 43 eggs July 7 (Ditmars, Gen., 1939). Size, 1.5x1.0 inches (Ditmars, Gen., 1939). Time of deposition, July 7 to Aug. 14. "All of the nests observed have been in an open, exposed, dry sandy field, and in the same portion of the field as that chosen by *Kinosternon, Chrysemys* and *Pseudemys* for their nests. The eggs are deposited in a large, oval cavity, 4 to 6 inches below the surface of the ground. One nest, 4 inches below the surface, was measured, and it was found that the cavity was 4 inches from top to bottom, 8 inches long and 6 inches wide. When found, this nest contained 33 egg shells, 3 hatchlings, and a number of shed skins. Spring plowing in April and early May has failed to reveal any nests. The only obviously gravid female collected was obtained on June 24, 1939. On dissection this specimen was found to contain 20 eggs, the shells of which were very thin and soft, apparently not quite ready to be laid. On July 15, 1944 a female was found in the act of laying eggs and on the same day 2 other nests were found with eggs which contained embryos 60 mm. long. Laying, therefore, probably starts about the first week in July" (Richmond, Va., 1945).

Young—Hatching, Sept. 15 (Ditmars, Gen., 1936); early Sept. to Sept. 18 and 23 (Richmond, Va., 1945). Size, 9–10.5 inches (225–260 mm.). About 8–11 inches (Richmond, Va., 1954). The U.S. National Museum has young 244 and 256 mm. long with tail lengths of 48 and 36 mm.

"The hatchlings shed before leaving the nest. Characteristically, the nest in late September contains egg shells, a tangled mass of shed skins, and a few hatchlings; the remainder of the hatchlings are scattered through the near-by soil" (Richmond, Va., 1945).

The most important recent contribution to our knowledge of this form is Richmond's study of hatchlings (Va., 1954). From two lots of eggs collected

August 22, 1952, he had 58 hatchlings. Usually two weeks after hatching they shed. The males were about 195–215 mm. in length; with ventrals 155–162; caudals 44–49; while the females were 205–224 mm. in length; ventrals 170–175; caudals 35–42. He found differences in the position of the umbilical scar in the two sexes and also differences in ventral tail pattern. Surprisingly he found 25 per cent of the hatchlings had the single anal plates.

Food: Fish, frogs, eels, *Amphiuma, Siren,* earthworms.

Field notes: June 28, 1928, St. Petersburg, Fla. Visited the veteran collector N. Fry. He says they catch the rainbow snakes when the snakes burrow for laying their eggs. The snake burrows down into a sandy area and makes a burrow 1 foot or more wide. The collector thrusts a stick down in the sand a foot or more. If the snake "winches" he knows she is there. She lays her eggs in such places. It reminds one of the way collectors locate cocooned *Protopterus* in the Nile region.

Authorities:

Brimley, C. S. (N.C., 1941–42)
Haltom, W. L. (Ala., 1931)
McCauley, R. H., Jr. (Md., 1945)

Richmond, N. D., and C. J. Goin (Va., 1938)
Richmond, N. D. (Va., 1945, 1954)
Van Hyning, O. C. (Fla., 1931)

GLOSSY SNAKES

Genus *ARIZONA* Kennicott (Fig. 19)

Size medium to large medium, 16–56 inches, of which the tail is 4–6 inches or $\frac{1}{7}$–$\frac{1}{9}$ the total length; form medium, head slightly distinct; anal entire; caudals paired; scales smooth and glistening with faint single pits and in 27–31 rows; snout rather pointed, rostral penetrates between internasals depressing prenasal; lower jaw is inset; preoculars 1 (2), postoculars 2 (1); temporals (1) 2 + 3 (4, 5, 6); posterior chin shields separated, narrower and sometimes shorter than anterior; several rows of gulars between tips of chin shields and ventrals; upper labials (7) 8 (9); lower labials 11–15. "There are several minor characters, not generic, which show that its affinities are not with the species of *Pityophis*" (Cope, Gen., 1900). The relationship however is close and the hemipenial characters are similar. Hemipenis (*A. e. elegans*)—"The hemipenis is single and widens outwardly. The inner half is almost covered with tiny points, although these are less evident on the side opposite the sulcus. At the middle of the shaft the organ widens rather suddenly and simultaneously the points increase in size. However, even the longest probably do not reach a millimeter in length and most are barely half that length, so can hardly be referred to as spines. They are very densely set and are smallest in size along the sulcus. At the outer end the points change to reticulated flounces. . . . At the outer end there is a truncated surface at an

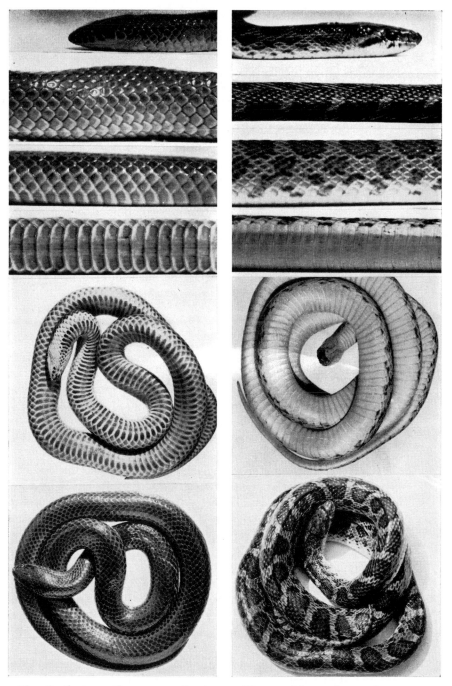

Fig. 26. *Abastor erythrogrammus,* Eureka, Marion Co., Fla., C. C. Tyler.

Fig. 27. *Arizona elegans elegans:* 1, 3–5, Brownsville, Tex., H. L. Blanchard; 2, San Antonio Reptile Garden, Tex.; 6, Poteet, Tex., Mrs. W. O. Learn.

angle with the shaft; this contains an unreticulated groove, which is reached by the sulcus passing over the outermost part of the organ" (Klauber). Transition to spines occurs in midshaft in *eburnata* and *occidentalis*. Ventrals 185–241, caudals 39–63. Synonyms: *Coluber, Pituophis, Pityophis, Rhinechis.*

KEY TO THE GENUS *ARIZONA* [1]

a. Scale rows 29 or 31, tail 14.2–15.7% of total length, ⅐ or a trifle over.

  b. Body blotches 42–56, crossing 13–15 scale rows, their length 2–4, most often 3–3½ scale rows, interspace 1–2 scale rows. Tail 14.9% in ♂, 14.2% in ♀. Preoculars 1 or 2. Anterior temporals long and slender, slanting upward posteriorly. Ventrals exceed 210 in ♂, 221 in ♀.

                                                      A. elegans elegans

  bb. Body blotches 47–66, crossing 12–13 scale rows, length 2–3 rows, interspace 1½ rows. Tail relatively long, 15.7% in ♂, 14.7% in ♀. Anterior temporals long and slender, parallel edged and directed upward posteriorly. Ventrals 210 or less in ♂, 221 or less in ♀.

                                                        A. e. blanchardi

aa. Scale rows 27 (occasionally 29).

  b. Tail longer, 16.1% of total length in ♂, 14.8% in ♀, over ⅐ of total length. Body blotches extreme range 52–72, usually 58–65, width 11 scale rows, length 2 rows, interspace 1 row. Anterior temporals attenuated and slant upward posteriorly.   *A. e. philipi*

  bb. Tail shorter, less than ⅐ total length, 13.9% in ♂ in *candida*, 12.5% in ♀ in *candida* and *occidentalis*. Body blotches extreme range 51–83, usually 56–72, width 7–11 scale rows, length 1¼–2, interspace 1½–2 rows.

    c. Body blotches equal or exceed interspaces in longitudinal extent.

      d. Body blotches 51–75; tail spots 13–25. Lowest lateral spots on ends of ventrals or scale row 1. Color darker. Spots often present on lower labials.   *A. e. occidentalis*

      dd. Body blotches 52–67; tail spots 15–23. No marks on ends of ventrals. Color lighter, lower labials clear, except occasionally spotted on last one.   *A. e. noctivaga*

    cc. Body blotches of less extent longitudinally than interspaces.

      d. Lowest lateral spots intrude on ventrals or are on scale row 1.

                                         A. e. occidentalis

      dd. Lowest lateral spots rarely touch a line below scale row 2. Color lighter.

        e. 1 preocular; dorsal blotches at mid-body rarely cross more than 7 scale rows. Blotches 55–83 on body; 15–29 on tail.

                                       A. e. eburnata

---

[1] Data mostly from Klauber: "Tail length, scale rows, ventral scutes and pattern most important characters in segregating subspecies."

ee. Usually 2 preoculars; dorsal blotches at mid-body cross 9 scale
rows. Body blotches 55–73; tail 14–24.   *A. e. candida*

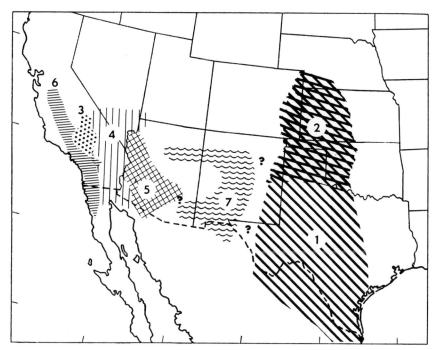

Map 11. *Arizona*—1, *e. elegans;* 2, *e. blanchardi;* 3, *e. candida;* 4, *e. eburnata;* 5, *e. noctivaga;* 6, *e. occidentalis;* 7, *e. philipi.*

Faded snake (6—Van Denburgh 1924), **Glossy snake**

Arizona elegans elegans Kennicott 1859. Fig. 27; Map 11

Other common names: [1] Arizona snake; elegant bull snake; Kennicott's
snake; mouse snake; sand snake; slender gopher snake; smooth-scaled Coluber; smooth-scaled gopher snake; Texas glossy snake.

Range: From longitude 98° in Texas to 104° in New Mexico and w.
Texas exclusive of the Panhandle, that is, s. of the Red River. In the lower
Rio Grande Valley it extends eastward to 97°. Klauber in 1946 meant Texas
west rather than Texas "east," of long, 98°.—U.S.A.: N.M.; Tex. Mex.:
Tamaulipas to Chihuahua, Coahuila. *Elevation*—100 to 4,000 feet. 3,800
feet (Klauber).

Size: Adults, 20–56 inches.

Distinctive characteristics: Large medium, wood brown or mouse gray
snake with fuscous-centered dorsal blotches with orange-cinnamon or snuff

---

[1] This topic is omitted under Klauber's new species (1946) which follow this account.

brown interspaces; under parts shining white or pale olive-buff—the darkest of the *Arizona* species.

"Thirty-one or 29 dorsal scale rows; and dark well-defined blotches, longer than the interspaces. *Elegans* can be segregated from all subspecies except *blanchardi* by its having 31 and 29 scale rows, while the other subspecies usually have 27 rows, although they may occasionally have 29. However, those western subspecies which have the highest frequency of 29 rows (*occidentalis, eburnata,* and *noctivaga*) still average well below *elegans;* also they have proportionally shorter tails and differ in various details of pattern. The subspecies most like *elegans* is *blanchardi,* which however has fewer ventrals and more body blotches on the average than *elegans*" (Klauber).

Color: A snake from San Antonio, Tex., May 21, 1925; recently shed. The general background color is light grayish olive. The back is marked with transverse bands of hair brown or mouse gray which become on the tail almost drab. These bands are bordered with fuscous black. The dorsal interspaces covering two scale rows are orange cinnamon or vinaceous cinnamon. Many scales on the sides between the dark spots are also marked with this color. On the sides, alternating with the dorsal bands, are round spots of hair brown or mouse gray, with darker borders almost absent. Alternating with these spots are smaller spots on the 3rd and 4th rows of scales. These lowest spots are not encircled with dark borders. Some of the scales of the 1st to 3rd rows are tinged with sulphur yellow, ivory yellow, or marguerite yellow. The general color of the head is hair brown or light drab, becoming a drab gray on the side. Two spots of deep brownish drab occur on the rear of the frontal, one on the front of the parietal, and one on the suture of the parietals. There is a postocular stripe of deep brownish drab and also a band of the same from eye to eye on the posterior edge of the prefrontals. There is another shorter stripe of deep brownish drab parallel to the postocular stripe and extending from the parietal backward. From the spot on the parietal suture a stripe extends for an inch or less along the neck. This stripe is at first deep brownish drab, becoming on the neck light vinaceous cinnamon. The upper labials are more or less white. The iris is hair brown or deep brownish drab with some fuscous dots. The pupil ring is terra cotta. The entire under parts are glistening white.

Habitat: For this best-known variety of the glossy snake the notes are few. Again we turn, as we have turned for a quarter of a century, to one of the San Antonio triumvirate (Mr. and Mrs. R. D. Quillin and A. J. Kirn). Excerpts from Kirn's letter to Klauber follow: "All the specimens taken by me were found in the daytime; I do not recall seeing them at night. . . . When I come upon any of these snakes they usually contract themselves into short bends or kinks for the entire length of the body. One, for example, had 11 kinks. I do not know if this is done for fright or if it is a method of defence; they never offer to strike. They do not coil, but remain in a traveling position. This is of course in the daytime. These snakes are frequently plowed up by farmers when breaking land. This would indicate that they do not go deep into the ground; probably they seek refuge in mole, kangaroo rat or possibly pocket gopher holes. Most of the specimens I have secured are from 7½ miles southwest of Somerset. The country round about is sandy to very sandy. There are woods and cultivated fields. The woods, on more sandy land, are 'black jack' oak, mixed with hickory and live-oak. The topography is gently rolling; there is little rock except in gullies, and some sandstone outcrops. I think *Arizona* well-dispersed throughout this region, especially in the more sandy areas."

At the beginning of the century Brown (Gen., 1901; Tex., 1903) doubtless saw more of them alive than anyone else. He thought of them as "brownish or reddish yellow above" or "reddish or pink on the dorsal line, between the spots." His largest from Pecos, Texas, measured 1,100 mm. (tail 510 mm.).

Period of activity: *First appearance*—Feb. 23, Mar. 4, Apr. 28, May 31 (Kirn in Klauber), May 5 (Marr, Gen., 1944); Mar. 12, Apr. 4, May 19 (Burt, Tex., 1935b). *Fall disappearance*—Sept. 5 (Kirn in Klauber).

Breeding: Oviparous. *Eggs*—Kirn wrote to Klauber: "One female I collected May 31, 1940, measured 42½ inches; it contained 12 eggs. Another laid 9 eggs." Conant and Bridges (Gen., 1939) mentioned "one record of 10." *Young*—"The smallest specimen measured 293 mm., and having been collected August 18, must have been but a few days old. . . . There is another specimen only 195 mm. in length, but its condition is such I cannot be sure it is an *Arizona*" (Klauber). In a letter Kirn wrote: "I do have a little *Arizona*, length 7.90 inches (191.5 mm.), collected Sept. 2nd, 1940, here at my station."

Food: Moles, rodents. Klauber, Kirn.

Field notes: May 7, 1925, San Antonio, Tex.: At Mrs. W. Odell Learn's establishment was one *Arizona elegans*. The boy called it a "sand snake." When she came she said that she had to have it for a previous order, seeing I had taken all her highly colored ones a few days before (coral snake, Le Conte's snake, copperhead, splendid king snake, and Schott's racer). This was sad, not to secure it and to have to yield it to a showman.

May 14, 1925, San Antonio, Tex.: In spite of good-natured nudging by my better half I stayed away from Mrs. Learn's place, but today returned to the *Arizona* quest. The lady says, "I have an elegant snake, let me wash it off." It is the *very same snake* I could not get May 7. It is now shedding but it never bites us. It is a very strong constrictor and is very willowy.

Authorities:

Blanchard, F. N. (Gen., 1924d) Klauber, L. M. (Gen., 1946)
Kennicott, R. (Tex., 1859)

Kansas glossy snake (2—Klauber 1946)

Arizona elegans blanchardi Klauber 1946. Fig. 28; Map 11

Range: Between 98° and 103° longitude, n. of the Red River; in panhandles of Texas and Oklahoma, n.e. New Mexico, w. Oklahoma and Kansas, s.w. corner of Nebraska, and n.e. corner of Colorado.—Colo.; Kans.; Neb.; N.M.; Okla.; Tex. *Elevation*—Mainly 1,000 to 4,000 feet, rarely 5,000 feet. 3,500 feet (Klauber).

Size: Adults, 16–47 inches.

Distinctive characteristics: "*Blanchardi* is a large blotched, dark-colored subspecies with 29 or 31 scale rows and a relatively long tail. While some western subspecies (*occidentalis, eburnata,* and *noctivaga*) occasionally have 29 scale rows, they have more blotches and shorter tails. *Blanchardi* has more ventrals than *philipi* or *expolita*. It is nearest to *elegans,* from which it differs in having, on the average, a lower number of ventrals and more blotches" (Klauber).

Color: A snake from 9 miles e. of Stinett, Tex., kindly furnished by W. F. Blair, July 26, 1950. The background color is light pinkish cinnamon, the dorsum marked with 53 body blotches and 16 spots on the tail. These blotches are snuff brown bordered with sepia on front and rear edges, the lateral ends mostly free of this border. The blotches are 10–13 scales wide and 2–3 scales long (scale tip to scale tip), with interspaces 1 + ⅔ scales in length and 8 scales wide, absolutely clear of dusky marks but heavily touched with zinc orange. Below these intervals and surrounding the ends of the blotches and lateral spots, each scale of the background is centered with dusky and many are marked with zinc orange flecks, some of which come on to rows 2 and 3. Rows 1–3 are naphthalene yellow, clear of dusky marks. There is a series of rounded lateral spots on rows 5–9 with but slight indication of a border of sepia. On the forward part of body are faint indications of a lower row alternating with the series on rows 5–9. These consist of dark smudges on rows 2 and 3. On the neck, somewhat back from the parietals, are 2 longitudinal spots like the dorsal saddles. From the lower edge of one of these longitudinal spots an oblique line of cinnamon-brown extends to the rear of the frontal and then obliquely back to the lower edge of the other longitudinal spot. Parallel with this and lower is a postocular band which starts at the last labial and passes through the eye and across the head, involving the cephalic edge of the supraocular and frontal as well as the rear half of the prefrontal. There is a slight vertical spot of dusky below the eye on the suture of upper labials 4 and 5. The iris is cartridge buff with touches of pale cinnamon-pink. The rostral, lower edges of upper labials, and entire under parts are clear glistening white. There is a tendency toward a square edge on the belly plates as in *Elaphe*. Scale rows 31. Length,

33 inches over all, tail 4⅝ inches. The anterior temporals are long and slender with parallel edges and directed upward toward the rear.

Habitat: This night-roving snake has been taken in sand dunes (Taylor; Smith and Leonard); in sandy sage-brush country and in pasture land above a large lake (Burt and Hoyle); near wheat fields (Burt, 1935); in "sandy areas, semi-arid regions on flat plains" (Smith).

Period of activity: *First appearance*—May 27, 28 (Marr); May 25, 29 (Burt, 1935). *Fall disappearance*—Sept. 10 (Marr).

Breeding: Oviparous. *Eggs*—Burt and Hoyle "took a female 6 miles east of Erick, Beckham County, Oklahoma, on June 10, 1933. . . . [It] was . . . with 10 large eggs in the right oviduct and none in the left." *Young*—"The shortest specimen measured 290 mm." (Klauber).

Food: Kangaroo rat. Marr.

Authorities: [1]

Burt, C. E. (Gen., 1935; Kan., 1933)
Burt, C. E., and W. L. Hoyle (Gen., 1935)
Hudson, G. E. (Neb., 1942)
Klauber, L. M. (Gen., 1946)
Marr, J. C. (Gen., 1927)
Smith, H. M. (Kan., 1950)
Smith, H. M., and A. B. Leonard (Okla., 1934)
Taylor, E. H. (Kan., 1929b)

Western Mojave glossy snake (2—Klauber 1946)

Arizona elegans candida Klauber 1946. Fig. 29; Map 11

Range: "The Antelope Valley and extreme western Mojave Desert, including the desert areas of southwestern Inyo County, southeastern Kern County, northeastern Los Angeles County, and western San Bernardino County, California." *Elevation*—2,490 to 4,000⁺ feet (Klauber).

Size: Adults, 17–35 inches.

Distinctive characteristics: "*Candida* is a subspecies characterized by its light color, narrow dorsal blotches and the high frequency of paired preoculars. It differs from all subspecies except *eburnata* in having dorsal blotches which are uniformly shorter (along the body) than the interspaces which separate them. From *eburnata* it differs in its high proportion of paired preoculars, and somewhat wider and fewer dorsal blotches which usually engage 7 scale rows in *eburnata* and 9 in *candida*. Also, the latter has

---

[1] 1955: Fouquette and Lindsay (*Texas Jour. Sci.*, 7:413–415) found that "two things are apparent . . . (1) the entire northwestern Texas series is intermediate between the races of *blanchardi* and *elegans*, and (2) there is a clinal increase in ventral scute counts evident from northern to southern populations. . . . It is probably safe to conclude that either (1) there is no restriction of gene flow between the proposed races, therefore they should again be considered as one; or (2) ventral count cannot be considered valid as a diagnostic character separating the proposed races."

Fig. 28. *Arizona e. blanchardi,* Stinnett, Tex., W. F. Blair.

Fig. 29. *Arizona e. candida,* Palmdale, Calif., W. Lasky.

fewer ventral scutes on the average, although there is considerable overlapping" (Klauber).

Color: A snake from Palmdale, Los Angeles Co., Calif., kindly furnished by Bill Lasky and Bob Goldfarb, June, 1940. The back is marked with dorsal saddles of deep olive-buff oulined with deep olive on a background of pale vinaceous-fawn to vinaceous-buff, 69 on body, 22 on tail. The lateral spots on the 4th and 5th scale rows are deep olive. The top of the head is vinaceous-buff. There is a dark band bordering prefrontals and frontal extending from eye to eye, and through the eye to the angle of the mouth. Across the head it is tawny-olive, back of the eye black or deep olive. There is also a bar from eye to upper labial margin across the 4th upper labial. A few spots mark the parietal suture. The iris is cinnamon buff with black tracery. The ventral color of pale olive-buff extends over 2½ rows of dorsal scales, above which for 2 or 3 rows the scale centers are washed with wood brown or avellaneous.

Habitat: Upon its describer, Klauber, we depend for our knowledge of this form. "Most specimens were collected at night when the character of the surrounding country could not be ascertained, but the classification would usually be light brushy desert. The following additional surroundings have been observed: heavy brush, medium brush, Joshua trees, and sandy desert. . . . It is my judgment that in the spring, when the desert cools quickly after sunset, the snakes seek refuge early; in summer they may be active all night, and then, in fact, the temperatures may be most suitable just before dawn. But on the cold and windy spring nights, one may readily infer from the presence of live snakes early in the evening and DOR's later, that the time of maximum activity is soon passed. At any rate, the nocturnal character of this desert snake is not to be doubted, for I have yet to find a specimen abroad in the daytime. Of the 44 snakes whose time of collection we recorded, the earliest was 7:15 P.M. (May 10, 1941) about one-half hour after sunset. The maximum seasonal activity I should place at about June 10, somewhat later than that of *eburnata* in the Colorado Desert, which at a lower altitude warms earlier. . . . In the section of the desert which it inhabits, *candida* is the second commonest snake."

Breeding: Oviparous. *Eggs*—"One specimen 856 mm. long contained 10 eggs; another 661 mm. in length 4 eggs" (Klauber). *Young*—"The smallest specimen measured 245 mm." (Klauber). Klauber (Gen., 1943b) gives 245 mm. female and 275 mm. male.

Food: Lizards and pocket mice. Klauber.

Authority: Klauber, L. M. (Gen., 1946)

Desert glossy snake (3—Klauber 1946)

Arizona elegans eburnata Klauber 1946. Fig. 30; Map 11

Range: From the head of the Gulf of California in n.e. Baja California and n.w. Sonora n. across Yuma Desert, and thereafter w. of Colorado R. to the center of the Mojave Desert, thence e. to s.w. Utah.—U.S.A.: Ariz.; Calif.; Nev.; Ut. Mex.: Baja Calif.; Sonora. *Elevation*—240 to 2,800 feet (Klauber).

Size: Adults, 17–46 inches.

Distinctive characteristics: "A desert subspecies characterized by small and narrow blotches, light color, and high ventral scale counts. It differs from all others except *candida* in having blotches markedly shorter than the interspaces which separate them. Other differences are as follows: From *elegans* and *blanchardi* it differs in having fewer scale rows and subcaudals; from *occidentalis* in its lighter color, narrower blotches, and immaculate infralabials and lower lateral scale rows; from *noctivaga* by its narrower blotches; from *philipi* and *expolita* by its greater number of body blotches. *Eburnata* can be segregated from *candida* since it has 1 preocular, while the Mohave Desert form generally has 2; also, the dorsal blotches of the latter usually engage 9 scale rows compared to 7 in *eburnata*" (Klauber, 1946).

Color: Snake from Coachella Valley, Calif., seen at California Serpentarium; kindness of C. M. Perkins and A. P. Artran, July, 1934. The spaces between the dorsal saddles are cream buff or cartridge buff. The dorsal saddles are drab or grayish olive. The lateral spots are the same. Sometimes the dorsal saddles break into 2 spots. The interspaces below the dorsal saddles have drab- or buffy-brown-centered scales. These transversal saddles are almost absent on the dorsum of the tail, where the vertebral band of cream buff or cartridge buff extends to the tip. The white of the belly extends on to the first 2½ rows of scales. There is a dark band bordering the prefrontals and frontal from eye to eye and through the eye to the angle of the mouth. Back of the eye this band may be almost black. (Van Denburgh: "These streaks are faded or absent in adults.") Two spots on either rear frontosupraocular suture. There is a band of drab or black on the occipital suture. There are two long drab or buffy brown nuchal spots, 8 scales long and 4 scales wide. The iris is cinnamon buff with heavy tracery of black over it. The ventral surfaces are glistening white.

Habitat: "The lowest temperatures at which this species was observed above ground were 14° and 18°C. . . . At 19°–20°C. appearances become more frequent, and it is probable that this constitutes a normal lower limit for voluntary surface activity. . . . Under laboratory conditions these snakes reached their critical maximum at 42, 42, 41, 42, 43°C., mean 41.8°C. Putative lethal temperatures were 43°–44°C. (6 observations)" (Cowles and Bogert).

"*Eburnata* occupies the largest area of the truly desert subspecies of *Ari-*

zona. It is found in a variety of surroundings, from an almost barren desert or sand dunes, to places where brush
cover is quite dense. While not absent
from rocky areas, it does not prefer
them, and is less plentiful in such situations than on the sandy flats. . . .
That *eburnata* is nocturnal can be
readily shown by a list of the hours
when specimens have been encountered on the road [list omitted]"
(Klauber, 1946).

Period of activity: *First appearance—*
Mar. 19. "The only snake of this kind
obtained, No. 33452, was dug out of a
hole in a sand hill east of Yuma, March
19, 1912" (Van Denburgh and Slevin);
May (Cowles and Bogert, Nev., 1936);
Feb. 20 (Cowles); May 26 (Linsdale);
Mar. 11 (Klauber, 1946). *Hibernation*
—These observations, together with a
few records on caged specimens, give
the impression that the species is one
of the most cold-tolerant snakes in
southern California and lead to the
belief that, if continuous hibernation
exists, it is probably of very short duration, possibly extending only from the
middle of December through January.

Breeding: Oviparous. *Eggs—*"A
large gravid female was captured in
Coachella Valley July 7, 1940, at 8 A.M.
in full sun. The day was cloudless
and hot, probably well over 38°C., in
the shade. To judge by the tracks in
the sand the snake had been very active, presumably during the night and
early morning, boring in and out of
the ground near a large hummock of
earth. It was probably seeking a suitable spot for oviposition. She deposited
23 eggs the following day, and these
hatched after 68 days of incubation at
room temperature, which fluctuated

Fig. 30. *Arizona e. eburnata,* Coachella,
Calif., C. M. Perkins and A. P. Artran.

between 25° and 32°C. At 8 days of age the young were tested for the critical maximum and responded at 38°–39°C." (Cowles and Bogert). *Young*—"The smallest specimen measured 213 mm." (Klauber). Blanchard's smallest is 294 mm. (Gen., 1924d).

Food: Lizards, mice, small birds. Van Denburgh, Perkins, Reynolds (Calif., 1943).

Authorities:

Cowles, R. B. (Gen., 1941a)

Cowles, R. B., and C. M. Bogert (Gen., 1944)

Klauber, L. M. (Gen., 1938, 1946; Calif., 1932)

Linsdale, J. M. (Nev., 1938–40)

Perkins, C. B. (Calif., 1949)

Tanner, W. W. (Ut., 1954)

Van Denburgh, J. (Gen., 1922)

Van Denburgh, J., and J. R. Slevin (Ariz., 1913)

Arizona glossy snake (2—Klauber 1946)

Arizona elegans noctivaga Klauber 1946. Fig. 31; Map 11

Range: "Arizona west and south of the Central Mountains, but excluding the Yuma mesa and Yuma Desert; also excluding Cochise County" (Klauber 1946).—U.S.A.: Ariz. Mex.: Sonora. *Elevation*—At least 1,000 to 3,500$^+$ feet. 3,500 ft. (Klauber, 1946).

Size: Adults. 18–42 inches.

Distinctive characteristics: *"Noctivaga* is a subspecies belonging to the short-tailed group, with body blotches slightly more extensive than the spaces which separate them, and usually with 27 scale rows. It has fewer scale rows than *elegans* or *blanchardi,* has more ventrals and a shorter tail than *philipi* or *expolita* and more body blotches than *pacata.* From *eburnata* and *candida* it may be distinguished by the relative longitudinal extents of the dorsal blotches and interspaces; in *noctivaga* the blotches exceed the spaces between, while the contrary is true of the others. Although *noctivaga* is territorially separated from *occidentalis* by the interposition of *eburnata,* they are superficially much alike and I know of no single character which will invariably separate them. *Noctivaga* has fewer ventrals on the average, fewer body blotches, and is usually lighter on the sides, with less regularly secondary spots, and with the lower lateral scale rows freer both of spots and the brownish ground color suffusion. It also lacks the brown marks on the lower labials which usually characterize *occidentalis,* although not those from the San Joaquin Valley" (Klauber).

Color: "The color of this specimen, about one foot in length, may be described as follows: General ground color of the 2 or 3 middorsal scale rows tilleul buff, that of rows 4 to 11 sorghum brown (with edges of scales white); rows 1 to 3 and scutes blue-white; dorsal blotches on anterior three-quarters of body mummy brown narrowly edged with fuscous black, this mummy

Fig. 31. *Arizona e. noctivaga:* 1, Organ Pipe Nat. Monument, Ariz., M. Hensley; 2,3, Wickenburg, Ariz.

brown changing on posterior blotches to clay color; sides of body on scale rows 3, 4, and 5 sparsely speckled with bone brown; small lateral blotches of mummy brown also present which lack the black outline present in the dorsal blotches; skin between dorsal scales mauve; general color of top of head bone brown as are also a stripe from eye to angle of mouth and line between 4th and 5th supralabials; an indefinite ventral light stripe of pale wistaria blue occupying middle quarter of scutes" (Ortenburger).

Habitat: "Creosote bush association on the plains east of Tucson" (Ruthven). "During the latter part of May and early June we worked the roads of the desert west of Superior almost every night. . . . Among the snakes [was] . . . the 'faded snake' (*Arizona elegans*)" (Gloyd). "*Noctivaga,* as the name implies, is nocturnal; this is shown by the following evening times of collection: 8:30, 9:20, 9:33, 9:40, 9:50 (2), 10:10, 10:37, 10:45, 11:00, 11:25, 11:30, 11:40. I have no daytime collection records. The following air temperatures in degrees F. were noted when specimens were found alive on the road: 70, 72 (2), 78 (2), 85 (2), 86, 90. . . . Other surroundings where specimens have been found were as follows: Fields (cultivated), grass, mesquite, brushy desert, rocky desert. . . . While *noctivaga* appears almost white in the glare of auto headlights against the black background of a paved road, the type specimen was collected on a dirt road and appeared darker than its background" (Klauber).

Breeding: Oviparous. *Young*—"The smallest specimen measured 272 mm." (Klauber). Blanchard (Gen., 1924d) has recorded a female of 270 mm.

Food: Flood and Wiklund on two Arizonas, collected June 20, P.M., and June 21, A.M., 31 and 24¾ inches respectively, observed that they ate: "7⁄16 —1 12-day old ratling; 7⁄20—4 rat hams; 7⁄25—1 rat ham (large); 8⁄9 shed skin; 8⁄9—2 rat legs; 8⁄16—2 rat hams."

Field notes: June 10, 1942, Wickenburg, Ariz., to Aquila, near Forepaugh: Took 2 *Arizona elegans occidentalis* (*noctivaga*), one half-grown and dead and one adult alive but skinned on side of the neck. Most of our snakes this night were taken on the open flat desert from Forepaugh westward.

Authorities:

Flood, W. A., Jr., and E. Wiklund (Ariz., 1949)
Gloyd, H. K. (Ariz., 1940)
Klauber, L. M. (Gen., 1946)

Ortenburger, A. I. and R. D. (Ariz., 1927)
Ruthven, A. G. (Ariz., 1907)

Western faded snake (11—Klauber 1928),
Faded snake (5—Van Denburgh 1897)

Arizona elegans occidentalis Blanchard 1924. Fig. 32; Map 11

Other common names: (California or western) glossy snake; smooth-scaled Coluber; southwestern smooth-scaled gopher snake.

Range: San Joaquin Co. through Central Valley to Tehachapi Mts.; coastal region from Los Angeles Co. s. in to Baja California. *Elevation*—Sea level to 3,132 feet (Klauber).

Size: Adults, 20–46 inches.

Distinctive characteristics: "Occidentalis is a subspecies inhabiting a territory having a considerable ecological variability and therefore it is subject in itself to considerable variation. It is characterized by a darker color than the other western subspecies. It may be distinguished from *elegans* and *blanchardi* by its usually having 27 scale rows compared with 29 or 31 in the eastern forms. Also, its blotches average higher in number and are narrower across the body. *Occidentalis* has more ventrals and a proportionally shorter tail than *philipi* or *expolita* and more blotches than *pacata*. It is darker in color and with lower spots and brownish suffusions on the sides than *eburnata* or *candida*. Although territorally separated from *noctivaga* by *eburnata* and *candida,* it is most like the Arizona form. However, *noctivaga* has fewer ventrals on the average, is usually lighter on the sides, and the lower lateral scale rows are freer of spots, as is also true of the infralabials" (Klauber).

Habitat: From Klauber: "I have never found a specimen abroad in the daytime, the earliest being 6:25 P.M. at La Posta." "*Occidentalis* is so much darker than *eburnata* and *candida* particularly from a lateral view, that it is relatively difficult to see at night. Thus, we have nothing like the success in collecting this subspecies that has attended our desert efforts [in San Joaquin Valley he had better success]." "In San Diego County it is known to occur in all ecological zones." "The relative frequency of surroundings where specimens have been found is shown in the following list: Grass (uncultivated) 12, Field (cultivated) 17, Light brush 7, Chaparral 7, Barren field 4, Orchard 3, Sand 1, Rocks 1, Total 62. This list indicates a definite preference for open areas."

Cook's note of 1930 is also pertinent: "Soon after sunset, when preparing to leave for home, a plank was overturned revealing an *Arizona elegans occidentalis* or western faded snake, nearly 12 inches long. It was nosing its way through the sand and did not seem disturbed by my presence."

Period of activity: *First appearance*—Feb. 23 (Cook); May 11 (Hanley); May 24 (Reynolds). "Seasonally, *Arizona* seems to be a trifle later than the other snakes of the area, for June slightly exceeds May as the peak month, whereas the contrary is true of most of the other species" (Klauber). *Hibernation*—"Specimens of *Arizona* are occasionally plowed out, showing that they hibernate at a comparatively shallow depth. I have records of specimens being plowed out on Feb. 10, 23, and 24. Paul Brese found one under a foot of sand in a vineyard. . . . L. H. Cook found one under a board; another was disclosed by turning over a rock, while a third was buried in sand" (Klauber).

Breeding: Oviparous. *Eggs*—"The female *Arizona* deposited three very

Fig. 32. *Arizona e. occidentalis,* McKittrick, Calif., collected by
K. Murray, photo by N. Cohen. *Arizona e. philipi:* 2, El Paso, Tex.,
M. L. Crimmins; 3, Organ Pipe Mts., N.M., T. H. Lewis.

elongate and cylindrical eggs July 22, 1940. The shells were white and had a leathery, flexible texture. The sizes of the eggs (in mm.) and the weight in grams were as follows: 57x17, weight 12.37; 60x17, weight 11.01; and 63x16, weight 11.40" (Reynolds). Klauber has recorded a female 731 mm. from Fresno containing 7 eggs. *Young*—"The smallest specimen is 248 mm. in length" (Klauber). Blanchard recorded a female 285 and a male 170 mm.

Food: Mice, lizards. Van Denburgh, Cook, Hanley, Reynolds, Linsdale (Baja Calif., 1932), and Perkins.

Authorities:

Blanchard, F. M. (Gen., 1924d)   Perkins, C. B. (Calif., 1949)
Cook, L. H. (Calif., 1930)   Pickwell, G. B. (Gen., 1947)
Hanley, G. H. (Calif., 1942)   Reynolds, F. A. (Calif., 1943)
Klauber, L. M. (Gen., 1946)   Van Denburgh, J. (Gen., 1922)

1949, C. B. Perkins: "This moderately rare snake, a large specimen of which would be about 3 feet long, is found from the ocean to the desert foothills, but not in the high mountains."

Painted Desert glossy snake (2—Klauber 1946)

Arizona elegans philipi Klauber 1946. Fig. 32; Map 11

Range: Painted Desert, Ariz. e. to Santa Fe, N.M.; s. to El Paso Co., Tex., and n. Chihuahua, Mex.; w. to Cochise Co., Ariz. U.S.A.: Ariz.; N.M.; Tex. Mex.: Chihuahua. *Elevation*—3,700 to 6,000 feet. 5,500 feet (Klauber).

Size: Adults, 16–37 inches.

Distinctive characteristics: "A subspecies characterized by a low number of ventral scutes and a relatively long tail. In the latter character it is like *elegans* and *blanchardi*, from which, however, it may readily be distinguished by its lower number of scale rows; *philipi* like the other subspecies farther west, usually has 27 rows, while *elegans* and *blanchardi* have 29 or 31. From *noctivaga* and the other subspecies farther west, *philipi* may be distinguished by its longer tail; thus it is seen to be a transition form between the eastern and western subspecies—like the former in tail proportionality and the latter in scale rows. Only *expolita*, a southern extension of *philipi*, occupies a similarly intermediate position, but *expolita* has fewer dorsal blotches than *philipi*" (Klauber).

Breeding: Oviparous. *Young*—"The Canyon Diablo specimen is a juvenile female evidently hatched but a short time before collection. It measures 249 mm. over all, with a 35 mm. tail" (Klauber). Blanchard has 2 females, 254, 272 mm., and 1 male, 299 mm.

Field notes: July 16, 1925, El Paso, Tex.; guests of Col. and Mrs. M. L. Crimmins: He was very anxious to take me to Mr. McLennan's taxidermy shop, where they had a very interesting exhibit. It was the original specimen of the photograph which Colonel Crimmins gave us. The photograph has on its back the following: "This chicken snake was found by Pvt. Gordon H. Spencer, 1st Signal Corps, 1st Cavalry Division, Ft. Bliss." It had a horned toad stuck in its throat and both were dead.

June 2, 1934, El Paso, Tex.: Just out of El Paso, northward, found in the road a recently dead *A. e. elegans* (*philipi*). It tends somewhat toward Blanchard's *A. e. occidentalis* in number and width of dorsal blotches.

July 17, 1942: On trip to Alamagordo from Las Cruces, about 9 or 10 miles toward San Augustine Pass, picked up an *A. elegans* (*philipi*).

Authorities:

Blanchard, F. N. (Gen., 1924d)   Klauber, L. M. (Gen., 1946)
Bogert, C. M. (Ariz., 1933)   Van Denburgh, J. (N.M., 1924b)

WORM SNAKES

Genus *CARPHOPHIS* Gervais (Fig. 21)

Size very small, 7–14.5 inches; slender cylindrical; head small, depressed, not distinct from body; tail moderate acute; anal divided; scales smooth, shining, without pits, in 13 rows; upper labials 5, lower 6 (5); large loreal and prefrontal enter orbit; no preocular; 1 postocular; supraocular small; internasals present or absent; frontal broad, almost equal to length; nasal single, entire; temporals 1 + 1 or 1 + 2; few or no gulars between posterior chin shields and ventrals; eye small; venter pink to carrot red or "salmon red" (Blatchley, Ind., 1900); maxillary and mandibular teeth very small, subequal, maxillary about 10. Hemipenis—undivided, sulcus forked, crown calyculate, calyces fringed (subfamily Dromicinae, see Cope, Gen., 1900, p. 733). Ventrals 112–146; caudals 23–28. Synonyms: *Brachyorrhos, Calamaria, Carphophiops, Celuta, Coluber.*

KEY TO THE GENUS *CARPHOPHIS*

a. Light color extending onto row 3 of dorsal scales; color above generally gray or black.   *C. a. vermis*

aa. Light color extending onto rows 1 and 2 of dorsal scales; color above generally brown.

    b. Prefrontals and internasals usually fused into 2 large shields.

                                                  C. a. helenae

    bb. Prefrontals and internasals separate.   *C. amoenus amoenus*

Worm snake (48—Baird and Girard 1853),
Ground snake (30—Baird and Girard)

Carphophis amoenus amoenus (Say) 1825. Fig. 33; Map 12

Other common names: Blind snake; blind worm; cricket snake; eastern ground snake; eastern twig snake; eastern worm snake; (little) red snake; milk snake; thunder snake.

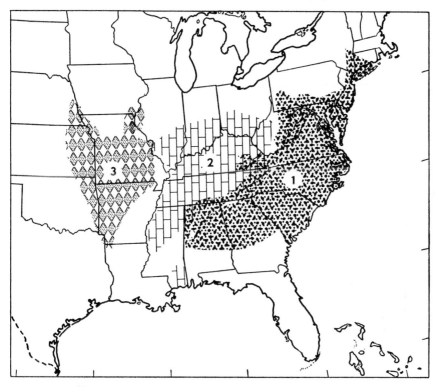

Map 12. *Carphophis—1, amoenus; 2, a. helenae; 3, a. vermis.*

Range: Coast and piedmont from Albany Co., N.Y., s. across Connecticut to cent. Georgia, penetrating Appalachians in w. Pennsylvania, West Virginia, and s.e. Kentucky and e. Tennessee.—Ala.; Conn.; D.C.; Del.; Fla.(?); Ga.; Ky.; La.(?); Mass.; Md.; Me.; N.C.; N.J.; N.Y.; Pa.; R.I.; Tenn.; Va.; W. Va. *Elevation*—Sea level to 4,300 feet (King). 2,500–3,000 (Dunn, N.C., 1917). "Upland forests to 300 ft." (Wilson and Friddle, W. Va., 1950).

Size: Adults, 7–13 inches.

Distinctive characteristics: Very small, cylindrical, solid, opalescent snakes, dark chestnut or mummy brown above; translucent belly, congo pink. Tail moderately short with sharp point. Prefrontals and internasals separate; light color extending to dorsal scale row 1 or 2.

Color: Snake sent to Trapido from New Jersey, May, 1936. The back is bister or mummy brown becoming on the upper sides olive brown. The ventral surface and 1½ rows of dorsal scales are congo pink. The rear edge of each ventral is heavily striated at right angles to the edge. The upper labials are congo pink except for the upper edges, which are like the dorsum. The iris is black. *Abnormal coloration*—Allard reports from his garden in Virginia a completely pink female with no hint of the normal chestnut brown dorsal coloration.

Habitat: See good accounts by Corrington, McCauley, Trapido, and Barbour. The habitats were recorded as follows: under logs 20, stones 16, leaves 7, bark slabs 5, rubbish 4, boards 4, rocks 3; in woods or wooded areas 13, open loose soft ground 8, gardens 5, rotten stumps 4, potato patch 1, weedy pasture 1, vegetation 1, rotten tree trunks 1, sawdust piles 1. Eight authors have them ploughed up, 4 speak of hoeing or spading them out. Road construction in wooded areas sometimes yields them.

Period of activity: *First appearance*—May 17, 1934 (Conant and Bailey, N.J., 1936); May 20, 1902 (Bishop). *Fall disappearance*—Sept. 7, 1935 (Conant and Bailey); Oct. 16 (Bishop, N.C., 1928). *Seasonal catch*—Brimley (N.C., 1925) caught 2 Jan., 1 Feb., 13 Mar., 16 Apr., 11 May, 4 June, 2 July, 3 Aug., 1 Sept., 9 Oct., 7 Nov., 1 Dec. This snake is one of two species recorded throughout the year at Raleigh (Brimley, N.C., 1925). *Hibernation*—Grizzell (Md., 1949) reported that while he was excavating a woodchuck den "on Feb. 8 a pink-bellied snake (*Carphophis a. amoena*) was found 24 inches below the surface. Later excavation produced *Haldea, Diadophis*, and *Plethodon c. cinereus*. None of the animals were curled up." Neill (Ga., 1948) found that this snake is "often dug out by road construction crews in wooded areas; also hibernates in rotting pine stumps." Barbour observed that "the 7 specimens from the potato patch . . . , according to the boy who found them, [were] 'in a ball, about 8 inches under the surface of the ground.' They were taken on August 24, 1948."

Breeding: Oviparous. *Sexual dimorphism*—Blanchard (1931) found that, in general, males above 192 mm. had keel-like ridges on the dorsal scales of the anal region. Are they seasonal or throughout the year?

Eggs—Number, 2–8. (2, 8) Fowler; (2, 8) Brimley; (2, 3, 5) McCauley; (3) Haltom; (4) Lamson; (8) Brimley. Time of deposition, latter part of June, early July. Size, 16 mm. There are records of 16 or 17 mm. long, 18 mm., 19x7 mm., 19x8 mm., 20x7 mm., 22x7 mm., 23 mm., 25 mm., 25x8 mm. Sometimes uniform or one end 1 to 2 mm. larger.

Two detailed accounts will suffice: "On July 12, 1902, two lots of snake's eggs were brought to me, different from any I had previously obtained. One lot consisted of 2 elongate, smooth, whitish eggs, 23 and 25 mm. long.

One was put up and the other kept until Aug. 14 (33 days later) when a young *Carphophiops amoenus* within a day or two of hatching was taken from the egg. The other lot consisted of 8 eggs, short, oblong in shape, just about the size and shape of the eggs of the lizard, *Sceloporus undulatus,* but smooth skinned and one-sided and about 16 to 17 mm. long. These were kept until Aug. 8, when two young snakes 185 mm. long, also *Carphophiops amoenus,* were hatched from the last eggs" (Brimley, 1903).

"On July 8, 4 eggs were found to have been laid in the center of the container at a depth of about 3 inches from the surface, probably deposited within the last week of June. These were about the size of a small capsule, very elongate and rather irregular in shape, one end being somewhat larger. The dimensions of these were as follows: 10x8 mm.; 22x7 mm. (middle), 8 mm. at the larger end; 19x7 mm. uniform in shape; and 20x7 mm. (middle), 9 mm. at the large end" (Allard).

Young—Hatching time, Aug. 1 to Sept. 15. Size at birth, 3–4 inches. 3½ in. according to Allard, Brimley (N.C., 1907), Fowler (D.C., 1945), Haltom (Ala., 1931), and McCauley.

McCauley gives us the longest and most pertinent comment. He found eggs 18.5x11 mm. to 23x10.5 mm. which hatched from the middle of August to the middle of September. "The number of eggs laid in most cases is 5 although clutches of 2 and 3 have been found. One clutch was found in rotting wood on the ground at the base of an old stump. The eggs were lying close together and no adult was found nearby. On July 22, 1936, 3 clutches were found in old sawdust piles, buried several inches below the surface. At the site where one of the latter clutches was found 3 adults were also uncovered. It does not seem likely that their presence there indicates any protective instinct. . . . The natal skin is shed during the first day after hatching. Of 6 newly hatched young the largest measured 104 mm., the smallest 88 mm. (the latter was one that hatched about September 15). The average length of the 6 was 98.6 mm."

Food: Insects, earthworms, slugs, snails. Abbott (N.J., 1868), Atkinson (Pa., 1901), Ditmars (N.Y., 1905), Surface, Trapido, Barbour, Uhler, Cottam, and Clarke (Vt., 1939).

Authorities:

Allard, H. A. (Va., 1945)

Allen, J. A. (Mass., 1868, 1871)

Barbour, R. W. (Ky., 1950)

Blanchard, F. N. (Gen., 1925a, 1931)

Brimley, C. S. (Gen., 1903, N.C., 1941–42)

Corrington, J. D. (S.C., 1929)

Ditmars, R. L. (Gen., 1939; Conn., 1896)

King, W. (Tenn., 1939)

Lynn, W. G. (Va., 1936)

McCauley, R. H. (Md., 1945)

Say, T. (Pa., 1825)

Surface, H. A. (Pa., 1906)

Trapido, H. (N.J., 1937)

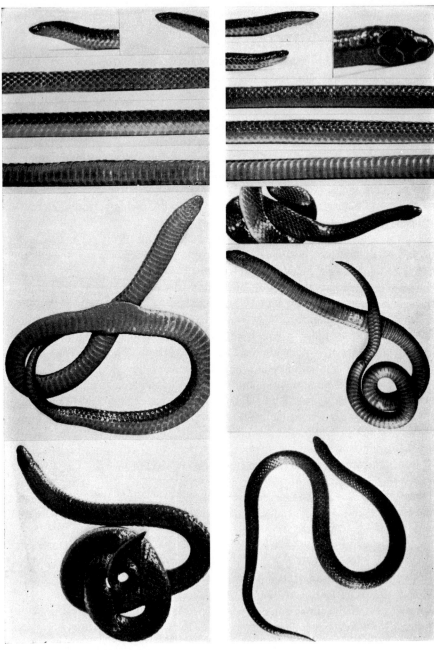

Fig. 33. *Carphophis amoenus amoenus,* Putnam, Conn., A. B. Klots.

Fig. 34. *Carphophis a. helenae,* Mammoth Cave Nat. Park, Ky., R. Dury through Miss E. G. Hutchinson, Cincinnati, O.

Worm snake (25—Smith 1882), **Ground snake**
(10—Jordan and Van Vleck 1874)

Carphophis amoenus helenae (Kennicott) 1859. Fig. 34; Map 12

Other common names: Central twig snake; central worm snake; Helen's snake; Helen Teunison's snake; Helen's worm snake; red snake.

Range: Between Appalachians and Mississippi Valley: Tennessee and Ohio River valleys and Mississippi embayment; from West Virginia to s. Illinois to n. Mississippi and Alabama.—Ala.; Ill.; Ind.; Ky.; Miss.; O.; Tenn.; W. Va. *Elevation*—100 to 2,000 feet, sometimes to 3,000 feet.

Size: Adults, 7–13 inches.

Distinctive characteristics: A very small opalescent burrower with sharp tail; chestnut or dark brown on the back; the light or vinaceous pink of the belly extends to 1st or 2nd rows of lateral scales; internasals and prefrontals fused into 2 plates.

Color: A snake from Mammoth Cave National Park in Edmonson Co., Ky., collected by Ralph Dury, Aug. 26, 1937 (kindness of Miss E. G. Hutchinson of Cincinnati, O.). The color of the middle of the back and top of the head is bister or prout's brown, becoming on the lower scale rows snuff brown. The iris is black. The venter is alizarine pink, venetian pink, or corinthian pink. This color extends on to the first row of scales and forms a clear-cut band on the lower two-thirds of the upper labials. The rostral is like the dorsal color.

Habitat: According to 15 authors, this inoffensive secretive snake occurs in moist situations, in wooded hills, sandy woods, and sparse woodlands, and among underbrush. Six authors found them under logs, 6 under stones or rocks, 4 under dead leaves, 3 under bark, 2 under boards and other moist covers.

Period of activity: *First appearance*—Apr. 14 (Blatchley, Ind., 1891); Mar. 26 (Hahn); May 23, 1946 (A. G. Smith). *Fall disappearance*—Aug. 26, 1937 (Dury); Oct. 25, 1946 (A. G. Smith).

Breeding: Oviparous. *Eggs*—Number, 2–6. In 1909 Hahn took a female which "contained 6 eggs. The eggs were subcylindrical and 14 mm. long." In 1926 Blanchard reported 4 clutches of eggs: 2 laid July 4–7, hatched Sept. 9–11; 2 July 7–11, hatched Sept. 16–17; 5 laid July 7–11, hatched Sept. 14–17; and 2 laid July 7–11, hatched Sept. 13–15. These eggs measured at deposition 17–27.5 mm., at hatching 19–31 mm. In width at deposition they were 7.5–9 mm., at hatching 10–12.9 mm. Two other females had 3 and 5 in their oviducts. Blanchard concluded: "The eggs, upon deposition, are not stuck to one another, as in many species of snakes, but are entirely separate, and lie nearly parallel to one another. . . . The period of incubation outside the body of the mother is about 2 months." Haltom's study (1931) for Alabama gave 3–5 eggs, probably applicable for *amoenus* and *helenae*. In

1944 Minton recorded a clutch of 3 eggs from a rotten log Aug. 18, hatching Sept. 1. He gave a range of 2–6 eggs. Time of deposition, June–July 15. Size, .66 or .68–1.1 inches (14–27.5 mm.)x.3–.36 inches in width (7.5–9 mm.).

Young—Size, 3.5–4.2 inches (87–105 mm.). "So small that they are easily mistaken for earthworms" (Funkhouser). Conant's smallest juvenile was 4 inches. Hatching period, late August–Sept. 17.

Food: Earthworms, insects, slugs. Hahn, Funkhouser, Bailey (Ky., 1933), Minton.

Authorities:

Barbour, R. W. (Ky., 1950a)	Hay, O. P. (Ind., 1892)
Blanchard, F. N. (Gen., 1925, 1925a; Ind., 1926)	Kennicott, R. (Gen., 1860)
	Minton, S., Jr. (Ind., 1944)
Blatchley, W. S. (Fla., 1899)	Morse, M. (O., 1904)
Conant, R. (O., 1938a)	Parker, M. V. (Tenn., 1948)
Cope, E. D. (Gen., 1900)	Piatt, J. (Ind., 1931)
Funkhouser, W. D. (Ky., 1925)	Smith, A. G. (Kans., 1948)
Garman, H. (Ill., 1892; Ky., 1894)	Smith, W. H. (O., 1882)
Hahn, W. L. (Ind., 1909)	Walker, C. F. (O., 1931)

F. N. Blanchard in 1925(a) found 89 per cent of his material had prefrontals and internasals fused; C. F. Walker over 60 per cent; R. Conant 71 per cent. R. W. Barbour made his material of e. Kentucky largely *C. a. amoenus* with that of central Kentucky *C. a. helenae.*

Worm snake (29—Mozley 1878), Western worm snake (6—Hurter 1893)

Carphophis amoenus vermis (Kennicott) 1859. Fig. 35; Map 12

Other common names: (Western) ground snake; western twig snake.

Range: In general, w. of the Mississippi River, rare in w. Illinois. E. Nebraska to n.e. Texas and n.w. Louisiana, n.e. to Illinois and Iowa.—Ark.; Ia.; Ill.; Kan.; La.; Mo.; Neb.; Okla.; Tex. *Elevation*—Mainly 500 to 1,200 feet, but known as low as 200 and as high as 1,500 to 2,000 feet.

Size: Adults, 7–14¾ inches.

Distinctive characteristics: Larger than *helenae;* the light coral red of under parts extend up onto the 3rd row of lateral scales; back a glossy black, blue-violet black, or gray. Internasals and prefrontals separate. Sharp tail ⅙–⅛ of total length.

Color: A snake received from D. L. Gamble, May 8, 1928. Seven rows and two half rows of scales across the back and sides are dusky violet or blue-violet black. The surface is very glistening and has bluish violet and emerald green or vivid green reflections. The top of the head is raw umber. The iris is uniform and of the same color as the dorsum of the body. The upper and lower labials are like the under parts. The color of the under parts which extends up on the body on either side for 2½ rows of scales is light coral red, grenadine pink, or carrot red, being brighter on the caudal than on the cephalic half of the body. The latter is coral pink.

Habitat: From 14 authors, we found that they frequent damp places, wooded hills near water, grassy hillsides near springs, rolling woods, the lower parts of bluffs, and shaded slopes. They seek cover under stones or rocks and in decaying bark, leaves, logs, and leaf mold.

Period of activity: *First appearance*—Mar. 23, May 2, 4, 19 (Hurter); Mar. 24, 1928 (Force); Mar. 25, 1928, Apr. 6, 1929 (Gloyd, 1928); Apr. 28, May 11, 16 (Gloyd, 1928). *Fall disappearance*—Oct. 30, 1891 (Test, Mo., 1894); Nov. 4 (Hurter); Dec. 16, 1933; Sept. 21 (Gloyd, 1928).

Breeding: Oviparous. *Sexual dimorphism*—Blanchard found males 190–290 mm. with anal ridges. *Eggs*—Number, 1–12. There are records of 1, 3, 4, 5, 8, and 12 eggs in the complement. Time, June 25–July. Size, 1.2–1.6 inches x.3 or .4 inch. Also 30x10 mm. and 40x9 mm. The records are: (1) "Small number of eggs (5) which are 30 mm. long and 7 mm. in diameter" (Hurter). (2) "It lays a few elongate soft-shelled eggs, from which young 3½ inches are hatched" (Guthrie). (3) "A female taken Apr. 28 contained 4 eggs which averaged 15x6 mm." (Gloyd, 1928). (4) "Two females taken May 2, 1927 contained respectively 12 and 8 eggs, 5 to 10 mm." (Force). (5) "A captive female laid 3 eggs which measured about 30 by 10 mm." (Hudson). (6) "A worm snake collected on May 23, 1936, laid 3 eggs on June 26. The eggs were thin shelled and pliant and measured 40x9 mm. Another laid a single egg June 25, 1938) (Anderson).

Young—As to size, we know of no records (except Guthrie's 3½ inches). Branson in 1904 had a 5-inch specimen; Gloyd in 1928 had two (135, 139 mm.), but they were not hatchlings.

Food: Earthworms, insects, small snakes. Hurter, Force, Hudson.

Authorities:

Anderson, P. (Mo., 1942)
Bailey, R. M. (Ia., 1939)
Blanchard, F. N. (Gen., 1931)
Branson, E. B. (Kan., 1904)
Force, E. R. (Okla., 1930)
Gloyd, H. K. (Kan., 1928, 1932)

Guthrie, J. E. (Ia., 1926)
Hay, O. P. (Ind., 1892)
Hudson, G. E. (Neb., 1942)
Hurter, J. (Mo., 1911)
Kennicott, R. (Gen., 1860)
Langebartel, D. A. (Ill., 1947)

SCARLET SNAKES

Genus *CEMOPHORA* Cope (Fig. 19)

Size small medium, 8–26 inches; slender; head not distinct from neck; tail rather short; anal entire; scales smooth with apical pits, in 19 rows; snout pointed; rostral large, projecting beyond lower jaw; frontal large, almost as

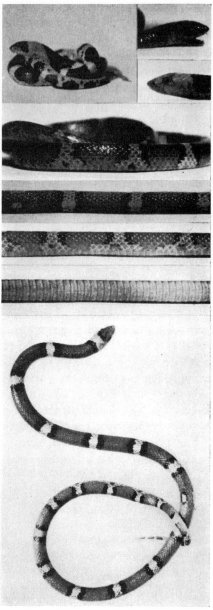

Fig. 35. *Carphophis a. vermis,* Arkansas, D. L. Gamble.

Fig. 36. *Cemophora coccinea:* 1, young, Eustis, Fla., O. C. Van Hyning; 2–8, Lake Co., Fla., A. Jackson.

broad as long; upper labials 6 or 7, lower 8; nasal normally single; loreal 1; preoculars 1–2; postoculars 2; 2–3 rows gulars between chin shields and ventrals; top of head red with black band behind eye, body red, yellow and black dorsal cross-bars, 16–20, venter glistening white; maxillary teeth smooth, posterior much longer, no interspace. Hemipenis—sulcus simple, calyces numerous, not fringed. Ventrals 156–188, caudals 35–45. Synonyms: *Coluber, Elaps, Heterodon, Rhinostoma, Simotes.*

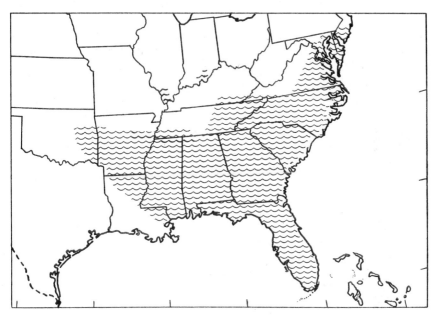

Map 13. *Cemophora coccinea.*

Scarlet snake (45—Harlan 1827), **Red snake** (2—Brimley 1907)

Cemophora coccinea (Blumenbach) 1788. Fig. 36; Map 13

Other common names: (False) coral snake; milk snake.

Range: S. New Jersey to Florida, w. to e. Oklahoma; w. of Appalachians in e. Tennessee and at New Albany, Ind.; introduced by airplane into Texas in 1948.—Ala.; Ark.; D.C.; Fla.; Ga.; Ind.; Ky.; La.; Md.; Miss.; N.C.; N.J.; Okla.; S.C.; Tenn.; Tex. (introduced—Auffenberg, 1948); Va. *Elevation:*—Sea level to 1,500 feet. 2,000 feet (King, Tenn. 1939). Many records are below 100 feet and surely below 500 feet.

Distinctive characteristics: A small medium sharp-snouted snake with red, black, and yellow dorsal bands—a red band bordered by pair of black ones, which are separated by a yellow or white interspace. Venter, mother-of-pearl white or pinkish or vinaceous on rear portions. Head, ahead of eyes, vermilion to pinkish white; black band behind eyes. Tail short.

Color: Snakes from Okefinokee Swamp, Ga., Apr. 25, 1921, and July 23, 1922. This snake is banded transversely across the back and upper side with red, black, and pale yellow or white rings. On mid-back, the red bands are 4 to 8 scales long, and the light bands 2½ to 3 scales long. The red areas are dragon's blood red becoming coral red or brazil red on the sides. The black, dusky slate-violet or blue-violet black bands outline both sides of both red and light rings. The light rings fork on the lower sides opening into the white, pallid purple drab, or pallid vinaceous-drab of the lower sides. Here the scales have white edges. Where the light bands end or fork, 3 or 4 rows of the yellow scales may have orange or orange-red centers. Opposite the end of each light band and producing the fork is a squarish spot of bay, hessian brown, or bone brown on the last 2 rows of scales of the sides and on the ends of 2 ventrals. The light rings are a pale olive-buff, olive-buff, or pale chalcedony yellow. The band across the back of the head is lighter than the other red areas. The iris is dragon's blood red, coral red, or brazil red. The pallid purple drab or pallid vinaceous drab of the lower sides extends more or less onto the white belly. The rear half of the venter has a pinkish or vinaceous cast.

Abnormal coloration—Albinism. "An albinistic individual was shown to me on July 26, 1931, by Wade Fox, which had been taken between Reidsville and Leaksville in Rockingham County. It was about 15 inches long and had the black bands replaced by white and the red spots reduced in size and the white (for black) and yellow ones widened" (Brimley).

Young—Scarlet saddles to 2nd or 3rd scale row, saddles separated from black bars by white interspaces. Venter and 1st and 2nd dorsal row white. Irregular row of black flecks at level of lateral border of red saddles. *Twelve-inch specimens*—White interspaces suffused with yellow. Ventrolateral black flecking reduced. Black bars extend to ventrals and red intensified. *Adults*—Deep transverse red bands to tips of ventrals bordered by black ones which reach ventrals. The black-bordered red bands separated by yellow interspaces which become white ventrolaterad. Color changes from youth to old age. In very old specimens, the scarlets become dark red brown, and the yellows turn to tan or light grayish brown. (See Neill, 1950.)

Habitat: Not until Loennberg's time did we have definite notes on this topic. From Loennberg (Fla., 1895), Brimley (N.C., 1895, 1941–42), Beyer (La., 1900), Deckert (Fla., 1918), Myers (N.C., 1924), Corrington (S.C., 1929), Force, Allen (Miss., 1932), Van Hyning (Fla., 1933), Hibbard, Carr, Gray (N.C., 1941), Minton, Auffenberg (Tex., 1948a), and Neill (Ga., 1950b), we cull meager notes about this secretive burrowing snake. This burrower in dirt, wood pulp, sandy soil, or even muck is often ploughed up in fields or dug up in earth foundations, grave diggings, and road constructions. It is found above earth under lumber piles, pieces of bark, stones, and logs. There are records of it near swamps, on rugged slopes, high banks of creeks, and open fields, and it has been found dead in residential areas.

Period of activity: *First appearance*—Apr. 1 (Corrington, S.C., 1929); spring, Apr. 10, 1928 (Force); Apr. 24, 1921 (A. H. W.): early May (Stejneger); Apr. 1, Apr. 17, May 3 (Dickson). *Fall disappearance*—Dec. 10, 1931 (Allen, Miss., 1932); Aug. 13, 15 (Deckert, Fla., 1918); Oct. 5 (Corrington); Aug. 17 (A. H. W.); Sept. 2 (Snyder). *Hibernation*—See Kauffeld).

Breeding: Oviparous. Males—823 mm.; females—650 mm. *Eggs*—Number, 3–8. 3 (Wright and Bishop); 8 (Carr, Ditmars). Time, June. Size, 34–35 mm. (1.3–1.4 inches) long. In 1915 Wright and Bishop reported a "specimen, taken June 21, 1912, had 3 white eggs which are very elongate and with a thin membranous integument. They were respectively 34, 35, 35 mm. long." Ditmars has recounted how a female on June 23 laid 8 long smooth eggs. Three weeks later one egg was examined. A week later the female was gorged with the remaining eggs. Carr on June 2, 1936, took a female "with 8 mature eggs in the oviduct."

Food: Lizards, small snakes, mice, insects, slugs, salamanders, turtle eggs. Ditmars, Force, Haltom, Minton, Snyder, Dickson, Neill (Gen., 1951).

Authorities:

Brimley, C. S. (N.C., 1941–42)
Carr, A. F. (Fla., 1940a)
Dickson, J. D. (Fla., 1948)
Ditmars, R. L. (Gen., 1907)
Force, E. R. (Okla., 1930)
Fowler, J. A. (D.C., 1945)
Haltom, W. L. (Ala., 1931)
Hibbard, C. W. (Ky., 1937)
Holbrook, J. E. (Gen., 1836–42)
Kauffeld, C. F. (N.J., 1935)

Kauffeld, C. F., and H. Trapido (N.J., 1944)
Klauber, L. M. (Gen., 1948)
McCauley, R. H. (Md., 1945)
Minton, S., Jr. (Ind., 1944)
Neill, W. T., Jr. (Ga., 1950)
Snyder, R. C. (Ala., 1945a)
Stejneger, L. (D.C., 1905)
Wright, A. H., and S. C. Bishop (Ga., 1916)

This strikingly colored snake has been dubbed a coral snake (*Elaps*) and a spreading adder (*Heterodon*), and various opprobrious terms have been used for it; but through most of its herpetologic history it has been *coccinea* or *coccineus*. On the confusion of this *Coluber coccineus* Blumenbach with Linnaeus' *Coluber doliatus* (*Lampropeltis doliata* of today), see Cope (Gen., 1900), or Klauber, or Stejneger (Gen., 1918).

Mittleman (Gen., 1952) has revived the old problem of *coccinea-doliata*. Stejneger, the master International Commission nomenclaturist, declares that *doliata* is probably *Cemophora*, but that it is useless at this date to change a well-established usage when the type is lost. (See our discussion of L. d. *doliata*.) Smith (Gen., 1952) sees no immediate need to petition the Commission.

BANDED BURROWING SNAKES

Genus *CHILOMENISCUS* Cope (Fig. 21)

Size very small, 6–11 inches; form stout, cylindrical, with a short tail; no constriction at the neck; snout broad, protruding, rounded, much depressed, and pointed in profile; rostral large, approaches or encroaches on prefrontals; internasal and anterior nasal merged and small posterior sometimes merged with anterior; loreal absent; scales smooth with apical pits and in 13 rows; anal divided; caudals paired; 1 preocular, 2 postoculars, temporals 1 + 1 (2); eye small, pupil round; 11 subequal maxillary teeth, those at posterior extremity feebly but distinctly grooved. Hemipenis—with numerous fringed calyces. Synonym: *Carphophis.*

KEY TO THE GENUS *CHILOMENISCUS*

a. 16–40 clear black or blackish brown crossbands on the body and tail, complete or incomplete across the venter.
  b. Clear interspaces, cadmium orange, orange chrome to red. *C. cinctus*
  bb. White interspace has each scale with a central grayish brown spot. A doubtful insular form. (Isla Partida, Espiritu Island, Baja Calif.)
                                              C. punctatissimus
aa. No clear crossbands. First and second rows free of dots.
  b. A black or brown dot on each brownish drab or yellowish cinnamon scale; venter yellowish white or straw color. (Cape region, Baja Calif.)　　　　　　　　　　　*C. stramineus stramineus*
  bb. Each scale with several scattered dots or blotches of verona brown; ground color vinaceous buff; venter white. (Estero Salina, Baja Calif.)
                                                C. s. esterensis

Banded burrowing snake (11—Grinnell and Camp 1917),
Burrowing snake (4—Van Denburgh 1897)

Chilomeniscus cinctus Cope 1861. Fig. 37; Map 14

Other common names: Arizona ground snake; horse snake; red and black ground snake; Sonora ringed snake.

Range: Guaymas, Sonora, to Phoenix, Ariz., w. to Colorado Desert, Calif., and s. to lat. 25°, Baja California.—U.S.A.: Ariz.; Calif. Mex.: Baja Calif.; Sonora. *Elevation*—Seacoast to 3,000 feet at least.

Size: Adults, 6–10 inches.

Distinctive characteristics: Sixteen to 40 black or blackish brown dorsal bands (complete or incomplete), the clear interspaces orange chrome or cadmium orange to almost red. Ventrals 109–120; caudals 22–28.

Color: This is one of the red-, black-, and yellow-ringed snakes. It has 24 black bands in all, 1 over the vent and 5 on the tail, which are complete rings crossing 3 subcaudals and 3 dorsal scale rows. Those from vent forward almost, but not quite, meet on the venter. These dark bands may be 2½, 3, or even 3½ scales wide, black, fuscous-black, or blackish-brown, the black most distinct toward the rear. The intervals orange chrome or cadmium orange on the 5 to 6 middorsal rows are somewhat wider, being 3½ to ½ + 3 + ½, occasionally 4½, scales in width. They are broadest on the

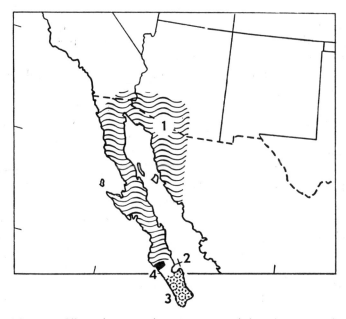

Map 14. *Chilomeniscus*—1, *cinctus;* 2, *punctatissimus;* 3, *s. stramineus;* 4, *s. esterensis.*

dorsum, and are only 2 scales wide where they go onto the belly on 2 ventrals. Below the orange chrome or cadmium orange, the intervals on the sides are pale greenish yellow and more prominent in the tail region. There is a slight wash of the orange in the band back of the head but none on the head ahead of the eyes. A dark head band extends from the rear half of the 3rd upper labial to the middle of the 7th, involving the first temporal, front edge of 2nd, and most of the parietal and leaving the outer tip yellow like the interspaces. The front of the band involves the preocular but leaves tip of supraocular and frontal cream color. The front of the snout, underside of rostral, and lower edge of upper labials are maize yellow or cream color. The eye is like the dark head band except for an area of light vinaceous-fawn around the pupil. The undersides of head, gulars, labials, and chin shields are white; the belly is pale viridine yellow.

Note: There is no sharp angle between belly and sides as there is in *Chionactis occipitalis*.

Note also that the orange chrome or cadmium orange of the mid-dorsum reaches from black ring to black ring, thus interrupting any yellow ring on the middorsum.

Habitat: Everyone calls this little snake a desert "burrower" or "digger" in sand, loose dirt, ground, or debris. Occasionally, it is under rocks or in stumps (see Cope; *Proc. Acad. Nat. Sci. Phila.*, **12** [1890]: 147 and Mocquard). In 1926 Vorhies (Ariz.) recorded that its captors reported "that two were seen in loose sandy soil near the creek and that they could travel so rapidly beneath the sand that difficulty was had in capturing them, one in fact being bisected by the shovel in the necessarily hasty digging." Mosauer, who found it common in loose sand in central and north central Baja California, wrote in 1936 that *"Chilomeniscus proceeds in the sand as easily as on it, and slips from sight as if there were no resistance whatsoever."*

Period of activity: *Appearances*—Apr. 23 to Nov. 2, 1910 (Van Denburgh and Slevin, Ariz., 1913); Apr. 9, 1927, Apr. 8, 10, July 27, 1931 (Linsdale).

Breeding: Oviparous. Nothing of record. The smallest we have seen was 110 mm. collected Aug. 8, 1919, by Slevin at Todos Santos, Baja Calif.

Food: Insects. Mocquard, Van Denburgh, Vorhies (Ariz., 1926), Mosauer.

Field notes: June 24, 1942. On the afternoon of June 23, 1942, we called on H. E. Weisner at his ranch 11 miles south of Tucson on the Nogales Road. We told him what we especially wanted, stressing *Phyllorhynchus d. nubilus* and discussing the *Chilomeniscus* he and Lee Arnold found in his cement tank. "Yes," he said, "I see them there every now and then. Two weeks ago we threw one out." This tank is one he uses in filling his 5-gallon honey cans. He has a honey ranch. That night about dusk we looked in his tank and sure enough, there was *Chilomeniscus*. He put it in a square can in dry sand. How quickly it disappears when dropped into the tin!! It is rather stocky in body with small head, small eye, and an "Andy Gump" profile because of a projecting upper jaw.

Authorities:

Bogert, C. M., and J. A. Oliver (Ariz., 1945)

Brown, A. E. (Gen., 1901)

Cope, E. D. (Baja Calif., 1862; Gen., 1900)

Ditmars, R. L. (Gen., 1939)

Gloyd, H. K. (Ariz., 1937a)

Klauber, L. M. (Calif., 1931a)

Linsdale, J. M. (Baja Calif., 1932)

Meek, S. E. (Baja Calif., 1905)

Mocquard, F. (Baja Calif., 1899)

Mosauer, W. (Baja Calif., 1936a)

Schmidt, K. P., and D. D. Davis (Gen., 1941)

Van Denburgh, J. (Gen., 1897, 1922)

Van Denburgh, J., and J. R. Slevin (Ariz., 1913; Baja Calif., 1921c)

In 1900 E. D. Cope recognized four forms of *Chilomeniscus* besides *stramineus* but K. P. Schmidt (Baja Calif., 1922), J. Van Denburgh (Gen.,

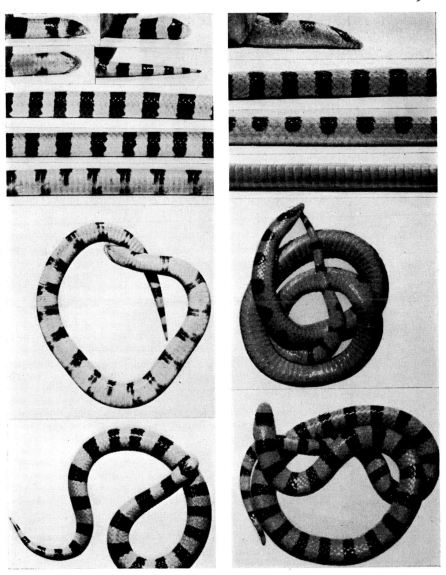

Fig. 37. *Chilomeniscus cinctus,* ranch of H. E. Weisner, south of Tucson, Ariz.

Fig. 38. *Chionactis occipitalis occipitalis,* Mojave, Calif., W. Lasky.

1922), L. M. Klauber, and J. M. Linsdale all consider there is but one species, the variable *cinctus*.

1922, K. P. Schmidt: "The forms of the genus *Chilomeniscus* are in considerable confusion and by no means well understood."

SHOVEL-NOSED GROUND SNAKES

Genus *CHIONACTIS* Cope (Fig. 23)

Size small, 6–17 inches; slender; head not very distinct; anal divided; tail short; abdomen angulate; nasal valve present; 3 maxillary foramina; snout flattened, spadelike, very pointed in profile and projecting far beyond lower jaw; upper labials 7 (8); lower labials 7; loreal present; nasal entire; 1 preocular; anterior margin of frontal angulate; scales smooth, without light edges, in rows 15–15; several rows of gulars between tips of chin shields and ventrals; pattern of 10–41 black dorsal crossbands ending at ventrals or crossing belly, and yellow intervals which are with or without red bands; 3–11 black rings usually encircle tail; maxillary teeth 8 + 3 or 9 + 3, the posterior 3 moderately enlarged and with lateral grooves. Hemipenis (after Stickel)— end of sulcus surrounded by calyces; no bare area at top of organ; no spines below zone of small spines except the 2 large basal ones; spines in upper part of spiny zone much enlarged just beneath the surface of the hemipenis. Ventrals 147–174, caudals 34–53. Synonyms: *Contia, Lamprosoma, Rhinostoma, Sonora*.

Our accounts of *Chionactis* were formulated before the appearance of Klauber's recent comprehensive résumé (Gen., 1951) of the genus. Except for the addition of the two new forms (we rely almost wholly on Klauber's material) and revision of the key, the accounts remain as originally written. Klauber gives much added material on every topic.

KEY TO THE GENUS *CHIONACTIS* [1]

a. Black body bands 10–20 and on tail 3–5; snout convex above; yellow ground color reduced to narrow rings between black bars and red saddles or between black bars.

  b. 10 crossbands on body and 3 on tail; middorsal interspace twice as wide as crossband. Ventrals 144 ♂ to 152 ♀; caudals 39 ♂ to 42 ♀. (W.-cent. Sonora.)   *C. palarostris palarostris*

  bb. 13–20 crossbands on body (13–16 ♂, 18–20 ♀) and 4 or 5 bands on tail; middorsal interspace less than twice band width. (Organ Pipe Cactus National Monument.)   *C. p. organica*

aa. Dark body band 21 or more (23–41) and on tail 5–13; snout flat above.

---

[1] See Klauber (Gen., 1951) and Stickel (Gen., 1943).

b. Definite secondary crossbands (often brown in preservative) present between the dark primary dorsal bands; these secondaries with scale centers spotted and sometimes crossing the dorsum.

    c. Bands (primary) black or very dark brown; bands (secondary) 1 scale in width or broken middorsally, 2 scales wide on side, extending to 2nd row as if the red dorsal interspaces of *annulata* had become narrower and impregnated with black, thus forming a double series of wide and narrow dark dorsal bands. Primary bands 23–32 on body, 7–11 on tail; ventrals 141–151 ♂, 153–159 ♀; caudals 42–47 ♂, 38–48 ♀. (Maricopa, Pima, and Pinal Cos., Ariz.)

C. o. klauberi

    cc. Bands (primary) brown; secondaries less distinct than c.; ventrals 152 ♂-162 ♀; caudals 44, 51 ♂; 43 ♀. (Nye, Esmeralda cos., Nev.)   *C. o. talpina*

bb. Interspaces without dark maculated secondary bands, clear or essentially so, primary bands 18–41 on body, 3–13 on tail; yellow intervals.

    c. Brown bars on body 25–41, av. 35, commonly terminating on 2nd row, not tapering on sides and intervals not greatly exceeding them; tail bands 6–13, av. 9; normally 12–24 dorsal bars not crossing abdomen, rings usually confined to the tail; interspaces without red saddles; dark headband almost straight between eyes; total number of bands on body and tail plus number of body bands not entirely encircling the body 52 or more; ventrals ♂ 146–170, ♀ 154–176; caudals ♂ 39–50, ♀ 34–48.   *C. occipitalis occipitalis*

    cc. Brown or nearly black bars on body 18–25, on tail 5–12; body bars widened on mid-dorsum and abdomen, tapering conspicuously to scale row 1, where it may be ⅕ width of interval; interspaces commonly with red saddles, usually narrower than black rings and ending on 2nd or 3rd row; normally 2–10 black bands not crossing the abdomen; headband crescentic in front and may extend forward to loreal region; total number of black bands on body and tail plus number of incomplete body bands 51 or fewer; ventrals ♂ 143–164, ♀ 153–178, caudals ♂ 40–57, ♀ 34–51.   *C. o. annulata*

Desert burrowing snake (3—Camp 1916), Mojave ringed snake

Chionactis occipitalis occipitalis (Hallowell) 1854. Fig. 38; Map 15

Other common names: Banded (ground) snake; (bicolor) spade-nosed snake; desert (ground) snake; Hallowell's ground snake; Mojave Desert shovel-nosed snake; Mojave (ground) snake; pencil snake; ringed ground snake; shovel-nosed ground snake; tricolor(ed) ground snake.

Range: Mojave district: Los Angeles and Riverside Cos., Calif., to Aquila, Maricopa Co., Ariz., n.w. to Clark Co., Nev., and thence w. across s. Inyo

Co. into Kern Co., Calif.—Ariz.; Calif.; Nev. *Elevation*—500 to 3,000 or 4,000 feet.

Size: Adults, 6–15 inches.

Distinctive characteristics: "The form typically has numerous (31 to 51) bands on body and tail. Few or none of the body bands encircle the trunk, and when they do they seldom broaden out on the abdomen. The bands are usually brown rather than black, and the interspaces are without vermilion or red saddles although orange or yellow may be present in the

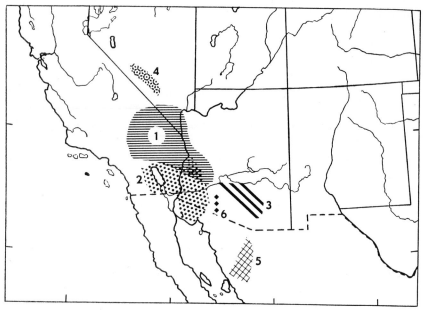

Map 15. *Chionactis*—1, *o. occipitalis;* 2, *o. annulata;* 3, *o. klauberi;* 4, *o. talpina;* 5, *palarostris;* 6, *p. organica.*

ground color to some extent. Combination of the two band counts (total plus incompletely encircling, as used in the key) gives a character that identifies all but 5 out of 99 available specimens of the subspecies. The qualitative color characters, though often quite apparent, are too variable for use alone" (Stickel, 1943).

Color: A snake from California (Mojave) received in June, 1940, through the kindness of Bill Lasky and Bob Goldfarb. This snake lacks the red rings of the other form described. The background of the back is straw yellow. It is crossed by brown bars 2½ scales wide, 33 on the body, 10 encircling rings on the tail counting the tail tip, the body bars not reaching the first scale row. These bars are bister or sepia. The interspaces are 3 scales longitudinally. There is a bister or sepia band across the parietals and rear portion of frontal and supraocular. The flat area across the top of the head is pale chalcedony yellow. The iris is bister or sepia. The under parts are naphthalene yellow.

Habitat: Sand or desert. This snake "is apparently not uncommonly observed in spring for there were several accounts of specimens which had been taken by boys (some of these may possibly have referred to the species following) who know it by the name of 'pencil snake,' an appellation presumably descriptive of its size" (Cowles and Bogert, 1936). "On March 28, 1938, 17 specimens were collected from 30 acres of ground, all from shallow soil, none of them deeper than 1 foot, and 2 from approximately 1 inch below the surface, both of these in relatively hard ground" (Cowles). See "Hibernation" below.

Period of activity: *First appearance*—June 1, 1941 (L. Cook, Jr.); Mar. 28, 1938, Mar. 26, 1939 (Cowles); Apr. 4, 1925 (Herms); Apr. 3, 1920 (Cowles, Calif., 1920); Apr. 4, 6, 1952 (Warren). *Hibernation*—Cowles made the following observation in the northern part of Coachella Valley (form close to borderline of *annulata-occipitalis*): "On February 23, 1938, four specimens of *Sonora occipitalis* were turned out of the soil on the Bell ranch during a single day of scraper operation. These comprised 3 adults, and 1 exceedingly small juvenile probably of the preceding year's hatch. One of the adult specimens was recovered from approximately 2 feet underground, the juvenile from a mound of wind-blown sand at a depth of about 18 inches. Of the other 2 specimens, one was tracked along a furrow and yielded no information as to hibernation site, while the other was severed at an unknown depth and the body exposed on the ground surface. The body temperature was obtained immediately and was verified by thrusting the thermometer through the length of the animal. The temperature throughout was 18°C. and the identical soil temperature at the site of capture was found at a depth between 28 and 30 inches."

Breeding: Oviparous. *Eggs and Young*—number 2–9. "On March 26, 1939, four specimens of *Sonora* were obtained. Four readings at four different parts of the body of one specimen gave consistent 19.5° temperature. The two largest specimens both measured 37.5 cm. and contained ova measuring 2 mm. in length. One specimen contained 6 visibly enlarged ova in the ovary, while the other contained 6 in one ovary and 3 in the other ovary. Both specimens showed abundant adipose tissue and appeared to be in very good condition" (Cowles).

The smallest we have seen was Tracy Storer's specimen of 124 mm. (tail 20) taken by W. B. Herms at Palm Springs, Riverside Co., Calif., Apr. 4, 1925 (39 dorsal bars, 8 on tail).

Food: Arthropods, insects, invertebrates. Cowles.

Field notes: In 1942 our examination of *C. o. occipitalis* in the Pacific and plateau state collections revealed the following: The total lengths varied from 167 to 348 mm., tail lengths from 27 to 64 mm. The tail lengths in body length ranged from 15–20%. The body dark bars were from 30–41, one 26, one 28, an average of 35 or 36. The tail bars were 6–10, average 8.5, mean 10. The total number of dorsal bars ranged from 33–51, an average of 41. Usually the first 12–24 (sometimes 8–11) dorsal bars did not encircle; often there were none on body except perhaps 2 or 3 in front of the vent. But when one approaches Blythe or Riverside County adjoining the Imperial and San Diego County lines one encounters difficulties.

Authorities:

Cope, E. D. (Gen., 1860–61 [Kennicott], 1900)
Cowles, R. B. (Gen., 1941a)
Cowles, R. B., and C. M. Bogert (Gen., 1944; Nev., 1936)
Hallowell, E. (Gen., 1859; Calif., 1856, 1857)

Klauber, L. M. (Calif., 1932)
Meek, I. (Baja Calif., 1905)
Stickel, W. H. (Gen., 1938, 1943; Ariz., 1941)
Warren, J. W. (Calif., 1953)

Shovel-nosed ground snake (7—Klauber 1932), Desert snake

Chionactis occipitalis annulata (Baird) 1859. Fig. 39; Map 15

Other common names: Banded snake; Colorado Desert shovel-nosed snake; tricolor ground snake; tricolor spade-nosed snake.

Range: Colorado and Yuma deserts: e. San Diego Co., Imperial Co., Calif., e. to Wickenburg, Ariz., s. to Gila Bend and Ajo, Ariz., and to Puerto Penasco, Sonora, Mex.—U.S.A.: Ariz.; Calif. Mex.: Baja Calif.; Sonora. *Elevation*—Sea level or lower to 1,000 feet.

Size: Adults, 7–17 inches.

Distinctive characteristics: "Bands on body and tail are fewer (22–46) than in typical *occipitalis,* but many of them meet across the abdomen, ringing the body and often widening out on the ventrals. The black bands are separated by interspaces having saddles of vermilion on a cream or ivory ground. The total number of bands added to the number of incomplete body bands gives a diagnostic figure varying from 26 to 57 (excluding data for the San Diego population discussed below). The range of variation, limited, as in the key to 26–51, includes 73 of the 78 non-San Diego specimens examined" (Stickel).

Color: Snakes from west of Benson's Dry Lake, San Diego Co., Calif., May 8, 1942; caught alive while crossing the road at night. The dorsal background color of one snake is chartreuse yellow becoming seafoam green or pale glass green on the head and back of the black half-moon and marguerite yellow on the tail. This is crossed by black or dark olive and salmon-orange bars. There is a black or dark olive band starting with the eye and involving the rear of the supraoculars, all the postoculars except the lowermost portion of the lowest one touching the upper edge of the first temporal and covering all the parietal except the rear tip and forward edge. This forms a crescent. Counting this head crescent, there are 22 black bars on the body and 8 black rings on the tail. The 9 caudal black bars of the body cross the abdomen, and the next 2 have black bars on the venter opposite but not connected with the dorsal bars. On the forward part of the body these black bands lack 2 scale rows of touching the ventrals. In their centers they are 2 to 2½ scales wide, and are separated by light intervals of 4 scales longitudinally. Each chartreuse yellow interval is crossed in its middle by a salmon-orange band, 11 scales transversely and 2 or only 1 longitudinally, which tapers to 1 at the side. The iris is black with a strong wash of rainette green. The belly is white.

Note: The sides and venter form a sharp angle.

The background of the dorsum of another snake caught at the same time and place is marguerite yellow. There are 31 black bars of which 8 are on the tail, and 10 body bands encircle it with 3 more dark belly spots cephalad.

Habitat: This snake is essentially a nocturnal desert form. Some of its habitats have been described as sand, desert, soft sandy ridges, base of bushes on a dune, desert sands, sand dune belt, and desert foothills. It is said to be virtually absent in irrigated areas. More unusual are comments that it is "mostly unearthed in grading" and in "little hills of firm soil."

1916, Camp: "Two of these docile little snakes were found on the gravelly, creosote-dotted plains south of Blythe Junction. One was taken late in the afternoon, the other early in the morning, and neither was active. One was caked with clay as though it had just emerged from the soil. Mr. H. A. Smith of Blythe Junction, to whom I showed one of the above examples, said he once found one of these snakes in the hard soil of his yard and some distance below the surface."

Cowles, to whom we owe more about this snake than to any other author, stated: "One specimen was taken at the grass-field between Blythe and Mecca, California. When taken it had been traveling out in the open and in the heat of the noon sun, April 3, 1920. It was found on a gravel wash and when approached it struck in all directions, though apparently it did not open its mouth upon striking the hand. It appeared to be blinded by the sun and unable to tell from which direction it was menaced."

Locomotion: Mosauer discussed its locomotion at length.

Period of activity: *First appearance*—Mar. 19, 1912 (Van Denburgh and Slevin, Ariz., 1913); Jan. 2, 1913 (F. Stephens); June 13, 1914 (C. L. Camp); Feb. 16, 1914, Apr. 18, 1922 (F. Stephens); Apr. 5, 1912 (Loye Miller); May 10, 1910 (J. Grinnell). *Hibernation*—Three miles west of Calexico, Calif., on Mar. 9, 1911, F. L. Weed found one about a foot underground in a canal bank; and in February, 1909, he found another about one foot underground beneath a mesquite.

Food: Insects, scorpions, lizards. Perkins.

Field notes: May 8, 1942, at night, on one of the San Diegan's favorite herpetological collecting roads: Perhaps 3 miles west of Benson's Dry Lake, we saw on the road in our headlights a small moving snake and picked up a *Sonora o. annulata* and very soon a second one. They look white in the car light. They are small, hence not hard to collect because they have some distance to go across the road. It was one of the forms desired. But a car approached in the dark. Charles Shaw and his friends. "That you, Dr. Wright?" One way for introductions! Incidentally they discovered we had a flat tire and repaired it for us. Herpetologic Samaritans!

In 1942 we saw most of the *C. occipitalis* collections of the west. The *C. o. annulata* material varied from 131 to 397 mm. in total length, the tail length from 20 to 72 mm. The tail length ranged from 15 to 20 per cent of the total length. The body dark bars range from 23 to 30, one 35, the average 26, the mean 26, the tail bars from 4 to 9,one 3, one 11, average 7.4, mean 7. The total number of dark dorsal bars is 25 to 36 except one 39, one 40, and one 46. Some have all dorsal spots encircling the venter except the first 3–6 bars. One had all except head and nape band encircling. Some begin encircling at the 9th and several at the 15th or 16th bar. A few began not until the 20th or 22nd bar. A few may not have encirclement until the 2nd or 3rd before the vent. Some of the dark bars when not encircling have corresponding ventral spots. The Sentenac Canyon material is very variable in respect to the supposed *annulata* and *occipitalis* characters.

June 11, 1942: Took a trip from Wickenburg to Aquila, Congress Junction, then back to Wickenburg. This morning 19 miles west of Wickenburg took a DOR *Sonora occipitalis occipitalis*.

1942: *Occipitalis-annulata* puzzles. At the three areas where the largest series have been taken, difficulties of identification appear:

1) Wickenburg, Ariz.—*occipitalis* + *annulata*.
2) East of Yuma, Ariz.—*annulata* + *klauberi*.
3) Sentenac Canyon, Borego, San Diego Co. in general—*annulata* + *occipitalis*.

Authorities:

Baird, S. F. (Tex., 1859)　　　　　Perkins, C. B. (Calif., 1938)
Camp, C. L. (Calif., 1916)　　　　Richardson, C. H. (Calif., 1910)
Cowles, R. B. (Calif., 1920)　　　Stickel, W. H. (Ariz., 1941)
Mosauer, W. (Calif., 1933; Baja Calif.,
　1936a)

1941, W. H. Stickel: "There is little doubt that *annulata* shades off into *klauberi* to the east and into *palarostris* to the south, but its relationship to *occipitalis* is rather *complicated*. The population of San Diego County, California, is represented by 143 specimens of which 23.7 per cent key out to *occipitalis,* although the group as a whole is referable to *annulata*. The range

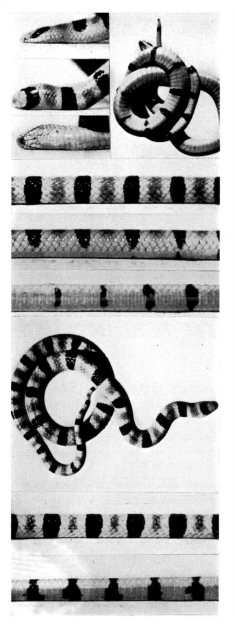

Fig. 39. *Chionactis o. annulata,* Benson Dry Lake, Calif.

Fig. 40. *Chionactis o. klauberi?,* Welton Mesa, Ariz., L. M. Klauber.

of variation in this county exceeds that of either subspecies and many specimens show odd combinations of the subspecific characters. For these reasons I believe this population to be of hybrid origin. Dr. Klauber concurs in this opinion and has suggested a reasonable explanation. At the site of the present Salton Sea there was until very recent geological times a much larger body of water, Lake Cahuilla, which completely covered the valley floor. As this receded, the northern and southern populations were able to migrate through the gap, mingle and interbreed. Possibly ecological factors operate to discourage the migration of *annulata* northward, for the *occipitalis* population of the Coachella Valley shows less indication of having interbred."

Two-banded ground snake, Tricolor ground snake

Chionactis occipitalis klauberi (Stickel) 1941. Fig. 40; Map 15

Other common names: Desert snake; (double-banded) spade-nosed snake; Klauber's ground snake; shovel-nosed ground snake; south-central Arizona shovel-nosed snake.

Range: From e. boundary of *Chionactis o. annulata* to e. borders of Pima and Pinal Cos., Ariz. Recorded specimens collected: Tucson, 3 miles n. of Florence, 5.5 miles s. of Florence Junction, 3 miles s.e. of Picacho. *Elevation* —1,000 to 3,000 feet.

Size: Adults, 11.25–12.2 inches. We have no data except Stickel's 3 males, 281, 282, 315 mm., and 1 female, 318 mm.

Distinctive characteristics: "Morphologically like the other forms of *S. occipitalis,* this subspecies is characterized by having a double series of dark bands: secondary brown bands occur in the spaces between the primary black bands. The heavy and distinct intercalated bands are not to be confused with the dark edging and mottling sometimes seen in the light areas of other subspecies" (Stickel, 1941).

Habitat: Zonally it is Arizonan (Cooper, Ecol., 1859; Smith, Ecol., 1941); of the desert or extreme desert (Shelford, Jones, and Dice, Ecol., 1926); of the Sonoran desert (Harshberger, Ecol., 1911); of the Basin and Range province (Fenneman, Ecol., 1931).

Authority: Stickel, W. H. (Gen., 1938; Calif., 1941)

Northern shovel-nosed ground snake

Chionactis occipitalis talpina Klauber 1951. Map 15

Range: "Fifty miles south of Goldfield in Nye County, Nevada, on the Beatty road; and from 10 miles north of Goldfield, Esmeralda County, Nevada, on the Tonapah road" (Klauber).

Size: Three known specimens, 2 males 284–335 mm., 1 female 340 mm.

Distinctive characteristics: "A subspecies differing from the subspecies of *palarostris* and from the other species of *occipitalis* except *klauberi,* in having, in the interspaces between the main series of crossbands, dark marks that give the effect of secondary brown crossbands. From *klauberi* it differs in having more ventrals, and in having brown, instead of black primary bands" (Klauber).

Color: "The colors in life (Ridgway) were as follows: the snout was Reed Yellow, the crescent Mummy Brown. The primary dorsal bands were mostly Warm Sepia, but Rood's Brown at their lower edges. The interspaces were Colonial Buff with spots of Light Ochraceous Salmon; the maculations were Rood's Brown. The ventral surface was Pale Olive-Buff and the rings Rood's Brown. There were Maize Yellow spots on the tail between the primary blotches. The eye was Black" (Klauber).

Breeding: The female contained 3 eggs.

Authority: L. M. Klauber (Gen., 1951)

Sonora shovel-nosed ground snake

Chionactis palarostris palarostris (Klauber) 1937. Map 15

Range: Has been found 5 miles s. of Magdalena, Sonora, Mex., and 50 miles s. and 40 miles s. of Hermosillo, Sonora.

Distinctive characteristics: Ten black body rings separated from red dorsal bands by narrow yellow rings, 1–1¾ scales wide; snout convex; 3 tail bars; red saddles twice the width of dark bars.

Organ-Pipe shovel-nosed snake

Chionactis palarostris organica Klauber 1951. Fig. 41; Map 15

Range: Organ Pipe Cactus National Monument, Ariz.

Size: Longest male, 308 mm.; longest female, 391 mm.

Distinctive characteristics: 13 to 20 body blotches; convex snout; red saddle interspaces shorter than or equal to body bars.

Color: A snake from Organ Pipe Cactus National Monument, Ariz., received May 16, 1946, from William R. Supernaugh through the kindness of J. R. Slevin.[1] The dorsum is crossed by bands of black and red separated

---

[1] Mr. Slevin wrote to us from Gila Bend, Ariz., on May 9, 1946, as follows: "Here we are! By express today I am forwarding a *Sonora* and trust it will be *klauberi.* Has lots of black like one I got before on Ajo road. I'm so used to telescopes I forgot any *Sonoras.* However this snake was given me by Mr. William R. Supernaugh, of the Organ Pipe Cactus National Monument. He was going to send it, so I told him I had boxes ready and would send it. If you do not want it for keeps, I can use it but it is your snake by rights. We found pickings at Potholes very poor—only 10 wormsnakes and Sonoras where we got loads before. Cruised roads from Alamo Canyon in the National Monument without seeing a snake. Yesterday went clear to Punta Penasco and drove back

by narrow yellow rings. There are 22 bands of scarlet, flame scarlet, or grenadine red, 4 of which are on the tail. These bands are 3–4½ scales long on mid-dorsum, do not taper on the side, and end along the tops of the 2nd row of scales. The yellow rings one scale in width that separate the black and red bands are sulphur yellow, chartreuse yellow, or seafoam yellow. The black to dull violet-black rings number 23 in all, counting the one on the head, of which 4 are on the tail and one over the vent. They are 4½–3½ scales long on mid-dorsum and taper suddenly on the lower scale rows to 1½–2 scales on the first scale row and cross the venter, usually on 2 ventrals, where from mid-belly backward each dark bar has a little extension backward and one forward. The first neck band of black does not cross the belly, but the second one does. The face, labials, and top of head ahead of the frontal are seafoam yellow, with a touch of grenadine red on top of the snout. The black head marking extends from front of eye to front of eye and back almost to rear of parietals, where there is a slight touch of seafoam yellow and scarlet. The rear edge of this black band is crescentic. The iris is black. The ventral background color is pale fluorite green to white on under side of head. The light areas on under side of tail have slight wash of shrimp pink to orient pink.

RACERS

Genus *COLUBER* Linné (Figs. 21, 24)

Size large, 22–78 inches; long and slender; head wide, its width .44–.52 in length; snout convex above and below; anal divided; scale rows 17 in mid-body, 15 at posterior end; scales smooth with apical pits; nasals 2; frontal concave on sides, anteriorly wider than supraocular; chin shields spreading at least at the tips with 2–3 rows gulars between tips and ventrals; lower preocular very small and wedged between adjacent upper labials; eye over upper labials 3 + 4 (4 + 5 in *C. stejnegerianus* and sometimes in *C. mormon*); upper labials 7 (8 in *C. mormon* and *C. stejnegerianus*) (when varied plate 2 involved); lower labials 9 (6–11); dorsal color uniform (aberrant form in Louisiana, spotted); juveniles, spotted, barred, or banded; venter gray, slaty blue, yellow, or greenish; preocular in adult without a

---

by night without seeing a snake—no dead ones on road either with one exception— way down towards the point we saw a very dead *atrox.* This A.M. picked up what I suppose is an *Elaphe,* though it is not unicolor. Looks more like a giant *Trimorphodon.* Have never collected one in Arizona, picked up dead on road but condition O.K. What is strange to both of us [his companion was the late Wallace Wood] is lack of lizards. Even *Callisaurus* and *Dipsosaurus* seldom seen. I took one nice *Chilomeniscus* in Alamo Canyon. It is not possible to reach Dripping Spring by car. Will you send name of snake to Mr. Supernaugh?"

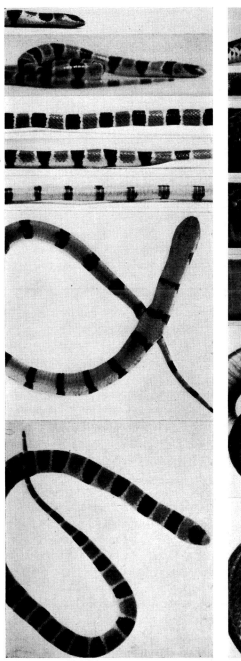

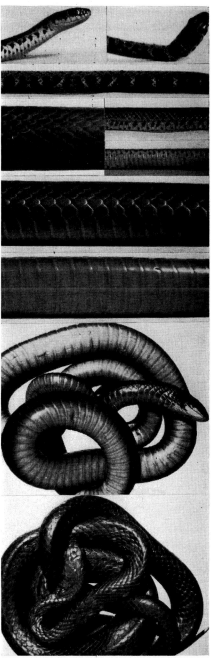

Fig. 41. *Chionactis palarostris organica,*
Oregon Pipe Cactus Nat. Monument, Ariz.,
W. R. Supernaugh.

Fig. 42. *Coluber constrictor constrictor,*
Enfield Falls, Ithaca, N.Y., W. Snyder,
W. Chapel.

white center; maxillary teeth 13–19. Hemipenis—stout, rounded, slightly bilobed; sulcus simple; 6–9 longitudinal rows of spines which number 90–135; 6–8 rows calyces, fringed, more basal ones spined; tip of organ smooth, basal ⅜ mostly smooth. Ventrals 151–193; caudals 72–120. Synonyms: *Bascanion, Bascanium, Coryphodon, Hierophis, Masticophis, Zamenis.*

KEY TO THE GENUS *COLUBER*

a. Dorsum spotted; back blackish green-gray, irregularly sprinkled with light scales of deep olive-buff to pearl gray and white; lower sides and ends of ventrals parula blue; mid-venter glaucous gray. Scalation like *C. c. flaviventris.* (W.-cent. Louisiana.)   *C. c. anthicus*

aa. Dorsum uniform in adults

    b. Belly dark gray. Dorsal surface black or very dark gray; chin and throat white. Caudals average 96 (80–120). Black racers. Young with 50–65 saddles.

        c. Proximal spines of hemipenes not enlarged into basal hooks. Eye color brown. (U.S. e. of Mississippi River exclusive of peninsular Florida.)   *C. constrictor constrictor*

      cc. Some of the proximal spines of hemipenes much enlarged into basal hooks. Eye: Pupil rim maize yellow or olive buff, surrounded by rufous, xanthine orange, or vinaceous tawny. (Florida.)

                                                C. c. priapus

  bb. Belly yellow or greenish. Green racers, Blue racers. Interscale color frequently black.

    c. Upper labials usually 7. Color dorsum predominantly blue-gray, slate, or olive. Caudal average 86 (66–105). Loreal may be divided longitudinally. (Young with 40–50 transverse bands.) Size large to 78 inches. (E. of Mississippi River [*foxi*]; w. of Mississippi River [*flaviventris*] according to some authors.)

                                            C. c. flaviventris

    cc. Upper labials usually 8 (7); size large medium, below 50 inches.

      d. Maxillary teeth 13–14. Ventral 163–193. Juveniles with 70–85 saddles; dorsum olive brown, brownish green, or grayish green. Lower labials usually 8; labials 3 + 4, sometimes 4 + 5 enter orbit.   *C. c. mormon*

      dd. Maxillary teeth 19. Ventrals 151–171. Juveniles with no saddles, but anteriorly 42–53 narrow crossbars (1–3 scales wide); Dorsum asphodel green and grape green, buffy olive on mid-back. Labials 4 + 5 enter orbit. (Subtropical s. Texas.)   *C. c. stejnegerianus*

Black snake (164—Glover-Clayton 1705),
Black racer (37—Garman 1877)

Coluber constrictor constrictor Linné 1758. Fig. 42; Map 16

Other common names: American black snake; American racer snake; black chaser; black runner; (Fox's) blue racer; blue runner; chicken snake; common black racer; common black snake; cow sucker?; eastern black snake; green racer; hoop snake?; horse racer?; pilot snake; racer; slick black snake; true black snake; white-throated racer.

Range: From Nova Scotia coastally to cent. New York, s.w. to mouth of Ohio River, down Mississippi River to Gulf coast and e. to Georgia. Roughly, e. U.S. s. of Ohio and e. of Mississippi Rivers, exclusive of peninsular Florida.—U.S.A.: Ala.; Ark.; Conn.; D.C.; Del.; Fla.; Ga.; Ind.; Ky.; La.; Mass.; Md.; Me.; Miss.; N.C.; N.H.; N.J.; N.Y.; O.; Pa.; R.I.; S.C.; Tenn.; Va.; W. Va. Can.: N.S.; P.E.I. *Elevation*—Principally from sea level to 1,000 to 2,000 feet. 2,250–3,900 (Barbour); 1,000–4,000 feet (King, Tenn., 1939); 2,000, 2,200, 4,100 feet (Dunn, N.C., 1917); 1,100–2,200 (Smith, Pa., 1945).

Size: Adults, 36–78 inches.

Longevity: 2–5 years (Kauffeld, Gen., 1951).

Distinctive characteristics: A long and moderately slender snake with glossy scales, the back uniformly black, the belly dark to medium gray, chin, throat, and neck white. Ventrals 161–181, caudals 72–107.

Color: We early (1928) described this common form from a snake from Florida which now has become *C. c. priapus,* which see.

Habitat: For New York, see Engelhardt, Nichols, Latham, and Murphy (1915); for New Jersey, Trapido; for Maryland, McCauley (1945); for D.C., Hay (1902a); for Virginia, Brady (1925); for North Carolina, Gray (1941) or Lewis (1946); for South Carolina, Corrington 1929; for Georgia, Wright and Bishop.

We accumulated 36 categories of habitat. Some of them are brushy country; undergrowths near streams; thickets of alders; wet wood growths; edges of woods, swamps, and marshes; margins of thick woods; wooded areas, regions, lots, lands; dry, thick, open upland; lowland forests; deciduous, pine, hardwood forests; open fields; clearings; meadows; grassy fields; old fields; glades; road borders; cultivated areas; around farms; stone walls; sandy regions; sandy hills or dunes; coastal plain environments; sparsely settled districts; and wild and unfrequented places.

Period of activity: Early appearances—Apr. 1, 2, 4 (Corrington, Miss., 1927); Mar. 20 (Harper, Ga., 1930); Apr. 6 (Cohen); May 9, 1908 (Fowler, N.J., 1908); May 15, 1912 (Engelhardt, N.Y., 1913).

Hibernation—In 1947 Cohen gave an extended account of the emergence of black snakes from hibernation. He found an old *Microtus* burrow be-

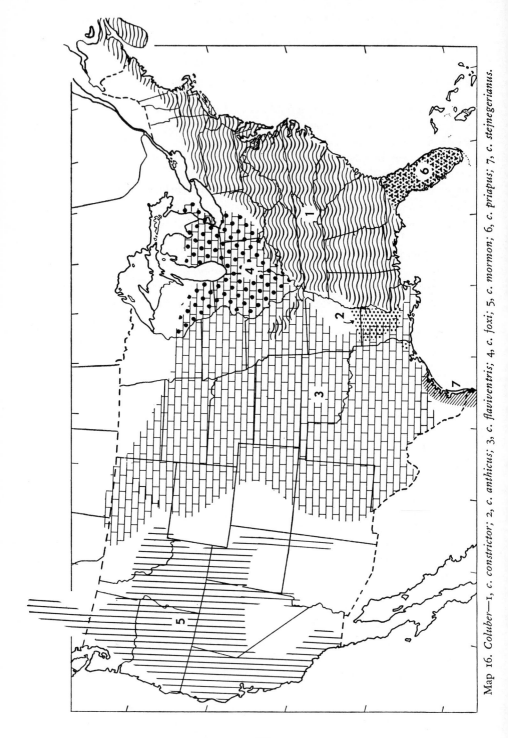

Map 16. *Coluber*—1, *c. constrictor*; 2, *c. anthicus*; 3, *c. flaviventris*; 4, *c. foxi*; 5, *c. mormon*; 6, *c. priapus*; 7, *c. stejnegerianus.*

tween two roots of a beech tree, 3 feet above the level of a nearby pond, whence the black snakes emerged. Owens (Mo., 1949a) on Mar. 3, 1949, took from an old cistern 8 blue racers and 7 black pilot snakes. They were concentrated near the top because the well was full of water except for the upper 3 feet. They doubtless went into hibernation when the well was dry. In 1949 Hudson (Pa., 1949) reported finding black snakes hibernating in a well 20 feet deep and 4 feet wide. Allen observed: "This species appears to be eminently gregarious, especially early in spring, when several (formerly scores) are often seen together sunning themselves. They probably collect in autumn, many hibernating together, sometimes alone, but not unfrequently associated with other species. A farmer in this vicinity turned up with his plow, quite early in May, 1868, a ball of them numbering between 70 and 80, and averaging between 4 and 5 feet in length. Another farmer, not long since, ploughed up at the same season a bunch of snakes, chiefly of the common striped species (*Tropidonotus sirtalis*), but including some . . . black snakes, numbering between 40 and 50."

In 1880 there appeared in the *American Naturalist* an article entitled "Bundles of snakes," from which we quote: "The second time I noticed a ball of black snakes (*Bascanion constrictor* L.) rolling slowly down a steep and stony hillside on the bank of the same river, but about two miles above Union Factory, Baltimore County, Md. Some of the snakes were of considerable length and thickness, and, as I noticed clearly, kept together by procreative impulses."

Unlike many other snake tales, those concerning bundles of snakes cannot be read out of court readily. One of our best Ph.D. students once saw near Ringwood Preserve, Ithaca, N.Y., a ball of snakes in the fall season. Such evidence cannot be ignored.

Breeding: Oviparous. Males 680–1,595 mm., females 710–1,683 mm. Miller (N.J., 1937) held the adult males to be 1,087–1,692 mm. and females 1,030–1,545 mm. For example, he called 831, 895, and 935 mm. males subadult and a female 924 mm. subadult.

Mating—May 8, 1921, Billy Island: A pair of black snakes was found. They were stretched out, more or less coiled, mating, the one below, or head and forward body below, being the male. It was longer from vent to head by 1 to 1½ feet. The rear parts of bodies from the vent were entwined. The female or smaller one seemed to have its tail around that of the male. There were contortions or quiverings from time to time. We caught both male and female. We were all surprised to find the larger one, the male, 1595 mm., and the female, 1200 mm. May 9, 1921: Jackson Lee saw black snakes mated, the male seizing the female by the top of the neck. Mating probably occurs until June 1 or later (A. H. Wright, Journal).

Eggs—Number, 3–40. Babcock (Gen., 1929a), Barbour, Brimley, Conant and Bridges (Gen., 1939); Conant and Downs, Ditmars (1907), Fowler

(D.C., 1945), Gadow (Gen., 1901), Lowe (Me., 1928), Minton (Ind., 1944), Stejneger (Gen., 1895), Surface, and Wright and Bishop (1916). Several records of 20–25 were reported in a clutch; possibly Surface's 40 may be an estimate. Time of deposition, June 1 into early July. Size, 1.1–1.8 inches x .64–1.1 inches in diameter. Conant and Downs have one record of 26.8 mm. x 20.4 mm. and one 46.5 mm. long. Wright and Bishop give 32–41 mm. x 16–23 mm. for 42 eggs (6 complements).

"Short, oblong in shape, often lumpy and one-sided and irregular and covered with thick skin with a rough surface to which dirt readily adheres so that the color is usually a dirty white. The eggs are free, not adherent" (Brimley). "Oval in shape—deposited 2 or 3 inches below the surface of loose soil into which the reptile burrows, or in piles of saw dust, hollow logs or decaying wood" (Surface). Ditmars described them as appearing as if sparsely sprinkled with grains of coarse salt.

Young—Most records of hatching from July 28–Aug. 15. One record of eggs hatching last of August or early September, one of hatching in October Size, 11–13.5 inches. The young are light gray with transverse dorsal blotches or spots. This livery they may retain for 1½–2 years or more.

Food: Small mammals, batrachians, snakes, lizards. Linsley (Conn., 1844), Bailey (Ky., 1933), Cope (Gen., 1900), Nash (Ont., 1908), Bateman, Wright and Bishop, Uhler, Cottam, Clarke (Va., 1939).

Authorities:

Allen, J. A. (Mass., 1868)
Barbour, R. W. (Ky., 1950)
Bateman, G. C. (Gen., 1897)
Brimley, C. S. (Gen., 1903)
Cohen, E. (Md., 1948)
Conant, R., and A. Downs, Jr. (Gen., 1940)
DeKay, J. R. (N.Y., 1842)
Ditmars, R. L. (Gen., 1907; N.Y., 1896, 1905)

Fowler, H. W. (N.J., 1907, 1908)
Funkhouser, W. D. (Ky., 1925)
Logier, E. B. S. (Ont., 1925)
Ortenburger, A. I. (Gen., 1928)
Surface, H. A. (Pa., 1906)
Thompson, Z. (Vt., 1842)
Trapido, H. (N.J., 1937)
Wright, A. H., and S. C. Bishop (Ga., 1916)

Spotted black snake (3—Strecker 1928), Ash snake

Coluber constrictor anthicus (Cope, 1862). Fig. 43; Map 16

Other common names: Blue racer; brown racer, Louisiana black snake; spotted racer; variegated racer; white oak racer.

Range: In Louisiana between Mississippi and Sabine Rivers n. of lat. 30° 30′ N. (Beauregard and Allen Counties), possibly extending into adjoining Arkansas and Texas.—La.; Tex. *Elevation*—Seacoast to 500 feet.

Size: Adults 24–48 inches certainly, and probably considerably larger. Cope described a 34-inch specimen. We have seen them at least 4 feet long.

Distinctive characteristics: Like *flaviventris* except for light, grayish, ashy gray, white, or yellowish white spots, scattered singly or clustered on a slate, olive, or black dorsum—a mottled *Coluber*.

Color: A snake loaned us by P. Viosca, of New Orleans. The background of the back is blackish green-gray, becoming on the sides bluish black or bluish slate-black, and finally becoming on the ends of the ventrals parula blue, a color sharply differentiated from the glaucous-gray of the mid-belly. All over the back is an irregular sprinkling of light scales. Along the mid-back, these are dark olive-buff or deep olive-buff. On the lower sides, they are pearl gray. As these spots enter the parula blue marginal band of the ventrals, they are almost pure white. The plates of the top of the head and face are deep olive-buff or grayish olive. The rostral and lower half of the upper labials are white. The upper part of the preocular upper labials is like the face, while the upper part of the postocular ones is bluish slate-black. The iris is bluish slate-black with a fawn band around the pupil and with the upper part of the pupil rim white. The main portion of the ventrals is glaucous-gray with a few scattered black dots which are absent on the first 30 ventrals and on the lower side of the head, which is white or seashell pink, as is the underside of the tail.

Field notes: May 12, 1950: Six miles east of Oakdale on route 22 saw dead on road a spotted racer which at first we called a rat snake (*Elaphe*) until we examined it. It was slaty on the back and the light spots and lighter color were pale yellowish gray. It was 3½ of my foot lengths (40 inches). The woods on either side of the road were dense and mixed forest. Two or 3 miles north of Oakdale near another woods [lay] a very dead spotted racer and another one almost too mashed to identify. In a wooded stretch between Leander and Leesville, La., found another *C. c. anthicus* dead on road, but there are very few light spots on it. Country from Leander to Leesville is largely cutover and as barren as the Cyber, Ala., cutover pine forests in 1917 or the stripped s.w. Oregon hills in 1942.

May 14, north of Benson, La.: As we approached a creek we saw a seeming grassy branch on road. It proved to be a spotted blue runner DOR. As I walked across the bridge I soon found another. When I came up to the car with these two trophies, Anna looked back in her mirror, and right where I found the first one a live one crossed the road.

We had considered this ash snake a very rare form, but our 1950 trip proved it the common *Coluber* of cent.-w. Louisiana in the old long-leaf-pine areas of Vernon and Rapides parishes.

Authorities:

Blanchard, F. (La., 1930)
Burt, C. E., and M. D. (Ark., 1929a)
Cope, E. D. (Gen., 1900; 1862 Proc., P.A.N.S., 338–339)
Dunn, E. R., and G. C. Wood (Gen., 1939)

Fitch, H. S. (La., 1949)
Ortenburger, R. I. (Gen., 1928)
Strecker, J. K., Jr. (Tex., 1927b, 1928c)
Strecker, J. K., Jr., and L. S. Frierson, Jr. (La., 1926)

1945, A. H. and A. A. Wright: For 20 years we have called it the *anthicum* phase and would still prefer to designate it a phase. Viosca has seen more of them alive than anyone else—and more than are in collections. Not until he or Meade or Cagle's group can give us more light are we inclined to designate this *Coluber constrictor anthicus* (Cope), a subspecies in good standing. In the light of Ortenburger's 6 forms (Gen., 1928, see map) in Louisiana and the tangled color phases we have overheard Viosca or Meade discuss, we prefer to hold the matter in abeyance pending a real field study of the problem.

1949, H. S. Fitch commented tersely: "Variegated racer *Coluber constrictor anthicus,* 17; all habitats, especially grassy uplands."

1950, A. H. and A. A. Wright: After we saw it in cent.-w. Louisiana, we wanted more study and evidence on its real status.

Blue racer (79—Mozley 1878), Yellow-bellied racer (18—Strecker 1908)

Coluber constrictor flaviventris (Say) 1823. Fig. 44; Map 16
(Includes *C. c. foxi,* of Schmidt's *Check List,* 1953, but see p. 142)

Other common names: Black racer; (common) black snake; (eastern) blue chaser; Fox's black snake; Fox's blue racer; green racer; olive racer; plains blue racer; (western) racer; (western) yellow-bellied adder; yellow-bellied black snake.

Range: Roughly, central lowland, great plains, and Ozark plateau of Fenneman (between long. 82° and 107°). Cent. Ohio, s.w. Ontario, and s. Michigan through s. Wisconsin and Minnesota to n.w. North Dakota and w. Montana, s. to cent. New Mexico and Big Bend of Texas, e. to Mississippi River.—U.S.A.: Colo.; Ia.; Ill.; Ind.; Kan.; La.; Mich.; Minn.; Mo.; Mont.; Neb.; N.D.; N.M.; O.; Okla.; S.D.; Tex.; Wis.; Wyo. Can.: Ont. *Elevation*—Seacoast to 5,000 feet.

Size: Adults, 24–78 inches. It has been reported 9 feet long (Clark, Mich., 1904), but we doubt it.

Distinctive characteristics: Large, smooth, lithe, uniform-colored serpent with back usually blue-gray or slate and belly yellow, greenish yellow, or white. Sometimes back may be "black gray, green, olive, yellow, and bluish" and belly "slate-colored, white, greenish, bluish, yellow" (Strecker); supralabials usually 7; average caudals 86 (range 66–105); ventrals 158–191.

Color: A young spotted racer from Riley Co., Kan. furnished by H. K. Gloyd, Apr. 28, 1928. On the back are 40 or 50 distinct transverse bands with light brownish olive centers encircled with chestnut brown or black edges. The space between the spots is white or pearl gray. Toward the vent the colors are broken into irregular markings. The dorsum of the tail is buffy brown. The scales of the sides are pearl gray on the edges with

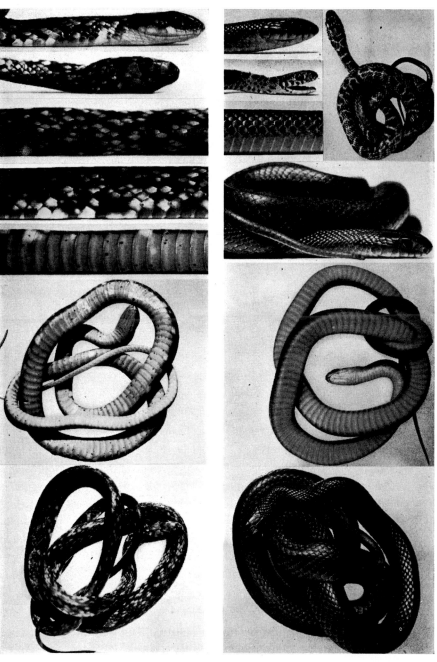

Fig. 43. *Coluber c. anthicus,* New Orleans, La., P. Viosca, Jr.

Fig. 44. *Coluber c. flaviventris:* 1,3,5,7, Franklin Co., Kansas; 2,4, Riley Co., Kansas, H. K. Gloyd. *Coluber c. foxi,* 6, Michigan, M. Pirnie.

centers of light grayish olive. Along the sides are about 3 irregular rows of chestnut brown or black spots with rufous or ferruginous edges.

A female green racer from Franklin Co., Kan. furnished by H. K. Gloyd, Apr. 23, 1928. The mid-back is deep olive, becoming, on the first 2 rows of scales, olive-citrine or dull citrine. The rear edges of these 2 lower rows of scales and the ends of the ventrals are pale glaucous green, deep lichen green, or pale olivine. The rear edges of most dorsal scales are black edged, or the interspaces are black. The color on the dorsum of the tail becomes fuscous. The top of the head, the side of the head ahead of the eye, and some of the scales on the back of the neck are brownish olive. The first row of scales on the neck is bright green-yellow. The lower part of the upper labials and the entire surface of the lower labials are straw yellow. The pupil of the eye is large with a cream or cartridge buff rim. This is followed in the iris by a narrow orange-cinnamon or vinaceous-rufous ring, while the main portion is liver brown to chestnut brown. The underside of the head is pale chalcedony yellow. The forward 6 inches or more of the under parts is primuline yellow or between lemon chrome and light cadmium. Rearward, the venter becomes pinard yellow, which finally in the rear under parts and underside of tail becomes baryta yellow, buff-yellow, or cream color.

Habitat: In 1823 the first specimens were taken in a stone quarry by James. Over 60 years elapsed before writers stopped copying life history and habitat notes on the eastern form. In 1886 Hughes (Ind.) found it frequently "about the barns and outhouses on the farm." Hahn (Ind.) in 1909 declared that it was "very abundant everywhere in the vicinity." No doubt in the very early days, when the first settlers annually burnt the prairie and plain districts, these snakes suffered badly. The habitat notes are numerous. We will content ourselves with the categories. Roadsides receive most votes because that is where we see them. They have been recorded in the timber zone, woods, woodland, wooded ravine, edge of woods, wooded hillsides, brambly thickets, trees, bushes, open woods, and brushy areas. They are also credited to cultivated areas or fields, such as: meadows 6, low grounds, grassy fields 4 or grassland 1, weedy areas 1, pastures 3, fields (wheat, grain, or hay fields) 6. Other places given are cover such as top of blackberry bushes, rocks, rock piles, debris, rotten logs, rock outcroppings. Still other miscellaneous places are sandy tracts; springs; foothills; borders of marshes, lakes, ponds; creek or river bottoms; glades; rocky hillsides. Sixty years or more ago it began to diminish; Hurter (Mo.) wrote in 1893: "This snake is getting rather scarce, owing to the cultivation of the low grounds and its preference for meadows."

Period of activity: *First appearance*—May 16 (Hankinson, Mich., 1908); Apr. 24, 1928 (Pope, Wis., 1927); Apr. 1 (Gloyd); Apr. 27, 1927 (Burt, Kan., 1927); last of March (Force, Okla., 1930); Apr. (Boyer and Heinze,

Mo., 1934); Apr. 17, 1926, Apr. 4, 1927 (Gloyd); Apr. 13, 1932 (Burt); Apr. 19, 1929 (Mann); Apr. 8, 15, 22, 27 (Hurter); Apr. 18, 1936 (Anderson, Mo., 1942). *Fall disappearance*—Sept. 11, 1913 (Ellis and Henderson, Colo., 1915); Oct. 29, 1926 (Pope, Wis., 1928); Dec. 15 (Gloyd); last of October (Force); Nov., 1931 (Boyer and Heinze); Oct. 1 to 17, 1932 (Burt); Oct. 3, (Hurter). *Hibernation*—The 1823 specimens were hibernators in a quarry. See Gaige (Ill., 1914), Boyer and Heinze, Loomis and Jones (Neb., 1941).

Breeding: Oviparous. *Mating*—Gloyd found a male and female under a stone Apr. 4, 1927, but not mated. Again, on May 12, he collected a larger pair together. Boyer and Heinze recorded 2 copulating pairs on May 3, 1921, and Anderson (Mo., 1945) observed 2 in coitus Apr. 18, 1936.

Eggs—Number, 1–28, average, 14–17. 8, 10, Force (Okla., 1930); 15, Guthrie (Ia., 1926); 19, Hay (Ind., 1892); 1, 24, Hudson and Davis (Neb., 1941); 26, 28, *Life* magazine; 18, Liner (La., 1949); 5, 8, 17, Marr (1944); 5, 14, Munro (Ark., 1948a); 13, 19, Ortenburger (Gen., 1928); 22, Ramsey (Ind., 1901). Time of deposition, June 1 (Ortenburger, 1928); June 9 (Guidry, Tex., 1953); July 4, 1948 (Munro, Kan., 1950a) to July 10. Size, 1.1–1.6 inches long x .5–1 inch. Force (Okla., 1930) gave us "the average size of 26 eggs 33.4x15.3 mm.; the extremes in length and diameter 29.0 to 39.8 mm. and 12.8 to 18.0 mm. Average number of eggs per brood 8.7."

Young—Hatching time, Aug. 1–Sept. 15 (Ramsey, Ind., 1901); Sept. 22 (Hankinson, Ill., 1917); Aug. 23, 24, 1948 (Munro, Kan., 1950a); July 22 (Guidry, Tex., 1953). Size, 10–12 inches or more. The young are lighter, grayish tan, greenish gray, yellowish, dark olive, or olive brown with spots and dorsal transverse blotches. Some authors say the young lose this coloration at 18–20 inches or 1½–2 years; others maintain they may keep the juvenile color to 25 or more inches or 3 years of age.

In recent years Munro (Ark., 1948a; Kan., 1950a) has given us the most detailed account of the breeding.

Food: Rodents, frogs, young birds, insects, poisonous snakes. Coues and Yarrow, Linsdale (Kan., 1927), Force (Okla., 1930), Garman (Ill., 1892), Notestein (Mich., 1905), Morse (O., 1904), Hughes (Ind., 1886), Hurter, Anderson (Mo., 1941), Guthrie (Ia., 1926), Over (S.D., 1923), Hudson, Gloyd (Kan., 1932), Strecker.

Authorities:

Blatchley, W. S. (Ind., 1891)

Branson, E. B. (Kan., 1904)

Brons, H. A. (Kan., 1882)

Coues, E., and H. C. Yarrow (Mont., 1878)

Ellis, M. M., and J. Henderson (Colo., 1913)

Evermann, B. W., and H. W. Clark (Ind., 1920)

Fitch, H. S. (Kan., 1951)

Garman, H. (Ill., 1890, 1892)

Garman, S. W. (Gen., 1876)

Gloyd, H. K. (Kan., 1928)

Hallowell, E. (Proc. Acad. Nat. Sci., Phila., 8: 241–242)

Hay, O. P. (Ind., 1892)

Hudson, G. E. (Neb., 1942)

Hurter, J. (Mo., 1911)

James, E. (Gen., 1822–23)

Liner, E. A. (La., 1949)

Marr, J. C. (Gen., 1944)

Munro, D. F. (Ark., 1948a; Kan. 1949b, 1950a, 1950b)

Ortenburger, A. I. (Gen., 1928)

Praeger, W. E. (Ill., 1899)

Shufeldt, R. W. (Gen., 1915)

Smith, H. M. (Kan., 1950)

Smith, W. H. (Mich., 1879)

Strecker, J. K., Jr. (Tex., 1927b)

Wied, M. zu (Gen., 1865)

1938, K. P. Schmidt (Gen.): "The range of the blue racer, *Coluber constrictor flaviventris,* is instructive. The species has been exhaustively studied (Ortenburger). While it is quite clearly a post-Wisconsin entrant into the prairie peninsula, its continuous range extends eastward beyond central Ohio. There could scarcely be a better example of correlation between existing range and the steppe peninsula hypothesis."

1951: H. S. Fitch reported that this species was frequently found in the funnel trap device he used for population studies. It was fourth in number caught.

Blue racer

Coluber constrictor foxi (Baird and Girard). Fig. 44; Map 16

Some prefer to think the blue racers east of the Mississippi River a separate subspecies, *C. c. foxi.* We therefore include a color description of the blue phase.

Color: A blue racer from Lansing, Mich., furnished by M. D. Pirnie, Aug. 5, 1928. The upper parts are bluish slate-black, dusky slate-blue, dark delft blue, or dusky green blue, becoming on the first row of scales and on the ends of the ventrals light medici blue, porcelain blue, or Alice blue. The top of the head is dark olive. The side of the head is black. The upper labials are ivory yellow, cartridge buff, or pale olive buff with black tips. Above the pupil the iris shows a patch of avellaneous or vinaceous buff which extends to the pupil rim. The pupil rim is tilleul buff in front and above, but deep olive below. The throat, chin, and lower labials are white. The ventrals are in general lighter than the dorsal scales, being sky gray, pale medici blue, or even lighter. The rear edge of each ventral is white with a deep medici-blue line ahead of it.

Western yellow-bellied racer (21—Van Denburgh 1897),
Blue racer (8—Van Denburgh 1897)

Coluber constrictor mormon (Baird and Girard) 1852. Fig. 45; Map 16

Other common names: Black chaser; (California) black snake; green racer; Mormon (blue) racer; western blue racer; yellow-bellied black snake; yellow-bellied racer; yellow coachwhip snake.

Range: The Great Basin from n.e. California, n. Nevada (above lat. 40°) e. to cent. Utah, n. across Snake River plains to e. Idaho, northern Rockies of w. Montana and n. Idaho, across Columbia plateau of e. Washington and Oregon to British Columbia and Cascades of Washington, then s. coastally to extreme s. California.—U.S.A.: Ariz.; Calif.; Ida.; Mont.; Nev.; Ore.; Ut.; Wash.; Wyo. Can.: B.C. *Elevation*—To 4,610 feet (Klauber, Calif., 1924a); 5,000 feet (Van Denburgh); 5,500 feet (Ruthven, Ut., 1932). Coast to divide (Klauber, Calif., 1931a); ocean to foothills (Perkins); 4,610 feet (Klauber, 1924a); 3,400 feet (Grinnell and Camp, Calif., 1917); 270, 600, 2,300, 3,300, 4,500, 5,300 feet (Grinnell, Dixon, and Linsdale); 4,000 to 6,000 feet (Linsdale, Nev., 1938–40); 5,500 (Ruthven, Utah, 1932); to 4,000 feet (Ferguson, Ore., 1952).

Size: Adults, smaller than black or blue racers, 27–51.5 inches.

Distinctive characteristics: A long, slender snake, smaller than *C. constrictor flaviventris;* back olive green, grayish green, or some tone of green or olive; belly some hue of yellow from cream or ivory to pale orange-yellow. Upper labials usually 8 (sometimes 7). Length 2–4 feet, while *C. constrictor* and *C. flaviventris* reach 6 feet. Juvenile saddles 70–85.

Color: A snake from San Diego Co., near Oceanside, Calif. furnished in May, 1940, by C. W. Kern. The middorsum is buffy olive, becoming on the 3rd and 4th scale rows yellowish olive. The belly is amber yellow.

A snake from Pullman, Wash., furnished by D. J. Leffingwell, May 22, 1929. The upper parts are deep grayish olive, becoming on the tail drab or olive brown. The first 2 rows of scales and the ends of the ventrals are deep glaucous gray or light celandine green. The top of the head is dark grayish olive or deep olive. The lower part of the upper labials is white. The iris is black with a light pinkish cinnamon rim to the pupil. The underside of the head is white, the under parts are sulphur yellow or light green yellow fading to seafoam yellow and white on the underside of the tail and becoming toward the tip pale pinkish cinnamon.

Habitat: Consult Cooper (Mont., 1869); Grinnell (Calif., 1907); Thompson; Ruthven and Gaige; Grinnell and Camp (Calif., 1917); Blanchard (Wash., 1921); Grinnell and Storer; Grinnell, Dixon, and Linsdale; Svihlas (Wash., 1933); Alcorn; Owen (Wash., 1940); Pack; Woodbury; and Klauber (Gen., 1939a) for notes on this topic, mostly subsequent to 1915. From this data, we record the following: all land habitats; mountains and basins at all altitudes; on margin of valley and mountain slopes; among grass and bushes of a valley; open washes; plains, hill slopes; dry hillsides; grasslands; meadows; amid water cress; bank of a ditch; swimming in a creek; barley fields; sandy ground; sedges of a small pool; irrigation ditch; wheatlands; conifer areas; sagebrush country; foothills; waste areas; canyon bottoms; orchards and vineyards—a widespread, common form.

Period of activity: In his census from 1923 to 1938 Klauber (Gen., 1939a) found 2 in Feb., 4 Mar., 11 Apr., 21 May, 26 June, 11 July, 2 Aug., 2 Sept., 1 Nov. *First appearance*—May 30 (Van Denburgh and Slevin); May 18, 1924 (Grinnell, Dixon, Linsdale); Apr. 28, 1934 (Alcorn); May 19, 1913 (Van Denburgh, Ut., 1915); May 10, 1927 (Shannon, Ariz., 1950). *Fall appearances*—Aug. (Cooper, Mont., 1869); Aug. 26, 27, 1916, Sept. 2, 1918 (Van Denburgh and Slevin); Oct. 6 (Pack). MVZ records it from Feb. 22 to Dec. 16. *Hibernation*—In the rattlesnake den which Woodbury has been watching for years, he and Smart (Ut., 1950) record 6 associated species, of which the mormon blue racer is 3rd in frequency.

Breeding: Oviparous. *Mating*—In 1937 Cottam wrote that he observed a pair of copulating western blue racers at midday June 10, 1927, at Moab, Grand Co., Ut. He wrote: "The snakes were encountered in a damp, grassy meadow near the banks of the Colorado River." *Eggs*—We have only 3 pertinent notes:

1) Bryant: "On June 22, 1923, I caught a western yellow-bellied racer, commonly called 'blue racer,' *Coluber constrictor mormon,* in Leidig Meadow in Yosemite Valley, California. The snake was carried to the Yosemite Museum and there placed in a terrarium. On June 26, upon being informed that the snake had laid some eggs, I went to investigate. In one corner were 3 cylindrical, white eggs and a fourth one was apparently ready for extrusion. The hour was 9:40 A.M. Occasionally muscular contractions which seemed to run almost the length of the snake's body were evident about every 5 minutes. An hour or so later, this fourth egg was in sight and was expelled within about 4 minutes, muscular contractions being evident 2 or 3 times per minute. About 1 o'clock, the fifth egg had been laid and by 2:40 another, making 6 in all. . . . An examination of the eggs showed that they varied in size from 38 to 48 millimeters in length, by actual measurement, but were rather uniform in diameter—about 10 millimeters. The end of the egg first extruded had an opaque, white color, whereas the other end of the egg was more transparent. To the touch, the egg membrane was of a rough, leathery texture, the surface of the eggs having a granular appearance."

2) Logier: "A *pregnant* female was taken at Marron Lake, southwest of Okanagan Lake [B.C.], on Aug. 15, 1930."

3) Storm and Pimentel (Ore., 1949): "One male and one female with three 32 mm. eggs were taken. . . . The female was taken on an open gravelly slope with scattered sage and sparse grass cover, and the male was taken in a grassy meadow. At least 2 others were seen in grassy situations."

Young—Time of hatching is presumably like *C. c. constructor* and *C. c flaviventris*. Size, no records of hatchlings. The smallest specimens we have seen are 175, 259, 275, 305 mm. long, the first of Sept. 10, 1910, and close to hatching size. Van Denburgh's smallest was 267 mm. Color, Perkins (Calif., 1949) uses "juveniles with 75-80 dorsal blotches" in separating this form from *C. c. stejnegerianus*. Van Denburgh and Ortenburger gave extensive accounts of juvenile coloration.

Food: Mice, insects, lizards, snakes, young snakes. Cronise (Calif., 1868), Ortenburger, Grinnell, Dixon, and Linsdale, Pack, and Woodbury.

Authorities:

Alcorn, G. D. (Wash., 1935)
Baird, S. F., and C. Girard (Gen., 1853)
Bogert, C. M. (Calif., 1930)
Bryant, H. C. (Calif., 1925)
Cottam, W. P. (Ut., 1937)
Grinnell, J., and T. Storer (Calif., 1924)
Grinnell, J., J. Dixon, and J. M. Linsdale (Calif., 1930)
Hawken, J. L. (Calif., 1951)
Klauber, L. M. (Gen., 1939a; Calif., 1934a)
Logier, E. B. S. (B.C., 1932)

Lord, J. K. (B.C., 1866)
Ortenburger, A. I. (Gen., 1928)
Pack, H. J. (Ut., 1930)
Perkins, C. B. (Calif., 1938)
Ruthven, A. G., and H. T. Gaige (Nev., 1915)
Stuart, L. C. (Mont., 1930)
Thompson, J. C. (Calif., 1914)
Van Denburgh, J. (Gen., 1922)
Van Denburgh, J., and J. R. Slevin (Ida., 1921b)
Woodbury, A. M. (Ut., 1931)

Florida black snake (4—Ballou 1919)

Coluber constrictor priapus Dunn and Wood 1939. Fig. 46; Map 16

Other common names: Black snake (of Florida); Dunn's black snake; Florida black racer.

Range: Peninsular Florida, roughly s. of a line from the mouth of the Suwanee River to the mouth of St. Mary's River. *Elevation*—Sea level to 500 feet.

Size: Adults, 22–56 inches. Few if any recorded maxima are at hand in scientific literature. We have seen specimens as large as 52 inches. Cone at the Florida State Museum measured one 4 feet 4 inches in August, 1928, C. C. Tyler collector. Blatchley in 1932 had a 4-foot specimen, but Loennberg's record was only 600 mm.

Distinctive characteristics: "Similar to *C. c. constrictor,* but with some of the proximal hooks of the hemipenis much enlarged as in *C. c. flaviventris* and *C. c. mormon.* Other characteristics those of *C. c. constrictor,* as differentiated from *C. c. flaviventris* by Ortenburger" (Dunn and Wood). Eye red or orange (Conant). Ventrals 174–193; caudals 98–116.

Color: A snake from Florida received through H. Axtell and described Mar. 10, 1943. A small snake about 2 feet long. The dorsal color is olivaceous black (3) to slate-black. The top of the head is deep olive. The facial plates, rostral, and front half of prefrontals are wood brown or buffy brown. The white of lower side of head extends onto upper labials, covering half in the rear, to the eye in the middle, the lower third on facial labials, and a rim on the rostral. This white has a slight wash of olive-buff. The first 3

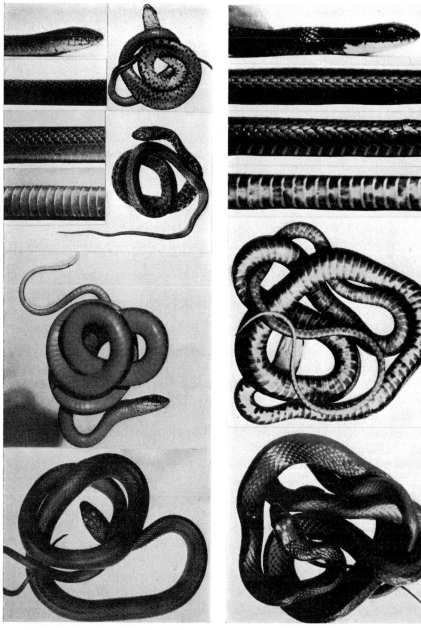

Fig. 45. *Coluber c. mormon:* 1,3,4,7,8, Pullman, Wash., D. J. Leffingwell; 2, Laguna Beach, Calif., C. M. Perkins; 5,6, Corvallis, Ore., K. Gordon.

Fig. 46. *Coluber c. priapus,* Fla., E. R. Allen.

ventral plates, all gulars except the last 2 rows, and the rest of the lower jaw are white. The pupil rim of the eye is olive-buff, surrounded by vinaceous-rufous to vinaceous-tawny. This color completely fills the upper portion of the iris, the rest being burnt umber or bone brown. Of the under parts, the tip or rear half of the tail is light brownish vinaceous merging into the ventral color with the edges of the subcaudals having a wash of pale brownish vinaceous. The middle of each ventral in the rear half of the snake is gull gray, the edges punctate with slate color. In the forward half of the body, the plates are olive-buff with scattered punctae of slate-gray. There is a tendency for the ventral plates to have toward either end on the rear margin a spot of black margined on its front edge with vinaceous-tawny to russet-vinaceous. The olive-buff ceases on the fourth plate.

Habitat: In 1894 Loennberg wrote: "The black snake is the commonest snake in South Florida and may be seen everywhere—in the dry pine woods, in the small prairies, at the borders of the lakes, on the ground, or climbing trees, or escaping down into the 'gopher' holes. At Acadia, De Soto County, I captured a small black snake which was crawling on the upper leaves of a palmetto." In 1918 Deckert (Fla., 1918) found it "the commonest snake hereabouts [Jacksonville]." In 1940 Carr had it "very extensively distributed; probably most abundant in open upland hammock or in old fields; limestone flatwoods. . . . Frequently seen near waters; I found one eating a leopard frog in shallow water at the edge of a pond. The Florida racers are much less given to tree-climbing than those in more northern regions; in Georgia and North Carolina they frequently ascend trees to escape capture, or glide about among the limbs in hedgerows while foraging, but Florida individuals almost never exhibit this tendency."

Bogert and Cowles wrote on temperature tolerance: "When placed in direct sunlight on a warm day, 4 of these snakes reached the critical maximum at temperatures of 43, 44, 44, and 44.5°C., respectively, and all of them subsequently recovered. Evidently therefore, the black snake can withstand slightly higher temperatures than the indigo snake. Moreover the latter loses moisture 5 times as rapidly as the black snake under conditions as extreme as those maintained in the thermal chamber. The advantage this gives to the black snake is apparent from the fact that it survived 10 times as long as the indigo snake under laboratory conditions, with the relative humidity at 37 per cent, and the air as well as the cage at 38°C."

Breeding: Oviparous. *Eggs*—Number, 7–16. Our first definite note came from Van Hyning: "In April, 1924, 16 eggs were given me by a farmer who had turned them up while plowing near Gainesville, Florida. Upon examination, these eggs were found to contain young snakes of this species, which were about to emerge." In 1942 Conant wrote: "Seven eggs of this racer were found May 14, 1941, in a cage containing a number of adults, all of which

had been collected 5 miles south of Brighton, Glades County, Florida, by
J. T. Sackett, a few days previously. It was not determined which female
laid the eggs, but it was presumed that all of them belonged to the same
clutch. Measurements and weights were: Length 39.7 to 50 mm., average 44.7.
Width 16.3 to 18.6 mm., average 17.9. Weight 8.1 to 9.6 gr., average 8.8."

Young—Hatchlings, 9–14 inches. Three of Conant's clutch of 7 hatched.
He wrote: "All the eggs were nonadherent and covered with coarse granu-
lations. Four spoiled but the others hatched between August 10 and August
14 (inclusive). Measurements and weights were: 332 mm., wt. g. 7.1; 320
mm., wt. g. 5.2; 248 mm., wt. g. 4.7; average 300 mm., wt. g. 5.7. . . . One
shed its skin August 23, another on August 30, and the last on September
2. All were brightly colored, the entire general tone being decidedly reddish.
In life they were as follows: dorsal blotches rich chestnut brown; lateral
ground color light bluish grey; spots on belly orange brown; ground color
of belly (posteriorly) bright pinkish orange; iris red (Brazil Red); pupil
black. The hatching of a clutch of eggs of *Coluber c. constrictor* a few
weeks later afforded an excellent opportunity to compare the young of that
form with the young of *priapus*. Fourteen eggs were laid June 23, 1941,
by a female caught near Philadelphia, Pa.; 10 of these hatched on August
30. The eggs, when laid, varied in length from 30.4 to 37.5 mm. (average
33.4); in width from 18.3 to 20.7 mm. (average 19.6); and in weight from
6.9 to 7.9 g. (average 7.4). The young varied in length from 245 to 287
mm. (average 268.9); and in weight from 4.3 to 5.8 g. (average 5.2). The
female *constrictor* weighed 253.7 g. and measured approximately 1,177 mm.
(part of tail was missing) immediately after laying. Nine of the young
were preserved. The juvenile specimens of *constrictor* were distinguishable
at a glance from the young *priapus,* and they can be separated readily after
several months of preservation. They are quite dark and much more dull
in appearance. In life they were: dorsal blotches dark brown; lateral ground
color medium bluish grey; spots on belly very dark brown or black; ground
color of belly bluish grey, darker posteriorly; iris very dark brown; pupil
black."

Food: Mice, rats, insects. Blatchley.

Field notes: May 5, 1950, Silver Springs, Fla.: Allen and Neill wonder
if the characters for the Florida black snake always hold.

Authorities: [1]

Blatchley, W. S. (Fla., 1932)
Bogert, C. M., and R. B. Cowles (Fla.,
 1947)
Carr, A. F., Jr. (Fla., 1940a)
Conant, R. (Gen., 1942; Fla., 1930)
Dunn, E. R., and G. C. Wood (Gen., 1939)

Hallinan, T. (Fla., 1923)
Loennberg, E. (Fla., 1895)
Robinson, R. G. (Fla., 1896)
Safford, W. E. (Fla., 1919)
Van Hyning, O. C. (Fla., 1931)

---

[1] 1955: P. W. Smith and J. C. List (*Amer. Midl. Naturalist,* **53**:121) interpreted their
Mississippi black runners as *C. c. priapus.*

1940, A. F. Carr, Jr.: "Specimens from the Eastern Rock Rim, the Upper Keys and the Cape Sable savannahs are much lighter in color than North Florida examples, the belly lacking pigment completely, and the dorsal surface usually having the coloration of *Coluber c. flaviventris*. Specimens from the Lower Keys have white bellies, but dorsally are just as dark as northern racers, while 2 from Tortugas are darker above and below than any other racers I have ever seen."

1942: R. Conant wrote: "Many adult racers from Florida, as first pointed out to me by Coleman J. Goin, of the University of Florida, have red or orange eyes." He concluded that possibly red eyes as contrasted to brown eyes in *C. c. constrictor* is an added character. Some workers in Florida in recent years have wondered if the red eye and even the hemipenial character will hold.

NEW RACERS

Coluber constrictor haasti Bell
Coluber constrictor paludicola Auffenberg and Babbitt

We have had no opportunity to appraise the two new forms of lower Florida, namely *Coluber constrictor haasti* Bell (*Herpetologica* 8 [1952]: 21) and *Coluber constrictor paludicola* Auffenberg and Babbitt (*Copeia* [1953], 44–45). As to *Coluber constrictor haasti*, Bell (Fla., 1952) wrote: "A subspecies of *Coluber constrictor*, similar to *C. c. priapus* except: venter black to very gray, not white as in *priapus*; no light color extending onto supralabials; snout dark brown; dorsum darker and shinier than in *priapus*; average length (about 3 feet) presumably less than *priapus*." *Coluber constrictor paludicola* Auffenberg and L. H. Babbitt is described as "a subspecies distinguished from *C. c. constrictor* and *priapus* by its considerably lighter dorsal and ventral coloration, and from *C. c. flaviventris, mormon*, and *stejnegerianus* by its higher number of subcaudal scales, a lesser number of dorsal saddles and a reddish cast to the general body colors when young. It differs from *C. c. anthicus* by its unspotted dorsal surface in the adult. The young of *anthicus* seem unknown."

Rio Grande green racer, Southern Texas racer
Coluber constrictor stejnegerianus (Cope) 1895. Fig. 47; Map 16

Another name: Stejneger's racer.
Range: Gulf coast from Matamoras, Tamaulipas, Mex., to n. San Patricio Co., Tex.—U.S.A.: Tex. Mex.: Tamaulipas. *Elevation*—Sea level to 500 feet.
Size: Adults, 25–37 inches.
Distinctive characteristics: A slender, medium-sized snake (less than 40 inches); back green, dark olive green, ivy green, sometimes greenish tan

posteriorly; belly yellow, yellow-green; throat peach blow, some with yellowish pink; upper labials 8; loreals bordering 2nd and anterior half of 3rd upper labials, not 3rd and 4th. Young with no saddles, but anteriorly with 42–53 narrow crossbars (1–3 scales wide).

Color: A snake received from S. Mulaik, Edinburg, Tex., June 14, 1934. The first row or two of scales are light grape green, becoming for the next 3 rows asphodel green. Down mid-back is a darker area, 5 scales wide, of buffy olive. On the tail, this color predominates down to the ventrals. The skin between the scales is slate-violet (2) or madder blue. The two front edges of the scales may be black or dusky slate-violet, which gives the animal in alcohol the appearance of having black-edged scales. The top of the head and the face are buffy olive or saccardo's olive. The temporal region is like the body. The rostral is primrose yellow. The lower portions of the upper labials are marked with primrose yellow. The lower labials are pale pinkish buff. The lateral gulars are reed yellow like the venter. The underside of the head is white or pale pinkish buff. The iris above and somewhat behind and particularly on the iris rim is light pinkish cinnamon. The rear of the eye on the lower one-third is black or bone brown. The venter is reed yellow, becoming marguerite yellow on the tail.

Habitat: This snake occurs in the subtropical Texan (Le Conte, Ecol., 1859), Tamaulipan (Cooper, Ecol., 1859), austroriparian (Cope, Ecol., 1873–81), Texas semidesert (Shreve, Ecol., 1921), and thorn savannah (Shelford, Jones, Dice, Ecol., 1926) regions or provinces. We have coursed over the area of this form several times since 1925, but Auffenberg's firsthand account is much better than anything we might write. We quote from him and the Mulaiks, for they have restored this form to validity. Of it the Mulaiks remark: "During 7 years of residence in the Lower Rio Grande Valley in Texas, in the Brownsville region, about 25 specimens of a *Coluber* approximating Cope's descriptions have been observed in captivity, and about half that number preserved. In the field, they are largely arboreal, gliding easily through the tops of bushes. When approached, they often remain quiet among the branches, relying on their coloration to help them escape notice."

From Auffenberg we quote: "Of the total number of specimens captured, or observed DOR, in various terrain, we find . . . that lightly wooded areas as well as scattered and sparse brush seem most populated. The heavy wooded and semiarid sections having the least representation. Although statistics are not shown, there seems to be a definite migration of females into the heavier vegetation during the months of June and early July. This seems to be in connection with the egg-laying period, for before and after those months there is no definite sex-terrain relationships."

Period of activity: "It can be noted . . . that the months of May, June, and July show the highest representation of total specimens observed, with a slight elevation again in October. It seems that it is during these months when the species is most active; September, March and April are the months least represented. In the sex-month relationships we find that the males outnumber the females in the months of March, April and May; yet the females are more numerous in the mid-season of June, July and August. . . . My figures correlate with theirs [Siebert, Hogen, and Blanchard], however, with reference to early fall when the sex ratio becomes almost equal" (Auffenberg).

Breeding: Oviparous. *Eggs*—Number, to 10. Time of deposition, June. Auffenberg recorded a batch of eggs June 5, 1947. *Young*—Time of hatching, mid-August. Size, "The young of the year averaged 273 mm." (Auffenberg).

Color: Perkins (Gen., 1949) used "juveniles with dorsal markings of small dark spots" to aid in separating this form from *C. c. mormon*. Auffenberg's detailed description is: "There are no saddle-shaped blotches on the young specimens' dorsums, the darker markings above being small spots considerably scattered on a dark olive, or greenish tan ground color. Laterally they are of a lighter coloration with the dark spots nearly covering some of the dorso-ventral scales or over half in most. The ventrals are yellowish white, with small bluish green spots near their lateral borders in the anterior portions. On the anterior dorsal surface, the young are barred with 42 to 53 fused rows of spots, forming narrow crossbars 1 to 3 scale lengths in width."

Food: Insects, lizards, frogs, rodents. Auffenberg.

Field notes: Apr. 16–18, 1925, Brownsville, Tex.: Should have taken some of the greenish racer snakes King had. The *stejnegerianus-conirostris* question is not settled. Do not believe it belongs in synonymy.

May 2, 1934, Edinburg, Tex.: With Stanley Mulaik visited his school and saw some of his New Mexican and Big Bend material. He has alive a dark greenish *Coluber* with 8 supralabials. It looks like Cope's *Z. stejnegerianus* or *Z. conirostris*. It has 17 rows of scales and is black between scales and yellow below. What are the relationships of these two forms to *M. t. ruthveni*, another greenish or grayish form?

May 5, 1934: We left Edinburg 11 A.M. Stanley gave me a *Leptodactylus* and the greenish racer. The green racer was secured from a *Drymarchon* which had swallowed one foot of the green racer. It's a fine specimen and as good a form as any other *Coluber*.

Authorities:

Auffenberg, W. (Tex., 1949)   Mulaik, S. and D. (Tex., 1942)
Cope, E. D. (Gen., 1895, 1900)

1950, A. H. and A. A. Wright: Since 1925 we have held this form a valid subspecies.

Fig. 47. *Coluber c. stejnegerianus,* Edinburg, Tex., S. Mulaik.

Fig. 48. *Coniophanes imperialis,* Harlingen, Tex., Mrs. I. Davis.

BLACK-BANDED SNAKES

Genus *CONIOPHANES* Hallowell in Cope (Fig. 22)

Size small-medium, 12–20 inches; moderately stocky; head not very distinct; tail moderate to long; anal divided; scales smooth without pits in 19–25 rows, first row wider than middorsal ones; (7) 8 (9) upper labials; lower labials 9; nasals 2; loreal 1; preocular 1; postoculars 2 (3); temporals 1 + 2, large; pinkish buff stripe from nostril to temporal; belongs in rear-fang group (opisthoglyphs); maxillary teeth subequal, 10–15, followed after an interspace by a pair of feebly enlarged grooved teeth, mandibular teeth subequal. "Hemipenis short, spinous and capitate (*fissidens*); . . . long and slender, without spines, deeply bifurcate, and calyculate but not capitate (*imperialis*)" (Bailey). Ventrals 111–174; caudals 59–115. Synonyms: *Dromicus, Erythrolamprus, Glaphyrophis, Homalopsis, Hydrops, Rhadinaea, Tachymenis, Taeniophis.*

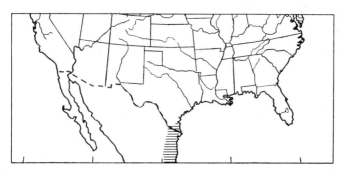

Map 17. *Coniophanes imperialis.*

Black-banded snake (6—Ditmars 1907),
Imperial snake (Yarrow 1882)

Coniophanes imperialis (Baird) 1859. Fig. 48; Map 17

Another common name: Black-striped snake.
Range: S. Texas to n. Veracruz, Mex.—U.S.A.: Tex. Mex.: Tamaulipas; Veracruz. *Elevation*—Sea level to 500 feet.
Size: Adults, 12–20 inches.
Distinctive characteristics: A small smooth snake with 19 (21) dorsal scale rows; a buffy brown dorsum with 3 dark stripes of purplish gray or dull bluish violet—a wide middorsal one (1 scale + 2 half scales), a lateral one on the 2nd to half of 4th row; a pinkish buff or cream line from muzzle over eye to the upper border of the 2nd upper temporal scale; belly, capu-

cine buff on chin to peach red on rear; anals never keeled; upper labials 8. "Hemipenis long and slender, without spines, deeply bifurcate, and calyculate but not capitate" (Bailey). Ventrals 118–143; caudals 67–94.

Color: A snake from Brownsville, Tex., furnished by H. C. Blanchard, Oct. 2, 1929. Recently dead. Colors intact. Kept on ice. A band, 3 whole and 2 half scale rows in width, buffy brown in color, extends down either side of the back to the tail tip. These bands are separated by a middorsal stripe, 1 whole and 2 half scales wide, of purplish gray to dull bluish violet. There is another stripe of the same color on the 2nd and 3rd and lower half of the 4th rows of scales. This stripe may be grayish blue-green. The 1st row has some of this color, but appears spotted or clouded, not unicolor. This is true also of the ends of the ventral plates. The irregular edge of this color on each ventral has in the rear corner an expanded spot of purplish gray or dull bluish violet (2). The top of the head is buffy olive or grayish olive heavily diffused or overlaid with purplish black or dull bluish violet (2). There is a stripe of pale pinkish buff, cartridge buff, or cream buff bordered above and below by clear lines of dull bluish violet (2) over the upper edge of the rostral and back over nostril to upper front edge of eye, resumed at the upper back corner of the eye and extending to the end of the upper temporal of the 2nd row. There is a border of the same on the upper edge of the upper labials. This pale pinkish buff eye stripe is broken in the rear for 2 or 3 scales and then resumed on either side of the middorsal body band, soon shading into the buffy brown band of either dorsal side. The iris of the eye is purplish gray, dull bluish violet, or black below. The upper third of the iris and the upper third of the pupil rim is dull pinkish cinnamon so that the forward and rear portions of the cream-buff oral stripe are connected through the eye. The lower edge of the rostral, the upper labials, the lower labials, and the chin are cartridge buff. From this color the venter shades through capucine buff to shrimp pink and la france pink in the cephalic half and peach red in the rear half.

Habitat and habits: To Brown we are indebted for most of what we know about this red-bellied form. In 1937 Brown wrote: *"Coniophanes imperialis,* which ranges from southern Texas to Vera Cruz, is found in much of Cameron and Hidalgo Counties in the Rio Grande Valley in Texas. Four adult specimens were taken during early mornings in March, 1936, within one block in Harlingen, Texas. They measured in cm. 49, 45, 42, and 31. Two of these had incomplete tails, which seem to break off easily in this species. They lived in captivity over 12 months, burrowing in the sand during the day and coming out at night or early in the morning. Though these opisthoglyph snakes never make an effort to bite when caught or handled, they are very restless and excitable. They readily take small toads which they grasp without striking. One snake was found holding a large toad by the leg. The toad escaped and appeared uninjured, but died in a few minutes. It is possible that the snake had injected sufficient venom to kill it."

In 1939 in "The Effect of *Coniophanes* Poisoning in Man" Brown wrote: "In April 1936, the author was bitten between the second and third finger of the left hand by a 15 cm. specimen of an opisthoglyph snake, *Coniophanes imperialis*. The bite caused an itching and burning sensation in the region of the punctures. A short time later the two fingers became numb and swollen, and a red discoloration was noticeable. The slight pain decreased in a short time, though the fingers remained swollen for nearly three days. No treatment or especial attention was given to the bite." (Two years later Brown induced one of these snakes to bite him and reported the results in considerable detail.)

Breeding: Oviparous. *Eggs*—Number, 4-5. The only evidence we have are two notes: "In June 1936, one of the snakes laid 4 granular capsule-shaped eggs. These average 18 mm. in length and 8 mm. at mid-section. They were placed in moist sand, but shrank and mildewed soon after. It is not known whether they were fertile" (Brown, 1937). "A 375 mm. female of this species, received May 3 from a dealer who collected it in the Brownsville area of Texas, laid 4 eggs en route to the zoo, and subsequently on May 4, a fifth egg was deposited at the zoo. These nonadhesive and nongranular eggs failed to hatch. Egg measurements: Length—width [in mm.]: 24-10, 25-10, 25-11, 26-13" (Werler).

Young—Not known. The smallest that Brown writes about is 15 cm. What is the size of a newly hatched young? We have a note of a 14-cm. specimen, but do not know its source.

Food: Small and transforming toads and frogs, small lizards, snakes, and young mice. Brown (Tex., 1937), Mr. and Mrs. Beimler, Conant (Tex., 1955).

Field notes: June 17, 1930, Brownsville, Tex.: Went to Rebb's palm grove to look it over for the Ecological Society of America. Under a log, found a mild-mannered snake, brown and purplish banded above and a beautiful pink below. It is *Coniophanes*.

May 2, 1934, Harlingen, Tex.: Mrs. Mulaik telephoned Mrs. Irby Davis of Harlingen to see whether they had killed their *Coniophanes imperialis*. Mr. Davis had tried to etherize it, but had not succeeded very well. We stopped at their house but did not then see the snake. Later we received the snake and photographed it.

Authorities:

Bailey, J. R. (Gen., 1937a)
Baird, S. F. (Tex., 1859)
Brown, B. C. (Tex., 1937, 1939)

Cope, E. D. (Gen., 1861, 1900)
Shannon, F. A., and H. M. Smith (Tex., 1949)
Werler, J. E. (Tex., 1949)

SHARP-TAILED SNAKES

Genus *CONTIA* Baird and Girard (Fig. 24)

Size small, 5–19 inches; slender, subcylindrical; head small, slightly distinct from body; tail medium, conical and sharp pointed; anal divided; scales smooth with apical pits and in 15 rows; upper labials 7 (6); lower labials 7; temporals 1 + 2; preoculars 1 (2); postoculars 2 (1); loreal 1; nasal entire, divided or half divided; anterior chin shields much larger than posterior ones; maxillary teeth small, equal; dorsal color brownish, ventral plates light each with a transverse black bar. Hemipenis—similar to *Carphophis* but "sulcus of *Contia* is forked for relatively less of its length" (Stickel, Gen., 1943, 1951). Ventrals 147–186; caudals 27–57. Synonyms: *Ablabes, Calamaria, Homalosoma, Lodia.*

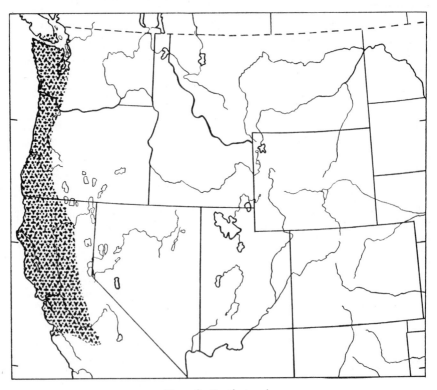

Map 18. *Contia tenuis.*

Sharp-tailed snake (12—Van Denburgh 1897),
Purple-tailed snake (2—Yarrow 1882)

Contia tenuis (Baird and Girard) 1852. Fig. 49; Map 18

Other common names: (Gentle) brown snake; Oregon worm snake; Pacific brown snake; Pacific ground snake.

Range: North Pacific coast—s. tip Vancouver Island, B.C., Puget Sound, Willamette Valley, Cascade and Sierra Nevada Mts., and Central Valley to lat. 36°N. (Tulare Co., Calif.).—U.S.A.: Calif., Ore., Wash. Can.: B.C. *Elevation*—Sea level to 1,500, sometimes 2,000 feet or more. 1,000 feet.

Size: Adults, 5–18.7 inches.

Distinctive characteristics: A small, nocturnal, light brownish olive or buffy olive snake with a sharp tail. Its striking mark is the slate-black bar across the front of each belly plate, followed by a light area of pale smoke gray or drab-gray. Few over 15 inches long.

Color: A snake received from J. R. Slevin of the California Academy of Sciences through S. C. Bishop of Rochester about June 2, 1936. The back is natal brown, sorghum brown, or verona brown, outlined on the edges of the 4th and 5th rows of scales, with vinaceous-fawn or light vinaceous-fawn. The 4th to 2nd rows of scales are natal brown or darker, with the front of each scale of the 4th row bearing a black spot. The 1st row of scales is like the 4th and 5th scale line. Under a lens, the dorsal scales are dotted with vinaceous-buff or light vinaceous-buff and black. On the back the light vinaceous-buff is more dominant, and there is less black, while on the sides the light vinaceous-buff dots are more widely separated, and there is more black intervening space. The top of the head is olive-brown. The upper and lower labials are pale smoke gray. There is a semicircle of black on the front of the rostral. The median suture of the chin shields is black, as are also the outer edges of adjoining lower labials. There is an indistinct black line in front of the eye, while back of the eye there is practically no black line except on the upper edges of 1 or 2 upper labials near the angle of the mouth. The back of the eye is dotted with pale smoke gray or pale vinaceous-fawn. In front of and above the pupil, Brazil red or burnt sienna appears. There is an outer ring of black. On the under parts there is, on the cephalic third of each ventral, a black bar extending wholly across the scale, the rear two-thirds being pale glaucous green or pale smoke gray. The anal plate and subcaudals are without the black crossbars. The black on the tail when present is confined to the ends of the plates.

Habitat: Habitat was little emphasized in the early records. In his 1883 discussion Garman reasoned that the "subcaudals are much lighter which suggests the possible existence of a habit of carrying the tail raised from the ground." After 1897 only Van Denburgh, Grinnell and Camp (Calif., 1917), Grinnell, Dixon, and Linsdale, Fitch, Slater, and Gordon gave habitat notes.

The snakes were taken among the redwoods, in hilly country, near irrigation ditches or streams, and from the basement of a house. They were found beneath stones, boards, and rotting logs. One of our snakes came from the Digger Pine area at Lucerne, Lake Co., Calif., in the lower transition zone, in 1941.

Period of activity. *Early appearances*—The California Academy of Sciences has 15 specimens taken Feb. 4, 1911, Feb. 12, 1911, Feb. 21, 1926, Mar. 2, 1904, Mar. 8, 1932, Apr. 18, 1909 to June. Stanford has them from Mar. 2 to June. Grinnell, Dixon, and Linsdale took it Apr. 6, Apr. 12, and June. *Fall captures*—In the fall Stanford has made captures from October to Nov. 30, CAS from Oct. 8, 1927, to Nov. 3, 1939. MVZ has material from Feb. 6 to Dec. 18.

Breeding: Oviparous. There are no records of eggs or hatchlings. The smallest specimens we have seen are 103 mm. (tail 14 mm.), Mar. 8, 1932; 112 mm., Oct. 8, 1927; 112 mm., Nov. 30; 121 mm., June, 1898; 122 mm., Mar. 2, 1904. All but one are early spring or late fall specimens. Are they near the hatching size? A student at Berkeley, Palo Alto, San Jose, or Corvallis could answer the question, for each of these regions has them in sufficient quantity.

Field notes: Feb. 23, 1942: Worked at Museum Vertebrate Zoology, Berkeley. Yesterday Rodgers and party went to Stockton. Fine trip. . . . Another boy or Storer (not Tracy) found a *Contia tenuis* above Strawberry Canyon where they occasionally have collected them before. (A day after its capture and escape the boys tore up the place trying to find for me the escaped treasure. So small it would be hard to find it.)

Mar. 22, 1942, Corvallis, Ore.: Prof. Kenneth Gordon planned a collecting trip to a wooded hilly area west of Corvallis and above the golf course. He said he wanted to take two students along, Messrs. R. Livezey and R. M. Storm. The latter Gordon assures me is almost a sure Sharp-tailed Snake man. He (Storm) feared he could not deliver but soon from a rotten log he produced a fine specimen of *Contia*. Two good collectors—from one huge log in the open we collected 75 *Aneides ferreus* rare to most herpetologists. (See Storm's later story of it.)

Mar. 30, 1942, Tacoma, Wash.: Went with Slater on a short trip. We had looked forward to the trip for we are quite certain that this is the lake (Spanaway Lake) about which he so gleefully said, "Near this lake is the type locality of Girard's *Lodia tenuis* and *Rana pretiosa*." It's exciting to feel oneself, 100 years later, on the spot where former naturalists of the U.S. exploring expedition of 1838–42 collected.

Authorities:

Baird, S. F., and C. Girard (Wash., 1854)
Brown, A. E. (Gen., 1901)

Carl, G. C. (B.C., 1950)
Fitch, H. S. (Ore., 1936)
Garman, S. (Gen., 1883)

Gordon, K. (Ore., 1939)

Grinnell, J., J. Dixon, and J. M. Lins-
    dale (Calif., 1930)

Gunther, A. (Gen., 1858)

Hawken, J. L. (Calif., 1951)

Slater, J. R. (Wash., 1939)

Stickel, W. H. (Gen., 1951)

Van Denburgh, J. (Gen., 1922)

1901, A. E. Brown: *"Lodia tenuis* B. and G. was based upon one example from Puget Sound, Oregon, agreeing with *C. mitis* except in having a small additional plate between the prefrontals and the loreal reaching the eye under the preocular. As no further specimen has come to light in 50 years, it seems safe to refer this unique example to the class of anomalies, the head plates being usually variable in these small burrowing forms."

RING-NECKED SNAKES

Genus *DIADOPHIS* Baird and Girard (Figs. 21, 24)

Size small to medium, 10–30 inches; slender; neck but little if any constricted; head flat; eye moderate, pupil round; snout broad and rounded; anal divided; scales smooth with single apical pits, in 15–17 rows (13–19); preoculars 2, postoculars 2; temporals 1 + 1 (2); loreal present; upper labials usually 7, some 8; lower labials 8 (7); maxillary teeth solid 9–21; usually a light nuchal collar (yellow or orange); venter yellow, orange, or red, spotted or unspotted, dorsum black to gray or green. Hemipenis: organ bilobed; spermatic sulcus forked; tip with numerous calyces; base with numerous spines. Ventrals 126–239; caudals 30–79. Synonyms: *Ablabes, Calamaria, Coluber, Coronella, Homalosoma, Liophis, Natrix, Spilates, Spiletes.*

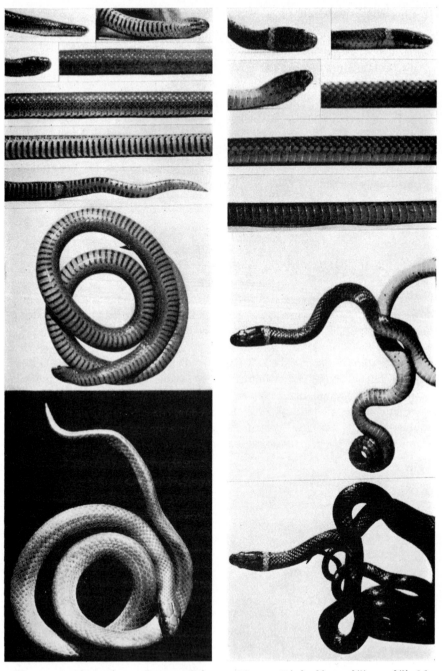

Fig. 49. *Contia tenuis:* 1–7, Lucerne, Lake Co., Calif.; 8, San Francisco, Calif., J. R. Slevin through S. Bishop; 9, Corvallis, Ore., K. Gordon.

Fig. 50. *Diadophis amabilis amabilis,* Madera Co., Calif., L. F. Hadsall.

KEY TO THE GENUS *DIADOPHIS* (After Blanchard)

a. Ventral color usually extending in anterior portion of body to one or more of the lowermost rows of dorsal scales.

   b. Difference between number of ventrals and number of caudals 139 or more in ♂ and 160 or more in ♀ (range in all 141 ♂ to 176 ♀); ventrals ♂ 204–225; ♀ 224–239, collectively 204–239. Size short to medium, maximum ♀ 443–749 mm. Neck ring absent or, if present, adult size medium to 750 mm., ventral color usually covers the lowermost dorsal scale row. Scale rows 17. (Rocky Mt. plateau section; long. 103°–114°. New Mexico-Texas boundary to Utah-Nevada boundary.)

      c. Neck ring distinct 2–4 scales in width, size medium—750 mm. (Arizona to New Mexico.)   *D. r. laetus*

     cc. Neck ring absent or greatly reduced.

        d. Size short, maxima 411 mm.–443 mm. (Schmidt). (Trans-Pecos Texas.) Ventrals 211–224; caudals 55–64.   *D. r. blanchardi*

       dd. Size medium (greater than *blanchardi*), maxima 490–726 mm. (6 authors). Nuchal ring absent, greatly reduced, or indistinct. Ventrals 204–236; caudals 53–79.   *D. regalis regalis*

  bb. Difference between number of ventrals and number of caudals 141 or less in ♂ and less than 160 in ♀ (range in all 111 ♂ to 159 ♀); ventrals ♂ 180–207; ♀ 188–215, collectively 180–215. Size short, maximum ♀ 470–533 mm. Neck ring present, ventral color covers 1/3–2 or more dorsal scale rows. (Pacific coast section; long. 115°–125°.)

      c. Scale rows 17–15, rarely 15–15.

        d. Ventral color not extending over more than 1st row of dorsal scales; belly usually conspicuously spotted with black. (San Bernardino Mts. and Los Angeles Co., Calif., including Santa Catalina Is. s. to extreme n. San Diego Co.)   *D. a. modestus*

       dd. Ventral color extending over 1 1/2–2 rows of dorsal scales; black spots on belly few and small. (Ventura Co. to Santa Cruz Co., Calif.)   *D. a. vandenburghi*

     cc. Scale rows 15–15 or 15–13 (rarely 17–15 or 15–17–15).

        d. Ventral color usually covering more than 2/3 of lowermost row of dorsal scales.

          e. Neck ring narrow, from 1–1 1/2 scale lengths in width, sometimes interrupted; ventral color covering 1/2–1 1/2 rows of dorsal scales; belly well sprinkled with small black spots; dorsal color usually dark. (San Francisco Bay region and San Joaquin and Sacramento River valleys.) *D. amabilis amabilis*

ee. Neck ring prominent 1 1/2–3 scales in width, not interrupted; ventral color covering from 1 1/2–2 or more rows of dorsal scales; belly rarely heavily spotted with black.

  f. First 2 rows of dorsal scales flecked with black; belly rather conspicuously, although sparsely, marked with small black spots. (Sonoma Co., Calif., n. through Oregon and along Columbia and Snake Rivers to Boise, Ida.) *D. a. occidentalis*

  ff. First 2 rows of dorsal scales not flecked with black; belly almost or quite unspotted. (W. slope of Sierra Nevada, s. perhaps to Tejon Pass in California and n. perhaps to Oregon.) *D. a. pulchellus*

dd. Ventral color usually covering 1/3–2/3 of lowermost row of dorsal scales.

  e. Scale rows 13 in posterior end of body in all males and 4/5 of females; typically a slender form; neck ring usually well defined. (S.w. San Bernardino Co. s. into the San Pedro Martir Mts., Baja California and San Martin Is.) *D. a. similis*

  ee. Scale rows 15 near posterior end of body in both sexes, larger and stouter bodied than the last; neck ring narrow and poorly defined; heavily marked below. (South Todos Santos Is., Baja California.) *D. a. anthonyi*

aa. Ventral color confined to ventrals (except rarely at extreme anterior end); neck ring present.

  b. Ventral plates 170 or more in ♂, 180 or more in ♀; ventrals 164–208, average in ♂ 176–186, in ♀ 200–202.

    c. Dorsal scale rows usually 15–15 (less often 17–15); ventrals 175–208, average in ♂ 186, in ♀ 200; generally only a single posterior (i.e., 2d) temporal; size to 422 mm. (Triangle from headwaters of Rio Colorado to mouth of Rio San Pedro [Devils River] to s.e. corner of New Mexico.) *D. p. docilis*

    cc. [Dorsal scale rows usually 17–17, occasionally 17–15; ventrals 164–206, average in ♂ 176, in ♀ 202; generally two posterior temporals; size 677 mm. (Mexico.) *D. dugesi*]

  bb. Ventral plates usually less than 170 in ♂ or 180 in ♀; ventrals 126–185, average in ♂ 133–156, in ♀ 142–168; size short to very short, maxima 361–517 mm. (East of long. 103°.)

    c. Chin generally without black spots; belly typically unspotted but sometimes with a more or less incomplete median line of small black spots (rarely with ill-defined, scattered spots); neck ring rarely interrupted; scale rows 15–15; ventrals ♂, 139–162, average 151; ♀ 146–176, average 160; size short, maximum 517 mm. (Appalachian and Great Lakes region.) *D. p. edwardsi*

cc. Chin with black spots; belly with black spots scattered or in a continuous median line; size very short, maximum 361–367 mm.

    d. Spots on belly usually scattered, but sometimes in a median line or absent; difference between number of ventrals and number of caudals usually more than 99 in ♂ and more than 115 in ♀; dorsal scales often in 17 rows (17–15). (Mainly trans-Mississippian steppe from s.w. Wisconsin, n. Illinois to Colorado and central Texas.)

D. p. arnyi

    dd. Spots on belly not irregularly scattered, but arranged in a more or less median line, or more or less confluent transversely on the ventrals; difference between number of ventrals and number of caudals usually less than 99 in ♂ and less than 115 in ♀; dorsal scales not more than 15 rows.

        e. A single median line of clearly-defined, half-circular, black spots on belly; upper labials usually 8, but occasionally 7. (Atlantic coastal plain, New Jersey to Mobile Bay.)   *D. punctatus punctatus*

        ee. Belly spots small and usually not perfectly regular in shape, often tending to form a median line, or more or less confluent transversely, or in pairs; upper labials 7, rarely 8. (Lower Mississippi Valley from s. Illinois to Mobile Bay and San Antonio, Tex.)

D. p. stictogenys

Western ring-necked snake (6—Ditmars 1907), Western ring-neck snake (6—Van Denburgh 1897)

Diadophis amabilis amabilis Baird and Girard 1853. Fig. 50; Map 19

Other common names: California ring-necked snake; Pacific ring-neck(ed) snake; red-bellied snake; ring-necked snake; spotted ring neck (Cooper 1869).

Range: Foothills of Central Valley of California between lat. 36° and 39° and San Francisco Bay region. *Elevation*—Mainly below 3,000 feet. 3,500 feet (Atsatt, Calif., 1912a); 3,600 feet (Blanchard, 1942).

Size: Adults, 6–20 inches.

Distinctive characteristics: "This form is characterized by a narrow neck ring that is sometimes interrupted; by 15 rows of scales, often changing to 13 at the posterior end of the body; by the ventral color extending usually onto the lower part of the 2nd row of dorsal scales; by numerous small black spots scattered over the belly; and by slender proportions and moderate length" (Blanchard, 1942).

Color: A snake from San Jose, Calif., received from K. S. Hazeltine, June 26, 1937. The dorsal color is deep olive, dark greenish olive, or olive, in some lights appearing yellowish olive to kronberg's green. The top of the head and side or face are dark olive, olive, or brownish olive. The neck ring of

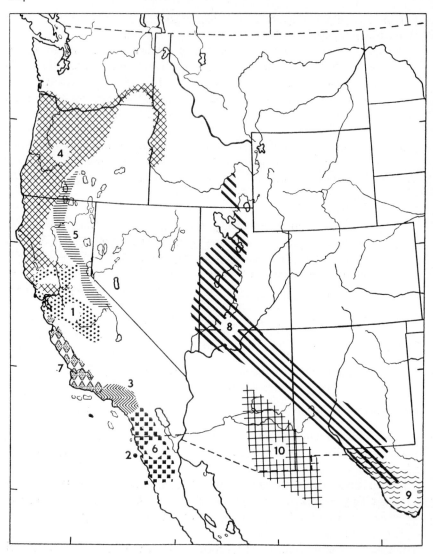

Map 19. *Diadophis*—1, *a. amabilis; 2, a. anthonyi; 3, a. modestus; 4, a. occidentalis; 5, a. pulchellus; 6, a. similis; 7, a. vandenburghi; 8, r. regalis; 9, r. blanchardi; 10, r. laetus.*

orange chrome or apricot orange is about 2 scales in width and is not interrupted by dorsal color. The iris is black or dark olive with a pupil ring of flame scarlet, bittersweet orange, or grenadine red. The lower half of the upper labials is, like the ventral color of the head, orange or cadmium yellow, more or less edged above with black. The mental plate, 4 lower labials, and anterior chin shields are heavily spotted with black dots, then a clear area occurs, but in the gular region several spots appear. There are only a few fine black spots on the rest of the ventral surfaces. The underside of the head and the forward ventral parts are orange or cadmium yellow, becoming on body cadmium orange or orange chrome. Before the vent is reached, the ventrals become scarlet. The underside of the tail is scarlet-red or even spectrum red. The ventral color extends up on the sides for 1½ rows of dorsal scales.

Habitat and habits: In 1897 Van Denburgh had it "under boards or logs in moist localities . . . even in salt marshes." In 1917 Grinnell and Camp (Calif.) said it "inhabits shaded cañons; lives in masses of dead leaves and beneath stones." In 1924, Grinnell and Storer found it in "shaded groves, keeping usually under leafy debris, logs or boulders." They also wrote: "An individual when suddenly uncovered, as when a stone or log is turned over, will sometimes lie with its brilliant undersurface uppermost and feign death. Under such circumstances, too, the tail of the snake is often curled in a tight spiral with the bright red undersurface exposed." (See Ditmars' [Gen., 1907] observations on this habit.) In Blanchard's paper of 1942 a few notes recorded with specimens are: "under rock, Indian burying ground, North Berkeley," "hill near Christy, 200 feet, Contra Costa County," "Chambers Ravine, 4 miles north of Oraville, Butte County, 600 feet," "Redwood Canyon, Contra Costa County," "La Loma and Cedar Streets, Berkeley," "Lagunitas Creek, 300 to 400 feet, Marin County."

In 1947 Pickwell wrote: "This little snake, which is truly 'friendly,' as the specific scientific name indicates, is common and is found frequently under rocks, under boards, and in fields throughout the state, except in deserts. When it is handled roughly, it may coil or spiral its tail to show the red undersurface—but gives no other reaction."

Breeding: *Sexual dimorphism*—Blanchard in 1942 found that males over 300 mm. long had ridges on the scales in the anal region.

Food: Insects, tree frogs, small snakes, earthworms, slugs. Van Denburgh (1897), Grinnell and Storer, Blanchard (1942), Pickwell.

Notes: In 1906 Dr. J. C. Bradley sent us our first *amabilis*. Our knowledge of live representatives of the various *amabilis* subspecies illustrates that if you live long enough at one institution (50 years), your students reward you with snakes.

In days when *D. amabilis* was not well known nor clearly allocated, good writers had it extending east into *edwardsi* territory. Let us not make similar mistakes in our interpretations of the southwestern *Diadophis*. In time, some of our records and interpretations may be outmoded. In the past there was little material and a great stretching of words and interpretations!

Authorities:

Baird, S. F., and C. Girard (Gen., 1853)

Blanchard, F. N. (Gen., 1923, 1942)

Cronise, T. F. (Calif., 1868)

Grinnell, J., and T. I. Storer (Calif., 1924)

Hawken, J. L. (Calif., 1951)

Pickwell, G. B. (Gen., 1947)

Van Denburgh, J. (Gen., 1897, 1922)

1944, A. H. and A. A. Wright: When we visited the San Francisco Bay region Prof. Trevor Cook, the physiologist, was studying the local *Diadophis,* and his son was collecting them assiduously. We hope he or his son will give us more light on the three subspecies which enter or point toward the Bay or, better, a review of the whole group of *D. amabilis*. Blanchard has given us a starting point, but much more awaits continued study.

1951, J. L. Hawken: This species makes us almost ¼ (155 specimens) of the 582 specimens of amphibians and reptiles (15 species) he collected in the flume system of the San Francisco water supply. Only *P. c. catenifer* with 165 specimens exceeded it. Is it so abundant or how should we explain it?

Los Angeles ring-neck snake (3), San Bernardino ring-necked snake (2—Ditmars 1936)

Diadophis amabilis modestus Bocourt 1886. Fig. 51; Map 19

Other common names: (Van Denburgh's) ring-neck snake; western ring-neck snake (2—Ditmars 1907); western ring-necked snake.

Range: N. San Diego Co. to Los Angeles Co., Calif., San Bernardino Mts.; Santa Catalina Is. *Elevation*—Coast to 6,400 feet. 4,000, 5,500, 6,400 feet (Grinnell, Calif., 1908).

Size: Adults, 8–21 inches.

Distinctive characteristics: "Features characteristic of this form are a moderately narrow neck ring, ½ to 2 scales in width; 17 rows of scales at the anterior end of the body, the ventral color extending only a little onto the first row of dorsal scales; the belly usually heavily spotted with black (in particular the ends of the ventrals generally each bearing a black dash); and bodily proportions distinctly stouter than *amabilis*" (Blanchard, 1942).

Color: A snake from Pacific Palisades, Los Angeles Co., Calif., received from C. M. Bogert, May 17, 1936. The upper parts are snuff brown, drab, or olive-brown or tend toward buffy brown. The top and sides of the head and the face are the same. The neck ring of fawn, cinnamon, or orange-cinnamon is 1½ scales wide and is partially obscured by dorsal color. The iris is black with a ferruginous or russet spot above the pupil. The forward ventral parts tend toward orange-buff and may be capucine buff to pale orange-yellow on the chin, lower head, and labials. On the chin, gular region, and lower labials, there is a central black spot on each scale, while the upper labials except the 5th and 6th lack this spot. The upper part of the upper labials is colored like the dorsum, while the lower half bears the ventral color. Ahead of the 5th, this region is faintly outlined by a dark edge, while back of the 6th, the black edge is prominent. The ventral parts are zinc orange, salmon-orange, or mikado orange, becoming on the rear of the belly light jasper red and on the lower side of the tail jasper red. This ventral color extends ½ scale onto the dorsal scales. On each ventral just below the lower point of the last row of scales is a spot almost black to the unaided eye, but under the lens dark madder blue or dusky violet-blue (2). These make a regular row from the neck ring to the tip of the tail. Except for this bordering row on either side of the venter, the tail is almost clear, and the last 2 inches of the belly bear few additional spots. Cephalad the spots are more or less regularly in 2 central rows.

The first good color description is that of 1907 by Grinnell and Grinnell (Calif.): "The color above, greenish or slate-gray, with no definite markings except a narrow white, yellowish, or reddish collar across the neck just behind the head. The top of the head is usually darker than the back. The lower surface is yellowish, rose, orange or coral-red, brightest toward the tail and more or less spotted with black."

Habitat and habits: The Grinnells in 1907 wrote: "This elegant little snake appears to be fairly common in the canyons and hilly country of many parts of the country. We have found it in August feeding on young tree-toads within a few feet of the stream in the Arroyo Seco Canyon. We have also found it in early spring coiled up in cavities under rocks. The gentle behavior and pleasing coloration of the snake render it one of the most attractive to handle alive."

In 1930 Bogert (Calif.) found that the "Ring-neck Snake [was] moderately common throughout the county except on the desert and desert slope. During the months from February to May, 1929, I secured 14 of these beautiful little snakes in my yard in Los Angeles by overturning rocks." In 1942 in the same general region Von Bloecker (Calif., 1942) wrote of it: "Quite common throughout the dune area, except on the strand. Frequently found under boards and rocks, and occasionally buried in loose sand, similarly to *Anniella pulchra.*" His largest specimen, 17 inches long, taken Apr. 2, 1939, was found "in the dune complex on top of the largest dune near a patch of tuna cactus (*Opuntia littoralis*)."

Period of activity: February to May, 1929 (Bogert, Calif., 1930).

Breeding: *Sexual dimorphism*—Blanchard finds that males over 300 mm. have anal ridges on the dorsal scales near the vent and none of the females have them.

Food: Insects, salamanders, lizards, small snakes. Bogert (Calif., 1930) Blanchard (Gen., 1942), Von Bloecker (Calif., 1942).

Authorities:

Blanchard, F. N. (Gen., 1923, 1942)   Van Denburgh, J. (Gen., 1922)
Perkins, C. B. (Calif., 1938)

1938, C. B. Perkins: "This snake is so similar to the San Diegan Ringneck that it would be hard to tell which was which without the use of a special key."

1942, F. N. Blanchard: "We may best regard *modestus* as a derivative of *laetus* and ancestral to all other forms of *amabilis*."

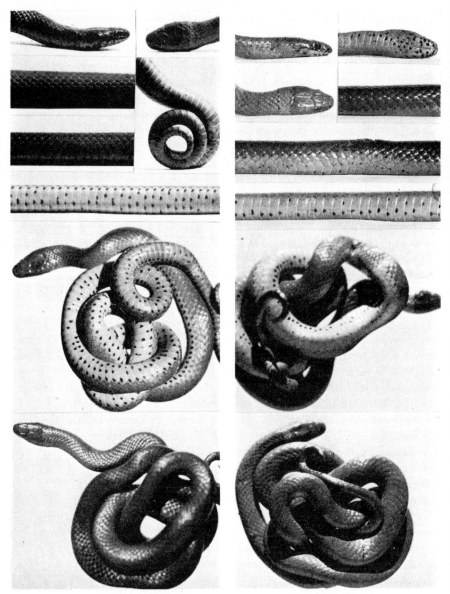

Fig. 51. *Diadophis a. modestus,* Pacific Palisades, Los Angeles Co., Calif., C. M. Bogert.

Fig. 52. *Diadophis a. occidentalis,* Red Bluff, Calif., A. Mead.

Northwestern ring-necked snake (3—Ditmars 1936),
Western ring-necked snake (3—Ditmars 1907)

Diadophis amabilis occidentalis Blanchard 1923. Fig. 52; Map 19

Other common names: Northwestern ring-neck snake (2); Sonoma ring-neck snake (1—Slevin 1934).

Range: W. Idaho, Columbia basin of s. Washington and w. Oregon, Pacific coast to Sonoma Co., Calif.—Calif.; Ida.; Ore.; Wash. *Elevation*—At least to 3,000 feet and doubtless much higher. 2,500 feet (Uhler).

Size: Adults, 8–24 inches.

Distinctive characteristics: "The chief characteristics of this form are a relatively broad, uninterrupted neck ring, 1½–2 scales in width, ventral color extending over 1½ to 2 of the dorsal scale rows, flecks of black on the first 2 rows of dorsal scales, belly lightly spotted with black, and the dorsal scales in not more than 15 rows. This form is intermediate between *D. amabilis vandenburghii* and *D. amabilis pulchellus*. From the former it differs in possessing not more than 15 rows of dorsal scales, in having a neck ring that averages slightly wider, and in having the ventral color extending on the average a little higher on the sides. From *D. amabilis pulchellus* it differs chiefly in having the light colored dorsal scales flecked with black; it also differs from this form in having on the average more black spots on the belly, a slightly narrower neck ring, and a lesser extent of ventral color on the sides" (Blanchard, 1923).

Color: A snake from Red Bluff, Calif., received in November, 1940, through the kindness of A. Mead of the University of California at Davis. The dorsum is slate-olive or deep olive-gray to vetiver green, including top of head, temporal scales, facial scales, and rostral except in the lower half. The neck ring of flame scarlet is unbroken and 2 full scales wide, with a broken caudal border made of 5 black spots. A thread of black crosses the middle of the upper labials, separating the vetiver green of the dorsum from the flame scarlet of the upper labial margin and thus forming a distinct black horizontal border. Each lower labial bears a large black spot, the anterior chin shields 2, posterior chin shields 1, and most gulars each 1. The iris is black with a pupil ring of flame scarlet. The under parts including the venter of the head and lower halves of the upper labials and rostral and also the 2 lower dorsal scale rows and a touch of the 3rd are flame scarlet. There is a delicate black spot on each scale of the 2nd dorsal row near the dorso-caudal edge. Usually each ventral bears 1 black spot, not necessarily in the middle; some have 2, rarely 3. The underside of the tail is Brazil red spotted with black. (For a detailed color description of an alcoholic specimen, see Blanchard, 1923.)

Habitat and habits: In 1933 the Svihlas (Wash.) took a specimen in Whitman Co., Wash., "at Wawawai, which is on the Snake River." In 1936 Fitch wrote: "All the snakes of this species that were seen were in low

Transition or Upper Sonoran life zones usually near water. At Belmont Orchard, 6 miles south of Medford one was taken as it was crossing a road, another was found in a dry irrigation ditch, a third was crawling under the edge of a bush of buckbrush (*Ceanathus cuneatus*). Near Dark Hollow, 7 miles south of Medford one was found coiled under a flat rock. Three snakes from lower Rogue River at Paradise Bar, 1 mile east of Lobster Creek, and 1 mile west of Lobster Creek, respectively, were found crossing trails at midday." In 1939 Gordon said that "it is usually found under boards, logs, and stones, in moist situations."

Breeding: The only pertinent note is one on Fitch's captive: "A large female (No. 17246) found near Burns Creek on May 15, 1934, contained 4 ova, averaging 20 mm. in length."

Food: Lizards, small snakes. Fitch, Darling.

Authorities:

Blanchard, F. N. (Gen., 1923, 1942)	Gordon, K. (Ore., 1939)
Darling, D. (Ore., 1939)	Uhler, F. M. (Ida., 1940)
Fitch, H. S. (Ore., 1936)	

1944, A. H. and A. A. Wright: At this moment we are moved by a spirit of levity. Why not *occidentalis* the parent of the *amabilis* complex instead of *modestus?* Why should not *regalis* and *occidentalis* kiss in mid-Idaho; they have each reached the Snake River drainage. Restricted *modestus* is widely divorced from its supposed progenitor *laetus,* of southeastern Arizona. Why the smallest range (*modestus*) except for the insular *anthonyi* should develop the whole *amabilis* group instead of the widest range (*occidentalis*) is hard to see, i.e., why isn't *modestus* incipient not relict from a bigger range, why isn't the widespread *occidentalis* ancestral, not merely a lusty youth? *Occidentalis* occupies the wide-open pioneer interstate spaces of northern California, Oregon, Washington, and Idaho, and *modestus* centers around intrastate urban Los Angeles. We are sure Dr. Blanchard would not allow Rotary pride to dictate the mother home of all *amabilis!*

Now to be serious! Almost every revisionist for 35 years has derived every snake group from Mexico, and that country ought to patent the idea. We query whether all these snake genealogies are genuine. Are they derived by people who have collected in and visited Mexico and the wide-open spaces or by neophytes following tradition in leaping their alcoholic material over space?

When we first began herpetologic work, Adams had convinced many that the southern Appalachians were the center of much of our eastern material. For mollusks, fishes, and salamanders maybe it is true. Do our Appalachian salamanders come from a psychological Oedipus complex or a real Central American Oedipus salamander? Or from some other general ancestor? Do some of our Floridian animals as well as plants come from West Indian hurricanes as Barbour postulated?

A student of Adams, Ruthven, began the procession, and his contemporaries held that he did as well with his material as anyone could to prove Mexico the home of the garter snakes. We considered he proved his case, but some more recent efforts are too strained in experience, effort, ease, and field work to convince us that Mexico is the universal Eden of snakes. Why at this stage derive all *punctatus* from *docilis,* which no living expert knows well, or all *amabilis* from still indefinite *laetus?*

Sierran ring-neck snake (3—Slevin 1934), California ring-necked snake (2—Yarrow 1882)

Diadophis amabilis pulchellus (Baird and Girard) 1953. Fig. 53; Map 19

Other common names: Beautiful ring-neck (Cronise 1868); coral-bellied ring-necked snake; western ring-necked snake.

Range: Tejon Pass along w. slope of Sierra Nevadas to extreme s. Oregon. —Calif.; Ore. *Elevation*—To 5,000 feet or more. 4,800 feet (Sequoia National Park, E. S. Herald).

Size: Adults, 8–19 inches.

Distinctive characteristics: "The salient features of this form are a broad, uninterrupted neck ring, 2 to 3 scales wide; the ventral color extended immaculately over the 2 lowermost rows of dorsal scales; black spots on belly few and small, or absent; and dorsal scales in only 15 rows" (Blanchard, 1942).

Color: Snakes from Swamp Lake, Tuolumne Co., Calif., received July 7, 1940, from Kitty Hemphill (Mrs. Stuart Brown) of the Yosemite School of Natural History. The dorsal color forward is dark medici blue, passing through green-blue slate and deep payne's gray to violet-slate on the tail. Really each scale is light medici blue, but this with its anterior black border produces dark medici blue. The neck color 2 to 2½ scales wide is an orange chrome ring. The row of scales back of the parietals borders it with black, and it is somewhat outlined with black in the rear. The parietals are also black. The black of the head extends across the 7th upper labial on to the 7th and 8th lower labials as one block of color. The upper labial margin is like the lower chin color. The edge of rostral and 1st 2 upper labials are orange-pink. The underside of the head is salmon-orange or orange chrome with the 1st to 5th lower labials each marked with a black spot. The iris color is like the top of the head, with the pupil rim a thin line of orange-pink. The belly is clear orange chrome, becoming flame scarlet, then scarlet ahead of the vent and under the tail. This color extends across the 2 lower rows of dorsal scales and onto the lower edge of the 3rd row. On the tail this color extends over the 1st row and somewhat on the 2nd.

Another snake has under parts in general scarlet or grenadine red, becoming in the rear almost spectrum red or Brazil red.

Habitat and habits: We have very few notes on this beautiful snake. In 1924 Hatt (Mich.) reported it in "dry pine forest." Grinnell and Storer (Calif., 1924) wrote of it as in "shaded ground, keeping usually under leafy debris, logs, or boulders."

Authorities:

Baird, S. F., and C. Girard (Gen., 1853)   Cope, E. D. (Gen., 1883–84)
Blanchard, F. N. (Gen., 1923, 1942)

1944, A. H. and A. A. Wright: This clean-cut, clear-bellied snake, like the coral king snake of the high Sierras, is the beauty of its group. As in the golden trouts (of Soda Creek and Volcano Creek), the high altitude of the Sierras brings out a high brilliant color type in this little gem, the Sierran ring-neck. We have seen several alive but know too little to philosophize about them.

San Diegan ring-neck snake (6—Klauber 1928),
Southern California ring-necked snake (2)

Diadophis amabilis similis Blanchard 1923. Fig. 54; Map 19

Another common name: Western ring-necked snake (2).

Range: San Pedro Martir Mts., San Martin Is., Baja Calif. to s.w. San Bernardino Co., Calif.—U.S.A.: Calif. Mex.: Baja Calif. *Elevation*—Coastline to the top of the divide (Klauber, Calif., 1931a); 5,500 feet (Atsatt, Calif., 1913); ocean to mountains (Perkins).

Size: Adults, 11–20 inches.

Distinctive characteristics: "Similar to *D. amabilis amabilis,* but with the light color of the ventral surface extending over only ⅓ to ⅔ of the lowermost row of dorsal scales. Other distinctive features are the moderate amount of black spotting on the belly, the dorsal scales in 15 rows throughout, or dropping to 13 toward the posterior end of the body, and the generally light olive color of the dorsal surface" (Blanchard, 1923).

Color: Some snakes from San Diego, Calif., sent by Klauber, May 20, 1928. The top of the head is deep olive, the neck with an orange chrome band, in which only 3 or 4 dorsal scales at the rear edge of the neck band have slight black margins. The area back of this ring is grayish olive, the next portion of the dorsum citrine-drab, and the rear parts deep olive. The scales of the dorsum have cadet gray, dutch blue to russian blue or endive blue edges. The iris is black with a patch of flame scarlet above and behind the pupil. The labials are cartridge buff. The underside of the head is cartridge buff, each scale with a black spot. This cartridge buff grades into pale orange-yellow on the forward parts, then light orange-yellow, next deep chrome in the rear half, and the underside of the tail jasper red or scarlet-red.

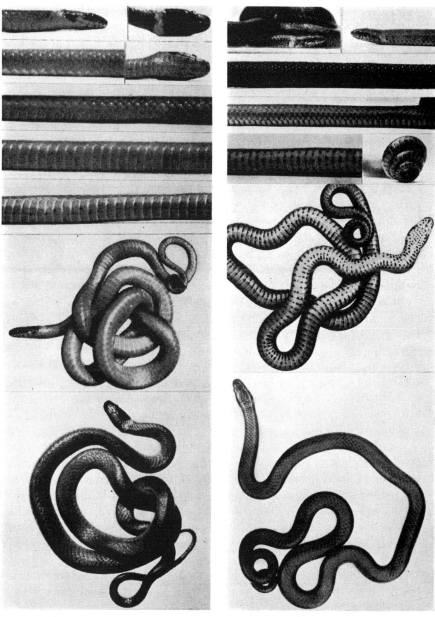

Fig. 53. *Diadophis a. pulchellus,* Swamp Lake, Tuolomne Co., Calif., C. H. Brown.

Fig. 54. *Diadophis a. similis,* 1,2,4,6–8, San Diego, Calif., L. M. Klauber; 3,5, Laguna Beach, Calif., C. M. Perkins.

This belly color extends up onto the 1st row of lateral scales. On the rear of each ventral may be 4 spots or 2 of each side may unite. Sometimes they are united on one edge and separated as 2 spots on the other half of the rear edge. Thus the venter may be marked with 2 rows of black spots on either side.

Notes on snakes recently dead, Apr. 27, 1928. The top of the head is deep olive or citrine-drab with black patches. On one, the under parts are capucine buff or even pale ochraceous-buff or cinnamon-buff; another is buff-pink or light vinaceous, cinnamon, salmon-buff, or salmon color. In one the upper parts are pale quaker drab. One has an irregular row of small faint black spots on mid-venter in the posterior half of the body.

Habitat and habits: Our knowledge of this topic came from Klauber and Perkins, each of whom said it was common in San Diegan gardens and in moist areas from ocean to mountain top. In 1929 Klauber (Gen., 1939a) in his "Sixteen Year Census" gave its distribution thus: "Coast, 395 specimens; inland valleys 54; foothills 29; mountains 9; undetermined 4."

Period of activity: "Because they are usually found by digging, Ring-necks are brought to the Reptile House every month of the year, although March, April and May rank highest" (Perkins). "Sixteen Year Census": "Jan. 14, Feb. 47, Mar. 84, Apr. 91, May 80, June 40, June 32, Aug. 23, Sept. 28, Oct. 23, Nov. 16, Dec. 13. Total 491. Rank 8. Per cent 3.79 of total of snakes" (Klauber, Gen., 1939a).

Breeding: Oviparous. *Sexual dimorphism*—"It is possible that adult females are in general larger than the males, at least this is suggested by the series of specimens examined" (Blanchard, 1942). *Eggs*—All we can find is that baby snakes come from eggs; in other words we know almost nothing of the breeding of this species.

Young—No one has recorded a brood of these snakes. Two pertinent notes are: "A very young specimen was noted as differing materially in coloration from the adults as the dorsal color was black throughout (not differing from the head coloration as in the adults), and the ring was brilliant coral red" (Klauber, Calif., 1924a). "The smallest specimen measured 142 mm., and in this specimen the umbilicus was not healed" (Blanchard, 1942).

Food: Insects, worms, salamanders, lizards, tree frogs. Klauber (Calif., 1934a), Perkins.

Field notes: We wish we could quote all of Klauber's published field-journal notes, which give the essential facts, in lively diction, even if terse and cryptic at times.

Authorities:

Blanchard, F. N. (Gen., 1923, 1942)

Klauber, L. M. (Gen., 1939a; Calif., 1924a, 1931a, 1934a)

Perkins, C. B. (Calif., 1938)

Schmidt, K. P. (Baja Calif., 1922)

1938, C. B. Perkins: This snake "might be confused with the California Black-headed Snake which is small and has a collar, but can be distinguished easily as the Black-headed Snake has a spotless, pinkish belly and under-tail."

Santa Barbara ring-necked snake, Van Denburgh's ring-necked snake (2—Ditmars 1936)

Diadophis amabilis vandenburghi Blanchard 1923. Fig. 55; Map 19

Other common names: Van Denburgh's ring-neck snake, Western ring-necked snake (1—Ditmars 1907).

Range: Ventura Co. to Santa Cruz Co., Calif. *Elevation*—Mainly below 3,000 feet.

Size: Adults, 7–19.7 inches. In 1942 Blanchard had males 175–475 mm. and females 205–486 mm.

Distinctive characteristics: "The distinctive features are: an uninterrupted, moderately wide neck ring (1½ to 2½ scales in width); 17 rows of dorsal scales anteriorly (at least near the head), becoming 15 posteriorly; the ventral color extending over from 1½ to 2 rows of dorsal scales; and the black spots on the belly unusually few and small" (Blanchard, 1923).

Color: A snake caught September 15, 1939, in San Roqul Canyon, Santa Barbara, Calif., and given us by W. G. Abbott of the Santa Barbara Museum of Natural History. The back is yellowish olive or saccardo's olive. The top of the head is olive or dark greenish olive. The 1st row of scales back of the parietals is of the body color, followed by a neck ring 1½ scales wide of orange-rufous. The iris of the eye is olive or dark greenish olive in the upper half and black in the lower. The pupil rim of orange-rufous is broadest above the pupil. The upper labials and rostral bear a row of black spots which more or less outlines the flame scarlet of the lower ⅔ of these labials, the upper third being like the top of the head. Lower labials are flame scarlet. The underside of head and neck are flame scarlet, the labials marked with dark sutures, the chin shields with black spots. The underside of tail and posterior part of body are brazil red with the forward half scarlet. The color of belly extends over the 1st row of scales and covers bases of 2nd row, leaving tips like dorsal color. The apices of most of the 1st-row scales in the middle of the body bear black spots. The spots of the underside are few, small, and not uniformly arranged. When first picked up, this form, like most *Diadophis amabilis,* will coil the tail, revealing its brazil red color.

A snake from a bluff overlooking the Pacific Ocean, about ½ mile s. of Point Sal, Santa Barbara Co., Calif., received June 23, 1940, from Clausen and Trapido. The back is deep olive with an unbroken neck ring of rufous 1½ scales wide. The top of head is black, upper labials black except for a little touch of rufous on the 5th and 6th; lower labials are clouded with deep olive. Iris is black. The belly color is apricot orange, scarlet in rear of body and tail. Apricot orange extends over gulars and chin shields and covers at least ⅔ of each scale of the 1st row. The venter is marked with 4 irregular rows of black spots except the rear half of the tail, which is clear scarlet.

Authority: Blanchard, F. N. (Gen., 1923, 1942)

1944, A. H. and A. A. Wright: Frankly, with the scanty material at hand we still hesitate to determine *vandenburghi* specimens. No one could have extracted more from such material than the masterly Blanchard. We speak thus because no live *Diadophis amabilis* we have seen from Santa Barbara County accords with the description of *vandenburghi,* yet these specimens are from the center of its supposed range. We also saw live material at the Santa Barbara Museum. The specimens of which we give color descriptions are debatable.

Southern ring-necked snake (6—Corrington 1929),
Ring-necked snake (17—Baird and Girard 1853)

Diadophis punctatus punctatus (Linné) 1766. Fig. 56; Map 20

Other common names: Eastern ring-neck snake; punctated viper (Kerr 1802); ring snake; southeastern ring-necked snake.

Range: Coastal plain and piedmont from s. New Jersey to Mobile Bay and Florida.—Ala.; Del.; Fla.; Ga.; Md.; N.C.; N.J.; S.C.; Va. *Elevation*—Coast to 1,000 feet. Sea level to 2,500 feet (McCauley, 1945).

Size: Adults, 7–18 inches.

Distinctive characteristics: "The leading characteristics of *punctatus* are 8 upper labials, 15 rows of scales throughout its length, an interrupted neck ring, a single line of dark spots along the belly, and a restriction in the number of ventrals between 127 and 155. It is best distinguished from *stictogenys* on the presence of a single median line of clearly defined half-moon shaped black spots on the belly. In *stictogenys* the ventral spots are more or less scattered, or imperfectly united in a median line. In addition the upper labials in *punctatus* are usually 8, instead of 7 as in *stictogenys*. There is no invariable distinction from *edwardsii*. The general sum of the ventral and caudal scutes is less than 191 in *punctatus* and from 190 to 228 in *edwardsii*. The median row of spots on the belly and the spotted chin are quite distinctive of *punctatus*" (Blanchard, Gen., 1942).

Color: A snake from Cypress Pond, Billy Is., Okefinokee Swamp, Ga. The back is dark olive in effect, but under the lens is seen to be bluish black, indigo blue, or dark dull violet-blue, each scale flecked with pale smoke gray, smoke gray, light olive gray, or tea green. The ring on the neck is interrupted on mid-dorsum by 1 scale. The dorsal portions of the ring are orange chrome, the side pale orange yellow. The chin and upper labials are cream color or

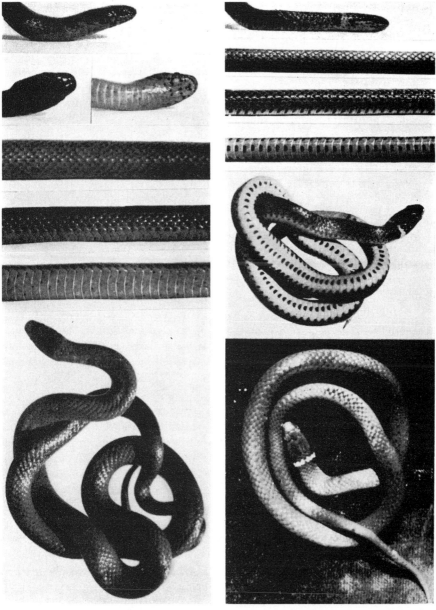

Fig. 55. *Diadophis a. vandenburghi,* San Roqul Canyon, Santa Barbara, Calif., W. G. Abbott.

Fig. 56. *Diadophis punctatus punctatus:* 1–4,6, Silver Springs, Fla., E. R. Allen; 5, Eustis, Fla., O. C. Van Hyning.

massicot yellow. The iris is black with an orange-rufous or xanthine orange pupil ring. The belly is ochraceous-orange or cadmium orange. There is a dark slate violet (1), dark dull violet-blue, or bluish black spot on the middle of each ventral and also on either end.

Abnormal coloration—Albinism. In 1941 Neill wrote: "While collecting at Augusta, Georgia, on Sept. 1, 1939, I found, beneath a pile of dead grass, an albino ring-necked, *Diadophis p. punctatus*. The specimen was very young, measuring only 140 mm. in length."

Habitat: From Loennberg, Brimley (N.C., 1895, 1909, 1941–42), Ditmars (N.Y., 1905), Fowler, Wright and Bishop, Deckert (Fla., 1918), Löding (Ala., 1922), Corrington (S.C., 1929), Van Hyning (Fla., 1933), Carr, Gray (N.C., 1941), McCauley (1941), Goin (Fla., 1943), Obrecht (S.C., 1946), Neill (Ga., 1951; Gen., 1951), we have assembled this summary. This snake is found in moist or damp places, near water, banks of brooks, cypress edges, and in creek bottomlands. Several authors mentioned woodlands, sometimes forest paths, thicker wood edges, edges of cultivated fields, and hardwood stands. Its cover may be logs, stones, fallen timber, bark of dead logs, trees or stumps, or any litter. Some have found it beneath sphagnum moss in moist situations, and one writer noted dry sphagnum beds.

Period of activity: *First appearance*—Apr. 17 (Harper, Ga., 1930); Apr. (Loennberg); Mar. 21, 1899 (Blatchley, 1902). *Seasonal catch*—Mar., 1; Apr., 7; May, 8; June, 6; July, 2; Aug., 1; Sept., 2; Oct., 12; Nov., 2 (Brimley, N.C., 1925). *Fall disappearance*—Oct. 20, 1926 (Bishop, N.C., 1928); Sept. 12, 1915 (Latham, N.Y., 1915); Sept. 16, 1936 (McCauley, 1941); Sept. 1, 1939 (Neill).

Hibernation—"This species is one of the few Florida snakes which are gregarious hibernators. Three or 4 are frequently found coiled together under a log or in sphagnum; a short rotten pine stick (not more than an inch in diameter) which I picked up to put on a fire, contained 6 *Diadophis*" (Carr).

Breeding: Oviparous. *Eggs*—Wright and Bishop reported taking, under a log, a ring neck, which "may have been seeking the sandy fields of the Lee family where lizards, snakes and turtles resort in great numbers to lay their eggs. The specimen had 5 unlaid eggs which measured as follows: 18x9 mm., 19x9, 20x9, 20x9, 21x10. The covering is thin and quite pinkish in alcohol. This species seems nocturnal in Okefinokee, as our experience with it elsewhere suggests. These specimens had insect and worm remains in their alimentary tracts." Several authors before Brimley in 1941 merely dubbed it "oviparous" without giving details. *Young*—McCauley (Md., 1941) collected "a newly hatched juvenile" Sept. 16, 1936. Blanchard's (Gen., 1942) 105–115 mm. female and 2 males 105–125 mm. were probably caught shortly after hatching.

Food: Insects, earthworms, salamanders, small frogs, and reptiles. Holbrook, Ditmars (N.Y., 1905), Fowler, Metcalf (Gen., 1930).

Authorities:

Barbour, T. (Fla., 1919a)
Blatchley, W. S. (Fla., 1902, 1932)
Brimley, C. S. (N.C., 1941–42)
Carr, A. F., Jr. (Fla., 1940a)
Fowler, H. W. (N.J., 1907)
Holbrook, J. E. (Gen., 1836–42)

Loennberg, E. (Fla., 1895)
McCauley, R. H. (Md., 1941, 1945)
Neill, W. T. (Ga., 1941b)
Say, T. (Gen., 1819)
Wright, A. H., and S. C. Bishop (Ga., 1916)

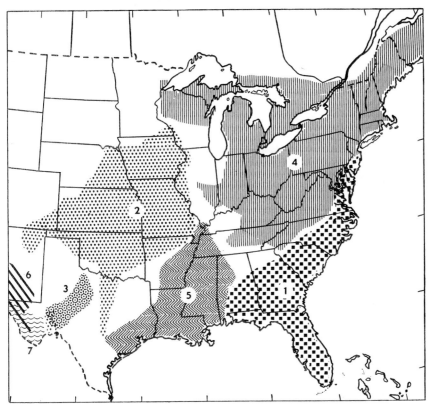

Map 20. *Diadophis*—1, *p. punctatus;* 2, *p. arnyi;* 3, *p. docilis;* 4, *p. edwardsi;* 5, *p. stictogenys;* 6, *r. regalis;* 7, *r. blanchardi.*

Prairie ring-necked snake (10), Arny's ring-necked snake (7—Yarrow 1882)

Diadophis punctatus arnyi Kennicott 1858. Fig. 57; Map 20

Other common names: Arny's ring-neck snake (2); blue racer (young); eastern ring-necked snake; Ozark ring-neck snake; ring-neck snake (13—Mozley 1878); ring-necked snake (14—Taylor 1892); Sonoran ring-necked snake; spotted ring-necked snake; western ring-necked snake.

Range: Central lowlands from Mississippi River in Wisconsin and Illinois s.w. through Ozark plateau to cent. Texas (however, Milstead *et al.* [Texas, 1950] record it in Terrell Co.), n.w. to s.e. corner of Colorado, n.e. across e. Nebraska and Iowa to s.e. Minnesota.—Ark.; Colo.; Ia.; Ill.; Kan.; Minn.; Mo.; Neb.; Okla.; S.D.; Tex.; Wis. *Elevation*—500 to 3,500 or 4,000 feet.

Size: Adults, 7 or 8 to 16 inches.

Distinctive characteristics: "Characteristic of *D. p. aryni* are the extension of the dark color of the head around or across the angle of the jaw and slightly forward on the lower jaw, scattered spots on the belly, usually 17 rows of dorsal scales, 7 upper labials and a moderate number of ventrals (142–185). There is little difficulty in distinguishing *arnyi* from any other member of the genus except *docilis* and *stictogenys*. Here the best distinction is on the number of ventrals. In *docilis,* considering the sexes separately, the number of ventrals is distinctly higher. . . . In *stictogenys*, except in the region of intergradation, males have fewer than 145 ventrals and females fewer than 150, while in *arnyi* males have more than 145 and females more than 150" (Blanchard, 1942).

Color: Four snakes received from E. H. Taylor, Department of Zoology, University of Kansas, Apr. 11, 1928. The back is hair brown. The neck band is obscure orange-pink, not normal. The upper labials are cartridge buff, capucine buff, or orange-pink. The iris is deep heliotrope-gray, with an area of grenadine above the upper edge of the pupil and somewhat on the rear edge. The throat is orange-pink or capucine buff, soon becoming on the venter capucine yellow, mikado orange, then salmon-orange around the vent, and scarlet-red or rose doree on the underside of the tail. On each ventral is a black spot at the end of each plate, with 2 or 3 spots in the central portion. The tail has 1 or 2 spots of hair brown on each subcaudal.

In the next snake, the dorsum is dark vinaceous-drab, dark grayish brown or deep purplish gray heavily marked with fine dots of pallid purplish gray, pearl gray, or pale olive-gray, giving the dorsum the effect of dark grayish brown. The neck band is orange chrome. The snout is ecru-olive. The iris is the color of the body with rufous or flame scarlet above the pupil. The throat is salmon-orange, spotted with dark, grading through orange chrome and flame scarlet in front of the vent and scarlet-red on the underside of the tail, which is unspotted.

Another snake has a black head and an orange-chrome neck band with a black margin behind. The dorsum is blackish brown (2).

The 4th snake is drab on the front portion of the dorsum, chaetura drab on the rear half, and dutch blue or slate-blue along the sides.

Habitat and habits: The records are numerous. These snakes have been found under rocks and stones; under logs, boards, sheet metal, debris, piles of driftwood; on shaded slopes; in decaying leaves; in gardens; on golf courses; in open meadows and pastures; in the gravel and sands of railroads. See Taylor, J. Hurter, Branson (Kan., 1904), Hurter and Strecker (Ark., 1909), Ellis and Henderson (Colo., 1913), Van Wagenan, Dice (Kan., 1923), Burt (Kan., 1927, 1933), Linsdale (Kan., 1927), Gloyd (Kan., 1928), Brennan (Kan., 1934), Burt and Hoyle, Hudson, Boyer and Heinze, P. Anderson (Mo., 1949); Owens (Mo., 1949), Force (Okla., 1926), Ortenburger and Freeman (Okla., 1930), Trowbridge (Okla., 1937), Smith and Acker (Okla., 1940), Bragg and Dundee, Langebartel, Over (S.D., 1923), and many others. In general this form is in the "rock-ground community" (Dice, Kan., 1923) and "under stones and rocks on hillsides covered with open woods" (Gloyd, Kan., 1928).

Period of activity: *Early appearances*—Apr. 11, 1928 (E. H. Taylor); Apr. 6, 1929 (Gloyd, Kan., 1932); Apr. 24, 1931; Apr. 9, 11, 13, 23, 30, May 1, 13, 1922; Apr. 4, 1926 (Burt, Kan., 1927); May 17, 1925, April 18, 1926; Apr. 28, 29, 1927 (Gloyd, Kan., 1928); Mar. 22; Apr. 14, 15, May 2, 6, 21, 24 (Hurter); Mar. 16, 29, 31, Apr. 1, 2, 3, 8, 9, 15, 16, 21, 1934 (Burt, Gen., 1935); Apr. 3, 4, 8, 22, 23, 1933 (Burt and Hoyle); Apr. 25, 1925 (Burt, Kan., 1927). "On April 13, 1932, 14 were taken under a flat rock near Schoenchen [by] Branson" (Burt, Kan., 1933). "They were most easily found in April and May and were seldom encountered in July and August. The earliest capture was March 26th, the last was November 22" (Anderson). *Fall disappearance*— Nov. 7 (Hurter); Sept. 23, 1928 (Gloyd, Kan., 1932); Oct. 14, 1917, Oct. 14, 1926, Oct. 19, 1930, Oct. 1, 1932 (Burt, 1933); Oct. 25, 1933 (Burt and Hoyle); Oct. 4, 1916 (Van Wagenan); Sept. 1, 1923 (Linsdale, Kan., 1927); Sept. 15, 1949 (Maslin).

Hibernation—"This subspecies was located in a snake den in Cowley County, Kansas, on March 29, 1934. Here ring-neck snakes were in company with numerous specimens of the larger snakes, *Elaphe laeta* and *Coluber constrictor flaviventris*" (Burt, Gen., 1935). Another note may have significance. Linsdale (Kan., 1927) observed that "several young were found in a hole in the ground at the side of a road by workers on Sept. 1, 1923."

Breeding: *Sexual dimorphism*—"Anal ridges in males indicate 210 mm. or higher as sexual maturity" (Blanchard, Gen., 1942). *Eggs*—Number, 1–7. Size, 16–52 mm. x 5.5 to 7.6 mm. or average of all records, 27x6.7 mm. Time of deposition, June to Aug. 16. In Tulsa Co., Okla., Force recorded that "on June 21, 1928, a female deposited 4 irregular deep yellow eggs, averaging 16 mm. in length by 6 mm. in diameter. Two other[s] deposited eggs each measuring 37 mm. by 7 mm. and 32 mm. by 7 mm." Data from Blanchard (Gen., 1942) based on deposited clutches and dissections show "one egg in 2 cases, 2 eggs in 5 cases, 3 eggs in 4 cases, and 4 eggs in 3 cases." "The eggs look much like those of *edwardsii* in being white with yellow ends or pale to deep yellow all over, but they are much longer and more slender." From his material, the normal range is from (16) 21–32.5 (52) mm. in length and

6–7.5 mm. in width. "They increase in size after being laid," e.g., 28x6.5 mm. at deposition, 33x9.3 mm. at hatching; or 21x6.7 mm. at deposition, 23.1x10.1 mm. at hatching. Blanchard's captives laid eggs on July 24, July 27, Aug. 16, and July 20, but he believes that June 20 is a more normal time. His times from deposition to hatching were 54, 55, and 70 days. In 1942 Hudson in Nebraska took "a large female . . . May 21 [containing] 7 eggs, the largest of which measured 18 by 5.5 mm." In 1947 Langebartel in Illinois related how "on July 23, 1945, one deposited 5 eggs averaging 27 mm. long; June 30th, 1945, another laid one egg."

Young—"The young are very similar to the adults except the ground color of the dorsal surface is more of a slaty-blue" (Taylor). "The young snakes at hatching look practically like the adults. Four specimens measured 98, 104, 105, and 108 mm. in total length" (Blanchard, Gen., 1942).

Food: Insects, earthworms, frogs, toads, small snakes, lizards, salamanders. Taylor, Guthrie, Force, Ellis and Henderson (Colo., 1913), Blanchard (1942), Hudson, Smith.

Authorities:

Anderson, P. (Mo., 1942)
Blanchard, F. N. (Gen., 1942; Tenn., 1922)
Boyer, D. A., and A. A. Heinze (Mo., 1934)
Bragg, A. N., and H. A. Dundee (N.M., 1949)
Burt, C. E. (Gen., 1935; Kan., 1927, 1933)
Burt, C. E., and W. L. Hoyle (Gen., 1935)
Cope, E. D. (Gen., 1900)

Force, E. R. (Okla., 1930)
Garman, S. (Gen., 1883)
Guthrie, J. E. (Ia., 1926)
Hudson, G. (Neb., 1942)
Hurter, J. (Mo., 1911)
Kennicott, R. (Gen., 1860)
Langebartel, D. A. (Ill., 1947)
Maslin, T. P. (Colo., 1950)
Smith, H. M. (Kan., 1950)
Taylor, W. E. (Neb., 1892b)
Van Wagenan, G. (Mo., 1917)

1942, F. N. Blanchard: "The differences between *dugesii* and *arnyi* are relatively slight; are less, in fact, than between *dugesii* and any other species in the genus; and these differences are in the nature of a specialization in *arnyi*. Therefore *arnyi* is to be regarded as a derivative of *dugesii* [through *docilis*], and as a progenitor of the other members of the *punctatus* group."

Texan ring-neck snake (Blanchard and Gloyd 1942), Ring-necked snake

Diadophis punctatus docilis Baird and Girard 1853. Fig. 58; Map 20

Other common names: Blue racer (young); Texas ring-necked snake.
Range: A crescentic area from Devils and Pecos Rivers n.e. almost to the Red River at the s.e. corner of the panhandle of Texas. *Elevation*—1,000 to 3,000 feet, possibly 3,500 feet.

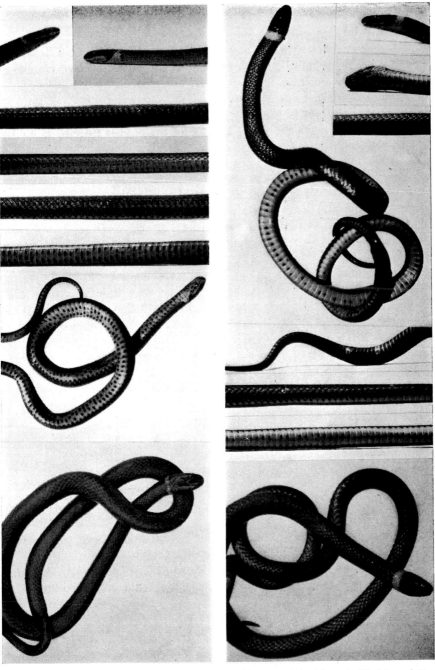

Fig. 57. *Diadophis p. arnyi:* 1,3–7, Imboden, Ark., B. C. Marshall; 2,8, Lawrence, Kan., E. H. Taylor.

Fig. 58. *Diadophis p. docilis,* Menard Co., Tex., A. J. Kirn.

Size: Adults, 7–17 inches.

Distinctive characteristics: "In general similar to *D. p. arnyi* but larger and with a distinctly higher number of ventrals and higher average number of caudals; dorsal scales usually in 15 rows" (Blanchard).

Color: A snake from Menard Co., Tex., received from A. J. Kirn of Somerset, Tex., June 6, 1946. The dorsal color is hair brown to deep mouse gray, all dorsal scales the same. The top of the head is fuscous, as are the face, temporals, and top of the supralabials. The ring across the neck is capucine buff. The eye is fuscous with a bar of capucine buff. The throat is pale yellow-orange. The under parts are capucine orange to capucine yellow, becoming on the tail and for 18 plates ahead of the vent rose doree. There is a row of midventral dots, one to a plate, but these are lacking on the tail. Each ventral bears a black dash on posterior lateral corner. *Remarks*—Eye of snake indicates it may soon shed. Ventrals 193; scale rows 15; single posterior temporal.

Field notes: After 1942 no one knew or saw more *docilis* alive than our dear friend, now departed, A. Kirn. The specimen from which our color description was written was accompanied by the following letter, which expresses the helpful spirit he showed toward many herpetologists: "May 31, 1941. Mailed you today a *Diadophis* from Menard County, Texas. Do not know if it is *docilis* or *arnyi* but hope it is the former. Had a good rain, a few nights ago. Spadefoots were out in force and now the *Bufos*." In a letter of July 5, 1945, he said: "I am including a Texan Ring-neck snake (*D. p. docilis*) that a friend just brought me from s.e. Taylor County, south of Abilene, Texas." And on Feb. 15, 1946 he wrote: "Sent preserved *D. docilis*. It was picked up in road, dead near Lawn, Taylor County, Texas."

Authorities: [1]

Baird, S. F., and C. Girard (Gen., 1853)	Coues, E. (Ariz., 1875)
	Cragin, F. W. (Kan., 1881)
Blanchard, F. N. (Gen., 1942)	Garman, S. (Gen., 1883; Tex., 1892)
Cope, E. D. (Gen., 1900; Okla., 1894)	

Shortly after its description, confusion began; it continued from 1875 to 1942 because of lack of material. See Coues, Cragin, Garman (Gen., 1883), Cope. Like some other central Texan forms (*Elaphe o. lindheimeri, Salvadoras*, racers, etc.), this snake was overlooked for many years; it is now being

---

[1] 1956: Mecham (*Copeia*, 51–52) still holds to the *D. p. arnyi* interpretation for the ringnecks of trans-Pecos and western Texas, and we have much sympathy with his arrangement. "The purpose here has been to point out the existence of only one species where two were thought to be present. Suffice it to say that the subspecies are largely artificial. . . . Of the racial units herein considered, *Diadophis punctatus docilis* seems to be the least justified. Set up almost solely on the basis of ventral count subject to clinal variation, it serves no practical purpose, and it might be discarded."

rediscovered in literature since several of the younger herpetologists have started to study and to visit Texas.

The recognition of new forms or the reallocation of the old is not the only solution of the question. Really there is a great scarcity of records, and even more of specimens, between New Orleans and Pecos, Tex. In view of the supposed meeting of *D. p. arnyi* and *D. p. stictogenys* in Helotes, in the light of the uncertain range of *D. p. docilis,* and in consideration of the new juxtaposed *D. regalis blanchardi,* which Schmidt and Smith establish in the Big Bend, one naturally wishes cent. and west. Texas to be thoroughly combed for *Diadophis* material before we accept the Texan allocations too religiously. It needs as much overhauling as Schmidt thinks ought to be done for the *regalis* group.

1950, Milstead, Mecham, and McClintock (Tex.): *"Diadophis punctatus arnyi, . . .* two specimens were collected about mid-morning [in Terrell County, one in the cedar-savannah association and one in the persimmon-shin oak association, each where there was a large amount of rock coverage]." This recent record emphasizes the previous comment. We do not necessarily question the allocation of *D. p. arnyi,* but the record is placed here to promote further work and collecting.

Eastern ring-necked snake (12—Ditmars 1907)

Diadophis punctatus edwardsi (Merrem) 1820. Fig. 59; Map 20

Other common names: Collared snake; eastern ring-neck snake (6); fodder snake; king snake; little black-and-red snake; northeastern ring-neck snake; northern ring-necked snake (4); ring snake; ringed snake (Storer 1838); ring-neck snake (15); ringed-necked snake; small black-and-red snake.

Range: Maritime Provinces across Quebec and Ontario to n. Michigan and extreme n.e. Minnesota; s.e. to cent. Tennessee and n. in Appalachian Mts. from South Carolina to Maine.—U.S.A.: Conn.; D.C.; Del.; Ga.; Ill.; Ind.; Ky.; Mass.; Md.; Me.; Mich.; Minn.; N.C.; N.H.; N.J.; N.Y.; O.; Pa.; R.I.; S.C.; Tenn.; Va.; Vt.; W. Va.; Wis. Can.: N.B.; N.S.; Ont.; Que. *Elevation*—Sea level upwards. Most records below 2,000 feet: reaching 720 feet (Lowe, Me., 1928); 1,800 feet (Necker, Tenn., 1934); 1,300–4,200 feet (Dunn, N.C., 1917); 1,000–5,800 feet (King, Tenn., 1939); 2,000–4,100 feet (Barbour, Ky., 1950).

Size: Adults, 10–20 inches.[1]

---

[1] On June 23, 1956, P. L. Litchfield and L. Adams found at Harford, N.Y., an aggregation of 16, of which 12 were females $13\frac{5}{8}$–22 inches long and 4 males $15\frac{9}{16}$–$17\frac{1}{2}$ inches in length. The females 21 and $22\frac{1}{2}$ inches laid eggs.

Distinctive characteristics: "The distinctive features of *edwardsii* are the generally unspotted belly and chin, uninterrupted neck ring, 15 rows of scales throughout the body length, 8 upper labials, and a high average number of ventrals (usually from about 145 to 170). The most constant distinctions from *punctatus* are the unspotted belly and chin, and the sum of ventrals and caudals lying between 190 and 228. When spots do occur on the belly in this subspecies, they are smaller and more irregular in form than in *punctatus,* and they are usually in an interrupted line" (Blanchard, 1942).

Color: A snake from Larch Meadows Hill at Ithaca, N.Y., caught by A. B. Klots and W. C. Herring, May 14, 1928. The forward part of the back appears grayish olive, drab, or light brownish olive. Toward the rear, the upper parts may be blackish brown (1), clove brown, or fuscous. Each scale is dusky slate-violet or black, with numerous pale smoke gray or pale olive gray specks close together. On the mid-dorsum and a few adjacent rows there is considerable drab in each scale. The neck band is pale yellow-orange, with a black margin 1½ scales wide on either side. The top of the head is deep grayish olive or dark grayish olive. Ahead of the eyes it is grayish olive, with the rostral and internasals drab, olive lake, or old gold. The iris is black or dark with a patch of dragons-blood red above and behind the pupil. In some snakes there is merely a thin rim of dragons-blood red around the pupil. Underside of head is white with labials of cream color, warm buff, or ivory yellow. At the ring, the venter becomes pale yellow-orange, then orange-buff, and ahead of the vent orange or capucine yellow. This last color is that of the underside of the tail.

In another snake, the under parts are capucine buff or even pale ochraceous-buff or cinnamon-buff. Another is buff-pink, light vinaceous-cinnamon, salmon-buff, or salmon color. In one snake, the upper parts are pale quaker drab. One snake has an irregular row of small black spots on mid-venter in the posterior half of the body.

For the color of an advanced embryo, see subtopic "Young" under "Breeding" below.

Habitat: Interesting samplings are found in the following: Storer, Latham (N.Y., 1915), Axtell (N.Y., 1947), Bishop and Alexander, Brown (Ont., 1928), Blanchard (Mich., 1928), Butler (Ind., 1887a), Conant (O., 1938a), Hibbard (Ky., 1937), King (Tenn., 1939), Dunn (N.C., 1917). A summation of about 75 accounts follows: This snake is undercover and nocturnal. It is recorded as found under bark of trees or logs 37, under stones 37, plus rocks 8, under or in fallen logs 28, under fallen timber 2, under fence rails 2, under stumps 2, under sheltering wood 1, under boards 1, rubbish 1, sticks 1, heaps of leaves 1, under top stones of broken dam 1, in sawdust pile 1, under wood 1. The kind of tree and the kind of stone are seldom mentioned.

This species frequents wooded areas. At least 35 records are of this sort:

wooded places 10, semiwooded places 2, heavily wooded places 2, heavy woods 2, dense woodlands 1, mossy woods 1, damp woods 5, moist woods 2, light woods 1, wood margins or edges 2, woodlands 1, woods 2, woods bordering a cranberry bog 1, forest cover 1, wooded slopes 1, wooded ridges 1. The last two categories suggest another requisite—rocky, wooded hillsides, characterized thus: hillside with southern exposure 1, hilly regions 1, wooded slopes 2, wooded ridges 1, side of an escarpment 1, damp shady hillside 2, dry hillside, drier hillside 1, dry, open hillsides 1, rocky areas 1, hillsides 1, rocky hills 1, ridges 1, shale outcropping 1, trap ridges.

There are few records of its roaming about by day or of open habitats, such as open areas 2, clearings 1, open pastures 1. The soil or ground is either "moist," "damp," "shaded," or the like. All in all, it is manifestly a wooded-area species whether its original habitat is now destroyed or not.

Period of activity: *Seasonal catch*—Apr. 19 (Wright and Allen, N.Y., 1913); Apr. 15–Oct. 15 (Wright, N.Y., 1919b); Mar. 18–Aug. (Necker, Ill., 1935); Mar. 31 (Hahn, Ind., 1909); May 6 (Small, Ont., 1884); May 12, 1889 (Blatchley, Ind., 1899). *Fall disappearance*—Sept. 7, 1863 (Jones, N.S., 1865); Oct. 16 (Wright and Allen); latter part of Sept., 1898 (Blatchley); Aug. 19, 1916 (Ellis, Mich., 1917). *Hibernation*—R. A. Grizzell (Md.) found a *Diadophis p. edwardsi* at a depth of 32 inches during February, 1949, when excavating a woodchuck den.

Breeding: Oviparous. Males 220–500 mm., females 220–550 mm. W. DeWitt Miller (Heyen, N.J., 1937) gives males 215–360 mm., females 250–365 mm. The first note we find is Bicknell's of 1882. One of the most definite early records is Blatchley's: "From the same hillside in the latter part of September 1898, Mr. J. S. Michaels took from the dirt thrown out from a quarry 8 eggs and one young of this species. The eggs were placed in a tool box and most of them hatched within a week. The young were about 5 inches in length and very lively." Minton in 1944 asserted that "the eggs of ring-necked snakes hatch in 4 to 6 weeks—a shorter period than is required for most snake eggs. There is some evidence to show that the eggs may in rare cases be retained until they are almost ready to hatch."

A very significant study is Barbour's: "Blanchard (1937) states that eggs are laid in late June or early July in northern Michigan. The smallest egg-laying female recorded by Blanchard was 317 mm. long. Twenty-seven females with a total length greater than 320 mm. were collected from Black Mountain. Of these 13 were taken between June 8 and June 24, and each of these females contained eggs. No egg-bearing females were collected after June 24, although 2 females were taken July 1 to 15, 3 from July 16 to 31, and 8 from Aug. 1 to 31. From these data, it is apparent that egg-laying occurs on Black Mountain in the latter part of June or early July, as reported for northern Michigan. . . . The larger number of eggs are generally laid by the larger females. The smallest and largest egg-producing females respectively taken from the Black Mountain area are 329 mm. and 486 mm. The average number of eggs contained by the 13 egg-bearing females was 3.77 ranging from 2 to 6."

A summary from one of the best snake life-history studies (Blanchard, Mich., 1930) follows: "1. Under natural conditions the eggs of the eastern ring-neck snake are laid in a moist (but not wet) place, preferably one exposed to the sun, where the moisture content is not likely to vary much during the summer. 2. The number of eggs in a clutch is most commonly 3. Two, 4 and 5 are less common numbers, and 1 and 6 are rare. Of more than 6 eggs to a set there is no conclusive evidence. 3. The eggs are normally deposited in a single series of layings, occupying about 5 minutes each and separated by about 25–50-minute intervals. 4. Laying dates in the laboratory (of eggs that hatched into normal young) have varied from July 8 to July 30. These dates are probably approximately like those obtaining in a state of nature. 5. The eggs are most commonly 21–34 mm. in length and 7–8 mm. in width. Extreme measurements are 20.5 to 41.6, and 6.0–10.6 mm. There is a tendency for the longest eggs to be narrow and the shortest ones to be wide. 6. Hatching of eggs under laboratory conditions has occurred chiefly from the last day or two of August through the first 3 weeks of September. 7. Eggs of a set kept under the same conditions ordinarily hatch within a day or two. 8. The length of the period from laying to hatching is determined largely by the temperature of the eggs during incubation. Under ordinary laboratory conditions this has varied about an average of 56 days. . . . 12. Young snakes vary from 105 to 143 millimeters in length. The average is 124. 13. The interval from hatching to first shedding of the skin has varied from 5 to 16 days, with an average of between 8 and 9 days. . . ." *Eggs*—Number, 1–10. 1, 7, Fowler (D.C., 1945); 1, 2, 3, 4, 5, 6, Blanchard (Mich., 1930); 2, 8, Minton; 2, 3, 4, 5, 6, Barbour; 3, Ditmars (Gen., 1907), Funkhouser (Ky., 1925); 3, 10, Lowe (Me., 1928); 5, Bicknell (N.Y., 1879); 6, 10, Wright and Allen (N.Y., 1913); 9, Blatchley (Ind., 1899); 10, Atkinson. Time of deposition, June and July. June (Miller, Minton, Fowler); June 10, July (Wright and Allen); June 12 (Bicknell); June 28 (Ditmars); July 3, 27 (Blanchard); July 8, July 30 (Blanchard); July 9 (Atkinson); midsummer (Funkhouser). Size, .8–1.6 inches x .25–.50 inches or 20–41 mm. x 6–12 mm.

Young—Time of hatching, Aug. 1–September. Surface gives September and October. Size at hatching, 4–6 inches or 100–125 mm., a few to 143 or 150 mm. In a soft gravelly slide brought down in 1947 near the top of the north bank of a gorge in Ithaca, N.Y., a group of 4 eggs was dug up on Sept. 1, 1950, by Dr. Elsa G. Allen.

Food: Insects, earthworms, toads, frogs, salamanders, other snakes, lizards. Funkhouser (Ky., 1925), Bishop and Alexander, Lowe (Me., 1928), Babcock (N. Eng., 1929), McCauley and East (Md., 1940), Trapido (N.Y.,

1937), Uhler, Cottam, and Clarke (Va., 1939), Minton, Barbour. Surface quotes Cope, Holbrook, DeKay.

Field notes: We have regretfully omitted a page of selections from the diaries of the master naturalist, W. DeWitt Miller. These selections came to mind because of the quotation of another meticulous naturalist, Dr. F. N. Blanchard, who wrote, "The question (*punctatus* on L.I.) seems, however, to be distinctly reopened by a *punctatus* from Matawan, Monmouth County, New Jersey, collected May 28, 1911, by W. DeWitt Miller (AMNH 43895)."

Authorities:

Atkinson, D. A. (Pa., 1901)
Barbour, R. W. (Ky., 1950)
Bishop, S. C. (S.C., 1928)
Bishop, S. C., and W. P. Alexander (N.Y., 1927)
Blanchard, F. N. (Gen., 1942; Mich., 1928, 1930)
Blatchley, W. S. (Ind., 1891)
Conant, R. (O., 1938a; Pa., 1942)

Ditmars, R. L. (N.Y., 1896)
Hay, O. P. (Ind., 1892)
Langlois, T. H. (Mich., 1925)
Miller, W. DeW. (*Diaries*)
Minton, S., Jr. (Ind., 1944)
Ruthven, A. G. (Mich., 1911)
Storer, D. H. (Mass., 1839)
Surface, H. A. (Pa., 1906)
Wagner, G. (Wis., 1922)

**Mississippi ring-neck snake (3—Ditmars 1936),
Ring-necked snake (8—Löding 1922)**

Diadophis punctatus stictogenys Cope 1860. Fig. 60; Map 20

Other common names: Common little ring-necked snake; eastern ring-necked snake; Mississippi Valley ring-neck snake; ring snake; (southern) ring-neck snake.

Range: Mississippi embayment; Gulf coast from Mobile, Ala., to Matagorda Co. Tex., n. to s. Illinois and s.e. Missouri.—Ala.; Ark.; Ill.; Ky.; La.; Miss.; Mo.; Tenn.; Tex. *Elevation*—Coast to 500 feet.

Size: Adults, 8–20 inches.

Distinctive characteristics: "This form is marked by 15 dorsal scale rows, 7 upper labials, generally less than 145 ventrals, belly more or less irregularly black-spotted, and neck ring narrow and often interrupted" (Blanchard, Gen., 1942).

Color: Three snakes from Henderson, Tenn., received from J. R. Endsley, April 7, 1938. The back of the largest snake is hair brown, mouse gray, or neutral gray. The lower scale rows are pale neutral gray. An orange neck band ½ scale in width extends down onto the 2nd scale row. This band then becomes white as it crosses the last upper labial and merges with the white underside of the head. All the upper labials are white in their lower portions. A black stripe extends around the nostril, through the lower portion of the nasals, along the edge of the upper labials, swinging across the neck to form a cephalic border to the orange neck stripe. The neck band

Fig. 59. *Diadophis p. edwardsi*, Ithaca, N.Y.: 2,4, A. B. Klots and W. C. Herring; 3,5, W. J. and H. Hamilton.

Fig. 60. *Diadophis p. stictogenys*, Henderson, Tenn., J. R. Endsley.

is bordered behind with black also. The top of the head is fuscous with a few black dots along the outer edges of the parietals, along the suture of temporals and parietals, crossing the head at the rear suture of supraoculars and frontal. The eye is black with a ring of orange-rufous or English red around the pupil. The underside of the head is white washed with pale yellow-orange. Each chin shield and almost every lower labial bears a black dot. The gulars are almost wholly without dots. The color of the ventral surface passes from orange-buff on the neck, through capucine yellow in the cephalic half to orange in the caudal half, heavily marked with black. In general, there is one row of compound black spots down the center of the venter. Frequently such a compound spot appears as 2 distinct but close-set black dots. These are almost absent on the underside of the tail. The ends of the ventrals are rarely marked with black dots in the cephalic half of the body, but such terminal spots become apparent in the caudal half.

Habitat: Records have been in pine forests, timbered hillsides, broken fields near water, bottoms of ravines and gullies, and in wooded hills. The cover has been logs, sphagnum, stones, loose bark of fallen pine trunks, damp leaves, leaf mats, and bark and loose litter around stumps and tree bases.

Period of activity: *Early appearances*—Feb. 21, Back Bay; Feb. 22, Soldiers Home; Mar. 3, Belmar (Corrington, Miss., 1927). "The ring-necked snake is commonly found during the entire year" (Allen, Miss., 1932a).

Breeding: Oviparous. *Eggs*—Parker (Tenn., 1937) gives us our first definite record: "On July 28, 2 eggs were found in a deep layer of damp leaves in a small side gully near the head of another ravine. The eggs were measured and kept in damp leaves. On July 29 egg number 1 measured 25.5x12 mm. and egg number 2, 23.5x9.5 mm. On Aug. 6 egg number 1 measured 26x11 mm. and egg number 2, 24x9.5mm. The larger egg was opened on August 6 and found to contain a fully-formed embryo beginning to pigment. A week later the other was opened and found sterile."

Young—Baird and Girard (Gen., 1853) have a young specimen 5 inches long which must be near hatching size. No doubt the 7 females of Blanchard of 1942, 105–155 mm., are newly hatched or just beyond, so also the 7 males, 105–155 mm.[1]

Enemies: In the stomach contents of one *Micrurus fulvius*, Schmidt found the "tail of *D. p. stictogenys, D. p. stictogenys, Storeria dekayi*, tail of *Storeria dekayi.*"

Field notes: Apr. 5–7, 1934: Examining Löding's ring-necks we guess they are nearer Blanchard's *stictogenys* than *punctatus*, but they are a varied lot. . . . To travel across the border lines of many races as we have fre-

---

[1] In 1955 P. W. Smith and J. C. List (*Amer. Midl. Naturalist*, **53**:121) recorded a clutch of 3 eggs hatching July 29. The young were 98, 102, and 103 mm. in length.

quently done leaves one dizzy at times—sometimes the specimens do not respect the definite separations first formulated.

Authorities:

Blanchard, F. N. (Gen., 1942, 1923; Tenn., 1922)

Cope, E. D. (Gen., 1900, 1860–61a)

Dellinger, S. C., and J. D. Black (Ark., 1938)

Haltom, W. L. (Ala., 1931)

Parker, M. V. (Tenn., 1937, 1948)

Schwardt, H. H. (Ark., 1938)

Sonoran ring-necked snake (7—Ditmars 1907),
Regal ring-necked snake (6—Yarrow 1882)

Diadophis regalis regalis Baird and Girard 1853. Fig. 61; Maps 19, 20

Other common names: (Arizona) ring-necked snake; ring snake; Sonoran ring-neck snake (2); southwestern ring-necked snake (4); thimble snake (4); western ring-necked snake.

Range: S.e. Idaho to s.w. Utah, n.e. Arizona to s. New Mexico.—Ariz.; Ida.; Nev.; N.M.; Ut. *Elevation*—2,800 to 5,000 feet (Bailey, N.M., 1913); 4,045–7,000 feet (Tanner, 1941a); from 4,300 feet to as high as 7,000 feet or more (Woodbury).

Size: Adults, 8–30 inches.

Distinctive characteristics: *"Diadophis regalis* B. & G.—Body above uniform greenish ash; beneath light yellow, scattered all over with small black spots. No occipital ring. Dorsal scales in 17 rows" (Baird and Girard).

Color: A snake belonging to A. M. Woodbury which was caught May 18, 1942, and came from the Cobblestone rattlesnake den near Grantsville, Ut. The back and top of head are tea green. The interspaces between dorsal scales are black. There is no neck ring. The rostral and upper labials except the last have lower edges of cadmium orange, which are separated from the dorsal and face color by black edges (sutures) of upper labials. The iris is tea green with some vinaceous-buff in the pupil rim. Each lower labial bears a black spot, each anterior chin shield 2, and posterior chin shield 1 at the rear. The gulars are almost clear cadmium orange, as is most of the belly and the 1st row of scales. On the belly are about 4 irregular rows of black spots, but the black spots below the scales of the 1st row and the ones on the front upper edge are faint. Through most of the tail length, the scales of the 1st row bear black edges which extend onto subcaudals as marginal bars. Just back of the vent are about 2 rows of black spots independent of the above-mentioned lateral margins. The color of undertail and for half an inch ahead of vent is between scarlet and brazil red. Notes: 7 supralabials, 9 infralabials, 17 rows of scales.

Habitat: The records of this unusual, beautiful, and secretive snake are not numerous. It has been taken according to Tanner (1941a) in the "Oak,

Juniper, Pinyon-Pine belts of our foothills" and in the "Aspen-Fir" belt of the higher elevations. These records are from beneath rocks, stones, or logs and often near water. See Woodbury (Ut., 1928), Presnall, Hardy, Tanner (1941a).

Period of activity: *First appearance*—Apr. 20, 1939 (J. S. Stanford); May 13, 1939 (R. Hardy).

Breeding: Oviparous. *Sexual dimorphism*—Blanchard held that tails of males were .180–.204, average .190 of the total length in males; in females .107–.167, average .154. *Eggs*—"The general belief that this species is oviparous can now be confirmed. A large specimen from Zion Canyon National Park No. 75 contained 5 eggs, which averaged 19.24 mm. long and 7.2 mm. wide. The largest eggs were located in the posterior portion of the body and measured in length 24.5 and 26.3 mm. respectively. The smallest measured 13.5 mm. and was the anterior egg. The 2 middle eggs were intermediate in size measuring 16 mm. each. In none of the eggs was there any indication of a developing embryo. The fact that this specimen was collected in May and contained 2 apparently fully developed eggs would lead us to believe that some of the eggs are deposited in late spring or early summer. The size of the above specimen is also noteworthy; it measured 726 mm. long and had a head width of 9.8 mm. and a body circumference at the middle of 36 mm. This I believe is the largest specimen of this species reported for Utah" (Tanner, 1941a).

Food: Insects, small snakes, small vertebrates. Ellis and Henderson (Colo., 1913), Woodbury, Tanner (1941a).

Authorities:

Baird, S. F., and C. Girard (Gen., 1942)

Blanchard, F. N. (Gen., 1942)

Hardy, R. (Ut., 1939)

Jameson, D. L., and A. G. Flury (Tex., 1949)

Presnall, C. C. (Ut., 1937)

Schmidt, K. P., and T. Smith (Tex., 1944)

Tanner, W. W. (Ut., 1940, 1941a)

Woodbury, A. M. (Ut., 1931)

1944, K. P. Schmidt and T. F. Smith: "We are unable to agree with Blanchard in the nomenclature proposed for the eastern and western subspecies of *regalis*, in which *regalis* is retained as the name for the eastern subspecies and the Arizonan form is referred to Jan's *laetus*, after having been described as *arizonae*. A specimen of *Diadophis* in Field Museum from Basuriachi, Chihuahua, collected by Robert M. Zingg, has a broad neckband, measures more than 700 mm. in length, and has 228 ventrals. In size and ventral count it accordingly agrees well with the type of *regalis* from Sonora, differing from it in the presence of a nuchal ring. Since this specimen, however, comes from a locality *east* of the type locality, we prefer to regard size and ventral count as more significant than the presence or absence of the nuchal ring, and regard *regalis* as applicable to the larger western race, proposing a new name for the Texan specimens. The geographic relations are not altered if the origin of the type of *regalis* is supposed to be in fact from southern Arizona. It does not seem possible to have *laetus* enclosing the type locality of *regalis*. Since *regalis* was described as without a nuchal ring, our arrangement assumes that this character may be an anomaly in the western race, and that *Diadophis r. arizonae* and *D. r. laetus* are synonyms of *regalis*. The alternative, that *laetus* is a valid form, and distinct from the Sonoran *regalis,* leaves our Chisos Mountain form still amply distinguished from both *regalis regalis* and *regalis laetus*. These notes do no more than reopen the problems connected with the taxonomy of *regalis,* for there appear to be significant differences between the Chisos population and the specimens from Utah reported by Tanner."

1949: Jameson and Flury describe their 2 ring-necks from the Sierra Vieja range as *Diadophis regalis regalis,* not *D. r. blanchardi*. See quotations from their work placed under the latter form. We incline toward their interpretation.

Arizona ring-necked snake (3—Klauber 1932),
Sonoran ring-necked snake (2—Ditmars 1907)

Diadophis regalis laetus (Jan.) 1863. Fig. 62; Map. 19
(*D. r. regalis* Schmidt, *Check List,* 1953)

Other common names: (Arizona) rink-neck snake; southwestern ring-necked snake.

Range: Cent. Arizona to e. Sonora and w. Chihuahua, Mex.—U.S.A.: Ariz.; N.M. Mex.: Chihuahua; San Luis Potosí; Sonora. *Elevation*—Most records probably from 3,000 to 5,000 feet.

Size: Adults, 12–30 inches.

Distinctive characteristics: "This form, like *regalis,* is distinguished from all other ring-neck snakes by a high number of ventrals (females more than 220, males more than 205), and from *regalis* it is marked by a broad, light-colored band behind the head" (Blanchard).

Color: A snake taken at Montosa Canyon, Santa Rita Mts., 11 miles above Amado, Ariz., about Aug. 25, 1933, and described at California Serpentarium July 18, 1934. (Kindness of C. M. Perkins and A. P. Artran.) The dorsal color is deep glaucous-gray, clear blue-green gray, or light glaucous-blue. Each dorsal scale, ahead, behind, and somewhat on the side is margined with black. The ring on the neck is orange chrome bordered with black.

A beautiful little snake 18 inches long collected by Orion Enzenberg near Total Wreck Mts., n. of Empire Ranch and s. of Pantano, Ariz., and sent to us by Mrs. Lyle M. Sprung of Diamond S Ranch. The back is olive-gray. The 1st scale row has the lower ⅔ orange, the rear of the upper 3rd body color with a black spot between it and the orange section. The top of

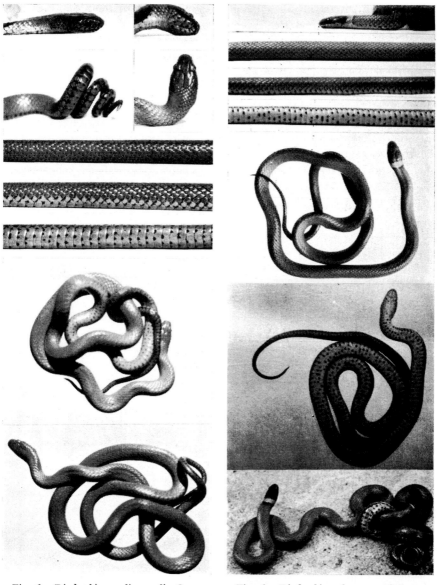

Fig. 61. *Diadophis regalis regalis,* Grantsville den, Salt Lake City, Utah, A. M. Woodbury.

Fig. 62. *Diadophis r. laetus:* 1–6, Laguna Beach, Calif., C. M. Perkins; 7, Madera Canyon, Santa Rita Mts., Ariz., photo by C. M. Bogert.

head from eye to collar is dark olive-gray with tip of snout and face deep olive-gray. The bright neck ring is apricot orange. It crosses the tips of scale row caudad of parietals, covers 3½ rows longitudinally, and has narrow black margins. The cephalad black margin on top of head is a narrow thread on the 6 median scales. The eye is mainly dark olive-gray with some black and a pupil rim of light-buff. The ventrals are orange, each scute with 3–6 inky spots becoming on underside of head and neck orange-buff. The labials are orange-buff, the upper tips of the upper ones dark olive-gray succeeded by a narrow thread of black below outlining the orange-buff. The lower labials are heavily spotted with black as are the chin shields and some of the gulars. The underside of tail and about 25 ventrals are solid scarlet-red, quite spotted ahead of vent, but on tail generally free in middle with black spots on 1st scale row and another a slight distance in from ends of plates.

Habitat and habits: Little is known of this species. Van Denburgh (Gen., 1897, 1922), Stejneger (Ariz., 1903), Van Denburgh and Slevin (1913), Quaintance, and Vorhies furnished this scant material. Most records were from old forts, canyons, and pine and oak belts, in a peach orchard, in fence holes, in mountainous regions. Quaintance and Vorhies frequently remarked the tail twisting and tail coiling of this form.

Food: Small snakes. Van Denburgh (Gen., 1902).

Field notes: July 18, 1934. At Laguna Beach, Calif. (Pomona College Biological Station), in the front room Messrs. C. M. Perkins and A. P. Artran have an exhibition hall known as the California Serpentarium. Am surprised at the large size of a ring-necked snake they secured at Montosa Canyon, Santa Rita Mts., 11 miles above Amado, Ariz., about August 25, 1933. Tried to get photos of the venters of it and a *Diadophis a. similis* together. The *D. r. arizonae* (*laetus*) in contrast was hard to manipulate because of its size.

Authorities:

Blanchard, F. N. (Gen., 1942)
Jan, G. (Gen., 1863–64)
Quaintance, C. W. (Ariz., 1935)

Van Denburgh, J., and J. R. Slevin (Ariz., 1913; Gen., 1902)

1953, A. H. and A. A. Wright: In the 1953 *Check List* Schmidt placed this form in the synonymy of *D. r. regalis*. We agree that the problem is not solved. (See *D. r. blanchardi.*)

PROBLEMATICAL FORM

Trans-Pecos ring-necked snake, Big Bend ring-necked snake

Diadophis regalis blanchardi Schmidt and Smith. Fig. 63; Maps 19, 20

Range: Trans-Pecos region, Texas from Pecos River to El Paso.

Distinctive characteristics: "Differs from *Diadophis regalis regalis* . . .

in smaller size [8–27 inches, A. H. W.], lower number of ventrals, and probably in the uniform absence of a nuchal ring" (Schmidt and Smith).

Color: A snake freshly killed on the road a mile outside Alpine, Tex., July 6, 1925. Upper color deep grayish olive or deep olive-gray; head dark grayish olive or iron gray; no nuchal collar. The belly is capucine yellow, cadmium orange, or orange chrome, in places geranium pink or eosine pink; the underside of tail and forward for 2 or 3 inches is nopal red, jasper red, or scarlet-red. The oranges or reds extend onto the 1st row of scales, forward scales orange, rearward red. Each scale in the 1st row is orange in the cephalic portion, the rear portion being spotted with the dorsal gray and with black edges, which extend onto ventrals, forming a dark spot on the caudal margin of each plate for $\frac{1}{16}$ to $\frac{1}{8}$ inch. On each ventral, 1 or 2 black spots appear between these caudal black end spots. Labials, gulars, and chin shields may be heavily spotted with black; their color may be orange or red. On the sides of the neck the oranges extend up for 5 rows of scales, but only at the base of the scales with black in front, and then deep olive-gray. I had to look hard for it, and from a dorsal view it scarcely shows. Two specimens that we saw in the Sul Ross Teachers' Normal College collection had no nuchal collars.

Habitat: We know almost nothing about the habits of this snake; all notes are about collections or specimens. Around 1903 or later Brown came to know this form, doubtless from Meyenberg. In 1905 Bailey in his *Survey of Texas* wrote: "A specimen of this little spotted-bellied snake was collected in the Chisos Mountains at 5,000 feet, June 3, 1901. The two previous recorded records for Texas—Fort Davis and Eagle Springs—are both close to 5,000 feet and, like the Chisos Mountain locality, at the edge of Upper and Lower Sonoran Zones."

Outside the Basin series of Schmidt and Smith, the most recent evidence has come from Jameson and Flury in the Sierra Vieja Range: "Two specimens [of the form here called *D. regalis regalis*] were taken, active at midmorning in the stream bed association of Z. H. Canyon. This species was probably restricted to the rocky associations of the area."

Authorities: [1]

Bailey, V. (Tex., 1905)
Blanchard, F. N. (Gen., 1942)
Brown, A. E. (Tex., 1903)
Jameson, D. L., and A. G. Flury (Tex., 1949)
Jan, G. (Gen., 1863–64)

Schmidt, K. P., and T. F. Smith (Tex., 1944)
Smith, H. M., and E. H. Taylor (Gen., 1945)
Strecker, J. K., Jr. (Tex., 1915)

---

[1] 1956: Mecham (*Copeia,* 51–52), probably quite properly, considers all the forms of western and trans-Pecos Texas one species. In 1950 he placed them in *D. p. arnyi* and apparently he still holds to that view. "If we disregard artificial species boundaries and consider instead character geography, the evidence at hand leaves no reason to suppose that *Diadophis regalis* and *Diadophis punctatus* are anything but elements of a single geographically variable species."

1944, A. H. and A. A. Wright (see our comment on *D. p. docilis*): Through the years we have seen new forms recognized in certain regions by non-visitors or first visitors only to have them reduced or changed by the authors themselves in after years or after familiarity with the region. For example, in view of the mixed *regalis, laetus, texensis, docilis, stictogenys, arnyi* scarcity from Texas to Arizona, we hated to see, in 1923, the establishment of *D. r. arizonae* on scanty material. We are glad it fell to the same author to place it in *D. r. laetus* until we learn more about it. Like Schmidt and Smith, we are troubled by the location of the type of *D. r. regalis* seemingly enclosed by *D. r. laetus*. We are not ready, however, to say that *D. r. laetus* is a synonym of *D. r. regalis,* as Schmidt and Smith suggest. In the same way, we are slow to accept *D. r. blanchardi,* though from experience we know the Big Bend ring-necks to be smaller than those of Utah or Arizona. Again we say, look at our distribution map for *Diadophis* and ask yourself if the two arrow points for Helotes, the beautiful triangle in Devils River country, the long sliver range of *D. r. regalis,* and the two cut-off southern ends for *laetus* and *blanchardi* actually represent the true state of affairs in *Diadophis.* It has to be admitted that *blanchardi* is based on material acquired by authors who visited the region and at least one of whom helped to collect it. This consideration ought more than ever to count. Most of the alcoholic material has been borrowed, counted, and published on. Revisions have helped considerably, but first-hand studies based on knowledge of the regions and the specimens involved count more. We who have published little on snakes but who have studied them many years would not dare to write thus about fine workers unless we had seen in its homeland fresh live material from Utah, Arizona, and Big Bend. What is the relation of *blanchardi* and *docilis?* Does *blanchardi* reach to Davis Mts., Guadalupe Mts., Franklin Mts., all of trans-Pecos Texas? What size will separate it from *r. regalis* near or in New Mexico? In any case, Blanchard's return from a new form *arizonae* to the old elusive *laetus* (type missing) and Schmidt and Smith's new *blanchardi* reopen the question, and no precipitate solution without much material will solve it correctly.

1945, H. M. Smith and E. H. Taylor: "In view of the paucity of data on these snakes, we feel justified in retaining Blanchard's arrangement as at least the most workable, if not the most nearly correct one, proposed to date."

1949, D. L. Jameson and A. G. Flury: "*Diadophis r. regalis* Baird and Girard. . . . Because of the great variation within the genus it seems best to describe these specimens. Both are males and neither has a nuchal ring. The total length measures 522 mm. and 259 mm., tail length 78 mm. and 37 mm.; ventrals 227 and 224, caudals 53 in both, scale rows 17-15-15 in both, supralabials 7-7 in both, infralabials 9-9 in the larger and 9-8 in the smaller, temporals 1-1-2 in both. In contrast to the type series of *D. r.*

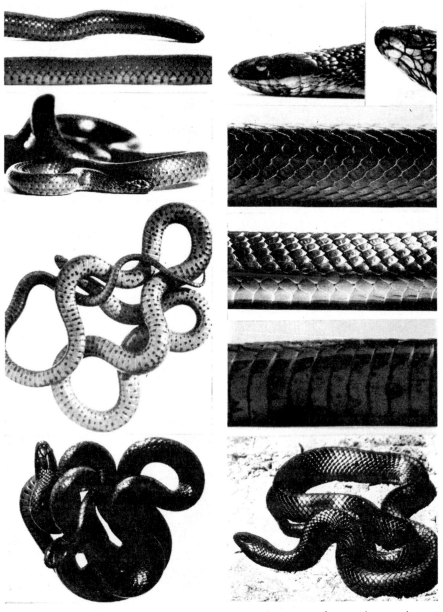

Fig. 63. *Diadophis r. blanchardi,* El Paso, Tex., M. L. Crimmins.

Fig. 64. *Drymarchon corais couperi:* 1,2,4, Anastasia Is., Fla.; 3, Sanibel Is., Fla., K. Palmer and N. Schuck; 5, Silver Springs, Fla., E. R. Allen; 6, Chesser Is., Ga.

blanchardi Schmidt and Smith (1944), the present specimens have a higher
ventral count and they have 2 temporals in the third row instead of one."

INDIGO SNAKES

Genus *DRYMARCHON* Fitzinger (Fig. 20)

Size very large, 36–102 inches; robust; head not distinct from neck; tail
⅙–⅛ total length; anal entire; scales wide, smooth with 2 apical pits, in
17 rows (15–14 at anus); dorsal head plates normal; preocular 1, postoculars
2; loreal 1; upper labials 8 (7), lower 8; temporals 2 + 2; posterior chin
shields shorter than anterior and spreading with a few gulars between their
tips and ventral plates; maxillary teeth smooth, subequal. Hemipenis, calyces
numerous, fringed. Ventrals 182–217; caudals 55–88. Synonyms: *Coluber,
Compsosoma, Georgia, Spilotes.*

KEY TO THE GENUS *DRYMARCHON*

a. Sixth upper labial (or the one behind the eye) separated from the temporals and postoculars by the meeting of the 2 adjacent labials in a
   suture above it; upper labials 8 (7 in 20%); 15 scale rows at anus; color—
   ground color of back uniform purplish, violet, or slaty blue, labials
   bittersweet orange to coral red; under parts uniform bluish or greenish
   gray except underside of head, which is buff and rose. (South Carolina
   to Florida reported west to e. Louisiana.) Ventrals 183–193; caudals 63–67.
   Drymarchon corais couperi
aa. Upper labial behind the eye (usually 6th) generally in contact with
   lower anterior temporal, or with a small scale cut off from it; upper
   labials 8; 14 scale rows at anus; color: ground color of back in cephalic
   half mixed brown and black (really sepia) with touches of light blue
   between scales, labials olive to drab; caudal half blue violet black; under
   parts—cephalic half salmon, caudal half passing from deep Payne's gray
   to bluish black. (Extreme s.w. Texas to n. Veracruz.) Ventrals 182–193;
   caudals 55–65.   *Drymarchon c. erebennus*

Indigo snake (29—Jones 1856), **Gopher snake**
(20—Robinson 1896)

Drymarchon corais couperi (Holbrook) 1842. Fig. 64; Map 21

Other common names: American corais snake; blue bull snake; blue
gopher snake; Couper's (gopher) snake; Georgia snake.
Range: Swampy coastal plain from South Carolina to Florida; reported
from Alabama and e. Louisiana (no specimens known).—Ala.?; Fla.; Ga.;
La.?; S.C. *Elevation*—Records give mainly sea level to 500 feet.

Size: Adults, 3–8½ feet.

We have seen one 7 feet 8 inches long at Gainesville, Fla., collected Sept. 20, 1928, by H. H. Camp.

Longevity: 11 years (Ditmars); 11 years 11 months (G. Wiley in Perkins, Gen., 1948); 3⁺ years (Kauffeld, Gen., 1951); 21 years 4 months (Perkins, Gen., 1954).

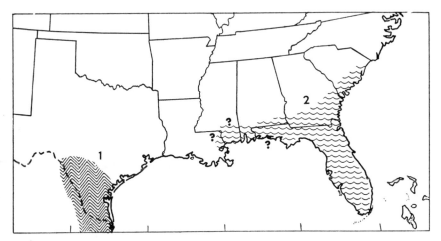

Map 21. *Drymarchon*—1, *c. erebennus;* 2, *c. couperi.*

Distinctive characteristics: "Adults uniform black above and below, except gular region; caudals less than 68; antepenultimate labial separated from temporal or postocular by contact above it of adjacent labials; 15 scale rows in front of anus" (Smith).

Color: Okefinokee Swamp, Ga., Aug. 18, 1922. The back is indulin blue, bluish slate-black, amparo purple, or hortense violet. Each scale is a soft bluish violet with a base of black, hyssop violet, slate-purple, or vinaceous-purple. The labial plates are bittersweet orange or grenadine with the rostral bay. Or the lower labials are old rose or coral red and the color of the body. On the ventral scales of the head, light buff occurs with old rose or coral red. The belly is olive-gray, tea green, light medici blue, or gnaphalium green.

Habitat: This gentle favorite of children and showmen is customarily thought to be an inhabitant of gopher turtle and other holes of high and dry land. It has been found on sandy, palmetto-covered hills, along roadsides of pine barrens, on sandy oak ridges, or in moist localities. Carr in his 1940 summary gave high pineland, dry glades, tropical hammocks, muck land fields, and flatwoods. Consult also Deckert (Fla., 1918), Löding (Ala., 1922), Metcalf (Gen., 1930), and Hallinan (Fla., 1923). Neill thought injured indigo snakes shed more frequently than normal ones, but Perkins concluded the opposite. In 1947 Bogert and Cowles wrote: "The third species of snake tested, *Drymarchon corais,* survived the extreme conditions of the experimental chamber for a relatively brief period and lost weight at an extremely rapid rate. These results offer some explanation for the abundance of the indigo snake in moist habitats, and because such habitats are more abundant in coastal plains of the United States [distribution] can be attributed, in part at least, to the physiological requirements of the species."

Breeding: Oviparous. Little else is known of the breeding of this former favorite of traveling shows. *Mating or combat dance*—"The park warden gave a vivid description of the mating of a pair, in which both the male and female strutted in front of each other, as though trying to show off to best advantage" (Safford). Were they male and female or two combat males? *Eggs*—Size, 3 or 4 inches x 1.1–1.3 inches. Carson has stated: "The length of time that spermatozoa may be stored in the genital tract of female vertebrates and still retain fertilizing capacity has been believed to be generally quite short. . . . An adult female indigo snake, *Drymarchon corais couperi,* 5 ft. 8 in. long, was purchased from a dealer in Merchantsville, New Jersey, on January 15, 1941. . . . On May 29, 1945, 4 years and 4 months after it came into the writer's possession this snake laid 5 eggs. The largest . . . measured 100 mm. long by 32 mm. at the greatest diameter, the smallest 75 mm. x 27 mm. The eggs were to all appearances normal, with turgid, leathery shells studded with elevations of calcification. The entire clutch weighed 27 grams and the snake after laying weighed 1219 grams. . . . At least one [egg] was fertile." *Young*—24 inches. In 1951 Neill (Gen., 1951) supplied much-needed facts. On Sept. 20 and 26, 1950, he recorded 2 babies, 599 and 616 mm. in length. On Sept. 18, 1948, he recorded one 668 mm. in length, and from October to January others were 698, 682, 688 mm., all with some umbilical scar evidence.

Food: Mice, rats, frogs, fish, lizards, snakes, birds, rattlers, turtle eggs Holbrook, Safford, Carr, Keegan, Carson, Babis.

Authorities:

Amaral, A. do (Gen., 1929a)
Babis, W. A. (Fla., 1949)
Bogert, C. M., and R. B. Cowles (Fla., 1947)
Carr, A. F. (Fla., 1940a)
Carson, H. L. (Gen., 1945)
Holbrook, J. E. (Gen., 1836–42)
Keegan, H. L. (Gen., 1944)

LeBuff, C. R., Jr. (Fla., 1953)
Loennberg, E. (Fla., 1895)
Neill, W. T. (Fla., 1949)
Perkins, C. B. (Gen., 1950)
Safford, W. E. (Fla., 1919)
Smith, H. M. (Gen., 1941k)
Tinkle, D. W. (Tex., 1951)

1842, J. E. Holbrook: "J. Hamilton Couper, Esq. of St. Simon's Island, Georgia, to whom I am indebted for a knowledge of this animal, says, 'The Indigo Snake, or Gopher, combines strength and activity. Its movements are confined to the surface of the ground, in which they are free, and, for so large a snake, rapid. It is perfectly harmless, frequenting the neighborhood of settlements, where it is usually unmolested, from its inoffensive character, and the prevalent belief that it destroys the Rattlesnake, which it attacks with courage. It is often found occupying the same hole with the Gopher (*Testudo polyphemus*), whence it receives one of its names. Although a harmless snake, it is a bold one, and when provoked, it faces its enemy with courage, vibrating its tail rapidly. It is, however, so mild in character that it may be domesticated; and an instance is mentioned of the negro children of a neighboring plantation being in the habit of holding on to the tail of one whilst it wandered about the yard.' "

1940, A. F. Carr, Jr.: "A consistent occupant of gopher holes in the hills of the peninsula. Below Lake Okeechobee, where it is most abundant, it is often ploughed up in damp soil in truck fields. It attains a tremendous size in the hammocks between Cape Sable and Paradise Keys. . . . I have been informed (by J. B. Tower of Homestead, and by an Indian in a camp in Collier County) that the Seminoles do not inhabit the Cape Sable country for fear their babies will be eaten by the Indigo snakes."

1953: C. R. LeBuff, Jr., supplies much-needed information on eggs and young. His captive 5-foot 5-inch female laid 6 eggs May 2, 1953. The average size is 2 inches long and 1¼ inch in diameter. The shortest was 1¾ inches, the longest 3 inches. On Aug. 8–10, 3 eggs hatched. The young's average length is 18 inches (15–20 inches range). On Aug. 16–18 the young molted and on Aug. 24 fed on six-lined race runners.

1953, A. H. and A. A. Wright: In our "List of the Snakes of the United States and Canada by States and Provinces" (*American Midland Naturalist,* 48:574–603), we gave *D. c. couperi* as accredited to Alabama and Louisiana. We called *D. c. erebennus* problematic for Alabama, and *D. c. couperi* problematic for Mississippi. In all our trips we never saw or located specimens from Alabama, Mississippi, or Louisiana. We believe the range of each very dubious, and feel each subspecies should now be pronounced problematic for these three states.

1941: H. M. Smith observed that "present records further demonstrate there is a hiatus between the range of *couperi* and that of the *Drymarchon* of Texas, this hiatus occurring in the region of Louisiana, eastern Texas and Mississippi."

Neither our friend H. P. Löding (Ala., 1922) nor W. L. Haltom (Ala., 1931) could catch this form in Alabama. Who has any positive, not escaped, material from Mississippi, Louisiana, or Texas above Corpus Christi? Probably Smith is nearly right, but he has it too far north in central Texas, where so many snake dealers live (San Antonio, New Braunfels, Floresville, etc.). As he remarks, "The apparent hiatus between the ranges of *erebennus* and *couperi* should be investigated."

Mexican indigo snake, Mexican black snake (2—Bailey 1905)

Drymarchon corais erebennus (Cope) 1860. Fig. 65; Map 21

Other common names: Black gopher snake; blue bull snake (2); blue gopher snake; corais; Cribo; indigo snake (Strecker 1928); Mexican gopher snake; (Mexican) rat snake; tropical indigo snake.

Range: S. Texas to n. Veracruz.—U.S.A.: Tex. Mex.: Coahuila, Hidalgo, San Luis Potosí, Tamaulipas, Veracruz. *Elevation*—Seacoast to 1,000 feet, possibly some to 2,000 feet.

Size: Adults, 3–8½ feet. We have seen in the cages of the "Snake King" in Brownsville, Tex., specimens larger than those of Florida

Longevity: 9 years (Cowles, Gen., 1949).

Distinctive characteristics: "Black above posteriorly, becoming spotted or banded on middle and anterior part of body in adults; subcaudals less than 68 (55 to 65); antepenultimate labial in contact with temporal or postocular or both; scale rows near anus usually 14" (Smith).

Color: Brownsville, Tex., April 24, 1925. The dorsal scales in the cephalic half of the body are sepia with dark edges, giving an impression of mixed brown and black. The spaces between the scales are pale forget-me-not blue and dusky or black. In the caudal half of the body, the upper parts are blue-violet black. The top of the head is fuscous or clove brown. The 4th, 5th, and 6th lower labials, and the 4th, 5th, 6th, and 7th upper labials are black-edged on the rear. The black on the 5th upper labial forms a prominent bar below the eye. The scales back of the angle of the mouth, the upper and lower labials, and the ends of the first few ventrals are drab, grayish olive, olive-brown, or buffy olive. The iris is blue-violet black. The underside of the chin is white or pale olive-buff. The cephalic half of the belly is ochraceous-salmon or light salmon-orange ranging to salmon-orange, with the ends of the ventrals marked with prout's brown. The under parts in the caudal half are clear payne's gray or deep payne's gray becoming near the vent bluish black. In this half, each ventral has the rear edge deep payne's gray or blue-violet black. Forward, the dark edges become less prominent; rearward the whole venter becomes blue-violet black.

Habitat and habits: We quote from Ruthven, though Smith might not consider the form *erebennus* today. "We found this snake [he calls it *Spilotes corais couperi.*—A. H. W.] quite generally distributed in the region. It was observed in the cane fields, on the savannah, in the woods (Lake Catemaco) and in the thickets about the shores of ponds and along the streams. It was nearly always observed on the ground, but it also climbs to some extent as we saw one sunning itself at full length on the tops of bushes along the Hueyapam River, 4 or 5 feet above the ground. It also enters water to some extent, as the writer observed 2 individuals hunting in the high grass and bushes about the margin of a pond, and the stomach of

Fig. 65. *Drymarchon c. erebennus:* 1,3–5, Brownsville, Tex., F. C. Favry; 2, San Antonio Reptile Garden, Tex.; 6, Brownsville, Tex., "Snake King."

Fig. 66. *Drymobius margaritiferus,* Tehuantepec, Oaxaca, Mex., loaned by C. M. Bogert and G. K. Noble.

one of these contained, besides 3 mice, 2 small snapping turtles and 2 toads (*Rhinophrynus dorsalis*). The latter were breeding in the pond."

Breeding: Oviparous. D. W. Tinkle wrote concerning a female *D. c. melanurus* and a male *D. c. couperi*: "Nearly every aggressive movement was made by the male, the female generally remaining placid unless attacked and then apparently biting only in self defense. At first the male and female went thru chin rubbing of the dorsum, neck sinuosities, tail twitching and body entwining, everything except copulation. At such a stage the female jerked free. After many tries the male began biting or seizing the female on neck, head or body. At times she bit back." (See also our meager field note.)

Field notes: Apr. 23, 1925, Brownsville, Tex., at the Snake King's (Lieberman): He has many large snakes which he calls "Black Snakes" which are gopher snakes, *Drymarchon*. Found 3 or 4 large eggs with some of them. They were dirty white, tough, rough eggs easily 4 inches long. They were if anything possibly larger than those I have seen in Florida.

Authorities:

Amaral, A. do (Gen., 1929a)

Bogert, C. M., and R. B. Cowles (Fla., 1947)

Ditmars, R. L. (Gen., 1939)

Perkins, C. B. (Gen., 1950)

Ruthven, A. G. (*Zool. Jahrb. Syst.*, 32: 324)

Smith, H. M. (Gen., 1941k)

Smith, H. M., and E. H. Taylor (Gen., 1945)

Taylor, E. H. (Tex., 1949)

Tinkle, D. W. (Tex., 1951)

We know little about this form. Its northern limit was never understood, and Smith had only 20 specimens, of which half were Mexican. None of his material is above the parallel of Eagle Pass, San Diego, Tex. The northern range needs clarification.

SPECKLED SNAKES

Genus *DRYMOBIUS* Fitzinger (Fig. 23)

Size large medium, 30–50 inches; long and slender; head distinct; anal divided; some scales feebly keeled with apical pits in 17 rows (15 at anus); head plates normal; frontal with sides evenly tapering and anterior margin straight; eye large, pupil round, no suboculars; upper labials (8), 9; lower labials 9–12; preocular 1 (small lower preocular fitting into labials, characteristic of *Coluber*, lacking), postoculars 2; temporals 2 + 2; chin shields contact 6 labials; 1 row gulars between chin shields and ventrals; angle on side of belly with black bars on vertical portion of ventrals; color (form in U.S.) green, each scale with central spot of yellow, blue, or orange; maxillary teeth 22–34 enlarged posteriorly; mandibular teeth equal. Hemipenis—with basal spines in 12 or 13 longitudinal rows, calyces flounced in more than 20 rows (after L. C. Stuart). Ventrals 142–168; caudals 85–126. Synonyms: *Coluber, Herpetodryas, Leptophis, Masticophis, Thamnophis, Zamenis.*

Speckled ground snake (3—Pope 1937), **Mexican speckled snake**

Drymobius margaritiferus (Schlegel) 1837. Fig. 66; Map 22

Other common names: Green-spotted racer (1—Ditmars 1936); Schlegel's snake (Strecker 1915).

Range: Extreme s. Texas to Central America.—U.S.A.: Tex. Mex.: Coahuila, Nuevo León, San Luis Potosí, Tamaulipas, and 7 other states of

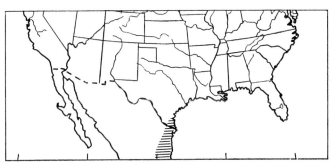

Map 22. *Drymobius margaritiferus.*

Mexico. *Elevation*—Coast to 4,500 feet. 0–4,000 feet (Gadow, Gen., 1910).

Size: Adults, 30–50 inches.

Distinctive characteristics: "Subcaudals black-edged posteriorly; a distinct dark (black) area in temporal region, much darker than any other part of head, darker than general tone of body anteriorly; posterior edge of each middorsal scale black, the anterior (concealed) edges blue (in adults; white in faded specimens, gray in young), middle yellow or light orange (white in faded specimens, light in young)" (Smith).

"Body black, each scale with a dashlike green or yellow-green mark; ventrals 146–149; subcaudals 109–117" (Taylor, Gen., 1951).

Color: A snake from Tehuantepec, Oaxaca, Mex., was loaned to us by C. M. Bogert and G. K. Noble of the American Museum, March 2, 1938. The background color of the back is black, fuscous-black, or olivaceous black (2). There is a brownish cast to the mid-back. Each scale is marked with a dart-shaped light spot. The broader base of the spot begins near the cephalic edge of the scale, and the point extends slightly caudad of the center. The spots of the 3 to 4 rows of the mid-back may be as deep as sulphin yellow or oil yellow but are mostly viridine green. About the 4th row of scales, these light centers become larger, broader, less spearlike or dartlike, with the color changing to opaline green, and give to the snake its predominant green color.

In the first row, they become pale turquoise green, and on the forward part of the body turquoise green. In the neck region, all the light spots may be turquoise green. These light spots are so regular as to appear in rows, a condition less conspicuous on the tail. The dorsal snout plates are buffy brown with black margins. There is a blackish brown (1) or fuscous-black vitta which involves the supraocular and the outer portion of the parietal, all the temporals, and the upper third of the last upper labial. The frontal and broad parietal sutures are water green, and this color swings around the rear of the black vitta to border it and the rear of the last upper labial. Each of the face plates is black-edged, and the upper labials have black rear borders. The ventral borders of the last 4 or 5 lower labials are edged with black, and the rear gulars have dark edges. The upper labials, rostral, and underside of the head have the color of the venter. The eye may seem to be black like the vitta, but close examination proves it to be warm sepia. The venter is white or seafoam yellow with a slight wash of chartreuse yellow toward the side. The sides meet the belly at almost a right angle, suggesting an arboreal habit. That portion of the ventral which enters the vertical side is bordered caudad with a prominent bar of black, with the intervening color strongly washed with pale turquoise green. Scale rows 17 in middle; 17 front; 15 at the tail. (This snake gasped or exhaled forcibly and audibly while held.)

Habitat and habits: Little is recorded about these. In 1905 Gadow (Gen., 1905) called it the "commonest snake" in Mexico. Perez's material from Veracruz was taken in December, 1886 or 1887. In 1937 Oliver (Gen., 1937) gave it as "common in the humid regions" of Colima.

Breeding: Oviparous. *Eggs*—Number, 7. Time of deposition, Apr. 22–August and later. In 1937 Gaige, Hartweg, and Stuart recorded that "one female No. 79759 collected in August contained fully developed eggs." "A female, 1339 mm. in length, was received from a dealer and bore only the data, 'Mexico.' On April 22, between . . . 9:40 A.M. and 5:45 P.M., this snake laid 7 eggs with non-adhesive, non-granular shells, measuring: *Length–Width:* 32-13, 34-14, 35-13, 35-13, 36-13, 37-13, 39-12. On June 9, one of the brood with a badly deformed tail and measuring 137 mm. in length emerged from its shell, and a second, measuring 123 mm. and possessing a deformity similar to the first, escaped from its egg on June 11th. Both died several days after hatching. The scales of the hatchlings were centered with small white spots, more vivid in color than those of the adult, but the young were otherwise similar to the adult in coloration and marking. The remaining 5 eggs failed to hatch" (Werler). "A female 940 mm. long, laid 2 infertile eggs on July 29, 1950. These had non-adhesive, non-granular shells. No. 1—43 mm. long, 15 mm. wide; No. 2—5 mm. long, 14 mm. wide" (Werler, Gen., 1951).

Young—We have seen juveniles from 242 or 251 to 384 mm., but have no impression of the size of newly hatched young. Taylor (Gen., 1951) describes a young specimen from Costa Rica thus: "A greenish white longitudinal mark on the frontal; a pair of greenish white lines curving behind last labial and extending to parietal; following this a large series of vertical greenish white and black lines running up on the sides to near the mid-line, a line occasionally meeting its fellow, but more commonly alternating with it. These lines gradually more indistinct on latter half of body where light and dark colors tend to form indefinite longitudinal lines, the most distinct being the greenish white line on the 2 outer scale rows that terminate at anus; ends of ventrals blackish; the free edge of the scales may be blackish for a greater or less distance, rarely crossing ventral; supralabials with black sutures; infralabials and chin greenish cream."

March 5, 1946: Mrs. L. Irby Davis of Harlingen, Tex., wrote us: "We caught the *Drymobius* in the native growth of palms down below Southmost (about 10 miles east of Brownsville and close to the Rio Grande). We have seen several of the speckled green snakes in that region but only tried to catch this little one which was crawling in the bottom of a little ditch. After chasing it some time, we finally ran it under a fallen palm leaf, and Irby pressed down on the leaf while I lifted up one edge and reached for the snake. After a heavy fall rain one year, we found another of this species near the river below La Feria in a hackberry woods. These are the only two places we've ever seen them."

Authorities:

Dunkle, D. H., and H. M. Smith (Gen., 1937)
Gaige, H. T., N. Hartweg, and L. C. Stuart (Gen., 1937)
Schlegel, H. (Gen., 1837)

Smith, H. M. (Tex., 1942a)
Stejneger, L. (Tex., 1891)
Stuart, L. C. (Gen., 1932)
Werler, J. E. (Tex., 1949)

RAT SNAKES

Genus *ELAPHE* Fitzinger in Wagler (Figs. 21, 25)

Size, large medium to very large, to 108 inches; long and slender; form compressed, many species with angulate ventrals indicating climbing habit; head distinct; anal divided; scale rows 25–33; scales smooth or weakly keeled, with apical pits; upper labials 8–11, lower 11–16; loreal 1; nasals 2; preocular 1, postoculars 2; temporals variable; internasals 2; 2–4 rows gulars between tips of chin shields and ventrals; posterior chin shields smaller and separated; maxillary teeth equal, smooth. Hemipenis—calyces numerous, fringed, sulcus single. Ventrals 190–281; caudals 45–105. Synonyms: *Callopeltis, Coluber, Elaphis, Natrix, Pantherophis, Pityophis, Scotophis.*

KEY TO THE GENUS *ELAPHE*

a. With subocular scales; dorsal interspaces 6–8 scales long; dorsal pattern black ⊢ on tan or gray with 2 stripes on neck; no head pattern; no lateral stripes on neck; lateral markings obscure; face oblique, labials below eye show in dorsal view; rear of jaw upcurved; upper labials (9) 10–11, clear; lower 14–16; scales in 31–35 rows, 15–29 faintly keeled. (Big Bend section of Texas into Mexico.)   *E. subocularis*

aa. Without suboculars; dorsal interspaces if present, 1–4 scales long.

  b. Some or all labials with prominent dark, black, or deep brown sutures; upper labials (7) 8 (9); venter heavily checkered, blotched, or spotted. Caudals 45–80, average 60–70.

    c. Not red snakes, usually gray or brown; body blotches 28–55.

      d. Head with distinct alternating light and dark marks; neck saddle arms cross parietals uniting on frontal; scale rows 27–29 on mid-body; upper labials 5 + 6 enter orbit; body blotches 29–55; venter variously spotted. Caudals 60–80, average 70.

        e. "Dorsal blotches 3–5 scales long; ventrals under body and tail more than 282; abdominals minus body dorsal blotches more than 170." (Ventrals 210–235; body blotches 31–50.)   *E. emoryi emoryi*

        ee. "Dorsal blotches 2–4 scales long; ventrals under body and tail less than 282; abdominals minus body dorsal blotches less than 170." (Ventrals 203–215; body blotches 42–55.)   *E. l. intermontana*

        "*E. l. intermontana* has fewer ventral plates but more and shorter dorsal blotches" (Woodbury and Woodbury Gen. 1942).

      dd. Head without stripes or, if stripes be present, not an alternation of light and dark; without arms of neck saddle extending forward across parietals to unite on frontal; scale rows 23–27; upper labials 4 + 5 enter orbit; body blotches 28–51; venter distinctly checkered. Caudals 45–70, average 50–60.

        e. Body blotches 33–51, average 40.9, with about 18 on tail, 3, 4, rarely 5 scales long; interspace 1 1/2 scales.   *E. vulpina vulpina*

        ee. Body blotches 34, average 34.5, with about 11 on tail, 4–6 scales long; interspace 2 scales or less; somewhat greater maximum length and more robust form than the above.   *E. v. gloydi*

   cc. Red, orange, or rosy snakes; head with distinct alternating light and dark marks; arms of neck saddle crossing parietals and uniting on frontal; upper labials 4 + 5 enter orbit; postorbital stripe bordered above with dark and light; 5 scale rows or fewer weakly keeled; scale rows 25–31; saddle spots russet or mahogany red with black borders and broken light ones. Caudals 79 or less.

      d. Venter heavily checkered with black; on white in cephalic portion, midsection orange-yellow, tail dark; Brady says ground color light buff and red saddles persist in preservation; ground color not as dominant as in *E. rosacea*. Caudals 61–79. (Florida mainland northward.)   *E. guttata guttata*

     dd. Venter tessellation or checkering not as distinct as in *guttata;* cephalic portion of venter white, middle pinkish cinnamon or cinnamon buff with small black spots on either end of each plate. Brady says ground color dark plumbeous becomes very pronounced in preservative, red saddles and lateral spots fade out. Caudals 61. (Florida keys.)   *E. g. rosacea*

bb. Labials without dark sutures or slight (except *o. williamsi* and *o. confinis*); venter more or less uniform, flecked or clouded (clouded, irregular checkers in *o. confinis*); head without distinct alternating light and dark marks; postorbital stripe normally absent or, if present, not bordered above by black and light. Caudals 68–120, average 75–95.

   c. Scale rows 31–39, smooth; upper labials 9–11, either 4 + 5, 5 + 6, or 5 or 6 entering orbit; dorsum more or less uniform with some green (gray in preservative). Caudals 83–120.

      d. Caudals 88–120; ventrals 247–281; scale rows 31–39; upper labials 9 (8); 2 labials enter orbit 5 + 6 or 4 + 5; lower labials 10–11 (12); dorsum yellowish green or grayish, 57–76 indistinct body bars indicating saddle spots (of young); old gold spots on top of head; venter clear buff or yellow.   *E. triasphis intermedia*

     dd. Caudals 83–88; ventrals 277–288; upper labials 10–11; 1 labial enters orbit 5 or 6 flanked on either side by small suboculars; lower labials (11) 12–14; color above uniform olive, reddish-brown, or tan becoming yellow or green toward ventrals; venter grayish or greenish yellow. (Baja California.)   *E. rosaliae*

   cc. Scale rows 29 or less; upper labials 8 (9 in *E. bairdi*).

      d. Posterior chin shields transversely divided; upper labials (8) 9, 4 + 5 entering orbit; scale rows 27; snout long; eye large; venter clouded; dorsal color drab with bittersweet orange scale edges; adults and intermediates uniform with indistinct or decided stripes; juveniles with dorsal spots. Our snake from the Big Bend had deep olive dorsal blotches on body connected at corners forming stripes. Caudals 85–99 ♀; 92–103 ♂ (ours 99).   *E. bairdi*

dd. Posterior chin shields not divided transversely; upper labials 8, 4 + 5 entering orbit; all juveniles with saddle spot pattern (see adult *spiloides* or *williamsi*).

  e. Dorsum black or brownish black, spots if present indistinct, a few areas with white-edged scales; rear of venter slate gray; upper labials usually 8 with inconspicuous narrow dark sutures; no head markings; scale rows 25–27, keels on 17 rows. Caudals 70–98.   *E. obsoleta obsoleta*
 ee. Dorsum not almost entirely black; a pattern of 4 stripes or stripes and spots (*quadrivittata* group) striped.

    f. Ground color dull gray; 4 stripes, each of lower lateral ones posteriorly a dark zone 3–3 1/2 scales wide; dorsum with inconspicuous "ladder like transverse bars." (Shackleford Banks, Beaufort, N.C.)   *E. o. parallela*
   ff. Yellow, tan, or orange conspicuous in ground color (buffy olive to orange rufous); no postocular stripe or if present narrow and interrupted; labials clouded in upper half, sutures like clouding. The intensity of the color within each subspecies, and of intergrades between groups, perhaps varying geographically, with habitat or age.

      g. Ground color light gray, buffy olive or yellowish; 4 sepia to mummy brown stripes; spots lacking or reduced to a few cloudy areas; venter: white throat, primrose yellow to brownish olive caudad, no bright orange spots; eye large, iris gray or yellow; tongue black. Ventrals 225–242; caudals 85–100.

                                                          E. o. quadrivittata
     gg. Ground color dull yellow or orange with brown or olive suffusion, 4 sharply defined stripes of auburn or hair brown, about 40 dorsal spots of auburn or dark gray flecked with ground color; venter: white throat, pinkish tan to gray toward tail, body venter with distinct orange areas or spots; eye moderate, iris pink or red; tongue black. "Scales lack a glaucous sheen." (Neill Fla. 1949a). Ventrals 240+; caudals 90+.   *E. o. deckerti*
    ggg. "Ground color of adults rich orange, orange-yellow, or orange-brown; dorsal and lateral stripes present, but not sharply defined, of a dull gray-brown shade . . . chin and throat bright orange; venter bright orange or orange yellow; scales with a glaucous sheen at least anteriorly; iris orange; tongue bright red" (Neill Fla., 1949a). Ventrals 236; caudals 93.

                                                          E. o. rossalleni
  fff. (The *obsoleta* group) saddle group. Gray to brown ground color; row of dorsal spots and alternating lateral series; venter olive-buff to yellow clouded or blotched; dorsal body blotches 27–40.

g. Ground color gray, fawn, or buff, light to very light to almost white; body blotches 30–35 very distinct, olive brown to mars brown; corners of anterior blotches tending to unite forming stripes; anterior lateral spots linear forming continuous or broken stripes; labials with dark sutures.

   h. Stripes on neck or anterior portion of body; postocular stripe broad, not black bordered, from eye to labial margin; top of head grayish olive; venter buff to yellow irregularly checkered with olive brown; body blotches about 33. Ventrals 231–258; caudals 70–89.

E. o. spiloides

hh. Stripes usually whole length of body; postocular stripe absent or vaguely indicated; top of head smoke gray, several plates with dark edges; venter buff with larger spots confined to ends of plate and scale row 1; body blotches 31, 4 scales long. Ventrals 230–240; caudals 86–93. "Black or very dark brown marking constituting a series of dorsal and lateral blotches (as in *confinis*) connected by 4 longitudinal stripes (as in *quadrivittata*)" (Barbour and Carr Fla., 1940).

E. o. williamsi

gg. Ground color with red or pinkish clouded with "lead color"; dorsal and lateral spots present, but not always clearly differentiated due to intermingling of ground color in the pattern; no stripes on the head; dorsal and lateral spots "lead-colored" (olive-brown, fuscous, mummy brown); ground color maize yellow, old rose, or rusty red clouded with brown; venter olive-buff clouded by deep grayish olive; labials dark in the upper half; body blotches clouded, 27–33, 5 or 6 scales long and 13–15 wide. Ventrals 218–237; caudals 76–89.

E. o. lindheimeri

(Our discussion of Elaphe was framed before the appearance of Dowling's [Gen., 1952] check list of *Elaphe*, and Schmidt's new *Check List*, 1953, which adopts Dowling's determinations. Being conservative, we ought to welcome Dowling's sending *deckerti, parallela, rossalleni,* and *williamsi* into *quadrivittata*. Maybe he is right, but we wish to know the reactions of the on-the-spot workers of Florida before we accept the new rulings. Therefore we retain the accounts as originally written. It is true that we are somewhat confused between *rossalleni* and *deckerti,* even though we saw live *deckerti* before the hurricane. Whether we can readily accept *williamsi* as *quadrivittata* is problematical. In the same way we feel that the *bairdi* and *lindheimeri* problem is not entirely solved, though we recognized *lindheimeri* before most other northern herpetologists—as early as 1917.

(We anticipate that Dowling's conclusions will be generally accepted, but we wish to provoke further work. Notwithstanding our retention of our pre-1952 drafts of *Elaphe,* our natural inclination is toward synthesis, i.e., 1 or 2 forms of *Coluber constrictor* in Florida instead of 3; or 4 or 5 forms of *Elaphe obsoleta* instead of 7.)

Baird's rat snake (5—Ditmars 1936), Baird's pilot snake (Strecker 1915)

Elaphe bairdi (Yarrow) 1880. Fig. 67; Map 24
(*E. obsoleta bairdi,* Dowling, "Check List" [Gen., 1952]; Schmidt, *Check List,* 1953)

Other common names: Baird's Coluber (Yarrow 1882); Great Bend rat snake.

Range: Big Bend country of Texas (Davis and Chisos Mts. to n. Coahuila, Mex.).—U.S.A.: Tex. Mex.: Coahuila. *Elevation*—3,000 to 6,000 feet.

Size: Adults, 15 (possible juvenile)—35 inches.

Distinctive characteristics: We can do no better than to quote Smith's note of 1938c: "*Elaphe bairdii* (Yarrow). One specimen (USMN No. 103692) was collected in Carbonero Canyon, Carmen Mts., Coahuila, by R. S. Sturgis, on September 23, 1937. It was found under a log in a pine and oak wooded canyon. The scutellation is as follows: scale rows 25-27-19; ventrals 241; caudals 98; supralabials 8-9; infralabials 13-14; oculars 1-2; temporals 2-4-5; total length, 845 mm.; tail length, 180 mm. The following color notes were taken by Dr. H. K. Gloyd: Ground color bluish-gray above; lower labials, chin and throat cream; belly cream with grayish-brown, squarish blotches about one scale wide along sides, and stippling and flecking of same color along middle, all becoming more dense posteriorly; midventral line of tail pinkish; spots of dorsal pattern very indistinct; pattern of 4 longitudinal stripes; one on each side of midline, 2 scales wide, and one, less distinct, slightly lower on each side, all extending faintly on tail. Head bluish-gray, with no distinguishable pattern; supralabials cream, clouded with gray. This species resembles *quadrivittata* in the development of a striped pattern in adults from a spotted condition in the young. The young are distinguished by the number of dorsal blotches, less than 50 occurring in *quadrivittata* and more than this number in *bairdii*. The adults may be distinguished by the position of the lateral stripes on the middle of the body; in *quadrivittata* they extend to the second scale row, while in *bairdii* they extend no lower on the sides than the third scale row. Specimens of *bairdii* of intermediate size may be more or less uniform bluish-gray, resembling *chlorosoma,* from which it differs in number of scale rows (31 to 37 in *chlorosoma,* 27 in *bairdii*). From *Elaphe obsoleta* the species differs in subcaudal count (92 to 103 in 7 males, 85 to 95 in 3 females of *bairdii;* usually less in *obsoleta*), in the number of dorsal blotches, when present (*obsoleta* has approximately the same number as *quadrivittata*), and in the presence in adults of a striped pattern."

The original description has posterior chin shields transversely divided. This condition showed plainly in our specimen in the Chisos Mts.

Color: Mrs. Wright's field notes made at the time are appended. May 21, 1934: We camped at 6,000 ft. in the Chisos Mts. above the Burnham ranch below the saddle that was just above the CCC camp, which was in a circular basin, Green Gulch. The country was dry as a sun-bleached bone and, although we saw lizards, we decided the snakes were all deep in their holes.

Early Monday morning, May 21st, just before breaking camp, we walked up and down the little wash beside our camp. At the moment I was searching for what might look like a ledge to a Say's phoebe I had watched preening its feathers on a large rock. I was going slowly when on the ground going through a low, loose-growing oak shrub I spied this snake. It was moving slowly and matched its surroundings beautifully, looking like a twisted, dead, gray branch among reddish orange stones.

The scales of most of the back are gray, but the base of each scale has an orange crescent. The scales toward the head take on a pinkish tone with orange on the sides of the neck.

The general appearance of the snake made me think of the rosy *Elaphe* from lower Matacumba. There are about 50 dorsal bars connected at their ends by 2 dorsal stripes. There is a row of spots on the side also connected by a faint stripe, narrower than the spots. These spots alternate with dorsal bars. The underside of the snake is very iridescent orange tan on the rear and yellow on the throat. The ends of the belly plates are indistinctly blocked with dusky purplish gray toward the tail, reddish brown in the middle body, with greenish yellow in the center of the plates and green gray spots on the neck. The head plates are gray with 3 dusky blotches; the nostril plates are pinkish orange.

Chisos Mts., Green Gulch, May 21, 1934: The background scales of back and sides are drab gray, becoming on the forward 5th of body ecru drab. Each scale has a basal crescent of bittersweet orange or carnelian red; toward the neck this color extends around the whole margin of the scale. The dorsal tail scales have practically no bittersweet orange and, as you approach the vent, the body scales have very little. The back of the body is marked with 52 saddles, the tail having faint indications of 6. The dorsal blotches are heaviest at their lateral ends, where they are connected with the dorso-lateral stripe. They are deep olive in color. The center of the dorsal saddles is lighter, actually being drab gray with black borders. The front and rear margins of these saddles are not straight but are sawtoothed, conforming with the dark edges of the scales. Beginning with the first dorsal saddle, a longitudinal dorso-lateral band extends well onto the tail, connecting the ends of the dorsal saddles. This band between the ends of the dorsal saddles has white-bordered scales. The skin between the scales is light purplish vinaceous. The dorsal saddles are about 9 scales wide and 2 scales longitudinally. On the sides, 3 scale rows below the dorsal saddles, are indistinct dark spots, actually drab gray scales with black borders. These spots may be from 1 to 4 scale rows deep, usually on the 3rd to 6th row or 4th to 6th row, alternating with the dorsal saddles. The dark gray between the dorsal saddles has less of the bittersweet orange cast than the scales of the sides, the last 3 rows of which are prominently bordered with bittersweet orange. This bittersweet orange becomes quite prominent on the side of the neck below the 1st dorsal saddle. There is a dash of bittersweet orange from the lower rear corner of the orbit along the upper borders of the 5th and 6th upper labials and along the front border of the 7th. On the upper portion of the 7th upper labial and on the 8th is a band of vertigo green. The prefrontals and internasals and face, except for lower part of upper labials, are avellaneous. The temporal scales and side of neck are light vinaceous fawn. The frontal, supraocular, and parietal plates are drab gray. The frontal and parietals are blotched with clustered dots of deep olive or olive brown. The first 2 or 3 dorsal saddles are drab or grayish olive. The 9 upper labials, except for their dorsal borders, are white, with rather indistinct dark borders. The lower labials are pure white with indistinct dark edges. The chin and lower side of head are pure white, except for the plates back of the chin shields, which have bittersweet orange apices. The posterior chin shields are divided. The iris is buffy brown or orange-buff with a crescent of buffy brown in the posterior lower quarter. The very front is margined with citrine-drab. Beginning with the neck, the ventral plates are light green-yellow or olive-buff with citrine-drab squares separated by 2 or 3 plates. Soon the light green-yellow or olive-buff is replaced by dark olive-buff or deep olive-buff, and this in turn on caudal half of body becomes wood brown. The citrine-drab squares are replaced by army brown blocks on either side of the deep olive-buff or wood brown center band. Outside the wood brown or deep olive we find the ends of 2 or 3 ventrals drab gray, then one with army brown or fawn. This gives a row of army brown spots on the ends of the ventrals.

Habitat: July 12, 1925: The snake from Ranger Canyon near Alpine was caught by Mrs. L. T. Murray, who wrote: "The rocks there are all volcanic, reddish and hard." In 1942 Borell and Bryant in *Mammals of the Big Bend Area of Texas* wrote concerning the mountain cotton rat (*Sigmodon ochrognathus*): A large red racer (*Masticophis flagellum*) was caught in a rat trap which had been set in a runway of a cotton rat. Two large chicken snakes (*Elaphe bairdi*) and a striped racer (*Masticophis taeniatus*) were collected within the area occupied by cotton rats." May 21, 1934: The *Elaphe bairdi* we found was in a region similar to that described above with sotol and bear grass, above the Government Spring area. Did it seek cotton rats or pigmy owls and woodpeckers, residents in holes in the tall old flowering stalks of sotol? Jameson and Flury, reporting on the reptiles of the Sierra Vieja region in 1949, noted that *Elaphe bairdi* was not obtained there.

Field notes: May 21, 1934; see color description.

1900–03: Brown through his collector Meyenberg at Pecos and others secured considerable material from western Texas. If from 1901–1903 8 specimens of *E. subocularis* (not common in collections yet) came under his ken, how did he miss *E. bairdi*? Is it possible there are some *E. bairdi* in his material?

1925–29, Myers and Murray specimens. "July 12, 1925. We left Ft. Davis via Toyahvale for El Paso after a fine week centering around Sul Ross Teachers' College, Alpine, Texas, Prof. R. A. Studhalter and Leo T. Murray helping us." In 1942 we visited Stanford University, and one day we said to Dr. G. S. Myers, "Might we see your two specimens of *Elaphe bairdi?*" He replied, "I'll put them on your desk. By the way one is a specimen borrowed from Sul Ross Teachers' College. To whom should I send it?" We replied, "Send it to Baylor University Museum, which is now the best in Texas. Besides, its curator, Dr. Leo T. Murray, is an old Sul Ross graduate and former guide for scientists in the Big Bend country for such as the botanist Palmer and others."

Imagine what I found the next morning on my desk! The Sul Ross specimen was collected by L. T. Murray and Charles Arthur in Ranger Canyon near Alpine, Brewster Co., Tex., and on *July 12, 1925,* the very day we left them in Davis Mts. We discover this miss 17 years later (1942).

We have seen the 1st (Yarrow), 3rd (Myers), 4th (Murray and Arthur), and 5th (Wright and Quillin) specimens and the Mulaik specimens (except the 3 in the Chicago Academy of Science).

1934, Wright and Quillin's specimen. We, transient visitors, had tried for 17 years, 1917–1934, to find *Elaphe bairdi*. When 17-year locusts come to a place it's hard to escape them. We were about to depart Chisos Mts. and decided to have one last look around camp when Mrs. Wright called, "Bert, what's this?" Last look and what a specimen! See color description May 21, 1934.

1949, A. H. and A. A. Wright: None of the recent authors remark on the

9 supralabials or divided postgeneials and they calmly ignore the name *lindheimeri.* Even if Cope's temporal formula distinctions for southeastern forms blew up, not until someone meets this supralabial and geneials problem and the *lindheimeri* question frankly can we accept all the *bairdi* discussions and extensions of range. First, what is *lindheimeri?* As good as any *Elaphe* form. Then were the type specimen of *bairdi* and our specimen aberrant in 9 supralabials and divided postgeneials? Our specimen does not look like *lindheimeri* eastward, and the Kerr County specimens look much like *lindheimeri* of Boerne and Helotes just east of Kerrville. Maybe *E. bairdi* as adults are striped, but are all striped so-called *E. bairdi, E. bairdi?*

Authorities:

Milstead, W. W., J. S. Mecham, and   Schmidt, K. P., and T. F. Smith (Tex.,
   H. McClintock (Tex., 1950)   1944)
Mulaik, S. and D. (Tex., 1941)   Smith, H. M. (Gen., 1938c)
Myers, G. S. (Letter)   Yarrow in E. D. Cope (Tex., 1880)

1901, A. E. Brown (Gen.): "The specimen remains unique and its relations are consequently doubtful."

1931, G. S. Myers, letter: "Do you have photos of *Elaphe bairdii* from the Davis Mts.? If not, you may be interested in having these. They are rather poor, but so far as I know, the only photographs of this species extant. You will note that, like *quadrivittata,* the species is striped, not banded, when adult. Traces of the 50 odd dark crossbars were evident when the specimen was closely examined. The data for the specimen are as follows—Head of Cherry Canyon, Davis Mts., Jeff Davis Co., Texas, May 20, 1929, G. S. Myers and G. M. Kranzthor, collectors."

1944, K. P. Schmidt and T. F. Smith: "Three specimens of *Elaphe bairdi* are available from the Chisos region, two collected by the junior author and one by A. E. Borell, and a fourth specimen was obtained by the junior author from Limpia Canyon, Jeff Davis County."

1950, W. W. Milstead, J. S. Mecham, and H. McClintock: "Two specimens were collected in the live-oak association on the Hicks Ranch [in Terrell Co., Tex.]. One was active shortly after dawn and the other was active about noon. Both specimens had typical *bairdi* coloration, but their supralabial counts seem to indicate that further work may prove *Elaphe bairdi* to be a western subspecies of *Elaphe obsoleta.*"

Emory's pilot snake (10—Strecker 1909),
Emory's snake (6—Yarrow 1882)

Elaphe emoryi emoryi (Baird and Girard) 1853. Fig. 68; Map 23.
(*E. guttata emoryi* Dowling (Gen., 1952); Schmidt *Check List,* 1953)

Other common names: Brown rat snake; chicken snake; eastern spotted snake; Emory's Coluber; Emory's racer (4—Cragin 1881); Emory's rat

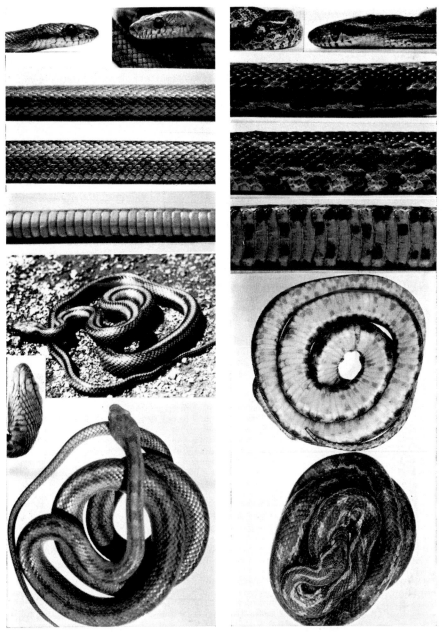

Fig. 67. *Elaphe bairdi:* 1–5, 7–8, Green Gulch, Chisos Mts., at elevations of over 6,000 feet. 6, Davis Mts., G. S. Myers.

Fig. 68. *Elaphe emoryi emoryi:* 1, San Vicente, Tex., T. Miller; 2–7, Brownsville, Tex., "Snake King."

snake (7); gray rat snake; mouse snake; (prairie) rat snake; spotted mouse snake; Texas rat snake; western pilot snake.

Range: From s.e. Nebraska to s.w. Illinois and cent. Missouri, s.w. through Arkansas, Oklahoma, and cent. Texas to Mexico. From Tamualipas to Chihuahua and n.e. across s.e. New Mexico and e. half of Kansas.—U.S.A.; Ark.; Ia.; Ill.; Kan.; Mo.; Neb.; N.M.; Okla.; Tex. Mex.: Chihuahua; Coahuila; Durango; Nuevo León; San Luis Potosí; Tamaulipas. *Elevation* —500 to 5,000 feet. 2,800–5,000 feet (Gilpin, N.S., 1875).

Size: Adults, 24–57 inches.

Longevity: 2 years 2 months (Conant and Hudson, Gen., 1949).

Distinctive characteristics: "Scales in 27 rows (occ. 29), all smooth or sometimes a few faintly keeled; ventrals 210–235; subcaudals 72–78. Ground color rather pale gray, with a dorsal row of olivaceous brown blotches with black borders, 3 or 4 scales long and 10 or 12 wide, separated by interspaces 1½ to 2 scales; a 2nd series of smaller alternating spots from the 3rd to the 7th rows, subcircular in shape; a 3rd indistinct series on the 2nd and 3rd rows, and a 4th indicated on the outer row and the ends of the ventrals; belly yellowish or white with irregular ashy blotches posteriorly; top of head much banded and a dark oblique postocular stripe. The number of the dorsal spots varies greatly, those now living in the collection of the Zoological Society ranging from 31 to 50 in number on the body, and from 17 to 21 on the tail" (Brown, Gen., 1901).

Color: San Antonio, Tex., Apr. 11, 1925. The dorsal color is pale drab-gray or ecru-drab. The edges of the scales are pale smoke gray with drab-gray centers. The large spots on the sides and the dorsal rhombs are olive-brown, black-encircled. Some of the lateral spots, the cephalic spots, and stripes on the head are buffy brown. The light stripes on the head are tilleul buff, drab, or deep olive-buff. The iris is fawn color, cinnamon, or pinkish cinnamon faintly specked with dark or black. The narrow rim of the pupil is cartridge buff. Outside the fawn color is a little hay's lilac and citrine-drab. The ventrals are white with rear edges of pale congo pink and checkered with deep dutch blue squares. *Abnormal coloration*—Ortenburger (Mass., 1922) recorded an albino.

Habitats: In this form, they are varied. Some called it a native of prairies, of mixed prairies, or of flat rock areas. It is found in breaks and canyons of the plains regions. Many other habitats are hilly country, woods, along rivers, on a mountain, in grassy lots, in residential districts, in a clump of oaks near a spring hole, on sunny slopes, in sparse woodland growth, or in open woods. They may be under ground cover or may climb trees. In 1880 Schenck discussed the vibration of the tail in *Elaphe*. Because he found it in *vulpina, confinis (spiloides)*, and *emoryi*, he believed it might belong to the whole genus.

Period of activity: *First appearance*—Apr. 30, 1932 Brennan (Kan., 1943); Apr. 10, 1927 (Gloyd); Apr. 21, 1928 (Gloyd, Kan., 1932); May 1927 (Strecker and Williams, Tex., 1927). *Fall disappearance*—Sept. 16, 1925, Oct. 8, 1927 (Gloyd); Oct. 2 (Marr). MVZ dates, March 6–July 21. *Hibernation*— "A den containing a dozen of these snakes (young to adult) was located on March 29, 1934, in a ravine 6 miles east of Winfield, Kansas, on a warm day following a cold period. The snake den was at the base of a south slope in a clump of oak trees above a small stream. A spring that flows all year was situated nearby and much rock was in evidence. At one point a vertical rock was scaled off to a height of about 4 feet and many snakes were revealed, including young *Coluber constrictor flaviventris* and some adults of *Diadophis punctatus arnyi* in addition to the present species" (Burt and Hoyle).

Breeding: Oviparous. Little is known about its habits. Males—1,200 mm., females—1,136 mm. *Eggs*—"Deposits considerable number of eggs in June and July" (Hudson and Davis, Neb., 1941). "A pair of *Elaphe laeta* was received in May 1937, from Willis Woolems of San Antonio. Mating was not observed, but the female laid one egg on July 8, 1940, and 13 more the following morning. These were divided into two batches, one of which became too moist and soon spoiled. In the other batch, hatching started 72 days later on September 18, 1940. Only 2 of these hatched. The other 5 were in perfect condition, but the snakes seemed to have been unable to slit the shells, which were exceptionally tough—much tougher than the shells of two other females which hatched a short time later. The young measured 242 mm. (about 9½ inches) at birth, and were fed a mouse apiece once a week. In November 1941, they were about 29 inches long" (Perkins, Gen., 1943). See Clark's recent article (Kan., 1953). His two females laid 4 and 5 eggs respectively, which were 51–61 mm. long by 20–22 mm. wide.

Young—Woodbury and Woodbury have a male 353 mm. and a female 328 mm. "A small specimen . . . taken in October is probably the young of the year" (Gloyd). It measures 328 mm. In Woodbury and Woodbury the young males 353 mm. (Edinburgh, Tex.) or 345 mm. (Mankato, Kan.) cannot be very old nor can the females 328 mm. (Lyte, Tex.) or 370 mm. (Edinburgh, Tex.). Strecker called his 400-mm. specimen a "young" female. In 1951 Werler wrote: "On June 14, 1950 a female 1,136 mm. long from near Brownsville, Texas laid 5 smooth adhesive eggs. Ten more were deposited the following day, June 15. (These were 40–50 mm. long by 27 to 31 mm. wide.) From Aug. 7–12, 7 emerged, 370–397 mm. in length." Then followed a good description of the color of the young.

Food: Mice, young birds, bats, insects, lizards. Hurter (Mo., 1911), Gloyd, Burt (1931), Burt and Hoyle, Boyer and Heinze, Marr, Uhler, Cottam, and Clarke (Va., 1939).

Authorities:

Baird, S. F., and C. Girard. (Gen., 1853)

Boyer, D. A., and A. A. Heinze (Mo., 1934)

Burt, C. E. (Kan., 1927, 1931)

Burt, C. E., and W. L. Hoyle (Gen., 1935)

Dowling, H. G. (Okla., 1951)

Gloyd, H. K. (Kan., 1928)

Marr, J. C. (Gen., 1944)

Schenck, J. (Gen., 1860)

Strecker, J. K., Jr. (Tex., 1910a, and others)

Woodbury, A. M. and D. M. (Gen., 1942)

Werler, J. E. (Gen., 1951)

Intermountain rat snake, Utah spotted rat snake

Elaphe emoryi intermontana (Woodbury and Woodbury) 1942. Fig. 69; Map 23

(*E. guttata emoryi* Dowling, 1952 [Gen.]; Schmidt, *Check List,* 1953)

Range: Colorado River basin (Colorado and Green Rivers of e. Utah and w. Colorado) s. into mountains of n. New Mexico.—Colo.; N.M.; Ut. *Elevation:*—2,000 to 5,000 feet or possibly 7,000 or 8,000 feet.

Size: Adults, 18–38 inches (Woodbury and Woodbury).

Distinctive characteristics: "A grayer smaller race, usually less than 1000 mm. in length with reduced scalation in numbers and increased pattern blotches. *E. l. intermontanus* has a grayish tinge (in alcohol) to the dorsal background which appears to be absent from the brown background of *laeta.* In the ventral color pattern, plates without spots are numerous enough to be conspicuous in the Texas specimens (*laeta*) which are rare in those from the Colorado Basin, which appear more densely spotted. . . . Dorsal blotches 2–4 scales long; ventrals under body and tail less than 282; abdominals minus body dorsal blotches less than 170. Intermountain Rat Snake, *E. l. intermontanus*" (Woodbury and Woodbury).

Habitat: "The 4 snakes taken from the type locality were occupying a streamside habitat of trees and cultivated fields. The specimen taken on Green River was found in late afternoon crawling about in streamside cottonwood trees on the bank of the river. The one from northern New Mexico was found under a dead log in ponderosa pine and boxelder forest" (Woodbury and Woodbury).

Period of activity: Early appearances—May 6, 1933, June 2, 1933, June 1937, May 1938 (Woodbury and Woodbury). *Fall disappearance*—July 18, 1927; July 27, 1933; Aug. 13, 1941 (Woodbury and Woodbury).

Field notes: In the summer of 1934 at Salt Lake City, one summer after Woodbury secured the Parrott Ranch specimens from Moab, Ut. (May 6, 1933), Woodbury laid them before me to await my surprise. I leaped. "There are no *Elaphe laeta* in Utah. Where did you get them?" He replied, "Moab, Utah." It was easy to see he had an interesting case of possible isolation.

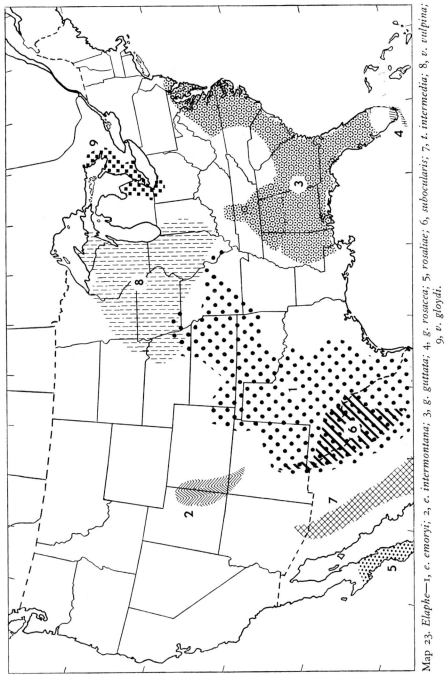

Map 23. *Elaphe*—1, *e. emoryi;* 2, *e. intermontana;* 3, *g. guttata;* 4, *g. rosacea;* 5, *rosaliae;* 6, *subocularis;* 7, *t. intermedia;* 8, *v. vulpina;* 9, *v. gloydi.*

Authorities:

Jameson, D. L., and A. G. Flury (Tex., 1949)

Woodbury, A. M. and D. M. (Gen., 1942)

1949: D. L. Jameson and A. G. Flury wrote: "Two specimens, a male and a female, were collected 5 miles north of Porvenir in the salt-cedar-mesquite association of the Rio Grande Basin district. They were active when found about 6 P.M. The male has a total length of 1054 mm. and a tail length of 189 mm. The ventral scale count is 207 and the subcaudal count is 72. There are 58 dorsal blotches on the body plus 19 on the tail."

We therefore depict *intermontana* in our range map as Woodbury and Woodbury originally gave it, despite Mosauer's and Jameson and Flury's records. We do so awaiting the "additional work" of which Jameson and Flury speak. We recognize the cogency of its allocation and the fact that Sierra Vieja is straight south of the Guadalupe Mts. Recently, Dowling (Gen., 1952) and Schmidt (*Check List,* 1953) relegated it to the synonymy of *E. guttata emoryi.*

Corn snake (59—J. Clayton 1705), Spotted racer
(10—Coues and Yarrow 1878)

Elaphe guttata guttata (Linné) 1766. Fig. 70; Map 23

Other common names: Beech snake; bead snake (Catesby); brown sedge snake; chicken snake; fox snake; house king snake; mole catcher; mouse snake; North American corn snake; pine snake; (red) rat snake; red chicken snake; red Coluber; red racer; red snake; scarlet snake; scarlet racer; spotted Coluber; spotted snake; spotted viper.

Range: Lower and upper coastal plains from s. New Jersey to Mississippi and s.e. Louisiana with a narrow arm through cent. Tennessee to Mammoth Cave. Ky.—Ala.; Ark.; Del.; D.C.; Fla.; Ga.; Ky.; La.; Md.; Miss.; Mo.; N.C.; N.J.; S.C.; Tenn.; Va. *Elevation*—1,000 to 2,500 feet (King, Tenn., 1939).

Size: Adults, 24–72 inches. The largest we have seen is 52 inches.

Longevity: 18 years 4 months, Philadelphia Zoo (Perkins, Gen., 1948); 19 years 4 months (Conant and Hudson, Gen., 1949); 21 years 4 months (Perkins, Gen., 1851); 8 years 2+ months (Kauffeld, Gen., 1951); 21 years 9 months (Perkins, Gen., 1954).

Distinctive characteristics: "Frontal a trifle longer than broad, rather broad behind, usually a little shorter than the snout; oculars 1–2; temporals 2–3 (4); upper labials 8, fourth and fifth entering the orbit; 11 or 12 lower labials, 5 touching anterior chin shields; scales usually in 27 rows (rarely 29), very slightly keeled on about 5 rows; ventrals 215–240; subcaudals 61–79. Length 1,200 mm. (tail 190). Light red, paler on sides; dorsal blotches darker

Fig. 69. *Elaphe e. intermontana,* Moab, Ut., paratype, D. W. Parriott to A. M. Woodbury.

Fig. 70. *Elaphe guttata guttata:* 1,8, Waverly, Ga.; 2–7, Washington, D.C., Zoo.

red with black borders and a narrow margin of dark red outside of the black; the dorsal spots reach to about the seventh row of scales; below these there is a second alternating series of smaller spots, which sometimes have a tendency to run together longitudinally, and a third series on the ends of the ventrals and the 2 outer rows. . . . The color beneath is yellowish white with quadrangular blotches of black on the outer ends of the ventrals. The head is usually but not always banded above" (Brown).

Color: Okefinokee Swamp, Ga., Aug. 18, 1922. The dorsal saddle spots are hay's russet or mahogany red. The intervals between the saddles vary from vinaceous-rufous to vinaceous-tawny. The spots along the side are orange-rufous in front varying to english red in the rear. The top of the head is burnt sienna. The iris is burnt sienna with a slightly lighter area of tawny near the pupil. The labials are white with dark edges. The venter is checkered with spots of slate-blue to deep slate-blue, on a background in the cephalic $\frac{2}{5}$ of white, in the caudal $\frac{3}{5}$ of ochraceous-salmon, flesh ocher, or light salmon-orange. The caudal portion may grow progressively brighter through light cadmium and light orange-yellow to deep chrome. *Abnormal coloration*—Albinism. Parker (Tenn., 1948).

Habitat: Clayton, the father of American botany, found these snakes most common in cornfields. This gentle, beautiful, and useful snake frequents roadsides, the neighborhood of settlements, barns, and outbuildings. It is also found in pine woods, prairies, fields, oak scrub, open areas, wooded uplands, and hills. Carr's summation had upland and tropical hammocks, high pine and dry flatwoods, fields and buildings. Neill (Ga., 1950b) found it in "tunnels and in old water mains, storm sewers, and abandoned pipelines," in basements of hotels and churches, in factories and in houses. For cover it uses bark of trees, rotting logs, holes in earth, or piles of litter, hay, or manure.

Period of activity: *First appearance*—Feb. 16, Apr. 3 (Corrington, Miss., 1929); Apr. 1, May 2 (Brimley, N.C., 1925); Apr., May (Cope, Gen., 1900); May, 1906 (Brimley, N.C., 1909). *Fall disappearance*—Nov. (Cope, Gen., 1900); Oct. 12 (Brimley, N.C., 1925). "Corn snakes are occasionally found at all seasons" (Allen, Miss., 1932). *Hibernation*—"They hibernate in hollow trees and rotten stumps" (Allen, Miss., 1932). Deckert (Fla., 1918) reported "several young taken from hollow trees in February." Neill (Ga., 1948) found that "it often hibernates beneath concrete floors of garages. . . . Specimens overwintering in stumps, move to the top of the stump on warm days, and lie beneath the bark on the sunny side. On cold days they retreat far below the surface along the tunnels formed by the decay of roots."

Breeding: Oviparous. *Eggs*—Number, 12–24. About the only definite record is Ditmars' (Gen., 1907) "one or two dozen." One uncertain record is: "On July 25, 1901 I found 17 eggs in a box in which I was keeping 2 species of Coluber (*guttatus* and *quadrivittatus*); these eggs were much like those of the King Snake but longer in proportion and contained very small embryos.

Nine eggs were stuck together in a cluster, 6 in another, and there were 2 free eggs" (Brimley, Gen., 1903). J. A. Fowler queried both the month and the number of eggs. In 1948 Parker in western Tennessee recorded that "a clutch of 18 eggs were reported found in early September 1937."

Food: Mammals, bats, young birds, insects. Brimley (N.C., 1941–42), Fowler, Wright and Bishop.

Authorities:

Bateman, G. C. (Gen., 1897)

Brown, A. E. (Gen., 1901)

Carr, A. F., Jr. (Fla., 1940a)

Corrington, J. D. (S.C., 1929)

Ditmars, R. L. (Gen., 1929)

Fowler, J. A. (Gen., 1947)

Holbrook, J. E. (Gen., 1836–42)

Loennberg, E. (Fla., 1895)

Neill, W. T. (Fla., 1949a; Ga., 1947)

Snyder, R. C. (Ala., 1945)

Wright, A. H., and S. C. Bishop (Ga., 1916)

1842, J. E. Holbrook: "The *Coluber guttatus* seems to have been a great stumbling-block to herpetologists, as may be seen by the great number of its synonyms. It is clearly described in the twelfth edition of the *Systema Naturae,* and no mention is made of it in any of the previous editions. Linnaeus described it from a specimen furnished him by Dr. Garden, and at the same time refers to Plate LX of Catesby, though with doubt. What he did doubtingly, others have done boldly. Plate LX of Catesby is the Bead-snake and not the *Coluber guttatus* of Linnaeus; but his Plate LV is the Corn-snake, and agrees with the *Coluber guttatus* in every respect."

Pink rat snake (5—Ditmars 1936), Rosy rat snake (Pope 1937)

Elaphe guttata rosacea (Cope) 1888. Fig. 71; Map 23

Other common names: Red rat snake; Key West rat snake.

Range: Florida keys. *Elevation*—0 to 50 feet.

Size: Adults, 18–60 inches.

Distinctive characteristics: "Color, rather than scalation and the pattern of the markings, will enable *rosacea* to be differentiated from *guttata*. The ground color of *rosacea* is a dark plumbeous in contrast to the light buff of *guttata*. The dorsal saddles, lightest anteriorly, are a darker red flecked with orange, differing from the even vermilion of the *guttata* saddles. The square black ventral spots are much the less distinct in *rosacea* which has the posterior ⅔ of the venter a bright orange, contrasting with the white ventral ground color of *guttata*. The species is characterized by 4 dark longitudinal stripes, a lateral and a median-dorsal pair. In the present specimen these stripes vary in intensity, being most pronounced immediately after sloughing of the skin. Since *guttata* have been known to bear, occasionally, similar stripes, the character is not infallible. Finally, preservation of *rosacea* is accompanied by marked fading of the red pigment of the saddles and lateral spots, as well as the longitudinal stripes. The dark dorsal ground color, however, remains quite pronounced—even in the type, after nearly half a century. This is quite the opposite from the case of *guttata* in which the red pigmented areas remain well defined" (Brady, Fla., 1933).

Color: A snake obtained from Caribee Colony, Upper Matecumbe Key, Fla., March 18, 1934. The outer part of the dorsal saddles is morocco red, the centers brazil red or english red. The saddles extend within 5 or 6 scale rows of the ventrals. There are alternating lateral spots which may be on the 3rd, 4th, and 5th scale rows or which at times may unite with spots similarly colored, located on the 2nd and 1st scale rows and on the ends of ventrals. This lateral row of spots plus those of the 1st and 2nd scale rows are orange-rufous or mars orange. Those on the ventrals may be xanthine orange. The dorsal saddles are black-edged in front and rear. There is a little indication of the same on the front and rear of the lateral spots. The intermediate area between the dorsal saddles is honey yellow to tawny-olive caudad as the background color of the sides becomes chamois or cream-buff. On the tail, this tends toward citrine-drab. The head has a band extending from the eye over the temporals to the angle of the mouth. This band is bordered above by black. Across the top of the head, on the rear of the prefrontals, is a transverse band, black-bordered behind. There are also 2 longitudinal bands which start at a common point on the rear of the frontal where they are outlined with a black border, and then extend backward across the parietals and along the top of the neck. These 5 bands, 2 postocular, 2 parietal, and the prefrontal are mars orange, or english red. The iris is xanthine orange. The upper labials are white, the first 5 with sutures of black or raw sienna. There are also dark sutures on the white lower labials. The chin is immaculate. The ground color of the venter, for the cephalic quarter, is pure white. From the neck backward there are small squarish spots like *Elaphe guttata*. For the last ⅔ of the venter, exclusive of the tail, the ventral plates are pinkish cinnamon or cinnamon-buff, with a small black spot on either end of most of the ventrals. The tail is immaculate cinnamon-buff or light vinaceous-cinnamon.

Another snake, a larger one, from Key West, Fla., came from M. G. Netting, May 1, 1941. It differs in several particulars from the specimen that we took at Upper Matecumbe Key, Fla. It is 40¼ inches overall of which 6¼ inches is tail. It has 27 rows of scales around middle; 245 ventrals; 61 pairs caudals; 8 upper labials; 12 lower labials. Dorsal spots 33 on body, 12 on tail. The background color between saddles and spots is drab-gray or smoke gray. The dorsal saddles are english red, bordered cephalad and caudad with black. They are not uniform blocks of solid color as the 2 central transverse rows of scales are partially edged with drab-gray or smoke gray.

Habitat and habits, with an outline of the literature:

1894, G. A. Boulenger (Gen., 1893–96): *g. rosacea,* "A color variety of *Coluber laetus.*"

1901, A. E. Brown (Gen., 1901): "One specimen 1720 mm. long, from Florida, now living at the Zoological Gardens, shows these spots quite plainly outlined on the back, 41 in number from head to vent, with the stripes running across them. There are also faint remains of lateral spots. This mixture of immature and adult characters probably accounts for *C. rosaceus* Cope."

1920, T. Barbour (Fla., 1920b): "This year my associate, Mr. W. S. Brooks, made a short and fruitful trip to Big Pine Key. He found there a beautiful *Elaphe* which is now before me, alive. It is distinct, agrees well with Cope's description and occupies, especially with respect to color pattern, a peculiarly intermediate position between *E. guttata* and *E. quadrivittata.* There is, therefore, no doubt that *Elaphe rosacea* should stand as a valid addition to the list with the habitat Lower Florida Keys."

1932, M. K. Brady (Fla., 1932a): "Concerning *Elaphe rosacea* (Cope) which has been confused with the present form, *E. q. deckerti,* I have seen but 2 specimens; the type U.S.N.M. No. 14418 from Key West, and M.C.Z. No. 14456, from Big Pine Key."

1933, M. K. Brady (Fla., 1933): "Since then many visitors to the Lower Florida Keys, myself among them, have searched in vain for this striking snake. I now have before me the third specimen, alive, and have compared it with *Elaphe guttata,* the widespread form whose range includes the area in which *rosacea* may be found."

1934, A. H. and A. A. Wright.

1940, A. F. Carr, Jr. (Fla., 1940a): "The Lower Keys. Hardwood hammocks; buildings. Rare. These snakes, along with *E. guttata,* while not common, are considered great pests by bird fanciers in Key West. I have talked with several individuals there who distinguished between the two. In my opinion, the affinities may possibly be with *quadrivittata* rather than with *guttata.* It seems quite likely that with the accumulation of more material, *deckerti* may prove to occupy a position intermediate between *quadrivittata* and *rosacea."*

1941, M. G. Netting (Gen., 1941).

1945, E. R. Allen and R. Slatten: Two on Cudjoe Key (Fla., 1945).

1949, W. T. Neill, Jr. (Fla., 1949a): "This rat snake is obviously a close relative of *guttata,* agreeing in general form, size, short tail, subcaudal count, reduced carination, general pattern, etc. . . . . *Rosacea* is a subspecies of *E. guttata.* Intermediate examples probably formed the basis for Cope's *Coluber guttatus sellatus,* which he characterized as being 'evidently annectent to the *C. rosaceus.'* "

L. H. Babbitt (letter): He took it at Key West Mar. 13, 1947, Mar. 20, 1948, Mar. 17, 1949 (2 spec.).

Field notes: We have seen most of the *E. rosacea* in collections and at least 2 alive.

Mar. 18, 1934: Came to the Caribee Colony on Upper Matecumbe Key because we missed the Ferry for Key West. . . . Went out to the pond near the water tank. There were countless small and half-grown *H. septentrionalis* in the pond. Many *Hyla squirella* calling. Are *H. squirella* the prey of the giant tree frog? From limbs higher than my head big tree frogs would leap into the pond with a pronounced "kerplunk" (like a toad). In looking for frogs in the bushes, Anna espied a pearly snake. She saw the rear of the belly. Then she saw the saddles. She called my attention and I picked it off from the branch. At first we asked, "Is it *E. guttata* or *E. q. deckerti* or *E. rosacea?*" A fine slender snake, not so black spotted on the underside of the belly. It is *E. rosacea.* On Matecumbe we hoped for *E. q. deckerti* and we drew *E. rosacea.*

Mar. 23, 1934: Went to Al Pflueger's place. He once had a large series of *Elaphes* from Lower Matecumbe Key. Most of them he lost. He said he had 2 more *E. rosacea* which he lost, i.e., besides the one M. K. Brady secured. Pflueger has seen many of these *Elaphe*. He said our specimen (Opalocka Zoo) tended toward *rosacea*. He believes they intergrade and that s. Floridan *Elaphe* forms are hardly worthy of specific rank or possibly subspecific rank. He has seen as many specimens as anyone. There may be much to his point of view and at times it has been ours. Certainly the 2 specimens, one at Opalocka Zoo and one at Aquarium, are quite divergent in appearance.

Pilot black snake (95—DeKay 1842), Pilot snake (37—Mozley 1878)

Elaphe obsoleta obsoleta (Say) 1823. Fig. 72; Map 24

Other common names: Alleghany black snake; black chicken snake (2); black Coluber; black pilot snake; black rat snake; black racer; black snake (25—J. Clayton 1705); blue racer; chicken snake; mountain black snake (17); mountain pilot snake; pilot; racer; rat snake; rusty black snake; scaly black snake; Schwartze schlange; sleepy John; white-throated racer.

Range: S. New England across New York and lower Ontario through middle Michigan and Wisconsin to s.e. Nebraska, s. to junction of Oklahoma, Arkansas, Texas, and Louisiana, thence to w. Kentucky and s.e. to n. Georgia.—U.S.A.: Ark.; Conn.; D.C.; Del.; Ill.; Ind.; Ia.; Kan.; Ky.; La.; Mass.; Md.; Mich.; Minn.; Mo.; N.C.; Neb.; N.J.; N.Y.; O.; Okla.; Pa.; S.C.; Tenn.; Va.; Vt.; W. Va.; Wis. Can.: Ont. *Elevation*—900 to 2,500 feet (Smith, Pa., 1945); 1,000–4,000 feet (King, Tenn., 1939); 3,500 feet (N.C., Dunn, 1917).

Size: Adults, 40–108 inches.

Longevity: 13 years 6 months (Perkins, Gen., 1951); 16 years (Perkins, Gen., 1954).

Distinctive characteristics: Black or blackish brown, very large, angulate-bellied (arboreal) snakes. If spots are present they are more or less indistinct

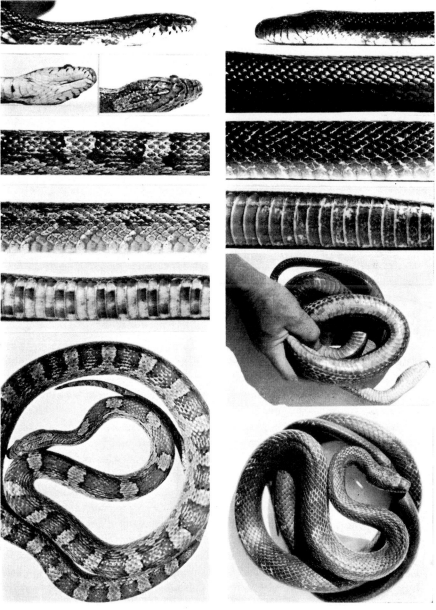

Fig. 71. *Elaphe g. rosacea,* Key West, Fla., loaned by M. G. Netting.

Fig. 72. *Elaphe obsoleta obsoleta:* 1,3,5,6, Enfield Gorge, Ithaca, N.Y., J. P. Porter; 2,4, Ramsay, N.J., L. Hook.

and indistinctly outlined with white. Interspaces between the faintly keeled scales are white. Posterior belly slate gray; throat, chin, and labials white. Young have the typical *Elaphe* dorsal saddles or spots with a grayish background.

Color: A snake from south of Enfield Gorge, Ithaca, N.Y., received from J. P. Porter, July 2, 1928. The color of the dorsum in the caudal half of the body is blackish slate, blackish violet-gray, or plumbeous black; in the cephalic half it is generally olivaceous black (3) to dark olive-gray. The cephalic half bears black or olivaceous black saddle spots about 12 scales wide. Alternating with these are lateral areas or obscure spots on the 2nd to 6th rows of scales. These obscure lateral and dorsal spots are indicated by the rose doree, old rose, or even eugenia red edges to the scales, the edges of the black scales in the interspaces being white, pale gull gray, lilac-gray, or pale quaker drab. The top of the head is dark olive-gray or mouse-gray. The labials are white except for the upper edges of the upper labials, which are pale olive-gray. The iris is slate-gray or purplish gray in the outer part, and neutral gray with flecks in the inner portion. In general, the eye is like the body color in appearance. The pupil rim is white. The chin is white, the underside of the head is clear white, then olive-gray comes in scatteringly so that the cephalic half is the lightest portion of the venter. Long before the middle of the body is reached, slate-gray begins to predominate and in the caudal half the ventrals are almost uniform slate-gray or slate color with a light line in the middle of the belly. The tail is self-color of slate-gray or slate color.

Color variations—Color patterns in various parts of the wide range of this snake are often very puzzling.

Habitat and habits: It is frequently called the most aboreal of our northeastern snakes. Some 25 or more writers mention this habit. Twenty-four or more ascribe it to trees (large 11, small 4, bushes 4, holes in trees 3, hollow 1, grapevines 1, etc.). Its climbing ability is recorded about barns 2, houses 3, granaries 2, schoolhouses 1, farm yards 2. It climbs to high places—an attic, a bat roost 1, cupola of a barn 2, top of a 30-foot grapevine 1, very highest point in cage 1, high in trees several. On the ground it is under rocks, under decaying logs, in ledges, in hollow logs, on fallen logs, along fence rows, in stumps, in dry stone stream beds, in fallen saplings, or in fallen logs. Several have ascribed it to hilly, rocky, or scrubby mountainous sections. Many place it in woods, oak-hickory woods, heavy oak woods, moist woodlands, heaviest forests, bottomland forest. Few if any call it a moist or semiaquatic snake. One author says: "uplands away from lakes and swamps."

Period of activity: *First appearance*—March 24, 1928; Apr. 6, 1926 (Gloyd, Kan., 1932); Apr. 17, 1925 (Gloyd, Kan., 1928); Apr. 4 (Hurter); Apr. 27 (Wright and Allen, N.Y., 1913). *Seasonal catch*—Mar. 1, Apr. 2, May 10, June 8, July 4, Sept. 2, Oct. 3, Nov. 1, Dec. 1 (Brimley, N.C., 1926). *Fall* *disappearance*—Nov. 2, 1915 (Logier, Ont., 1925); Nov. 29, 1909 (Lindsey, Ont., 1931); Nov. 12, 1926 (Gloyd, 1928). MVZ dates are Apr. 6–Nov. 26.

Hibernation—"The pilot black snake is common in the rocky lands of Leeds County [Ontario, Canada] and has several times been noted on the islands of the St. Lawrence River. A number of specimens were taken during 1934. Two live ones from Gananoque Lake were sent to Mr. Logier. There is a small area near this lake which has never been burnt or cut over, with a talus slope close to the water that makes an ideal wintering den. Farmers of the vicinity have told me that they have seen as many as 15 or 20 black snakes in the spring, sunning themselves near the talus slope" (Toner, Ont., 1934). In the forested Missouri River bluff region of s.e. Nebraska Loomis and Jones collected 1 milk snake (*Lampropeltis d. syspila*), 2 racers (*C. c. flaviventris*), and 3 pilot snakes (*E. o. obsoleta*) "It was beneath rocks at the opening of a 30-foot, partially covered well. This well evidently served as a hibernating place" (Neb., 1949). "Eight specimens preparing to hibernate in a well in company with 2 blue racers, *Coluber constrictor flaviventris* and a small little *Pituophis sayi* were taken November 12, 1926. They were resting in crevices of the rocks, less than 12 feet below the surface of the ground. The well was carefully walled up and closed at the top" (Gloyd). See article on the hibernation of *Coluber c. flaviventris* by Owens (Mo.) in 1949, when he took 7 pilot black snakes and 8 blue racers from an old cistern on March 3, 1949.

Breeding: Oviparous. Size data are meager. We have only males 1,095–1,835 mm., females 715–1,800 mm. Most of Miller's specimens were 1,285–1,3600 mm. *Mating*—There are several records from May 25 or the last of May to June 12 or later. The duration may be short. There are records of 17 minutes to 6 hours.

Eggs—Number, 6–24. 6, 13, Minton; 8, Johnson (La., 1950), Wilson and Friddle (W.Va., 1950); 8, 10, Slack (Ky., 1944); 9, Rathvon (Pa., 1879); 10, Fowler (D.C., 1945), Bishop and Alexander (N.Y., 1927), Corrington (S.C., 1929); 10, 24, Wright and Allen (N.Y., 1913); 11, Piatt (Ind., 1931); 11, 14, Gloyd; 11, 12, 22, Conant and Downs (Gen., 1940); 12, Littleford and Keller, Evans (N.Y., 1947); 12, 14, Atkinson (Pa., 1901); 16, Boyer and Heinze (Mo., 1934); 17, 44, Netting; 19, Hurter; 22, Cope (Gen., 1864), Conant and Bridges (Gen., 1939), Schmidt and Davis (Gen., 1941). Time of deposition, June and July (Boyer and Heinze, probably premature); June, July (Wright and Allen); July (Fowler); July 2, 17 (Littleford and Keller); July 5 (Johnson); July 11 (Gloyd); July 20 (Slack); July 21 (Mansueti); July 26 (Netting); July 26, last of July (Minton); July 30 (Piatt, Gloyd). Size, 36–60 mm. (1.4–2 inches) x 20–26.5 mm. (.8–1.1 inch). The May 23d eggs measured 32.5x26.5 mm. and 29x25 mm. Were they premature?

Young—Hatching time, Aug. 22–Oct. 2. Aug. 22 (Gloyd); Sept. 13–16, Sept. 15–17 (Atkinson, Pa., 1901); Sept. 16–18, Sept. 30, Oct. 2 (Littleford,

Md., 1946a); Sept. 19 (Minton); Sept. 20 (Slack, Kan., 1944). Size, 11–16 inches. There are records of 273–324 mm., 297–331, 351, 360, 361, and between 300–400 mm. On May 3 and 13, Gloyd collected several under 400 mm., presumably hatched the preceding fall.

Food: Mammals, nestling birds, lizards, amphibians. Recent writers include Uhler, Cottam, and Clarke (Va., 1939) and Barbour.

Field notes: During the thirties a CCC camp was established in the upper portion of the Enfield, New York, State Park. One of our students was a councilor there. From time to time he brought us black pilot snakes, often headless. He had a hard time persuading the boys that the snakes were useful. When the boys saw the snakes in the park paths, they killed them, thinking they were saving ladies from frights and children from dangers, and doing mankind a favor.

Once when we were about to start for a month's trip, a lady called up from near Enfield and said she had a black snake. We asked her to keep it until we returned. She did. The instant we returned she reminded us of it. On our first class trip we went to her house. My associate, Prof. W. J. Hamilton, Jr., was along and in his best humorous form. The lady was only 4 feet 8 or 9 inches tall with short arms. Against the background of the hill she spread her arms and said, "The boys saw one on the hill 15 feet long." Prof. Hamilton soberly remarked to the students, "What a pity she isn't bigger."

Authorities:

Axtell, H. H. (N.Y., 1947)
Barbour, R. W. (Ky., 1950)
Branson, E. B. (Kan., 1904)
Brimley, C. S. (N.C., 1941–42)
Burt, C. E. (Kan., 1933)
Conant, R. (O., 1938a)
Gloyd, H. K. (Kan., 1928)
Holbrook, J. E. (Gen., 1936–42)
Hurter, J. (Mo., 1911)

Littleford, R. A., and W. F. Keller (Md., 1946, 1946a)
McCauley, R. H. (Md., 1945)
MacCoy, C. V. (N.E., 1931)
Mansueti, R. (Md., 1946)
Minton, S., Jr. (Ind., 1944)
Netting, M. G. (Pa., 1927b)
Say, T. (Gen., 1822–23)
Surface, H. A. (Pa., 1906)

1899, W. S. Blatchley (Ind.): "It is my opinion that a careful examination of a large series of specimens will show that *C. confinis,* as well as *C. spiloides* Dam. Bibr., are but forms, perhaps the young, of *C. obsoletus.* In fact, the young of most if not all of our dark colored snakes are spotted, and as they grow older and shed their skin a number of times, they gradually grow darker, until finally they become almost wholly black. This has, in the past, been the cause of much confusion in the naming of the reptiles, many of the young having been thought to be distinct species."

Deckert's chicken snake (2—Carr 1940),
Deckert's rat snake (Ditmars 1939)

Elaphe obsoleta deckerti Brady 1932. Fig. 73; Map 24
(*E. obsoleta quadrivittata* Dowling [Gen., 1952]; Schmidt, *Check List,* 1953)

Other common names: Four-lined rat snake; southern Florida rat snake; Matecumbe rat snake.

Range: Tip of Florida from Princeton to Cape Sable and s. on the keys to Lower Matecumbe. *Elevation*—Below 50 feet, coast line.

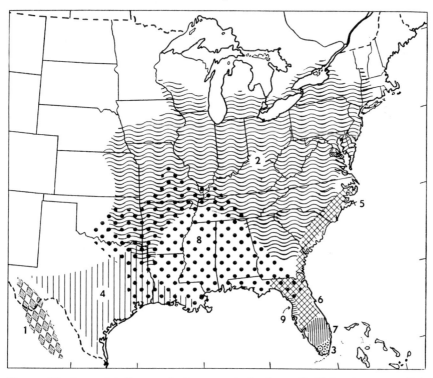

Map 24. *Elaphe*—1, *bairdi;* 2, *o. obsoleta;* 3, *o. deckerti;* 4, *o. lindheimeri;* 5, *o. parallela* 6, *o. quadrivittata;* 7, *o. rossalleni;* 8, *o. spiloides;* 9, *o. williamsi.*

Size: Adults, 27–72 inches. Brady's largest specimen was 968 mm. We have seen specimens from 26–66 inches long.

Distinctive characteristics: "A slender, orange-red *Elaphe,* having 4 brownish longitudinal stripes on the body, about 40 plumbeous saddles on the dorsum between the median stripes, a bright orange, distinctly spotted venter, chin and throat bright yellow, ventral scales usually more than 240, caudals normally 90 or more" (Brady, Fla., 1932). "In *E. o. deckerti,* the ground color is a dull yellow with a brown or olive suffusion of variable intensity; the stripes are blackish, narrow, and well defined; a sublateral stripe is better defined than in *rossalleni;* the chin and throat are yellow, often with a large white gular patch; the venter is pinkish, flesh, or tan, occasionally spotted with orange-yellow; the scales lack a glaucous sheen; the iris is pink or red; the tongue is black. Usually some trace of dorsal spots remains evident throughout life. *Deckerti* is smaller than either *quadrivittata* or *rossalleni"* (Neill, Fla., 1949a).

Color: A snake in the Opalocka Zoo at Miami, Fla., came from Matecumbe Key and was described Mar. 23, 1934. The body is marked with dorsal saddles between median stripes and with a lateral stripe on either side. The ground color between the saddles and between the upper and lower stripes is orange-rufous or mars orange, and the 4 stripes, upper and lower, and the saddles are auburn. The saddles are spotted with orange-rufous. About 2 rows of scales below the lateral stripe are of the ground color edged in front with light cadmium and in the rear with white. Many of the scales of the orange stripe have white edging or interspaces. The top of the head is antique brown. The upper labials are primuline yellow; the lower ones are edged with the same or with light cadmium. *The lower side of the head and the immediate neck region are white.* The iris is english red with the outer edge nigrosin violet. The pupil rim is white. The iris is dotted all over with whitish flecks, so that the brazil red iris appears to the naked eye english red. The ventral surface in the forward part of the body is light cadmium, becoming in the middle capucine orange.

(See Fig. 73. We are surely confused. The specimen was reputedly from Matecumbe Key, yet orange-rufous or mars orange sounds like Neill's *rossalleni.* Note, however, the white of lower side of neck and head in our specimen. Unfortunately we didn't describe the color of the specimen collected by E. Ross Allen from Matecumbe in 1939.)

Habitat: "Widely distributed in tropical Florida; most abundant in hardwood hammocks and in old buildings. Fairly common. Habits—similar to those of *quadrivittata.* I have seen 2 in mangroves over salt water; they frequent Jamaica dogwood trees with surprising regularity" (Carr, Fla., 1940a).

Period of activity: *First appearance*—Apr. 17, 1932 (Brady, Fla., 1932). *Fall disappearance*—Nov., 1931.

Field notes: In 1934, two years after Brady's description, we sought to get *E. q. deckerti,* but had to come back to Opalocka Zoo, Mar. 23, before we saw it alive. Since then we have seen several alive. The first 2 were young and, like the plate, showed the saddles quite distinctly (never like *confinis* or *williamsi*). At the present we have alive 1 large *deckerti,* 2 *confinis,* 2 *quadrivittata,* 1 *obsoleta,* and 1 *guttata.* The large *deckerti* in a photograph shows the saddles not at all, yet in a certain light some areas of the dorsum reveal the indistinct saddles. As Carr explains, the ground color is not so clearly uniform, being more reddish or orange, and the stripes not so clean-cut as in *quadrivittata*. In the early stages after its description we were somewhat skeptical. But *Elaphe* of the southeast will not alone be solved by a tyro borrowing all the museum material. Someone in the center of its distribution, preferably Florida, with countless live specimens, can best satisfy the requirements.

Mar. 17, 1934, Opalocka Zoo, Miami, Fla.: They have a nice *Elaphe q. deckerti* and several *E. quadrivittata*. The *deckerti* is a beautiful snake. Went to Florida Tropical Reptile Society. Here met Mrs. Frampton. They have a good collection, 1 nice *E. q. deckerti*.

Mar. 22, 1934: At Ferry, Lower Matecumbe Key, Mr. C. L. Craig, Islamorda, Fla., said he found these snakes (*E. q. deckerti*) in the hammock back of his store.

Mar. 23, 1934, Opalocka Zoo: Photoed *E. q. deckerti*. It came from Lower Matecumbe Key and is in fine color.

Mar. 24, 1934: Went to see Deckert. He says *E. q. deckerti* may have stripes or not.

Apr. 1, 1934, at Eustis, Fla.: Jay A. Weber took *E. q. deckerti* from Lower Matecumbe Key.

Authorities: Morphologically like other *Elaphes,* there are no cardinal differences to emphasize; hence we give only Brady's original diagnosis and other coloration paragraphs.

1932, M. K. Brady (Fla.): *"Range.* Lower Matecumbe Key, Monroe Co., Florida. *Coloration* (in life). Above 4 hair brown longitudinal stripes, extending from neck along body, dorsal stripes extending to tip of tail, lateral stripes ending at vent. The stripes cover 2 scale rows anteriorly and posteriorly, widening to cover 3 rows mediad. Forty dark grey to plumbeous, somewhat concave saddles between dorsal stripes on body. Saddles on tail represented by an indistinct plumbeous clouding. Dorsal ground-color a rich orange-ochraceous, slightly clouded with grey. Scales in longitudinal stripes frequently tipped with white. Ventral color a bright wax yellow mottled with white on the chin and throat, changing to orange, spotted with grey posteriorly. The ventrals are upturned at their ends and are a rosy grey over the posterior $\frac{2}{3}$ of the animal, forming a less distinct third pair of longitudinal stripes. The iris is strongly suffused with red, the pupil is black. The more anterior dorsal saddles have faint suggestions of black borders. The top of the head is more of a buff than the dorsal ground color of the body and has no pattern."

1940a, A. F. Carr, Jr. (Fla.): "The only constant characters distinguishing this form from *quadrivittata* are the slightly darker and more reddish ground-color; the tendency toward lessening and diffusion of pigment in the longitudinal stripes, and an orange- or lemon-yellow bloom, which, anteriorly at least, is striking in living examples, but which may disappear entirely in preservative. Scutellation, size, and pattern (persistence of the juvenile dorsal saddles) are not consistently diagnostic of the race. In view of the facts, it seems necessary to extend the range of *deckerti* somewhat farther north to embrace the whole region in which the peculiarly colored individuals occur. I have examined specimens from localities covering most of Florida south of the lower end of Lake Okeechobee, and Wesley Clanton and I collected a fairly typical specimen on the northeast of the lake. We saw 6 in 2 days at Cape Sable."

1940, T. Barbour and A. F. Carr, Jr. (Fla.): *"Elaphe q. deckerti* appears to be the least stable of any of the forms, and is only feebly differentiated from *quadrivittata* in south-central Florida, roughly at about the latitude of the north shore of Lake Okeechobee."

A. H. and A. A. Wright: In collections we have seen several specimens. In a small one, 690 mm., it seemed as if the saddles were more prominent than the stripes. Some over 900 mm. have the 4 marked stripes but also saddles present. Others have the saddles very indistinct. (We are speaking solely of Matecumbe populations, though Carr's interpretation may be correct.)

1949a, W. T. Neill (Fla.): To his new form (*rossalleni*) Neill gives a ground color of rich orange, orange yellow, or orange brown, and he departs from the bright orange in Brady's description in his description of *deckerti*. He thus discusses his interpretation: "Much of the confusion surrounding *deckerti* is due to the fact that Brady's material (insular examples from the extreme limit of the range) was not particularly typical; and most subsequent reviewers have quoted or paraphrased Brady's description. The ground color of *deckerti* is seldom orange, never the bright orange of *rossalleni*. In the material I have examined, the ground color was straw, tan, dull orange with a dingy brown suffusion, wood brown, or sepia. The lighter specimens are reminiscent of *quadrivittata*, but are much less attractive. Some examples are nearly as dark as *obsoleta*. The stripes are gray-brown, rosy brown, or blackish, better defined than in *rossalleni*. Usually dorsal spots are distinct. . . . A sublateral stripe is present posteriorly. The iris is pinkish-orange or red. The tongue is black, even in lighter examples. I suspect that the topotypical Lower Matecumbe Key population was slightly aberrant, as is very frequently the case with isolated Key West populations. Unfortunately, we may never know whether this is true. During recent hurricanes, the ocean completely covered the island. Mr. Allen and his collectors have been unable to secure specimens there in recent years. During the summer of 1947 I visited the island, collecting *Hyla squirella* but no *Elaphe*. A single topotype collected in 1940 differed from the mainland *deckerti* in displaying sharply defined dorsal spots and gray mottlings on the posterior portion of the venter."

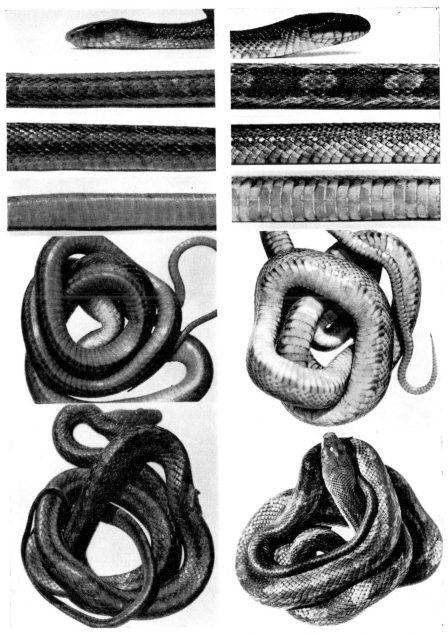

Fig. 73. *Elaphe o. deckerti,* Matacumba Key, Fla., G. F. Sirman.

Fig. 74. *Elaphe o. lindheimeri,* Brownsville, Tex., H. C. Blanchard.

Lindheimer's pilot snake (3—Strecker 1908),
Texas pilot snake (2—Strecker 1908)

Elaphe obsoleta lindheimeri (Baird and Girard) 1853. Fig. 74; Map 24

Other common names: Black Coluber; black snake; checked pilot snake; eastern Texas rat snake; (gray) pilot snake; Lindheimer's Coluber; Lindheimer's rat snake; Lindheimer's snake (Yarrow 1882); mountain black snake; red-headed Coluber; spotted chicken snake.

Range: Roughly from Pecos River to Sabine River, Texas, possibly extending into Oklahoma, Arkansas, and Louisiana.—Okla.; Tex. *Elevation—* Coast to 2,000 or 3,000 feet.

Size: Adults, 28–61 inches.

Longevity: 4 years 11 months (Conant and Hudson, Gen., 1949); 2 years 9 months, 2 years 3 months, 2 years 2 months (Kauffeld, Gen., 1951).

Distinctive characteristics: We quote from the two, Garman and Brown, who knew *lindheimeri* best: "Dorsals 27 rows; ventrals 232; tail mutilated. About 30 transverse blotches of brownish on the back, in a reddish ground color; smaller alternating blotches on the outer rows; belly yellowish, clouded with brownish. Corpus Christi" (S. Garman). "Yellowish above with a dorsal series of dark lead-colored spots. . . . The bases and margins of many scales in the light interspaces are rusty red in every living specimen I have seen; this fades rapidly in alcohol. Top of head uniform lead color without bands. The eye is rather large" (Brown).

Color: A snake from west of Rio Medina Lake near Blue Wing Lake, San Antonio, Tex., Feb. 28, 1925. The top of the head is olive-brown, mummy brown, bister, or even fuscous. The spaces between the spots of the dorsal row, the lateral row, and the row on the ends of the ventrals are baryta yellow or maize yellow with many of the scales tipped or clouded with the brownish colors. On the dorsum and on the sides, in the baryta yellow interspaces, are light touches of light salmon-orange or bittersweet pink. On the sides, considerable of this latter color is revealed if the scales are stretched, and the color may be old rose, begonia rose, or deep vinaceous. The same color is evident in the interspaces and in the lateral spots when the skin is stretched. The chin is white, and the upper labials are largely white. The iris is fuscous, mummy brown, bister, and black, with a white pupil ring. (Do you suppose the ring would be yellowish if the animal were not so cold?) The under parts are olive-buff with deep grayish olive rear edges to ventrals and subcaudals, the dark edges being broader under the tail.

Abnormal coloration—Albinism. "May 22, 1926, a very peculiar snake was killed on the Elkhart road, about 4 miles out from Palestine, Anderson County, Texas. The ground color, in the freshly-killed snake, was pure white above and below, but the skin now has a slightly pinkish cast" (Strecker, Tex., 1926d).

Habitat and habits: This common snake of Texas, the "witch snake" of folklore, is abundant in wooded tracts.

Period of activity: *Early appearances*—It was abroad early on our 1925 trip (Feb. 28, Mar. 18, May 1), and in 1934 we saw it Apr. 19 and Apr. 25. Feb. 28, 1925 (R. D. Camp); Apr. 1, 1905 (Bailey, Tex.). *Fall disappearance* —Bailey gave it as late as Nov. 21, 1891. *Hibernation*—"In central Texas, the pilot snake hibernates about 3 months of the year. I have found a number of fairly lively specimens as late as the last week of November, and as early as the second week in February. December 18th of an unusually mild winter, I captured, in a hollow rotten stump, one that was still able to show fight. After winter sets in in earnest, they find hibernating places in holes under large fallen trees and usually go down to a depth of several feet. They often share their winter quarters with copperheads, brown snakes, leopard frogs, and toads" (Strecker, Tex., 1926a).

Breeding: Oviparous. Males to 1,520 mm., females 764–1,374 mm. *Mating*— "The breeding season extends from April to the middle of June" (Strecker, Tex., 1926f). *Eggs*—Number, 8–15, probably to 24 as in *E. o. obsoleta*. "In central Texas, from 8 to 12 eggs are the usual number laid by this snake" (Strecker, Tex., 1926f). "A large female collected within the city limits of San Antonio, Texas, deposited 15 eggs on June 11. These nongranular eggs were separate after laying, but since they were covered with an adhesive substance would undoubtedly have adhered in a cluster, had they been laid one against the other" (Werler). Size, 1.55–2.2 inches long x 1–1.25 inches in width. "Large specimens sometimes lay eggs fully 50 mm. in length" (Strecker, 1926f). "The egg measurements follow: Length-width: 39-31, 40-27, 40-28, 41-29, 42-28, 43-27, 44-26, 44-31, 45-27, 45-30, 46-27, 47-30, 47-30, 48-24, 54-27" (Werler).

Young—Time of deposition, June; hatching time, August. Size, 13.8– 15.7 inches. "On July 29, one of the eggs of this clutch was opened and examined, and disclosed a living, and nearly completely developed embryo. Eggs slits were seen to appear in most of the group on August 1, and on August 2, 13 of the snakes escaped from their shells; the last egg of the clutch hatching August 3. The hatchling snakes measured: Length [in mm.]: 345, 352, 356, 359, 361, 364, 366, 368, 369, 373, 374, 381, 391, 392" (Werler). Recently, Werler (Gen., 1951) reported 4 depositions: (1) a female 762 mm. on June 24 laid 5 eggs 67–76 mm. long by 18–21 mm. wide. These hatched Aug. 15–17, 418–448 mm. long; (2) 14 eggs found July 19, 1950, in the top of a rotted standing tree trunk, 43–47 mm. long by 28–32 mm. wide (they hatched July 27–29, 387–510 mm. in length); (3) a female 1,374 mm. long laid 7 eggs, 61–71 mm. long by 24–27 mm. wide, which hatched Aug. 7, 451–463 mm. long; (4) a female June 13–16 laid 9 eggs, 41–47 mm. long by 22–25 mm. wide, which hatched from Aug. 8–9, 415–442 mm., a runt 227 mm. long.

Authorities:

Brown, A. E. (Gen., 1901)
Garman, H. (Tex., 1892)
Garman, S. (Tex., 1892)

Strecker, J. K., Jr. (Tex., 1915, 1926a,
    1926f, 1928b, 1928c)
Werler, J. E. (Tex., 1949)

1901, A. E. Brown: "The distinctness of the color pattern at all ages, the red on the scales of the flanks, the slight but, as it appears to me, very general difference in the shape of the frontal, with an apparently circumscribed geographic range, are quite enough, in my opinion, to compel recognition of this subspecies." Brown in his time knew Texan forms best.

From 1900 to his death, J. K. Strecker gave us most of the information we have on this form. By 1901 Brown knew it from many specimens alive and dead. Thereafter confusion reigned. In the San Antonio region alone, the out-of-the-state authorities had *obsoleta, lindheimeri, spiloides,* and *confinis.* There is only one form there besides *E. emoryi.* No wonder Strecker was confused. Great names who hadn't visited Texas kept it *confinis* for 30 years.

1944, A. H. and A. A. Wright: One cannot properly solve so difficult a genus as *Elaphe* without collecting or living in the centers of troublesome *spiloides* and *lindheimeri* or the Florida races. Of the 4 authorities from 1900–1943 who dominated our *Elaphe* thinking, none thus qualified before 1930 or thereabouts. With difficult specimens they often went on *geographical probabilities.* From preserved material we need geographical data. Dr. Liberty Hyde Bailey sent a South Pacific specimen (without locality) to his friend William Trelease, the world's authority on the genus. That authority returned it immediately because it had no data.

Baird and Girard, Cope, the Garmans, and Brown recognized *lindheimeri.* Then Hurter became one of our vigorous collectors, and he used *spiloides.* From 1922 to 1930 Blanchard used *confinis.* Therein lie the vogues. Does it mean that Strecker, who from 1901 to 1930 had seen spotted chicken snakes alive, was vacillating or nondiscriminative? Far from it. He was perplexed by the variety of his material determined by far-off nonresident authorities. We vividly recall our confusion with the first 6 specimens of *confinis* in Okefinokee Swamp, Ga., when Cope's temporal formula distinctions for 6 forms were revealed on one or the other side of these 6 specimens. Our friend Strecker followed for a time his dear collector-friend Hurter and then Blanchard. Blanchard, master though he was, had never lived in the center of *confinis* (*spiloides*) or *lindheimeri* when he made them synonymous. This is a genus for the expert alone—and only after a long term of residence or oft-repeated visits to the center of the species and its intergrading areas. This is a southern U.S. genus. Go there and live a while and get confused, as Strecker and we did. Borrowed pickles will help, but not solve the problem. Get 600 live specimens from one area as Klauber did for one species. Above all go into the field and find some of your keys and inspiration there, while at the same time you grow cautious and hesitant. The first trip you will describe a lot of new species, but the problem is only beginning, and the snakes of the second trip will not all head for your new stalls. *Lindheimeri* may possibly stretch from Texas to Arkansas or Missouri. We feel that it is a neglected form.

Chicken snake (24—Bartram 1791), **Striped chicken snake** (9—Brimley 1903)

Elaphe obsoleta quadrivittata (Holbrook) 1836. Fig. 75; Map 24

Other common names: Banded chicken snake; four-banded Coluber; four-banded rat snake; four-lined chicken snake; four-lined Coluber; four-lined rat snake (2); four-lined snake; North American chicken snake; red racer; striped house snake; white oak runner; yellow chicken snake (Wachtel); yellow rat snake (4).

Range: Lower or swampy coastal plain from Albemarle Sound, N.C., to Apalachicola River and Lake Okeechobee, Fla.—Fla.; Ga.; N.C.; S.C. *Elevation*—0 to 500 feet, mainly below 100 feet.

Size: Adults, 24–84 inches. The largest we have seen was 5 feet 7 inches.

Longevity: 13 years 7 months (Perkins, Gen., 1951); 2 years 10 months, 2 years 5 months (Kauffeld, Gen., 1951); 16 years 7 months (Perkins, Gen., 1954).

Distinctive characteristics: "In *E. o. quadrivittata,* the ground color varies from light gray (near the region of intergradation with *E. o. obsoleta*) through yellowish-gray to clear yellow to tan; the stripes are blackish, narrow, and well-defined; a sublateral stripe is occasionally evident; the chin and throat are white; the venter is whitish, mottled with gray posteriorly; the scales lack a glaucous sheen; the iris is gray or yellow; the tongue is black. Some trace of juvenile spots is often retained until the individual is quite large" (Neill).

Color: A snake from Eureka, Fla., came from Tyler, June 20, 1928. The 3 dorsal rows of scales are isabella color or buffy olive in the forward portion and dark olive-buff in the rear. On the 6th to 9th rows of scales is a stripe of dark olive-buff, deep olive-buff, or olive-ocher. The 1st or 1st and 2nd rows of scales are the same color. On the 3rd to 5th rows and also on the 10th to 12th rows are bands of brownish olive, sepia, or mummy brown. The top of the head is ecru-olive. The iris is orange-cinnamon with a pupil rim of light pinkish cinnamon. The lower edges of the upper labials, the underside of the head, and the forward venter are white or cartridge buff. Caudad, the venter becomes colonial buff, then primrose yellow. One-third of the way caudad it becomes quite clouded with brownish olive, and in the caudal half, but not in the tail, this color predominates. The underside of the tail is deep colonial buff.

Habitat and habits: The food accounts place this snake in barns, houses, schoolhouses, cabins, trees, caves; it is mainly a domestic form about farms and poultry grounds. Beginning with Coues and Yarrow in 1878 in N.C., we learn that it is "very numerous in woods of islands and mainland." Ditmars in 1907 gave it as arboreal, living in a large live-oak tree, in rafters of cabins, on the surface of swamps, or in cypress swamps. Deckert (Fla.) in 1918 took several specimens "in oak thickets on high ground." Van Hyning (Fla.) in 1933 reported them common in woods and outbuildings. In 1939 Stabler (Gen.) wrote that he had *E. q. quadrivittata* 36 months under observation. He gave rest periods and sheddings. In 1940 Carr (Fla.) wrote: "Very widely distributed; most numerous in Upland Hammock and about rat infested buildings. . . . Quite arboreal; expert climbers. They scale limbless pine and oak trunks with ease; one which I kept in the laboratory slowly climbed from floor to ceiling in the angle at the corner of the room with no support other than the rough surface of the plaster." In 1946 Lewis (N.C.) found it in sandy areas set with scrub palmetto.

Breeding: Oviparous. Of this very common zoo snake there are few breeding records. We, like many others, have seen their eggs but have not recorded them.

Eggs—Number, 8–41. "On August 17, 1901, a striped Chicken Snake (*Coluber quadrivittatus*) from Georgia laid 9 eggs in confinement, 2 lots of 2 each were adherent, the rest free. The eggs were long and narrow with a tough white skin and measured 37 to 43 mm. long by 17 to 20 wide" (Brimley). "During the night of June 16, 1941, 2 female *Elaphe quadrivittata quadrivittata* laid a total of 19 eggs. Eight more had been laid a day or so before, making a total of 27. They were divided into 3 batches, and all spoiled in a short time. Both females have been here since 1937, the male since 1940" (Perkins). "Available for comparison was a clutch of 41 eggs deposited by a female *E. o. quadrivittata*. These eggs were smaller than those of *E. o. rossalleni*, the length ranging from 30.0 to 38 mm., average 32.5 mm.; and the diameter from 18.0 to 21.1 mm., average 19.5 mm." (Allen and Neill, Fla., 1950). Time of deposition, June 1–Aug. 17, mainly June. Zoo specimens are often delayed. Size, 1.2–1.8 inches x .75–.9 inches. Ditmars gave 1¼x⅞ inches as the dimensions of the egg.

Young—Time of hatching, August and early September. If eggs hatch 6–8 weeks (Ditmars) after deposit, then dates of hatching of late eggs would become Sept. 9–23 or Oct. 1–15.

Size, 12–15 or more inches. The Myers (N.C., 1924) specimen, 15 inches, must have been near hatching. Ditmars gave 12.5 inches as hatching size. We have seen young 323, 327, 344, 353, 360, 379, 380 mm. shortly after hatching with no evidence of stripes; in the same lot was one 621 mm. with 4 dorsal stripes beginning to appear. "The young ones are spotted, and sometimes these spots remain conspicuous in older specimens too. I once saw quite a large specimen shot in a packing house, where it had been a regular guest for some time. This snake measured nearly 2 meters and had large yellow saddle blotches on its back" (Loennberg). Ditmars gave the length of the newly hatched young as 12½ inches.

Food: Rats, mice, bats, small mammals, birds and chickens and their eggs, tree frogs, snakes. Higgins (Gen., 1873), Boulenger (Gen., 1914), Bartram (Gen., 1791), Kingsley (Gen., 1885), Loennberg, Carr (Fla., 1940a).

Authorities:

Bateman, G. C. (Gen., 1897)

Brimley, C. S. (Gen., 1903)

Cope, E. D. (Fla., 1889)

Ditmars, R. L. (Gen., 1907)

Garman, S. (Gen., 1883)

Holbrook, J. E. (Gen., 1836–42)

Loennberg, E. (Fla., 1895)

Neill, W. T. (Fla., 1949a)

Perkins, C. B. (Gen., 1943)

1942, C. S. Brimley (N.C., 1941–42): "The North Carolina specimens show a strong tendency to blacken and become almost indistinguishable from the Black Chicken Snake and apparently the 2 species grade into one another where their ranges meet in this state."

1949a, W. T. Neill: "*E. o. quadrivittata* ranges from the lower Coastal Plain of the Carolinas southward into Florida and westward into the Gulf Coastal Plain. . . . Authentic records from Alabama and Mississippi are lacking. . . . The form is lacking throughout most of the western portion of the Georgia Coastal Plain."

Everglades rat snake, Orange rat snake

Elaphe obsoleta rossalleni Neill. Fig. 76; Map 24

(*E. obsoleta quadrivittata* Dowling, 1952 [Gen.]; Schmidt, *Check List,* 1953)

Other common names: Allen's rat snake; Everglades chicken snake.

Range: From s. Sarasota Co. and Glades Co. and s. of Lake Okeechobee to n. Monroe and Dade Cos., Fla. *Elevation*—Below 100 feet.

Size: Adults, 3–7 feet.

Distinctive characteristics: "A large snake, allied to *E. obsoleta quadrivittata;* ground color of adults rich orange, orange yellow, or orange-brown; dorsal and lateral stripes present but not sharply defined, of a dull gray-brown shade; a vague sublateral stripe, evident posteriorly, on the tips of the ventrals; chin and throat orange; venter bright orange or orange-yellow; scales with a glaucous sheen, at least anteriorly; iris orange; tongue bright red. The diagnostic coloration is assumed at an early age; the smallest specimen examined, 605 mm. total length, was readily identifiable as *rossalleni*" (Neill).

Fig. 75. *Elaphe o. quadrivittata:* 2, St. Petersburg, Fla., N. P. Fry and Son; 1,4,6,7, Eureka, Marion Co., Fla., C. C. Tyler; 3,5, Washington, D.C., Zoo.

Fig. 76. *Elaphe o. rossalleni,* s. of Lake Okeechobee, Fla., E. R. Allen.

Color: Three snakes from below Lake Okeechobee, Fla., received from E. R. Allen, Sept. 22, 1949. First snake: The middorsal band covering 4–5 scale rows is buckthorn brown with touches of ochraceous-orange. It is outlined by stripes 1–1½ scales wide of dresden brown to saccardo's umber. Below this is a lateral band crossing 4 scale rows of ochraceous-buff. The lower lateral stripe on rows 3 and 4 is olive-brown to snuff brown with the keels dark, differing in this last respect from scales of rows 1 and 2 and the upturned ends of the ventrals, which are uniformly buffy citrine with touches of primuline yellow. The side of the neck is aniline yellow and raw sienna to light cadmium. The top of the head from the front of the frontal back is antique brown, with the prefrontal and tip of head orange-citrine, which is the general color of the face. The lower half of upper labials and some of lower labials are aniline yellow to yellow ocher. The iris is tawny to ochraceous tawny. The undersides of rostral and chin shields are white, sparsely flecked with yellow. The belly is absolutely clear yellow except for a few cloudy spots on 20–30 plates ahead of vent. The cephalic portion of venter is strongly primuline yellow becoming caudad ochraceous-buff with touches of orange and, under the tail, orange-buff. The base and tip of tongue are mahogany red while the mid-portion is spotted with black.

Second snake: Male. The middorsal band is tawny-olive to sayal brown. The stripes outlining this area are 2–2½ scales wide, dresden brown. Below this each dorsolateral stripe is a lateral band of isabella color, honey yellow, or old gold. The lower lateral stripe, 2–3 or 3½ scales wide, is raw umber. All 4 stripes are marked at intervals with darker and slightly wider areas 2–3 scales long and 2–3 scales deep suggestive of spots, those of the dorsal stripe alternating with those of the lateral ones. The top of the head is sudan brown, the top of the snout, orange-citrine to buckthorn brown. The iris is tawny. The chin shields are white. The rear third of belly and underside of tail are cinnamon, passing cephalad through cinnamon-buff to yellow ocher. Side of neck below lateral stripe is ochraceous-orange or zinc orange. The tip, base, and underside of tongue are chestnut or mahogany red, the remainder black.

Habitat: Several botanists and others, such as Safford (Fla., 1919), have discussed the Everglades, but we restrict ourselves to Allen and Neill: "The greater part of the range lies within the Everglades and the adjoining Big Cypress Swamp. Within this area the form seems to reach its maximum abundance in northern Broward and southern Palm Beach Counties, in the Everglades. . . . The area given near the western end of Broward-Palm Beach County line is mostly one of saw-grass marsh, the characteristic habitat of the Everglades. Here the saw-grass (really a sedge, *Cladium Jamaicensis*) stretches monotonously for mile on mile. Farther east, the saw-grass marsh is interspersed with numerous clumps and thickets of wax-myrtle (*Myrica* *cerifera*) and beyond that one encounters marshy 'prairies'—areas overgrown with grasses and forbs than can tolerate considerable fluctuation in water level. Eastward of the 'prairies' are more saw-grass marshes, wax-myrtle thickets, deep water holes, cypress stands, and finally salt marsh. In this region, the rat snake's choice of habitat is as varied as the Everglades itself. The herpetologist who is familiar only with the more northern subspecies of *E. obsoleta* may be surprised to find *E. o. rossalleni* in the well-nigh treeless saw-grass marshes. It is even more surprising to find the snake in abundance about the 'prairies,' which fluctuate between extremes of flood and drought, and where the only shelter from the blazing sun is an occasional palmetto clump. Everglades rat snakes are also commonly found in wax-myrtles over the water and upon the branches of trees and shrubs bordering canals and roadways. Many are discovered by night in the 'Australian pine' trees (*Casuarina equisetifolia*) which have been planted along the highways of the area; others are found in roadside sheds, and also in the vicinity of bridges, where they secrete themselves in crevices between the road bed and the bridge supports."

Breeding: Oviparous. *Eggs*—The only record we know is from the source from which we have quoted freely, Allen and Neill: "A captive female *E. o. rossalleni* deposited 21 eggs on August 6, 1949. Three of the eggs were unusual in being pointed at one end, and also in being noticeably larger than any of the remainder, measuring 44.3x23.7, 42.4 by 24.4, and 43.5 by 24.1 mm. respectively. One of the eggs was unusually small, measuring only 28.7 by 19.7 mm. The remaining 17 eggs ranged in length from 19.1 to 23.0 mm., average 21.1 mm. The egg shells were mostly smooth and whitish in color, but bore light purplish mottlings upon which small granules or crystals could be seen. Apparently calcification of the shell was incomplete in this instance. . . . On several occasions the eggs of *E. o. rossalleni* were discovered in the wild, buried beneath leaves and debris on canal banks or islands —places generally affording protection from rising waters."

Young—According to Allen and Neill, they are readily identifiable at hatching but with the same basic pattern that all subspecific *obsoleta* young have. These young have ground color pinkish buff, first 3 dorsal blotches H-shaped. "The light pinkish orange or pinkish-buff ground color of the young *E. o. rossalleni* foreruns the brilliant orange of the adult and is unique among the species of *E. obsoleta*."

Food: Tree frogs, frogs, lizards, rats, mice, young rabbits, birds and their eggs, young ducks and chicks, hens' eggs. Allen and Neill.

Authorities:

Allen, E. R., and W. T. Neill, Jr.   Neill, W. T., Jr. (Fla., 1949a)
   (Fla., 1950)

1950, E. R. Allen and W. T. Neill, Jr.: "The above observations suggest that *E. o. rossalleni* is a form specifically adapted for life in the Everglades or regions of comparable habitat. Possibly as a result of its thorough adaptation, it is a common snake throughout much of its range. Thus, during the course of one night's canoe trip, 47 specimens were found lying in the branches of trees along a canal bank. Recently a professional collector brought 200 specimens to the Reptile Institute; other large consignments have been received in the past."

Gray pilot snake (12—Strecker 1915), Spotted chicken snake (12—Ditmars 1907)

Elaphe obsoleta spiloides (Duméril, Bibron, and Duméril) 1854. Fig. 77; Map 24

Other common names: Black snake; blotched chicken snake; blotched rat snake; checked pilot snake; (gray) chicken snake; gray Coluber; gray pilot; gray rat snake (10); live oak snake; racer; red-headed chicken snake; red-headed Coluber; (southeastern) rat snake; southern chicken snake; spotted gray snake; spotted pilot snake; white oak snake; wolf snake.

Range: Gulf Coast: w. Florida, s.w. Georgia, n. in Mississippi embayment to w. Kentucky, s. Illinois, and cent. Missouri s. through Oklahoma to e. Texas.—Ala.; Ark.; Fla.; Ga.; Ky.; La.; Miss.; Mo.; N.C.; Okla.; S.C.; Tenn.; Tex. *Elevation*—Seacoast to 1,000 feet; 2,000 feet (Dunn, Ala., 1920).

Size: Adults, 28–84 inches. Allen gives its length as 6 feet for n. Florida, and 4 other authorities give the same. There are 2 records for 5 feet, 2 for 7 feet, and others from 3 to 6.3 feet. Not until we understand this form better will we expand this topic. The longest we have seen was 4 feet. In 1953 Guidry (Tex., 1953) reported one 6 feet 11 inches.

Longevity: 4 years 6 months (Conant and Hudson, Gen., 1949); 12 years 5 months (Perkins, Gen., 1954).

Distinctive characteristics: Haltom's characterization is as good as any description: "Pale gray, with a series of large brown saddles on the back; on the neck these blotches are long and send out extensions at their corners, thus assuming an H-shaped formation. On each side of the body is a series of smaller blotches, and beneath this another, smaller series, at the edges of the abdominal plates. On the back and the sides, numerous scales show white edges when the skin is distended. . . . The head is gray, dotted with black. There is often a dark band in front of the eyes and usually a wide dark band from behind the eye to the angle of the mouth. . . . On the forward part of the body the abdomen is white irregularly blotched and peppery with gray; on the latter part of the abdomen is uniform, dark gray."

Color: A snake from Auburn, Ala., furnished by H. Good, May 1, 1928. Additional data are taken from a snake from Okefinokee Swamp, Ga., June 6, 1921. The background color is smoke gray, light olive-gray, or deep olive-buff, some of the scales with faint orange edges. The back is marked with 33 black-edged saddles of olive-brown, mars brown or verona brown. Alternating with these are elongate spots of the same on the 2nd to 6th row of scales. Alternating with this lateral row are squarish spots of deep olive-buff or hair brown, located on the 1st row of scales and extending onto the ends of the ventrals. These spots are usually spaced with intervals of 3 plates. On the neck and for 6 inches along the side, the 2nd row of spots is more or less linked, forming a stripe or band. The head is grayish olive. There is a vitta of deep grayish extending obliquely downward from the eye. The iris is pale vinaceous fawn, pale cinnamon pink, or pale pinkish buff with a network of lines just outside the pupil, but not covering the whole iris. The iris rim is shell pink. The cephalic under parts are clear cartridge buff, white, chalcedony yellow, or marguerite yellow. In the rear, they are heavily blotched with olive-brown, hair brown, or olive-buff, or may be clouded with blackish.

Abnormal coloration—Albinism. In 1946 Meacham (N.C., 1946) reported a pure white, red-eyed *E. o. obsoleta* from Stanfield, Stanley Co., N.C. It was 1,153 mm. long and a complete albino, according to Brimley.

Habitat: Many of the numerous habitats recounted are damp situations, water courses, swamp lands, alluvial lands, edges of streams, levees, cypress swamps, or dry flood plains. There are records of wooded areas, open woods, open or wild overgrown meadows and fields. Some have called it our most arboreal snake, finding it in bushes, in large trees, in tops of tall grasses and canes, and also in buildings.

Period of activity: *First appearance*—"On a warm day, Feb. 4, 1930, one was taken from the top of a high stump" (Allen, Miss., 1932). MVZ dates are April 18–Nov. 16. *Fall disappearance*—Oct. 25, 1925 (Force, Okla., 1930). *Hibernation*—"During the winter occasional specimens are to be discovered beneath bark and in hollow trees" (Allen, Miss., 1932).

Breeding: Oviparous. *Mating*—"On June 10, 1943, during troop movements on the Camp Sibert Military Reservation near Gadsden, Alabama, the writer noticed 2 gray rat snakes, *Elaphe obsoleta obsoleta* Baird and Girard, in a copulating position. Both were good sized individuals of approximately 4 feet" (Snyder).

In many ways one of the most interesting papers that has appeared on this form is "Mating activities between two subspecies of *Elaphe obsoleta*" by Johnson. Unfortunately we cannot include the whole paper. Excerpts follow: "A 62 inch male *Elaphe obsoleta confinis* (Baird and Girard) collected near Gramercy, Louisiana, March 26, 1948, and a 52 inch female *Elaphe obsoleta obsoleta* (Say) collected near Delaware, Ohio, April 9, 1948, were kept as cage mates from Apr. 9 to May 21 before evincing any interest in each other. On the night of May 21 both snakes were removed from the cage for approximately half an hour. Shortly after being returned to the cage, the male became very alert and began to court the female. . . . Courtship began at

9:30 P.M. and was continuous until 10:35 P.M. when coitus was effected. . . . Courtship and copulation were observed on subsequent occasions [May 22–May 28]."

Eggs—There are no distinct records except for 2 or 3 on its border intergrade areas. These are included under *E. o. obsoleta.* The habits of this form need attention. Whether our observation belongs in this subspecies or in *E. o. quadrivittata* (as Neill believes) may be questionable. "This is an oviparous snake, and 3 specimens taken June 1, 3, and 15, 1912 [in Georgia] had the eggs quite immature. One had 18 on the left side and 15 on the right side; another had 14 in all, 8 on the right side and 6 on the left side" (Wright and Bishop). Was Parker's Tennessee (1937) record of a small adult laying 7 eggs on July 11 an *E. o. spiloides?* The eggs were "53.8x22 mm. at beginning, later 52.8x25.6 mm. . . . The remainder hatched the middle of September." Guidry (Tex., 1953) gives 14 eggs July 30, hatching Oct. 3.

The mating of a male *E. o. spiloides* with a female *E. o. obsoleta* resulted as follows: "On July 5, 1948, the female deposited 8 eggs. The shells were white, faintly striated longitudinally and some of them had a narrow constriction encircling the shell at right angles to the long axis of the egg. . . . All the eggs were turgid. Measurements, plus or minus 1 mm., were: 45x24, 47x24, 48x22, 50x22, 50x24, 51x22, and 57x22. An accident prevented the hatching of these eggs" (Johnson).

Food: Mice, lizards, birds and their eggs, tree frogs. Funkhouser (Ky., 1925), Allen (Miss., 1932), Hurter (Mo., 1911), Meade, Wright and Bishop.

Authorities:

Beyer, G. E. (La., 1800)
Carr, A. F., Jr. (Fla., 1940a)
Corrington, J. D. (S.C., 1929)
Haltom, W. L. (Ala., 1931)
Hay, O. P. (Ind., 1892)
Johnson, R. M. (La., 1950)
Meade, G. F. (La., 1940)

Neill, W. T., Jr. (Fla., 1949a; Ga., 1947)
Rhoads, S. N. (Tenn., 1896)
Snyder, R. C. (Ala., 1944)
Welter, W. A., and K. Carr (Ky., 1939)
Wright, A. H., and S. C. Bishop (Ga., 1916)

We close this account with the period of great inquiry, 1890 to the present.

1892, O. P. Hay: "I conclude that *C. spiloides* is not more than a variety of *C. obsoletus,* and *C. confinis* is probably an individual variation with respect to its temporals."

1895, S. N. Rhoads: "A study of Professor Boulenger's diagnosis of this species corroborates my own observations and belief that individuals which may be severally classed under the varietal synonyms *alleghheniensis, lindheimeri,* and *spiloides* may be found associated in both Carolinian and Austroriparian districts."

1949a, W. T. Neill, Jr.: "Excluding temporarily certain Texan specimens, the gray rat snake ranges from Louisiana northward through the Mississippi

Fig. 77. *Elaphe o. spiloides,* Auburn, Ala., H. G. Good.

Fig. 78. *Elaphe o. williamsi,* Gulf hammock, Fla., D. Swindell to E. R. Allen.

Valley, filling in the territory not occupied by *obsoleta*. It also ranges eastward in the Gulf Coastal Plain to northwestern Florida, and is said to reach the Carolinas. . . . I doubt that it ranges much farther east (of Aiken and Barnwell counties, S.C.) . . . I feel certain *confinis* does not enter the Piedmont."

Gulf hammock rat snake (4), Gulf hammock chicken snake

Elaphe obsoleta williamsi Barbour and Carr 1940. Fig. 78; Map 24
(*E. obsoleta quadrivittata* Dowling, 1952 [Gen.]; Schmidt, *Check List,* 1953)

Other common names: West Florida chicken snake; oak rat snake.
Range: Gulf hammock of Levy Co. and s.w. Alachua Co., Fla. *Elevation*—Sea level to 100 feet.
Size: Adults, 41–60 inches.
Distinctive characteristics: "Apparently related to both *E. confinis* and *E. q. quadrivittata,* in squamation agreeing more closely with the latter (ventrals: *quadrivittata* 225–242, av. 235, *williamsi* 230–240, av. 235, *confinis* 234–250, av. 238; subcaudals: *quadrivittata* 85–100, av. 91, *williamsi* 86–93, av. 89, *confinis* 70–89, av. 81). Distinct in coloration and pattern; ground color white or gray (instead of tan as in *quadrivittata*), with black or very dark brown markings constituting a series of dorsal and lateral blotches (as in *confinis*) connected by 4 longitudinal stripes (as in *quadrivittata*)" (Barbour and Carr).
Color: Two snakes furnished by R. Conant of the Philadelphia Zoo and collected by Hyatt Verrill in Chiefland, Levy Co., Fla., in April and May, 1940. One snake was 45½ inches in body with tail of 11½ inches. The other was 48 inches in total length, of which 8¾ inches was tail. In the latter one, the background color of the back is vinaceous-buff, marked with 30 saddle spots on body and 14 on the tail. These dorsal spots are olive-brown, 10 or 11 scales wide and 4 scales long. The first 4 are connected at outer corners by olive-brown lines. The lateral spots on the 3rd to 6th rows, or more commonly 4th to 6th, are buffy brown. They break up toward the rear and tend to be linked in a linear row in forward parts. The top of the head bears no prominent bars or bands and is light grayish olive or smoke gray with most of the scales having narrow dark edges. The underside of the head and the labials are white or olive-buff, the labial sutures being black. The iris is vinaceous-buff. The venter is pale vinaceous-buff with blocks of vinaceous-fawn in the rear half. In the cephalic half the center of the venter is olive-buff flanked on either side by deep olive-buff spots located on 1st row of scales and on ends of ventrals in blocks of 2 ventrals.

Notes on the larger snake, May 2, 1941. The background is pale drab-gray with dorsal and lateral spots of benzo brown, fuscous, or clove brown. There are 31 dorsal spots on body and 17 on tail, connected at their corners with lines of brown for the full length of the body.

A snake from the Gulf Hammock in Florida, collected by David Swindell, July 2, 1950, and loaned us by E. R. Allen. Background pale olive-buff with dorsal saddles of wood brown to army brown, drab or snuff brown, 35 on body and 12 on tail. Those on the neck are 4 scales long, near the vent 2–2½ long. The intervals between saddles are in the cephalic half 5–6 scales long, in midbody 4–5, and toward the vent 3. On scale rows 9, 10, and the edge of 11 are clear-cut, continuous dorso-lateral stripes of warm sepia passing through the outer edges of the dorsal saddles, from neck to tip of tail. On scale rows 6, 7, 8, and the edges of 5 and 9 is a lateral band of pale olive-buff. On rows 3, 4, and 5 is the lower lateral stripe of natal brown, more intense where it crosses the lateral spots, with interval scales for about 3 scale lengths edged on the rear with ivory yellow. The top of head and face are between light drab and tea green. The iris is mineral gray. The underside of the head is ivory yellow with lower labials thinly edged with brown, as are the sutures between the upper labials 4–5 and 5–6. The forward half of the belly is ivory yellow with a few flecks of buffy brown for the first foot; mid-area heavily flecked with the same and the rear half of body solid olive-brown to the vent. The subcaudals are deep olive-buff flecked and edged with buffy brown.

Structure—Scale rows, 27. Body length 44½ inches plus 8-inch tail. Is the sharp horn on the end of the tail regenerated or natural? It is glistening bone brown.

Habitat: "The new snake seems to be restricted to the great Gulf Hammock, a well defined area of forest roughly 15 by 100 miles in area, situated in the counties from Levy to Pasco, which border the Gulf of Mexico in northwestern peninsular Florida. . . . The type series is from Lebanon in the south-central section of the county (Levy). In addition to these preserved specimens the author has seen 2 live individuals in the collection of Mr. Harold Williams from the mouth of the Withlacoochee River, and a badly mashed specimen on the highway about 12 miles north of Lebanon" (Barbour and Carr).

"Gulf Hammocks. A region of alternate hammocks, flatwoods, and swamps. The hardwood forests are not suitable for grazing as there is very little grass in them, and fire does not go through easily on account of a large part of the vegetation being the large leaf evergreens, and a consequent absence of a layer of pine needles and grass on the ground. Furthermore the dense shade keeps the forest floor so moist that fire does not readily run through it. The open pasture lands have been grazed and some of them burned over. The hardwoods, however, are almost in their natural condition, except for the relative scarcity of the larger game. Wild turkeys are common. Deer and bear are still found in the region, but of course they are not as abundant as they originally were. The region is but little settled and developed" (Watson).

Food: In 1954 Paul G. Pearson in his "Mammals of the Gulf hammock, Levy County, Florida" (*American Midland Naturalist,* **51**: 468–480) reported *E. o. williamsi* as an enemy of the flying squirrel; he also gave an instance of one of these snakes 4⅓ feet long which had eaten a cottontail rabbit, 11 inches long from "tip of snout to tip of hind foot."

Field notes: May 3, 1950: As we approach Lebanon, quite hammocky. Very dry. Hammock from Lebanon to Gulf hammock densest yet. Some *Magnolia grandiflorum* in blossom near Gulf hammock. We understand that it is about Gulf hammock where most of the specimens of *E. o. williamsi* have been taken. From Otter Creek northward the country is more open, piney, and barren, not so beautiful and hammocky as around Gulf hammock to Lebanon. We were told by some one that Chiefland was the center of this form's range, but we hold that the Lebanon-Gulf hammock country has its densest population.

Authorities:

Barbour, T., and A. F. Carr, Jr. (Fla., 1940)

Neill, W. T., Jr. (Fla., 1949a)

Watson, J. R. (Gen., 1926)

1949(a), W. T. Neill, Jr.: "There is no evidence that it occupies all the Gulf Hammock. It is not restricted to the Hammock in Levy County [Fla.]; specimens were collected in the eastern portion of the county. Mr. Allen also secured a specimen in southwestern Alachua County, and suggests that the Levy and Marion County records of *confinis* may have been based on *williamsi. Confinis* and *williamsi* are known from adjoining counties (*confinis* from Union and *williamsi* from Alachua County). The 2 forms can be distinguished by no morphological feature, and both display a whitish ground color and dark markings. In many eastern *confinis,* a lateral stripe is well developed along the entire length of the body. A dorsal stripe is often evident on the neck, and sometimes on the entire anterior half of the body. Furthermore, the more northern specimens of *williamsi* display short stripes, thus closely approaching *confinis.* The gap between the 2 forms is virtually bridged. I believe that *williamsi* is a derivative of the closely similar *confinis,* replacing it geographically; and that the two are conspecific. Further evidence of intergradation should be found in the region between northern Alachua and southern Taylor County, Florida."

Davis Mountain rat snake (4—Ditmars 1936),
Davis Mountain pilot snake (Strecker 1915)

Elaphe subocularis (Brown) 1901. Fig. 79; Map 23

Other common names: Davis Mt. Coluber; Trans-Pecos rat snake.
Range: Organ Mts., N.M., s.e. through Apache, Davis, and Chisos Mts.

to Valverde Co., Tex., and into Coahuila, Mex.—U.S.A.: N.M.; Tex. Mex.: Coahuila. *Elevation*—Most records 1,500 to 3,000 feet, possibly to 5,000 feet, 4,000 feet (Schmidt); 4,100 feet (Lewis, N. Mex., 1950).

Size: Adults, 20–72 inches.

Distinctive characteristics: *"Coluber subocularis* sp. nov. Plate XXIX. Specific characters: Head broad and flat on top. Body stout. Tail short. Rostral broad and low. A row of small accessory plates below the eye and preocular. Preocular in contact with the frontal. Temporals small and numerous. Scales in 31–35 rows. Anal divided. Body color yellow, with a series of black H-shaped dorsal blotches with pale centres, the lateral arms being continued by a paler shade, and forming a pair of longitudinal stripes. Head and belly unmarked" (Brown, Tex., 1901).

"Head and venter are without markings. There are 28 dark H-shaped spots on the back, and 11 dark markings on the tail. The first 5 of these are connected, forming a pair of lines on the neck, and the first 2 are recognizable only as slight expansions of these lines, not connected across the back. These lines are on the eleventh to thirteenth scale rows. Caudad the dark markings are shorter, more widely separated, and they may enclose a pair of light spots" (Schmidt).

Color: A snake caught amongst vegetation along the Rio Grande at San Vicente, Tex., May 23, 1934, died en route to Alpine, Tex., and was brought to us by T. J. Miller. The head plates are light grayish olive or citrine-drab. The neck and forward quarter of the body is clear deep olive-buff, and there the normal H-shaped saddles become 2 longitudinal black bands separated by 5 rows of scales. At intervals of about 1½ inches, these longitudinal bands widen as if to make H spots, and the intervening deep olive-buff scales are faintly outlined with the longitudinal stripe color. On the remainder of the body, the ground color of the sides becomes pale ecru-drab or vinaceous-buff. On the rear ⅔ or ⅘ of the body, there are about 24 H-shaped saddles, which are clove brown toward the head and more dusty or bone brown toward the tail. The bar of the H is formed by dark-edged interline scales, not solid black ones. The arms of the H of some of the middle and rear saddles may be 3 scales wide. The centers of these arms are white-edged scales. The end of one arm is connected with the next to form the longitudinal stripe of buffy brown. The areas between the bars of the H's are clear tilleul-buff patches, which may be margined at their bases with avellaneous or pinkish cinnamon. Alternating with the H spots and also opposite them in the almost clear lateral color are a few faint indications of lateral bars formed by dark edges on the lower sides of scales. The lateral scales are flecked with wood brown. The iris may be benzo brown or deep grayish olive with a smoke-gray pupil rim and a wash of pale smoke gray. The throat and underside of the neck are pure white; the rest of the venter is an opalescent olive-buff. The underside of the tail is somewhat blotched with clusters of buffy brown specks, which, in the rear half of the tail, become localized on the sutures between the two rows of subcaudals.

Habitat: (See "Authorities" below, in this account.) The best discussions of habitat and of plants and animals associated with this snake are by Lewis of Las Cruces, N.M.: "It was collected September 15, 1947, in an outbuilding near the eastern slope of the Organ Mountains, a few miles from San Augustine Pass, Doña Ana Co., New Mexico. The elevation is approximately 4100 feet, the annual rainfall less than 10 inches. The desert here is composed of coarse alluvial sands and gravels, with a sparse cover of grass. The prominent large plants are *Yucca elata, Prosopis juliflora* and various *opuntia*" (1948).

In 1950 Lewis gave a more detailed account of this habitat: "From the edges of the alluvial fans a gentler and smoother slope extends between the 4300 and 4000-foot contours. These slopes are also stream built and show yucca-mesquite-ephydra-grassland associations . . . interspersed between areas of creosote bush desert. The creosote (*Larrea divaricata*) forms pure stands on bare gravelly soil and is virtually devoid of associated reptiles except where diluted by other plants." In the noncreosote portions of this zone he gives 18 distinctive plants besides grasses as well as 4 lizards and 5 other snakes. "At about the 4000-foot contour, dunes of fine loose sand appear, . . . mostly fixed in place by crowns of mesquite or salt bush (*Atriplex canescens*)."

In 1950 Milstead, Mecham, and McClintock wrote: "This species appears to prefer the associations which have a large amount of rock coverage. Three specimens were collected: 2 males from the persimmon-shinoak and 1 female from the cedar-savannah association."

Authorities:

Bailey, V. (Tex., 1905)
Brown, A. E. (Tex., 1901, 1903)
Jameson, D. L., and A. G. Flury (Tex., 1949)
Lewis, T. H. (N. Mex., 1948, 1950)
Milstead, W. W., J. S. Mecham, and H. McClintock (Tex., 1950)

Schmidt, K. P. (Tex., 1925)
Schmidt, K. P., and D. W. Owens (Tex., 1944)
Schmidt, K. P., and T. F. Smith (Tex., 1944)
Smith, H. M. (Gen., 1939, 1941i)

1901, A. E. Brown: "On June 18, a large and handsome *Coluber* was received at the Zoological Gardens from Mr. E. Meyenberg, a resident collector of the Society at Pecos, Texas, which both in color and scutellation differs greatly from any species of the genus previously collected in the United States."

1903, A. E. Brown: "*Coluber subocularis* A. Brown. Eight specimens of this species have been collected, as far as is known. In addition to the 4 on which the original description was based, 2 more were received at the Zoological Gardens in 1902, and the New York Zoological Society has also received

2, one of which was courteously sent me after death by Mr. R. L. Ditmars. The 3 now in my possession have the scales in 33 rows, and the upper labials 10–11. All seem to have come from the Davis Mountains."

1905, V. Bailey: Under *Crotalus confluentus* Bailey says: "In 1902 at a place 75 miles northwest of Pecos, I met one of his men bringing in a wagon-load of live animals, among them numerous snakes and lizards which had been collected along the base of the Guadalupe Mountains, mainly in Upper Sonoran zone, but probably also in Transition. As these specimens apparently were sent out as collected at Pecos, in Lower Sonoran zone, the difficulty of using Meyenberg's material for zonal work is apparent."

1925, K. P. Schmidt: "The present specimen comes from McKilligan's Canyon, altitude about 4000 feet, Franklin Mts., El Paso County, Texas, collected May 5, 1924 by Col. M. L. Crimmins, who has done much to further our knowledge of the snakes of western Texas."

1944, K. P. Schmidt and T. F. Smith: "Two specimens of this little-known species were collected by the junior author in 1937, one at Wilson Ranch, at the west base of the Chisos, the other in Juniper Canyon on the other side of the range."

1949, D. L. Jameson and A. G. Flury: "Collections were made in the following rocky associations of the Plains belt: catclaw-tobosa, 1; catclaw-cedar, 4. In the Roughland belt specimens were taken in 2 associations as follows: catclaw-grama, 6; and stream-bed, 1. . . . In view of the scarcity of published records, it seems worthwhile to note some characters evident in our series of 8 males and 4 females. . . . All our specimens were taken between sunset and about 10 P.M. while they were apparently foraging; none was found with obvious food lumps in it. These snakes seemed to prefer rather calm nights, and surprisingly none was found on the several moist or rainy nights of the trip. The light from the gasoline lanterns did not seem to disturb them, and they made little attempt to bite or escape when captured. One specimen was first located by the reflection of the rays of an electric headlight from its eyes."

Green rat snake (3—Ditmars 1936), **Mexican green snake** (Van Denburgh 1922)

Elaphe triaspis intermedia (Boettger) 1883. Fig. 80; Map 23
(Formerly *Elaphe chlorosoma*)

Another common name: Mexican green rat snake (Pope 1934).

Range: Mountains of Pacific drainage from Santa Rita Mts. to Isthmus of Tehuantepec.—U.S.A.: Ariz. Mex.: Chihuahua and 6–9 other states. *Elevation*—In Arizona 2,000 to 6,000 feet. Colima City, Mex., 1,600 feet (Oliver); above 7,000 feet (Gadow, Gen., 1905).

Size: Adults, 24–50 inches.

Fig. 79. *Elaphe subocularis:* 1–4, San Vicente, Tex., T. Miller; 5, Organ Mts., N.M., photo by T. H. Lewis. The black specks on 3 and 4 are due to warm developer.

Fig. 80. *Elaphe triapsis intermedia,* Ruby, Ariz., D. H. Fairchild to C. T. Vorhies.

Distinctive characteristics: A medium to large, smooth (median scales faintly keeled), olive, gray, green or citrine snake; adults unspotted; young have 57 or 58 dorsal spots (Smith and Taylor) or 66 (Hall); under parts mainly colonial buff or cream with some yellow, dorsal scales 31–39 rows; ventrals 247–281, caudals 88–120; 1 preocular; 2 postoculars; 8 or 9 upper labials; 10–11 (12) lower labials; eye over 4–5 or 5–6 upper labials; temporals 2 + 3 + 4. (See "Structure" below.)

Color: A snake caught by D. H. Fairchild near Ruby, Ariz., one or two days before Sept. 28, 1934, and sent to Vorhies, University of Arizona, Tucson, Ariz. It had just shed. The cephalic fifth of the dorsum is olive lake or sulphine yellow, becoming thereafter buffy citrine or dull citrine. This is the general ground color. On the first 4 rows of scales is a row of indistinct spots of olive-ochre or wax yellow. This row alternates with a row of larger spots on 7th to 13th rows of scales. This second row in turn alternates with faintly dark-edged dorsal saddles about 12 scales in transverse diameter and 1 or 2 scales longitudinally. There are about 76 of these indistinct saddles on the body proper, and very indistinct ones on the tail. The dorsal saddles have black cephalic margins. Toward the rear for ⅓ the body, not counting tail, these saddles are broken in the middle and come to be 2 rows of staggered (or alternating) spots about 4 scales wide transversely. Where these saddles are broken, there is an ill-defined vertebral of citron yellow. The 2 lateral rows of spots are not black-edged in front. The throat and neck are white, so also are the lower labials and upper labials except for their dorsal edges and the front 4, which are the color of the dorsum of the head. The top of the head, olive lake or sulphine yellow, is marked with rather typical *Elaphe* spots. The prefrontal bar is old gold. The longitudinal band from the frontal angle onto the supraocular is old gold. The most conspicuous mark is a small rectangular block of old gold or buckthorn brown on the rear of the frontal; this block is dark-edged in front. On the rear end of the median parietal suture, a bar of old gold or buckthorn brown extends forward ⅛ or ¼ inch, dividing and forming a Y, each arm of which extends obliquely forward onto each parietal plate. This Y-shaped spot is somewhat dark-edged, and, with the posterior frontal spot, makes up the most distinctive marks of the snake. Obliquely downward in a posterior direction from the rear end of the parietal plate is a spot 2 scales wide. Then beginning less than ¼ inch caudad of the parietals are 2 longitudinal neck spots about 16 scales long. The iris is ecru-olive or deep olive-buff. The venter is barium yellow near the vent, straw yellow at the tip of the tail. The rest of the venter has a colonial buff wash. The lowest row of lateral spots usually expands over onto the end of one belly plate and the edge of another, forming ecru-olive areas. There is usually between these areas one white-ended gastrostege, which bears further in on the belly—a squarish spot of ecru-olive. This gives an indistinct checkered arrangement on the sides of the belly. In the middle of the belly plates may be 1 or 2 faint, transverse, colonial buff washes. The whole belly is iridescent.

Günther's description—upper parts greenish olive, each scale being black-edged—does not apply to all of the scales. No doubt he had alcoholic specimens for his description.

Structure: A slender yellowish green snake with a conspicuously slender neck and elongate head and a long and square snout. The eyes are quite protuberant; pupils round. The scales are smooth; even the dorsal scales have hardly any trace of keel. Prefrontals more than half the frontal. The internasals about half the prefrontal; loreal longer than deep; preocular very large with an upward forward hook, contacts frontal; postoculars 2; temporals 2 + 3 + 4; upper labials right 8, left 9; eye over 5 and 6 on each side; lower labials right 10, left 11; anal divided; ventrals 279; caudals 103.

Field notes: (We have exposed ourselves to *E. triaspis intermedia* country from Ruby, Ariz., through the Santa Ritas to the Huachuca Mts., but never found one ourselves. We've quizzed Dr. Pilsbry and our Arizona friends and correspondents on how to find one, but it has not been our good fortune to succeed.)

June 9–13, 1934, Ramsay Canyon, Ariz.: Mr. James has seen green bush snakes 3 or 4 times in the heat of the day and on hot days. One was gliding over an agave and over into the tops of some lower bushes. Once he set a trap for a squirrel which was eating chicken feed. In the trap he caught one of these chicken snakes. Was it *Elaphe chlorosoma?* I doubt that he meant *Oxybelis.*

July 27, 1946: Mrs. Dorothy Sprung of Sonoita writes that a neighbor, Orion Enzenberg, brought in a small snake to be sent us and told them of a large green snake which goes through the tops of the trees "like a bat out of hades."

Authorities:

Günther, A. C. L. G. (Gen., 1885–1902)

Hall, C. W. (Gen., 1951)

Oliver, J. A. (Gen., 1937)

Smith, H. M. (Gen., 1941i; Tex., 1943a)

Smith, H. M., and E. H. Taylor (Gen., 1945)

Stone, W. (*Proc. Acad. Nat. Sci. Phila.,* 43)

Taylor, E. H. (Gen., 1940b)

Taylor, E. H., and I. W. Knobloch (Ariz., 1940)

1885–1902, A. C. L. G. Günther: *"Coluber chlorosoma,* sp. n. . . . Hab. Mexico, Atoyac in Vera Cruz, Amula in Guerrero (H. H. Smith), San Ramon 1500 feet (A. C. Buller)." (We regret that we were not in college early enough to know the peerless tropical collector, H. H. Smith, who later was a friend of Löding and others in Alabama. He came from a very talented family of Manlius, N.Y.)

1911, W. Stone (p. 231): First U.S. record. "17,895. Santa Rita Mountains,

Arizona. 1910. Dr. H. A. Pilsbry. 17,909. Agua Caliente Cañon, Santa Rita Mountains, Arizona, 6,000 feet. 1910. Dr. H. A. Pilsbry. The identity of these specimens was confirmed by Dr. Leonard Stejneger who kindly examined one of them. The species was not previously known from north of the Mexican boundary."

1941(i), H. M. Smith: "It is my belief that this specimen (E.H.T.-H.M.S. No. 5193—spotted) represents the juvenile pattern of *chlorosoma,* the young of which were previously unknown. In *Elaphe* pattern changes such as are indicated in *chlorosoma* are known in *bairdii* and *quadrivittata,* although in these species the spots are replaced by stripes (which may be faint) in adults. . . . This conclusion has been reached also by Dr. Taylor, who writes, 'I have examined the *chlorosoma* specimens and find, as you presume, that the youngest shows spots on the body, and likewise traces on the head of the markings of the specimen I recently discussed as *E. mutabilis.* I believe you are correct in assuming that specimen is the heretofore unidentified young of *chlorosoma.'*"

1945: H. M. Smith and E. H. Taylor recorded it from Chihuahua, Colima, Guanajuato, Guerrero, Jalisco, Michoacán, Oaxaca, Zacatecas, and perhaps Querétaro and San Luis Potosí.

1952: H. G. Dowling (Gen.), following R. Mertens, pronounces *E. chlorosoma* to be *E. triaspis intermedia* (Boettger).

Western fox snake (4), Fox snake (66—Cragin 1881)

Elaphe vulpina vulpina (Baird and Girard) 1853. Fig. 81; Map 23

Other common names: Bull snake; copperhead; corn snake; Fox racer; Fox's black snake (Smith 1879); hardwood rattler; pine snake; prairie fox snake; pilot; racer; red-headed Coluber; spotted adder; timber snake.

Range: E. Indiana, through Illinois to n. peninsula of Michigan, w. to s.e. South Dakota and e. Nebraska.—Ill.; Ind.; Ia.; Ky.; Mich.; Minn.; Mo.; Neb.; S.D.; Wis. *Elevation*—500 to 1,500 feet.

Size: Adults, 32–63 inches.

Distinctive characteristics: "A large *Elaphe* with a reddish or reddish-brown head. Pattern consisting of a medium series of large chocolate or black blotches 33 to 51 (av. 40.9) in number and flanked on each side of body by 2 alternating rows of smaller blotches. Ground color above yellowish or light brown; belly yellow, checked with black. Distinguished from *E. v. gloydi* by the greater number and smaller size of the dorsal blotches (av. 34.5 in *gloydi*); from *E. o. obsoleta* by its different coloration and smaller number of ventrals (216 or less in *vulpina;* 221 or more in *obsoleta*); and from *E. laeta* by the lack of forward extensions from the 1st dorsal blotch which traverse the parietals and unite on the frontal" (Conant).

Color: A snake from Cedar Falls, Iowa, sent by H. G. M. Jopson, May 29, 1936. This handsome snake, at first appearance, in the color of the top of the head, and in its vigorously shaking tail, reminds one of a darkly colored pine snake. The back is marked with 41 saddles on the body and 18 on the tail if the tip is counted. These dorsal saddles, which are mummy brown or raw umber, cover 13 scales transversely and $3\frac{1}{2}$ longitudinally. There are 2 longitudinal spots just back of the parietals before the transverse saddles begin. The intermediate body color is dark olive-buff, isabella color, or buffy olive. On the sides it becomes lighter and grayer, namely deep olive-buff, and almost olive-buff in the neck region. The skin between the scales of this intermediate background area is light pinkish cinnamon or pinkish buff. On the sides, on the 3rd to 7th rows of scales, is a series of spots which alternate with the dorsal saddles. They are about $1\frac{1}{2}$ scales longitudinally and 5 scales deep, and are orange-citrine or dresden brown. Again alternating with this lateral row and located on the 1st and 2nd or 1st to 3rd rows is a row of indistinct but similarly colored small spots, less than 1 scale longitudinally. On the forward part of the body, the dorsal saddles extend to this lower lateral row, the extensions being orange-citrine or dresden brown. The top of the head is buffy olive or isabella color. The rim of the pupil is massicot yellow or ivory yellow surrounded by a circular band of honey yellow, which merges into an outer circle of buffy olive or isabella color. The upper labials bear a few dark punctae, and the edge of the rear ones is honey yellow or chamois. The lower labials are cream-buff and have a few dark punctae at the sutures. The underside of the head is cartridge buff or cream-buff. The chin and the first 4 or 5 ventrals are immaculate. The spots of the lower lateral series become blackish in the lower portions, and form square spots, each covering the ends of 1 or 2 ventrals. Besides these lateral rows of black spots on the belly, there extends down the middle about 2 rows of square or rectangular spots. These more or less alternate in the forward part, become grouped in more or less irregular pairs in the middle, less regular toward the rear, till on the tail there is just 1 spot to each subcaudal. The effect is a prominently checkered belly. The ground color is barium yellow or citron yellow in the neck region, becoming straw yellow or massicot yellow on the rear parts.

Abnormal coloration—Albinism. In 1944 Keegan recorded an albino from Iowa.

Habitat: This inhabitant of prairies, open country, building yards, briar patches, and copses has been called essentially a ground snake, rarely a tree climber. It is harmless, although its tail vibration in dead leaves has frightened many. In his well-known paper of 1938 Schmidt considered this form "a postglacial spread, favored by the impoverishment of the fauna of the coniferous forest during the glacial retreat." A hasty review of habitat notes since 1925 reveals "high side of a hill," "rolling prairie habitat," "partial to the vicinity of marshes and bodies of water," "coiled on a mouse nest in a rotten stump near the edge of a shallow pond," "grain fields," "edges of woods," "near houses and barns," "dune country of Lake Michigan," "stream valleys," and a variety of other places.

Breeding: Oviparous. *Mating*—"On the second of June 1940, in a roadside park near Hermansville, Michigan, I noticed a pair of fox snakes. . . . That evening, while I was holding the pair (one in each hand), the male, with a sudden movement, grasped the female by the back of her neck with his jaws and began to coil himself about her until their anal regions were together. . . . Again on June 14, 1940, at 7 p.m., as I was observing the snakes in their cage, the male became rather excited and grasped the female at the back of the head. . . . During the copulation the male continuously held fast to the posterior head region of the female. . . . On July 7, a very similar copulation between the pair was observed" (Carpenter, Mich., 1948). This is not unlike the observations of A. S. Winder of Chicago, as related to Davis (Gen.) in 1936. Therein at first the male had the female's head in his maw, but afterwards seized the female behind the head. No copulation was observed.

Eggs—Number, 7–29. We give 6 excerpts: "Fox snakes lay eggs to the number of 18–20 in rotten stumps and hollow logs and in sawdust piles" (Funkhouser). "One of these snakes in our cages laid 13 eggs on July 24. They were white in color and of a firm, leathery texture and adhered firmly together, with the exception of one that had been deposited separately. The shape was elongate, and somewhat variable. The width of the eggs was, in all cases, $\frac{7}{8}$ of an inch but the length varied as may be seen. The eggs were plump when laid, but the dry air caused them to shrink before being photographed. The young hatched in 54 days and were from $9\frac{1}{2}$–11 inches long" (Guthrie). Schmidt and Davis (Gen., 1941) report a female laying 8 eggs in the first week of July. They give the eggs as $1\frac{3}{4}$x1 inch, the eggs adherent. Hatching came in September and October with the young $10\frac{1}{2}$ inches long. "During late June and early July a considerable number of eggs are deposited; generally in hollow of a rotting stump" (Hudson and Davis, Neb., 1941). "The number of eggs in a clutch may vary from 15–29 and average about 44 by 24 mm." (Hudson). "The only 3 clutches on record were laid by captive females and had 7, 7, and 13 eggs in them" (Pope). Time of deposition, last of June to July 24.

Size, 1.6–2.4 inches x .8–1.1 inch. Until July 24, 1950, we gave the size as 1.6–1.9 inches x .8–1.1 inch, but 6 of 7 eggs we had in our home on that date were 51x28 mm., 49x24, 50x22, 50x22, 55x23, 60x20 mm., respectively. These eggs, the only ones we have seen laid, were those of a small female sent us by Dr. Hobart M. Smith. This snake was taken 4 miles s.e. of St. Joseph, Champaign Co., Ill., and by July 23, 1950, the day of its arrival, it had laid 3 eggs in transit and it laid 4 more through the next day. The snake and eggs

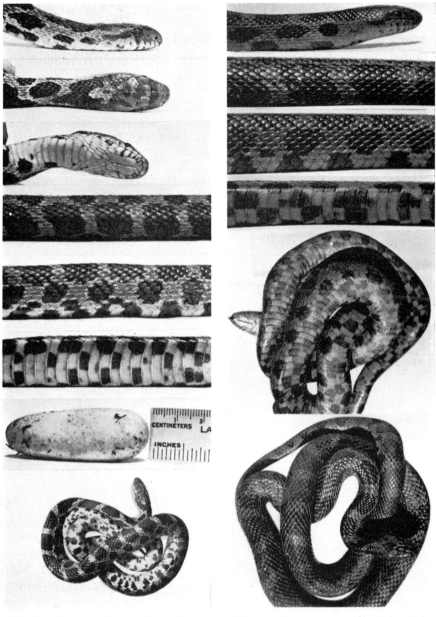

Fig. 81. *Elaphe vulpina vulpina,* St. Joseph, Ill., H. Smith.

Fig. 82. *Elaphe v. gloydi,* Cedar Point Marsh, Toledo, Ohio, R. Conant.

were returned to Dr. Smith. These eggs were marked with no concretions of any sort. Two were separate, 4 agglutinated. The last 4 had surfaces somewhat crackled on one side. The same summer we also received a small female from T. B. Tebo, Jr., Ames, Ia., who received the snake July 29. On July 20 this female had laid 9 eggs and since then had refused food.

Young—Hatching time, Aug. 25 (Minton, Ind., 1944); through September into October (Schmidt and Davis, Gen., 1941). Size, 9.5, 10.5, 11, and 12 inches. We ourselves have seen August and September captures from 300 to 330 mm. long.

Food: Small vertebrates, young rabbits, rats, mice, gophers, ground squirrels, insects; eggs and young ground birds. Higley (Wis., 1889), Hay, Blatchley, Evermann and Clark, Over, Funkhouser, Guthrie, Metcalf (Gen., 1930).

Authorities:

Blatchley, W. S. (Ind., 1899)

Conant, R. (Gen., 1940)

Evermann, B. W., and H. W. Clark (Ind., 1920)

Funkhouser, W. D. (Ky., 1925)

Guthrie, J. E. (Ia., 1926)

Hay, O. P. (Ind., 1892)

Hudson, G. E. (Neb., 1942)

Keegan, H. L. (Ia., 1944a)

Over, W. H. (S.D., 1923)

Pope, C. H. (Ill., 1944)

Schmidt, K. P. (Gen., 1938)

Eastern fox snake, Fox snake

Elaphe vulpina gloydi Conant 1940. Fig. 82; Map 23

Other common names: Ontario fox snake; hardwood rattler.

Range: N. Ohio, s.e. Michigan and Ontario bordering Georgian Bay, Lake Huron, and Lake Erie.—U.S.A.: Mich.; O. Can.: Ont. *Elevation*—Mainly 500 to 1,000 feet.

Size: Adults, 36–66 inches; somewhat larger than *E. v. vulpina*.

Longevity: 4 years 2 months, 4 years 1 month, 3 years 1 month (Gen., Kauffeld, 1951).

Distinctive characteristics: "A large snake, similar in pattern and scutellation to *Elaphe vulpina vulpina* Baird and Girard, but differing chiefly in the smaller number and larger size of its dorsal body blotches. These average 34.5 as compared with 40.9 in *vulpina*, and anteriorly they are 4, 5, or 6 scales in length, as compared with 3 or 4 (and more rarely 5) scales in length in *vulpina*. The number of tail blotches also is less in *gloydi*. Specimens of *gloydi* attain a somewhat greater maximum length and appear to be more robust in form" (Conant, 1940).

Color: A snake from Long Point, Ont., Can., collected by R. M. Roecker, and described Aug. 11, 1949. It has 34 black dorsal saddles on the body and 11 on the tail. They are 3½–4 scales longitudinally and cross 15 scale rows in the cephalic portion, and 10–12 toward the tail. A few on the neck region may be 5 to 5½ scales long, and from the 1st saddle, 2 black bars extend forward, but do not reach the parietals. The interspaces between the saddles are 2 scales or less longitudinally, and are flecked with capucine orange to mikado orange on a barium yellow to chalcedony yellow ground, while the center of each scale is black or heavily and closely flecked with black. Below the ends of the dorsal saddles the interspaces have little of the orange and are largely deep olive-gray. The sides bear 2 alternating rows of large black spots, the lower one on scale rows 1 and 2 and extending onto the ventrals. The upper lateral row extends from the upper edge of the 2nd scale row to half or more of the 7th row. These spots cover 6–8 scales and in a few cases merge into the spots of the lower row. The interspaces of the lower lateral series bear few dark flecks, being almost clear barium yellow to chalcedony yellow like the background color of the belly. The top of the head is buffy citrine or isabella color to buffy olive with an obscure dark bar on the rear of the prefrontals and an irregularly rounded dark spot on the rear of frontal and near the interparietal suture. On the side of the head, the upper labials are flesh ocher, with their sutures except for the 6th unmarked with black; the face and back of eye ochraceous-tawny or cinnamon-rufous. There is a cloudy area on the upper edge of the 6th upper labial and lower 1st temporal, making an obscure postocular spot. The eye is yellowish citrine with a cream pupil rim. Ventrally, the neck, lower chin, and lower labials are white to cream with flecks of mikado orange. The anterior chin shields, mental, and first 2 lower labials bear a few fine flecks of black. The sutures of the first 6 lower labials are black, and opposite the 6th a black line extends as an upper labial suture to the eye. The background color of the belly is barium yellow to chalcedony yellow, which caudad of the midbody is washed with orange-pink, becoming on the underside of tail orient pink. The whole venter bears black rectangular spots arranged in an irregular checkerboard, a spot often being on 2 or 3 adjoining plates.

Notes: The body of the snake is 47 inches long, the tail 10½; the circumference at midbody 4½ inches.

Habitat: This harmless timid snake has been taken in sandy areas, pine lands, lake beaches, and marshes. Though generally considered a ground snake, several have recorded it as a splendid climber in trees.

In 1938(a) Conant (O.) gave the habitat and habits of this form: "The fox snake is abundant in and near the extensive lake marshes from Toledo to east of Sandusky and it also occurs on the Lake Erie Islands. In the marshes it was taken among the reeds, on muskrat houses and on the nearby dikes and beaches. It often entered the water and appeared to be able to take care of itself in an aquatic environment. . . . It was also found in fields, along the streams which flow into the marshes and on the highways. . . . At Catawba Island, Ottawa County, and on the islands it was taken in woods and on the cliffs. Most were discovered in the open, but a number were beneath rocks, boards and other shelter. One or two were in low bushes."

Breeding: Oviparous. *Eggs*—Number, 7–29. 7, 17, Logier; 9, Evans and Roecker, Triplehorn; 10, 11, 29, Conant and Bridges; 11, 14, 21, Conant and Downs; 11, 15, 17, 29, Conant; 13, Evans; 21, Schmidt and Davis. Time of deposition, June 20 to Aug. 5; June 24, 1933; July 17, 1929; July 19, 1930; July 21, 1938; July 23, 1938; July 29, 1929; July 30, 1938. Size, 1.2–2.0 inches. 29 to 58.5 mm. x 14.5–30 mm.; 36–47.7 mm. x 24–27 mm.; 38.1–58.5x22.3–25.8 mm.; 29.1–47.2x27.3 mm. (Conant and Downs); 44x24 mm.; 40–50x20–30 mm. (Conant, O., 1938a).

"Common on the beaches, where the eggs are deposited under the dead wood. Apparently several individuals place their eggs in the same site, as on one occasion 3 specimens and half a bushel of eggs were found in a section of log. On emission the eggs are coated with an adhesive fluid which causes them to adhere and form masses" (Patch). This half bushel of eggs reminds us of the Hechts' experience of 1949 (see "Field notes" below).

Conant (1938a) gave notes on 5 females: (a) ♀ July 29, 1929, laid 15 eggs averaging 44x24 mm. These hatched Oct. 19, 1929; young 10½–11 inches long. (b) ♀ laid 17 eggs July 17, 1929. (c) ♀ laid 15 eggs July 17, 1929. (d) ♀ laid 11 eggs July 19, 1930. ♀ s 51, 49, 50, 45½ inches long. (e) ♀ laid 29 eggs June 24, 25, 1933, eggs 40–50 mm. x 20–30 mm.

Conant and Downs: ♀ s collected by R. H. Mattlin. (a) ♀ laid July 20, 1938; 14 eggs 36–47x24–27 mm. (b) ♀ laid July 21, 1938; ♀ 1229 mm. 11 eggs. 38.1–58.5 mm. x 22.3–25.8 mm. 5 hatched Sept. 15. 300–333 mm. long. (c) ♀ July 23, 1938 laid 21 eggs. 29.1–47.2x22.9–27.3 mm.

Mattlin: ♀ 1,381 mm. laid 20 eggs Aug. 5, 6. On Sept. 18–20 45 days later hatched; no egg tooth. Sizes 264–309 mm.

Logier (Ont., 1939): "Reproduction is by eggs which are deposited in decaying logs, manure heaps, sawdust piles, etc. in July. The number of eggs in a clutch varies and we have counts ranging from 7 to 17. Often a large number of eggs may be found together in one nest, the product of several females. . . . Hatching requires about 7 or 8 weeks."

Evans and Roecker: "On July 31, 1949, the writers found 2 clutches of eggs under logs on the sand dunes approximately 25 feet from the lake shore and about 5 feet above water level. The cover is very limited on the dunes and other egg clutches were found destroyed by predators. . . . Of the 2 undisturbed clutches found one contained 9 eggs, the other 13. The eggs adhered to one another in an irregular pattern, and an average egg measured 20 mm. in diameter and 39 mm. in length. . . . The advanced clutch hatched the last week of August and the newborn snakes averaged 320 mm. in length. The other clutch hatched on Sept. 19 and the snakes averaged 270 mm. in length."

Young—Hatching time, last of August–Oct. 19. Records of 45–78 days from deposition to hatching. Size, 10–14 inches.

Food: Vermin, rats, mice, young rabbits, frogs, toads, earthworms, birds (fledglings, adults, eggs). Cope (Gen., 1900), Surface (Pa., 1906), Logier (Ont., 1925, 1931), Conant (1938a), Hay (Ind., 1892).

Field notes: Aug. 25, 1949, Ithaca, N.Y.: Max and Bessie M. Hecht just arrived with a large package of snake eggs in the process of hatching. They are *E. v. gloydi,* which they found near the northern shore of Lake Erie, in Ontario, at Robineau Bay Point. They were in and under a rotting log, and more or less attached to each other. The mass must have contained clutches of several snakes. We await a more complete report from the lucky finders.

Authorities:

Conant, R. (O., 1938a; Gen., 1940)

Conant, R., and A. Downs, Jr. (Gen., 1950)

Evans, H. E., and R. E. Roecker (Ont., 1951)

Hecht, M. and B. M. (unpublished)

Logier, E. S. (Ont., 1931, 1939)

Mattlin, R. H. (O., 1948)

Patch, C. L. (Ont., 1919)

Ruthven, A. G. (Mich., 1911)

PROBLEMATICAL FORM

North Carolina Banks rat snake, Barbour and Engels chicken snake

Elaphe obsoleta parallela Barbour and Engels 1942. Fig. 83; Map 24
(*E. obsoleta quadrivittata* Dowling, 1952 [Gen.]; Schmidt, *Check List,* 1953)

Range: Shackelford Banks, Carteret Co., N.C.

Distinctive characteristics: "There is nothing peculiar about the squamation. Its color, however, is very distinct. The straw-color of the typical form, is replaced by a dull gray; the bands are evident, the lower lateral band on the posterior part of the body becoming a broad, dark zone 3 to 3½ scales wide; along the dorsum the upper lateral bands are connected by cross commissures which give the specimen in life a distinctly ladderback appearance, very like the aspect of *Elaphe williamsi.* Unfortunately, although the specimen was received in Cambridge alive, it was just about to shed and the peculiar and conspicuous pattern is much less evident now, since a considerable portion of the body has desquamated" (Barbour and Engels).

Field notes: We have never collected on the "banks" or "bars" of North Carolina. When we examined *Lampropeltis g. stictoceps, Natrix s. engelsi, E. o. parallela,* and *Natrix c. taeniata* for photographs in Cambridge, we made several notes on this form. The only notes we now find are "Gray; truly an *E. quadrivittata* derivative; the dark of back not in conspicuous saddles like *E. o. confinis;* cross commissures show slightly; will it prove eventually to be a good form?"

Authorities:

Barbour, T., and W. L. Engels (N.C., 1942)

Engels, W. L. (N.C., 1942)

Neill, T. W. (Fla., 1949a)

1942, T. Barbour and W. L. Engels: "The junior author writes under date of May 18, 1942, as follows: 'I agree that the differentiation of these forms must have been rapid, perhaps even more rapid than you suggest. As nearly as I can make out from a study of the Johnson and de Beaumont theory of development of these shore bars, these islands must be post-Pleistocene in origin, and probably never were part of the mainland, or at most indirectly connected as now through Cape Henry and probably formerly also at the southern end of the series just below Beaufort, North Carolina. This is the view I am expressing in my paper on the Okracoke vertebrate fauna which is now ready to send away. It will appear in the *American Midland Naturalist,* probably in November.' The senior author had suggested the possibility that these barrier islands had received their fauna at the time of the last glacial episode, when there was sufficient water tied up in the polar ice cap to have reduced the level of the ocean sufficiently to have made all these islands part of the mainland. In either event we have evidence here of how rapid may be distinct and fundamental changes of coloration and, in one case, modification of habits within a relatively short period of time."

1949: T. W. Neill under *obsoleta-quadrivittata* intergrades wrote: "A single such intergradient specimen from Carteret County, North Carolina, evidently afforded the basis for the description of *E. quadrivittata parallela* (Barbour and Engels 1942; 103). The type differs in no way from Georgia-Carolina intergradient material. The name *parallela* is to be relegated to the synonymy along with *lemniscatus.*"

In 1950, through conversations and the kindly offices of William L. Engels at the University of North Carolina, we secured a better idea of the environment of this form and the circumstances of its description. He, Dundee, and Loomis tried to secure us a live specimen in the summer of 1950. We honestly believe it should stay in the problematical category, though we agree with Neill and Dowling that it will finally reside within *C. o. quadrivittata.*

HORN SNAKES

Genus *FARANCIA* Gray (Fig. 22)

Size, very large, 20–84 inches; form cylindrical, heavy; head not distinct from neck; tail short ending in horny spine; anal divided; scale rows 19 at midbody, smooth, without pits, almost square; labials 3 and 4 contact orbit; no preocular; loreal and prefrontal contact orbit; postoculars 2 (1–3); nasal single, semidivided; upper labials 6–8; lower labials (7) 8–10; internasal *single* (see *Abastor*); several rows of gulars between chin shields and ventrals; ventrals 168–208; caudals 31–55. Hemipenis—"bifurcate with moderate number of dentate calyces, and numerous spines" (Cope, Gen., 1900). Synonyms: *Callopisma, Calopisma, Coluber, Helicops, Homalopsis, Hydrops.*

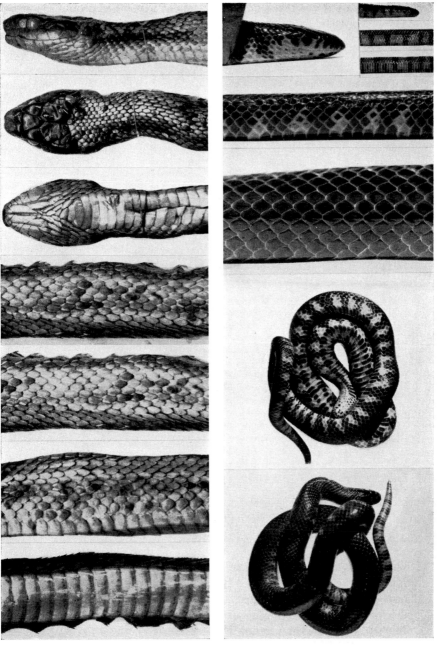

Fig. 83. *Elaphe o. parallela,* MCZ, photos of type by G. Nelson.

Fig. 84. *Farancia abacura abacura:* 1,5,7,8, Gainesville, Fla., O. C. Van Hyning and A. H. Wright; 2,3,4, young, Auburn, Ala., H. G. Good; 6, Everglades, Fla., N. P. Fry.

KEY TO THE GENUS *FARANCIA*

a. Ventral color extending onto sides of body as narrow bars which become gradually narrower and terminate in points or diffuse into the darker color of the dorsum; light bars on neck separated by no more than 3 or 4 median scale rows. 　　　　　　　　　　　　　　　*F. abacura abacura*

aa. Light bars extending up sides, at least anteriorly, abruptly terminated dorsally; posterior one sometimes pointed, but not diffusing into the darker color of the dorsum; light bars on neck separated medially from each other usually by 8–9 rows of scales (hence shorter). *F. a. reinwardti*

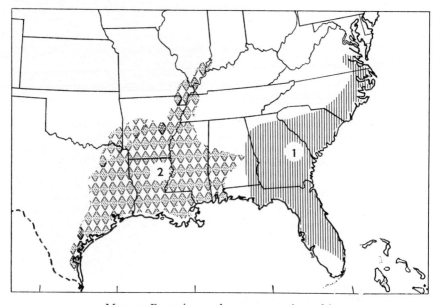

Map 25. *Farancia*—1, *abacura;* 2, *a. reinwardti.*

Horn snake (23—Clayton 1705), **Mud snake** (9—Löding 1922)

Farancia abacura abacura (Holbrook) 1836. Fig. 84; Map 25

Other common names: Checkered snake; dart snake (Clayton 1705); eastern horn snake (1); eastern mud snake (2); hoop snake (6); horned snake; North American red-bellied snake; rainbow snake; red-bellied horn snake; red-bellied snake (11); stinging snake; thunder snake.

Range: Atlantic coastal region from Amelia Co., Va., to e. Alabama and peninsular Florida.—Ala.; Fla.; Ga.; N.C.; S.C.; Va. *Elevation*—Seacoast to 500 feet.

Size: Adults, 20–84 inches. One of our notes reads: Gainesville Museum,

♀ 6 feet 3 inches, U. R. Parker, July 29, 1931; 8 feet 5 inches reported by Carr.

Distinctive characteristics: Recently reviewed by Smith: "Distinguished from *reinwardti* by having the ventral color extending onto sides of the body in the form of narrow bars not abruptly terminated dorsally, but becoming gradually narrower and terminating in a point or diffusing into the darker color of the dorsum; light bars on neck separated by usually no more than 3 or 4 median scale rows; distal light bars on tail frequently uniting medially; young with numerous complete or nearly complete light bands about body, especially anteriorly; usually (70%) 53 or more light bands on body; males usually (90.5%) with 13 or more light tail bars, females usually (68.4%) with 11 or more."

Color: A snake from Billy Is., Okefinokee Swamp, Ga., described June 21, 1921. The back is a dusky purplish gray, blackish violet-gray, blue-violet black, or bluish slate-black. The scales are glossy, enamellike, and at times with a metallic sheen. This color extends down the sides to the belly as 55 to 60 vertical bars separating, on the lower sides, interspaces of shrimp pink, la france pink, or cameo pink, the ground color of the ventrals. The upper and lower labials, mental, gulars, and chin shields are pale greenish yellow, each marked with a black spot in the middle. The edges of the scales in front of the eyes are pale greenish yellow, but the temporals are edged with shrimp pink. The iris bears a circle of orange chrome, orange-rufous, or xanthine orange around the pupil. The rest of the iris is blackish with fine specks of the above-mentioned orange shades. The ventrals are coral pink or jasper pink with the caudal third of their number light jasper red. The dark vertical bars of the sides meet 2 rows of bluish slate-black or dusky purplish gray spots on the venter. For the first 13 ventrals, these extend entirely across the plates. Then they split in the middle, leaving a long spot on either end of each ventral. These rows of spots extend to the tail tip, but past the cephalic third are less regular. The spots on the sets of 2 ventrals where the dark vertical bars join the belly are the largest; those between are smaller.

Young—A baby snake from Paine Prairie, Alachua County, several miles s. of Gainesville, Fla., collected by Kauffeld, Bassler, and Trapido, April 2, 1941. It is 10%16 inches long, of which 1¼ inches is tail. The dorsum is black, crossed by faint broken lines of brazil red. All scales on the top and sides of the head are edged with the same except the interparietal suture and rear of the frontal. The eye is black and brazil red. The belly is between brazil red and scarlet-red, becoming on lower side of head peach red or strawberry pink. This color extends as narrow triangular bars up the sides about 4 scale rows. Across the back, between the tips of these bars and on the 6th and 7th rows of scales, are 2 scales partly tipped with brazil red. Occasionally, particularly in the rear half of body, there is an intermediate series of the same.

Abnormal coloration—(1) White bellied. "Curiously enough, the 2 specimens which we first took alive, one 151.7 cm. long and the other 43 cm. were *white beneath, and not red*. The other preserved specimen has also the whitish appearance" (Wright and Bishop). (2) Partial erythrism. Etheridge (Fla., 1950) described one in which dorsally there was a black line for ⅓ the length anteriorly, followed by a shorter line posteriorly. The rear half had transverse dorsal bands. The interspaces were red.

Habitat: Some of its habitat preferences appear to be bayheads, marshes, alluvial swamps, drainage ditches, sphagnum bogs, wet lowlands, dense muddy marshes, and salt marshes. It is abroad briefly during rains or at the mating season; it is nocturnal and a burrower in aquatic situations (Deckert, Corrington, Van Hyning, Carr, Grimshawe, Brimley, Goin, Neill, Loennberg, Wright and Bishop).

"The largest specimen was taken in a dark cypress thicket wherein a Florida barred owl had retreated. In water ankle deep or more our guide accidentally stepped on the snake, thinking it at first a moccasin. He recoiled and then quickly shot it. The smallest specimen was secured in the most difficult tangle (Minne Lake trail to Minne Islands) of the whole swamp, where the magnificent cypress trees and associated undergrowth were thickest. On a mat of sphagnum it rested, and when alarmed quickly shot down into it. . . . From all that we observed of the living snakes of this species, we would consider them timid, harmless burrowers. They are decidedly inhabitants of the twilight parts of the swamp, and their eyes suggest such a habitat. . . . We discovered no superstitions regarding its horny tip" (Wright and Bishop).

Period of activity: *First appearance*—Apr. (Carr); Apr. 14 (Bragg, S.C., 1912); Apr. 26, 1950 (Wright and Wright); May 14, 1923 (Brimley, N.C., 1927a); May 16, 1902 (Brimley); May 1906 (Brimley, N.C., 1909); May (Deckert, Fla., 1918). *Fall disappearance*—Oct. 4, 1935 (Bass, Fla., 1935); Oct. 6 (Goldstein); Nov. 10, 1886 (Ridgway); Dec., 1913 (Needham and Bradley).

Breeding: Oviparous. Males 600–1,090 mm., females 920–1,875 mm. *Sexual dimorphism*—Blanchard (Ind., 1926) reports keel ridges on dorsal scales of anal region of males.

Eggs—Number, 15–104. 15, 20 eggs, Conant and Downs; 25, Brimley (N.C., 1941–42); 35, Grimshawe; 40, Goldstein; 43, Wright and Bishop; 50, Brimley; 54, Reynolds and Solburg; 104, Van Hyning. "On July 23, 1929 a female horn snake 235 cm. in length was found, freshly killed, on the highway near Payne's Prairie about 5 miles south of Gainesville, Florida. From this specimen were taken 104 eggs averaging 21 mm. x 30 mm. which were covered with a tough white skin and which filled the body cavity for about two thirds of its posterior portion" (Van Hyning). Size, 1.2–1.4 inches long x .8–1.0 inches in depth. May reach length of 40–50 mm. at hatching.

Time, April–July. "The eggs are laid in April, May, and June in moist sand or under heaps of dead hyacinths and other vegetable debris" (Carr). "A large female was found about August 20, 1937, coiled around her eggs under a large log on St. Simon's Island, Georgia" (Conant and Downs).

Excerpts from two reports of the early forties concerning this beautiful but much maligned snake follow:

"Investigation disclosed . . . a 6 foot specimen of the mud snake, *Farancia a. abacura,* coiled in a hole in one of the mounds. When she was removed the excavation proved to be a shallow affair, 10 to 12 cm. deep, 20 long and 7 or 8 wide. As we were about to leave, several rounded objects were noticed in the walls and upon close examination they were seen to be eggs. Forty were found. The eggs were imbedded in the walls of the cavity in three layers. Two of these were completely buried, while the outermost jutted slightly from the earth. . . . They were taken home, examined and measured. They were creamy-white prolate spheroids, parchment like in texture, averaging 35x25 mm." (Goldstein).

"Early in the morning of July 9 the mudsnake (56 inches, ♀) crawled from the water to the rocks above the pool and appeared to be nervous and in search of a suitable place to deposit her eggs, finally coiling in a level spot some 2 feet directly behind and above the pool. On the following morning several eggs were observed beneath her coils. When the cage was opened the snake paid no attention to the intruder. She was left coiled about her eggs until the next morning, July 11, when it was found she had left the clutch and was moving about the cage. The eggs were then removed and found to number 54. The eggs were not adherent, white in color, elliptical in shape and with shells of a smooth leathery texture. The average weight per egg of 30 that were weighed was 12.3 grams" (Reynolds and Solberg).

Young—Hatching time, Sept. 7–Oct. 9. We received from Auburn, Ala., on Apr. 10, 1928, an egg which hatched en route. Was it an early egg laying or a carryover from fall? Size, 182–234 mm., average 209.7 mm. (Goldstein); 202–230 mm. (Reynolds and Solburg); 204–231 mm. (Conant and Downs). "The natives relate how the thunder snake (*L. getulus*) digs beneath rotten logs and other cover for the adults and young of this species" (Wright and Bishop). "Young [have] numerous complete or nearly complete light bands about body, especially anteriorly" (Smith). "The young may occasionally be found in great numbers among the roots of water-hyacinths growing in shallow water" (Carr). "The first young snake cut its egg on the morning of October 6. It stayed inside occasionally protruding its head but withdrawing it at the slightest disturbance. At 6 P.M. on the following day it came out and immediately burrowed into the earth-sphagnum medium in which the eggs lay. The others left the eggs between 7:30 P.M. and 8 the next morning. . . . When they were 5 days old their skins became cloudy and they finally moulted on the 8th day" (Goldstein).

Food: Sirens, congo eels, small salamanders, earthworms, frogs, fishes. Van Hyning (Fla., 1932), Carr, Goldstein, Reynolds and Solberg, Neill (Gen., 1951).

Field notes: Fondness of children for our *Farancias*. Each wanted a picture taken with it across his or her neck. One child played with it as with a doll, put it in corner of couch, covered it up and seemed to take satisfaction in knowing it was quiet there. The snake made no effort to get away. How about the so-called instinctive fear of snakes in children?

May 5, 1950: At the Allen-Neill Museum they have a *Farancia-Abastor* hybrid 237 mm. Dark band down belly almost to vent. Light stripe down back somewhat scalloped in front. Light band on either side somewhat scalloped above. They question generic differences between *Abastor* and *Farancia*.

Authorities:

Carr, A. F., Jr. (Fla., 1940a)
Conant, R., and A. Downs, Jr. (Gen., 1940)
Goldstein, R. C. (Fla., 1941)
Grimshawe, F. M. (Fla., 1937)

Reynolds, F. A., and A. N. Solberg (Gen., 1942)
Smith, H. M. (Gen., 1938)
Van Hyning, O. A. (Fla., 1931)
Wright, A. H., and S. C. Bishop, Jr. (Ga., 1916)

Western horn snake (1—Smith 1938), Mud Snake (16)

Farancia abacura reinwardti Schlegel 1837. Fig. 85; Map 25

Other common names: Horn snake (17); hoop snake (10); horn tail; red-bellied horn snake; sting(ing) snake; stingaree; thunder snake; wampum snake; western mud snake (2).

Range: Cent. Alabama, extreme w. Florida to Corpus Christi, Tex. and n. as a Mississippi embayment form to s. tips of Illinois and Indiana.—Ala.; Ark.; Fla.; Ill.; Ind.; Ky.; La.; Miss.; Mo.; Okla.; Tenn.; Tex. *Elevation*—Coast to 500 feet.

Size: Adults, 20–72 inches.

Distinctive characteristics: "Distinguished from *abacura* in certain details of coloration: at least the anterior light bars abruptly terminated dorsally; posterior bars sometimes terminated in a point, but not diffused into general darker color of dorsum; light bars on neck separated medially from each other by usually 8 or 9 scale rows; distal tail bands not united medially (except sometimes that on tip); young similar to adults without complete light bands on body; usually (71.6%) 52 or fewer light bands on body; males with usually (81%) 12 or fewer light bars on tail; females with usually (94.5%) 10 or fewer light bars on tail" (Smith).

Color: A snake from Gramercy, La., received from G. Meade and described March 31, 1941. The dorsum is black with a bluish cast. There are 47 light lateral areas on the body and 10 on the tail. *The first 2 light areas on the neck are blocks, not triangles, and are 2½ to 3 scales wide and 4½ scales deep with the intermediate dorsal black crossing 11 scales.* These light areas are coral red or jasper red, as is the ground color of the belly. This color extends up on the sides as distinct triangles 1½ scales longitudinally and 2 scales vertically. These triangles of the 2 sides are not directly opposite, and their belly extensions may be abruptly terminated at the center by a block of black which usually covers 2 ventrals, thus giving the belly a checkerboard of black and coral red. On the tail, the ventral color becomes a series of black and coral red bands becoming solid coral red toward the tail tip. The dorsal head plates are not marked with light except for a preocular spot on the rear of the prefrontals and a light border on the rear of the internasals. The ventral side of the head is bittersweet orange, becoming on the upper and lower labials light cadmium. Each lower labial except the last 2 bears a distinct large black spot in its center, and in the same way the upper labials are centered. The first 3 or 4 ventrals bear transverse bars of black, and the gulars each have a black spot. Thus 4 or 5 rows of spots appear. The chin shields are bittersweet orange each with a black spot toward the forward end. The iris is flame scarlet except for the upper third, which is black.

Abnormal coloration—Albinism. "An albino horn snake was captured in May by a farmer living about 10 miles west of Houston, Texas" (Heiser). *Aposematic coloration*—See the article by Davis for an account of the behavior and display of *Farancia* when annoyed or molested.

Habitat: From Hurter (Mo., 1903), Dabney, Viosca (La., 1923), Parker (Tenn., 1948), Burger, and Burger, Smith, and Smith we assembled these habitats: on shores of stagnant waters, beneath logs, in morasses and cypress brakes and low basins, in wooded alluvial swamps, in tupelo swamps, in river bottoms, in debris in shallow water, and in ditches in a palmetto grove.

Period of activity: *First appearance and fall disappearance*—Most of the records of appearance come in late March or in early April. Hurter (Mo., 1903) has Apr. 18, 19, and 24. Strecker gives a Nov., 1905, date but the species usually goes into hibernation in October. "A dead specimen was found March 10, 1947, in Shelby County [Tenn.], presumably killed by cold weather following a warm period. No others have been found before April" (Parker, Tenn., 1948).

Hibernation—Meade's 1937 observations are excerpted: "The snake ate the last 'eel' on Oct. 4. . . . By this time (Oct. 24) the snake showed an evident desire to dig into the ground whenever opportunity offered. . . . On all warm days the hibernating box was examined but there was no sign of the reptile until Feb. 14. . . . March 6 when the snake was again above ground it was taken up and found to weigh 3 lbs. 10 oz., only one ounce less than the weight 4 months and 10 days before. [It reappeared Mar. 18 but refused food.] . . . The snake was taken up [Mar. 26] and sprayed with water after which it attacked and ate a 14 inch *Amphiuma,* the amphibian biting the reptile several times during the struggle. This was the first meal in 5 months and 22 days."

Breeding: Oviparous. Males 725–982 mm., females 852–1,790 mm. *Mating*—"The mating was first observed about 7 A.M. on July 11 [in Louisiana]. The paired snakes were then in the water but they moved onto the concrete soon afterward where they remained coupled throughout the day. During much of this time the female was in a loose coil with a male in a fairly straight line at right angles to the posterior part of her body. The other snakes in the cage showed no interest in the mating. At 10:30 P.M., the snakes, observed with a flashlight, were again in the water still coupled but the following morning they had separated and no further inclination to mate was noted. There were no courtship activities seen on the days previous to the mating although the occupants of the cage were under frequent observation" (Meade, 1937).

Eggs—Number, 11–50. There are records of 11, 15, 18, 24, 25, 28, 28, 29, 48, 50 eggs in a clutch. As early as 1883 Ridgway found the snake with 11 eggs at Wheatland, Ind. The eggs measured 34 mm. x 19½ mm., 33.5x22, 31x22, 32.5x22, 32x24, 30.5x21.5, 32.5x25.5, and 32.5x22.5. (See Meade under "Hatching time" below.) Time, from July 10, to July 31, through Aug. 10 to Sept. 5, which is rather a late date. Size, 1⅝–1⅞ length x $^{13}/_{16}$–$^{15}/_{16}$ of an inch diameter (Meade, 1937). He observed: "The eggs were obviously increasing in size and toward the end of October they appeared as large as small hen's eggs. On October 22 (7 weeks' incubation), one measured 2⅛ inches long and 1⅛ inches in diameter, an increase of about 250% in volume since the day it was laid." He described the eggs as "cream-white elongated spheroids, smooth, nonadhesive, regular in size and shape. . . . The shells, which are flexible and leathery, were marked with numerous small rod-like flecks in groups of 2 and 3 and lying parallel to the elongated axis." We have an undocumented note of eggs 30½ to 34 mm. x 19½ to 24 mm., and Meade gives another measurement of 20x33 mm. to 21x35 mm. Maternal care of eggs, Meade (1940a) shows that the female remains coiled about the eggs from deposition to hatching except for feeding, moulting, or defecation.

Young—Hatching time, Sept. 1–Oct. 30. Meade's late hatching date, Oct. 30, came 8 weeks from ovulation and 16 weeks from mating. Some of his clutch of 18 eggs, Aug. 10, hatched away from the female on Oct. 2–6, or 7 weeks after deposition. Size, 6¼–9 inches (Meade). Smith uses the juvenile character as one of his differentiating characters: "Young similar to adults, without complete light bands."

Food: *Amphiuma, Siren,* frogs. Meade (1934, 1940), Buck, Tschambers. In many a zoology class or other groups of onlookers, the sight of *Farancia* subduing and eating an *Amphiuma* causes great excitement. To George P Meade belongs the credit for suggesting this zoological thriller.

Authorities:

Auffenberg, W. (Tex., 1948)
Buck, D. H. (Tex., 1946)
Burger, W. L., Jr. (Okla., 1948)
Burger, W. L., P. W. Smith, and H. M.
 Smith (Tex., 1949)
Dabney, T. G. (Miss., 1919)

Davis, D. D. (Tex., 1948)
Heiser, J. M., Jr. (Tex., 1931)
Meade, G. P. (La., 1934, 1935, 1935a,
 1937, 1940, 1940a)
Smith, H. M. (Gen., 1938a)
Tschambers, B. (La., 1948)

HOOK-NOSED SNAKES

Genus *FICIMIA* Gray (Fig. 22)

Size from our records 10–19 inches. Like *Gyalopion* except that rostral makes broad contact with frontal; internasals small or absent; loreal absent; 1 preocular; 1–2 postoculars. Ventrals 128–160; caudals 30–42.

Rostral in contact with frontal, internasals absent, 1–2 postoculars; prefrontal contacts labial 2; no loreal; black dorsal bands 38–47, very narrow (a scale length or less) separated by about 3 times their length of hair brown or grayish olive scales, and often broken posteriorly and evident only as small middorsal spots. Ventrals, ♂ 128–154, ♀ 142–157; caudals, ♂ 34–40, ♀ 29–34.   *Ficimia olivacea streckeri*

Strecker's hook-nosed snake (4—Ditmars 1936),
South Texas hook-nosed snake (2)

Ficimia olivacea streckeri (Taylor) 1931. Fig. 86; Map 26

Other common names: Dog-nosed snake (Strecker) 1915; hook-nosed snake.

Range: Extreme s. Texas to n. Veracruz, Mex.—U.S.A.: Tex. Mex.: Hidalgo, Nuevo León; San Luis Potosí; Veracruz. *Elevation*—Seacoast to 1,000 feet.

Size: Adults, 10–19.3 inches. In 1943 Mulaik and Mulaik reported them 115–325 mm. "Excluding the two smallest the average for the others is 264 mm." In his series of 10 specimens from the Xilitla region Taylor (1949) has specimens from 250–483 mm. (one 139 mm.), or 10–19.3 inches long.

Distinctive characteristics: Rostral in contact with the frontal; one preocular, one postocular in Texas series, 2 in most of Xilitla series; ventrals 128–157; caudals 28–40; 17 scale rows in midbody (from 21–19–17–19–17–17); supralabials 7; infralabials 7 (8); no loreals and normally no internasals; temporals 1 + 2; very narrow bars 38–47 (sometimes dorsal spots 30 or more in number, or spots on posterior only).

Color: A snake from Brownsville, Tex., furnished by H. C. Blanchard, Aug. 13, 1931. The ground color of the back is hair brown, deep grayish olive, grayish olive, or light grayish olive and continues to the tip of the

Fig. 85. *Farancia a. reinwardti,* Grammercy, La., G. Meade.

Fig. 86. *Ficimia olivacea streckeri,* Brownsville, Tex., H. C. Blanchard.

tail. These scales under the lens are grayish olive with white or cartridge buff rear edges. The 2 front edges of the diamond are often thinly dark rimmed. Down the back are 49 transverse dorsal spots of chaetura black, 38 spots on the body and 11 on the tail. On the body, these spots are 2 to 3 scales transversely and 1 to 2 scales long. The dorsal ground color extends down the sides to the 2nd row of scales, which have a light color intermediate between that of the dorsum and that of the belly. These 2 lower rows of scales are olive-buff or a color intermediate between the grayish olive of the dorsum and the buffy tints of the labials. One might easily say that in alcohol or formal the belly color extends up on 2 rows of scales, as it does in *Carphophis*. The head plates are hair brown or mouse gray. Obliquely down from the rear of the eye is a spot of chaetura black. The upper edge of the first upper labial, the upper half of the postocular, almost the whole of the 1st temporal, and a few specks on the upper portions of the last 2 upper labials are like the head plates, hair brown or mouse gray, with fuscous, olive-brown, or brownish olive on the upper edges of the 4th and 5th upper labials. The upper labials are, on their lower edges, seafoam green, and on the upper portions of the 3rd and 4th and the middle of the 5th, colonial buff. The lower labials are seafoam yellow edged with the light color of the belly. The iris in general is fuscous or olive-brown with touches of the lighter dorsal color. The lower portion of the iris is almost solid olive-brown. The upper half of the rim of the pupil is seafoam green or white. The under parts of the chin and belly are pale purplish vinaceous or pale brownish vinaceous, with the center of the ventrals showing pale bluish lavender or pale verbena violet opalescent reflections.

Habitat: This snake is a burrower. In 1931 Taylor wrote: "While collecting in southern Texas in the summer of 1930, I captured a specimen of a small snake which I believe to be an undescribed species of the genus *Ficimia*. It was found 3 miles east of Rio Grande City along the highway, about midnight of the night of July 13, 1930."

In 1943 Mulaik and Mulaik told how they came to secure their good series: "The largest number of specimens was secured in the spring and summer of 1935 in concrete canals [in the Edinburg region]. At that time government agencies made funds available to irrigation districts to keep the concrete canal banks clear of overhanging grass and weeds. Such cleaning up has since been discontinued so that the snakes can readily climb out after getting in the water."

Breeding: Oviparous. Males 251–483 mm., females 250–450 mm.

Food: Spiders. Mulaik and Mulaik (Tex., 1943).

Authorities:

Axtell, R. W. (Tex., 1931)

Mulaik, S. and D. (Tex., 1943)

Shannon, F. A., and H. M. Smith (Tex., 1949)

Smith, H. M. (Tex., 1944)

Smith, H. M., and E. H. Taylor (Gen., 1941)

Taylor, E. H. (Tex., 1931, 1949, 1950)

1943, S. and D. Mulaik: "Over 30 specimens have been examined; the above figures are based largely upon 10 males and 6 females in the personal collection of the authors and on several males and females in the collection of L. Irby Davis."

1949, E. H. Taylor: "A series of 10 specimens of this burrowing species was acquired in the Xilitla region. It is important since it gives a better idea of the range of variation in the form."

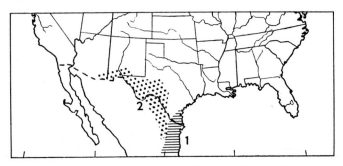

Map 26. *Ficimia* and *Gyalopion*—1, *F. o. streckeri;* 2, *G. canum.*

HOOK-NOSED SNAKES

Genus *GYALOPION* Cope (Fig. 22)

Size, very small, 5½–14 inches; body cylindrical, stout; tail short; anal divided; head slightly distinct from neck; snout projecting, acute; rostral enlarged, flattened, and concave, recurved in a sharp point, separated from frontal by prefrontals; prefrontal touches 2nd labial; scales smooth with apical pits in 17 rows; usually no loreal; internasals present, small; nasal fused with first labial; 1 preocular, 2 postoculars; 7 upper labials; (6) 7 (8) lower labials; temporals 1 + 2; posterior chin shields very small, 3–5 rows of gulars between them and ventrals; maxillary teeth 12–15 subequal, some with shallow lateral depressions, mandibular teeth small, equal; hemipenis undivided, sulcus simple, numerous fringed calyces in distal two-thirds, small area of spines, then basal sixth ridged. Ventrals 125–146; caudals 23–36. Synonyms: *Ficimia, Gyalopium.*

Hook-nosed snake (6—Ditmars 1936), **Pug-nosed snake** (3—Van Denburgh 1922)

Gyalopion canum Cope 1860 [1] Fig. 87; Map 26
(*Ficimia cana* Schmidt, *Check List,* 1953)

---

[1] Following the *Check List,* 1st to 4th eds., we normally used *Ficimia cana.* In 1941 we changed our manuscript to follow Taylor and Smith. We have no aversion to a change again to *Ficimia.*

Other common names: Dog nose snake (Yarrow 1882); dog-nosed snake; western hook-nosed snake.

Range: Mexican boundary form; from Nuevo León, Mex., to Tom Green Co., Tex., w. to Santa Cruz Co. in s. Arizona.—U.S.A.: Ariz.; N.M.; Tex. Mex.: Nuevo León. *Elevation*—1,000 to 3,000 feet. 2,800–5,000 feet (Bailey, N. Mex., 1913).

Size: Adults, 5.5–14 inches.

Distinctive characteristics: "Background pale pinkish cinnamon, crossbars tawny-olive. Rostral separated from frontal by prefrontals; no loreals; anal divided; spots on body 30 to 39, on tail 9 to 12; spots brown, black edged, broken laterally or continuous with lateral spots, reaching nearly to ventrals; irregular, small spots scattered on body" (Smith and Taylor).

Color: A snake caught Sept. 3, 1947, 15 miles north of El Paso, Tex., and sent to C. F. Kauffeld by Lt. L. W. Feagin of El Paso. It reminds one of a small *Arizona elegans* or of a *Hypsiglena*. The background is pale pinkish cinnamon except for 2 lower scale rows which are almost clear white on the forward part of the body with touches of black where the dorsal bars extend toward the venter. This background is clear in mid-back for about 5 scale rows, then washed with tawny-olive and faint specks of black for 4 scale rows. Beginning with the neck-spot, the body is crossed by 32 tawny-olive bars and 9 on the tail. In the cephalic region the bars are 2 scales long and 7 scales wide with anterior and posterior edges jagged and irregularly bordered with black, and below their lower ends the scales are lighter with a black longitudinal bar crossing the middle, forming irregular lateral spots. From midbody caudad the dorsal bars are loosely joined to the lateral spots. The neckband of tawny-olive bordered in front with pale pinkish buff is about 8 scales transversely and 3 scales longitudinally except in the middle, 9 scales, where its point extends to the rear of the parietals. Beginning on the 3rd and 4th rows of temporals just above the angle of the mouth, a tawny-olive oblique bar, dark-edged front and rear, crosses the parietal to meet mate of other side. Back of the eye, a straight avellaneous bar extends across the rear half of the supraoculars and frontal, with a tawny-olive band, black-bordered on both edges, in front of it. Front half of frontal, rostral, and upper parts of labials are avellaneous. The iris is cinnamon. The entire venter from tip of chin to tip of tail is glistening white.

Structure—Total length 12½ inches; tail 2 inches; 17 scale rows around middle, 21 rows at neck, 15 at anal; 135 ventrals on body with 38 on tail. The anal is divided. The tail has obtuse tip. The rostral is concave above near its tip. The snake throws out vent in protest and, Max Hecht said, popped it with a noise and extruded a drop of moisture. Attention was called to this habit by Kauffeld, to whom this rare snake belongs.

Habitat and habits: In 1860 Cope described this new form thus: "It is an extraordinary serpent, resembling, at first sight, a diminutive *Heterodon*." Ruthven's discovery in 1907 was very important and yielded the fourth specimen. Excerpts are: "The single specimen of this snake taken was found, as before stated, on the shore of Lake Walters to the east of the White Sands. This makes it evident beyond question that the species occurs in the *Atriplex* association. A small specimen (No. 123) of this species was found dead on the shore of Lake Walters, at the White Sands, west of Alamogordo, N.M. The specimen is immature and was undoubtedly bred in the immediate vicinity. Whether or not it occurs elsewhere is as yet an unsettled question. *Range*—As far as I know but 2 other specimens of this species have been recorded. One of these is listed simply 'Southern Arizona,' the other, the type, came from Fort Buchanan in southeastern Arizona. This, the 3rd specimen [actually the 4th; Brit. Mus. Cat. specimen was 3rd], therefore, extends the range of the species across the Proplateau to the East Front Ranges in New Mexico."

In 1931 Taylor gave us the best summary to date. He and J. S. Wright had taken a pair, and Taylor wrote: "The male snake when first found remained motionless, perhaps blinded by the light which I carried; but immediately on being touched it began to writhe and to throw its body in strange contortions, as if in agony, sometimes almost throwing itself off the ground. It would continue these actions for several seconds and at the same time it would extrude and retract the cloaca rather rapidly, for a distance of a half an inch or more, which resulted in a popping sound. Wright tested the female and found that she reacted in practically the same manner as the male. These tactics were repeated time and again by the 2 specimens and even when in the collecting sack they continued these strange gyrations and jumping movements, as well as the continued extrusion and retraction of the cloaca. The terrain where they were found was a large flat, covered with short, very sparse grass, the soil largely free from sand or gravel. A large number of mounds thrown up by rodents (probably a species of *Dipodymus*) were scattered about the terrain. A rain had fallen, probably sometime in the morning, and the surface of the ground was still moist." (This was 10 miles north of Florida, Luna Co., N.M.)

In 1948 Kauffeld gave us some valuable "Notes on a Hook-nosed Snake from Texas": "The Staten Island Zoo has had the good fortune to receive a specimen of the rare hook-nosed snake, *Gyalopion canum* Cope, probably only the ninth known specimen of this species, from Lt. L. W. Feagin of Biggs Field, El Paso, Texas. Lt. Feagin found the little snake while road cruising for snakes 15 miles north of El Paso, between El Paso and the Dona Ana firing range on the east slope of the Franklin Mts., El Paso County, Texas, at 8:10 P.M., September 3, 1947; weather clear; surrounding soil of mixed sand and gravel. The specimen was loaned to Dr. A. H. Wright, and while in his possession apparently ate a garden spider. Predilection for an arachnid diet was confirmed subsequently on its return to the zoo when it ate 4 more spiders and a centipede. It refused millipedes consistently, also lizards, small snakes, frogs, and newborn mice. Due to the difficulty of obtaining the proper food, the specimen was killed and preserved while still in good condition, and is No. 106 of the Staten Island Zoo's study collection. It shows the following characters: length 302 mm.; tail 51 mm.; head 12 mm. long, 8 mm. wide; 30 body blotches and 9 tail blotches; scale rows 19-17-17; ventrals 135; subcaudals 33; anal divided; sex male. The peculiar 'cloacal popping' described by Taylor (*Copeia* 1931: 4–7) was produced by our specimen every time it was handled in the early days of its captivity, but ceased later. This snake used its specialized rostral to good advantage in burrowing in the sand of its cage."

Several years ago Mr. and Mrs. Bryce Brown told us of the finding of *Gyalopion canum* by Mrs. Brown, 9 miles north and a bit east of Menard, Tex., under a small flat stone. (A.H.W.) In 1950 Milstead, Mecham and McClintock recorded 2 in western Texas: "One of these snakes, partially digested, was removed from the stomach of a *Crotalus lepidus* collected on the rimrock. Another specimen was found in September DOR on highway 290, 22 miles west of Sheffield, Pecos County in the mesquite-creosote association." This same year Curtis recorded that "Barger Sullivan collected one female specimen on August 14, 1941, 1 mile west of Alpine, Brewster County, Texas. It was taken about 6:15 P.M. as it crawled among rocks on a hillside."

Breeding: Oviparous. Males 168–302 mm., females 205–325 mm. Three different years we have made one-day hurried trips to Lake Walters (once no water, once a good pond, and once just about dried up), but never any luck. Every station given for U.S.A. we have visited, still no specimens. Measured by *G. canum,* we are total failures. Other collectors take courage or satisfaction! Night trips would be best. Much time afield in southwest might bring this form. To one of the 4 or 5 best field collectors of U.S.A. (E. H. Taylor) has fallen the best success.

Finally, in 1948, through Kauffeld, we were enabled to study a living snake of this rare species.

Authorities: [1]

Boulenger, G. A. (Gen., 1893–96)
Cope, E. D. (*Proc. Acad. Nat. Sci. Phila.,* 12:243)
Curtis, L. (Tex., 1950)
Kauffeld, C. F. (Tex., 1948)
Milstead, W. W., J. S. Mecham, and H. McClintock (Tex., 1950)

Ruthven, A. G. (Ariz., 1907)
Schmidt, K. P., and T. F. Smith (Tex., 1944)
Smith, H. M., and E. H. Taylor (Gen., 1941)
Taylor, E. H. (Tex., 1931)
Van Denburgh, J. (Gen., 1922)

1875: E. Coues (Ariz., 1875) quoted Cope, but gave a plate (XVIII 2, 2a) of *Gyalopium canum.* Unfortunately for separation of *Gyalopium* from

---

[1] 1955: W. E. Duellman (Ariz.) reported one from near the Chiricahua National Monument, Cochise Co.

Ficimia, the figure shows the tip of the rostral just touching the frontal.

1915: J. K. Strecker, Jr. (Tex., 1915), said that a specimen from Duval Co., Tex., was recorded by Boulenger in his catalogue. Boulenger gives El Paso as the place of origin and Forrer as his collector or donor. Strecker must have known that Taylor of San Diego, Duval Co., Tex., shipped Texas material to the British Museum. Was this specimen from Duval Co. or El Paso? Has anyone seen the specimen to determine whether it is *canum* or *streckeri?* If the latter, possibly Strecker was right in ascribing it to Duval County.

1931: H. M. Smith and E. H. Taylor with 7 specimens gave a review of *Gyalopion* and *Ficimia.*

1944: K. P. Schmidt and T. F. Smith reported a specimen from Green Gulch, Chisos Mts. Dorsal blotches 34 + 11.

1944: H. M. Smith (Tex.) took a specimen in Galeana, Nuevo León, and mentioned another male specimen from Mount Livermore, Jeff Davis Co., Tex. by Schmidt and Schmidt.

GROUND SNAKES

Genus *HALDEA* Baird and Girard (Fig. 24)

Size very small, 4-12 inches; body cylindrical, moderately stout; head small, neck not distinct or slightly so; tail short, tapering to a point; anal divided; scale rows 15 or 17; scales smooth or keeled; no preocular, loreal and prefrontal contacting eye; 1 or 2 (3) postoculars; nasals 2, temporals 1 + 1 or 1 + 2; upper labials 5 or 6; lower labials (5) 6 (7); few or no gulars between chin shields and ventrals; dorsum light brown, venter greenish yellow or pink; maxillary teeth smooth, 16-20, subequal; mandibular 19-22 small; hemipenis spinous. Ventrals 111-135; caudals 22-50. Synonyms. *Amphiardis, Calamaria, Celuta, Coluber, Conocephalus, Natrix, Potamophis, Virginia.*

KEY TO THE GENUS *HALDEA*

Preocular absent; scale rows 15-17; venter uniform; anal divided; loreal present; nasal divided; small snakes.

a. 6 upper labials; postoculars (1) 2 (3); scales smooth or weakly keeled posteriorly; 2 internasals (*Virginia*)

    b. Scales in (13) 15 rows, usually smooth.   *H. valeriae valeriae*

    bb. Scales in 17 (19) rows, usually keeled posteriorly.   *H. v. elegans*

aa. 5 upper labials; postocular 1; scales strongly keeled.

    b. One internasal (*Potamaphis*)   and⎫

    bb. Two internasals (*Amphiardis inornatus*)⎬*H. striatula*

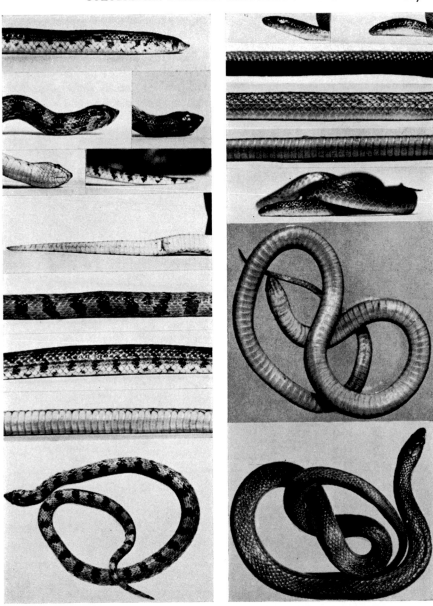

Fig. 87. *Gyalopion canum*, 15 miles north of El Paso, Tex., L. W. Feagin to C. F. Kauffeld.

Fig. 88. *Haldea striatula*, Arkansas, D. L. Gamble.

Brown snake (38—Baird and Girard 1853),
Southern ground snake (3)

Haldea striatula (Linné) 1766. Fig. 88; Map 27

Other common names: Brown ground snake; ground snake (8); little brown snake; little striped snake; small brown viper; small-eyed brown snake; striated viper; worm snake (3).

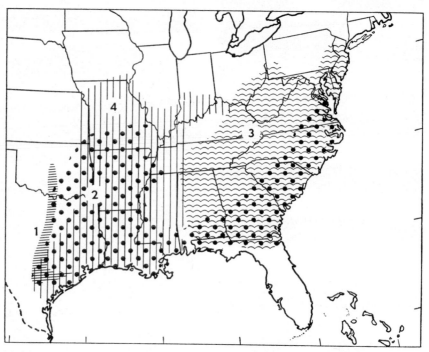

Map 27. *Haldea*—1, (*Amphiardis inornatus*); 2, *striatula*; 3, *v. valeriae*; 4, *v. elegans*.

Range: Delaware to n.e. Florida, Baker and Duval Counties, w. to cent. Texas and n. to s.e. Kansas and s. Missouri.—Ala.; Fla.; Ga.; Ill.; La.; Miss.; Mo.; N.C.; Okla.; S.C.; Tenn.; Tex.; Va. *Elevation*—Sea level to 1,000 feet.

Size: Adults, 6–12 inches.

Distinctive characteristics: A small burrowing ground snake, olive brown, or dull grayish brown above, and glass green below; 17 rows of keeled scales; 1 postocular; upper labials 5.

Color: A snake from Arkansas received from D. L. Gamble, May 4, 1928. The upper parts are light brownish olive or olive-brown. On the lower sides and extending somewhat onto the ventrals, pale vinaceous-fawn or light vinaceous-fawn occurs. At times the dorsal scales are opalescent with purples and blues, and under the lens the dorsal scales are seen to be marked with fine punctae. The top of the head is deep olive or grayish olive. The upper and lower labials are pale drab-gray. The pupil rim is cinnamon or orange-cinnamon. The iris is olive-brown with touches of pale drab-gray or pallid mouse gray. The underside of the head is white, pale olive-buff, or pale vinaceous-fawn. The rest of the under parts are pale glass green, which becomes on the caudal half of the body and on the underside of the tail glass green.

Habitat and habits: Hurter (Mo., 1897, 1911), Strecker (Tex., 1902, 1927b), Gray (N.C., 1941), Brimley (N.C., 1941–42), Deckert (Fla., 1918), Carr (Fla., 1940a), Löding (Ala., 1922), Snyder (Ala., 1945), Allen, Force, Burt and Hoyle (Gen., 1935), and Parker (Tenn., 1948) recorded the following habitats: sunny slopes under rocks; under decaying logs; among masses of decayed wood and dead leaves; under logs in thickly timbered bottoms; under leafy carpets of woods; under fallen branches; under rubbish piles near dwellings; in gardens; in city plots as well as woods; under bark in a dried-up bayou; in flatwoods; in upland and mesophytic hammocks; in swampy fields, in moist sand in a prairie ledge; and in wooded uplands and valleys.

Period of activity: *Early appearances*—Hurter has them Mar. 22, May 13, 30. Allen took many Feb. 12, 1930, and Corrington in S.C. spotted them Feb. 21. Peterson gave Mar. 23–Apr. 6, 1946 (Tex., 1950). *Hibernation*—"Favorite lurking places for small specimens are along the edges of dead vines which are partly sunken among fallen leaves. Here a whole brood will remain near together until cold weather compels them to seek hibernating places under ground. At Victoria, Mr. J. D. Mitchell found these snakes in clustered hibernating masses with copperheads, ribbon snakes, lizards, leopard frogs, and toads; at Waco, I found, in addition to the gray pilot snake, approximately the same condition. Brown snakes are not as susceptible to cold as the larger species of ophidians and they are the first snakes to liven up in the spring, and usually the last to disappear below ground in the winter. Some writers think it is doubtful whether they hibernate more than a period of 4 or 5 weeks" (Strecker).

Breeding: Viviparous. Males 180–260 mm., females 192–298 mm. *Young*—Number, 3–13. In 1892 O. P. Hay discovered a female with 5 embryos. Ditmars in 1907 reported a female giving birth to 7 young Aug. 20. In 1908 Strecker said that Mr. Mitchell recently had sent him an adult female containing 7 embryos. Brimley in 1910 said very young specimens often have a white crossband or half collar on nape. Wright and Bishop reported a female of June 15, 1912, with 6 embryos. In 1926 Guthrie said the young are produced alive. Force wrote: "A female (WJH 172) collected April 9, 1928, carried 4 large and 9 small ova in the anterior oviduct and 2 large and 4 immature in the posterior oviduct. The larger ones averaged 5 and 6 mm. by 2 and 3 mm. Another (WJH 177), collected Mar. 3, 1928, contained 3 ova each 1 to 3.5 mm. by 1 to 2 mm. in size." In 1939–1941 Conant and Bridges and Schmidt and Davis gave 6 to 8 young. In 1953 Guidry (Tex.)

reported 3, 4, 5 young. Size, 4–5 inches. "When first born, brown snakes are nearly 4 inches in length" (Strecker). The smallest specimen of *H. striatula* we have seen is 122 mm. long. Strecker and Williams' small snakes for the study of juvenile coloration were 112–139 mm. except for one of 100 mm. Time, August. "The number of young produced at a birth by this species is from 6 to 8. I have several records of pregnant females. One of these [was] captured in the month of July at Victoria, Texas, by the late J. D. Mitchell. She contained 7 young. . . . In Mann's woods, near Waco, I found a large female with 8 foetuses and in Gurley's park, a smaller one with 6. Both were captured early in August. While she is heavy with young, the female retires into a hole at the base of a stump or inside a hollow tree" (Strecker).

Food: Beetles, ants, earthworms, sowbugs, mollusks, small anurans, young lizards. Surface (Pa., 1906), Hurter, Guthrie (Ia., 1926), Strecker.

Authorities:

Allen, M. J. (Miss., 1932)

Corrington, J D. (S.C., 1929)

Force, E. R. (Okla., 1930)

Hay, O. P. (Ind., 1892)

Hurter, J. (Mo., 1911)

Strecker, J. K. (Tex., 1927b)

Valeria's snake (16—Yarrow 1882), Eastern ground snake (8—Gloyd, Conant, Pope)

Haldea valeriae valeriae (Baird and Girard) 1853. Fig. 89; Map 27

Other common names: Blaney's snake; brown (worm) snake; eastern gray snake (2); gray snake; ground snake; smooth brown snake (1—Ditmars 1929); spotted ground snake; Valeria Blaney's snake (Jordan 1876); Virginia('s) snake.

Range: From New Jersey and e. Pennsylvania s. to n. Florida, w. to Alabama and n. to s. Ohio and s.w. Pennsylvania.—Ala.; D.C.; Del.; Fla.; Ga.; Ky.; Md.; N.J.; N.C.; O.; Pa.; S.C.; Tenn.; Va.; W. Va. *Elevation*—Most records below 500 feet, some to 1,000–1,500 feet. 1,000–1,500 feet (King, Tenn., 1939); 850–2,900 feet (Wilson and Friddle, W. Va., 1950); 2,300 feet (Smith, Pa., 1945).

Size: Adults, 6–11 inches.

Distinctive characteristics: "Head small, narrow, and relatively high; snout pointed and the sides of the head perpendicular; upper labials, 6, and fifth largest, eye over third and fourth; lower labials, 6; scales in 15 rows, those on the tail feebly keeled, all the others smooth; ventral plates, 111 to 128; subcaudals, 24 to 37. Yellowish or grayish brown above, with usually scattered dots forming a faint line on each side of the back; a faint light line along the middle of each scale; beneath, the color is uniform dull yellow. Length, 8 to 10 inches" (Hay, D.C., 1902a).

Color: A snake from Auburn, Ala., received from H. G. Good, Sept. 25,

1928. The dorsal color is benzo brown, deep brownish drab, mars brown, or light brownish drab. Under the lens, the scales are light vinaceous-fawn with many fine dark speckings. The first row of scales is like the belly and is light vinaceous-fawn, pale vinaceous-fawn, pale grayish vinaceous, or pale vinaceous-pink. The top of the head is hair brown or like the dorsum with many dark spots on the large plates. The upper labials are ecru-drab or lighter, and some of the labials are marked with drab-gray spots. There is a small ring of black around the eye with little present on the supraocular and upper postocular. The iris is a vinaceous-tawny ring with an outer ring of black. The vinaceous-tawny ring is interrupted in the lower right corner by black, and again by black extending inward from the lower preocular. The under parts of the head are white and the rest of the venter light vinaceous-fawn, pale vinaceous-fawn, pale grayish vinaceous, or pale vinaceous-pink.

Habitat: Some think its habits are like those of the burrower *Carphophis amoenus* (see Atkinson, Pa., 1901, and M. Morse, Ohio, 1904). This fossorial species has been ploughed up in soft ground in spring in dry pasture fields or meadows and dug up in gardens. It has been found in vacant city lots and about abandoned dwellings. Its cover may be rubbish, paper, debris, surface layer of dead leaves or leaf mold, stones, dead logs, boards, and other litter. It has been taken in thick woods, dry deciduous woods, pine woods, trapridge woods, and wooded pastures. It has also been recorded in upland hammocks and lowland wet meadows, and often in urban localities.

Period of activity: Most of the records of this species are in the summer, mainly from Aug. 13 to 27. *First appearance*—Apr. 3, 1948. There are a few early records in February and a few later in the spring. *Hibernation*—"During February 1949, several hibernating reptiles and one salamander were found, incidental to the excavation of a woodchuck den, though not in the burrow. The den site was located on a terrace between a river flood plain and a cropped field. On February 8 a pink-bellied snake, *Carphophis a. amoena* was found 24 inches below the surface. . . . Further excavation of the same area on February 15 unearthed a brown snake, *Haldea v. valeriae,* 212 mm. long, which was located 30 inches below the surface, and a 280 mm. ringnecked, *Diadophis punctatus edwardsii,* which was found at a depth of 32 inches" (Grizzell, Md., 1949).

Breeding: Viviparous. Males 190–255 mm., females 183–280 mm. In 1906 Surface (Pa.) wrote, "We at present are unable to state how, when or where this species reproduces, as these facts are not known to anyone." And in 1942 Brimley (N.C., 1941–42) wrote, "Like its relatives it is viviparous giving birth to small broods of living young in late summer."

Young—Number, 7 to "fewer than 10" (Schmidt and Davis, Gen., 1941); 18 (Sinclair). The only definite data of recent times come from McCauley: "Very little material concerning the breeding habits of this snake is available. The number of young in 5 specimens examined by me and reported to me by other observers were 4, 6, 7, 7, and 8. Information concerning the birth of young has been made available to me by two observers. A specimen collected by Mr. Elias Cohen in Baltimore County gave birth to a litter of 4 young August 13, 1936. Another specimen collected by Father McClellan in St. Mary's County gave birth to 6 young. These he described as dark gray in color, and about 2.5 inches long."

Size and hatching time—2.5 inches in mid-August. Very recently Willson and Friddle observed (W. Va., 1950), "A female, collected August 10, 1941, was pregnant." Sinclair recorded a 261-mm. female with 18 ovarian eggs.

Food: Earthworms, insects, snails.

Field notes: In lieu of our own notes we give a résumé of this form in New Jersey as portrayed by our students, their friends, and ours.

1916: The following is all that was published about the form by Miller: "*Virginia valeriae*. Some years ago I came across several individuals of this small snake on the trap ridges immediately north of Plainfield. With one exception, they were on the north side of the First Mountain at Watchung, a single individual being found on Second Mountain less than a mile further north. All were hiding under boards or stones in dry deciduous woods. The single specimen preserved was collected on May 30, 1903. This species has not, so far as I am aware, been found elsewhere in New Jersey and the above locality is its northernmost known station."

In 1937 Trapido resumed the *Haldea* story, and in 1942 he and Kezer carefully examined Miller's notes and recorded observations on the species. Their concluding paragraph was: "In the extensive collecting of Mr. Carl Kauffeld and his associates on the coastal plain of southern New Jersey and the widespread collecting of Miller and others over New Jersey generally, *Haldea v. valeriae* has not been found outside the trap rock ridges (Watchung Mountains) of the Piedmont Plateau, where an isolated colony of this species apparently exists."

Authorities:

Blanchard, F. N. (Gen., 1924a)
Fowler, H. W. (N.J., 1907, 1908)
Kezer, J., and H. Trapido (N.J., 1943)
Lynn, W. G. (Va., 1936)
McCauley, R. G. (Md., 1945)
Miller, W. D., Jr. (N.J., 1916)

Richmond, N., and C. J. Goin (Va., 1938)
Sinclair, R. M. (Tenn., 1951)
Trapido, H. (N. J., 1937)
Walker, C. F. (Ohio, 1931)

Virginia's snake (17—Yarrow 1882),
Western ground snake (3)

Haldea valeriae elegans (Kennicott) 1859. Fig. 90; Map 27

Other common names: Brown snake; elegant snake (2—Brimley 1910); elegant Virginia; gray snake; ground snake; Kennicott's brown snake

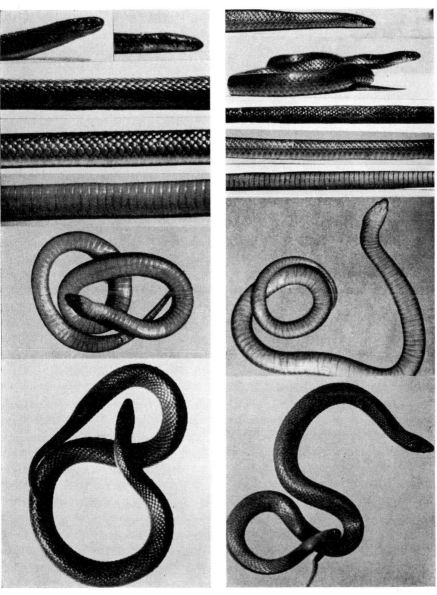

Fig. 89. *Haldea valeriae valeriae,* S. Aquasco, Prince George Co., Md., A. D. Jones.

Fig. 90. *Haldea v. elegans:* 1,2,4,6,7, Arkansas, D. L. Gamble; 3,5, Imboden, Ark., B. C. Marshall.

(Jordan 1876); Valeria's snake; Virginia brown snake; Virginia snake (4); worm snake.

Range: From s. Indiana s. to the Gulf, w. to Corpus Christi, Tex., and n. to e. Kansas and s.e. Iowa.—Ala.; Ark.; Ill.; Ind.; Ia.; Kan.; Ky.; La.; Miss.; Mo.; Okla.; Tenn.; Tex. *Elevation*—Sea level to 2,000 feet.

Size: Adults, 6–12.6 inches.

Distinctive characteristics: A small light brown to russet brown burrower with dorsal scale rows 17 (rarely 19), usually keeled at least posteriorly. No dorsal spots. Collectively the ventrals are 113–132 (males 113–125, females 118–132), the caudals 27–45 (males 35–45, females 25–36). Other characters are supralabials 6, infralabials 6 (5, 7), loreal 1, oculars 0–2 (3).

Color: A snake from Helotes, Tex., found May 2, 1925. The mid-back is brick red shading into hay's russet or carrot red on the first 2 or 3 scale rows. Head plates in the rear are auburn or rood's brown, becoming forward buffy brown. Each prefrontal is marked with 1 or 2 dark spots, the frontal with several and the parietal and temporal regions with a few. The upper and lower labials, rostral, and scales just back and below the angle of the mouth are flesh pink or coral pink. The iris in the cephalic lower quarter is chocolate or liver brown, the rest is flesh pink or coral pink spotted with vinaceous-rufous or hay's russet. The lighter color forms a crescent over the round pupil. The chin is pale grayish vinaceous with a wash of flesh pink or coral pink. The belly is sulphur yellow with the sides and ends of the ventrals vinaceous-rufous. The underside of the tail is warm buff or pale orange-yellow.

A snake received from Gamble, May 8, 1928. The back is hazel, cinnamon-brown, or verona brown with the 2 middorsal rows of scales tawny-olive. The top of the head is snuff brown spotted with black. The upper and lower labials are pale cinnamon-pink.

Habitat and habits: Most writers agree that this burrower is a rare snake. Indeed it is a "not common snake." "Rare," "very rare," "seldom seen," "only 2 for the state," "never seen alive," 1 to 4 at the most for any collector, express its status. Most of a dozen or more authors agreed that they occurred in heavily timbered regions whether river bottoms, sandstone woods or shaded rocky woods. They have been taken under rocks; under logs throughout the year; in narrow wooded paths; in thick piles of dead leaves and other cover.

Period of activity: "Occasionally found . . . throughout the year" (Allen, Miss. 1942). *First appearance*—Alabama: Apr. 15, 1912 (Löding, 1922); Missouri: Apr. 4, May 4, 13 (Hurter, 1911); Apr. 3, 8, 18 (Anderson, 1942); Oklahoma: Apr. 28, 1928 (Force, 1930); Kansas: May 9, 1926 (Gloyd); Tennessee: May 5, 1945 (Sinclair). *Fall disappearance*—Missouri: Sept. 6 (Hurter, 1911), Oct. 24, 1937 (Anderson, 1942); Tennessee: Sept. 20, 1900 (Blanchard, 1922).

Breeding: Viviparous. Males 199–256 mm., females 183–280 mm. *Number*—6–12. "I am indebted to Mr. Fred Payne for the first record of this comparatively rare snake from this locality. I took a second specimen in the edge of the woods near the house on August 30. The body was swollen to such an extent that the tail was sharply demarked. Dissection revealed 6 perfectly formed embryos, one of which was examined and found to be 95 mm. in length and similar in squamation and color to the adult except that it is slightly darker and the markings more obscure" (Hahn, Ind., 1909). "WJH 153, collected in the fall, contained 12 ova from 2 to 4 mm. long and 1 to 3 mm. in diameter" (Force, Okla., 1930). "A Lawrence County specimen contained several well developed embryos in its oviducts" (Minton, Ind., 1944). "This snake was dissected and found to contain 6 elongated eggs measuring from 10.5 to 12 mm. with an average length of 11.5 mm. All were 6 mm. in width" (Sinclair).

Food: Insects, earthworms. Hay (Ind., 1892), Blanchard, Guthrie (Ia., 1926), Gloyd, Minton (Ind., 1944).

Authorities:

Blanchard, F. N. (Gen., 1924a)   Kennicott, R. (Gen., 1860)
Gloyd, H. K. (Kan., 1928)   Sinclair, R. M. (Tenn., 1951)

PROBLEMATICAL FORM

Garman's snake

Amphiardis inornatus (Garman) 1883. Map 27
(Scale variant of *Haldea striatula* called *Virginia inornata* by Garman in 1883)

Range: Coastal Texas (Matagorda County), central Texas (San Antonio, Dallas) to central Oklahoma (Sapulpa).

Distinctive characteristics: "The types from which this species was described were secured near Dallas. Their principal difference from *Potamophis striatula* appears in the divided internasal, lack of an occipital ashy band, and in a stouter form" (Garman, Tex., 1892).

Color: A snake taken May 2, 1925, from a shaded pecan-oak bottom near Helotes, Tex. Ends of ventrals and sides vinaceous-rufous becoming on back hay's russet or coral red on first 2 or 3 rows of scales to brick red on dorsum. Labials and rostral flesh pink or coral pink, as are scales just back of and below angle of mouth. Head plates in rear auburn or rood's brown becoming forward buffy brown. Prefrontals each with 1 or 2 dark spots. Frontal with several and occipital with a few spots; temporal region with a few dark spots. Chin pale grayish vinaceous with wash of flesh pink or coral pink. Belly sulphur yellow; underside of tail warm buff or pale orange yellow

Authorities:

Blanchard, F. N. (Okla., 1924d   Schmidt, K. P. (Okla., 1919)
Brown, A. E. (Gen., 1901)   Strecker, J. K., Jr. (Tex., 1915, 1922)
Cope, E. D. (Tex., 1889, 1900)   Van Denburgh, J. (Tex., 1922)
Garman, S. (Gen., 1883)

HOG-NOSED SNAKES

Genus *HETERODON* Latreille (Fig. 25)

Size medium, 12–48 inches; body stout; head slightly distinct from ex-
pandable neck, anterior ribs capable of spreading to flatten that portion of
body like a cobra; tail short; anal divided, frequently double; scales keeled
with pits in 23–25 rows; rostral projecting, upturned, recurved and keeled
above; usually 1–20 accessory scales (azygous) separating internasals and
prefrontals; subocular ring present; oculars 8–12; upper labials 7–8, lower
9–13; temporals 2 (3) + 3 (4); 4 + 4 or 4 + 5 (in *kennerlyi*); loreal 1;
nasals 2 (sometimes an extra subnasal); venter frequently blocked light
and dark, or largely black; maxillary teeth 6–11, diastema, 2 posterior
maxillary teeth much enlarged, mandibular teeth subequal; "hemipenis bifurcate, the apices with numerous papillose calyces, and separated by a free
margin from the spinous portion. Spines numerous, hooked" (Cope, Gen.,
1900). Capitate. Ventrals 114–152; caudals 27–60. Synonyms: *Boa, Coluber,
Natrix, Oxyrhina, Pelias, Scytale, Scytalus, Vipera.*

KEY TO THE GENUS *HETERODON*

a. Rostral straight; no accessory scales about azygous plate; prefrontals in
   contact; frontal longer than broad, sides straight or concave; eye larger
   (1.5 in snout); top of head flatter (depth of head at eye about equal
   depth at angle of mouth); length of head approximately normal; upper
   labial outline elliptic; rostral narrower dorsally (2 or more in space between eyes); scale rows 23–25; about 2 rows of gulars between chin
   shields and ventral plates.
  b. Internasals separated by single median azygous plate; series of dark
     saddle spots and 20–31 light crossbars on body with 1 row of large
     lateral spots to dorsum totally black. Ventrals 119–150; caudals 37–60.
     H. platyrhinos platyrhinos
  bb. Internasals in contact, no azygous plate (sometimes present); dark
     saddle spots and 16–19 light crossbars. Ventrals 114–141; caudals 42–53.
     H. p. browni
aa. Rostral sharp and abruptly upturned; accessory scales about azygous

plate; prefrontals separated by small scales and often reduced; frontal width equal to or greater than length; sides rounded or convex; eye smaller (2 in snout); top of head very rounded to an abrupt snout; head stubby, depth at eye contained 1.5 in depth at angle of mouth; upper labial outline semicircular; rostral broader (1.5-1.8 in space between eyes); scale rows 23–27; 4 to 5 rows gulars between chin shields and ventrals.

b. Scale rows 23; 24–55 dorsal body spots; 2 rows lateral spots; venter with considerable black; rostral as broad as space between eyes. (No inferior nasal plate.—Cope.)

   c. 2 or 3 scales accessory to azygous plate; belly black and yellow checkered or quadrate blotched; loreal very small or absent. Ventrals 128–144; caudals 29–47.   *H. n. kennerlyi*

   cc. 8–20 small scales accessory to azygous plate; belly almost entirely black with a few yellow spots; loreals 2–5. Ventrals 125–152; caudals 27–47.   *H. nasicus nasicus*

bb. Scale rows 25 rarely 27; 35 dorsal body spots; 1 distinct row of lateral spots; 3–12 small scales accessory to azygous; rostral narrower than space between eyes; venter light, may be clouded or punctate. (Inferior nasal plate.—Cope.) Ventrals 115–150; caudals 32–55. *H. simus*

Hog-nosed snake (17—Yarrow 1875), Western hog-nosed snake (21—Ruthven 1910)

Heterodon nasicus nasicus Baird and Girard 1852. Fig. 91; Map 28

Other common names: Blowing adder; blowing viper (Baird 1854); blow snake; bluffer; common western hog-nosed viper; (western) hog-nose snake; North American long-nosed snake; prairie hog-nosed snake; puff(ing) adder; sand viper; spoonbill snake; spreadhead snake; spreading adder (Baird 1854); spreading viper; Texas hog-nosed snake; Texas rooter; western spreading adder; western hog-nosed adder.

Range: S.w. Manitoba, Can., s.e. to w. Illinois and s.e. Missouri, s.w. to cent. Texas, thence n.w. to n. New Mexico (a spur to cent. Arizona and n. Sonora), n. across e. Colorado, extreme e. Wyoming and Montana to s.e. Saskatchewan, Can. Reported in Indiana.—U.S.A.: Ariz.; Colo.; Ia.; Ill.; Kan.; Minn.; Mo.; Mont.; Neb.; N.M.; N.D.; Okla.; S.D.; Tex.; Wyo. Can.: Alta.; Man.; Sask. Mex.: Sonora. *Elevation*—300 to 8,000 feet. 4,000–8,000 feet (Bailey, Tex., 1905); 330 feet (Evans).

Size: Adults, 16–32 inches.

Ellis and Henderson's 13 records range from 170 mm. to 790 mm. or an average of 419 mm., or if the 170–255-mm. specimens are eliminated, the average is 513 mm. (or about 20.5 inches).

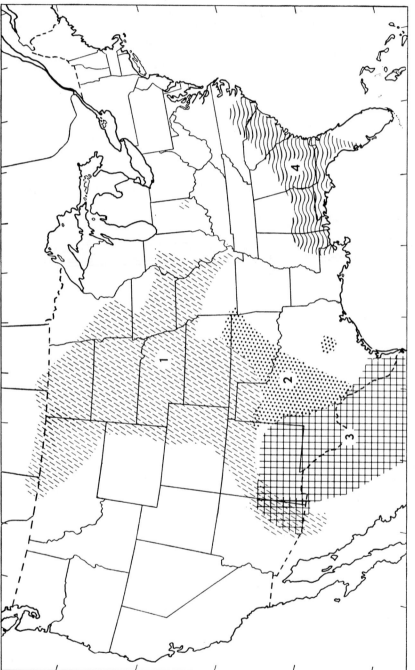

Map 28. Heterodon—1, n. nasicus; 2, n. gloydi; 3. n. kennerlyi; 4, simus.

Distinctive characteristics: A small medium to medium, sand-loving snake with an upturned snout; 2 to 3 rows of lateral spots, black belly, no inferior nasal and 23 rows of dorsal scales (not 25 to 27). Many small accessory scales around azygous and rostral therefore separated from frontal. Dorsal color deep olive buff to buff, or grayish brown; dorsal spots (average 40 spots) buffy olive.

Color: A snake from Brule Co., S.D., 7 miles east of Pukwana on U.S. 16, furnished June 14, 1940, by Mrs. Stuart M. Brown, Jr. The back is marked with dorsal saddle spots of buffy olive, 40 on body, 12 on tail. There is an upper lateral row of brownish olive spots and a lower row alternating with it of yellowish olive ones. The background between the dorsal saddles is deep olive-buff, that of the sides above the 1st scale row, grayish olive. The background color of the tail is more intense, being dark olive-buff. The lower half of the 1st row of lateral scales and the extreme ends of the ventrals are ivory yellow. The top of the head and neck are marked with bars of buffy citrine. There is a V on the neck with apex on the parietal plates and a narrow mesal band back of the parietals, a band from eye to eye across the rear of the frontal which extends obliquely back of the eye to angle of the mouth, and another such band between the forward corners of the eyes across the accessory scales. There is a sharp outline between the 2 eye bands and in front of the first one of straw yellow. The top of the rostral is like the eye bands. The background between these markings is grayish olive. The lower labials, gulars, and chin shields are white or ivory yellow. The upper labials are straw yellow with suture lines punctate with buffy citrine, while the underside of the rostral is clear naphthalene yellow. The iris is straw yellow around the pupil, and above it is an expanded area of the same with a wash of xanthine orange, but the front and rear of the iris are buffy citrine. The belly background is black with 2 irregular rows of small clear spots of amber yellow, spaced about every third ventral and located near the edge of the black portion of the plate. These spots are practically absent in preanal region and tail. The anal plate is mustard yellow. This black area extends onto the neck, the 7 anterior plates being straw yellow.

Habitat and habits: Some 18 or 20 authors have alluded to its habitat. Beginning in 1880 with Cragin (Kan., 1881), we find that the blow snake is usually found in dry, sandy locations. Distinctly a prairie species, almost every writer refers it to sandy tracts such as sandy hills, sand dunes, sandy flood plains, sandy prairies, sandy areas, and sandy fine loam. Whether upland, river, or open and grassy meadows, sandy soil or gravel enters the conditions.

Period of activity: MVZ has dates Jan.–Sept. 19. Evans recorded May 15–Oct. 10. Ellis and Henderson gave June 1–August.

Breeding: Oviparous. Males 385–550 mm., females 430–660 mm.

Eggs—Number, 5–24. "A large female taken July 20 laid 5 eggs on August

4, but died shortly afterward without passing the rest of those in the oviducts" (Ruthven). "Deposits about 2 dozen eggs late in July" (Hudson and
Davis, Feb., 1941). "Eggs were found in May and June in 9 individuals. In
these and other snakes, there often occurred numerous small eggs very distinct in size from the larger eggs and distributed in the ovaries with these
larger eggs that were obviously to produce young shortly. Either these small
eggs had started to develop and for some unknown reason were being re-
sorbed, or they represent a group of eggs that would mature the following
year or later in the same year. In all egg counts the small eggs have been
omitted. Kansas specimens from Ford Co. taken on May 27 had 14 eggs;
on May 29, 23 eggs; on May 29, 11 eggs; on June 2, 17 eggs; on June 3, 7
eggs; from Gray Co., on June 18, 13 eggs" (Marr). "On the night of July
5–6, the above-mentioned *Heterodon nasicus nasicus* laid 11 fairly uniform
eggs which had a smooth, soft rubbery feel." The eggs were (in cm.) 3.4x2.0,
3.5x1.9, 3.4x1.9, 3.55x1.85, 3.15x2.0, 3.3x2.0, 3.5x2.0, 3.2x1.9, 3.2x2, 3.2x1.95,
3.4x1.9; they hatched August 30 to Sept. 4. The hatchlings were about seven
inches long (Munro, 1949e). In Alberta, J. E. Moore reported a 22⅛-inch
female laying 4 eggs July 19–23. On dissection it had 7 more. The deposited
eggs were 1⅛x½ inch in dimensions.

Young—Our most definite record of the size of hatchlings is 7 inches
(Munro, 1949e). We wonder how far from hatching were Anderson's
Missouri specimens—a female of 188 mm. and a male of 195 mm. They were
within the range of hatching in *H. p. platyrhinos,* namely 6.5–8.4 inches.
Were Ellis and Henderson's 13 records of 170 mm. (June 26) and 190 mm.
(July 17) near hatching size?

Food: Toads, frogs, shrews, sparrows, rats, mice, lizards, garter snakes.
Guthrie (Ia., 1926), Burt and Burt (Ariz., 1929), Marr, Munro (1949d),
Swenson (Colo., 1950), Swenson and Rodeck (Colo., 1948).

Authorities:

Coues, E., and H. C. Yarrow (Mont., 1878)
Ellis, M. M., and J. Henderson (Colo., 1913)
Evans, P. D. (Mo., 1940)
Hudson, G. E. (Neb., 1942)
Kilpatrick, J. W. (Mo., 1893)
Marr, J. C. (Gen., 1944)
Moore, J. E. (Alta., 1953)

Munro, D. F. (Kan., 1949d, 1949e)
Ortenburger, A. I., and B. Freeman (Okla., 1930)
Over, W. H. (S.D., 1923)
Ruthven, A. G. (Ia., 1910b)
Schmidt, K. P. (Gen., 1938)
Smith, H. M. (Kan., 1950)
Stanley, W. F. (Ill., 1941)
Stansbury, H. (Ut., 1853)

1878, E. Coues and H. C. Yarrow: "This is the most abundant and wide-
ranging species of the genus, occurring throughout the West east of the
Rocky Mountains. . . . Mr. Allen procured it on the Yellowstone, and it appears to increase in numbers southward, being one of the more common serpents of New Mexico and Arizona."

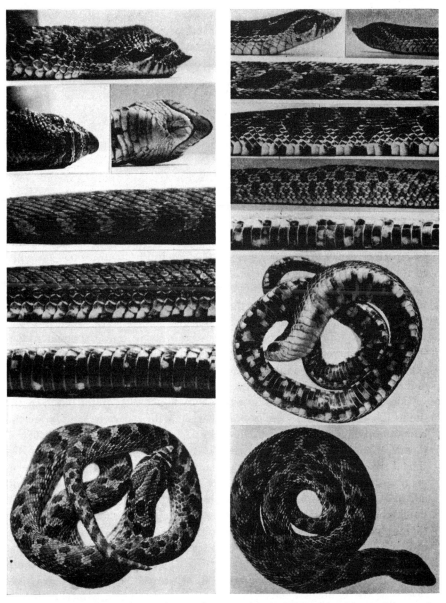

Fig. 91. *Heterodon nasicus nasicus,* Puke-vana, Brule Co., S.D., C. H. Brown.

Fig. 92. *Heterodon n. kennerlyi:* 1,3,4,6,7, Brownsville, Tex., H. C. Blanchard; 2,8, Brownsville, Tex., "Snake King"; 5, Vaughn, N.M.

Kennerly's hog-nose snake (Yarrow 1882), South-western hog-nosed snake

Heterodon nasicus kennerlyi Kennicott 1860. Fig. 92; Map 28

Other common names: Blowing hog-nosed snake; western hog-nose(d) snake.

Range: Tamaulipas, Mex., and s. Texas n.w. to cent. New Mexico and extreme e. Arizona, s. through Chihuahua, Durango, and Zacatecas e. to San Luis Potosí, Mex.—U.S.A.: Ariz.; N.M.; Tex. Mex.: Chihuahua; Coahuila; Durango; San Luis Potosí; Zacatecas. *Elevation*—2,000 to 8,000 feet. 4,000–8,000 feet (Bailey, Tex., 1905).

Size: Adults, 16–24.5 inches. The largest that Brown (Gen., 1901) ever saw was 610 mm. in length.

Distinctive characteristics: "Head broad, very short anteriorly. Rostral plate very large. Loral plate very small, sometimes absent. Only 2 supplemental plates behind the azygous; the latter is sometimes replaced by 2 symmetrical contiguous plates, and without any supplemental. The prenasal and prefrontal [are] in contact with the posterior process of the rostral. Dorsal row of scales 23, all carinated except the first and second, which are perfectly smooth. Ground-color light yellowish gray; a dorsal series of rather indistinct, rounded or subquadrate, brown blotches; a second series of smaller, circular spots, much darker and more distinct; below this a third and more indistinct series" (Coues and Yarrow).

Color: A snake from 30 miles east of Vaughn, N.M., 1925. It had recently been killed in the road. The back is marked with transverse saddles of cinnamon-brown, outlined behind the black. The skin between the scales in these transverse spots is black. There is a row of alternating spots on the side of the same color as the dorsal spots and with the black most prominent on the upper edges. Here, too, the skin is black. On the 3rd, 4th, 5th, and 6th rows of scales is another row of spots located directly below the dorsal saddles. These spots have no black edges and are ochraceous-tawny or buckthorn brown. The interspaces between the dorsal saddles are tawny-olive or avellaneous. The rest of the interspaces are drab in the centers or light drab with white edges. There are stripes of cinnamon-brown or snuff brown and white on the side of the head. There is a bar of black below the eye. The iris is burnt sienna followed by a ring of black, which in turn is followed by olive lake. The pupil rim is orange-buff. The mental, chin shields, and gulars are white. The first 10 belly plates are white, their centers washed with pinkish cinnamon or zinc orange. The ends of the ventrals are usually white, except for every 4th or 5th plate where the end is light grayish vinaceous or drab-gray. After the first 10 white plates, the middle of the ventrals is dull violet-black (2). Interspersed are spots of zinc orange which may go all the way across the dull violet-black band, or which may appear as squares. The last 2 plates in front of the vent are zinc orange. The underside of the tail is dull violet-black or bluish slate-black.

In another snake, which is larger, the belly has no zinc orange.

Habitat and habits: Bailey (Tex., 1905) found that the hog-nosed snake "is not a common or conspicuous species." In 1915 Strecker (Tex.) recorded the western spreading adder as in "western Texas, extending eastward in the Rio Grande Valley as far as Cameron County. Common in the trans-Pecos counties. . . . In the Rio Grande valley this species seems to be found only in the border counties and does not range northward into the interior for any distance." In 1937 Gloyd (Ariz.) stated that "a small hog-nosed snake was found in sand beneath a piece of tin on the plain east of the Huachuca Mountains." Jameson and Flury (Tex., 1943) wrote: "We have 2 specimens of this species, both from the Miller ranch. One specimen, a female, was collected by Miller in 1947 from the tobosa-gramma association. The other specimen was taken in the catclaw-cedar association. This species may be restricted to the Plains belt."

Breeding: Oviparous. Adults, 16–24.5 inches. Our only note is Werler's (Gen., 1951) observation of a female, 656 mm., depositing 7 small white nonadhesive eggs on June 3, 1950.

Food: Toads, frogs, small mammals. Little and Keller (N.M., 1937), Boulenger (Gen., 1914), Gloyd (Tex., 1944).

Field notes: July 17, 1942, Alamogordo, White Sands, N.M.: At 7 P.M. Dr. R. H. Deniston (Tucson, Ariz.), the ranger, went with us to Lake Walters to look for *Ficimia cana*. Anna at the south end of Lake Walters in a weedy green area espied a moving snake near the White Sand first dune. It went into a clump. She pinned it down to determine whether it was a rattler or not. Seeing it wasn't, she picked it up hoping for *Ficimia*. It proved to be a fine *Heterodon n. kennerlyi*.

In the fall of 1946, a beautiful little *Heterodon nasicus* came to us from Mrs. Dorothy Sprung of Sonoita, Ariz., of the Diamond S ranch. It is *H. n. kennerlyi*, with only 1 loreal and with a total of 3 azygous scales. It looks much like the one from White Sands, N.M., except that the spots at the middorsal row are more barlike, the interspaces narrower, and this barlike condition extends close to the neck. There are 3 rows of the lighter spots on the sides below the row of darker ones that occur at either end of the light dorsal interspace bar. There are 37 dark bars on body + spot at neck + 13 on tail; the large spots just back of the parietals are round, not narrow oblique, bars as in the one from White Sands.

Authorities:

Coues, E., and H. C. Yarrow (N.C., 1878)

Kennicott, R. (Gen., 1860–61)

Smith, H. M. (Tex., 1943a)

Smith, H. M., and E. H. Taylor (Gen., 1945)

1878, E. Coues and H. C. Yarrow: "This species differs from *H. simus* in many of the same features as does *H. nasicus*. These, together with the small or absent loral and small number of supplemental plates, will readily distinguish it."

1943, H. M. Smith: "A specimen from 'Sonora' (collected by Jenkins and Everman, No. 61954) has 3–4 loreals and 16 azygous scales, and accordingly cannot be considered *kennerlyi*. I have examined several similar Arizona specimens. I cannot observe readily definable differences between these and typical *nasicus,* to which I refer them. The area occupied by them in Sonora and Arizona no doubt borders the western edge of the range of *kenneryli,* and it is conceivable that the southwestern and northern ranges of *nasicus* are continuous through northern New Mexico."

Gloyd's hog-nosed snake

Heterodon nasicus gloydi Edgren. Map 28

In December, 1952, R. A. Edgren (Gen., 1952) published his synopsis of *Heterodon*. He sent *H. p. browni* into synonymy, with which we agree. He also recognized a new form, *H. n. gloydi*. His three *nasicus* forms, arranged in key form, are:

2   Belly black with small yellow blotches.   3
3   Generally less than 7 scales in azygous area.   *kennerlyi*
3a Generally more than 9 scales in azygous area.   4
4   Generally more than 35 blotches anterior to vent in males; more than 40 in females.   *nasicus*
4a Generally less than 32 dorsal blotches in males; less than 37 in females.
                                                                                       gloydi

The range of the three forms he gave thus:

H. nasicus nasicus. Texas panhandle and adjacent New Mexico n. through w. Oklahoma and Kansas to s.w. Manitoba and s.e. Saskatchewan in Canada; prairie portions of Minnesota, and prairie relicts in Illinois.

H. n. gloydi. S.e. Kansas and s.e. Missouri, e. Oklahoma, and all of Texas except for the panhandle, trans-Pecos Texas and extreme southern Rio Grande Valley.

H. n. kennerlyi. Mexico from Tamaulipas and cent. San Luis Potosí n. and w. along the Cordillera Occidental, invading the United States in extreme s. Rio Grande Valley, trans-Pecos Texas, s.w. New Mexico, and s.e. Arizona.

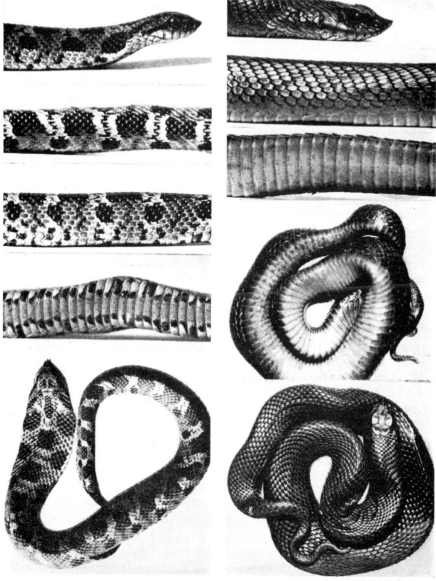

Fig. 93. *Heterodon platyrhinos platyrhinos* (spotted phase), Lake Alfred, Fla., L. E. Dills.

Fig. 94. *Heterodon platyrhinos platyrhinos* (black phase), Mobile, Ala., H. P. Loding.

Spreading adder (93—De Kay 1842), Hog-nosed snake
(86—De Kay 1842)

Heterodon platyrhinos platyrhinos (Latreille) 1801. Figs. 93, 94; Map 29

Other common names: Adder; bastard rattlesnake; black adder; black blowing viper; black hog-nosed snake; black viper snake (Beverly 1722); blauser; blower; blowing adder; blowing snake (Clayton 1705); blow(ing) viper; blow snake; buckwheat-nose snake; calico snake; checkered (or checquered) adder; chunk head; common hog-nosed snake; common spreading adder; deaf adder; eastern hog-nosed snake (3); flat-head; flat-head(ed) adder; hay-nose snake; hissing adder; hissing snake; hog-nosed adder; hog-nosed rattler; hog-nose snake (Catesby 1731–43); hog-nosed viper; hissing viper; (mountain) moccasin; North American adder; North American hog-nosed snake; pilot; poison viper; puff(ing) adder; red snake; rock adder; rossel bastard; sand adder; sand viper; spotted (spreading) adder; spread-head moccasin; spread-head snake; spread-head viper; (spreading) viper.

Range: E. United States. From New Hampshire to lower Hudson Valley across s. and cent. Pennsylvania to n.e. Ohio and s. Ontario, w. through lower peninsula of Michigan and s. Wisconsin to cent. Minnesota and s.e. South Dakota, thence s. to Del Rio, Valverde Co. Texas, down the Rio Grande to Brownsville, along Gulf coast to tip of Florida and n. to New England.—U.S.A.: Ala.; Ark.; Conn.; D.C.; Del.; Fla.; Ga.; Ill.; Ind.; Ia.; Kan.; Ky.; La.; Mass.; Md.; Mich.; Minn.; Miss.; Mo.; N.C.; Neb.; N.H.; N.J.; N.Y.; O.; Okla.; Pa.; R.I.; S.C.; S.D.; Tenn.; Tex.; Va.; W. Va.; Wis. Can.; Ont. *Elevation*—Seacoast to 2,500 feet, mostly below 1,000 feet. 1,000–2,500 feet (King, Tenn., 1939).

Size: Adults, 18–48 inches.

Distinctive characteristics: This stocky hog-nose is the largest and most widespread of his clan, and comes in varying patterns and colors, spotted and uniform, in red, gray, and black. In some the pattern is reduced to broken tracery, in others to clear-cut saddles. The rostral is approximately straight, but sharply pointed; the top of the head is quite flat, of the same depth at eye as at angle of mouth; the internasals are separated by a single scale—the azygous plate; ventrals 119–150; caudals 37–60.

Color: A snake from Spanish Creek, Folkston, Ga., July 16, 1922. The mid-dorsal spots are pecan brown toward the head and light brownish olive toward the tail. All these spots are separated by black bars alternating with lateral spots of black. The lowest 4 rows of scales are specked with black on a pale vinaceous-fawn ground. The interspaces around the lateral spots are vinaceous-buff from within an inch of the head to the region of the vent, though the color is somewhat lighter toward the tail. The interspaces just back of the head are pinkish cinnamon, ochraceous-salmon, flesh ocher, or bittersweet orange.

A snake from Auburn, Ala., furnished by Good, Apr. 16, 1928. Down the back are 19 large transverse bars of black separated by narrower transverse bars of clay color or honey yellow, which on the tail become prominent bars of ecru-olive with reed yellow edges. Below each end of the honey yellow bar is a black spot alternating with the dorsal black saddles. This lower spot is almost surrounded with clay color or light cadmium. The first 3 or 4 rows of scales are black, lemon chrome and yellowish glaucous, or olive-buff. The top of the head is black. Back of the eye is an oblique black band bordered below by antimony yellow. In front of the eye is a colonial buff spot. Below the eye is a black bar. The upper labials are straw yellow to cartridge buff. The iris in general is hay's maroon or bay, and above the pupil are a little vinaceous-rufous and 2 or more patches of olive-buff. The lower head parts are chamois spotted with black. The neck for 2 or 3 inches is reed yellow. The belly is olive-buff or ecru-olive down the center with dottings like the violet-slate margin on either end of each ventral. Somewhat in from the end, or on the end, each ventral bears a violet-slate spot, set off by the light color of the lowest lateral rows.

Resemblances—"It was of the banded type, in color and markings mimicking *Ancistrodon contortrix*" (Strecker, Tex., 1909a). "Inasmuch as the residents generally confuse those snakes which even in a slight respect resemble a rattler, it was impossible to get other certain records of its occurrence in the region" (Thompson, Mich., 1911).

Abnormal coloration—Melanism: By 1940 this phase had been remarked on by at least 20 writers, including Abbott, 1868; Higley, 1889; Hurter, 1893; Brimley, 1895; Beyer, 1900; Morse, 1901; Eckel, 1901; Street, 1914; Engelhardt, 1915; Ellis, 1917; Patch, 1919; Löding, 1922; Strecker, 1926; Strecker and Frierson, 1926; Klots, 1930; Snyder and Logier, 1931; King, 1939. It is not an old-age phase; see Evans on immature black (N.Y., 1947). Albinism: "I send this photograph of an albino snake because its occurrence may be worth recording as the only hog nose albino snake ever reported in the United States. It was captured by a farmer in a field near Amherst, New Hampshire, last July and aside from being an albino, it is one of the most northern records of the species in New England" (Newton, N.J., 1940). Yellow: We have heard of yellow hog-noses with spots, but not uniform. Gray: "Of the three Samburg specimens one adult is noteworthy in having the body and tail a uniform grayish olive above and ashy white below, without markings. The head and neck have the normal black markings" (Rhoads, Tenn., 1896). Brown: "Uniform brown without spots" (Higley, Wis., 1889). Slate: "Mr. W. T. Davis has a specimen which was of 'uniform slate color' collected at Yaphank, July 14, 1907" (Engelhardt *et al.*). Red (Erythrism): We have seen pure red hog-nose snakes from southeast of San Antonio, Tex.

Habitat and habits: This species is distinctly a sandy-habitat one (55), liking dry (18) rather than wet or marshy ground. It likes open or thinly wooded tracts better than dense forests; it prefers uplands, hillsides, and hammocks to lowlands. One author says it is never about habitations, but two say it is. It has been recorded in greenhouses (1), ferneries (1), dwellings (1), barns (1), cultivated fields (5). It has been taken in fields (15), cornfields (1), orange groves (2), high fields (1), outbuildings (1), barns (2). One author says it is not found under rocks or logs and does not swim. Of rocks and logs we have no record, but two have been reported as swimming—one in surf and one in a flooded river—and several as living on islands. If woods are described, they are usually pine or deciduous. On this topic we accumulated 130 records, but we forbear to give them all to you. For two extended accounts, we recommend Engelhardt, Nichols, Latham, and Murphy and Wright.

"Feigned death"—More has been written about this antic or habit than any other. We give only one quotation: "When disturbed it flattens its head, hisses, throws its mouth wide open, giving it the appearance of a dislocated lower jaw (which remains fixed for some time), and darts at the object. If unable thus to frighten away its foes, and is in turn a little roughly treated, such as being pushed with a stick, it will feign death, as was observed by Troost and also by Prof. Steere of Michigan University. The former . . . was so far deceived that he laid down his snake for a short time, when it made its escape, and was found again with difficulty" (Smith, O., 1882). Those who wish more information about this habit may read: Abbott (N.J., 1868); Smith (Ohio, 1882); Bumpus (Gen., 1885; R.I., 1885); Garman (Ill., 1892); Kilpatrick (Mo., 1893); Spaid (Gen., 1903); Morse (Ohio, 1904); Surface (Pa., 1906); McAtee (Ind., 1907); Dury (Ohio, 1910); Hurter (Mo., 1911); Boulenger (Gen., 1912); Bartlett (Gen., 1920); Evermann and Clark (Ind., 1920); Logier (Ont., 1925); Funkhouser (Ky., 1925); Proctor (Gen., 1926); Guthrie (Ia., 1924); Ortenburger, best account (Gen., 1930); Bailey (Kan., 1933); Brimley (N.C., 1941).

Burrowing behavior—Davis (Ill., 1946) has described this aptly, graphically, and in great detail.

Period of activity: *First appearance*—Mar. 31 (Hahn, Ind., 1909); Mar. 22, 1890 (Blatchley); May 9, 1908, Apr. 21, 1902 (Fowler, N.J., 1908); Apr. 5 (Harper, Ga., 1930); May 7, 1927 (Strecker, Tex., 1928); Apr. 16, 1928 (Pope, Wis., 1928); May 15 (Engelhardt); Apr. 12 (Hurter); Apr. 29, 1939 (Anderson, Mo., 1942). *Fall disappearance*—Sept. 26, 1936 (Crowell, N.H., 1937); Nov., 1871 (Coues and Yarrow, N.C., 1878); Oct. 14 (Hurter); Oct. 3, 1928 (Force, Okla., 1911); Sept. 28, 1926 (Anderson); Dec. 2, 1926 (Netting, Pa., 1927b). *Seasonal catch*—Jan. 1, Mar. 2, Apr. 1, May 12, June 6, July 3, Aug. 6, Sept. 1, Oct. 8, Nov. 4 (Brimley, N.C., 1925). "A serpent that is frequently encountered throughout the summer and occasionally in the winter during the high temperatures" (Allen, Miss., 1932).

Breeding: Oviparous. Males 400–1,050 mm., females 450–1,200 mm. *Sexual dimorphism*—Edgren (Gen., 1951) records dimorphism in the umbilical scars of males and females: "The actual range for the anterior end of the scar in the males varies from ventral 98 to ventral 108, in females 107 to 120. The posterior end varies from the 99th ventral to the 111th in males and from the 109th to the 121st in females."

Mating—Gaines (Ind., 1894) reported a pair (one uniform black, one spotted) copulating. Blatchley wrote: "The var. *niger* is almost as frequent as the typical species, and, in the writer's opinion, is but a mere form. On April 13, 1889, a specimen of *niger* was found in copulation with one of the typical *platyrhinus,* while but a foot or two away was another *platyrhinus."* In Hay's article (Gen., 1893), the mating of black and spotted phases was mentioned. Medsger (N.J., 1927) wrote: "Two males, both alive, and uninjured, had mated with the dead female. They were both fastened at the vent of the female and when we took a stick and picked her up and tossed her about, they did not pull loose. Without doubt the males were not around when the female was killed or they would have met the same fate that she did."

For male *Heterodon p. platyrhinos* crossed with *H. simus,* see Neill (Gen., 1951).

Eggs—Number, 6–42. 6 eggs (Minton, Ind., 1944); 7 (Conant, O. 1938a, Guidry, Tex., 1953); 8 (3 authors); 10 (1); 11 (1); 12 (3); 13 (1); 15 (1); 16 (1); 18 (1); 19 (1); 20 (1); 22 (2); 24 (2); 25 (3); 26 (1); 27 (2); 28 (1); 30 (1); 34 (1); 35 (1); 37 (1); 40 (2); 42 (1). Time of deposition, mainly June, some July, few in early August. Most records are June 3–June 27. There are some July 1–12 and 2 in August (Clark, Conn., 1952). "I have seen a female of this species buried in the soft earth of a cornfield, apparently guarding her eggs among which she was coiled" (Hahn, Ind., 1909). "During the next 3 days [after deposition] she twice coiled about her eggs for a short space of time" (Strecker, Tex., 1926). Size, 1 (24 mm.)–1.5 (39 mm.) inches x.5 (12.5 mm.)–1.2 (30 mm.) inches; average 29 mm. x 19 mm. "The eggs of this species are about the same size and shape as those of the Black Snake, but the skin of the egg is smooth and very thin, much thinner than in any other species whose eggs I have handled. Like those of the Black Snake, the eggs of this species are free, not adherent to one another in clusters" (Brimley).

Young—Hatching time, last of July to early September. Most records in August from Aug. 5 through 27. There are records of eggs hatching after deposition as follows: 39 days, 52 days, 60 days, 2 months. Size, 6½–8.4 inches; most hatchlings near 8 inches. Dubious accounts: S. S. Rathvon (100 young); J. Schenck (87 young); H. C. Bumpus (111 young). Doubtless these were water snakes.

Food: Toads, salamanders, fish, snakes, lizards, insects, worms, birds, frogs, mice, chipmunks. Many authors; Uhler, Cottam, and Clarke (Va., 1939).

Authorities:

Bartlett, W. E. (Gen., 1920)

Blatchley, W. S. (Ind., 1891)

Brimley, C. S. (Gen., 1903)

Engelhardt, G., J. T. Nichols, R. Latham, and R. C. Murphy (N.Y., 1915)

Hay, O. P. (Gen., 1893)

Hurter, J. (Mo., 1911)

Kilpatrick, J. W. (Mo., 1893)

McAtee, W. L. (Ind., 1907)

Minton, S. J., Jr. (Ind., 1944)

Ortenburger, A. I. (Gen., 1930)

Strecker, J. K., Jr. (Tex., 1926f)

Wright, A. H. (Ga., 1926)

(and many more)

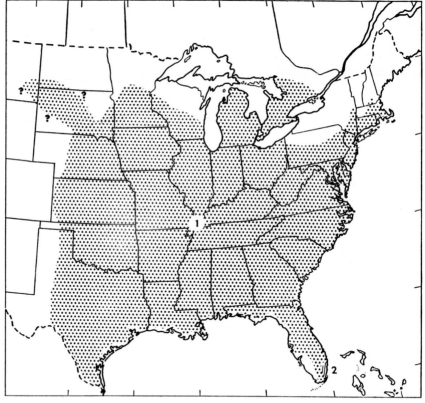

Map 29. *Heterodon*—1, *platyrhinos; 2, p. browni.*

Florida hog-nosed snake (4), Brown's hog-nosed snake
(4—Ditmars 1936)

Heterodon platyrhinos browni Stejneger 1903. Fig. 95; Map 29 (Variant of *H. p. platyrhinos*)

Other common names: Hog-nose snake (1—Stejneger 1903); hog-nose(d snake); puff adder.

Range: Eastern Dade Co., s. Fla. *Elevation*—Seacoast to 50 feet.

Size: Adults, 18–30 inches. Such as we have seen alive average about the same size as *H. p. platyrhinos.*

Distinctive characteristics: Similar in appearance to many *p. platyrhinos.* The one we described had 17 black saddle bars and colonial buff interspaces, the bars being a bit larger and fewer than those of the *p. platyrhinos* we had. "Maxillary teeth 8 + 2; *no azygous shield between internasals or prefrontals;* rostrals narrower than distance between eyes; scale rows 25; ventrals 114–127; anal divided; subcaudals 47–53 pairs" (Stejneger).

Color: A snake in Opalocka Zoo, Miami, Fla., Mar. 23, 1934. The back is marked with 17 black saddles on the body and 8 on the tail, with small rounded alternating spots on the 5th to 9th rows of scales. The intervals between the saddles and the skin between the scales of the interspaces between the lateral spots are colonial buff. Below the lateral row of spots is a light area. The iris is black except for the upper quadrant, which is white. In the center of the quadrant, on the pupil rim, is a black spot. The ends of most of the ventrals are marked with white, while down the middle of the venter lime green or ecru-olive appears, becoming a little brighter whenever this color extends to the ends of the ventrals.

Habitat and habits: See *H. p. platyrhinos.* We give only Carr's note: "Palmetto and limestone flatwoods; hothouses and truck fields; occasionally ploughed up in muckland. Fairly common locally."

Field notes: June 10, 1928, Jacksonville Zoo: Three spreading adders—one of which is black and apparently without azygous plate.

June 16, 1928: Went to Opalocka Zoo, Miami, Fla. Mr. Sirman there showed me his snakes. He had 3 *Heterodon.* They have the rostral sending back an extension in place of an azygous cutoff plate. One has an azygous, but it is very irregularly cut off. Am not yet wholly satisfied. Later saw R. F. Deckert. He wonders about *Heterodon browni.*

March 17, 1934: Visited Opalocka Zoo. G. F. Sirman, Quimby Sirman have two *Heterodon*—one without an azygous and one with a very minute one. Went to Florida Reptile Society. Here we met Mrs. Frampton. They have a fine collection. They have a *Heterodon browni* with a small azygous plate.

Mar. 23, 1934, Opalocka Zoo: Took a few pictures of *Heterodon browni.* Chose one without an azygous plate. We had a pleasant afternoon at the aquarium. Met Mr. Frampton, whom O. C. Van Hyning recommended to me. He, like myself, queries about *Heterodon browni.*

Authorities:

Barbour, T. (Fla., 1919)

Carr, A. F., Jr. (Fla., 1940a)

Safford, W. E. (Fla., 1919)

Stejneger, L. (Fla., 1903)

(We yield to no man in our admiration of Stejneger, the man or the scholar, but we are still very doubtful about this form. It should be placed with the problematical species.)

1940(a) A. F. Carr, Jr.: "In a series from Central Florida I found every condition of the scale, from non-existent to normal in size and shape. I have also examined specimens with an intermediate number of transverse dorsal bars. There seems little doubt that these 2 forms are races of one species."

Southern hog-nosed snake (14—Wachtel), Hog-nosed snake (11—Davis and Rice 1883)

Heterodon simus (Linnaeus) 1766. Fig. 96; Map 28

Other common names: Blowing adder; blowing viper; flat-nosed snake (Shaw 1802); hog-nose adder; hog-nosed viper; puff(ing) adder; sand viper; shovel-nose spreading adder; snubby viper (Kerr 1802); spread-head snake; spreading adder; southern hog-nose; viper.

Range: Cent. North Carolina s. to Pinellas Co., Fla., w. to e. Louisiana. —Ala.; Fla.; Ga.; La.; N.C.; S.C. *Elevation*—Seacoast to 500 feet.

Size: Adults, 12–27 inches. The largest we have seen was 20 inches long.

Distinctive characteristics: A small medium digger with 25 (27) dorsal scale rows (like *platyrhinos*) but with better developed rostral; unlike *platyrhinos* with prefrontals separated by small scales and the azygous plate back of rostral surrounded by 4–10 or 12 accessory scales. Venter cream, white to pinkish buff, punctate in rear. One distinct lateral row of dorsal spots. Unlike *nasicus* with its black or black-checkered belly, 23 dorsal scale rows, and 2–3 rows of lateral spots, and no inferior nasal. General ground color drab or light drab.

Color: A snake from Alligator Farm at South Jacksonville, Fla., June 10, 1928. The middorsal background for about 7 rows of scales is drab or light drab. The back is marked with saddles of clove brown outlined in front and rear with black. On the 6th to 8th rows of scales and alternating with the dorsal saddles is a line of smaller spots of the same sort. The interval color on the sides is avellaneous, vinaceous-buff, or ecru-drab. On the 3rd and 4th rows of scales, there is a row of obscure spots, each spot covering only 1 or 2 scales. These spots are opposite those of the regular lateral row. There is a long bar which is black or of the color of the dorsal saddles on either side of the neck. These 2 nuchal spots unite forward on the meson just back of the line of the eyes, and between them is a narrow dorsal stripe of the same color. Some of the scales of the interval areas of this region may have vinaceous-fawn edges or interspaces. There is a black vitta from the angle of the mouth to the rear of the eye and from the angle of the eye to the azygous plate. The iris is clove brown with a deep olive-buff area above the

Fig. 95. *Heterodon p. browni,* Opalaka Zoo,·Miami, Fla., G. F. Sirman.

Fig. 96. *Heterodon simus:* 1, 7, alligator farm, Jacksonville, Fla.; 2–6, Silver Springs, Fla., E. R. Allen.

pupil. The pupil rim is olive-buff. The lower side of the rostral and the general under parts may be cream colored, white, pale cinnamon-pink, or pale pinkish buff. The rear half of the venter is more or less clouded or punctate with drab and clove brown.

Habitat and habits: In general, this is a sand-inhabiting snake. The information on it is scant. In Louisiana, Beyer (1900) secured one sand viper in Washington Parish; in Mississippi, Allen (1932) had 4 specimens, one "in a thick woods." In Florida, Van Hyning (1933) wrote that its "habits [are] similar to those of the preceding species [*platyrhinos*]; moderately common." Carr (Fla., 1940a) placed it in "upland hammocks; dry flood plains of rivers; wire grass flatwoods; fields and groves."

As late as 1941–42 Brimley wrote: "I know nothing of its habits which presumably resemble those of the Spotted Adder. Only 6 specimens are on record from North Carolina, 2 taken in Wake County, Oct. 5, 1907, another in June, 1930; 1 at Havelock, June 20, 1905 (J. J. Ballard); 1 at Wilmington (Myers), and 1 in Goldboro (U.S. National Museum)."

Breeding: Oviparous. To the discredit of herpetologists this is one of the numerous forms which still travel under the familiar phrase "similar to" or "presumably resembles" to cover our ignorance. Previous to 1951 we knew little of its breeding. Thanks to Neill (Gen., 1951) we have two notes. "On May 29, 1950, a female southern hog-nosed snake, *Heterodon simus,* was brought into the Reptile Institute. The snake was unusually large, but otherwise was typical of the species in Florida. It was placed in a cage with several common hog-nosed snakes, *H. p. platyrhinos.* Some time later, the large *simus* was found to be in copula with a small male *platyrhinos.* Coitus lasted for about 3 hours and perhaps would have continued longer had not the pair been disturbed." The female died later. The other note is of how, "on May 23, 1951, a female of this species was noted in copula with two males simultaneously. One male had inserted its right hemipenis, the other its left."

Food: Toads, frogs, lizards, spadefoots. Deckert (Fla., 1918), Van Duyn, Goin. *Hyla gratiosa, Pseudacris ornata*—tree frogs (Neill).

Authorities:

Brimley, C. S. (N.C., 1941–42)
Goin, C. J. (Fla., 1947)
Holbrook, J. E. (Gen., 1832–42)
Kerr, R. (Gen., 1802)
Say, T. (Gen., 1819)
Shaw, G. (Gen., 1802)
Van Duyn, G. (Gen., 1937)

1937, G. Van Duyn: An interesting account.

NIGHT SNAKES

Genus *HYPSIGLENA* Cope (Fig. 24)

Size, small to small medium, 6.2–26 inches; slender cylindrical; tail less than ⅕ total length; head distinct; temporal region swollen in old adults; snout projects beyond the mouth; anal divided; scales smooth, but with spines above anus in males, apical pits single (usually); scales in 19–23 rows —(23) 21–21 (23)–17 (15); temporals conspicuously larger than dorsal neck scales; supraoculars narrow; frontal wide; preoculars (1) 2 (3) (upper may be very large and corner on labial with lower inserted between labials);

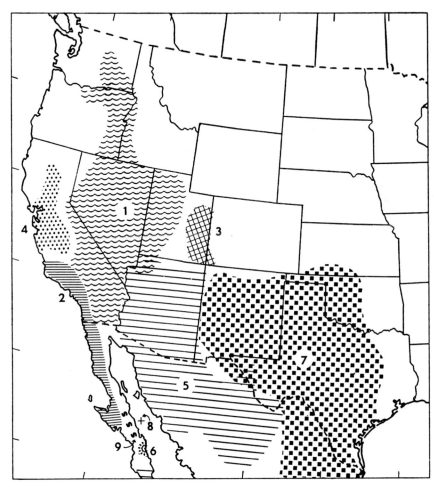

Map 30. *Hypsiglena*—1, *t. deserticola;* 2, *t. klauberi;* 3, *t. loreala;* 4, *t. nuchalata;* 5, *t. ochrorhyncha;* 6, *t. slevini;* 7, *t. texana;* 8, *t. tortugaensis;* 9, *t. venusta.*

postoculars (1) 2–3; upper labials (7) 8 (9); lower labials 10 (9, 11); loreal 1; temporals 1 + 2 + 3; parietals, latero-cephalic point may contact or come close to labial; chin shields contact 5–6 lower labials; anterior and posterior about equal; posterior chin shields with outer sides straight and parallel with 3–4 rows of gulars between their tips and first ventral; eye small to medium, pupil vertical and elliptical; ventrals not angulate; dorsal background cinnamon-buff or cinnamon-drab with about 50 brown dorsal spots on body, venter white or cream-buff; maxillary teeth 7–10, diastema, $+2$ (1) ungrooved fanglike teeth in upper rear; "hemipenis—apical calyces present, calyces not furnished with spines except inferior marginal ones, hemipenis capitate" (Cope, Gen., 1900). (Adult males have keels on dorsal scales and anal region; see Fig. 6.) Ventrals 154–204; caudals 36–71.

We follow Dunn, also Bogert and Oliver, in calling all forms discussed *torquata,* but we use Tanner's key to distinguish subspecies until further material clarifies our understanding of these puzzling forms. Synonym: *Leptodeira.*

KEY TO THE GENUS *HYPSIGLENA*

a. Dorsal scales in 19-19-17-15 rows; supralabials 7-7; preoculars 2-2; nape without a light nuchal band but with dark nuchal blotch; ventrals 179–201.   *H. t. nuchalata*

aa. Dorsal scales in 21 or more rows at midbody; upper labials rarely less than 8-8.

    b. Dorsal scales in 23 rows at or near midbody; parietals in contact with lower postoculars; caudals 68. (Puerto Escondido, Baja Calif.)

                                                H. t. slevini

  bb. Dorsal scales in 21 rows at midbody; parietals not in contact with lower postoculars; diameter of the orbit equal to or less than distance from orbit to nostril.

    (c. Nape with light nuchal band 4–5 scales across, not or rarely interrupted medially or laterally, and followed by a large nuchal blotch; 7 or 8 upper labials; caudals 38–47. [Pacific coast of Mexico.]

                                       H. torquata torquata)

    cc. Nape without light nuchal band; nape variously blotched, that is, spotted or with single blotch covering nape.

      d. Loreals 2-2, scales between dorsal spots distinctly lighter in color than those laterad.   *H. t. loreala*

      dd. Loreals 1-1, rarely more, but when present small.

        e. Dorsal rows of spots separated by a lighter median stripe varying from a scale or less in width; dorsal spots small involving 4–5 scales and occupying a space of 2 or 3 scales; 1st lateral row of spots separated from dorsal ones by at least 1 row of scales; ventrals 174–190. (Central Baja Calif.)

                                            H. t. venusta

        ee. Two dorsal rows of spots rarely separated, often a few alternating; spots larger involving 7 or more scales and occupying a space of 4 or more scales.

          f. Nape with 3 distinct spots, 2 lateral and 1 medial, the

medial occasionally divided near the middle, but always in contact with parietals, or the scale immediately posterior to parietals.

g. Medial nape spot greatly enlarged posteriorly, the anterior narrow 1–3 scales wide, and extending back from parietal 4–7 scales, where it immediately enlarges to cover nearly all of nape; lateral nape spots complete and reaching anteriorly at least to the eye; ventral-caudal totals 229–261; rarely more than 16 dorsal scale rows at vent.　　　　　　　　　　　*H. t. deserticola*

gg. Medial nape spot uniform, or nearly so, for its entire distance (varying only a scale or so in width).

　　h. Ventral-caudal total 245 or more; caudals high, 52–59 in 2 females, medial nape spot 12 scales long or more. (Tortuga Is., Baja Calif.)　*H. t. tortugaensis*

　hh. Ventral-caudal total rarely more than 240; caudals in female 54 or less, in males up to 60.

　　　i. Top of head usually rounded; 6th upper labials about half pigmented; dorsal spots extending from 7th to 15th scale row, and each spot when complete involving 22 or more scales; spots separated by one scale or less, usually about ½ scale; first row of lateral spots large involving 6 or more scales and extending from 4th to 7th or 8th row; lateral nape spots complete; dorsal scales rarely less than 17 rows at vent; ventrals 154–177.
　　　　　　　　　　　　　　　　H. t. texana

　　　ii. Top of head usually flattened; 6th upper labial less than half pigmented; dorsal spots smaller, usually extending from 8th to 14th row and each involving less than 22 scales; lateral spots smaller, separated from dorsal ones by 1 scale or more; ventrals 161–188.　　　*H. t. ochrorhyncha*

ff. Nape with 3 distinct spots, the medial 1, 2, or more scales posterior to the parietals, lateral nape spot divided at angle of mouth or posterior to it; dorsal scales 17 or 15 rows at vent.　　　　　　　　　　　　　*H. t. klauberi*

fff. Nape without 3 distinct spots, but with 2 or a narrow nuchal blotch which extends entirely across the neck region; this nuchal band 1–6 scales across; dorsal spots medium to small, usually involving fewer than 21 scales and 1 or more scales apart; dorsal scales at vent 17 or 15 rows.　　　　　　　　*H. t. ochrorhyncha*

Desert spotted night snake, Great Basin spotted night snake

Hypsiglena torquata deserticola (W. W. Tanner 1944). Fig. 97; Map 30

Range: Colorado and Mojave Desert areas of s. California, n. through Nevada and e. Utah, w. Idaho, e. Oregon to cent. Washington.—Ariz.; Calif.; Ida.; Nev.; Ore.; Ut.; Wash. *Elevation*—1,000 or 2,000 feet to 4,000 feet at least, possibly 6,000 feet. 5,000 feet (Johnson, Bryant, and Miller, Calif., 1948).

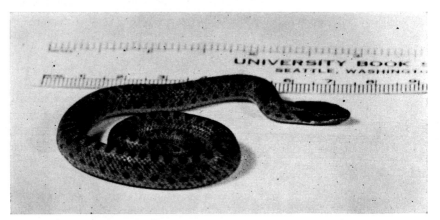

Fig. 97. *Hypsiglena torquata deserticola,* Vantage, Wash., photo by T. H. Lewis.

Size: Adults, 6.5–26 inches, average 322 mm. (Tanner, Calif., 1943).

Distinctive characteristics: "Related to *H. o. ochrorhynchus,* but differing from it in the following color and scale characteristics: medial nape spot greatly enlarged posteriorly, as wide as half its total length or more, lateral nape spot complete, the number of dorsal spots high, 49–75. Dorsal scales mostly in 15 rows at the vent. Ventrals high, male 177–195, female 186–204; caudals male 49–66, female 44–57; spots medium to small" (W. W. Tanner).

Habitat and habits: Most of the 15 authorities listed treated habitat and habits in their discussions of this wide-ranging species. In addition, Hardy (Ut., 1939), Smart (Ut., 1950), Cowles (Gen., 1941), and Pickwell (Gen., 1947) have contributed to the picture. Three writers found it beside a river, at a ferry, or on stony river flats; three remarked little or scattered sagebrush, in hot sagebrush areas, or in grassy sagebrush growth; two took them in snake dens; two in creek canyons. Localities in the open were: on a hill of a cattle range, dead among basaltic fragments, coiled on top of a potato pit. Their cover has been rocks, logs, boards, dead Joshua tree limbs, holes or burrows, and moist sand.

Period of activity: *Early appearance*—Apr. 20 (Erwin); Apr. 29 (Svihla and Knox); May 1 (Smart, Ut., 1950); May 19 (Hardy, Ut., 1939); May 22

(Bentley, Nev., 1918); May 26 (Johnson, Bryant, and Miller, Calif., 1948). *Fall disappearance*—Sept. 25, 28 (Hardy, Wash., 1939). *Hibernation*—In 1941 Cowles in his "Observations on winter activities of desert reptiles" showed an illustration of the tracks of *Hypsiglena ochrorhynchus, Sonora occipitalis,* and *Phyllorhynchus d. perkinsi.* In his discussion he said, "The smallest marks are those of *Hypsiglena."*

"Recently, in the afternoon of November 7, we took a specimen from under a dead Joshua Tree in the upper end of Antelope Valley of the Mohave Desert. When handled and photographed, the snake exhibited the extreme nervousness of other Night Snakes that we have handled" (Pickwell, Gen., 1947).

Food: Lizards, tree frogs, arthropods, centipedes, insects. Tanner, Klauber, Cowles (Gen., 1941), Lewis (Wash., 1942).

Venom: "The evidence for the possession of an effective venom by *Hypsiglena ochrorhynchus* is limited, but it is the writer's belief that there can be no question as to the presence of a highly toxic venom" (Cowles, Gen., 1941). Cowles's interesting account prompted T. H. Lewis in Washington to make his experiments: On July 2, July 6, and Aug. 19, 1941, Lewis introduced *Utas* into his *Hypsiglena* cage and recorded their attack on the introduced lizards. "After ten minutes, the lizard [*Uta*] seemed dead, with no respiration, no response to stimulus with a needle, no response to pulling the limbs, massage, opening of the eyes or jaws. The wounds on the nape were quite superficial, and a mechanical explanation for the cause of death seems difficult." From his experiments he concluded: "Although poison glands, ducts or other structures connected with venom production and use in *Hypsiglena ochroryncha* Cope . . . remain to be demonstrated, and no toxin has actually been demonstrated or isolated, the manner in which this small and little known snake overcomes its prey indicates a venom of rather low virulence, of but minute quantity, and of peculiar physiological properties." Lewis, like countless herpetologists the country over, offered to us his illustrations of *H. t. deserticola,* of which we had none. Goodman gives further evidence.

Field notes: May 30, 1942: For 2 or 3 days have had visits with Tanner and his *Hypsiglena* material. Beginning to feel that possibly some order may come out of this difficult genus in spite of our doubts expressed at different dates and places. Await his study with great interest.

Authorities:

Anderson, O. I. (Ore., 1940)
Bentley, G. H. (Nev., 1918, 1919)
Erwin, R. P. (Ida., 1925)
Goodman, J. D. (Calif., 1953)
Klauber, L. M. (Calif., 1932)
Lewis, T. H. (Wash., 1942, 1946)
Pack, H. J. (Ut., 1930)

Presnall, C. C. (Ut., 1937)
Storm, R. M., and R. A. Pimental (Ore., 1948)
Svihla, A., and C. Knox (Wash., 1940)
Tanner, V. M. (Ut., 1929)
Tanner, W. W. (Gen., 1944)
Woodbury, A. M. (Ut., 1928, 1929, 1931)

San Diegan spotted night snake

Hypsiglena torquata klauberi (Tanner 1944). Fig. 98; Map 30

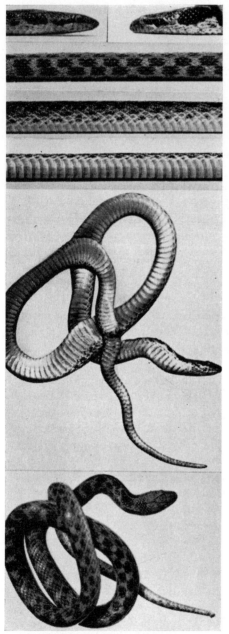

Fig. 98. *Hypsiglena t. klauberi,* Miramar, San Diego Co., Calif., B. C. Marshall.

Range: Coastal from Santa Barbara, Calif., to San Ignacio, Baja Calif., Mex.—U.S.A.: Calif. Mex.: Baja Calif. *Elevation*—Sea level to 5,000 feet or more.

Size: Adults, 6.2–16 inches.

Distinctive characteristics: "A subspecies of the *ochrorhynchus* group which varies from other forms in having a median spot which is 3–5 scales posterior to the parietals; the dark line extending posterior from the eye rarely contacts the lateral nuchal blotch, nor does it extend anteriorly beyond the eye; the eye is moderate, its diameter less than ½ the interorbital space" (Tanner).

Habitat: "It was found about 4 o'clock in the afternoon of Aug. 21, 1907, in a clover patch within a few feet of the margin of the upper Santa Ana, near our Cedar Cabin camp 5,500 feet altitude" (Grinnell). "Nocturnal. Usually taken in rocky sections" (Klauber, Calif., 1928b). "Rare. Specimens have been collected on the Mount Wilson Trail near Sierra Madre. In all probability it also occurs on the desert" (Bogert, Calif., 1930). "Under rocks" (Klauber, Calif., 1931a; Perkins). Klauber found 2 in heavy brush chaparral, 6 in rocks, boulders, 6 in rocky desert, 1 in brushy desert (Klauber, Gen., 1939a).

Period of activity: Klauber recorded 11 live snakes found on the roads (not restricted to desert roads) all at nighttime—3 in April, 3 in May, 4 in June, 1 in July. These he found active 7:40 P.M.–12:45 P.M. In his

"Sixteen Year Census" he gave 6 snakes in Jan.; 7, Feb.; 18, Mar.; 19, Apr.; 35, May; 22, June; 11, July; 19, Aug.; 8, Sept.; 5, Oct.; 3, Nov.; 4, Dec. (Klauber, Gen., 1939a).

Food: Insects, lizards. Klauber (Calif., 1934a), Perkins.

Authorities:

Grinnell, J. (Calif., 1908)

Klauber, L. M. (Gen., 1939a; Calif., 1928b)

Perkins, C. B. (Calif., 1938)

Tanner, W. W. (Gen., 1944)

Utah spotted night snake

Hypsiglena torquata loreala (Tanner 1944). Map 30

Range: Green, Colorado, and San Juan River basins of e. Utah and s.w. Colorado.—Colo.; Ut. *Elevation*—4,000 to 6,000 feet.

Size: Adults, 6.5–20 inches (Tanner).

Distinctive characteristics: "A subspecies of *ochrorhynchus* closely related to *deserticola* in that it has a similar color pattern and a high ventral and caudal scale count. Distinct from all *ochrorhynchus* in having 2 large loreals on each side" (Tanner).

Habitat: Little is known. Only Hardy has given definite types of places such as in shad-scale area near a pond, in rubbish near a river, beneath a rock at the edge of the piñon-juniper pigmy forest.

Breeding: Oviparous. *Eggs*—Number, 3–12. "This very fat specimen contained 3 large and 4 small eggs which vary from 2 to 19 millimeters . . . in length" (Hardy, Ut., 1939). "The type specimen was gravid at the time of collecting. Three eggs were felt soon after she was collected. The specimen was placed in a separate bag and placed in the car, but in spite of careful handling, the 3 eggs and 9 shells were produced before we returned to camp. Two eggs were fully distended while the third was soft and not entirely filled; the 9 shells appeared normal and were folded together in a cluster" (Tanner).

Food: Lizards, tree frogs. Hardy, Ditmars (Gen., 1936), Tanner (Ut., 1929).

Venom: "Because of the fact that the fangs in the rear upper jaw can be used in puncturing the skin of *Phrynosoma* and *Sceloporus* lizards to allow the entrance of a substance into the blood stream, and because lizards so treated die sooner than lizards badly injured without having been chewed, this species may be considered as being closely related to *Dipsadomorphinae*" (Hardy).

Field notes: 1944: The Utah group (particularly Hardy and Turner) have added as much as anyone to the live notes and accumulation of specimens of this species. In 1939 the latter modestly remarked, "Only a start has been made on the gathering of data on the distribution of this secretive little snake." A year before the publication of Tanner's *nuchalatus,* he showed us samplings of the *Hypsiglena* material of the U.S. The glance was too hurried for us to formulate any conclusions. Our natural inclination at this moment is to make his *Hypsiglena nuchalatus* a subspecies of *torquata.*

Authorities:

Barry, L. T. (Colo., 1932, 1933)
Hardy, R. (Ut., 1938)
Tanner, W. W. (Gen., 1944)

Woodbury, A. M., and E. W. Smart
(Ut., 1950)

Fig. 99. *Hypsiglena t. nuchalata,* O'Neals, Calif., photo by N. Cohen.

Sierra Nevada spotted night snake

Hypsiglena torquata nuchalata (Tanner 1943). Fig. 99; Map 30

Range: Slopes bordering Central Valley of California from Tulare and Monterey Counties to Tehama County. *Elevation*—500 to 2,500 or 3,000 feet.

Size: Adults, 6.4–14 inches.

Distinctive characteristics: "A subspecies characterized by having a dark nuchal band and a narrow head. The orbit is equal to or greater than half the interorbital space, rarely less; dorsal formula normally 19-19-17-15; supralabials 7-7; body and tail spots distinct. Ventral count high 179–201" (Tanner, Gen., 1944).

Color: "The ground color in this individual is a very light tan and the spots are light brown. The larger spots on the dorsal and lateral sides posterior to the head are darker brown in color. Where the largest spots on each side of the back coincide with their counterpart on the other side the convergence results in a saddle-shaped pattern. The degree of coinciding is irregular. The smaller spots alternate with the central series. The ventral scales in the individual photographed are very light yellow and have no markings" (letter from Nathan W. Cohen, San Joaquin Experiment Range, O'Neals, Calif., Aug. 9, 1951).

Habitat. Before 1951 our knowledge of this secretive snake came largely from Van Denburgh, Grinnell and Camp, and Fitch (Calif., 1949). Recorded habitats are: in rocky places, under small granite rocks, under boulders, under a pile of recently cut hay. These covers have been near edges of creeks and streams at the water's edge, in the warm belt of foothills or other foothill belts, in granite outcrops, and in the open woods of the blue oak and digger pine belt.

After 1951 we have the account given by N. W. Cohen as resident zoologist at O'Neals, Calif. "From June 1950 to 21 March 1951 I have found only 3 *Hypsiglena* on this 5,000 acre site. The first 2 were adults and were collected on 9 August 1950 and 2 September 1950 in the evening. The collecting site was nearly exactly the same for both of them. This site was at the water's edge in a board-covered well, the water level of which was about 4 feet below the ground surface. The snakes apparently entered the well at will through cracks in the well wall. From the top of the well and extending down about 3 feet the well is walled with rock and below this it is lined by a smooth, but slightly rusted, metal casing. The water level at both times of collecting was about 1 foot below the top of the metal casing. On the two separate occasions, the snakes were at the same spot, both hanging onto the well wall, just at the water level. At the time of finding the first *Hypsiglena* I thought that it may have fallen into the water and was just barely hanging on at the water level, but finding the second one at the same spot makes it appear unlikely that both snakes were there by accident. The third snake, from which the black and white and color shots were taken, is a juvenile and was collected on 21 March 1951. This individual was taken from under a small granite rock (6" diameter) lying on the ground surface and not more than 10 feet from the edge of a small stream. This individual weighed 2.2 grams and measured 165 mm. in total length" (letter, Aug. 9, 1951).

Period of activity: MVZ dates may possibly apply to other subspecies. They are Feb. 8–July 18.

Food: So far as known, this snake is saurophagous.

Authorities:

Bogert, C. M., and J. A. Oliver (Ariz., 1945)

Fitch, H. S. (Calif., 1939a, 1949)

Grinnell, J., and C. L. Camp (Calif., 1917)

Tanner, W. W. (Gen., 1944; Calif., 1943)

Van Denburgh, J. (Calif., 1906)

1945, C. M. Bogert and J. A. Oliver: "In this paper Tanner (1943, pp. 49–54) proposed two names, 'Hypsiglena nuchalatus' and 'Hypsiglena slevini.' The former is based upon specimens from central California, the type locality being Lemon Cove, Tulare County. Whereas he calls this form a 'species,' he follows his descriptions by a discussion of 'relationships and intergradations (sic)' and proceeds to list intergrades from three localities and to discuss areas of intergradation. It seems obvious that his nuchalatus, if the pattern characters described by him serve to differentiate it, should be placed as a subspecies of torquata."

Spotted night snake (44—Van Denburgh 1907),
Rock snake (9—Ditmars 1907)

Hypsiglena torquata ochrorhyncha (Cope 1860). Fig. 100; Map 30

Other common names: Irwin's snake (Yarrow 1882); Sonoran spotted night snake; Texan rock snake; Xantus' snake (Yarrow 1882).

Range: Arizona, trans-Pecos Texas, Mexico (Chihuahua, Sonora, and s. Baja California).—U.S.A.: Ariz.; N.M.; Tex. Mex.: Baja Calif.; Chihuahua; Durango; Sonora. *Elevation*—500 to 3,000 or 4,000, possibly 5,000, feet.

Size: Adults, 7–20 inches.

Distinctive characteristics: "The typical *ochrorhynchus* is distinguished from *texana* by its light pigmentation between and lateral to the dorsal spots, and by the smaller and less extensive dorsal and nuchal blotches. In scalation 70% of the *ochrorhynchus* specimens studied possessed less than 17 rows above the vent. From *janii* it differs in having 3 nuchal blotches and by smaller dorsal spots. From *venusta* it differs by its larger and fewer dorsal spots which are not divided medially and by fewer ventral and caudal scutes. From *klauberi* by reason of its complete lateral nape spot, and the extension of the medial spot to or within a scale of the parietal. From *deserticola* by its low ventral and caudal counts and also by its elongate medial nape spot. From *unaocularus* and *lorealus* because of its single loreal and from *tortugaensis* because of a much lower caudal count and a complete lateral nape spot" (Tanner).

Color: A snake from east of Vail, Ariz., Aug. 1, 1925. The upper parts are light cinnamon-drab, cinnamon-drab, wood brown, or drab-gray. Each scale is covered with fine specks except for the very edge. The top of the head to the nape spot is light drab or drab-gray with spots of benzo brown, some of which on the parietals have light drab centers. The benzo brown nape spot has a forward prong. Back of the nape spot are 6 transverse dorsal spots, which are followed to the tail, with 2 rows of more or less paired or alternate spots. On top of the tail are 3 rows of dots. On the 6th row of scales is a row of small spots alternating with the dorsal saddles, and on the 3rd and 4th rows in a series of small spots alternating with the above series. These rows extend but slightly or not at all onto the tail. The first 3 rows of scales are pale drab-gray. From the eye to beyond the angle of the mouth there is a band which is drab in the center and bordered with benzo brown or natal brown. The face plates and upper labials have in part natal brown edges. The lower labials, chin, and gulars are specked with natal brown. The iris is olive-buff specked as the scales and upper head plates are. There is some grayish olive around the vertical pupil. The eye is very protuberant. The under parts are white with an opalescent or silvery sheen.

Habitat: Beginning in 1921 with Van Denburgh and Slevin, we have from Allen, Campbell (Ariz., 1934), Taylor (Gen., 1936a), Little (Ariz., 1940), and Burger and Hensley (Ariz., 1949) the following accumulation of places in which this night-roaming snake lives. As reported chronologically, they are: under a pine log in a mountain meadow, beneath loose stones, in a mesquite bush near a large mass of rocks, in a sandy place in a canyon bottom, under a rock under any overhanging cliff near a bay, and in semidesert-woodland zones. "It is a female with 190 ventrals, 47 caudals, and 16 dorsal scale rows above the anus. It was taken alive on the road on August 8, 10:30 P.M." (Burger and Hensley).

Period of activity: Early appearances—Apr. 6, 1910; Mar. 23, 1912; May 3, 1912; Apr. 16–22, 1912; Mar. 28, 1892 (Van Denburgh, Baja Calif., 1895a). *Fall disappearance*—Oct. 7, 1890; Sept., 1893; Oct., 1893; Sept., 1894 (Van Denburgh, 1895a).

Breeding: Oviparous. *Young*—The smallest rock snake we have seen is about 4 inches long. There are few, if any, records below 142, 150, 154, 156 mm.

Food: Lizards, insects, toads, small frogs. Perkins (Calif., 1938), Bogert and Oliver, Flood and Wiklund (Ariz., 1949).

Authorities:

Allen, M. J. (Ariz., 1933)
Bogert, C. M., and J. Oliver (Ariz., 1945)
Brown, A. E. (Gen., 1901)
Cowles, R. A. (Gen., 1941)
Hensley, M. M. (Ariz., 1950)
Johnson, D. H., M. D. Bryant, and A. H. Miller (Calif., 1948)

Klauber, L. M. (Gen., 1938)
Stejneger, L. (Calif., 1893)
Tanner, W. W. (Gen., 1944)
Taylor, E. H. (Gen., 1936a, 1938)
Van Denburgh, J. (Gen., 1922)
Van Denburgh, J., and J. R. Slevin (Ariz., 1913; Baja Calif., 1921c)

This form is one of our most vexing problems.

In 1893 L. Stejneger recognized two new forms, *H. chlorophaea* and *H. texana*. In 1899 F. Mocquard proposed *H. venusta*. In 1938 L. M. Klauber believed *H. venusta* invalid.

1901, A. E. Brown: "The convexity of the head attributed to *H. texana*

Stejn. appears to be abnormal, and the difference in the lateral head stripe is trivial."

1936, E. R. Dunn (Gen.): "Leptodeiras without grooved fangs are usually considered a different genus (*Hypsiglena*), and by some authors placed in a different subfamily."

1938, L. M. Klauber: "Concerning the desirability of combining these two genera I have no opinion to offer."

1944: W. W. Tanner revised the genus *Hypsiglena*. He kept *H. torquata* and *H. ochrorhynchus* patterns distinct and felt they should not be merged, yet he appended a paragraph: "It is quite possible that more collecting may produce enough evidence to justify the uniting of *ochrorhynchus* with *torquata*. In fact I consider this is a real probability. But as yet enough data are not at hand and such a procedure would provide us with an unreal conclusion."

1945, C. M. Bogert and J. A. Oliver: *Hypsiglena torquata-ochrorhyncha* (intergrades?). Because they found representatives of the *torquata* and *ochrorhynacha* patterns in Guirocoba, Sonora, they query whether they are two species.

Texas spotted night snake

Hypsiglena torquata texana Stejneger 1893. Fig. 101; Map 30

Range: New Mexico to s. Kansas, s. across w. Oklahoma and cent. Texas to Nuevo León, Coahuila, and Chihuahua, Mex.—U.S.A.: Kan.; N.M.; Okla.; Tex. Mex.: Chihuahua; Coahuila; Nuevo León; Tamaulipas(?). *Elevation*—Sea level or 100 feet to 1,000 or 2,000 feet, a few to 3,000 and 4,000 feet. Mainly 500–5,000. 2,350 feet (Hibbard); 2,800–5,000+ feet (Bailey, N.M., 1913).

Size: Adults, 6.2–19 inches.

Distinctive characteristics: "Similar to *H. o. ochrorhynchus* but with the upper surface of the head convex, the lateral outline of the frontal curved outward, and the dark eye stripe covering much more than half of the 6th supralabial. Scale rows 21; gastrosteges 175; urosteges 45; supralabials 8, preoculars 1; pseudoculars 1; postoculars 2; temporals 1. Type—U.S. Nat. Mus. No. 1782; between Laredo and Camargo, Tex.; U.S. Mex. Bound. Surv., Arthur Schott, coll. Habitat—Southwestern Texas. In addition to the type the museum possesses 2 other specimens, one collected by Mr. W. Taylor at San Diego (U.S. Nat. Mus. No. 15672) and one by Mr. Butcher at Laredo (No. 7124). Both agree in every respect with the type" (Stejneger).

"*Texana* is a variation from *ochrorhyncha* from which it differs in having larger spots, and a long median nape spot which extends from the parietals posteriorly for a distance of 9–13 scales and varies in width only 1 or 2 scale rows for the entire distance. Because of the large dark spots the ground

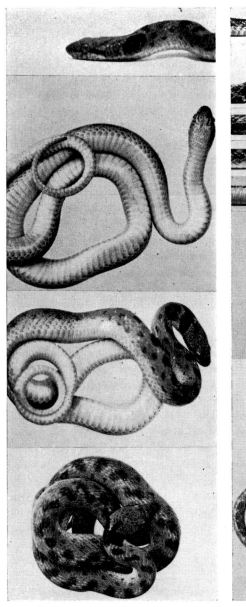

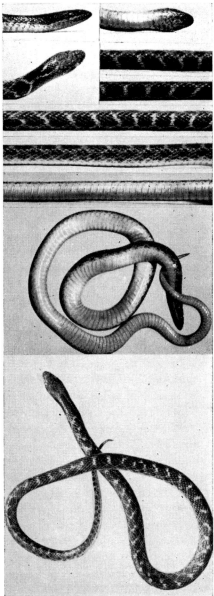

Fig. 100. *Hypsiglena t. ochrorhyncha,*
East Vail, Ariz.

Fig. 101. *Hypsiglena t. texana,* Palo Pinto,
Tex., P. Harter.

color is darker than in typical *ochrorhynchus;* fewer ventrals and a ventral-caudal total which rarely exceeds 224 scutes, upper half of the 6th labial in the lateral spot" (Tanner).

Color: Two snakes from Palo Pinto, Tex., received from Philip Harter, May 25, 1938. First, a female, the lighter colored of the two. The background color of the sides is cinnamon-buff, becoming in the interval bars of mid-dorsum, light pinkish cinnamon. The dark spots on the back are isabella color and are 3 scales longitudinally and 7 or 8 wide. There are 49 on the body, 16 on the tail. Below these dorsal spots is a similar lateral row of alternating spots on the 3rd to 7th scale rows. On the 2nd and 4th rows is another series of alternating similar small spots opposite the ends of the middorsal ones. The top of the head is buffy olive, as is also the iris. There is a dark vitta from the eye across the upper half of the upper labials and 1st temporal, narrowing at the last upper labial and there joining the lateral nape spot which is 11 scales long and 7 scales deep. These 2 lateral spots are separated from a narrow dorsal one of similar color by thread intervals of light pinkish cinnamon. There is a cream-buff upper labial stripe to the eye. The ventral surfaces are cream-buff with the underside of the head, lower labials, and lower half of the upper labials spotted with light brownish olive.

The second, also a female, the darker colored of the two. The background color of the sides is wood brown, becoming, where it crosses the back as light bars, vinaceous-buff or tilleul buff. The middorsal region is marked with 52 dark roughly rectangular spots on the body and 14 on the tail. These spots are saccardo's umber, 3 scales longitudinally and 7 or 8 scales wide, breaking in 1 or 2 places into 2 alternating spots.

Habitat: Strecker (Tex., 1928b) took it under stones on hill and mountain side. Hibbard found it under flat stones on a small rocky slope facing southeast, also on the top of a canyon under a pile of stones. Koster found it in a rabbit burrow in typical mesa land at the base of a fairly high cliff. Kuntz's locality was under granite boulders on the western slopes of small stream valleys. The most extensive observations are those of Dundee. He took them in mesquite-savanna areas which had many outcrops of gypsum and dolomite and in rocky situations bordering Wichita Mts., but not in the mountains proper. Eight were taken several days after a rain while the ground was moist.

"Nearly all specimens appeared as if surprised when discovered and made many motions as if they were looking for a place to burrow. One specimen flattened the head and struck in such a way as to appear quite vicious. A similar display was reported by Fitch (1949) for *H. t. nuchalata*" (Dundee).

Period of activity. Early appearances—Kansas, June 12, 1936 (Hibbard); Oklahoma, Apr. 23, 1938, June 14, 1938 (Kuntz); New Mexico, May 9 (Marr), Feb. 2, 1939 (Koster). *Hibernation*—"The specimen at hand was taken February 2, 1939, about 5 miles southwest of Las Lunas in Valencia County, New Mexico, from the mouth of a rabbit burrow by Mr. Pearce Beach. It was probably hibernating in this situation until disturbed by the heat and smoke of the smudge. The rabbit burrow was described as being in the typical 'mesa' land at the base of a fairly high clay bluff. The ground was partially covered by a snow of the previous night" (Koster).

Breeding: Oviparous. Females, to 488 mm. *Eggs*—The evidence as to number is scanty. "The female taken June 12 was skeletonized and was found to contain 4 eggs" (Hibbard). "On July 7 one female from Beckham County laid 6 eggs. . . . [They] were measured on July 8 and the range in length determined as 22–28 mm. averaging 24.7 mm. The median diameters ranged from 10.0–11.5 mm. One egg was kidney-shaped and another had a hump in the middle. The weights ranged from 1.6–1.9 grams, the average being 1.75 grams. . . . It is interesting to note that the smallest egg was 25% greater in diameter than the snake. The total combined weight of the eggs was 10.5 grams, about 91% of the weight of the parent. The total combined length of the eggs, which apparently had been arranged linearly in the body, was 148 mm., about 44% of the total body length" (Dundee). On Apr. 25, 1950, Werler (Gen., 1951) recorded a 488-mm. female laying 4 smooth nongranular eggs 27 to 32 mm. long by 9–11 mm. wide. Some of these hatched June 18, the young being 146–153 mm. long. (Werler then described the young.)

Food: Lizards, worms, snakes. Ditmars (Gen., 1907), Schmidt and Owens (Gen., 1944), Dundee, Werler (Gen., 1951).

Field notes: Two of our notes remind us how easily *Hypsiglena* species may be confused with the young of other species. Other snakes with which *Hypsiglena* has been confused include the following: (1) *Leptodeira septentrionalis annulatus* (Cope, Baja Calif., 1862); (2) *Arizona elegans elegans;* (3) *Coluber flagellum flavigularis;* (4) *Pituophis c. affinis x deserticola* (Dodge, Ariz., 1938); (5) *Crotalus;* (6) *Coluber constrictor mormon* (Anderson, Ore., 1940).

Authorities:

Brown, A. E. (Gen., 1901)
Dundee, H. A. (Okla., 1950)
Hibbard, C. W. (Kan., 1937)
Koster, W. J. (N.M., 1940)
Kuntz, R. E. (Okla., 1940)
Marr, J. C. (Gen., 1944)

Stejneger, L. (Ariz., 1893)
Strecker, J. K., Jr. (Tex., 1915, 1927b, 1928b)
Tanner, W. W. (Gen., 1944)
Taylor, E. H. (Gen., 1938)

1915, J. K. Strecker, Jr.: "Dr. Brown refuses to recognize *texana.* . . . However, as Dr. Stejneger distinctly says that the other specimens from Texas examined by him agree in every respect with the type, I shall here recognize it."

1927, J. K. Strecker, Jr.: "Dr. Van Denburgh precedes the reference to *texana* with a question mark. Dr. Blanchard, in Key to the Snakes, . . . reduces *texana* to the rank of a synonym of *ochrorhynchus,* for it is still questionable whether the characters assigned by Dr. Stejneger to certain Texas specimens from the Rio Grande Valley are sufficiently constant to entitle them to even subspecific rank."

1938, E. H. Taylor: "I have hesitated to venture an opinion on the validity of the supposed species, *Hypsiglena venusta* Mocquard, *Hypsiglena chlorophaea* Cope, or *Hypsiglena texana* Stejneger, because of insufficient specimens. It is likely that when sufficient material is available, certain of these will be recognized as subspecific forms."

1945, A. H. and A. A. Wright: A glance at our three plates (Texas; Vail, Ariz.; California) shows much variation in pattern. For 25 years we have vacillated on *Hypsiglena texana* and we still incline to the negative. We have never tried hard to believe *chlorophaea* or *venusta* acceptable and readily follow Klauber's pronouncement. Until far more material appears, we retain *Hypsiglena* for the genus but accept Dunn's suggestion concerning *torquata* for the species. In the light of recent discussions, our specimen from Vail, Ariz., is of considerable interest. It retains a suggestion of the *torquata* pattern. We are glad Tanner has ventured an elucidation of this difficult group.

KING SNAKES

Genus *LAMPROPELTIS* Fitzinger (Fig. 20)

Size, small medium to large, from 7 to 24 inches in the smaller scarlet king snakes to 77 inches in large Florida king snakes; body moderate to stout; head normally not distinct from neck (exceptions: *alterna, blairi, pyromelaena*); anal entire; scales smooth, 2 apical pits, in 17–27 rows, cephalic plates normal; lower labials 9–11, upper 7; nasals 2; preocular 1, postoculars 2–3; loreal 1; temporals usually 2 + 3 + 4; pattern various—dorsum uniform; with dorsal saddles; transverse (2–4 colors) or longitudinal bands; venter, blocked, checkered, ringed or plates dark edged or almost entirely dark; maxillary teeth 12–20 subequal; hemipenis—"Organ rounded, bilobed or forked at end; sulcus spermaticus single; calyces continuous across end of the organ or leaving there a small bare space, apical, few with short processes . . . passing into spines which increase in size gradually toward the base; . . . basal portion . . . smooth or with numerous minute spines" (Blanchard, Gen., 1921). Types differ in *doliata, calligaster,* and *getulus* groups. Ventrals 152–254; caudals 31–79. Synonyms: *Ablabes, Anguis, Bellophis, Calamaria, Coronella, Herpetodryas, Natrix, Ophibolus, Osceola, Phibolus, Pseudoelaps, Zacholus*

KEY TO THE GENUS *LAMPROPELTIS*

a. No pattern, black or brown head and dorsum; no scales with light centers; belly washed with yellow; lower labials 8–10; scale rows 23–27 midbody.

   b. Color black.   *L. calligaster calligaster* (black phase)

  bb. Color brown.   *L. c. rhombomaculata* (uniform phase)

aa. Pattern of bands, stripes, or spots.

   b. Pattern of 4 colors, gray, white, black, and red or orange; about 14–20 red bands, gray dorsal areas edged with white which crosses 1st row of scales and ends of ventrals; rest of venter mainly black or dark brown with some white; temporal scales larger than those on mid-dorsum of neck; scale rows 25; lower labials 10 or 11.

     c. Head distinct from neck; head shields black mottled with gray; broad postocular band; regular series of prominent, approximately equal red and gray bands; red ones distinctly bordered on either end by a black ring (2 blacks to a red); gray ones on either end by white. Ventrals 227–229; caudals 63.   *L. blairi*

    cc. Head broad, crown flat, neck narrow (1.5–1.6 in width of head); head almost uniform gray with postocular band absent or broken; general effect gray crossed irregularly by narrow black bars, alternate ones centered or split with red or xanthine orange; red band narrow and confined as zigzag split within a black band; alternate black areas without red and more or less broken. Ventrals 213–221; caudals 58–64.   *L. alterna*

  bb. Pattern of 2 or 3 colors; head not conspicuously wider than neck (1–1.2, rarely 1.3, in width of head); crown rounded; if gray interspaces present, they are less than dorsal saddles or bands and confined to the light bars separating them.

     c. Pattern of 2 colors, without red, without black-bordered brown or red dorsal blotches. When black or dark brown dorsum is crossed by light bars, the dark color is 2–4 times width of light.

       d. Dorsal areas of solid black or brown scales; dominant color black or brown.

         e. Top of head back of eyes heavily spotted white or yellow; face quite oblique; head flatter and broader (neck in width of head 1.33) than *L. g. getulus;* anterior light middorsal blotches 3–4, widely spaced; typical *getulus* bar pattern begins well back on body, bars 2 1/2–3 times *getulus* bars; (37 middorsal light spots and bars on body and tail); labials with large white spots; some lateral scales with light spots; scale rows 21; food habits neither ophiophagous nor constrictor. (Suggestive of mixed patterns studied by Klauber in *L. g. californiae-boylii.*)   *L. g. sticticeps*

ee. Top of head back of eyes not heavily spotted white or yellow, black predominating; face hardly oblique; head rounded not much broader than neck (neck 1.0–1.1 in width of head); none with anterior middorsal light blotches; food habits ophiophagous and constrictor.

    f. Middorsum black without conspicuous bars, spots, or stripes, sometimes few faint partial light lines evident; light spots distinct on lower scale rows to 3 or 4; scale rows 21.   *L. g. niger*

   ff. Middorsum black or brown with light transverse bars or middorsal light stripe.

      g. Light middorsal stripe on red-brown to black ground color; lateral light stripe on rows 1–3 or 4. [Middorsal stripe highly variable, so also lateral areas—Klauber, Calif., 1936b.] Venter usually light; upper labial suture below eye prominent dark spot; scale rows 19–27.   *L. g. californiae (californiae* phase)

      [Or the following peculiar variations according to Van Denburgh (Gen., 1922):

     "h. Dorsal stripe white or yellow sharply defined on a dark brown or black ground color. Fresno Co., Calif., to northern Calif. . . .
                                            L. getulus californiae

    "hh. Dorsal stripe poorly defined of light brown or cinnamon on a dark brown ground color; belly uniform brown. . . .
                     L. getulus nitida" (Blanchard, Gen., 1921)[1]

    hhh. "Longitudinal dorsal band purplish brown like the ground color; lateral scales all with light centers; lower surfaces chiefly black. *L. catalinensis*" Van Denburgh, Gen., 1922. (Baja California.)]

   gg. No light middorsal stripe; light dorsal transverse crossbars from neck to tail; zebra pattern of black and white lines on labials and facial plates frequent.

      h. All lateral scales to row 5 or 10 spotted; ventral plates black, spotted light on ends; back crossed by 41–85 short bars of light-centered scales; black predominates on facial plates, temporals and rear upper labials. Scale rows 23 or 25 (19–25) in midbody.
                                       L. g. splendida

     hh. White on the sides restricted to lateral extensions or expansions of dorsal bars (28–50).

        i. Venter mostly black with few spots of light. 23–52 light dorsal bars narrow, dividing on sides in inverted V's ending in irregular collections of white-spotted scales; black predomi-

---

[1] Probably *nitida* is only an aberrant form or pattern phase of *conjuncta*—Klauber, Calif., 1936b. (Baja California.)

nates on facial plates, temporals, and rear upper labials; black labial suture below eye not an expanded spot. "Posterior chin shields nearly as long and nearly as wide as anterior, in contact or separated by not more than 1 small scale." Blanchard. Sometimes really 2 scales; scale rows 21 (17–23).

L. getulus getulus

ii. Venter largely light or in blocks of black or brown and light, the black seldom more than half the venter; white dorsal bands 1–3 scales wide, very distinct; upper labial suture below eye as prominent black spot. "Posterior chin shields generally much shorter and narrower than anterior and separated by 1 or 2 small scales" (Blanchard). Scale rows 19–27.

j. Light dorsal bands of clear white scales widen on scale rows 1–3, cross belly as large blocks of white, the black areas also crossing venter as blocks of black (a ringed pattern); under head mostly light scales; white predominates on facial plates, temporals, and rear upper labials; anterior upper labials light with or without dark edges.

L. g. californiae (boyli phase)

jj. Dorsal light bands or lateral expansions usually of spotted scales; black of dorsum crossing belly directly or as block opposite light dorsal bar produces a V pattern like getulus; ventral gulars heavily spotted black. Black predominates or equals white on facial plates, temporals, and rear upper labials.

L. g. yumensis

k. ["White scales mostly brown at their bases. White bars on prefrontals occupying less than half of the area of the scutes; frontal plate uniform black or with white restricted to a narrow transverse bar at its anterior end; no white on parietals; infralabials usually 9   yumensis

kk. "White bars on prefrontals occupying more than half of the area of these plates; frontal with prominent white markings or at least with a central spot of white; each parietal with one or more white spots; infralabials usually 10.

g. c. conjuncta" (Blanchard, Gen., 1921.)[1]]

dd. No dorsal areas of entirely black scales, all scales partly or largely light; top of head back of eye uniformly speckled; predominant color yellow or brown; scale rows 21–23.

---

[1] Recognition of conjuncta as a valid subspecies is not warranted.—Klauber, Calif., 1936b. (Baja California.)

e. Distinct deep brown saddles, each scale bearing a vaguely defined light spot; 21–24 light dorsal areas broad and 4–8 scales long, each scale light anteriorly and dark in posterior half; venter largely dark, rich brown with light streaks on ends of plates. *L. g. goini*

ee. Dorsum more or less uniformly speckled; light bands if present narrow, 46–100, no more than 1 and 2/2 scales long; venter mainly light or blocked with dark.

f. Color of dorsum overspreading most of each scale; scales with darkened tips; crossbands if present 46–85; scale rows on midbody usually 23 (sometimes 19–21).

g. Color of snake yellow; each scale mostly light with dark tip, all scales the same; dorsal crossbars absent or very faintly visible; venter mostly yellow blocked with cinnamon. *L. g. brooksi*

gg. Color brown or drab, back crossed by more than 50 olive-buff or dirty white crossbars extending well down the sides; under parts yellow blocked with slate. *L. g. floridana*

ff. Color pattern due to distinct yellow or green-yellow spots on black scales; crossbands if present 50–100; under parts pale yellow checkered with black; scale rows midbody usually 21 (17–23). *L. g. holbrooki*

cc. Color pattern with red rings or bars (red rings obscured by black in black and white *L. multicinctus*), or with black-bordered dorsal blotches or brown or red; form medium to slender, size medium.

d. With faintly dark-edged dorsal blotches of red or brown above scale rows 5 to 7; light intervals close to width of dark (.8–1.4 x); narrow, faint black borders of dorsal saddles not perceptibly widened at mid-dorsum and contained in light interval 5–10 times or more; venter buff; scale rows 21–27; size long (to 4 1/2 feet).

e. 46–78 dorsal spots with concave anterior-posterior margins; upper lateral spots roughly round; lower labials 9–10; scale rows 25–27 midbody; some individuals uniform black. Size to 4 feet, 7 inches. *L. calligaster calligaster*

ee. 48–64 dorsal spots with convex anterior-posterior margins. Upper lateral spots vertically elongate; lower labials commonly 8; scale rows 23–21 midbody; some individuals uniform brown. Size to 3 feet, 8 inches. *L. c. rhombomaculata*

dd. Pattern in rings or, if in saddles, of red or brown reaching to scale row 5 or below; light rings less than dark intervening area (1.5–7 times in dark interval); black borders in saddle forms contained 1–3 times in light rings; black borders at middorsum usually broader than near venter. Form slender; size medium, to 3 1/2 feet.

e. 2-color pattern of black or brown and light rings; light rings not widening at venter; black rings slightly wider than light ones and extending onto or across venter; anterior upper labials black.   *L. z. multicincta*

(f. Similar to *L. multicincta*, but with the red of that species represented only by a few small lateral blotches or spots of very pale pink usually evident only on the neck; snout black. . . . (Van Denburgh and Slevin, Baja Calif., 1923.)   *L. z. herrerae*

(Banded wide black and narrow white or cream extending across belly; black top of the head; first light stripe across rear of parietals; no other white on head; reminds us of rare individuals of *L. z. multicincta* in Yosemite, but California Academy has 4 jars of these all alike from this island, and it seems a good race.—A.H.W. and A.A.W., 1941.) (Baja California.)

ee. 3-color pattern with red rings or with red or brown dorsal saddles.

f. Light rings same width dorsum to venter or if widened at venter (1.1–1.4 middorsal width); red of dorsum normally crosses belly; temporals 2 + 3; no red on snout.

g. Snout light (white or olive buff), sometimes all labials white, tip of lower jaw white; black of dorsum goes 1 1/2–2 times into red; dorsal red area much less than yellow + 2 blacks on middorsum; first black ring back of head does not encroach on lower side of head, going from angle of mouth to angle of mouth; 1st red ring crosses venter; light rings (buff on body) 35–71, sometimes interrupted on venter by black; scale rows 23–25 midbody.
          L. pyromelaena

gg. Snout almost entirely black, tip of lower jaw black; 1st black ring back of head extends onto ventrals and is back of angle of mouth.

h. Light rings 23–57; black rings about equal to or slightly less than red bands; black rings frequently encroach on red dorsally; 1st red bar usually confined as a dorsal saddle; light rings not wider at venter.   *L. zonata zonata*[1]

---

[1] The following analysis of *h* was given by Klauber in 1943(c):

"A. More than half of the triad rings of the body include transverse red bands which cross the dorsum.

  B. Top of snout back to frontal black; or if predominantly red or pink, total body triads less than 40.   *L. multicincta multifasciata*
          (= *L. zonata zonata*)

  BB. Top of snout back to the frontal predominantly red or pink, and with body triads exceeding 39.   *L. multicincta agalma*
          (= *L. zonata agalma*)

"AA. More than half of the triad rings of the body entirely black, or with lateral red areas which are not confluent dorsally.

hh. Light rings 19–26; red area equal to or wider (1.2–1.7) than 1 yellow + 2 black rings, black 3–4 times into red band; light rings, orange-yellow to deep chrome on body, sometimes widen slightly at venter (1–1.4 times dorsal width) cross belly on 2–3 unmarked ventrals; 1st red ring crosses venter as a long area. The red of belly irregularly encroached on by black, frequently as black bars or broad areas in mid-venter; scales of red areas not black tipped.

L. d. annulata

ff. Light rings expanded at venter (2–3 1/2 times dorsal width); snout not totally black, usually red, ecru-olive, or oil yellow.

g. Red crosses venter; black bars wider on dorsum than at venter, often very narrow on scale row 1.

h. Temporals 1 + 2; scale rows 17–19; light rings 15–25; top of head ahead of eyes scarlet, frontal and parietals black, chin and most of lower labials scarlet. *L. doliata doliata*

hh. Temporals 2 + 3; scale tows 19–21; light blotches 18–25; top of head rufous and black, snout oil yellow, black sutures on light labials, underside of head buff or yellow. *L. d. amaura*

gg. Red not crossing venter; temporals 2 + 3.

h. Red or brown saddle spots not normally reaching ventral plates, usually extending to row 3; 3–5 rows of dorsal blotches; scale rows 21–23.

i. Black line from eye to angle of mouth, more or less bordered with russet, top of head with black-bordered Y or V and band of saddle color, rostral band of olive buff, labials white with dark sutures, a black-bordered longitudinal spot on neck; body blotches 28–62; belly rather evenly checkered with sharply edged blocks of bluish gray. *L. d. triangulum*

C. Usually some red areas laterally or dorsally; last supralabial untouched by black posteriorly. *L. multicincta multicincta* (= *L. zonata multicincta*)

CC. No red or pink laterally or dorsally except a few lateral spots; last supralabial touched with black posteriorly; supraoculars often fused to parietals. *L. multicincta herrerae* (= *L. zonata herrerae*)"

"May be yellow, cream or buff in preserved specimens, but must not be confused with the really white rings between triads. A black ring even though unsplit by red is considered a triad if bordered on either side by a truly white ring" (Klauber, Calif., 1943c).

ii. Black line from eye along upper labials, turning at right angle to cross head; head markings separated from blotch by light collar, bordered front and rear by black, top of head faun, labials gray, those ahead of eye with dark sutures, rostral band of grayish olive, a light crossband on neck bordered behind and in front at edge of parietals with black; body blotches 23–36, the 1st one long with black edge on scale row 2 except for brief extension on 2 or 3 scales; belly gray, checkered spasmodically with broken-edged patches of black. *L. d. syspila*

hh. Red or brown dorsal saddles reaching or extending onto ventrals; a single row of dorsal saddles; head markings separated from 1st blotch by light collar bordered front and rear by black.

    i. First dorsal saddle terminating on scale row 2; black borders not perceptibly widened on mid-dorsum; dorsal head color distinctly marked off by anterior black border of white collar; parietals burnt umber; light bars 18–32. *L. d. temporalis*

    ii. First dorsal saddle on neck extending onto ventrals; black borders not perceptibly widened on mid-dorsum; dorsal head color wholly black or rufous and yellowish spotted with black, not distinctly marked off by anterior black border of white collar (rather of *pyromelaena-multicincta* type).

        j. Head black, snout ecru-olive; saddles 25–40. *L. d. gentilis*

        jj. Head vinaceous-rufous spotted black to black, snout oil yellow, later grayish black; russet or rufous saddles 18–26; anterior black border of neck band evident when head is rufous. *L. d. amaura*

Davis Mountain king snake (5—Ditmars 1907),
Davis Mountains king snake (Pope 1937)

Lampropeltis alterna (Brown) 1901. Fig. 103; Map 31

Range: In s. trans-Pecos Texas (Pecos, Jeff Davis, Presidio, and Brewster Cos.), s. to the old Cruz Verde Mt. near Saltillo, Coahuila, Mex.—U.S.A. Tex. Mex.: Coahuila. *Elevation*—1,500 to 5,000 feet.

Size: Adults, 21.7–34 inches. Only 5 specimens known. Lengths (in mm.) are: 710 (Brown); 848 (Murray); 810 (Smith, Tex., 1941f); 542 (Jameson and Flury); 773 (Mecham and Milstead).

Distinctive characteristics: In general appearance, it looks like a gray "little green rattlesnake" (*Crotalus lepidus*) except for the orange-rufus patches on mid-dorsum within alternate black crossbands. The head is very distinct, triangular with a sharp snout and large eyes, making the snake look more like a *Trimorphodon* than a *Lampropeltis;* temporal scales enlarged.

Five good descriptions have been given. Jameson and Flury's follows: "The

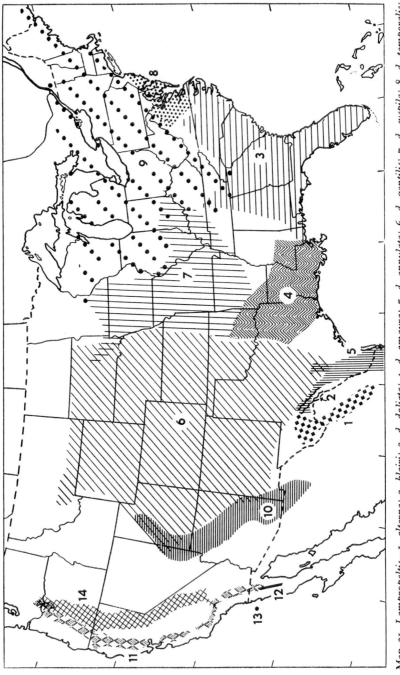

Map 31. Lampropeltis—1, alterna; 2, blairi; 3, d. doliata; 4, d. amaura; 5, d. annulata; 6, d. gentilis; 7, d. syspila; 8, d. temporalis; 9, d. triangulum; 10, pyromelana; 11, z. zonata; 12, z. agalma; 13, z. herrerae; 14, z. multicincta.

dorsal color is gray. On the body there are 36 black transverse bands narrowly edged with white. Complete bands, 2 to 3 scales wide (middorsally), alternating with a narrower band 1 to 2 scales wide. The narrow bands are broken dorsally, dorso-laterally, or both, by the ground color. Of the wider bands, the 3 most anterior bands and the last one just anterior to the anus are split transversely by a rather definite red band. The remaining wide bands and a few of the narrowed ones have scattered red flecks on the black scales. Small black spots, mostly lateral, are irregularly scattered between the bands. The head is gray, irregularly mottled with black. A dark stripe passes from the eye to the angle of the mouth. Immediately behind the head, there is a red-centered black spot and other scattered black spots which probably represent broken bands. On the tail there are 5 wide bands which form rings around the tail. The first band posterior to the anus is split dorsally by a red band. The narrow bands are represented on the tail by round middorsal spots. The ventral surface is dark gray with an indefinite midventral stripe of white. Along the lateral edges of the ventral plates there is a white stripe which is broken by the extension of the dorsal bands into the dark ventral color."

Remarks—We received a snake from Murray, Aug. 23, 1938. He secured it in the Chisos Mts. The rostral is twice as broad as high, hardly visible from above, and concave on the lower side. Internasals are slightly broader than long and about half the length of the prefrontals, which are also slightly broader than long. The frontal is longer than the suture of the parietals. Nasals 2; loreal 1; preocular 1; upper labials 7–7; lower labials 11–11; temporals left side 3 + 4; right side 2 + 2 + 3. On each side there is a temporal that extends deeply between the 6th and 7th upper labials. Anterior chin shields are twice as long as the posterior ones, which are not separated by scales. The scale rows are 23-25-19. Anal entire. Ventrals 221; caudals 64. Pits on scales inconspicuous. Total length, 818 mm. (32.7 inches), body 700 mm. (28 inches), tail 118 mm. (4.7 inches).

Color: The background of the back is olive-gray or mineral gray. The lower edges and tips of the lateral scales are pale olive-buff. The back is crossed at intervals of 7 to 8 scale rows by composite bands, 20 usually complete ones on the body and 5 on the tail. They range in length from 2 to 3 scales on mid-back and taper on the sides to 1½ to 2 scales. These bands have dorsal centers crossing 10 to 12 scales of orange-rufous, xanthine orange, or apricot orange. This orange becomes longer and more conspicuous as the tail rings are approached, the first 3 of which are with orange, the last 2 without. These orange areas are bordered with black, which is outlined with pale olive-buff or white. On the sides below the orange these bands become chestnut-brown or mummy brown and connect with the dark areas of the belly. Alternating with these xanthine-orange-centered bands are narrower, often broken, black bands (1 to 1½ scales longitudinally) also outlined with pale olive-buff. In the middle third of the body, the dorsal transverse section is usually separated from its lateral extension, while in the rear third, it becomes reduced to a median dorsal spot far removed from its lateral vertical segment. On the forward third of the body, in the illustration of the type specimen, the orange-centered rings seem to extend to the neck, with the regular alternation of narrower solely black bands. In this specimen the first 13 orange-centered bands ahead of the vent have alternating narrow black bands. Ahead of the 13th xanthine orange spot, the arrangement is: 3 narrow black bands followed by a xanthine-orange-centered one. This succession occurs 4 times with a xanthine orange center replaced by black. In the neck region, for about 3 inches, only irregular black specks appear. About ½ inch caudad of the parietals is an indefinite xanthine orange spot. The top and sides of the head are light olive-gray to light mineral gray, with a tea green or grayish olive tint ahead of the eyes where also the plates are heavily spotted with small black specks. There is a U-shaped black patch on the front of the prefrontals, the arms of the U pointing backward. The dorsal head plates have few black spots back of the eyes, and some of the dark centers on the temporal scales are faint. There is a black line from the eye to the angle of the mouth, continuous on one side and somewhat broken on the other. The iris is light mineral gray or light olive-gray with a pupil rim of white. The underside of the head is white with a wash of tea green on the gulars. The ventral surface is white, heavily marked with mummy brown or chestnut-brown. Where the lateral portions of the dorsal bands come onto the venter, the centers of 2 or 3 ventrals are prominently light. Each lateral bar connects with a succeeding one by a band of mummy brown on the venter, thus more or less forming gray saddles. Down the mid-belly is a white irregular line, separating the 2 irregular bands of mummy brown. On the tail, the xanthine orange-centered bands are complete rings, the intervening ventral area having brown only on the median sutures of the subcaudals.

Habitat: In the light of recent records maybe Meyenberg did get his first specimen in much the same locality as *E. subocularis*. The range of each species is being expanded in much the same way. Murray found his specimen in a "horizontal fissure in the face of a mass of igneous rock." Smith (Gen., 1942) and his wife found their specimen "in a crack in a large boulder on the northern side of a barren hill." Mecham and Milstead's specimen "was found DOR on U.S. Highway 290 about midnight on September 17, 1949" in the mesquite-creosote association (see Mecham and Milstead). In the Sierra Vieja Mts., Presidio County, Jameson and Flury found one in the "catclaw-grama association."

Field notes: 1934: In our files we have an envelope with the caption, "L.

alterna. Precious Photo. Only photograph of this snake in existence. Only one snake of this kind ever found. Mrs. Ellen Schulz Quillin to A. H. Wright, May 12, 1934." Among the numerous kindnesses Mr. and Mrs. R. D. Quillin have extended to us was the privilege of looking over their pamphlet and reprint collection. One time Mrs. Quillin said to us, "Some time ago I bought a collection of papers here in San Antonio, and you might wish to look them over." Soon we came to a brown-covered reprint entitled "A New Species of *Coluber* from Western Texas" by Arthur Erwin Brown. That meant the library was probably 50 years old. But soon we had the family assembled. "Everybody come! Look at the inside of the back cover." What did it have? Here was a print of the lone live specimen of *L. alterna* in the center of the page with a note above the print "Photographed at the Philadelphia Zoological Gardens by R. D. Carson with whose compliments it is sent to Mr. E. Meyenberg." Below the print occurs: "Meyenberg's *Second* New Snake. Note—The broader dark rings are *black* on the edges with *red* in centers."

This meant Mrs. Quillin must have bought Meyenberg's pamphlets. How did they get from Pecos to San Antonio? Who knows the life of Meyenberg, Brown's collector? We do not know the handwriting of Brown or that of the photographer, R. D. Carson. Doubtless one or the other sent the pamphlet to Meyenberg and made the notation. The article was about *Elaphe subocularis,* but for Meyenberg's pleasure and information the print of *L. alterna* was pasted on the back cover.

When we returned to Ithaca, it began to dawn on us that we had seen the photo before, and when we consulted the original description, we found this print reproduced. Nevertheless for 6 months we traveled on rarefied air, and even yet this special reprint is valuable for historical reasons (A. H. Wright, Journal).

June 17, 1939, letter from Murray: "Dr. and Mrs. Gloyd spent the night with us a week or so ago. He was much interested in the *L. alterna*. His first words were almost the same as my first when I saw it, 'That is not a king snake.' It looks like a *Trimorphodon* but with specimens so rare I can't bring myself to cut into the head to see the teeth. I showed him the pictures."

Authorities:

Brown, A. E. (Tex., 1901–02)
Jameson, D. L., and A. G. Flury (Tex., 1949)

Mecham, J. S., and W. W. Milstead (Tex., 1949)
Smith, H. M. (Gen., 1942; Tex., 1941f)
Murray, L. T. (Tex., 1939)

1902, A. E. Brown: "Type, No. 14,977 Academy Coll. From the Davis Mountains, Jeff Davis County, Texas. Collected by E. Meyenberg. The snake here described was received alive at the Zoological Gardens, on October 22, and came from the same locality and collector as the lately described *Coluber subocularis.* . . . The species is perhaps intermediate between *O. zonatus* and *O. leonis* Gunth., the type of which came from Nuevo León, Mexico."

1939, L. T. Murray: *"Lampropeltis alterna* (Brown). B.U.M. 6444, west side of Casa Grande Park, Chisos Mts. As far as I have been able to discover, there is no published record of any other specimen of this species save that of the type specimen, which was collected in the Davis Mountains in 1901. This second specimen is a female, 73.5 cm. in length; tail, 11.3 cm. . . . Since nothing is known of the natural history of this species, our meager notes seem worth reproducing. The snake was captured about 8 A.M. by Rudolph Hikel and Tom Turner. They found it in an horizontal fissure in the face of a mass of igneous rock. This rock mass appears to be a portion of a dike that has weathered out. It now rises 30–50 feet above the surface soil. Boulders and smaller pieces have accumulated about the base of the mother rock. This habitat is one that would seldom be visited by anyone except a collector; and one in which it is usually difficult to take a snake. This snake very likely would have escaped, but she was attempting to swallow a large specimen of *Sceloporus torquatus poinsetti* (B.U.M. 6428). This so hindered her movements that she was taken before she could retreat further into the crack."

1941, H. M. Smith *"Lampropeltis alterna* from Mexico.—A specimen of *Lampropeltis alterna* (H.M.S. Field No. 11505) was found in a crack in a large boulder on the northern side of a barren hill (the old Cruz Verde Mountain) just west of Saltillo, Coahuila, on October 15, 1939."

1949: D. L. Jameson and A. G. Flury, of Blair's party in the Sierra Vieja region of Texas, published the following valuable data on this little-known form: "One female specimen was collected near the mouth of Fox Hollow on the Miller ranch. It was active about 10 P.M. in the catclaw-grama association. According to Schmidt and Davis (1941) only 5 previous specimens have been reported. The specimen agrees in general with Brown's (1901b) description of the species but the variable characters seem worthy of description."

1949, J. S. Mecham and W. W. Milstead: "A recent collecting trip to West Texas by J. A. Herrmann and the writers yielded 1 specimen of *Lampropeltis alterna* from the Stockton Plateau in Pecos County, Texas, approximately 15 miles west of Bakersfield. The specimen was found DOR on U.S. Highway 290 about midnight on September 17, 1949. This record extends the known range of *Lampropeltis alterna* eastward in Trans-Pecos to the Stockton Plateau and indicates a wider distribution for the species than has been previously indicated. The remains of a *Sceloporus undulatus consobrinus* were contained in the stomach of the specimen."

Blair's king snake

Lampropeltis blairi Flury 1950. Fig. 102; Map 31

Range: In s. Terrell Co., trans-Pecos region, Tex. *Elevation*—Approximately 2,200 to 2,800 feet.

Size: 35.4 inches.

Distinctive characteristics: "Dorsal scale rows 25 anteriorly; infralabials 11; subcaudals 63; annuli on body 14, the anteriormost red one about 3 times as wide as the others; gray annuli separated from black ones by narrow bands of white; red annuli in form of saddles completely enclosed ventrally by black; red scales not black tipped. . . . The four-color dorsal pattern, low number of annuli and the enlarged nuchal blotch are distinguishing characters of *Lampropeltis blairi*" (Flury).

Fig. 102. *Lampropeltis blairi,* Devil's River bridge, 11 miles n.w. of Del Rio, R. W. Axtell, photo by D. Darling and J. E. Werler of San Antonio Zoological Society, Tex.

Color and description: "Head distinct from neck; general proportions of *doliatus* (Klauber, 1948) group; total length 885 mm.; tail length 138 mm.; tail divided by total length 0.156. Dorsal scale formula (Clark and Inger, 1942) as follows: 25, . . . 23, . . . 21, . . . 19. . . . Ventrals 229; anal entire; subcaudals 63, in 2 rows. Dorsal scales with 2 apical pits.

"Snout rounded; rostral about twice as wide as high with a low, wide notch below; internasals and prefrontals paired, symmetrical; nasals divided, nares lying equally in each scale; loreal single, small, twice as long as high; preoculars and supraoculars single; postoculars ⅔, lower one extending forward to median point of orbit; temporals ⅔ in 1st row, lower more than twice as large as other 2, ¾ in 2nd row and ⅘ in 3rd; supralabials 8, 3rd and 4th entering orbit, 6th much smaller than 5th or 7th. Eye 4.3 mm. long. Mental small, triangular; infralabials 11, anterior pair meeting on midventral line and separating anterior ⅓ of 1st pair of chin shields; a very small scale on midventral line between posterior ends of anterior chin shields; 3 scale lengths between posterior end of chin shields and 1st ventral plate; 8 scale rows separate posterior chin shields from infralabials.

"Dorsal pattern of alternating black-bordered red saddles and white-bordered gray saddles. Head shields black, mottled with grays; anterior 4 supralabials white, flecked with gray; a broad black band from eye to angle of mouth; temporals, posterior part of head and sides of neck covered by 1st gray dorsal saddle.

"Dark gray dorsal saddles 14 on body, one above anus and 3 on tail; range (including white border) 6–9 scale lengths (middorsal), average 7. Anteriormost saddle covering posterior part of head (7 scale lengths behind parietals); extending obliquely to 2nd scale row opposite 9th ventral. White borders narrow, irregular, about ½ scale wide middorsally; widening (at expense of black borders) to 2–3 scales on 1st to 3rd scale rows; white usually extending along 1st scale row and lateral edges of ventrals to enclose gray saddles.

"Black bordered red saddles 14 on body and 3 on tail; posteriormost one completely black; next anterior one only flecked with red; average width of red saddles on body 6.7 scale lengths (middorsally), range 4–19 (4–9 aver., 5.8 if anteriormost saddle is discounted); red narrowing laterally, usually reaching 1st scale row for 1–4 scale lengths; red scales with irregular black flecks along edges; color of the apparently typical 7th red saddle seems to agree with Maerz and Paul's (1930) Plate 3, color A-11. Black borders 1–2 scales wide middorsally; narrowing to 1 scale on 1st and 2nd scale rows; uniting with black on ventrals to enclose red saddles.

"Ventral surface with black borders of red saddles uniting laterally and forming a band 4–8 ventrals wide across belly; bands interrupted or mixed with white midventrally on anterior half of body. Irregular blotches of black and white opposite gray saddles; 2nd and 3rd of these blotches with lateral extensions of black invading gray saddles up to 5th scale row; 8th and 9th blotches with similar extensions reaching 1st scale row; blotches restricted to midventral region on tail. White borders of gray saddles usually 1–2 ventrals wide across belly but often mixed with black from irregular blotches" (Flury).

Habitat: In Terrell Co., Tex., there is a considerable area of Austin chalk in thin-to-medium-bedded white chalky limestone flags and ledges. The point of collection for *L. blairi* was 8.8 miles west of Dryden, Terrell Co., at an elevation of about 2,400 feet. This point is 67 miles east of Marathon, and about 30 miles east of the eastern edge of the Marathon Basin with its uplift of Pennsylvania, Devonian, and Ordovician rocks. The country rises to 4,000 feet at Marathon. "The old Rio Grande embayment enters Trans-Pecos Texas in southern Terrell Co." (Blair, Ecol., 1950). This is now an arid region within the range of creosote bush. About 6 miles west of the collecting point of this *blairi,* we found *Elaphe subocularis* and *Masticophis f. testaceous* near a rocky knoll, in a land of sotol, brushy oak, and oregon-grape.

Food: "The *blairi* in the photo sent you . . . is now at the Zoo where we keep it under almost constant observation. It feeds on both white mice and lizards, seeming to prefer the latter. The snake has taken *Sceloporus oliva-ceus, Sceloporus v. marmoratus,* and *Holbrookia texana,* seizing the lizards with a sudden forward thrust, much the same as *annulata* when feeding upon *Cnemidophorus.* Most feeding is done at night as it prowls about the cage. During the day it is seldom active, remaining hidden beneath the moss in the cage. A very quiet snake, it seldom resents handling" (letter from J. E. Werler, Aug. 26, 1950).

Shortly after this letter was written, Axtell reported on an additional speci-men of *Lampropeltis blairi* from Texas: "This snake was taken about 79 miles southeast of the type locality. During a collecting trip with W. W. Milstead and Glen Fry, the writer found the snake active about 10 P.M. on June 9, 1950, 200 yards east of the Devil's River bridge on U.S. Highway No 90. This individual has been kept alive at the San Antonio Zoo."

Authorities:

Axtell, R. W. (Tex., 1951)   Flury, A. (Tex., 1950)

1950, A. Flury: *"Lampropeltis blairi* apparently belongs in the *Mexicana* subgroup of Smith" (Tex., 1942).

1951, R. W. Axtell: This and the original specimen are some of the most fortunate discoveries in Texas in the last half century.

Yellow-bellied king snake (17—Ditmars 1907), **Evans'** king snake (12—Yarrow 1882)

Lampropeltis calligaster calligaster (Harlan) 1827. Fig. 104; Map 32

Other common names: Blotched king snake (6); brown king snake (2); Kansas king snake; Kennicott's chain snake (Jordan 1876); king snake; milk snake; prairie king snake (8); (Say's) chain snake.

Range: From w. Indiana to cent. Kentucky, w. Tennessee to Dickson Co. (Sinclair, Tenn., 1951a), Mississippi to Gulf coast in w. Louisiana w. along

Fig. 103. *Lampropeltis alterna,* Chisos Mts., Tex., L. T. Murray.

Fig. 104. *Lampropeltis calligaster calligaster,* Washington, D.C., Zoo.

Gulf to Matagorda Bay and w. to Pecos River, Texas, n. into Oklahoma, e. Kansas, and s.e. Nebraska, e. through s. Iowa and cent. Illinois.—Ark.; Ill.; Ia.; Ind.; Kan.; Ky.; La.; Minn.; Miss.; Mo.; Neb.; Okla.; Tex. *Elevation*—500 to 3,000 feet, mostly below 2,000 feet.

Size: Adults, 11–50 inches.

Longevity: 2 years 9 months (Conant and Hudson, Gen., 1949); 2 years 10 months (Kauffeld, Gen., 1951).

Distinctive characteristics: A medium, 25- (27-)rowed, brown, grayish, or black snake with lower labials (8) 9 or 10. Venter light yellow or buff with quadrate areas on ends of ventrals. "Body color pale grayish brown; a dorsal series of subquadrate blotches, dark brown with narrow black borders, 2 to 3 scales long, 8 to 10 wide, somewhat emarginate before and behind; the interspaces are about equal to the spots; a smaller alternating series on the sides, which often form irregular vertical bars, and a third on the outer row of scales and ends of the ventrals; belly yellowish, with or without square black blotches on the centre; the head markings are sometimes very elaborate" (Brown, Gen., 1901). This snake may be wholly black or may be somewhat like *Elaphe quadrivittata, E. obsoleta spiloides,* or *E. emoryi.*

Color: A snake from the St. Louis, Mo., Zoo loaned by R. M. Perkins, Nov. 21, 1928. From the 3rd and 4th rows of scales to the 6th and also on the 11th and 12th rows are longitudinal bands of raw umber, prout's brown, or mummy brown, giving this animal a 4-banded appearance somewhat like that of *Elaphe quadrivittatus.* The ground color between the bands is a light brownish olive, buffy brown, or drab. Across the back are transverse saddles, 43 on the body, or olive-brown outlined with mummy brown. They are about 6 scales transversely as they extend between the 2 dorsolateral stripes. The interspace between the spots is deep grayish olive. The first 3 rows of scales are smoke gray. There is a faint suggestion of a row of spots which alternate with the saddles located on the first 5 or 6 rows of scales and extend onto the belly plates on the adjoining edges of 2 ventrals as a line or spot of olive-brown. The top and sides of the head are without spots and are grayish olive or deep grayish olive. The upper labials are smoke gray or pale smoke gray. The iris is light yellowish olive above with a honey yellow or clay color iris rim. The lower portion of the iris contains much olive-brown. The throat is white or pale pinkish cinnamon. The belly is marguerite yellow, ivory yellow, or olive-buff with quadrate areas on the ends of the ventrals. These areas are light grayish olive or a lighter gray and are more or less alternate with the lateral spots.

A snake from Arkansas received from D. L. Gamble, May 4, 1928. Black phase. The upper parts, including the top of the head, are dark olive, fuscous-black, or black. The first 3 rows of scales have white forward edges, and the interspaces in general are white if the skin is stretched. The under parts are tilleul buff, white, or pale olive-buff, with various parts washed with ochraceous-buff, or honey yellow.

A snake from Washington, D.C., Zoo, used through the kindness of Wetmore, Mann, Norris, and Godwin, June 14, 1933. The saddle spots of the back, the 2 longitudinal nuchal spots, a postvittal stripe, the Y on top of the head, and a frontal-prefrontal suture band between the eyes are drab or buffy brown. The spots on the rear half of the snake are olive-brown. On each side is a row of vertical spots 3 to 5 scales deep of the same color. These stop in the 4th scale row.

Abnormal coloration—Melanistic and striped phases. In our experience with this form we have seen more black individuals than one nicely conforming to the color pattern described in Blanchard's excellent Ph.D. thesis. In his treatment, however, he clearly recognizes this situation. Brown (Gen., 1901), Branson, Hurter, Gloyd, Force (Okla., 1930), and others have noticed these two color phases. Some have ascribed the darkening of specimens to age.

Habitat: This form occurs on the prairies, in pastures, in ploughed or cultivated fields, along roadways, in rock ledges, in hayfields, hay shocks, haystacks, or under shocks of grain. Other habitats recorded include open and mixed woods, upland meadows, bottom lands, semiopen uplands and savannas, cornfields, and several other types of places.

Period of activity: *Early appearances and seasonal catch*—Missouri, Apr. 2, 22, 24, May 26 (Hurter); Iowa, Apr. 23, 29, May 13, 14 (Bailey); Kansas, May 1, 14, June 1, 16 (Gloyd); Mississippi, Apr. 19–Oct. 29, 1937 (Cook, Miss., 1945). *Fall disappearance*—Missouri, Sept. 9 (Hurter); Iowa, Oct. 12, 1936 (Swanson in Bailey); Kansas, Sept. 9, 20, 22 (Gloyd). MVZ dates, Apr. 20–May 31.

Breeding: Oviparous. Males 537–1,254 mm., females 434–1,105 mm. *Eggs* —Number, 4–13. For a long time we had only a record of 11 eggs ploughed up in early August, 1918. They hatched 1 month later (Blanchard, Conant and Bridges, Gen., 1939; Schmidt and Davis, Gen., 1941). "This snake deposits a small number of eggs during July" (Hudson and Davis, Neb., 1941). "A cluster of 13 eggs of this species was plowed from a field in Little Blue River bottom land about 1 mile west of Lake City on August 6, 1939. The eggs were so badly desiccated when received that the embryos were dead, but probably would have hatched within a week, had they remained in the ground. One collected June 2, 1940, laid 6 eggs on July 13. The eggs averaged 50 mm. in length and 20 mm. in diameter" (Anderson, Mo., 1942). "A 40-inch female king snake of this type laid 11 eggs on July 22. The eggs were moderately elongated, and several were adherent. They were almost ready to hatch on September 14 when they were accidentally destroyed" (Minton, Ind., 1944). "One specimen dissected on June 17, 1951, contained 8 eggs" (Guidry, Tex., 1953). In Kansas, Clarke (1954) reported a female 994 mm. in length, laying 9 eggs. Size, 2 inches x .8 inch (Anderson). Time, July and August.

Young—"Four new hatched young . . . which seemed to be no more than 2 or 3 days old, judging from the condition of the egg membranes from which they emerged were received from a farmer August 21 without any data. . . . Three were females and 1 a male. Their lengths in millimeters were as follows: 273, 269, 275, and 280" (Gloyd). In 1927 Burt recorded a female of 290 mm. and in 1931 a 270-mm. specimen. We have seen young specimens 246 (tail 34), 248, 252 (tail 34), 277, 358 (tail 45), and 367 (tail 48) mm. In the Stanford University collection we saw 320-mm. (Myers) and 347-mm. (Regnery) specimens.

Food: Mice, rats, moles, gophers, lizards, frogs, small fish, toads, smaller snakes. Taylor, Hurter, Schmidt (Okla., 1919), Blanchard, Boyer and Heinze (Mo., 1934), Grant, Branson.

Field notes: May 16, 1950: Near Boothe, Ark., saw a 4-foot snake we thought *Elaphe o. obsoleta,* with pattern visible. With snake in hand, it finally dawned on us that we had *Lampropeltis c. calligaster.* We fear this mistake has occurred in the literature of the *Elaphe* species such as *E. emoryi.*

Authorities:

Bailey, R. M. (Ia., 1939)
Blanchard, F. N. (Gen., 1921)
Branson, E. B. (Kan., 1904)
Burt, C. E. (Kan., 1931)
Dury, R., and W. Gessing, Jr. (Ky., 1940)

Gloyd, H. K. (Kan., 1928)
Grant, C. (Kan., 1936a)
Hallowell, E. (Kan., 1857)
Hibbard, C. W. (Ky., 1937)
Hurter, J. (Mo., 1911)
Taylor, E. W. (N.M., 1892a)

Brown king snake (15—Brimley 1905), Mole snake (8)

Lampropeltis calligaster rhombomaculata (Holbrook) 1840. Fig. 105; Map 32

Other common names: Blotched king snake (3—Yarrow 1882); brown snake; ground snake; house snake (?); king snake; mole catcher (3—Dunn 1915).

Range: Upper coastal and piedmont areas from cent. Maryland to Lake Co., n. cent. Fla., n. and w. to Pearl River, Miss., n. in e. Mississippi to s.e. Tennessee, thence northward e. of the mountains.—Ala.; D.C.; Fla.; Ga.; La.; Md.; Miss.; N.C.; S.C.; Tenn.; Va. *Elevation*—Sea level to 2,000 feet. 400–600 feet (Barbour, N.C., 1942).

Size: Adults, 8–48 inches.

Distinctive characteristics: A medium-sized brown (olive-brown to prout's brown) snake. Sometimes, in adult state, uniform; but some adults, almost all immatures, and all young have 42–60 transverse dorsal saddles (deep red to russet) edged with black. These saddles, 10–12 scales wide, alternate with a narrow vertical row on first 5 rows of body. Top of head bister. Venter clouded, areas alternating with lateral spots fawn and white on front half of venter and cream buff on rear half. It is a (19) 21- (23) dorsal-rowed, short-headed snake, with dorsal blotches convex or straight on anterior and posterior margins. It has infralabials normally (7) 8 (9), ventrals 186–213, caudals 36–55.

Color: A snake at Washington Reptile House made available through the kindness of Messrs Wetmore, Mann, Norris, and Goodwin, June 15, 1933. The back between the saddle spots is snuff brown, olive-brown, drab, brussels brown, or prout's brown. The saddle spots, covering 11 scales transversely, are morocco red or occasionally, when scales are off, peach red, brick red, or hay's russet. They are edged with black. The brown of the sides below the lower ends of the saddle spots is light drab or with other vinaceous tints. The scales of the first 5 rows and also those in the saddle interspaces

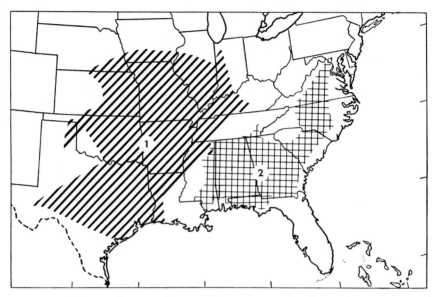

Map 32. *Lampropeltis*—1, *calligaster*; 2, *c. rhombomaculata*.

of the forward part of the body have light edges of deep olive-buff, olive-buff, or white. Alternating with the saddle spots are vertical lateral bars of the same color. These bars are 5 scales deep and about 1 scale wide. They extend onto the end of 1 or sometimes 2 ventrals. The color on top of the head and to the upper edge of the upper labials and the rear of the interspace between the saddle spots is bister. On either side of the neck dorsum there is an elongate spot which is morocco red like the saddle spots. An obscure spot of the same color occurs on the inner edge and suture of the parietals. The labial edges are faintly darkened with dark specklings, and the plates of the underside of the head are speckled. The iris is the color of the saddle spots. On the venter, alternating with the vertical lateral spots, are areas of avellaneous or vinaceous-fawn with white on the cephalic half of the body and with cream-buff or cartridge buff on the rear half.

A snake from Avon, Nelson Co., Va. loaned us by H. M. G. Jopson, May

27, 1950. The belly is primrose yellow to marguerite yellow with spots of verona brown to snuff. The underside of the tail is almost clear with a little spotting paler than that of the belly.

Habitat: Brimley early called this snake a subterranean burrower. Dunn reports 7 plowed up in a 12-acre field in middle Virginia. From the labels, Blanchard gives a "grassy bank," "dry road," "cut-over pineland with more or less scrub oak," "light soil, sandy loam," "near water." In North Carolina, Gray (1941) wrote: "Although not common this snake has been frequently found crossing highways and wooded roads. Farmers sometimes mistake it for the copperhead." Allen found it in fields not far from stands of timber, along the highway, or under logs.

Period of activity: *Seasonal catch*—North Carolina, 1925, Feb. 3, Mar. 1, Apr. 2, May 10, June 7, July 4, Aug. 2, Sept. 3, Oct. 4, Nov. 4 (Brimley, N.C., 1925). Mississippi, Sept., 1930, Apr. 1931 (Allen); Cook has it from Mar. 21, 1938 to Oct. 30, 1940. *Fall disappearance*—Sept., 1926 (Brimley, N.C., 1927a); Sept., 1930.

Breeding: Oviparous. Males 508–1,131 mm.; females 512–1,042 mm. *Eggs* —Even if this is Washington city's very own snake, we know next to nothing of its breeding habits. As late as 1948 Fowler queried: "Months Eggs Found? Number of Eggs?" Earlier Brimley (N.C., 1941–42) had written: "The eggs are much like those of the larger species (*getulus* and *doliata*), but smaller and are as usual in the genus more or less attached to each other in clusters." *Young*—We do not know the hatchling time or size. The smallest we have seen were 206, 222, 226, 235 mm. Blanchard had males as low as 228, 229, 231, 238 mm. and females 201, 212, 220 mm.

Food: Lizards, young snakes, mammals and birds, mice, rats. Brimley, Shufeldt, Ditmars (Gen., 1907), Lockwood.

Authorities:

Allen, M. J. (Miss., 1932)
Blanchard, F. N. (Gen., 1921)
Brimley, C. S. (N.C., 1941–42)
Cook, F. A. (Miss., 1945)
Holbrook, J. E. (Gen., 1836–42)
Lockwood, R. A. (N.C., 1954)

Löding, H. P. (Ala., 1922)
Miller, G. S., Jr. (Va., 1902)
Shufeldt, R. W. (Gen., 1915)
Stickel, W. H., and J. B. Cope (Gen., 1947)

Scarlet king snake (15—Wachtel), **Red king snake** (13—Beyer 1897)
Lampropeltis doliata doliata (Linné) 1766. Fig. 106; Map 31

Other common names: Coral king snake; eastern milk snake; (false) coral snake; garter snake; house king snake; Osceola snake, red snake, scarlet snake; thunder snake.

Range: Extreme s.e. Virginia along coast to tip of Florida, w. to s. Mississippi, n.e. (with tongue into s.e. Tennessee) to extreme s. cent. Virginia.—

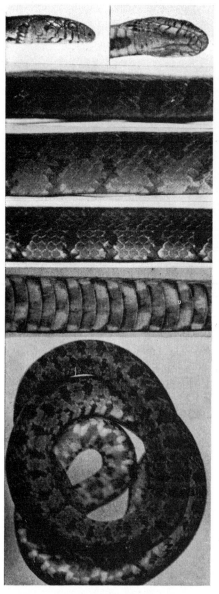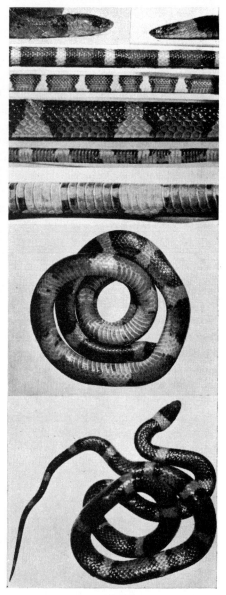

Fig. 105. *Lampropeltis c. rhombomaculata:* 1,2, Avon, Nelson Co., Va., H. M. G.
Jopson; 3–7, Washington, D.C., Zoo.

Fig. 106. *Lampropeltis doliata doliata:*
1,2,4,5,6,7,8, St. Petersburg, Fla., N. P. Fry
and son; 3,9, Eureka, Marion Co., Fla., C. C.
Tyler.

Ala.; Fla.; Ga.; Ky.; La.; Miss.; N.C.; S.C.; Tenn.; Va. *Elevation*—Mainly 500 to 1,000 feet, but sometimes to 2,000 feet.

Size: Adults, 7–24 inches.

Longevity: 3 years or more (Kauffeld, Gen., 1951).

Distinctive characteristics: "Red above crossed by rings of black and white or yellow, every alternate ring being black; these rings cross under parts in typical *elapsoides,* but are interrupted in *virginiana.* Scale rows usually 19, occasionally 21, and often only 17 in far southern specimens" (Brimley, N.C., 1941–42). The red rings vary from brazil red, dragon's-blood red, scarlet, or morocco red to hay's russet or rufous. The light rings range from white, cartridge buff, pale lemon yellow to strontian yellow.

Color: A snake from St. Petersburg, Fla., furnished by N. P. Fry and Son, Aug. 7, 1928. On the back, the red rings or bands, which are usually 4 to 6 scales wide, but occasionally only 3, are scarlet or scarlet-red. These bands, crossing the venter, are rose doree or geranium pink, and are bordered at either end by rings of blue-violet black or dull violet-black, which are slightly broken on the venter. The light rings are olive-buff, white, cartridge buff, or sulphur yellow. These rings are complete across the belly, but become pure white there with jasper pink edges to the ventrals. The top of the head ahead of the eyes, the supraocular, the face, and the postocular regions are scarlet or scarlet-red. The frontal and parietals are blue-violet black or dull violet-black. The chin and most of the lower labials are scarlet. The eye is vinaceous-rufous or carnelian red.

Habitat: Deckert found one in a sweet potato field and commonly saw them plowed up in fields. One was found on the frame of an old building 4 feet above the ground, others under the bark of dead pines, under logs in wooded sections, and as a burrower removed in road building. One was seen in high pine upland mesophytic hammocks, in loose soil. This snake is partly nocturnal. Brimley (N.C., 1941–42) pronounced it the most subterranean in habits of any of the genus.

Meade's record, one of the farthest west in origin, is pertinent: "This beautiful little 5-inch snake was ploughed up in a field on a cold day and evidently was in its first year. At present, in its 4th year, the length is about 12 inches. The brilliant red snout is in sharp contrast to the gray-black snout of *amaura,* and the coloration generally more vivid. This specimen has fed readily on skinks from the time of its capture, refusing to take even small specimens of other lizards until quite recently. The feeding preference continues to be for skinks. Schmidt and Davis (1941: 173) say of the scarlet king snakes, 'Captives are gentle, rarely attempting to bite,' but this one has always been pugnacious and invariably bites when handled."

Period of activity: *Early appearances*—North Carolina, Mar. 11, 19, 25, Apr. 26, 1901; May 10, 1905 (Brimley, N.C., 1941–42). "Seasonal catch"—

Feb., 1 snake; Apr., 5; May, 4; June, 5; July, 3; Aug., 1; Oct., 3; Nov., 1. Total, 23 (Brimley, N.C., 1925).

"Winter and spring are the seasons in which this species is occasionally found in the crevices and hollows beneath the bark of pine stumps and logs. During the winter of 1929–1930 about 15 individuals were taken from these situations. The capture of a specimen on May 25 appears to be the latest record for this type of habitat. On a night in June a large female containing eggs was discovered crawling across a street on the outskirts of Biloxi and this is the only instance in which a specimen has been found in any situation other than the one described. What becomes of it during the summer months remains unknown. Large areas of stumps and logs have been worked over in this season with no success. The example of the capture in June might possibly indicate that with the advent of warm weather it assumes a roving disposition" (Allen, Miss., 1932).

Breeding: Oviparous. Males 397–827 mm., females 399–520 mm. *Eggs*— The breeding data is scanty. "On July 28, 1903, three eggs measuring 30 to 31 mm. long were received. These were long and slender, and were attached to one another on the side, so that their long axes were parallel. . . . The probability is that they were the eggs of the Red King Snake (*Ophibolus coccineus*)" (Brimley, Gen., 1904). *Young*—There are no records of hatchlings. The smallest we have seen was 211 mm., but Blanchard examined males 182, 185, 190, 193, and 201 mm. and females 165, 187, and 197 mm.

Food: Lizards, snakes, insects, earthworms, fish, mice. Wright and Bishop, Haltom (Ala., 1931), Carr, Meade, Allen (Miss., 1932).

Authorities:

Brimley, C. S. (Gen., 1904, 1905; N.C., 1941–42)
Carr, A. F., Jr. (Fla., 1940a)
Cope, E. D. (Gen., 1900; Fla., 1889)
Ditmars, R. L. (Gen., 1907)
Holbrook, J. E. (Gen., 1836–42)
Loennberg, E. (Fla., 1895)

Meade, G. P. (La., 1945)
Mittleman, M. B. (Gen., 1952)
Nehrling, H. (Fla., 1905)
Smith, H. M. (Gen., 1952b)
Stejneger, L. (Gen., 1918)
Wright, A. H., and S. C. Bishop (Ga., 1916)

1836–42, J. E. Holbrook, applying the name *Coronella doliata:* "Schlegel received this animal from Professor Troost, of Nashville, and described it under the name of *Coronella coccinea;* at the same time he refers doubtingly to the *Coluber doliatus* of Lacépède. I have not the least doubt that this animal is identical with the *Coluber doliatus* of Linnaeus (whose specific name I have retained) which he received from Dr. Garden. . . . in Bosc's description . . . the rings are represented encircling the body, as in *Elaps fulvius*, with which the animal seems to have been confounded, but from which it is entirely distinct in the arrangement of its teeth; there being in *Calamaria elapsoidea*, palatine and maxillary teeth, but no fangs."

(1898) 1900, E. D. Cope: (At this period we began systematic biology.

Osceola elapsoidea, with a loreal, was a delightful name and form for us. When we grew older in the field and discovered Cope had *Osceola elapsoidea, Osceola doliata doliata, Osceola doliata parallela, Osceola coccinea,* each in Florida, we became doubting Thomases. In addition when he populated the Carolinas with *clerica, doliata, syspila, coccinea,* and *elapsoidea* we thought he had another *Natrix compressicauda* spawning bee.)

1905, H. Nehrling: Some Floridian should translate this German article by one of Florida's most helpful and constructive citizens.

1918, L. Stejneger: "As for *Coronella coccinea* of Schlegel, 1837, it must first be noted that he described it as having 17 scale rows, being undoubtedly the same form which Holbrook the following year described as *Coluber elapsoides.* This would give Schlegel's name the priority, but the name is not original with him, as he quotes *Coluber coccineus* of Latreille, 1802. This name, however, is antedated by Blumenbach's *Coluber coccineus* (1788). Latreille's and Blumenbach's name, however, undoubtedly refers to the same species, Schlegel's statement to the contrary notwithstanding. Thus the name which has caused so much confusion fortunately drops out as unavailable." Stejneger's discussion of the proper name for this form concluded with the observation that probably Linnaeus described a *Cemophora coccinea* as *Coluber doliatus,* and, with the type gone, he did not wish to disturb our present usage.

Scarlet king snake (11—Yarrow 1882), Red king snake (5—Strecker 1915)

Lampropeltis doliata amaura Cope 1860. Fig. 107; Map 31

Other common names: Cope's milk snake (4); coral (king) snake; corn snake; Louisiana milk snake (3—Ortenburger 1927); Lower Mississippi Valley milk snake; Mexican king snake (Yarrow 1882); (red) milk snake; red snake; scarlet (house) snake; thunder snake.

Range: S.e. Oklahoma to Mobile Bay along Gulf to Houston, Tex., n. through e. Texas.—Ark.; La.; Miss.; Okla.; Tex. *Elevation*—Seacoast to 750 feet, few above 500 feet.

Size: Adults, 10–25 inches.

Longevity: 7 years (Meade, La., 1940). 14 years 7 months (Perkins, Gen., 1951). In Christmas greetings for 1951, Meade wrote us: "My little *L. d. amaura* captured close to our house in June 1936 continues to thrive. She is now at least 16 years old, about 23 inches long and slender as a lead pencil." 17 years 7 months (Perkins, Gen., 1954).

Distinctive characteristics: "This form may be distinguished from *elapsoides* (*doliata*) by the greater number of ventral plates (nearly 200), a maximum of 21 instead of 19 rows of scales, the usually greater extent of black on the head, the fact that the snout is usually more or less mottled with black instead of being a uniform red; from *syspila* it may be distinguished by the fact that (1) the pattern is in rings, or, when in blotches of red, there is no ventro-lateral series of dark spots alternating with the dorsal blotches, (2) the head is black with a red snout, instead of red with a posterior black band and various dark edged light markings between the eyes, and (3) the number of transverse yellow bands is commonly above 23; and from *gentilis* it is best known (1) by the smaller number of yellow cross bands, usually not more than 25, (2) by the fact that the black rings show but slight tendency to encroach dorsally upon the red, and (3) the black of the belly in *gentilis* is usually concentrated between the black rings opposite the dorsal red areas, instead of being divided with red, as in *amaura*" (Blanchard).

Color: A snake received from B. C. Marshall, June 23, 1929. There are on the body 26 and on the tail 6 vinaceous-rufous, hay's russet, or terra cotta saddles which extend onto the ventrals about the width of a row of scales. These saddles are bordered ahead and behind by transverse black rings which also border the vinaceous-rufous saddle on the belly. Between the 2 black rings is a sulphur yellow ring 2 scales wide above and 3 to 5 scales wide on the 1st row. This yellow area extends onto the belly. There is no lateral row of spots alternating with the saddles, opposite the red, the yellow, or the black rings. The neck is sulphur yellow bounded in front and rear with black. The black ring in front passes from angle of mouth to angle of mouth across the posterior part of the parietals. The top of the head to near the front of the prefrontals is vinaceous-rufous with black spots. The snout is oil yellow or light yellowish olive, and there is some of the same on the postoculars. The underside of the head is cartridge buff or at times sulphur yellow. The eye is grenadine red or carnelian red spotted on the outer parts with dark. There are very few spots of black on the middle of the ventral surface.

Habitat: So far as the recorded material is concerned this is a Texas and Strecker story. Strecker has recorded it in 6 or more articles. In Louisiana in 1900 Beyer said: "Of the red, black and yellow-ringed king snakes, this species is the most common, occurring in almost every part of the state. Burrowing in the sandy soil, it is frequently brought to notice by the plow." Then followed the 6 notices by Strecker. He found it in cotton fields, in a crevice of a log near a sawmill, and in cornfields in bayou bottoms. Others have taken it at the edge of a cypress swamp, in a hilly region, and also in lowlands.

Period of activity: *Hibernation*—"Winter and spring are the seasons in which this species [*elapsoides,* but in s. Miss. probably equally true of *amaura*] is occasionally found in the crevices and hollows beneath the bark of pine stumps and logs. During the winter of 1929–1930 about 15 individuals

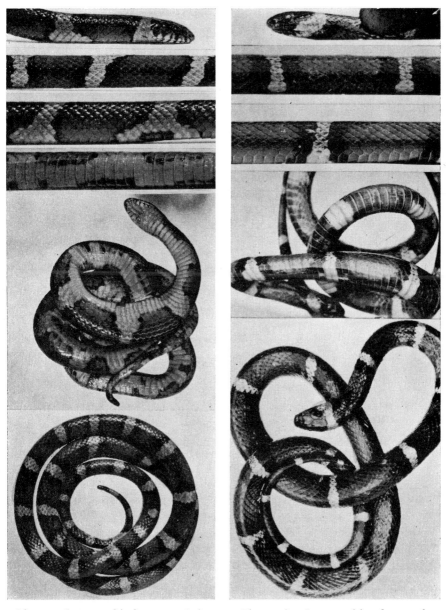

Fig. 107. *Lampropeltis d. amaura,* Irving, Kan., B. C. Marshall.

Fig. 108. *Lampropeltis d. annulata,* Brownsville, Tex., "Snake King."

were taken from these situations. A capture of a specimen on May 25 appears to be the latest record for this type of habitat" (Allen). "They feed occasionally during the winter, not oftener than once a month from November to March, during which time they are in a cool pantry away from steam heat.

They spend most of their time in a brown cardboard box in their cage into which is stuffed a flannel cloth in the winter months" (Meade, La., 1940).

Breeding: Oviparous. Males 413–622, females 425–629 mm. Meager indeed are our data on this topic. *Eggs*—"On a night in June a large female containing eggs was discovered crawling across a street in the outskirts of Biloxi" (Allen). *Young*—The smallest specimens Blanchard recorded were females 193, 221 mm., a male 202 mm. In the light of Meade's record these are beyond hatching. "A small specimen, apparently freshly hatched, was captured in August 1937, the brilliant pattern being striking in this 5-inch snake" (Meade, La., 1940).

Food: Lizards, small snakes, blind snakes. Meade (La., 1940), Allen, Curtis (Tex., 1949).

Authorities:

Allen, M. J. (Miss., 1932)

Blanchard, F. N. (Gen., 1921)

Cope, E. D. (Gen., 1860–61, 1875)

Curtis, L. (Tex., 1949)

Meade, G. P. (La., 1940, 1945)

Strecker, J. K., Jr. (Tex., 1915), 1922, 1926, 1928c, 1930)

In 1940 G. P. Meade gave us our most important picture of this form. One snake he had for 7 years. It was 14 inches when captured and 21 inches at the end of the period. He observed that the oyster-white light bands of the baby snake changed to light brownish yellow and that the snout became grayish black.

Ringed king snake (3—Yarrow 1882), **Mexican milk snake** (2)

Lampropeltis doliata annulata Kennicott 1860. Fig. 108; Map 31

Other common names: Ring king snake; ringed milk snake (1—Ditmars 1936).

Range: Kerr Co., Tex., s. to Mexico (Coahuila, Nuevo León, Tamaulipas). —U.S.A.: Tex. Mex.: Coahuila, Nuevo León, Tamaulipas. *Elevation*—Seacoast to 2,000 or more feet. 1,500 feet.

Size: Adults, 14–39 inches.

Longevity: 10 years 5 months (Perkins, Gen., 1951); 13 years 5 months (Perkins, Gen., 1954).

Distinctive characteristics: "These snakes show the following color characters: Body and tail marked with a series of 22–25 yellow rings and these bordered by slightly wider black rings which become narrower near the ventrum. In one specimen the black rings are so widened as to nearly completely crowd out the red on the dorsum. The red rings on the body are just as wide as the combined yellow and two adjacent black rings, and do not extend onto the ventral surface. Yellow bands extend onto the ventrum where they are separated by broad areas of black. Head, from snout to posterior edge of parietals, entirely black" (Werler). See diagnosis in Smith.

Color: A snake from Brownsville, Tex., furnished by "Snake King," Apr. 22, 1925. The red areas bounded by black rings may be hay's russet on the dorsum, vinaceous-rufous on the upper part of the side, and carrot red on lower sides and belly; or coral red on the dorsum varying to light coral red on lower side and belly. The dark rings are dull violet-black (2), becoming on the sides violet-slate and on the belly violet-plumbeous, where some light coral red may be intermixed. The bands between the black rings are light orange-yellow or deep chrome on the body and orange-buff on the tail. On the belly these bands become ivory yellow, seafoam yellow, or white. The top of the head is black or dull violet-black (2). The facial plates are marked with white spots. The iris is brazil red or in the rear, violet-slate, marked with some blackish specks.

Breeding: Oviparous. Males 353 up, females 345–950 mm. *Eggs*—The only records are those of Werler: "A female 749 mm. in length, collected July 2, 1948, in northern Cameron County, Texas, laid a clutch of 5 eggs on July 12. The eggs were non-granular, and adherent in a cluster, showed signs of collapse on August 18 and this condition increased, until, on the day before hatching, the eggs had lost all semblance of their original full shape. Egg measurements follow: Length-width: 36-22, 37-20, 39-20, 40-18, 43-19. On August 8, one egg of this cluster was opened, for it was thought the egg masses had solidified and the eggs would not hatch, but examination revealed a living, apparently normal embryo. The first snake of the 4 remaining eggs began to slit its shell on the morning of August 25 and had emerged from the egg on the afternoon of August 26. This hatchling, which measured 218 mm. long, was badly deformed by a series of 9 sharp bends or kinks, the length of its body and tail and because of this deformity remained coiled with much of its ventrum turned upward and exposed. On the evening of August 27, 2 more snakes hatched from their eggs and these were normal and measured 230 mm. and 241 mm. respectively. The last snake of the clutch, a 228 mm. hatchling which escaped from its eggs on the morning of August 28, was deformed in the same manner as the first hatchling, exhibiting a series of kinks along the posterior fifth of its body."

On June 5, 1949, according to Werler, a female of 712 mm. laid 5 eggs, smooth, adhesive, and 48 to 52 mm. long by 18 to 21 mm. wide. On July 24 and 25, 3 hatched, the young being 231–237 mm. long.

Field notes: 1942, Salt Lake City, Ut.: Worked at the collection of S. and D. Mulaik. On June 23, 1941, they took a fine *L. t. annulata* at Raven's Ranch, Kerr Co., Texas. This is a very important definite record for this subspecies.

Letters from A. J. Kirn: Sept. 26, 1947—"I made a nice find when I picked up a dead *Lampropeltis triangulum annulata* in the road about 4 miles from the Bexar Co. line in Bandera County, road from Helotes to

Bandera." Apr. 5, 1949—"I took a *Lampropeltis triangulum annulata* just north of San Geronomo, northern Bexar Co. A specimen in the Old Scientific Society's collection, now at St. Mary's University, is also of that form. This must be the subspecies occurring in this area."

Authorities:

Brown, A. E. (Gen., 1901)
Cope, E. D. (Gen., 1860–61a, 1893)
Kennicott, R. (Gen., 1860–61)
Kirn, A. J. (Letters in "Field Notes" above)
Milstead, W. W., J. S. Mecham, and H. McClintock (Tex., 1950)

Mulaik, S. and D. (Tex., 1945)
Smith, H. M. (Gen., 1942)
Stejneger, L. (Tex., 1891; Gen., 1918)
Taylor, E. H. (Gen., 1940b)
Werler, J. (Tex., 1949)

1950: W. W. Milstead, J. S. Mecham, and H. McClintock took one in the cedar-savannah association in Terrell Co., Tex.

Western milk snake (10—Ellis and Henderson 1913), Western king snake (9—Van Denburgh)

Lampropeltis doliata gentilis (Baird and Girard) 1853. Fig. 109; Map 31

Other common names: (Arkansas) king snake; banded king snake; chicken snake (Mozley 1878); coral snake; corn snake; house snake (Mozley 1878); milk snake (Mozley 1878); prairie painted king snake; red king snake; ring snake; ringed king snake (6—Ditmars 1907); scarlet snake; southern milk snake; thunder snake.

Range: N.e. Arizona, n. in Utah to s. Montana, e. across South Dakota, s. through most of Nebraska and Kansas to n. cent. Texas, w. avoiding trans-Pecos area, Texas through New Mexico.—Ariz.; Colo.; Kan.; Mont.; Neb.; N.M.; Okla.; S.D.; Tex.; Ut. *Elevation*—2,000 to 8,000 feet. 4,000–8,000 feet (Bailey, N.M., 1913); above 6,000 feet (Ellis and Henderson, Colo., 1915).

Size: Adults, 7.5–36 inches.

Distinctive characteristics: A medium tricolored (scarlet or red, white or sulphur yellow, black or brown) snake of the customary *doliata* scutellation; 25–40 light bands. The black and light bands contact across the back and belly sometimes (they may not contact ventrally or dorsally). Normally the head is black or black with flecks of red or white; labials are often flecked with white. Sometimes the red bands are wide dorsally or ventrally, or more often the black dorsally may encroach on the red, making the red bands into red lateral blotches.

Color: A snake from Greenwood, Colo., 50 miles from Pueblo, taken May 12, 1937, by Brayton Eddy, who having had it in his zoo for the summer, loaned it to us. The back is marked with red, black, and yellow or white rings. There are 29 light rings on the body and 10 on the tail. The red does not cross the belly. The light annulus is sulphur yellow as it crosses 10 middorsal scale rows with longitudinal width of 2 to 2½ scales. It then becomes white as it narrows to 1½ scales and then widens to 3, 3½, or 4 scales longitudinally on the 2nd row of scales. On the tail the complete ring is sulphur yellow. This white annulus on the 1st to 6th scale rows has each scale marked with a dusky or black spot on its cephalic end. Then the white annulus crosses the venter as a clear white area about 3 scales in longitudinal width. These white annuli are bordered on either side by black or mummy brown rings 2 scales long on mid-dorsum and ¼ scale long on the 2nd scale row. This black or mummy brown extends onto the venter for 3 to 4 scales' width and encloses the red areas of the dorsum. These black ventral bars are 4 scales wide on the ends of the ventrals and 2 or 3 scales wide on the middle of ventrals, or the middle of a group of ventrals may form a longitudinal median white band. Of the red bands, the one on the neck and one or two succeeding ones are rufous. Then they grade through cinnamon-rufous to orange-cinnamon, and mostly cover 3 scale rows on mid-dorsum and 3½ to 4 scale rows on the sides. The first band of feruginous or rufous is 9 to 10 scales long. It is bordered in front by a black or mummy brown band, which is succeeded in turn by a sulphur yellow band 3 scales long, which crosses on its cephalic edge the tips of the parietals. This sulphur yellow extends to the angle of the mouth. This band below the angle of the mouth enters the white of the lower side of the head. Crossing the head between the eyes and extending from the top of the 5th to 7th upper labials is a band of black or mummy brown. The rest of the head and face and a spot over the eye are ecru-olive or deep olive-buff with a few spots of black or mummy brown. The upper and lower labials are olive-buff or seafoam yellow with black or mummy brown sutures. The underside of the head is white or seafoam yellow. The iris is black or mummy brown with a pupil rim of rufous or english red.

Another snake from laboratory of Vasco M. Tanner at Provo, Ut. The body is crossed by 30 composite bands of red bordered with black and by 8 on the tail. The red on dorsum is scarlet, becoming on sides flame scarlet or english red.

Habitat and habits: In 1904 Branson wrote: "These snakes are very gentle. They never bite unless very much aggravated. When they do bite they do not strike like other snakes, but take the offending object in their mouths and shut down on it. Their teeth are so small that they can do little injury." Linsdale (Kan., 1927) found one in a hole beside the road, while Taylor (Kan., 1929b) had one taken in the bluffs of a river. In 1935 Burt and Hoyle (Gen.) took them on limestone ledges and in treeless prairie, while in 1938 Brennan (Kan.) recorded them in "mixed prairie, flat rock hillside." Tanner (1940) reported: "Specimens have been collected in 11 of the 29 counties of Utah, extending from Tooele on the northwest to Washington on the southwest and to Uintah on the northeast. From our records it appears that this species, which while not numerous or common in any part of the state, has a statewide distribution."

Period of activity: *First appearance*—At Provo, Ut., the earliest date we recorded is Apr. 30, 1939. Ellis and Henderson's (Colo., 1915) earliest record is May 18, 1914. *Fall disappearance*—At Provo, Ut., we saw records of Sept., 1931, Sept. 26, 1933, to Dec. 14, 1940. The latest we discover for Colorado is Burnett's Nov. 15, 1921, and Sept. 15, 1925. *Hibernation*—"Several specimens of this snake have been collected during its hibernation, and it seems noteworthy to report them at this time. One specimen in Cedar Valley, Dec. 10, 1940, was taken while digging for power line poles. The snake was found in sand gravel pit near Helper, Utah, December 15, 1940. . . . This specimen was 6 feet under ground. Another specimen was taken from a gravel pit near Mt. Pleasant, Utah" (Tanner).

Breeding: Oviparous. Males 355–736, females 412–748 mm. *Mating*—"One of a pair observed was collected 8 miles south of Price on the Hiawatha road near the Carbon-Emory County gravel pit May 15, 1938" (Hardy). *Eggs*—Number, 8–12. Time, June, July. Size, 1x.6 inches. "Deposits 8–12 eggs in July" (Hudson and Davis, Neb., 1941). On May 30, 1944, "a large individual measuring 28⅞ inches . . . contained 12 eggs about 14x24 millimeters" (Marr). *Young*—The smallest that Ellis and Henderson (Colo., 1913) reported were 190 mm. (July 22, 1904) and 210 mm.; the smallest Tanner mentioned were 200, 202, 205 mm., all females; Blanchard's smallest were 213 and 220 mm.

Food: Insects, earthworms, young snakes, small mammals, lizards. Taylor, Ellis and Henderson (Colo., 1913), Over (S.D., 1923), Hudson and Davis (Neb., 1941), Tanner.

Authorities:

Baird, S. F., and C. Girard (Gen., 1853)
Blanchard, F. N. (Gen., 1921)
Branson, E. B. (Kan., 1904)
Brown, A. E. (Gen., 1901)
Burnett, W. L. (Colo., 1926)
Cope, E. D., and R. Kennicott (Gen., 1860–61a)
Coues, E., and H. C. Yarrow (Mont., 1878)
Ellis, M., and J. Henderson (Colo., 1913, 1915)

Garman, S. (Gen., 1883)
Hallowell, E. (Kan., 1857)
Hardy, R. (Ut., 1939)
Hudson, G. E. (Neb., 1942)
Marr, J. C. (Gen., 1944)
Nelson, D. J. (Mont., 1948, 1950)
Smith, H. M. (Kan., 1950)
Stejneger, L. (Tex., 1891)
Tanner, W. W. (Ut., 1941a)
Taylor, W. E. (Neb., 1892a)

Fig. 109. *Lampropeltis d. gentilis,* Green-wood, Colo., B. Eddy.

Fig. 110. *Lampropeltis d. syspila,* Imbo-den, Ark., B. C. Marshall.

Red milk snake (12—Blanchard 1921),
Milk snake (10—Garman 1892)

Lampropeltis doliata syspila (Cope) 1888. Fig. 110; Map 31

Other common names: Calico snake; chequered adder; chicken snake; (coral) king snake; corn snake; painted king snake; red (king) snake; red snake (Kirtland 1838); scarlet king snake (2); scarlet snake; spotted adder; thunder-and-lightning snake.

Range: South Dakota, s.e. Nebraska, extreme e. Kansas to n.e. Oklahoma, n.e. through Arkansas to s. Indiana, n.w. through s. Illinois, thence w. of Mississippi River to s. Minnesota.—Ark.; Ia.; Ill.; Ind.; Kan.; Ky.; Minn.; Mo.; Okla.; S.D.; Tenn. *Elevation*—500 to 2,000 feet.

Size: Adults, 15–42 inches.

Longevity: 4 years 10 months (Conant and Hudson, Gen., 1949).

Distinctive characteristics: A medium-sized snake with red, black, and light bands on the back, the red being any of various kinds, or rufous, or brown, and the light being white or olive buff. The 23–43 dorsal saddles extend to the 3rd row or lower. There is one series of alternating spots heavily mixed with black. The top of the head is various, an incomplete *triangulum* pattern with light black-bordered superciliary spot. Saddles completely closed at bottom, though more thinly so than in *triangulum*. Light half collar behind head.

Color: A snake from Imboden, Ark., furnished by B. C. Marshall, Apr. 18, 1929. The saddles are hay's russet, vinaceous-rufous, or burnt sienna and extend at the lowest lateral point to the 1st to 3rd row of scales. They are bordered with black. There is an alternating series of small spots of the same color heavily intermixed with black located on the 1st and 2nd scale rows and on the ends of the ventrals. The intervals between the saddles on the dorsum are pale olive-buff or tilleul buff, becoming, on the widened lateral portion, pallid purplish gray or even white. The top of the head back of the eyes is vinaceous-fawn or darker, while ahead of the eyes, it is light grayish olive or light olive-gray. The upper and lower labials are pallid purplish gray or white, the upper labials ahead of the eye having more or less black on the sutures. There is a black upper margin on the upper labials extending from the postnasal to the rear of the temporals, where it turns at right angles and crosses the neck as a black front margin to the 1st light dorsal interval. The iris is grenadine red or flame scarlet. The belly is pallid purplish gray or white, more or less checkered with black. On the belly marking 2 or 3 ventrals are irregular black patches located opposite the dorsal saddles, and alternating with the spots of the lower lateral row.

Habitat: This species has been found under flat rocks, decaying logs, loose bark, boards, scrap metal, lime flakes, around spring houses, on the open crest of a hill, about prairie ledges, in open woods and fields, in dense woods, rocky shaded spots, limestone ledges of treeless prairie, copperhead dens, and on suburban lawns and in wooded hills and uplands.

Period of activity: *Early appearances*—Apr. 6, 1929, Apr. 21, 1928 (Gloyd, Kan., 1932); May 14, 1932; May 3, 12, 29, 1927 (Gloyd, Kan., 1928). For Missouri, Hurter gives Apr. 4, 12, 15, May 2, 24. "All but one were caught in April and May" (Anderson, Mo., 1945). *Fall disappearance*—For Missouri, Hurter gives Oct. 4, Nov. 8. *Hibernation*—"In the forested Missouri bluff region . . . it was beneath rocks at the opening of a 30 foot, partially covered well. This well evidently served as a hibernating place for the milk snake, 2 blue racers, *Coluber constrictor flaviventris,* and 3 pilot black snakes, *Elaphe obsoleta obsoleta*" (Loomis and Jones). On Oct. 18, 1942, August Napier and Paul Anderson had the unique experience of watching prairie rattlesnakes assemble at their hibernating quarters in Tripp County, S.D. At the entrance to the den, "with the sunning aggregation were 6 bull snakes (*Pituophis sayi sayi*), 4 blue racers (*Coluber constrictor flaviventris*), 2 western hog-nosed snakes (*Heterodon nasicus nasicus*) and 1 banded king snake (*Lampropeltis triangulum syspila*)" (Anderson).

Breeding: Oviparous. Males 355–726, females 412–800 mm. *Mating*—"A boy killed one in the woods, and I went out to examine it, and found beside the dead snake a live one of the same species. It was examining the body and showed fight when disturbed" (Gaines, Ind., 1894).

Eggs—Number, 6–12. Time, June, July. Size, 1.25–2x.4–1.25 inches. The evidence is scanty. "I have taken eggs of this species in Illinois that were buried in a pile of manure and more or less glued together. The egg is 2 inches long and little less than 1¼ inches in diameter. The covering is parchmentlike. It contains a young snake 10 inches long" (Hay). "It is oviparous, laying in June about a dozen eggs which hatch in September" (Funkhouser). "The eggs, numbering about a dozen, measure about ½ inch by 1¼ inches and are creamy-white, elongate and rather slender. They are placed under stones, and in similar places for incubation" (Guthrie, Ia., 1926). "Another of Mr. Clanton's specimens collected May 29 deposited 6 eggs July 3. They averaged 35x10 mm. in size and were not hatched" (Gloyd). "A large female measuring 32 inches laid 8 eggs in captivity" (Loomis).

Young—See above. The smallest specimens Blanchard measured were 196, 203, 211, 212, 213, 220, 224 mm., which are beyond hatching. The smallest young we have seen are 211 and 212 mm.

Food: Lizards, snakes, rats, mice, moles. Hurter (Mo., 1893, 1911), Funkhouser, Force (Okla., 1926, 1930), Schwardt (Ark., 1938), Anderson (Mo., 1942).

Authorities:

Anderson, P. (S.D., 1947)
Blanchard, F. N. (Gen., 1921)
Blatchley, W. S. (Ind., 1891, 1899)
Cope, E. D. (Gen., 1893; Fla., 1889)
Dury, R., and W. Gessing, Jr. (Ky., 1940)
Funkhouser, W. D. (Ky., 1925)
Gloyd, H. K. (Kan., 1928)
Hallowell, E. (Kan., 1857)

Hay, O. P. (Ind., 1892)
Hurter, J. (Mo., 1911)
Loomis, R. B. (Ia., 1948)
Loomis, R. B., and J. K. Jones (Neb., 1949)
Rhoads, S. N. (Calif., 1936b)
Smith, H. M. (Kan., 1950)
Swanson, P. L. (Ind., 1938)

Coastal plain milk snake (5), Virginia red king snake (3—Brimley 1926)

Lampropeltis doliata temporalis (Cope) 1893. Fig. 111; Map 31

Other common names: Blanchard's red king snake; calico snake (Abbott 1868)?; Cope's milk snake; East Shore milk snake; northern scarlet king snake; red king snake (4—Brimley 1899); scarlet snake; Virginia red snake.

Range: S. New Jersey across s.e. Pennsylvania, Delaware, and Maryland to Shenandoah Valley and southeast to extreme n. North Carolina near Raleigh.—D.C.; Del.; Md.; N.C.; N.J.; Pa.; Va. *Elevation*—Coast to 1,000 feet, mainly below 500 feet; 2,000 feet (King, Tenn., 1939). This last is probably *L. d. triangulum*.

Size: Adults, 10–38 inches.

Longevity: 3 years 4 months plus (Kauffeld, Gen., 1951).

Distinctive characteristics: "Dorsal pattern a series of 24 to 31, average (7) 28 black-edged, red bands, upon whitish, light grayish, or buff ground color, red color of bands extending to 1st row of scales or upon the gastrosteges, [and] a series of alternating blotches present on less than half the total body length or absent; belly white, marked laterally by the ends of the dorsal bands, a single median series of black blotches alternating with ends of bands, or more than 1 series where alternating blotches are present on the sides; top of head more or less immaculate red, typical *triangulum* markings absent or only indicated, supralabials and infralabials white, edged with black, chin and throat white" (McCauley, Md., 1945).

Color: A snake from the New Jersey pine barrens, loaned to us by C. F. Kauffeld of Staten Island Zoo, May 3, 1949; collected from a lath pile at Upton, Burlington Co., N.J., by Asa Pittman, Aug.–Sept., 1948. The back is marked with dorsal saddles of brick red, 3½–5 scales long, outlined with black at least 1 scale long on middorsum and ½ scale on lower side. The cephalic saddles extend to within 1½ scale rows of the venter. There are intermediate dark blotches on scale rows 1 and 2 which extend onto ends of 2 or 3 ventral plates. The cephalic ones may have some brick red in the center, while those in the rear are entirely black. The saddles are separated by pale gull gray intervals 1 and 2 half scales or 1½ scales long. There is a clear-cut black-edged collar 2 scales long of pale gull gray. Below the first saddle is a clear straight-edged white area ½–¾ inches long which joins the collar. From the base of the collar an irregular white area extends diagonally forward to the supraocular. The parietals are burnt umber bordered caudally with black, and with a suture spot of white edged with black. From eye to angle of mouth is a band of burnt umber, with prefrontals more or less the same. The eye is dragon's-blood red. The nose and side of the face are gray flecked with black. Most of the labials are dark edged; chin shields and gulars white. The venter is white, marked in front with the black extensions of the lateral blotches on the ends of the ventral plates. From middle of body backward, it is irregularly marked with squares of black. This snake shows its relationship to *Lampropeltis doliatus doliatus.*

"A darker than usual example, but the pattern is especially typical. Most are more brilliant red" (Kauffeld letter).

Habitat: This coastal-plain form has been taken in bogs in the New Jersey pine barrens. McCauley gives loose sandy soil where it probably burrows. He has one ploughed up in a field, one from a cellar where it was between the foundations of the house, one inside a log on the edge of a cornfield near woods.

Period of activity: *Early appearances*—Brimley (N.C., 1920b) gave Jan. 2, 1911, Apr., 1899; June 20, 1901. *Fall disappearance*—Several of Brimley's true *d. doliata* were found in October. Quite likely *d. temporalis* continued out until that month. Fowler's (N.J., 1907) dates for the season are May 12, 1902–Oct. 7, 1906.

Breeding: Oviparous. Males 473–581, females 471–745 mm. *Eggs*—Not noted. Even one of the two who know it best wrote, "The general habits of this snake *probably* resemble those of its very close relative, the common milk snake" (McCauley, Md., 1945).

Food: Small mammals, snakes, frogs. Abbott (N.J., 1868), Fowler (N.J., 1907).

Field notes: 1921–1943: Conant spoke of the milk snakes as perennial puzzlers. Shortly after Blanchard's description of *L. e. virginiana* we queried if he had not had material from the periphery of a good race. We examined the Washington material and seldom could find a specimen to match the description.

In 1938 our kind and excellent student, Miss Frankie Culpepper of the Newark Museum, sent us a specimen received from Greenbank, Burlington Co., N.J. At this period Robert H. McCauley, Jr., was struggling with two specimens he had received from high-school collections of e. Maryland. For years we had thought *Lampropeltis t. temporalis* might be revived, and he independently came to the same conclusion. These 3 specimens represented *L. t. temporalis,* and his paper is a distinct contribution to the solution of the question.

Later, in 1943, Conant with 383 *Lampropeltis triangulum* specimens from the Atlantic coastal plain, piedmont, and Appalachians redefined this form. He outlined the ranges of *L. t. elapsoides, L. t. temporalis,* and *L. t. triangulum* with intergrade areas.

1943–1949: The current concept is one species, *doliata* (formerly called *triangulum*), of which we have several races. Now we have all in the one *doliata* species and the Atlantic coastal material from N.J. southward 2 forms, *L. d. temporalis* northern and *L. d. doliata* (old *elapsoides*) southern.

Authorities:

Blanchard, F. N. (Va., 1919)
Conant, R. (Gen., 1943a; Del., 1945)
Hallowell, E. (Kan., 1857a)

Hay, W. P. (D.C., 1902a)
McCauley, R. H. (Del., 1941a; Md., 1945)

Milk snake (139—Pierce 1823), **House snake** (54—Williamson 1832)

Lampropeltis doliata triangulum (Lacépède) 1788. Fig. 112; Map 31

Other common names: Adder; *blatschich schlange;* chain snake; checkered (or chequered) adder; checkered (or chequered) snake; chicken snake; common milk snake (many); cow-sucker; eastern milk snake; highland adder; horn snake; house moccasin; king snake; leopard-spotted snake; milk sucker; pilot; red snake; sachem snake; sand-king; scarlet milk snake; spotted adder; thunder-and-lightning snake.

Range: E. of Mississippi River from cent. Wisconsin, s. peninsular Michigan to Nova Scotia, down coast to New Jersey and s.w. in the mountains to n. Georgia, n. to West Virginia and Ohio, w. through cent. Indiana and Illinois.—U.S.A.: Conn.; D.C.; Del.; Fla.; Ga.; Ill.; Ind.; Ky.; Mass.; Md.; Me.; Mich.; Minn.; N.C.; N.H.; N.J.; N.Y.; O.; Pa.; R.I.; S.C.; Tenn.; Va.; Vt.; Wis.; W. Va. Can.: N.B.; Ont.; Que. *Elevation*—Seacoast to 4,600 feet. 900–2,400 feet (Smith, Pa., 1945); 1,800–4,600 feet (King, Tenn., 1939); 3,500, 3,800 feet (Dunn, N.C., 1917). "Not limited by altitude in this county" (Wilson and Friddle, W. Va., 1950).

Size: Adults, 10–54 inches.

Longevity: 8 years 9 months (Conant and Hudson, Gen., 1949).

Distinctive characteristics: "Five (or 3) rows of dorsal blotches, these composed 1 row of large middorsal, and 1 or 2 alternating rows of smaller blotches on each side of the body. Middorsal blotches 24 to 52, mean 36.6 in number. Usually a light Y or V on the neck. Belly checkered with white" (Conant, Gen., 1943a).

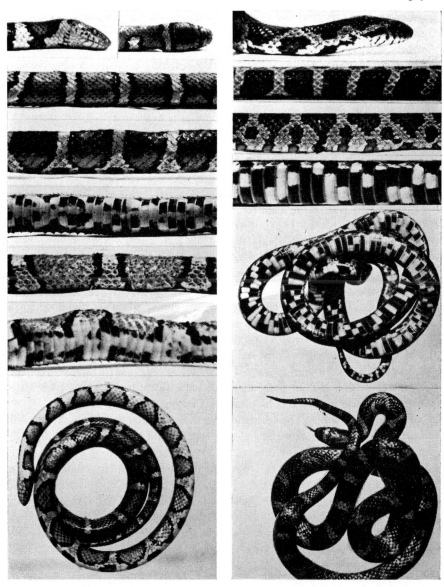

Fig. 111. *Lampropeltis d. temporalis:* 1–5,8, Philadelphia Zoo, Pa., R. Conant through R. H. McCauley (♂ 2,3,8, ♀ 1,4,5); 6,7, Washington Twp., Burlington Co., N.J., D. Thomas and W. J. Koster.

Fig. 112. *Lampropeltis d. triangulum,* Ithaca, N.Y.: 1,4–6, A. B. Klots.

Color: A snake from Danby Creek, near Ithaca, N.Y., taken July 20, 1928. The saddle spots extend down to the 3rd or 4th rows of scales and are cinnamon-brown, warm sepia, walnut brown, or rood's brown, edged with black or chestnut-brown. The intervals between saddles on the dorsum proper are pale vinaceous-fawn or vinaceous-buff. On the 3rd to 5th row of scales is a row of dark-edged spots, alternating with the saddle spots and colored either like them or hazel. Opposite the ends of the saddle spots and located on the 1st and 2nd scale rows and on the end of the ventrals is another series of black or chestnut-brown spots which occasionally have centers like the saddles. Sometimes these spots merge with the saddles. The lateral interval space is light mineral gray, pale smoke gray, pearl gray, or pale olive-gray. On the top of the neck is a light buff spot surrounded by black. On the rear of the head is a heart-shaped spot of cream color bordered with brown or black. The rostral, and a band from eye to eye across the head, are deep olive-buff. From front of eye to front of eye is a band colored like the saddles and with a black border. A black-bordered spot of saddle color marks the rear end of frontal and front of parietals. Another occurs on the parietals, uniting on the sides with the brown border of the heart-shaped spot. There is a black vitta from the eye to angle of mouth which is more or less bordered with hay's russet. The labials are white, their sutures marked with black or hay's russet. The throat and chin are white. The iris is dragon's-blood red or coral red around the pupil, and flesh color or salmon color toward the outer rim. The venter is checkered in the center with blocks of russian blue or deep delft blue on a light ground, these spots alternating with the dark spots of the lowest lateral row.[1]

Habitat and habits: The fable that this snake sucked cows or stole the milk from the dairy, we heard when young. Although a testy creature, it does not deserve to be called "house moccasin," for it is not venomous. It searches the abode of man for mice and rats. Some of the places ascribed as its haunts are: buildings 5, dwellings 4, barns 4, outhouses 3, dairies 3, cellars 3, an old cellar, a stable, a granary, an icehouse, a woodshed, a pig house, a spring house—about all of man's buildings. It searches bogs and hills, a wide choice of habitat, in search of its prey. Some of the country it frequents is: prairie 1, woods 3, beaches 2, pine ridges 2, aspen country 1, open woods 3, high pine 1, upland hammock 1, sand plains 1, upland situations 1, bog forests 1, second-growth pine 1, hardwood land 1, edge of salt water 1, gorges 1, shores of lakes, ponds, streams, and other diverse places. In the daytime, we have seen it as often in the open as under cover. If under cover, it may be in decaying logs, stumps, or rock piles, or under stones, rocks, boards, bark, rub-

---

[1] In 1955 (*Copeia*, 257) Condit and Woodruff recorded a female albino milksnake from Licking Co., O.

bish, tar paper, sheet iron, rotting logs, or any other cover. All in all, it is widespread in local distribution.

Period of activity: In 1919 we (in New York) gave it as Apr. 15–Oct.; whereas Conant in 1918 (Ohio) gave Apr.–Nov. *Fall disappearance*—There are many Oct. and Nov. records in the literature. *Hibernation*—Workmen grading the abandoned Miami and Erie Canal bed at Maumee, Lucas Co., O., found 2 hibernating specimens buried 2 or 3 feet in a clay bank on Jan. 26, 1934 (Conant, O., 1938a). "The well in which the snakes apparently (March 3) hibernated was approximately 20 feet deep and 4 feet wide. The sides were lined with large stones which were placed in such a manner as to allow the snakes an easy passage between them. A large heavy concrete block served as a cover" (Hudson, Pa., 1949).

Breeding: Oviparous. Males to 1,115 mm., females 404–966 mm. Miller's series is: males 840–1,106 mm., one 815 specimen possibly immature; females 820–1,007 mm., one 815 and one 795 possibly mature.

Eggs—Number, 6–24. 5 (Davis); 6 (Babcock); 6, 8, 9, 11 (Ditmars); 6, 11, 16 (Schmidt and Davis); 6, 16 (Fowler); 6, 12 (Bishop and Alexander); 8, 11, 16 (Pope); 8, 13 (Trapido); 8, 20 (Wright and Allen); 11 (Noble); 12 (Atkinson); 13 (Blanchard, Barton); 15 (Brimley); 16, 17 (Conant); 20 (Ditmars, Lamson, Miller); 24 (Ditmars). Time of deposition, late June and July. One author gives August. Size, 1.6x.5 to .7 inches. Various measurements, such as 1¼x⅝ inches (Schmidt and Davis, Gen., 1941); 1 inch (Babcock, Gen., 1929a); 24 to 31x17 mm. (Blanchard, Mich., 1928); 1½x½ inches (Bishop and Alexander); 1⅕x1⅗ inches (Trapido, N.J., 1937); 1¼x ⅝ inches (Pope); 25, 30, 35x16 mm. (Conant, 1938a), have been given. Blatchley in 1899 gave 2 inches x 1 inch. Was he right? Eggs are laid in sawdust piles, manure piles, and rubbish piles, under logs, boards, old planks, and other cover, in loose soil and sand. They are smooth, tough, leathery-white opaque, adherent sometimes in one cluster. Surface, Noble, Bishop and Alexander, Conant (1938a), and Pope gave exceptional accounts.

Young—Size, 6.75–10.2 inches. Records include 6¾ to 8¾ inches, 8 or 9 inches, 8⅜ to 9⅞ inches, 9 inches, 254 mm., and 198–230 mm. Time of hatching, August and September. Surface gave late September to Oct. 25 as hatching time. Some authors feel that 2 months elapse from deposition to hatching; some give 6 weeks. Several think that eggs are sometimes far in development when deposited. Most authors believe the young are more vivid and active than the mature; the dorsal blotches of the young are red or bright chestnut red with black margins and white or clear ash intervals.

Food: Small mammals, snakes, lizards, amphibians, birds and their eggs, insects. Uhler, Cottam, and Clarke (Va., 1939) and many other writers.

Field notes: June 11, 1915, Duck Lake, N.Y.: In Featherbed swamp, Ludlow Griscom and I found milk snakes mating.

Authorities:

Axtell, H. H. (N.Y., 1947)

Bishop, S. C., and W. P. Alexander (N.Y., 1927)

Blanchard, F. N. (Gen., 1921)

Conant, R. (Ohio, 1938a; Gen., 1943a)

Cope, E. D. (Gen., 1893)

Dunn, E. R. (N.C., 1917)

Medsger, O. P. (N.Y., 1922)

Miller, W. D. (N.J., 1937)

Noble, G. K. (N.Y., 1920)

Pope, C. H. (Ill., 1944)

Storer, D. H. (Mass., 1839)

Surface, H. A. (Pa., 1906)

Thompson, Z. (Vt., 1842)

King snake (68—Baird and Girard 1853), Chain snake (43—Catesby)

Lampropeltis getulus getulus (Linné) 1766. Fig. 113; Map 33

Other common names: Bastard horn snake; black king snake; black moccasin; common chain snake; common king snake (frequent); cow sucker; eastern king snake; horse racer; master snake; North American king snake; oakleaf rattler; pine snake; racer; rattlesnake pilot; thunder-and-lightning snake; thunderbolt; thunder snake (14); wamper; wampum snake.

Range: S. New Jersey and s.e. Pennsylvania to the e. panhandle of West Virginia, s.w. to Mobile Bay, thence e. through n. Florida.—Ala.; D.C.; Del.; Fla.; Ga.; Md.; N.C.; N.J.; Pa.; S.C.; Va.; W. Va. *Elevation*—Mainly coastline to 1,000 feet, a few records to 1,500 or 2,000 feet. 1,500–2,500 feet (King, Tenn., 1939); 2,300 feet (Dunn, N.C., 1917).

Size: Adults, 24–72 inches. Our longest snake is 4 feet 5 inches.

Longevity: 6 years (Blanchard); 9 years (Flower, Gen., 1937); 3 years 7 months; 3 years (Kauffeld, Gen., 1951).

Distinctive characteristics: A large, solid, glossy black snake with 23–52 crossbands of white, buff, or yellow bifurcating on the flanks and joining on the sides in semichain pattern. There are several spots of yellow on head plates. Underside of head, labials, and throat are light yellow, rest of under parts dark grayish brown with some light crossbar color. Scales 21 (23) dorsal rows; ventrals 203–238; caudals 38–58.

Color: A snake from Hammonton, N.J., furnished by Mr. Yehl, May, 1933. The background of the upper parts is black, with a wash of the purplish cast of the under parts. The back is crossed by bars of olive-buff, deep olive-buff, or cream color, which become, on the sides, pale dull green-yellow or pale chalcedony yellow. These crossbars are about 1 scale wide, but are usually formed by light-colored parts of 2 or more scale rows with the bases of the scales next to the black area buffy brown. These bars cross about 10 dorsal scale rows, then fork obliquely downward for 4 or 5 scale rows, where the color widens to cover 2 scale rows. This lateral patch extends onto the ends of 1 or 2 ventrals. There are spots of pale chalcedony yellow on parietal, frontal, supraocular, internasal, and rostral plates. The upper part of the

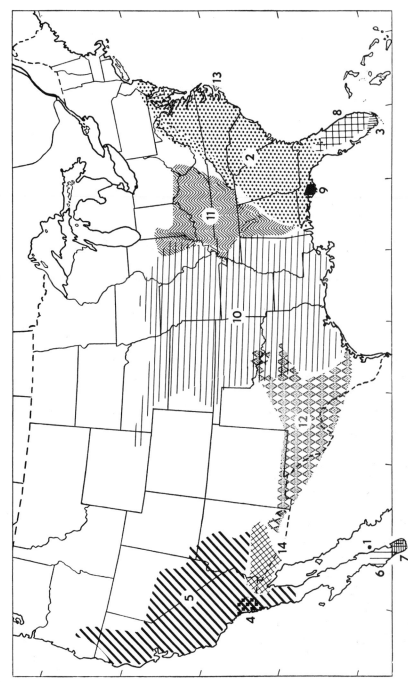

Map 33. *Lampropeltis*—1, *catalinensis*; 2, *g. getulus*; 3, *g. brooksi*; 4, *g. californiae* (*californiae*); 5, *g. c.* (*boyli*); 6, *g. c.* (*conjuncta*); 7, *g. c.* (*nitida*); 8, *g. floridana*; 9, *g. goini*; 10, *g. holbrooki*; 11, *g. niger*; 12, *g. splendida*; 13, *g. sticticeps*; 14 *g. yumensis*.

iris partakes of the light color of the transverse chain. The scales of the side of the head, the upper and lower labials, and the ventral head plates are also each marked with pale chalcedony yellow. The under parts are deep mouse gray, deep quaker drab, or dark grayish brown marked with scattered subdued spots of the crossbar and vertical bar colors.

A snake from near Gallberry Is., Okefinokee Swamp, Ga., caught by Harrison Lee and Francis Harper, June 23, 1921. The light crossbars are sulphur yellow, naphthalene yellow, barium yellow, or marguerite yellow, becoming on mid-back olive-yellow. The light spots on the head are light yellowish olive. The dark areas of the back are brownish olive or saccardo's umber with tips of warm sepia, which is the color of the ventral spots. *Abnormal coloration*—In 1920(a) Brimley in North Carolina reported a snake in which crossbars were almost all oblique.

Habitat: This large, handsome, harmless serpent, though aggressive with other snakes, is a favorite pet. Authors have placed it in moist woods and shady places, in pine woods, brush plains, pine barrens, forest glades, under tree trunks, in palmetto and heath covers, along roadsides, borders of creeks and bayous, in hayfields, about farm buildings, in dry woods, in upland hammocks, in the vicinity of aquatic habitats, in thickets between grove land and lakes, in upland pastures and lowland meadows.

Period of activity: *First appearance*—North Carolina; Apr. 8, 1886 (Spaunhorer); Apr. 17, 1938 (King, Tenn., 1939); May 9, 1899 (Seal). *Fall disappearance*—Virginia, Nov. 11, 1893 (Silver); West Virginia, Sept. 14, 1935 (Netting); North Carolina, Oct. 13, 1920 (Brimley, N.C., 1920a). *Seasonal catch*—Mar., 1 snake; Apr., 7; May, 17; June, 8; July, 4; Aug., 2; Sept., 1; Oct., 4; Nov., 4 (Brimley, N.C., 1925).

Breeding: Oviparous. Males 531–1,752, females 550–1,747 mm. *Mating*— "Mr. Harper reports a pair of them mating on May 19, 1912, and says another king snake was watching the pair" (Wright and Bishop). "In Maryland the breeding of king snakes occurs in the spring. On May 18, 1937, Miss Lois Booth observed a recently captured pair in copulation. They lay coiled close to each other; the male, united with the female, was seen to move the posterior part of his body in a caressing lateral movement over that of the female. This was observed for a period of about 15 minutes, though it may have been in progress for some time previously" (McCauley, Md., 1945).

Eggs—Number, 5–24. At the beginning of the century a wealth of herpetological material came out of the supply bureau of C. S. and H. H. Brimley, Raleigh, N.C. Then the authors began teaching, and one of the best notes of the breeding of this species comes from those days: "The eggs of the King Snake (*Ophibolus getulus*) are long, oblong in shape, with a smooth tough skin and are more or less adherent to one another in clusters. A lot was brought in July 11, 1900, some of which were put up from time to time till 3 young snakes, 275 mm. long, were hatched from the last eggs on Aug. 14, 34 days later. These eggs were about 40 to 43 mm. long by 24 to 26 wide. In July, 1900, a King Snake in my possession laid 17 eggs in confinement; these eggs were like the foregoing lot, but smaller, and were also adherent in clusters. One egg of this lot contained an embryo with 2 heads, and 2 bodies, the bodies separate for the anterior ⅓ of their length. Another lot of 10 eggs laid in confinement in July, 1901, were stuck together in 2 clusters, 4 in one lot and 6 in the other, and measured 31 to 35 mm. in length" (Brimley, Gen., 1903).

From Ditmars to Knepton, 10 authors contributed to our knowledge of the breeding of this favorite snake. 1907, Ditmars gave 10–24 eggs, hatching 5 or 6 weeks later; 1908, Davis in N.J., July 8, 16 eggs; 1916, Wright and Bishop, June 13, 7 eggs, 39 or 40 mm. x 22 or 23 mm.; 1939, Conant and Bridges 6–24 eggs; 1941, Schmidt and Davis 7–11 eggs, 1⅝x⅞ inches, young 11 inches; 1942, Brimley 17 eggs, young 11 inches long; 1945, Fowler 6–24 eggs; 1945, McCauley, July 14, 12 eggs, 37.5 to 29x22 or 23 mm., young averaging 238.7 mm.; 1951, Knepton, May 17, 7 eggs, 61–69 mm. x 25 mm., hatching on July 15 and 16, mating having been on March 18.

Time, June to mid-July. Size, 1.15–1.6 inches x .9–1.1 inches.

Young—Time of hatching, Aug. to Sept. 10. Size, 9–11 inches. We have seen specimens from Maryland 248 mm., from District of Columbia 265, 266, 270 mm., from Virginia 275 mm., from North Carolina 250, 265 mm., from South Carolina 302 mm. Brimley (Gen., 1903) has newly hatched young 275 mm. long. In 1942 he gave young as about 11 inches. Probably King's (Tenn., 1939) specimen of 287 mm. was recently hatched. Conant and Bridges (Gen., 1939) gave the size as 10¾ inches.

Food: Snakes, turtle eggs, rats, mice, sparrows, lizards, amphibians, any vertebrate eggs, insects, centipedes, millipeds, spiders. Wright and Bishop, Carr, Wilson and Friddle (W. Va., 1946).

Field notes: June 10, 1912, Billy Island. After our thrilling experience with the white-bellied *Farancia,* Dave Lee said that he once saw a thunder snake digging under a log which had rotted and flattened out on dry land. Presently, where the thunder snake had been digging, he found a mother *Farancia abacura* (red underneath) and with her 43 young, which were surely red underneath. This was in the spring or early summer.

June 18, 1912, west side of swamp at Turpentine Still or Commissary: On way over caught a king snake. While I was talking to the men we saw a black snake. We caught it. I held the king snake loosely in my right hand and the black snake in my left. Like magic the king snake behaved nicely and was across the gap in a twinkling, the head of the black snake in the maw of the king snake. One of the best demonstrations of my life.

July 30, 1921: On July 28 Mr. Lemuel Quarterman found at No. 4 set on main line east, where a skidder was formerly, a chain snake. It was in the ashes and charcoal left by the skidder. Not in the water. It was with its eggs, one of which he brought in.

Authorities:

Bateman, G. C. (Gen., 1897)

Blanchard, F. N. (Gen., 1921)

Boulenger, E. G. (Gen., 1914)

Brimley, C. S. (Gen., 1903; N.C., 1941–42)

Carr, A. F., Jr. (Fla., 1940a)

Corrington, J. D. (S.C., 1929)

DeKay, J. E. (N.Y., 1842)

Ditmars, R. L. (Gen., 1907, 1929)

Holbrook, J. E. (Gen., 1836–42)

Knepton, J.C., Jr. (Fla., 1951)

Netting, M. G. (W.Va., 1936)

Say, T. (Gen., 1819)

Shaw, G. (Gen., 1802)

Wilson, L. W., and S. F. Friddle (W.Va., 1946, 1950)

Wright, A. H., and S. C. Bishop (Ga., 1916)

Brook's king snake (5—Ditmars 1936), **South Florida king snake**

Lampropeltis getulus brooksi Barbour 1919. Fig. 114; Map 33

Another common name: Yellow king snake.

Range: Extreme s. Florida in Dade, Collier, and Monroe Cos. Babbitt (in letter) extends it to Collier City Island off the w. coast of Florida. Here he took one Feb. 15, 1949. *Elevation*—o to 50 feet.

Size: Adults, 15–44 inches (Barbour) and 52 inches (Brady).

Longevity: 10 years (Perkins, Gen., 1947).

Distinctive characteristics: "Similar to *L. getulus floridana* Blanchard, in squamation, but differing widely in coloration. Pattern so reduced as to be almost everywhere undiscernible. Each scale dull chrome yellow with a conspicuous very dark brown apical spot" (Barbour). A beautiful chalcedony yellow, greenish yellow, or sulphur yellow snake with rear edge of each scale brown or black and practically no crossbars.

Color: A snake from Dade Co., Fla., furnished by E. R. Allen, Apr. 27, 1935. Its general color is light chalcedony yellow. The 10 to 12 scale rows of the mid-dorsal region are reed yellow, chalcedony yellow, or light greenish yellow, with the 10 central rows outlined on the rear of the scale with broad, prominent edges of snuff brown, verona brown, or black. The lateral scales are light chalcedony yellow, sulphur yellow, or primrose yellow, the first 6 or 7 scale rows having narrower edges of brown than the dorsal ones. At about 5 scale intervals, there are faintly indicated crossbars of pale pinkish cinnamon or tilleul buff. These are more or less visible transversely for 7 to 9 dorsal scale rows. Where these intervals are indicated, the brown rear edges of a scale spread to cover half of the scale. Each plate of the head is light in color, with each suture marked with brown. The side of the head is colored like the body, while the top of the head bears a wash of cinnamon as well. The lower half of the iris is black. Immediately over the pupil is a longi-

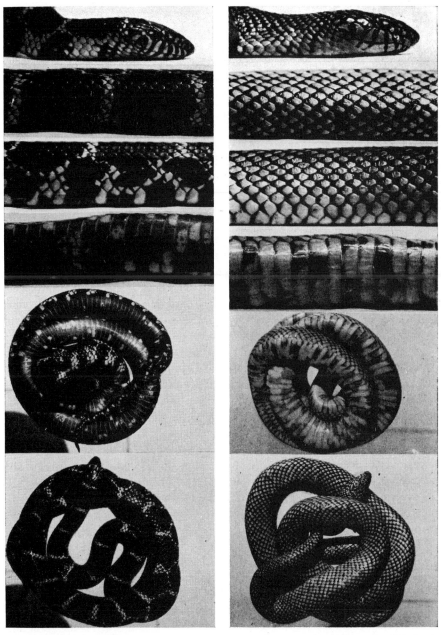

Fig. 113. *Lampropeltis getulus getulus,* Hammonton, N.J., H. Yehl.

Fig. 114. *Lampropeltis g. brooksi,* Dade Co., Fla., E. R. Allen.

tudinal line of seafoam yellow with pale vinaceous-fawn above it. The ventral color is seafoam yellow or pale chalcedony yellow. First on one side of the venter, then on the other, are alternating blotches, 2 scales longitudinally and half a ventral transversely, of pinkish cinnamon, ochraceous-tawny, or cinnamon, thus blocking the belly with light and dark. The subcaudals are seafoam yellow or light chalcedony yellow with the inner sutures marked as a zigzag line of light pinkish cinnamon, ochraceous-tawny, or cinnamon down the middle of the tail.

Habitat and habits: Carr (Fla., 1940a) writes of the yellow king snake: "Extreme southern Florida. Known from Collier, Dade, and Monroe Counties. Tropical hammock, limestone flatwoods, and glade land; fields and edificarian situations. Apparently about equal in abundance to *L. g. getulus*. Habits probably those of *getulus*. Feeding—I saw a very large individual chasing rats in a shed in J. B. Tower's fruit grove near Homestead."

Field notes: March 17, 1934, Royal Palm Park: On the chimney of the house was a snake shed. One person said they were king snakes. Mrs. Atkinson said they crawled through the chimney and came out under the mantel of the fireplace when she had company. The boys of the company liked it, but not the ladies. Mr. Atkinson says that once they left the snake shed across the face of the fireplace. Were they *L. g. floridana* or *L. g. brooksi?* Maybe the latter.

Authorities: 1919, T. Barbour (Fla., 1919b): "The limestone area of extreme southern Florida is inhabited by still another race, as distinct in coloration from *floridana* as this is from true *getulus;* but it is like its neighbor in the high number of scale rows."

1944, A. H. and A. A. Wright: Maurice Brady's specimen from Pine Crest, Monroe Co., Fla., Jan. 13, 1932, is 1,550 mm., a male with the tail 175 mm.

1954: E. R. Allen and W. T. Neill (Fla., 1954) recorded a juvenile, 517 mm. in length. It had a third color, red. Their descriptive paragraph is worthy of inclusion. "The dorsal ground color is black. There is a nuchal crossbar of pale yellow (10F2 straw), 47 similar bars on the dorsum of the body, and 13 on the tail. Some of the scales of these crossbars are light tan (12C, old ivory). Eight of the black dorsal interspaces of the body and all the tail interspaces, bear scales centered with yellow (10F1), suggesting incipient crossbars. All the other dorsal interspaces of the body bear scales centered with reddish brown (5A10, rose beige). The sides are marked with irregular upright yellow bars, which approximately alternate with the dorsal bars, but which are more numerous, 54 on the left and 63 on the right side of the body (excluding the tail). Most of these lateral light bars are centered with bright red (3D11). Commonly, each lateral light bar bears a cluster of three, four or five red scales. Red areas are present on the lateral light bars from head to tip of tail."

California king snake (11—Ditmars 1907),
California milk snake (3—Van Denburgh 1897)

Lampropeltis getulus californiae (Blainville) 1835. Fig. 115; Map 33
(Striped *Californiae* phase Blainville 1835)

Other common names: Banded king snake; Blainville's king snake (Yarrow 1882); (California) striped king snake; Fresno king snake (Yarrow 1882).

Range: S.w. California and Baja California, Mex.—U.S.A.: Calif. Mex.: Baja Calif. *Elevation*—Seacoast or 500 to 2,500 or 3,000 feet. Coast to the desert foothills, stopping at about 2,500 feet on the eastern slope (Klauber, Calif., 1931a); ocean to desert foothills (Perkins, Calif., 1938).

Size: Males and females of this phase have been recorded from 12 to 50 inches.

Longevity: 3 years, 2 years 2 months (Kauffeld, Gen., 1951).

Distinctive characteristics: Structurally like the *boyli* ringed phase of *L. g. californiae*. A prominent middorsal line of some yellow color often breaking into spots on tail. Under parts may be clear yellow to ventral edged rearward with dark to some blotching with dark. Usually the centers of the last 3 or 4 rows of lateral scales have longitudinal yellow centers, making 3 or 4 broken lines of spots. Parietal usually with prominent spot; face and labials yellow with prominent dark sutures. Dark color of animal may be sepia, auburn, brown to black.

Color: A snake from San Diego, Calif., was furnished by L. M. Klauber, May 6, 1928. There is a dorsal stripe, 1 scale and 2 half scales wide, of pale orange-yellow, maize yellow, or baryta yellow. So also are 5 disconnected middorsal spots on the tail, and a middorsal spot an inch back of the occiput. The general color of the upper parts is warm sepia, mars brown, or auburn. On the front of the body, the 4 lowest scale rows have pale lemon yellow or picric yellow centers encircled with one of the above browns. In the middle length, there are 3 such rows and ahead of the tail 2, except that in the middle of the body, the 2 longest rows are entirely picric yellow. Each parietal spot, the top of the head ahead of the eyes, and the sides of the head are massicot yellow. The upper and lower labials are pinard yellow. The under parts of the head are amber yellow, but soon the under parts become naphthalene yellow or pale chalcedony yellow, and become green-yellow near the tail. The underside of the tail is natal brown or benzo brown. A few inches back of the head starts a line of warm sepia that crosses the ends of the ventrals. Toward the middle of the body, this line sends transverse bars along the posterior edges of the ventrals, those of opposite sides not meeting however. In the caudal half of the body, these ventral bars of color leave a uniform light space in the middle of the belly.

Abnormal coloration—"The second albino was a small specimen of *Lam*-

propeltis californiae californiae collected April 28th 1924 in San Diego. . . . In this specimen the yellow dorsal stripe and side markings were normal, but the areas ordinarily dark brown were translucent white. The eyes were pink" (Klauber, Calif., 1924a).

Habitat and habits: See under *L. g. californiae* (*boyli* phase) below.

Period of activity: "Sixteen Year Census"—Jan., 3 snakes; Feb., 7; Mar., 21; Apr., 108; May, 190; June, 176; July, 109; Aug., 60; Sept., 34; Oct., 10; Nov., 4; Dec., 3. Total 725 (Klauber, Gen., 1939a). MVZ gives Apr. 27 to July 27.

Breeding: Oviparous. Males to 1,189 mm., females to 1,142 mm. *Mating*—"A pair, both typical *L. g. californiae,* were found mating May 22nd, 1924" (Klauber, Calif., 1924a). *Eggs*—Number, 4–10. Time, June 23–Aug. 2. *Young*—Hatching time, Sept. 5–Oct. 10. Period of incubation, 71–86 days, average 76 (Klauber, Calif., 1939). Size, no records. We have never seen newly hatched young. The smallest specimens we have seen are 308, 375, and 406 mm. Doubtless 306 mm. is near hatching size. Since 1925 eggs have been recorded, and since 1935 broods, but no description (appearance, etc.) of eggs or size of hatchlings is of printed record.

Food: A few samples from Klauber's diary indicate mice, gopher snakes, alligator lizards, and racers as preferred food.

Authorities:

Klauber, L. M. (Calif., 1924a, 1931a,   Smith, H. M. (Calif., 1943)
  1936b, 1939, 1944c)   Van Denburgh, J. (Gen., 1897)

1897, J. Van Denburgh: "This is a very peculiar snake, which may prove to be a mere variation of *Lampropeltis boylii,* from which it does not differ in size, form, or scale characters. There is an immense amount of variation in the color pattern; indeed it is rarely alike in any 2 specimens."

1901, A. E. Brown (Gen.): "The relations of this snake to *O. g. boylii* are uncertain, and it is quite possible that specimens known are but abnormal color variations of that species."

1921: F. N. Blanchard (Gen.) treated it as a separate species with no intergradation or aberrant color patterns.

1924(a): L. M. Klauber (Calif.) reported and figured a specimen with mixed markings of *L. g. boyli* and *L. g. californiae.* In 1931 he stated: "From these considerations separate species are indicated, the mixed specimens being considered hybrids." In 1936(b) Klauber concluded: "The problem has now been solved by the hatching of 2 broods, one from a mother of each form; and each brood contained young of both forms, although in one instance not typical of one pattern. Therefore the 2 forms are merely pattern phases of a single species which should be known as *Lampropeltis getulus californiae.*" From 11 or more broods Klauber still held in 1939 that the 2 forms were mere pattern phases of one species. He found 5 patterns: "Two of these comprise about 90 per cent of the population. The other 3 are inter-

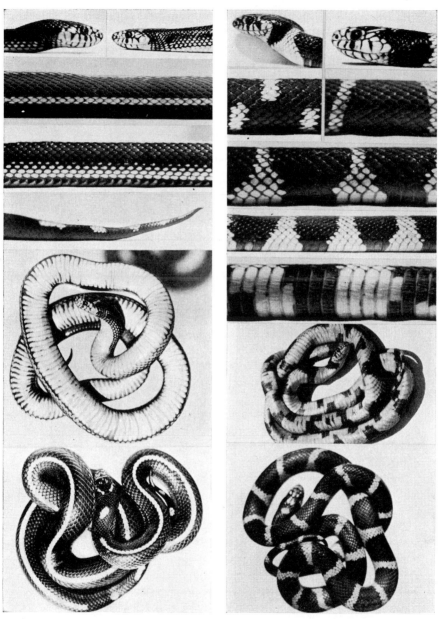

Fig. 115. *Lampropeltis g. californiae* (striped, *californiae* phase), San Diego, Calif.: 1,4, C. B. Perkins through R. H. McCauley; 2,5–7, L. M. Klauber; 3, Washington, D.C., Zoo.

Fig. 116. *Lampropeltis g. californiae* (banded, *boyli* phase): 1,6,8, s. of Phoenix, Ariz., C. L. Evans; 2,3,7, San Diego Zoo, Calif.; 4,5, Fresno, Calif., L. F. Hadsall; 9, San Diego, Calif., C. B. Perkins through R. H. McCauley.

mediates. . . . The mother of any phase can produce young of any other phase, but tends to produce a high proportion of young of her own phase."

1944: E. Mayr (Gen.) summarized this discussion "by saying that no one of Smith's arguments in favor of a specific status for the striped phase of the California king snake seems to be valid."

Boyle's king snake (24—Meek 1905), Boyle's milk snake (8—Cooper 1869)

Lampropeltis getulus californiae (Blainville) 1835. Fig. 116; Map 33

(Banded *boyli* phase Baird and Girard 1853)

Other common names: Banded milk snake (Conise 1868); black and white king snake; Boyle king snake (7); Boyle milk snake; California king snake (7); (California) milk snake; chain snake; (Pacific) king snake; western milk snake.

Range: S. cent. Oregon to n. Baja California, Mex., e. to cent. Arizona, s.w. Utah, and the s. half of Nevada.—U.S.A.: Ariz.; Calif.; Nev.; Ore.; Ut. Mex.: Baja Calif. *Elevation*—0 to 6,000 feet, mainly below 3,000. From the coast to the edge of the desert (Klauber, Calif., 1931a); 1,700, 2,200, 4,400 feet (Atsatt); 250, 260, 600 feet (Grinnell, Dixon, and Linsdale); 2,000, 2,000, 3,500, 4,060, 4,400, 4,500 feet (Van Denburgh, Gen., 1922); below 6,000 feet (Grinnell and Camp, Calif., 1930); below 5,000 feet, Nevada; 5,000 feet (Johnson, Bryant, Miller, Calif., 1948); 2,000 feet (Grinnell and Camp, Calif., 1907).

Size: Adults, 15–50 inches. The largest we have seen was 1,239 mm. (CAS 63776). Klauber's (Gen., 1943b) measurements of 278 males and 249 females are: over-all 540.51 mm. males, 539.10 mm. females; maxima, 1,301 mm. (tail 161) males, 1,233 mm. (tail 143) females.

Longevity: 6 years (Tanner, Ut., 1935); 11 years 1 month (Perkins, Gen., 1948); 14 years 1 month (Perkins, Gen., 1951); 14 years 10 months (Perkins, Gen., 1954).

Distinctive characteristics: A large medium, stout black or brown snake with 28–49 clear uniform white or yellow rings widening on the sides. These white or yellow, yellow green, or buffy rings are usually without dark edges, are 1½–2 scales wide on dorsal meson and 4 scales wide next to ventrals and go across venter on 4 or 5 ventrals. The dorsal fuscous or black bands 6–7½ scales wide on mid-dorsum narrow to 3 or 4 scales at ventrals, go across venter on 2 or 3 ventrals, or are interrupted on the venter. Ventrals 206–254; caudals 41–62. Dorsal scale rows 23-21-19 to 23-25-21-19.

Color: A snake from Arizona Reptile Gardens, Aug. 11, 1925. The dark of the upper parts is fuscous or fuscous-black. The light parts are seafoam yellow, seafoam green, or olive-buff. The iris is fuscous, fuscous-black, or dull violet-black (2) with an irregular area of seafoam yellow or seafoam green in front of the pupil. The dark of the under parts is green-blue slate except on the underside of the tail and the first 2 or 3 rings back of the head, where it is fuscous or fuscous-black.

Abnormal coloration—In 1946 Walker (Calif.) reported an albino *L. g. californiae, boyli* phase.

Habitat: One author said it knew no special restrictions. Another held it did not frequent open grass lands. Records are varied. These snakes have been found along streams where brush or trees occur, in short grass among boulders, in open prairies, on the roadsides, in damp spots, in dense thickets of *Atriplex torreyi,* over dry leaves, in foothills and upland regions, in chaparral of Lower and Upper Sonoran zones, amongst rocks in a canyon bottom, in low willows, along small streams, and on shaded ground with mixed vegetational cover. In recent times the best account of its activities is that of Fitch (Calif., 1947), from whose "Study of snake populations in central California" we have drawn under several topics. He calls it a secretive, slow-moving snake, quick to retreat into cover.

Period of activity: "Sixteen Year Census," Jan., 8 snakes; Feb., 12; Mar., 37; Apr., 133; May, 303; June, 256; July, 173; Aug., 76; Sept., 48; Oct., 20; Nov., 10; Dec., 1. Total 1,077 (Klauber, Gen., 1939a). MVZ dates, Mar. 28 to Oct. 19. *First appearance*—Apr. 19, 1934, Apr., 1935 (Fitch, Ore., 1936); May 6 (Stejneger); May 18, 1934 (Linsdale, Nev., 1938-40); May 25, 1924 (Grinnell, Dixon, and Linsdale); Apr. 26 (Cooper, Calif., 1869).

Breeding: Oviparous. Males 520–1,301 mm., females 525–1,233 mm. *Mating* —A pair mated in captivity, June 1, 1925 (Klauber, Calif., 1931a). "In May 1946, mating behavior was observed when several king snakes were held in confinement for a few days. A male would glide over the female, with chin pressed against her back and would grasp her body anteriorly with his jaws" (Fitch, Calif., 1947). *Eggs*—Number, 3–10. Time of deposition, June, July, a few in early August. "July 19, 1925. Nine eggs laid by a specimen caught June 28, 1925. July 30, 1928. A captive specimen laid eggs" (Klauber, Calif., 1931a).

Young—Number, 1–10. Size, 6, 8, 10–12 inches long. We have seen specimens taken Mar. 19, 297 mm. long, May 2, 327 mm. Were they from the late summer or fall before? We have measured specimens taken Sept. 13, 302 mm., Sept. 25, 307 mm., Oct., 329 mm. in length. Were they just after hatching? The smallest we have seen were 290, 294, 297, and 299 mm., all from different places. "I can add that a single egg from a set laid by *Lampropeltis getulus boylii* on June 25, 1924, hatched 118 days, nearly 4 months later (October 20)" (Blanchard, Okla., 1932). By 1939 Klauber and Perkins had 13 broods from females mated in the wild (fathers unknown)—1 brood of 3, 4 of 4 each, 2 of 6, 3 of 7, 1 of 8, 1 of 9, and 1 of 10 (Klauber, Gen., 1939). Seemingly, Fitch's (Calif., 1949) smallest male is about 285 mm. and smallest female 262 mm. Klauber's (Gen., 1943b) minimal measurements are 205 (tail, 29) mm. for males and 210 (tail, 25) mm. for females.

Growth—"A small Boyle's King Snake 6 inches long was collected near Santa Clara on June 3, 1929 by Doyle Liddle, Antone Bentley and the writer while we were doing field work in this region. The specimen was brought to the university where it has grown until it is 25 inches long. It has been fed on water snakes and lizards. It has escaped from the cage 3 different times. The first time it was gone 5 months and was found in a basement room, where it had just had a meal of 3 small mice. It is now past 6 years old and seems to be as healthy as ever" (Tanner, Ut., 1935).

Fitch (Calif., 1947) observes: "The king snake may have smaller broods with greater survival expectancy at the time of hatching; secretive tendencies in the small young may also be involved. Three marked males recaptured 72–75 months later had gained from 978 to 1,160 mm., 885 to 1,118 mm., and 920 to 1,050 mm. or 182, 233 and 130 mm. additional."

Food: Snakes, mammals, birds, lizards, vertebrate eggs. Fitch (Calif., 1949) and many more, such as Pack, Klauber, Perkins.

Authorities:

Atsatt, S. R. (Calif., 1913)

Baird, S. F., and C. Girard (Gen., 1853)

Camp, C. L. (Calif., 1916)

Grinnell, J. and H. W. (Calif., 1907)

Grinnell, J., J. Dixon, and J. M. Linsdale (Calif., 1930)

Grinnell, J., and T. Storer (Calif., 1924)

Hallowell, E. (Calif., 1854)

Hawken, J. L. (Calif., 1951)

Stejneger, L. (Calif., 1893)

Yarrow, H. C. (Calif., 1883)

Florida king snake (9—Wachtel), **King snake** (6—Loennberg 1895)

Lampropeltis getulus floridana Blanchard 1919. Fig. 117; Map 33

Another common name: Rattlesnake pilot.

Range: Peninsular Florida from Alachua and Putnam Cos. s. to Collier and Dade Cos. *Elevation*—Seacoast to 500 or fewer feet.

Size: Adults, 16–77 inches. Most records are between 3½ and 5¾ feet.

Longevity: 2 years 3 months (Conant and Hudson, Gen., 1949); 10 years 6 months (Perkins, Gen., 1954).

Distinctive characteristics: "Characters in general like those of *L. getulus getulus* from which it differs in having double the number of transverse light bands, about 60; by a basal lightening of the scales of the dark areas; by a degeneracy of the chain pattern; and by an increase of 1 row of scales on each side, making 23" (Blanchard, Ariz., 1919). In his 1921 paper (Gen.) he gave the transverse bands as 46 to 85.

Color: A snake from St. Petersburg, Fla., furnished by N. P. Fry and Son, April 16, 1928. In general the dorsal scales are benzo brown, hair brown, or black, with centers of drab. On the body are 67 transverse bars of pale olive-buff or dirty white. These bars are 1 scale wide, covering 2 half scales longitudinally and 12 scales transversely. On the side many scale centers and the vertical bars are olive-buff or seafoam green. The top of the head is vermiculated with deep olive-buff, and each of the upper and lower labials is olive-buff with plumbago slate sutures. The iris is heliotrope-slate or plumbago slate with the upper rim of the pupil deep colonial buff and with some of the same color dotted in the plumbago slate. The under parts of the body are blocked with primrose yellow, marguerite yellow, or chartreuse yellow and plumbago slate. The underside of the tail is heliotrope-slate or dark vinaceous-gray.

Habitat: Carr commented that its habitat is "generally similar to that of *getulus;* numerous cypress ponds in savannah pine lands and prairies. Fairly common, perhaps locally somewhat more abundant than *getulus.*" In 1943 Goin in "The lower vertebrate fauna of the water hyacinth" held that "the Florida King snake is widespread but not particularly abundant. Recorded for February, March, April, September and October." Before J. L. Williams' time (1837), it was known as an enemy of the rattlesnake and called rattlesnake pilot.

Breeding: Oviparous. Males 842 to 1,753 mm., females to 1,155 mm. *Mating*—"A pair of king snakes was discovered in copulation on April 19, 1930, near a ditch along the highway 6 miles southwest of Gainesville, Florida. . . . They remained in this position for 20 minutes, when they were placed in a bag; at 8:20 P.M. when removed from the bag they had separated. Unfortunately, they both were killed during my absence a short time later" (Van Hyning, Fla., 1931).

Eggs—Number, 7–11. Time, May, June. Size of young, 11–12 inches long. "I have seen eggs laid by an *L. getulus* in captivity. They were rather large, whitish with soft skin" (Loennberg). This may possibly apply to *L. g. floridana.* "♀ 1,047 mm. deposited May 19, 11 eggs, 33–50x22x23.8 mm., average 41.7x23 mm. Plain cream white, with smooth parchmentlike shells. Hatched July 26 and 27, size of young 277–300 mm. Some began eating DeKay's snakes and one another almost at once" (Conant and Downs). *Young*— The smallest specimen we have seen is 305 mm., most certainly near hatchling size.

Food: Similar to that of *L. g. getulus.* There are records of diverse snakes, mice, and small eggs in the diet. Hurter had a 4-foot-6-inch king snake which swallowed a 5-foot-3-inch rat snake. He remarked that the king snake remained in a rigid half circle for several days.

Authorities:

Blanchard, F. N. (Fla., 1919)
Carr, A. F. (Fla., 1940a)
Conant, R., and A. Downs, Jr. (Gen., 1940)

Cope, E. D. (Fla., 1889)
Goin, C. (Fla., 1943)
Hurter, J. (Mo., 1893)
Loennberg, E. (Fla., 1895)

Before F. N. Blanchard, E. Loennberg noted the varied coloration. Others like A. E. Brown in 1904 and R. L. Ditmars in 1907 also remarked these variations. Blanchard found enough essential characters to make it a separate variety of *L. getulus*.

Chipola River king snake

Lampropeltis getulus goini Neill and Allen 1949. Map 33

Range: Chipola River and Apalachicola River valleys in Gulf and Calhoun Cos., Fla. *Elevation*—Sea level to 500 feet.

Size: Adults reach 5 feet in length.

Distinctive characteristics: "Light transverse bands reduced in number (1 on the nape, 15 to 17 on the body, 5 or 6 on the tail). Light bands very wide, covering the length of 4 to 8 scales dorsally and further widening on the sides. Each scale of the light bands light on its anterior half but dark on its posterior half. Dark ground color, between the light bands, formed of deep brown scales, each bearing a vaguely defined light spot. Venter rich brown with light streaks on the ends of the ventrals, groups of these streaks roughly alternating from side to side of the abdomen. A wide light band crossing back of the head; remaining light head markings, except those of the labials, reduced to narrow lines or dots" (Neill and Allen, Fla.).

Habitat: We wanted to see the countryside of *Lampropeltis g. goini* and would of course have welcomed the snake, but he did not appear as we rode up and down the road just west of the Chipola River and back and forth from Wewahitchka to Panama City. The land of Torreya, the stinking cedar (*Tumion taxifolium*), is a geologically complicated one. Stinking cedar is on the chalky Tampa limestone hills bordering the Apalachicola River in Florida with streams flowing in from the phosphatic sandy limestone to the east and crossing the Duplin marl around Bristol. The nearby land of *Lampropeltis g. goini* offers no fewer complications as the Chipola River crosses the Mariana region of subterranean streams and large springs, the red loam, and the occasional pure-white chalky limestone outcrops, passes through a band of iron-stained yellowish limestone, a bit of the chalky Tampa limestone, a stretch of Chipola formation of marine sandy shell marl merging into micaceous and phosphatic Duplin marl. The water at Wewahitchka is heavily impregnated with iron. From there to Scott's Ferry is a realm of gray sandy loam uplands with clay subsoil usually within 3 feet of the surface, a long-leaf pine and wiregrass country with many cypress ponds in shallow depressions and in swamps along branches of the Chipola and Apalachicola Rivers and the tangles of Dead Lakes. *Lampropeltis getulus goini* lives in the nearby drier, upland "piney woods."

Authorities: Neill, W. T., and E. R. Allen (Fla., 1949)

Fig. 117. *Lampropeltis g. floridana:* 1,2,4,6, St. Petersburg, Fla., N. P. Fry and Son; 3,5, Silver Springs, Fla., E. R. Allen; 7, Tamiami Trail, Fla., Willie Willie (Indian chief).

Fig. 118. *Lampropeltis g. holbrooki:* 1-4,6,7, spotted, Little Rock, Ark., C. L. Shilladay; 5, with bars, Marshall, Tex., D. L. Gamble.

1949, W. T. Neill and E. R. Allen: "Variation. The chief pattern variations are shown in the . . . photographs. In all specimens, the scale row count was 21-19. In No. 19212, a female, the ventrals number 214; the tail tip is missing and no subcaudal count can be made. In No. 19213, the ventrals number 216; the tail tip is missing; the anal is divided. In No. 19214, a female, the ventrals number 216, the subcaudals 53. . . . Affinities. Apparently the range of *goini* is completely surrounded by that of typical *getulus*. We have examined many *getulus* from Calhoun, Wakulla, Jefferson and Escambia Counties, Florida. Even from Calhoun County, *getulus* showed little approach to *goini*. However the latter is evidently a member of the *getulus* complex and we think it likely that intergrades will be found eventually. Thus the new form has been given subspecific rank. The Apalachicola and Chipola River Valleys support a remarkable number of endemic plants and animals such as Florida yew, *Taxus floridana;* stinking cedar, *Tumion taxifolium;* the camel-crickets, *Centhophilus umbrosus* and *C. rogersi;* the rare katydid, *Hubbellia marianifera;* the wingless grouse-locust, *Tettigidea empedonepia;* the peculiar opilionid, *Siro americanus;* the sawback turtle, *Graptemys barbouri,* etc. Most or all of these are generally considered to be relict forms and so we are inclined to consider *L. g. goini."*

Speckled king snake (22—Mitchell 1903), Say's king snake (16)

Lampropeltis getulus holbrooki Stejneger 1902. Fig. 118; Map 33

Other common names: Chain snake; chicken snake; dotted black snake; egg snake (Mozley 1878); guinea snake; Holbrook's (king) snake; milk snake; salt-and-pepper (king) snake; southern king snake; speckled adder; spotted king snake; western king snake; yellow-speckled king snake; yellow-spotted black snake; yellow-spotted king snake.

Range: From w. Alabama n. to w. Illinois, w. through s. Iowa to s.e. Wyoming and s. through cent. Texas to the coast.—Ala.; Ark.; Ia.; Ill.; Kan.; Ky.; La.; Miss.; Mo.; Neb.; Okla.; Tenn.; Tex.; Wyo. *Elevation*— Sea level to 2,000 feet, rarely higher.

Size: Adults, 15–64 inches.

Longevity: 3 years 2 months (Conant and Hudson, Gen., 1949); 10 years 8 months (Perkins, Gen., 1954).

Distinctive characteristics: A large handsome snake (salt and pepper), every black scale of which has a sulphur or greenish yellow center; with or without 41–85 narrow cross bars. Head is generally spotted with yellow. The under parts are various hues of yellows, the black checkers few in cephalic half, more prominent in rear half, the yellow, however, being the more dominant. Scale rows 21 (23); ventrals 200–220; caudals 38–55.

Color: A snake from Marshall, Tex., furnished by D. L. Gamble, May, 1928. It is marked with short small dorsal bars of sulphur yellow or pale green-yellow extending transversely across 6 or 7 scale rows. The other dorsal scales are black with centers of pale green-yellow or sulphur yellow; or some of the scales of the first 3 rows may be wholly pale chalcedony yellow or light chalcedony yellow. The stripes and spots on the top and the sides of the head are light green-yellow. The iris is black. There is a cartridge buff patch above the pupil. The pupil rim is pale ochraceous-salmon except as it is broken in the lower front quarter by black. The belly is pale chalcedony yellow or light chalcedony yellow checkered with black rectangular spots. Toward the tail, almost every ventral is marked with a spot, but forward the yellow interspaces are more extensive.

A snake from Little Rock, Ark., furnished by G. L. Shilladay, fall, 1929. The scales of the back except those of the first 3 rows are black with sulphur yellow or pale chalcedony yellow centers, which are generally nearer the front than the rear of the scale. There are no dorsal crossbars. The scales of the first 3 rows are, like the belly, sulphur yellow, pale green-yellow, or barium yellow; or they may be light yellow-green or light green-yellow with black edges. Each scale of the head is marked with some sulphur yellow, pale chalcedony yellow, lumiere green, or even apple green. The side of the head and the labial plates are almost solely light dull green-yellow with dark sutures, the suture marks on the lower labials being narrow or short. The eye is entirely black except for the iris ring (incomplete in its lower front quarter) of naples yellow, ochraceous-buff, or warm buff. The under parts are sulphur yellow, pale green-yellow, or barium yellow marked particularly in the posterior half and on the tail with squarish blocks of black. These checkers are more widely separated in the cephalic half.

Habitat and habits: It has been recorded in open pine woods and along edges of swamps, in mixed prairie, on flat rock hillsides, in oak woods, grassy borders of a lagoon, hilly places with sunny glades, open situations. It has been under cover of logs, limestone rocks, pieces of tin, bark of stumps or logs, fallen trees. It has been recorded in tunnels under rocks, ploughed up. Two notices will suffice. In 1932 Allen wrote: "This species is common at all seasons and is usually found in the open pine woods and along the edges of swamps. A large example, discovered in the summer beneath a piece of tin, quickly disappeared down a hole upon removal of the shelter, but it was necessary to dig only about a foot to secure it. During the winter no large specimens have been seen, small ones alone having been taken from under the bark of stumps and logs. It is not until spring that mature individuals make their appearance." Regarding the fighting abilities of the king snake Meade (La., 1940) has written: "In an attempt to obtain motion pictures of a fight between a speckled king snake, *Lampropeltis getulus holbrooki,* and a canebrake rattlesnake, *Crotalus horridus atricaudatus,* it was found that the defense reaction of the rattlesnake was somewhat similar to that described by Cowles for some western rattlesnakes in the presence of

L. g. californiae. The rattlesnakes observed by Cowles (*C. v. oreganus* and *C. cerastes*) are described as forming a broad loop or bend of the body which is lifted from the ground, and the loop is then used as a human being might use an elbow in striking a heavy blow. . . . Motion pictures were also taken of king snakes in the presence of two pit-vipers common in this region, *Agkistrodon mokasen* and *A. piscivorus.* The copperhead, a 42-inch specimen, showed no attempt at defense whatever, merely keeping as far away from the king snake as possible. The cottonmouths, several specimens, did not appear to be afraid of the king snakes and one specimen struck a king snake, imbedding its fangs."

Period of activity: Early appearances—Missouri, Apr. 2, 4, 15, 26, May 13 (Hurter); Mar. 28, 1938, Apr. 15, May 2, 1939 (Anderson, Mo., 1945). Kansas, May 14, 1921, May, 1925 (Gloyd); May 5, 1927 (Burt, Kan., 1927). Mississippi, Mar. 2–Apr. 8 (Corrington, Miss., 1927). *Fall disappearance—*Oct. 1, 1911 (Hurter); Oct. 22, 1932 (Burt, Kan., 1933); Oct. 1, 1926 (Gloyd). *Hibernation—*"Lloyd collected 2 specimens at Matagorda in January and February 1892" (Bailey, Tex., 1905).

Breeding: Oviparous. Males 610–1,202 mm., females 600–1,006 mm. *Eggs* —Number, 6–14. "There is no record of breeding observations" (Blanchard, Gen., 1921). "A female in the museum laboratory deposited 10 eggs June 22 sometime before 1:00 P.M. When first noticed 5 had become white and opaque but the remaining 5 were still soft and translucent. . . . Their average length was 37 mm. and average diameter 18 mm. . . . A slit about 4 mm. long was noticed on one egg August 24. This opening was lengthened the following day and 2 days later a very active little snake emerged. It caused its tail to vibrate energetically whenever approached. In appearances it was unusually 'plump' because of the large amount of unassimilated yolk. Two days after hatching it shed its skin. The other egg was cut August 27 and hatched, it shed its skin. Both individuals were males, length 270 and 202 mm.; the tail lengths 38 and 30 mm." (Gloyd).

"A set of 8 eggs was deposited on June 2, between 4:45 and 9 P.M. The process was timed, and the results recorded. . . . In general the eggs were oblong, about twice as long as wide, with parallel sides and rounded ends. The first was somewhat larger and more irregular in shape than the others. The ends of each, soon after emergence, were a deep cream color, while toward the center they were almost white. The texture was smooth and parchment-like." For the first 8 eggs the time required for deposition varied from 2 minutes to 4 minutes 30 seconds, the intervals between deposition 15 minutes to 1 hour 5 minutes. The average size of 16 eggs, 36.7x19.2 mm. Extremes of length and diameter 32.4 to 43.3 mm. and 10.5 to 29.1 mm. (Force).

"The female specimen was kept and laid 9 eggs on July 17th, 73 days after the mating. The eggs were cyclindrical in form with rounded ends, all very much of one size, about one and a quarter inches (32 millimeters) in length and half an inch (13 millimeters in diameter). . . ." (Some eggs hatched 69 days later, the young about 10 inches long—Meade, La., 1932).

Blanchard (Okla., 1932) received a snake from Force. It deposited 6 eggs July 17. Eggs varied in length 42.1 to 44.8 mm. and in width from 17.8 to 19.9 mm. The eggs hatched Oct. 3 and 4, interval 77–78 days from deposition to hatching. Young measured 260, 265, 267, 270, 272 mm. Egg teeth were shed in 3 or 4 days after hatching. "A female taken near Kimmswick on June 29, 1931, laid 14 eggs on July 1" (Boyer and Heinze). "Common; set of 7 eggs removed from muskrat house on August 1" (Penn, La., 1943).

Young—"The young snakes were agile and slender, about the size of a lead pencil, and as brilliantly colored as green and gold enamel" (Meade, La., 1939). Conant's smallest newly hatched young is 9¼ inches; Baird and Girard's specimen from Kemper Co., Miss., is 9½ inches. The smallest specimens we have seen are 244, 277, 328 mm.

Food: Poisonous and other snakes, small birds, lizards, mice, rats. Branson (Kan., 1904), Strecker (Tex., 1908c), Hurter, Löding (Ala., 1922), Guthrie (Ia., 1926), Gloyd, Force, Boyer and Heinze, Taylor (Ark., 1935), Anderson (Mo., 1942), Howell (La., 1954).

Authorities:

Allen, M. J. (Miss., 1932)
Baird, S. F., and C. Girard (Gen., 1853)
Blanchard, F. N. (Gen., 1921; Okla., 1932)
Boyer, D. A., and A. A. Heinze (Mo., 1934)
Conant, R. (Calif., 1938a)

Force, E. R. (Okla., 1930)
Gloyd, H. K. (Kan., 1928)
Hurter, J. (Mo., 1903)
Meade, G. P. (La., 1932, 1940)
Stejneger, L. (Ariz., 1903)
Strecker, J. K., Jr. (Tex., 1908c, 1915, 1926, 1928c, 1930, etc.)

1915, J. K. Strecker: "The speckled king snake inhabits the greater portion of the area of Texas, but some of the published locality records doubtless refer to *Ophibilus splendidus* Cope, and on this account it would be a difficult matter at this time to define the limits of its Texas range."

Black king snake (13—Myers 1926), King snake (7—Hay 1887)

Lampropeltis getulus niger (Yarrow) 1882. Fig. 119; Map 33

Other common names: Black (chain) snake; chain snake; mole snake; Ridgway's king snake (Yarrow 1882); thunder snake.

Range: From w. West Virginia w. to e. Illinois and s. to s.e. tip of Missouri, thence s.e. to w. Alabama and northeastward w. of the mountains.— Ala.; Ark.; Ill.; Ind.; Ky.; O.; Tenn.; W. Va. *Elevation*—Mainly 500 to 1,000 feet; some to 2,000 feet; 1,500–2,500 feet (King).

Size: Adults, 15–56 inches.

Distinctive characteristics: A glistening, large-to-medium black snake rarely totally black, but usually with traces of 50–95 faint crossbars or rows of yellow or white spots. Some lateral scales are yellow centered. Throat white; infralabials with prominent black sutures; much yellow in forward belly and much black in rear half of venter. Ventrals 199–216; caudals 41–54.

Color: A snake from the Zoo at Memphis, Tenn., received from Malcolm Parker through Harold Trapido, Mar. 6, 1937. The first impression of the back is that it is a uniform glistening black. Close examination shows 6 slightly indicated threadlike crossbands of pale chalcedony yellow in the cephalic 4 inches. Thereafter, the scales on the back are generally black with a scale here and there marked with a pinpoint of pale chalcedony yellow. In the first 3 scale rows are many light-centered scales. These extend diagonally upward beginning above the light intervals of the belly and ending opposite the black ones. Above these 3 rows are faintly traced lines of pinpoints of light chalcedony yellow. The top of the head is mostly black with a few points of yellow. All the scales of the side of the head are light-centered. The upper labials have vertical centers of pale chalcedony yellow and broad sutures of black. The rostral is pale chalcedony yellow broadly rimmed along the sutures with solid black. The iris is black with the upper and rear of the rim of the pupil pale chalcedony yellow or pale yellow green. The belly is checked with pale chalcedony yellow and black. The chin and throat are pale chalcedony yellow except for the black sutures of the lower labial plates and the black rear margins of the gulars. The same yellow predominates for 4 to 6 inches. Usually, the ends of 2 ventrals are yellow with an interval of black ranging from 1 to 3 ventral ends. The light intervals on one side of the belly plates alternate with the light areas of the opposite side. Thus also the black intervals. Caudad of the first few inches, the black becomes increasingly predominant until on the tail there are only a few minute light points on the ends of subcaudals indicating the alternation of light and dark of the cephalic region.

Abnormal coloration—For a long time this form was held comparable to the black phase of *Heterodon niger;* see, e.g., Hay (Ind., 1892): *"Ophibolus getulus niger* is a so-called variety of this species [*L. g. getulus*]. . . . [The Wheatland, Ind., specimen] was 4 feet 6 inches long. This form is reported to be common in that region. We have in the king-snake another illustration of the phenomena seen in *Heterodon platirhinos, Natrix sipedon,* and some others, a gradual transition from very spotted specimens to those which are of a plain black color. We cannot give a distinct name to every stage in the change." In 1899 Blatchley declared: "This [black phase] is especially true of *Bascanion constrictor* and *Ophibolus getulus sayi,* as shown above, also of *Coluber obsoletus.* The form *niger* of *Heterodon platyrhinos* has never been seen by the writer in the juvenile stage, though hundreds of the young of the more common form have been noted. *Niger,* therefore, is, we believe, but a mature form of the species. The same is probably true of the form *niger* of *Ophibolus getulus.*" [It is, of course, a separate subspecies.]

Habitat: From Hay (Ind., 1897), Garman (Ky., 1894), Blatchley (Ind., 1899), Blanchard (Gen., 1921; Ind., 1926), Funkhouser, Conant, Swanson (Ind., 1939), Welter and Carr (Ky., 1939), King, Minton, Smith (Ill., 1947), Parker (Tenn., 1948), and other writers, one assumes that the black snake frequents the following niches: open woodlands and borders of moist thickets, timberland uplands and lowlands, rocky hillsides, rocky thickets, holes beneath sandstone slabs, rocky hillside pastures, dry rocky slopes in the hills, small dry prairie, dry woodland, wooded areas, wooded ravine, wood's clearing, bottomlands, area above flood plain, land along or near rivers, lakes, ponds, and sloughs, fields and roadsides. One author asserted they never were in open fields or roadsides, and another held they had no penchant for swimming, but that is hardly the true situation.

Period of activity: *Early appearances*—May 6, 23, 1933 (Conant, O., 1934a); Apr. 24, 1927 (Walker); June 10, 1934 (Hallowell, Kan., 1857a); May 8, 10 (Minton). *Fall disappearance*—Oct. 22, 1888 (Blatchley, Ind., 1891).

Breeding: Oviparous. Males 591–1,471 mm., females 673–1093 mm. *Eggs*—Number, 3–24. Size, 1.1–1.9 inches long x .7–.9 inches wide. Time, June. "It lays from 1 to 2 dozen eggs in the early summer. These hatch in about 2 months, the young snakes resembling the parents" (Funkhouser).

The data on this form is so scanty that we give part of Conant's (O., 1934a) definitive "Observations on the eggs and young of the black king snake": "The first female, secured May 6, 1933, 10 miles southwest of Portsmouth, Scioto County, Ohio, laid 10 eggs June 22, 1933. These were capsule shaped, except for 2 which were pointed at one end, and were nonadherent save for 2 pairs cemented together along their long axes. They were cream white at first, but became yellowish in a few hours. The lengths varied from 28.1 to 36.2, average 31.4 mm., the widths from 17.4 to 19.6, average 18.5 mm.; the average weight was 6.25 g. . . . The remaining 8 hatched during the afternoon of September 9 and when examined a few hours later no egg teeth could be found. The young ranged in length from 235 to 258, average 242 mm., and showed an average weight of 5.8 g. . . . The second female was collected May 29, 1933, near Lynx, Adams County, Ohio, and deposited 9 eggs June 25, 1933. All were adherent and were arranged roughly in the same plane. In color and shape these were similar to those of the first clutch even to having 2 with pointed ends. Those of the second clutch were larger, however, varying from 31.7 to 47.0, average 41.5 mm., in length, from 21.0 to 22.6, average 21.6 mm., in width and having an adult weight of 11 g. . . . A comparison of the dates of laying and hatching shows that the period of incubation for the first clutch was 78 days and for the second 80 to 81 days. All the young showed a tendency to hide under the objects occupying the cage floors. Most were aggressive when teased, vibrating their tails rapidly and striking repeatedly to the accompaniment of a sharp hiss. Both groups shed 10 to 14 days after hatching and 2 of the second brood shed again 55 to 57 days respectively after hatching. Twenty-five days after the appearance of the first snake it was found that the specimens of the second group had gained an average of 14 mm. in length and had lost an average of 0.7 g. in weight. About the middle of October 2 specimens began feeding upon young *Storeria dekayi* and *Thamnophis butleri*. At the age of 2 months they had attained lengths of 285 and 310 mm. and weights of 8.4 and 10.1 g. respectively."

Food: Small mammals, amphibians, snakes, birds, poisonous snakes. Blatchley, Funkhouser, Conant, Minton.

Field notes: July 6, 1931, Dunbar, Kanawha Co., W. Va.: Just out of and opposite the camp Dr. W. J. Hamilton, Jr., and his class found on a hillside of the golf links a very recently killed king snake.

June 27, 1933, Reelfoot Lake, Tenn.: The other day when one of the men went to get turtle eggs for fish bait he found a king snake eating one of the eggs. The snake is glistening black with little white specks (*L. g. niger*).

May 19, 1950, Wheatland, Ind.: Quite cultivated. Hickories, oaks, button-woods, ashes, walnuts, maples, soil light colored. Just after we left Wheatland we recalled it was the type locality for the Black king snake. Within 10 miles—just east of Montgomery, Ind., we discovered DOR the finest specimen of *L. g. niger* we ever saw. On the back the light bars were barely indicated by tiny flecks. Areas on back between these bars are absolutely black for a width of 10 scales. On the sides for about 3 rows of scales there are little oblique lines. Then an area of 2 or 3 scale rows where slight white fleckings occur. The belly is beautiful—throat and under head prominently white, made more striking by the black sutures of the infralabials; forward quarter of belly considerable yellow; next 2 quarters yellow as crescents; rear quarters and underside of tail almost no yellow. The yellow of the belly is pale chalcedony yellow, becoming in places pale lumiere green. The snake is 3½ of my foot lengths (40 inches).

Authorities:

Blanchard, F. N. (Gen., 1921)
Blatchley, W. S. (Ind., 1899, 1900)
Burt, C. E. (Gen., 1935)
Conant, R. (O., 1938a)
Dury, R., and W. Gessing, Jr. (Ky., 1940)
Funkhouser, W. D. (Ky., 1925)
King, W. (Tenn., 1939)
Minton, S., Jr. (Ind., 1944)
Parker, M. V. (Tenn., 1937, 1948)
Trapido, H. (Tenn., 1938)
Walker, C. F. (O., 1931)
Yarrow, H. C. (Gen., 1882–83)

Fig. 119. *Lampropeltis g. niger,* Memphis, Tenn., M. V. Parker through H. Trapido.

Fig. 120. *Lampropeltis g. splendida:* 1–4,7, Brownsville, Tex., H. C. Blanchard; 5,6, San Antonio, Tex., Mrs. W. O. Learn.

Sonoran king snake (5—Strecker and Williams 1927),
Splendid king snake

Lampropeltis getulus splendida (Baird and Girard) 1853. Fig. 120; Map 33

Other common names: Boundary king snake; king snake (6—Bailey 1913); Mexican king snake; Sonora king snake; Sonoran milk snake.

Range: S.e. Arizona, extreme s. New Mexico to Red River (exclusive of panhandle of Texas), s. to Matagorda Bay, w. through w. Tamaulipas, Mex., to n.e. Sonora, Mex.—U.S.A.: Ariz.; N.M.; Okla.: Tex. Mex.: Chihuahua; San Luis Potosí; Sonora; Tamaulipas. *Elevation*—Seacost or 500 to 5,000 feet, mainly from 2,800 to 5,000 feet (Bailey, N. Mex., 1913); 7,000 feet (Taylor, Gen., 1952).

Size: Adults, 14.5–60 inches, the smaller lengths seldom being recorded.

Longevity: 2 years 2 months plus (Kauffeld, Gen., 1951).

Distinctive characteristics: A handsome, glistening, medium stocky snake of a deep brown color, normally 23 (25) dorsal rows, seldom 21; narrow (41–85) crossbars of mustard or lemon color which fork and join to make dorsal rhombs; very dark with each scale very lightly marked with yellow; lateral scales with yellow centers; chin yellow, belly solid blue gray (black in alcohol) with blocks of rich yellows at the sides of ventrals. Each plate of side of head is yellow centered. Ventrals 207–225; caudals 43–56.

Color: A snake in Texas May 7, 1925. The general dorsal color is mummy brown, fuscous, or slightly darker than olive-brown. The interspaces when the skin is stretched are violet-plumbeous or hair brown. The back is crossed at intervals of about 5 scales by transverse bars of primuline yellow or lemon chrome centered scales. These bars are ½, 1, or 2 scales wide, forking at about the 9th row of scales and there widening into 2 or even 3 full rows of scales. These forks thus leave clear spots covering from 1 to 3 scales of mummy brown which alternate with the dorsal rhombs. Except for these lateral spots, all the scales of the side have light centers. Each plate of the side of the head has a sulphur yellow center. In the rostral, internasal, and prefrontals, the yellow tends toward buff-yellow. The labials are sulphur yellow with mummy brown sutures. The chin in general is sulphur yellow. The iris is sulphur yellow above and below while the rest is mummy brown. The belly color is pale violet-plumbeous, clove brown, or from green-blue slate to pale green-blue gray in unshed skin, marked with blocks of barium yellow or sulphur yellow.

In Lewis' snake from the Organ Mts. region of New Mexico, forks of the light lines are not evident since the lateral ends of the dorsal rhombs are cut off squarely due to the straight line of light spots on the 9th or 10th scale row. This regularity also makes the black dorsal rhombs a bit smaller and the light lateral spots more uniform and more conspicuous. A similar condition was noted in the snake of W. A. Flood, Jr. (Cornell University) from

Bisbee, Ariz. *Young*—Palo Pinto, Tex., Aug., 1938, from P. Harter. Back with distinct squares of black separated by yellow. There is considerable yellow on the forward venter.

Habitat and habits: Notes on this aspect are very rare. In 1897 Van Denburgh (Ariz.) recorded that "2 specimens of this handsome snake were taken, one of which was 'shot in a tree in the river-bottom near Fort Lowell May 28, 1893.'" In 1937(a) Gloyd (Ariz.) recorded that "a king snake fairly typical of this sub-species was found beneath a pile of boards at the 'Circle J' Ranch, 10 miles southeast of Wilcox, July 19, 1931." In 1950 Milstead *et al.* (Tex.) recorded it from the mesquite-creosote association of Terrell Co., Tex. In 1900 Cope called this a Sonoran, Chihuahuan snake; Brown in 1904 dubbed it Texan; Bailey in 1913 called it Lower Sonoran.

Breeding: Oviparous. Males 752–1,250 mm., females 751–1,432 mm. *Eggs*—Number, 9–12. Until 1950 the only record we knew was the following field note by ourselves: A female which was secured from Mrs. Learn on May 5, 1925, laid 9 eggs May 26, 1925. These eggs are sulphur yellow or naphthalene yellow, sometimes greenish yellow on the ends. This female came from a place on the Corpus Christi road 6 miles out of San Antonio. On July 24, 1950, a female deposited 12 eggs, 35–41 mm. long x 19–30 mm. wide (Werler, Gen., 1951).

Food: Mice, rats. Flood and Wiklund (Ariz., 1949).

Authorities: [1]

Baird, S. F., and C. Girard (Gen., 1853) • Stejneger, L. (Ariz., 1903)
Blanchard, F. N. (Gen., 1921)   Strecker, J. K., Jr. (Tex., 1922 and 5
Cope, E. D. (Gen., 1900)   more articles)
Lewis, T. H. (N. Mex., 1950)

1853, S. F. Baird and C. Girard: "This species forms a connecting link, as to color, between the blotched varieties of *O. sayi* and *O. getulus.*"

1903, J. Stejneger: "This form, consequently, seems to skirt over Mexican border pretty closely. It probably extends some distance south into Mexico, how far we can only conjecture."

1903, A. E. Brown (Texas): "The only comment to be made is that these gentlemen [Stejneger and Cope] cannot have counted the scale rows in any large number of specimens. I have before me at this moment 5 living examples from Pecos, showing more than an 'approach' to the pattern of *splendidus,* one at least even having the head unspotted except on the snout; 3 of these have 23 rows, and 2 have 21. The case seems analogous to that of *Crotaphytus baileyi,* already discussed, and does not strengthen the evidence

---

[1] 1955: W. E. Duellman wrote about *Lampropeltis getulus* sp. because his central and southeastern Arizona material to Chiricahua had as many *yumensis* as *splendida* characters. One individual (Cochise Co.), he said, "combines the color pattern characters of both *yumensis* and *splendida.* . . . At the present time it is impossible to delimit the ranges of the two subspecies in southern Arizona."

for *splendidus,* unless selected individuals with 21 rows and usually spotted heads are to be called *O. g. sayi,* and those with 23 rows and usually unspotted heads are *O. splendidus,* even when they occur side by side—which would not commend itself as a conception of specific difference."

1921, F. N. Blanchard: "There can be no doubt, even from this brief summary, that *splendida* bridges the gap between *holbrooki* and *yumensis,* in structural and color pattern features as well as in geographic position."

Desert king snake (3—Klauber 1931),
Yuma king snake (Klauber 1934)

Lampropeltis getulus yumensis Blanchard 1919. Fig. 121; Map 33

Other common names: Arizona king snake; desert milk snake; king snake (Blanchard 1921).

Range: From Imperial Valley n.e. to Blythe, Calif., e. almost to Phoenix, Ariz., thence s.w. to the head of the Gulf of California (Sonora and Baja California), Mexico.—U.S.A.: Ariz.; Calif. Mex.: Baja Calif.; Sonora. *Elevation*—500 feet or lower to 1,000, 2,000, or 3,500 feet. Along the bank of Colorado River in Imperial Co., Calif. (Klauber, 1931a); 3,500 feet (Little, Ariz., 1940).

Size: Adults, 13–50 inches.

Distinctive characteristics: "White bars on the prefrontals occupying less than half the area of these scutes; frontal plate uniform black, or with the white restricted to a narrow transverse bar at its anterior end; no white on parietals; lower labials usually 9" (Schmidt, Baja Calif., 1922). A large medium deep brown or black snake, with top of head dark except for 2 bars across prefrontals and internasals; body with narrow white or light yellow crossbars on anterior part, often alternating with vertical bars on posterior half; face and under parts of head white with black; light rings expand into lateral triangular areas; dark bands cross belly or extend half way across it, the ventral interval white forward, light yellow rearward —a distinctive striking animal.

Color: A snake from Pinal, Ariz., collected June 21, 1941, 10 miles s.e. of Komatke, and received from L. W. Arnold of Komatke. The background color of the back is chestnut-brown, mummy brown, or clove brown, crossed by light bars. For the first 11 spaces these light bars, 9 to 11 scales deep, end on mid-dorsum, and those of opposite sides are alternately spaced, hence not forming complete rings. Then follow 26 rings on body and one complete one on the tail, then 5 bars on right side and 4 on the left, alternating in position. These light rings are white on the 4 to 5 lower rows of scales and primrose yellow across the dorsum in the forward half of body and seafoam yellow in the caudal half. In width the ring crosses 2 half-scales the bases of which are clove brown. Forward, the alternating vertical bars are 1 scale and 2 half scales wide. The light rings expand on the sides into triangular areas 3 or 4 scales long at base, and cross the belly on 3 of 4 ventrals. The scales of these triangular areas are dark edged as are also the light ventrals. The light areas on the underside of tail do not completely cross the subcaudals. The background color is 6 scales long on the dorsum and 3 scales long on the side, and passes as solid color across the venter on 3 ventrals. Occasionally, this dark color is irregular with only 1 or 2 plates completely dark—i.e., the 3 dark plates of one side do not exactly meet the 3 dark ones of the other side. This gives a series of dark blocks. The top of head is black except for 2 very narrow white bands across front of prefrontal and internasal. Each of the labials has a vertical white band, which is most conspicuous on the 4th, 5th, 6th, and 7th upper labials. The first temporals, postocular, preocular, loreal, nasal, and rostral have white centers. The throat is white, but every gular scale has dark caudal or caudal and lateral border. Back of the angle of the mouth the gulars and side and top of neck are black. The chin shields are white with dark caudal tips. The iris is black.

Habitat and habits: In 1931(a) Klauber recorded it on a "river bank." In 1932 Linsdale, who had taken this snake in Baja California, wrote: "One of the specimens from near Cerro Prieto was found crawling at the margin of tules; the other one was caught inside an old house. Both the individuals from El Cajon Cañon were caught near a creek, one of them on sandy ground." In 1934 Klauber (Calif.) wrote: "The Yuma King Snake has not yet been found in the Imperial District, but will no doubt eventually reach there from the river by way of irrigation canals." Gloyd (Ariz., 1937a) stated: "In the western foothills of the Catalina Mountains during the late evening of August 3, 1930, a specimen of this king snake was found among the underbrush of mesquite and catclaw near a small group of cottonwoods at the mouth of a little cañon." Then Klauber (Gen., 1938) wrote: "On May 14, 1937, I found a specimen run over on the road, but fortunately still suitable for preservation, 4 miles west of Blythe, Riverside County, California. Blythe is in an irrigated area on the Colorado River, about 60 miles above Yuma. Also, through the courtesy of Mr. A. C. Koller, I have secured specimens from Holtville and 2½ miles west of Seeley, Imperial County. Both of these points are in the Imperial Valley irrigated area. Since this district has now been under irrigation for about 35 years, and the king snake was not previously found there, despite some intensive collecting, it is probable that it has increased its range westward by following the irrigation canals and the bordering fields. Seeley is about 70 miles west of Yuma." Little (Ariz., 1940) reported it from the Roosevelt Reservation "in semi-desert 3,500 ft. Lower Sonoran." (For Wood's [Calif., 1945] account, see *Leptotyphlops humilis cahuilae* and *Sonora miniata linearis*.)

Period of activity: *Early appearances*—Cooper in 1869 gave Apr. 26. Slevin

and Wood collected it Apr. 22, Apr. 24, May 28, 1941. *Fall disappearance*—
Oct. 30, 1939 (Potholes, Calif., Wallace F. Wood). MVZ has records Apr.
6.–Oct. 30.

Breeding: Oviparous. Males 932–1,394 mm., females 1,005–1,204 mm.
Eggs—Numbers, 10–20. On Aug. 22, 1930, with Prof. W. A. Riley of the
University of Minnesota we visited Mrs. Olive Wiley's Museum on an upper
floor of the library building, Minneapolis, Minn. An interesting attraction
here that worried some of the librarians below was a fine Arizonian *Lampropeltis*. It was *L. getulus yumensis* female. It was coiled about its eggs,
the typical *getulus* type, about 15 or 20 of them. She laid them several days
before Aug. 22. We tried to take some photos, but they were very poor. We
find no breeding notes in the literature.

Young—In MVZ the smallest we recorded is No. 32099 (taken Oct. 30,
1939, at Laguna Dam, Potholes, Imperial Co., Calif., by Wallace F. Wood),
which is 321 mm. (tail 42) in total length. In the CAS No. 80758–807761
(Potholes, Apr. 22, 1941, Slevin and Wood) are small specimens, one of
which is 406 mm. Except for the preceding, the smallest we have seen is
380 mm., which is doubtless considerably past hatching size. Blanchard had
a male 345 mm. and a female 391 mm.

Authorities:

Blanchard, F. N. (Gen., 1921; Ariz., 1919)

Camp, C. L. (Calif., 1916)

Grinnell, J., and C. L. Camp (Calif., 1917)

Hensley, M. M. (Ariz., 1950)

Klauber, L. M. (Gen., 1938, 1939a; Calif., 1931a, 1934a)

Linsdale, J. M. (Baja Calif., 1932)

Van Denburgh, J. (Gen., 1922; Calif., 1912a)

1921, F. N. Blanchard: "It appears that *yumensis* is not an intergradational
condition between *splendida* and *boylii,* nor yet, as will be more clearly
brought out further on, is it identical with *conjuncta* of the Cape Region
of Baja California, but a recognizable distinct form having a definite range
that lies between the ranges of *boylii* and *splendida,* and the intergrading
with both of these forms where their ranges meet its own."

1950: M. M. Hensley in the Ajo region took 2 males DOR, the longer
1,120 mm.

1955: K. F. Murray and R. Zweifel (*Herpetologica,* **11**:44) recognized the
San Pedro Martin *yumensis* to be actually *Californiae.*

Arizona king snake (13—Yarrow 1882),
Arizona coral king snake (3)

Lampropeltis pyromelana (Cope) 1866. Fig. 122; Map 31

Other common names: (Arizona) coral snake; Arizona milk snake;
(Arizona) ringed snake (2—Ditmars 1907); banded king snake.

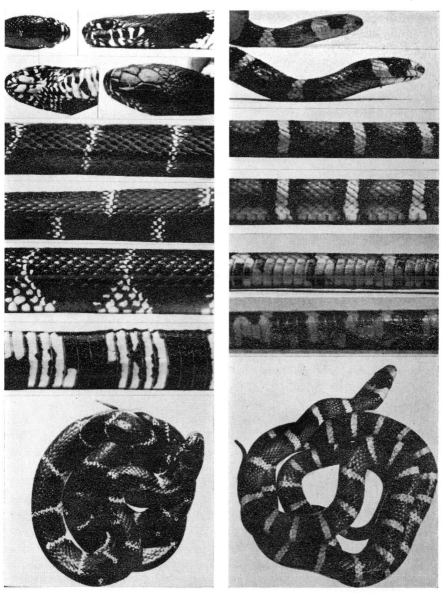

Fig. 121. *Lampropeltis g. yumensis,* Komatke, Pinal Co., Ariz., L. W. Arnold.

Fig. 122. *Lampropeltis pyromelana:* 1,6,7, Arizona; 2–5, Jacob's Lake, Ariz., sent to W. Rundle.

Range: N. cent. Utah, s. through extreme s.e. Nevada, through cent. Arizona and extreme s.w. New Mexico to e. Sonora and cent. Chihuahua.—U.S.A.: Ariz.; Nev.; N.M.; Utah. Mex.: Sonora, Chihuahua. *Elevation*—2,800–5,000 feet (Bailey, N. Mex., 1913). About 7,000 feet, Nevada. Some to 5,500–6,000 feet (Grinnell and Camp, Calif., 1917); 6,000 feet (Van Denburgh, Gen., 1922); 3,500–6,000 feet (Little, Ariz., 1940); 7,000 feet (Van Denburgh and Slevin, Ariz., 1913); 5,400–7,000 feet (Dodge); 5,400–6,500 feet (A.H.W., 1942).

Size: Adults, 11–41 inches.

Longevity: 2 years 3 months; 2 years 2 months (Kauffeld, Gen., 1951).

Distinctive characteristics: A medium-sized snake with 23 (25) dorsal rows with ventrals 216–235 and caudals 62–79. A tricolored snake with red (coral red or brazil red) and yellow (olive-buff to marguerite yellow) rings bordered by black (bluish black)—the yellow rings on body 38–47 and on tail 10–16, or 48 to 63 in all. Snout or in front of eye "yellowish" (dark or deep olive buff, often white in preserved material). Underside of head variable yellows. Color of dorsum imperfectly or diversely carried onto belly.

Color: A snake found at the Recreation Area, Madera Canyon, Santa Rita Mts., Aug. 6, 1925. The red rings are brazil red on the back, dragon's-blood red or coral red on the sides, and light coral red or carnelian red on the belly. The yellow rings are deep olive-buff on the back, olive-buff on the sides, and cartridge buff or marguerite yellow on the belly. The edges of these rings are seafoam yellow or sulphur yellow, and on the back and sides the scales are marked with numerous punctae. Bordering both sides of both red and yellow rings are black, bluish black, or blue-violet black rings which appear on the dorsum triangular in outline. Often this black ring is absent on the first 2 or 3 scale rows forward of the deep olive-buff ring. On the belly in the cartridge buff or marguerite yellow areas are usually 2 to 4 or 5 squarish, bluish black spots. On the tail, the black or bluish black dorsal bands unite with the squarish black or bluish black spots. The snout and head cephalad of the eyes is dark olive-buff or deep olive-buff. From the top of the 4th upper labial, through the eye, and across the frontal, supraocular, and forward half of parietals and postoculars extends a plumbeous-black or blue-violet black area. Then follows a band of dark olive-buff or deep olive-buff across the nape and rear of parietals, temporals, and labials. From angle of mouth to angle of mouth is another black or plumbeous-black band 3 scales in width. The underside of the head except below the angle of the mouth is cartridge buff, sulphur yellow, or pale green-yellow.

Habitat: Most of the records come from high elevations. Pine regions, coniferous forests, and pinyon, sycamore, and walnut associations; chaparral woodland and pine forests; lower branches of *Cercocarpus* (mountain mahogany); canyons, rocks on canyon sides, and canyon mouths; rock slides; mountain trails; and mountains in general are all desirable points of search.

Period of activity: *First appearance*—Hinds gave May 20, 1920, in Pinery Canyon, Chiricahuas. *Fall disappearance*—Records are scanty: Oct., 1938

(Wood and Thorne, Vernal, Ut.) and Oct. 1, 1919, Cane Creek, Chiricahuas (Hinds).

Breeding: Oviparous. Males 424–1,067 mm., females 519–840 mm. *Young*— The smallest specimen we ever saw is 205 mm. (tail 27½ mm.) (CAS No 30352) taken at Vernal, Uintah Co., Ut., by Wallace F. Wood and Leo C. Thorne. We suspect it is a hatchling of 1938. Other specimens are: Brigham Young University, No. 634, Santa Clara, Washington Co., Ut., D. E. Beck, Oct. 1937, total length 281 mm. (tail 46); and No. 278, Museum of Northern Arizona, Flagstaff, which is 10⅝ inches, of which the tail is 2 inches.

Food: "Nothing is known of the habits of this snake" (Van Denburgh, Gen., 1922). "Very little is known regarding the food or habits of this rather uncommon reptile" (Dodge). "The writer is aware of no information on the habits of this snake" (Tanner).

Field notes: Aug. 25, 1925: At Flagstaff, Ariz., learned D. M. Eldredge had 2 live Arizona king snakes. One he took at Mt. Elden, Ariz., July 26, 1925. They occur on creek banks, among ferns, oaks, in heavy underbrush. Another live specimen he took at Oak Creek near a spring, marshy like the above locality. Bought them (Cat. Nos. 663, 664).

Authorities:

Blanchard, F. N. (Gen., 1921)
Cope, E. D. (Ariz., 1866)
Dodge, N. N. (Ariz., 1938)
Gloyd, H. K. (Ariz., 1937a)

Stejneger, L. (Ariz., 1903)
Tanner, W. W. (Ut., 1941a)
Van Denburgh, J., and J. R. Slevin
    (Ariz., 1897, 1913)

NEW CORAL KING SNAKES

Lampropeltis pyromelana infralabialis subsp. nov.; *Lampropeltis pyromelana knoblochi* Taylor; *Lampropeltis pyromelana woodini* subsp. nov.

Zweifel's paper on *L. zonata* presaged a similar analysis of *L. pyromelana*. Tanner (Gen., 1953) has just issued a study of the latter species wherein he recognized 4 color patterns or subspecies. We record merely his key, which follows:

"A. Infralabials 9-9, white annuli complete across the ventrals in 50 percent or more of the body annuli—*pyromelana infralabialis* subsp. nov.
"AA. Infralabials 10-10, white annuli not complete across the ventrals in 50 percent of the body annuli . . . . B
    "B. White annuli not extending as transverse bars to the ventrals, terminating or joining a lateral zig-zag white line on the 3–5 dorsal rows on each side; orbit reached by the white of the first annulus . . . .
        . . . . *pyromelana knoblochi* Taylor
    "BB. White annuli normally extending to ventrals, no zig-zag lateral line; orbit not reached by first annulus C

"C. White body annuli low, usually less than 43, average 39; ventrals 222–233, average 227; caudals minus the total white annuli equals 17 or more, average 20. . . . . *pyromelana woodini* subsp. nov.
"CC. White body annuli higher, usually more than 43, average 48.2; ventrals 214–288, average 221; caudals minus total white annuli equal 17 or less, average 9. . . . . *pyromelana pyromelana* Cope."

The ranges of these 4 forms are: *L. p. knoblochi* Taylor, Majarachic, Chihuahua; *L. p. pyromelana,* s.w. New Mexico, Chihuahua, and Arizona except extreme southern border; *L. p. woodini* W. Tanner, Huachuca Mts. to Penna Blanca, Ariz., and Chihuahua; *L. p. infralabialis* W. Tanner, Grand Canyon, Ariz., through Utah to e. Nevada.

Coast-Range coral king snake, California king snake

Lampropeltis zonata zonata (Lockington) 1876. Fig. 123; Map 31

Other common name: Coral (king) snake.
Range: Coast range from n. Baja California to state of Washington.—U.S.A.: Calif.; Ore.; Wash. Mex.: Baja Calif. *Elevation*—Mainly 4,000 to 8,000 feet. "The mountains above 4,500 feet with an occasional specimen on the higher foothills" (Klauber, Gen., 1931a). 6,000 feet (Van Denburgh, Gen., 1922); 6,400 feet (Linsdale); 6,000 feet (Atsatt, Calif., 1913); 8,000 feet (Meek).
Size: Adults, 10–37 inches. "Two feet is large, but specimens over 33 inches long have been taken" (Perkins). The Grinnells (Calif., 1907) have specimens 25, 26, and 27¾ inches, while Meek has a 26.4-inch one from Hot Springs, Calif.
Longevity: 13 years 6 months (Perkins, Gen., 1954).
Distinctive characteristics: This medium-sized tricolored snake is characterized by Klauber (Calif., 1943c) thus: "In the Coast Range form the 2 black boundary rings of each triad are generally well separated so that the central red ring crosses the dorsum." More than half of the triad rings of the body include transverse bands which cross the dorsum. Top of snout back of frontal black; or if predominantly red or pink, total body triads less than 40. ("Any black ring or pair of black rings, completely or partially split with red, is considered a triad, provided it is bounded on either side by a white ring.")
Color: A snake from San Diego, Calif., received from C. B. Perkins, July, 1944. The pattern is one of rings red, black, and white, the black separating the red and white. The white rings are of uniform width from meson to venter, the black ones wider on the meson, sometimes breaking the red rings

into lateral areas. In this specimen there are 33 red rings on the body and 6 on the tail. The first 6 red rings are not interrupted on the dorsum by widening of the black ones; the next 2 are interrupted, followed by 10 unbroken ones, then 6 interrupted, 1 not interrupted, and 3 broken, with the last 2 before the vent clear red rings crossing 6 or 7 scale rows. The first 3 rings on the tail are not interrupted; the others are broken. In the forward part of body, the red medially is broader than the black or white and laterally is as broad as 2 blacks and 1 white combined. The forward red bands are scarlet or grenadine red, those toward the rear brazil red. The first red ring covers 6 scales medially and 6 laterally. Thereafter the red is laterally 4 scales wide and in the caudal half 3 scales, while on the meson it is reduced to 1 or 2. The cephalic bordering black rings may cover 2 to 2½ scales and caudally tend to meet on the meson. The first black ring, 3 to 3½ scales wide, crosses the last upper labial and rear half of 8th lower labial and is a complete ring crossing 3 rows of gulars and the 2nd, 3rd and 4th ventrals. The cephalic white rings cross 2 scale rows, others 1 or 1½ to 2. These light rings are white laterally with the median 10 to 12 scale rows pale olive-buff, except the first light ring which is marguerite yellow. This yellow ring crosses the tips of parietals, some of the temporals, the posterior ¾ of the 6th upper labial, and the anterior half of the 7th. It is twice as wide laterally as dorsally and extends as a white band ventrally across the 1st abdominal plate, gulars, posterior chin shields, and 3 lower labials with a white prong on the anterior chin shields, extending into the solid black lower labial border. This ring therefore sharply outlines the black of the head. The eye is black. Ventrally, the first 5 or 6 red bands are not interrupted by black; thereafter black speckles and spots grow increasingly prominent.

Habitat and habits: Grinnell and Grinnell (Calif., 1907) state: "This brilliantly-colored snake is of very general distribution in the large canyons all through our mountains. In most of its range it appears the commonest snake; at least it is the one to most often attract attention. Many are the stories we have heard of the animosity existing between this species and the rattlesnake, and of how the king snake always succeeds in coming out of an encounter victorious. All of this *may* be true, but we have never had an opportunity to verify by personal observation. Hence we are skeptical. The coral snake is a relatively small snake, of slow movement and perfectly harmless. Yet when roughly handled it bites to the best of its strength. The senior author has allowed himself to be bitten on two different occasions by king snakes and although the needle-sharp teeth sank deeply enough into his hand to draw blood, the resulting wounds healed promptly, with no unpleasant complications whatever. The snake is very similar to the poisonous coral snake of Mexico and the adjoining parts of the United States; hence it, too, is often supposed to be venomous."

In 1930 Bogert (Calif.) found it "moderately common in the canyons of both the Santa Monica and San Gabriel Mountains, occupying only the Upper Sonoran and Transition Zones."

Several notes have come from Klauber. In 1931(a) he placed it in the "forest." In 1934(a) he said: "It is essentially a mountain species, being seldom found below an altitude of 4,000 feet; it has been collected on all our peaks above this contour, except the desert range of the Santa Rosas. It has usually been called the Coral King Snake; but this name is objectionable because of possible confusion with the true Coral Snake, a venomous genus which does not occur in California." Later he (1943c) found one "in a dry farming habitat—a most unusual habitat for this snake." "Mountains," "high mountain areas," "timber in the mountains," "mountains above 4,500 feet" are some of his characterizations of its habitat.

Period of activity: "Sixteen Year Census"—Jan., 1 snake, Apr., 1; May, 8; June, 16; July, 12; Aug., 10; Sept., 1; Oct., 1. Total 50. Rank 21. Per cent catch 0.39. "A spring peak of seasonal activity is indicated for every species. This is seen to be earlier in Upper than in Lower Sonoran forms, since the former are, in their centers of dispersal, more accustomed to moisture and lower temperatures. But mountain species (e.g., *Lampropeltis multicincta*) have late peaks, since their habitat has a late season, even in this southern country" (Klauber, Gen., 1939a).

Breeding: Oviparous. Males 530–919 mm., females 583–917 mm.

Food: Lizards, snakes, mice. Van Denburgh (Gen., 1897), Bogert (Calif., 1930), Perkins.

Authorities:

Klauber, L. M. (Gen., 1939a; Calif., 1931a, 1934a, 1943c)
Linsdale, J. M. (Baja Calif., 1932)
Meek, S. E. (Calif., 1905)
Mosauer, W. (Calif., 1935)
Perkins, C. B. (Calif., 1938)
Van Denburgh, J. (Gen., 1897, 1922)

(See *L. z. multicincta* below for *zonata* versus *multicincta*.)

We add here L. Stejneger's (Ariz.) reaction of 1903. "It will be seen that I have ignored Blainville's name *Coluber zonatus,* which Boulenger, following Lockington's example, has recently revived for the present species."

1938, C. B. Perkins: "This is the most beautiful snake in San Diego County. It is often called Coral King Snake and is moderately rare and found in the timber in the mountains. . . . Often someone comes into the Reptile House saying that he has killed a poisonous Coral snake. It is explained that this poisonous snake does not occur in California, and although known to be in several states east of the Mississippi, is found only in Texas, New Mexico, and Arizona in the Southwest. Although both snakes are ringed with the same colors, the *order* of the rings is different. In the non-poisonous King snake there is a black ring on each side of the white ring (twice as many black rings as white), the colors being in this order—red, black, white, black, red, etc. In the *poisonous Coral snake,* the order is red, white, black, white, red, etc."

NEW COASTAL MOUNTAIN KING SNAKES

Lampropeltis zonata multifasciata Zweifel; *Lampropeltis zonata parvirubra* Zweifel; *Lampropeltis zonata pulchra* Zweifel

Zweifel (Calif., 1952) has divided the coastal mountain king snakes into 4 subspecies: *L. z. zonata, L. z. multifasciata, L. z. parvirubra,* and *L. z. pulchra.* Quite likely our plate of *L. z. zonata* is Zweifel's *pulchra.* In the light of his imposing list of acknowledgments to western herpetologic scholars and advisers, we should instantly accept this analysis. It seems to be a careful study, but being conservative we wonder whether the *Diadophis amabilis* complex was the model or whether some student will ever submit *L. z. multicincta* to the same fragmentation. What about the black and white Sierran *L. z. multicincta* with no red rings? A California scientist can best answer these questions. For this reason and for the sake of completeness, we quote Zweifel's key:

"A. Posterior margin of first white ring back of angle of mouth.   B.
    Posterior margin of first white ring on or anterior to last supralabial. D.
"B. Sixty per cent or more of body triads with lateral red areas dorsally confluent, splitting triads.   C.
    Less than 60 per cent of body triads with red areas dorsally confluent, snout black.   *multicincta*
"C. Snout with red markings, especially on internasals and prefrontals; black of triads greatly restricted laterally.   *multifasciata*
    Snout dark, without red markings; black of triads usually more than one scale wide laterally.   *zonata*
"D. Snout with red markings, especially on internasals and prefrontals. E.
    Snout dark, without red markings.   F.
"E. Usually less than 41 body triads.   *multifasciata*
    More than 40 body triads.   *agalma*
"F. No red in pattern.   *herrerae*
    Red in pattern.   G.
"G. 36 or fewer body triads.   *pulchra*
    37 or more body triads.   *parvirubra.*"

South of the northern intergradation with *L. z. multicincta* Zweifel's 4 regions are roughly these:

zonata zonata: North of San Francisco Bay in Lake, Mendicino, Napa, and

Fig. 123. *Lampropeltis zonata zonata,*
San Diego, Calif., C. B. Perkins.

Fig. 124. *Lampropeltis z. multicincta,*
Yosemite Nat. Park, Calif., C. A. Harwell.

Sonoma Cos. *z multifasciata:* South of San Francisco Bay from Santa Clara
Co. to Ventura Co. or extreme w. edge of Los Angeles Co. *z. parvirubra:* Los
Angeles Co., s.w. San Bernardino Co., and n. cent. Riverside Co. *z. pulchra:*
Coastal Los Angeles Co., border of Orange and Riverside Cos., and San Di-
ego Co.

Coral king snake (20—Atsatt 1913), **Sierra coral king snake** (Klauber)

Lampropeltis zonata multicincta (Yarrow) 1882. Figs. 124, 125; Map 31

Other common names: Arizona king snake; (California) coral snake; California king snake (4—Van Denburgh 1897); corral snake; (Eisen's) king snake (Yarrow 1882); harlequin snake; mountain king snake (3— Klauber 1934); red milk snake (3); ringed king snake (3—Klauber 1934); red milk snake (3); ringed king snake; ring snake; Sonoran king snake; western coral king snake (3).

Range: Sierra Nevada Mts. of Kern Co., Calif., n. to Washington state. Intergrades with *L. z. zonata* at its n. and s. ends.—Calif.; Ore.; Wash. *Elevation*—400 to 8,000 feet, mostly 4,000 or more feet. Some of the numerous records are : 100 feet (Johnson, Wash., 1939); 1,410, 4,900, 5,500, 5,600, 6,000 8,000 feet (Van Denburgh); 3,600 feet (Wright, Calif., 1921); 6,000 feet (Hall and Grinnell, Calif., 1919).

Size: Adults, 13.5–40 inches.

Longevity: 11 years 4 months (Perkins, Gen., 1951).

Distinctive characteristics: A medium-sized, tricolored (scarlet or grenadine red, black, white, or deep olive-buff) snake. Klauber (Calif., 1943c) characterizes it thus: "In the Sierra pattern the 2 black boundary rings usually coalesce dorsally, thus restricting the red marks to paired lateral blotches, or the red may even be completely suppressed." Also: "More than half of the triad rings of the body entirely black or with lateral red areas which are not confluent dorsally. Usually some red areas laterally or dorsally; last supralabial untouched by black posteriorly."

Color: A snake from Mather, Calif., received from G. Streisinger, Aug. 16, 1945. The pattern is one of rings—red, black, white, the black separating the red and white. The white rings are of uniform width from meson to venter; the black ones widen on the meson. In this specimen there are 32 red rings on the body and 8 on the tail (not counting the tip). The first 4 red rings are not broken by black on the dorsum, the next 4 are broken by black, and successively thereafter 4 are clear, 4 broken, 3 clear, 7 broken by black, 2 clear, 2 broken, 2 clear. On the tail, all but one are broken by black encroachments on the meson. The red rings are scarlet or grenadine red in the cephalic portion and brazil red caudally, crossing the belly on 3 ventrals or sometimes 2 and only rarely flecked or broken with black. The black rings are mostly 2–2½ scales wide on the dorsum, narrowing to 1 scale at the venter, which it crosses on 1 ventral plate or may be interrupted by white on mid-venter. Two black rings often widen dorsally, meeting occasionally, and may sometimes pinch out the red entirely on one or both sides. When entirely, one has the condition which Dr. Klauber described. The first black ring is 3–3½ scales wide on the dorsum, crossing the head 2 scales caudad of the last upper labial and crossing the venter as a narrow caudal border of the second ventral. In the light rings, the scales are white-edged with deep olive-buff centers and bases for about 12 scale rows and then entirely white on lower sides, crossing the venter on 2 plates or sometimes on 3. The first light ring is olive-buff, covers 2½ scale rows on the meson, crosses the lateral edge of parietals extending to the 2nd row of temporals, involving them and the 6th and 7th upper labials. The same color extends forward about to the front margin of the anterior chin shields and on to the posterior 4 lower labials. This area is much wider laterally, covering the gulars and crossing the 1st abdominal plate. The lower edges of the 3rd, 4th and 5th upper labials and the cephalic lower labials are white heavily clouded with black. The eye is black.

Habitat: Authors have ascribed them to forests, coniferous forests, forest floors, and chaparral-covered hillsides. Johnson (Wash., 1939) described the place of a capture: "The immediate environment of the place is as follows: Columbia River, one eighth mile to the south, railroad paralleling highway, above which is a spring, which is dry in summer, comes over a high basaltic cliff and rock slide; much poison oak, scrub oak and general brush, between cliff and road" where it was killed.

Grinnell and Storer (Calif., 1924) wrote of it in Yosemite thus: "Inhabits chiefly shaded slopes beneath golden oaks. . . . Our Coral King Snake is of quiet, sluggish behavior, so that it is likely to excite interest only by reason of its brilliant coloration. If a person happens to come upon one of these snakes while the latter is resting on the soft dust of a trail, the reptile is prone to remain motionless, with its body in a series of rounded loops. If disturbed it will glide away slowly into the cover of nearby rocks or leafy litter. If picked up, its demeanor is docile; in other words, it can be handled, according to our experience, with absolute impunity."

Period of activity: *First appearance*—Gunnison gave Apr. 4, 1935, in Sequoia National Park; Johnson, May 13, 1938, in Washington. MVZ gives Mar. 21 to Dec. 17.

Breeding: Oviparous, males 507–850 mm., females 547–973 mm.

Eggs, Young—We know of no records of its eggs or young. The smallest specimen we have seen measured 257 mm., which may be beyond hatching. At MVZ we observed 4 of approximately the same size at different dates as follows: 350 mm., June 15, 1928; 345 mm., July 5, 1908; 360 mm., Sept. 16, 1932; 350 mm., Oct. 9, 1926.

Food: Snakes. Van Denburgh, Grinnell and Storer (Calif., 1924). "The King Snake is said to destroy many rattlers and other snakes. I have never been able to verify this, although I have tried with captive specimens" (Van Denburgh, Gen., 1922).

Field notes: (The first of this form that we saw were live specimens shipped to us from the first Yosemite-ranger school years.)

July 22, 1934: Made Yosemite Valley floor, went to the Museum. Met Harwell. They had 2 *Clemmys marmorata* from lower levels, 1 *Rana boyli sierrae*, 3 *Lampropeltis multicinctus*, and 3 of the black and white phase of *multicincta*. They also have *L. getulus boyli* that one can compare with the odd black and white *multicincta*.

Read David Starr Jordan's "Old rattler and the king snake," *Popular Science Monthly,* **56** (Jan. 23): 371, and for a California quail-and-king-snake story, R. H. Ellis' "Snakes and their meals," *Blackwood's,* **136** (1935): 325.

Authorities:

Blainville, H. D. de (Baja Calif., 1835)   Lockington, W. N. (Calif., 1871)
Burt, C. E. (Calif., 1936)   Peters, J. L. (Calif., 1938)
Gordon, K. (Ore., 1935)   Van Denburgh, J. (Gen., 1922)
Klauber, L. M. (Calif., 1942b, 1943c)   Yarrow, H. C. (Calif., 1883)
Linsdale, J. M. (Baja Calif., 1932)

For an understanding of the names of this form before 1943, consult De Blainville, *Coluber (Zacholus) zonatus;* Lockington, *Bellophis zonatus;* Yarrow; Linsdale; Burt; and Peters.

1876, W. N. Lockington, *Bellophis zonatus:* "The difference in number between the red and white rings arises from the fact that the red rings die out upon the hinder part of the tail which has white rings only. . . . The red rings in many cases do not cross the back, but are divided by the junction of a pair of black rings. The black rings become wider on the centre of the back, approaching and in most cases, joining each other in pairs, but always at the expense of the red rings, the white rings being invariably continuous with the white of the abdomen. There are traces of red on parts of the abdomen, and the black rings can generally be partially traced across the abdominal scutellae."

1943, L. M. Klauber: "The question whether the specific name of the coral king snakes of the Pacific Coast should be *multicincta* or *zonata* has been the subject of considerable argument, hinging upon the uncertainty of identification of the type specimen of *Coluber (Zacholus) zonatus* Blainville 1835, and the alternative applicability of *Bellophis zonatus* Lockington 1877. I shall not review this question, which will be found fully discussed in the papers by C. E. Burt (1936) and J. L. Peters (1938). Personally, I have adopted the view that the identity of the Blainville specimen is indeterminate and that Lockington's name cannot be used for reasons advanced by Peters. Those who disagree may assign to the coastal form, *L. zonata zonata* to the coastal form, *L. zonata multicincta* to the Sierran, and *L. zonata agalma* to that of the San Pedro Martirs."

1944: We have seen all the *agalma* and *herrarae* materials and know from life the typical *multicincta* and *multifasciata* races and the extreme black and white Yosemite form from 1925 onwards. Neither school entirely satisfies us. We employ nomenclatorially the Stejneger–Peters–Klauber–Schmidt *multicincta,* but zoologically we are quite well satisfied that Blainville's and Lock-

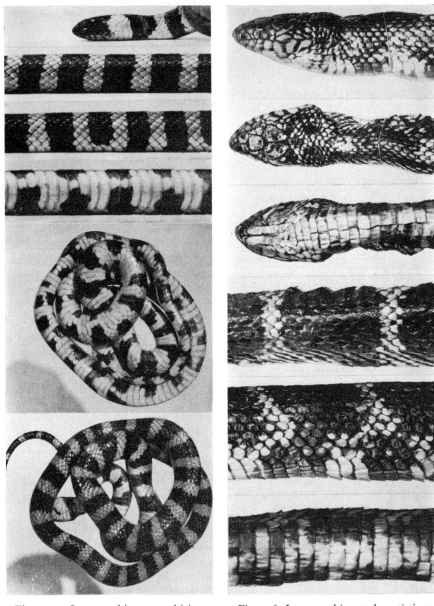

Fig. 125. *Lampropeltis z. multicincta,* Yosemite Nat. Park, Calif., C. A. Harwell.

Fig. 126. *Lampropeltis getulus sticticeps,* MCZ, photos by G. Nelson.

ington's *zonatus* and Yarrow's *multicincta* are the same. We are old enough to recall that Van Denburgh employed *L. zonata* and quite likely saw Lockington's types in the California Academy of Science. We are very glad the three authorities (Blainville, Lockington, Yarrow) did not accidentally have for their types *herrarae, agalma,* or the aberrant black and white Yosemite variations, or the argument might even involve *boyli–californiae* or *nitida–conjuncta.*

1949: C. B. Perkins (Gen.) in his key employs *Lampropeltis zonata multicincta* (Yarrow) for the Sierra form and *Lampropeltis zonata zonata* (Lockington ex Blainville) for the coastal form.

PROBLEMATICAL FORM
Banks king snake, Okracoke king snake

Lampropeltis getulus sticticeps (Barbour and Engels) 1942. Fig. 126; Map 33
(Probably *L. getulus getulus*)

Range: Knoll midway between Okracoke Inlet and Hatteras Inlet, Okracoke Island, N.C. *Elevation*—Sea level.

Size: The sole specimen measures 1,152 mm. or 46$^+$ inches.

Distinctive characteristics: "This form may be distinguished at once from *Lampropeltis getulus getulus* by it broader and flatter head, heavily marked with white; large white spots are to be found on the labials and along the sides of the body; the interior rings appear in form of spots, and the chain-like pattern does not begin until well down the body, and from then on the familiar pattern is composed of white bands averaging 2½ to 3 times as broad as the bands in the typical form; the 3 anterior spots are shown in the figure. These are followed by 24 bars on the body, whereas there are 1 bar and 9 spots on the tail. There are 21 rows of scales, 104 ventrals, 44 caudals, although we suspect that the tip of the tail has been lost" (Barbour and Engels).

Field notes: 1944: Through Barbour and Norton, we examined and secured photos of the lone type. At that time we observed that this specimen was seemingly thinner and more steep-sided than normal; the head flatter, possibly the face more oblique. There are first 3 dorsal spots, then 24 dorsal saddles, then 9 dorsal spots on the tail. The dark interspaces behind white spots are 6 scales wide, the white saddle is more than half of 2 scales. The tail tip is gone.

1950: In the light of Coues and Yarrow's observation in 1878 that it was "very common," we are hesitant to pronounce on one specimen. We have talked with Engels, and he has given us the circumstances of its discovery and description. Also in view of the indeterminate position of the rat snake and water snakes of the bars we await more evidence. If we cannot possibly pronounce on the water snake which we have seen alive from the type locality and a northern bar, we must not pass on this form yet.

Authorities:

Barbour, T., and W. L. Engels (N.C., 1942)

Coues, E., and H. C. Yarrow (N.C., 1878)

Engels, W. L. (N.C., 1942)

1878, E. Coues and H. C. Yarrow: We have not examined their material. Did they save any? This account may have some pertinence to this new form. "*Ophibolus getulus sayi,* Holbrook. King Snake. Corn Snake. Thunder Snake. Very common on islands and on mainland. This serpent is called 'King Snake' by the residents, who state that it frequently destroys both rattlesnakes and moccasins, eating its victims after the conflict is over, and for this reason it is held in great esteem and carefully protected. The fight which takes place between *Crotalus* and *Ophibolus* has been seen by several persons, and was described as follows: So soon as the rattlesnake sees his enemy, he endeavors to escape, if possible, and failing to effect his retreat, instantly throws his body into coils. The king snake approaches swiftly, and moves around the rattlesnake in a circle, gradually drawing nearer and nearer, the rattlesnake following his motion with his head. This circular movement of his antagonist appears finally to disconcert him, for after a time it is noticed his movements are less energetic and finally, in an unguarded moment, *Ophibolus* throws himself with lightning rapidity upon him and chokes him to death, pulls his body apart, and devours him. In captivity they are very gentle, and it requires very severe provocation to induce one to bite. Several specimens which were kept in a large box could not be induced to eat either mice, frogs, or toads, but as several fine specimens of *Ophisaurus ventralis* (Daud.), kept in the same box, soon disappeared, it was easy to account for the apparent want of appetite. In fact, a large male was found in the act of devouring one of the 'glass snakes.' It is believed that other species of *Ophiboli,* such as *O. doliatus* and *triangulus,* live upon the islands as well as the mainland, but none have been noticed."

1942, T. Barbour and W. L. Engels: "As is well known, the sandy, almost waterless, islands off the Carolina coast have a very limited and naturally somewhat highly specialized fauna and but relatively few forms have been able to adapt themselves to this highly rigorous environment. The first of the novelties may be called *Lampropeltis getulus sticticeps.* . . . At first sight this might seem slender evidence for describing a new race, but the evidence that we deal here with a well-marked physiological form is so interesting that this fact alone would warrant its being named. For this snake, unlike all its allies, is not ophiophagous. Kept in captivity for a long time, as it was, it refused every sort of snake offered it for food and fed regularly on mice. Probably it was forced to do this on an island where, as far as is known, other snakes are absent and beach mice swarm. A glance at the figures will show how extraordinarily *Pituophis*-like is the head of the new form, and *Pituophis,* of course, is a rodent feeder. Whereas king snakes normally twine about their prey, this snake has acquired the *Coluber*-like habit of seizing its prey and then dragging it to some position where it may be pressed to death with the body against some firmly set object. Thus its feeding habits are those of a Black Snake, and not a King Snake. This fact was confirmed by repeated experiments of the junior author."

1942, W. L. Engels: "Nothing more definite can be said at present regarding the age of these bars than that they are almost certainly post Pleistocene in origin. It is probable that they are not more than 20,000—nor less than 5,000—years old. . . . Thirty-five species of tetrapod vertebrates . . . occur on the island. By comparison, more than 200 species of the same group breed in the Coastal Plain of North Carolina."

ANNULATED SNAKES

Genus *LEPTODEIRA* Fitzinger (Fig. 25)

The United States form: Size medium, 10–32 inches; head distinct with a large bulge just back of eyes where temporal scales are much larger than on dorsum of neck; tail less than ¼ total length; anal divided; scales smooth with apical pits usually paired, in rows 21–23 (26 (25)–21–23–15), with row 1 much wider than others; preoculars contact frontal, thereby separating supraocular and prefrontal; supraoculars wide so that frontal covers about ½ interocular space; chin shields contact 6 labials; anterior and posterior chin shields about equal, posterior spreading with outer margins following line of lower labials and with 1 row of gulars between tips and ventrals; eye has large vertical and elliptical pupil; labials 8 upper and 10 lower; preoculars 3; postoculars 2; loreal 1; temporals 1 + 2 + 3; dorsal background ochraceous-orange to apricot buff crossed by 21–24 dark brown saddle spots on body, 9–15 on tail; venter orange; maxillary teeth 15–18 with 2 enlarged strongly grooved fangs in rear; "hemipenis undivided with bifurcate sulcus spermaticus and numerous spines below and calyces above. The latter present a free margin to the superior spinous region, that is, the organ is capitate" (Cope, Gen., 1900). Ventrals 177–207; caudals 63–82. Synonyms: *Dipsas, Eteirodipsas, Leptodira, Sibon.*

Annulated snake (5—Ditmars 1907), **Ringed snake** (3—Yarrow 1882)

Leptodeira annulata septentrionalis (Kennicott) 1859. Fig. 127; Map 34

Other common names: Bush snake; nocturnal tree snake; (northern) cat-eyed snake.

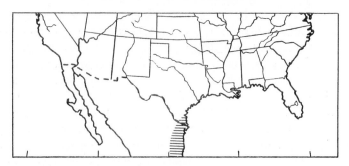

Map 34. *Leptodeira annulata septentrionalis.*

Range: Extreme s. Texas into Tamaulipas and Nuevo León, s. to n. Vera-cruz, Mex.—U.S.A.: Tex. Mex.: Hidalgo, Nuevo León, Querétaro, San Luis Potosí, Tamaulipas, Veracruz. *Elevation*—Sea level to 2,000 or 3,000 feet.

Size: Adults, 15–32 inches.

Longevity: One snake lived 10 years before its escape; 3 years 6 months (Conant and Hudson, Gen., 1949); 4 years 11 months 21 days (Flower, Gen., 1925).

Distinctive characteristics: "This large robust form is represented in our collection by 3 specimens. . . . This form may be diagnosed by the presence of 3 preoculars (presuboculars); by the large black blotches touching or reaching near the 1st scale row; the high number of ventrals and subcaudals (186 to 197; 63 to 79, combination of data given by Dunn [1936] and my own data), and by the presence of more or less pigment on the posterior edges of the ventrals; the scale count reduces to 15 in front of the anus. There is a black spot on the posterior edges of the parietals, usually confluent with an indistinct head pattern" (Taylor, Tex., 1938).

Subsequent papers revise the scalation to ventrals 186–206; caudals 63–94; scale formula 21-23-17; spots on body 22–33, spots on tail 12–19.

Color: A snake taken Jan. 2, 1939, one mile from Raymondville, north of Edinburg, Tex., and received from S. Mulaik. The background of the back is ochraceous-orange to apricot buff, this showing as clear spots on the mid-dorsum covering 5 or 6 scales transversely and 1½ to 2 scales longitudinally. As this background widens on the sides to cover 5 or 6 scales at the 1st rows, it is washed with dark, thus becoming buffy olive for 7 or 8 scale rows. The back is crossed by 21 saddles on the body of which 2 are doublt spots form-ing long hourglass-shaped saddles crossing 17 scale rows. One of these is on the neck, the other on the mid-portion of the body. These dorsal spots are mostly rhomboidal with the lower corners rounded, and extend onto the upper edge of the 1st row of scales, but sometimes reaching the ventrals. These spots are raw umber with narrow black borders which are broadest on middorsum. The neck spot is entirely black. There are 9 spots on the tail.

The light band across the rear of the head is 3½ to 4 scales broad. Back of the interparietal suture line it is clear ochraceous-orange to apricot buff. The same color extends over the whole temporal region, the upper temporals each marked with a black center. The whole of the 1st temporal, the front border of the lower temporal of the 2nd row, and the upper borders of the 7th and 8th upper labials are crossed by an irregular black vitta. The plates of the head back of the eye are tawny-olive, becoming saccardo's umber ahead of the eyes. These plates are heavily flecked with black. The 1st and 2nd rows of scales on the neck and the rearmost upper and lower labials are clear antimony yellow. The first 6 upper labials are yellow ocher very heavily clouded with raw umber or mummy brown. The eye is old gold with a vertical pupil. The lower side of the head is pure white, the color grading caudad through ochraceous-buff and ochraceous-orange to solid ochraceous-salmon which extends to the vent. The central part of the venter is immaculate, the ends of the ventrals bearing a few flecks. The underside of the tail is light ochraceous-salmon quite heavily flecked with dark.

Habitat: Our pet came from a caliche pit. This form occurs from the southern tip of Texas southward in a district dubbed Tamaulipan, northern Mexican, subtropical, Texas semidesert, thorn savannah, coastal plain, and temperate rain forest.

Breeding: Oviparous. Males to 818 mm., females to 825 mm. Haines in 1940 published a paper on delayed fertilization in *Leptoderia annulata polysticta*. To us this is very interesting because 30 or more years ago we began to think that delayed fertilization, autumnal matings in turtles and snakes, turtles approaching adulthood with both sexual parts, and many more such nonrecognized phenomena might be possible. Since then some of our students—Rahn, Trapido, Wimsatt, and others—have expanded these topics. But in many ways the observations of Haines were the most startling. In short, his conclusion was that the female studied produced fertile eggs at least 5 years after the last possible copulation.

Eggs—Noguchi (Gen.) in 1909 called the form oviparous. The only record from earlier literature that we can find is from Ditmars in 1907; he has a captive laying 12 eggs in a sandy hollow under a stone. In 1949, Taylor recorded a 825-mm. female from San Luis Potosí which had 9 eggs in the oviducts. *Young*—We know of no records of newborn young. The two smallest we ever saw are Lt. Couch's (USNM 4267) 183-mm. and G. Wurdemann's (USMN 1312) 237-mm. specimens.

Food: Frogs, snakes, lizards, mice. Ditmars, Kapp. (see below).

Field notes: Mrs. Kay Kapp, who has cared for our pet snake several years, gave us the following two manuscript accounts: "We have had this snake for about 7 years this spring [1946]. It eats readily whenever food is offered unless it should be a day or two immediately after eating. Actually, we feed about once every 3 or 4 weeks during the winter, when frogs are not so easily obtained. In the summer it may be fed as often as once a week. So far, none of the mice or small rats offered have ever been eaten. Amphibians are the usual diet, *Rana pipiens* being the species most easily obtained, especially during the winter. Tadpoles are also relished, but after consuming half a dozen, it will eagerly accept a large frog. A few odd salamanders have been fed at intervals and eaten, but not as eagerly, perhaps because they are not as active and not as quickly noticed. Some lizards have also been taken. This snake seems to have no difficulty with a large *Rana pipiens,* although occasionally several different positions are tried before swallowing is accomplished. I believe the first food given was either a small lizard or salamander; no record was kept of it. It will stay curled in the water dish for days at a time, but whether there is water in the dish or not does not seem to matter. Shedding takes place every 2 or 3 months on the average, and is accomplished quite easily, although when the cloudiness is most evident, wet paper towels are usually placed in the cage to supply sufficient moisture. We have observed that there is a period in the latter part of the summer when food is refused. This is a time when food is most plentiful and easiest (for us) to obtain. Does this mean that in nature this species is one that goes into aestivation during the hottest part of the year? Most often, snakes kept here have refused food during the winter months, if at all, but the *Leptodeira* eats throughout the winter. We have been unable to detect any effect of its poison on the animals eaten."

"The Cornell Zoology Laboratory has had a *Leptodeira septentrionalis* from Texas for the past 10 years [1938–1948] which is a most satisfactory reptile pet. On the occasion of his recapture after he had escaped and had been at large in the laboratory for several weeks he showed mild resentment, but that is the only time in his history here that he hasn't been most amiable. At first, while attempting to discover what food was acceptable, we had a near tragedy when a small mouse put in his cage for food chewed him badly so that he still carries some scars after nearly 10 years. In that way we discovered, contrary to the records, that mammals were not acceptable. The main diet has turned out to be frogs and tadpoles, although an occasional lizard, salamander, or fish has been eaten. Unlike most snakes, he often eats a day or so before shedding and always takes food eagerly except after recent heavy feeding. The skin is shed frequently and seems to have direct relationship to feeding; the more food consumed, the more often shedding takes place. During the hottest two months of the year, this snake invariably refuses all food."

Authorities:

Ditmars, R. L. (Gen., 1936)
Dunn, E. R. (Gen., 1936)
Haines, T. P. (Gen., 1940)

Kennicott, R., in Baird (Tex., 1859)
Taylor, E. H. (Gen., 1940; Tex., 1938, 1949, 1950)

MUD SNAKES

Genus *LIODYTES* (Fig. 22)

Size small medium, 9–26 inches; body short and stout; head slightly distinct; tail short; maxillary teeth 16–18, posterior ones longer, with diastema; mandibular teeth 18–20; scales in 19 rows, first 3 rows larger, smooth on body (or slightly keeled), pits normally absent, 5 or more scale rows on tail keeled; anal divided; cephalic plates normal except the single internasal, the nasals meeting behind the rostral; oculars 1–3; loreal 1; labials upper 8 (7), lower 11 (10); temporals 1 + 2; ventrals 121–129; caudals 58–63; venter salmon with or without midventral row of spots; hemipenis—sulcus undivided; "transversely plicated (divided) (Flabellati), plicae not papillose; diacranterian. *Helicops*." (Cope, Gen., 1900). Synonym: *Helicops*.

KEY TO THE GENUS *LIODYTES*

a. Ventral surface from throat to tail tip clear, light ochraceous-salmon.

L. alleni alleni

aa. Ventral surface with distinct row of midventral black spots or an indistinct line there on salmon-buff ground.   *L. a. lineapiatus*

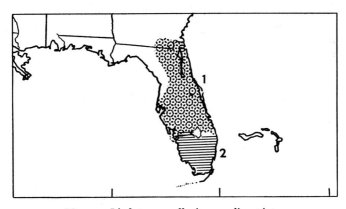

Map 35. *Liodytes*—1, *alleni*; 2, *a. lineapiatus*.

Allen's snake (6—Yarrow 1882), **Allen's mud snake** (6—Wachtel)
Liodytes alleni alleni (Garman) 1874. Fig. 128; Map 35

Other common names: Allen's helicops; (Florida) swamp snake; mud snake.

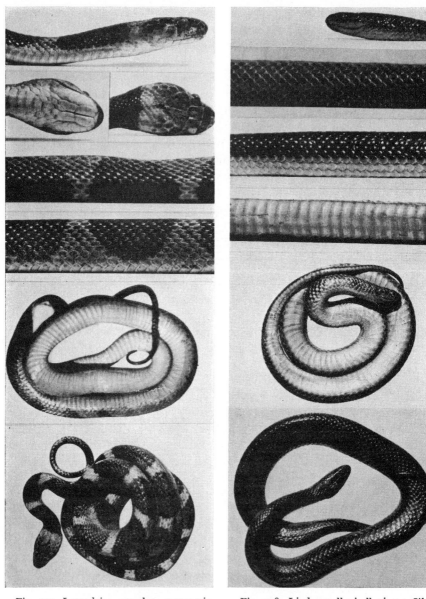

Fig. 127. *Leptodeira annulata septentrionalis,* Raymondville, Tex., S. Mulaik.

Fig. 128. *Liodytes alleni alleni:* 1,3, Silver Springs, Fla., E. R. Allen; 2,4–6, Eustis, Fla., O. C. Van Hyning.

Range: Okefinokee Swamp, Ga., to Charlotte and n. Dade Cos., Fla.—Fla.; Ga. *Elevation*—Sea level to 150–250 feet.

Size: Adults, 9–26 inches.

Distinctive characteristics: A small-medium iridescent aquatic burrower with buffy or salmon-orange belly. Down the back are 3 stripes of olive or natal brown with bluish or violet reflection. The head and neck are dark olive; labials and lower head surfaces yellow.

Color: A snake taken from Billy Lake, Okefinokee Swamp, Ga., June 20, 1921. Like other burrowers, the back of this snake is very glossy. There is a dorsal band of olive-brown or natal brown, and also a lateral stripe 2 scales in width of natal brown and a scale's width above of dark olive-buff. These darker stripes are iridescent with a metallic cornflower blue, soft bluish violet, methyl blue to spectrum violet, or even violet-purple. The first 3 scale rows of the side are deep olive-buff with rear edges of olive-buff. The head and upper neck are deep to dark olive. The upper labials, part of rostral and lower head surfaces are yellow ocher to primuline yellow. The iris is heavily spotted with old gold or olive-yellow. The ventral surface of the snake from throat to tail tip is light ochraceous-salmon.

Habitat and habits: Cope (Fla., 1889) reported *Liodytes alleni* "not uncommon throughout the peninsula." See also Loennberg under "Enemies." Referring to Alachua County, Van Hyning in 1933 (Fla.) very tersely wrote: "In aquatic vegetation and burrowing in muck; locally common." The next person to know it well was Carr, who in 1940 summarized thus: *"Habitat—* marshes and bayheads; sloughs and sphagnum bogs; among water-hyacinth roots in shallow water. *Abundance—*Fairly common locally; half a dozen or more are often taken in an afternoon from masses of water hyacinths along the shore of Payne's Prairie. *Habits—*Probably the most aquatic Florida snake; I believe many of them remain permanently in the water. While wading along a little bay head ditch in Lake County I saw an *alleni* withdraw its head quickly into the mass of *Utricularia* which choked the stream; locating the hole through which the head had protruded, I felt around and found a well-defined tunnel in the tightly packed vegetation, connecting with another tunnel in the mucky bank a foot beneath the surface. Forcing my hand nearly the length of my arm along this second tunnel, I found the snake coiled in a little cavity at the end. Six other specimens were taken on the same afternoon under almost identical conditions." In his study of the water hyacinth habitat Goin (Fla., 1943) said that *L. alleni* is "probably the most aquatic snake in Florida and is fairly common among the water hyacinth roots in shallow water." Finally, Auffenberg wrote: "I have occasionally caught them under rotten cypress logs in Volusia County, Florida. Fresh water marshes, canals, sloughs, open hyacinth 'prairies,' shallow lakes, and drainage ditches are the most frequent habitats, although they are occasionally taken in larger lakes, cypress ponds, streams of varying sizes, and flatwoods ponds."

This form falls in the peninsular Floridan part of Sargent's Coast Pine belt. It is in the Florida section of Fenniman's Coastal Plain. Other ecological characterizations are temperate rain forest, southeast coniferous area, pine barren strand vegetation, southeastern mesophytic evergreen forest, and Sabalian zone.

Period of activity: "They are frequently found deep in sphagnum bog in winter" (Carr).

Breeding: Viviparous. Males (401)–600 mm., females (401)–652 mm. *Sexual dimorphism*—Blanchard (Gen., 1931) holds that the males have keellike ridges on dorsal scales of the anal region. *Young*—6–34. The only record we know before 1950 is Brimley's (Gen., 1903) of 6 young in August, 1899. This was in the period when C. S. and H. H. Brimley were in the natural-history supply business with collectors all over the south to Texas. We have seen 3 young specimens, one 136 mm. (tail 33), one 164 mm. (tail 39), and one 176 mm. (tail 40). In 1950 Tschambers (Fla., 1950) gave the following data: "A gravid female measuring 25¾ inches was caught crawling about the bank of a drainage ditch during the evening following a late rain near Okeechobee City, Florida, by R. Marlin Perkins on the 20th of March. . . . Dissection revealed 34¾-inch embryos in the oviducts."

In 1951 Neill (Gen., 1951) reported that "dissection of these specimens gave the following embryo counts of 6, 6, 7, 9, 9, and 12."

Food: Crayfish, *Pseudobronchus*. Van Hyning, Carr.

Field notes: June 20, 1921: *Liodytes alleni* (*Helicops alleni*). Like other burrowers it is glistening or glossy in back scales. It will wrap its tail around my finger and then draw its body very close.

June 21, 1921: To No. 60 to collect maiden cane, sphagnum, *Eriocaulon*, and floating mats of *Polygonum*. We rowed to the edge of Billy Lake. Then we hurriedly pulled into the boat all the maiden cane we could. In the bottom of the boat we took . . . one fine snake *Liodytes* (*Helicops*) *alleni*. At first I didn't know but that it might be *Natrix grahami*. This species was never taken north of Florida before. In the boat it opened its mouth, and we thought it was about to bite. We noticed the same tendency when we handled it or photoed it.

About this same period we found that they were in isolated mats in mid-pond in cypress ponds. We would bring a net up under such a mat, catching frogs, *Amphiuma*, *Siren*, *Pseudobranchus*, several fish, and *Liodytes alleni*.

Authorities:

Auffenberg, W. (Fla., 1950)

Brimley, C. S. (Gen., 1903; N.C., 1941–42)

Carr, A. F., Jr. (Fla., 1940a)

Cope, E. D. (Fla., 1877)

Garman, S. W. (Fla., 1874)

Loennberg, E. (Fla., 1895)

Van Hyning, O. C. (Fla., 1932)

Everglades swamp snake

Liodytes alleni lineapiatus Auffenberg 1950. Map 35

Another common name: Mud snake.

Range: "Southern Florida; central Glades County to extreme south Florida, excluding the Floridian keys. It has been recorded from the following counties: Dade, Glades, Broward, and Collier. Further collecting in Monroe, Palm Beach and Hendry Counties should show that the form inhabiting those areas is *lineapiatus*. Carr records *Liodytes* from Charlotte, Okeechobee and Palm Beach Counties. The 2 former counties are probably in the area of intergradation. The latter county is within the range of the new form" (Auffenberg). *Elevation*—Sea level to 50 feet.

Size: "For *lineapiatus* I have taken the following measurements: largest female 532 mm., largest male 420 mm. and an average length for the subspecies of 356 mm. In the head—total length measurements of *alleni* and *lineapiatus* have approximately the same ratio" (Auffenberg).

Distinctive characteristics: "Differs from typical *alleni alleni* in having a row of very distinct midventral black spots, or an indistinct line as in the specimens from the vicinity of Royal Palm State Park" (Auffenberg).

Habitat: Quite manifestly Barbour's observations near West Palm Beach must refer to this form. They are: "A few specimens of *Liodytes alleni* were secured all at exactly the same spot. They were found sunning themselves in the road where the Okeechobee Road runs past a small pond about 2 miles back of West Palm Beach. No examples were observed in hundreds of other similar situations where they might have been expected to occur. The species is very rare and local."

Breeding: Viviparous. Males (356)–420 mm., females (356)–532 mm.

Authorities:

Auffenberg, W. (Fla., 1950)   Barbour, T. (Fla., 1920a)

1950, W. Auffenburg: "In May 1948, I received from Mr. L. H. Babbitt of Petersham, Mass., a specimen of *Liodytes alleni* from the southern portion of the Florida peninsula which appears sufficiently distinct to warrant subspecific designation. Since then 10 more specimens have come to my attention, 3 of which I have used as paratypes. The new form may be termed: *Liodytes alleni lineapiatus* subs. nov."

WHIP SNAKES

Genus *MASTICOPHIS* Baird and Girard (Fig. 23)

Size large to very large, 20–96 inches; long and slender; head narrow in proportion to its length, .41–.44; anal divided; scale rows 17 or 15 in midbody and 13, 12, 11 at posterior end; scales smooth with apical pits; nasals 2; frontal concave on sides, not wider or but slightly wider than supra-oculars; posterior chin shields spreading at least at tips with 2–3 rows of gulars between tips and ventrals; lower preocular very small and wedged between adjacent upper labials; eye over upper labials 4 + 5; upper labials

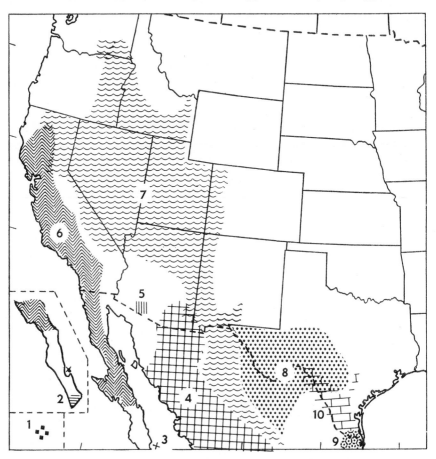

Map 36. *Masticophis*—1, *anthonyi;* 2, *aurigulus;* 3, *barbouri;* 4, *b. bilineatus;* 5, *b. lineo-latus;* 6, *l. lateralis;* 7, *t. taeniatus;* 8, *t. ornatus;* 9, *t. ruthveni;* 10, *t. schotti.*

8 (when varied plate 3 involved); lower labials 9 (*M. bilineatus* 10, rarely 11 or 8); a throat pattern of dark spots often extending forward on head (some heads of *M. flagellum* and *M. f. piceus* black); dorsal color striped, banded, dotted, and some uniform; venter usually with some pink to coral red in life; preocular with a central white spot except in some individuals in *M. flagellum* group; maxillary teeth 16–23; hemipenis—stout, rounded, slightly bilobed; sulcus simple; tip smooth; 9–14 rows fringed calyces; 2–5

rows of spines numbering 30–75. In *taeniatus* group *ruthveni* and *schotti* are deeper lobed, *taeniatus* slightly so; the rows of spines 3–5, rows of calyces 8–10. In *flagellum* group hemipenis varies less than in *taeniatus* group; (*f. piceus*) spines 30–37 in 2–3 rows; calyces in 13–14 rows, much more strongly fringed near the spinous tract. Ventrals 183–214; caudals 94–160. Synonyms: *Bascanion, Bascanium, Coluber, Coryphodon, Drymobius, Herpetodryas, Leptophis, Liophis, Natrix, Psammophis, Zamenis.*

KEY TO THE GENUS *MASTICOPHIS*

Scale rows 15 or 17; head narrow in proportion to length; scale rows at posterior end of body 13, 12, 11; upper labials 8; throat usually spotted; venter usually with some pink to coral red; long slender snakes. Ventrals 183–214. Caudals 94–160.

a. With 1 or more lateral stripes; white spot on loreal in adults; snout prominent, rather pointed, somewhat flattened above and below; rear ventrals and tail with pink.

  b. Scale rows 15; formula 15–13–12–11.

   c. Pattern of 2 or more light longitudinal stripes on each side interrupted or continuous; ventral plates with dotting, flecking, mottling, or bars of gray to vinaceous-rufous; white to buffy line on ends of ventrals and adjacent edges of scale row 1.

    d. Lateral stripe interrupted; head plates with light edges; dorsal color satiny black or dull purplish black, crossed by 8 indefinite transverse areas of light-edged scales; lateral stripe on rows 3 to 5 white and hair brown, broken in 8–9 places.   *M. t. ornatus*

    dd. Lateral stripe not interrupted.

     e. Plates on top of head with light edges; except anteriorly, a solid median dorsal band 5 and 2 half scales of sepia or brownish olive to drab or drab gray on tail; 5 white to ivory yellow lateral lines, most prominent on ventral tips and 1st row and a double bead-like one on rows 3 to 5.   *M. taeniatus taeniatus*

     ee. Plates on top of head without light edges; dorsal color glaucous gray, clear green-blue gray, and over green, olive to wood brown; pale green yellow stripe on row 4, and on tips of ventrals and adjacent edges row 1, the last bordered above and below by orange to brazil red in anterior portion; venter pale mission blue to pale salmon, tail coral pink.   *M. t. schotti*

   cc. Faint single lateral stripe on adjacent edges of scale rows 3 + 4; dorsal color olivaceous black, deep slate olive to grayish olive.

M. t. ruthveni

  bb. Scale rows 17, formula 17–15–14–13; venter cream or yellow to rose, generally clear.

   c. Dorsal color bluish gray to dark brown with 2 white or reed yellow and 2 dark stripes on either side of body anteriorly. Lower labials 9 or 10; upper labials white, bordered at top with black.

    d. Middorsal color light celandine green to deep glaucous gray. Light lateral stripe 2/2 scales in width originates on 4th scale caudad of labials. Facial dark stripe splits conspicuously bordering with black the lateral light line above and below. A slight indication of dark stripe on ends of ventrals 4–20, the ends then becoming buff pink for 25 ± scutes and then indication of stripe ceases. Lower labials 10 (9).   *M. bilineatus bilineatus*

    dd. Middorsal color very dark brown; light lateral stripe 2/4 scales wide originates on 8th scale caudad of labials, upper dark border less conspicuous because of dark back. Two dark sublateral stripes, one on scale rows 3 + 2, the other on ends of ventrals which fuse into one on anterior 30 scutes. Lower labials 9.

                                        M. b. lineolatus

  cc. Dorsum black, fuscous black to dark brown or gray with single light stripe on either side on rows 3 + 4 from neck to vent; lower labials usually 9; lateral scales without central brown lines.

                                          M. lateralis

[Van Denburgh's analysis (Gen., 1922) follows:

  "cc.² A single light yellow or white line along scales of 3rd and 4th lateral rows; lateral scales without central brown lines.

    "dd.² Lateral light line not broken anteriorly.

      "e. Lateral line yellowish, of uniform width from neck to tail; dark markings present on lips, chin, and throat.   *M. lateralis*

      "e.² Lateral line pure white, with slight enlargements at intervals of from 4 to 7 scales; no dark markings on lips, chin, and throat.   *M. barbouri* (Espiritu Santo Is. Racer)

    "dd.² Lateral light line yellowish, broken up anteriorly, absent or indefinite posteriorly.   *M. aurigulus* (Cape San Lucas Racer)."]

aa. No lateral stripes; pattern if any of dark cross bands.

  b. Scale rows 15–13–11; dorsal color olivaceous black, deep slate olive to grayish olive; many scales with cream edges.   *M. t. ruthveni*

  bb. Scale rows 17; light loreal stripe present or absent; young with crossbands or saddles; snout intermediate.

    c. Dorsal surface black, extending across ends of ventrals; head and throat may be entirely black. Venter pink (red vanishing in preservative); young with white loreal stripe and conspicuous dark crossbands wider than light intervals and extending to venter; neck bands much darker than succeeding bands.

                                    M. f. piceus (*piceus* phase)

"c.[2] Color above walnut brown, deepest toward the tip of each scale, and with blackish brown narrow linear spots, never longer than a scale, sparsely and irregularly scattered over the back and sides. Stejneger 1901. (Clarion Is., Baja Calif.) *M. anthonyi*"

cc. Dorsal surface of body and tail not black; scales of tail sharply outlined by dark borders, in appearance a braided whip-lash.

    d. Dark crossbands or transverse areas on neck and body, usually 6 or more.

        e. Distinct longitudinal white stripe on loreal; adults with 3–8 neck bands, often many more, 2–4 times width of lighter intervals and color in strong contrast; dorsal ground color tawny olive to pale olive-buff, bars of russet, walnut brown, pompeian red. Venter coral red to flesh pink with geranium pink on tail; throat speckled; young with conspicuous dark crossbands extending to the venter; neck bands darker than succeeding ones.

M. f. piceus (*frenatus* phase)

        ee. No longitudinal white stripe through loreal; typical adult color olive-brown, tawny olive, isabella, drab, or smoke gray with inconspicuous bands of olive-brown, cinnamon brown, or bister; seldom more than 6–8 anterior cross bands; venter usually white, light or deep yellow (pink or red present in some western specimens, red being lost in preservative) (see: ee-ff). Young with very narrow dark cross bands not in striking contrast to wider lighter intervals.   *M. f. testaceus*

  dd. No dark crossbands on neck and body in adult; no light loreal stripe.

    e. Anteriorly, dorsal color black with green or violet reflections, dark brown or light brown fading through sepia, army brown or light drab in mid-body to fawn or clay color, to deep olive-buff on tail; venter wood brown, olive-buff, buff; underside of head and neck may be entirely black or white clouded on the edges.

M. flagellum flagellum

    ee. Anterior portion of body little if any darker than posterior; in young, neck bands not greatly darker than those following; in adults, if bands are visible, they are narrower than spaces between them.

       f. In adults, a dark line through center of each scale at least on anterior part of body and at least subcaudal surface salmon red (persistent in preserved specimens); in young, dark bands broader than light interspaces, which are incomplete and irregular.   *M. f. lineatulus*

ff. No dark lines through centers of scales; in western portion of range
may have pompeian red head and neck; mid-body tawny olive scales
edged with pink; venter coral red to pink under tail. (Red ventral color
very transient in preservative.) Young have dark crossbands narrower
than light interspaces, which are complete.   *M. f. testaceus*

Sonoran racer (4—Van Denburgh 1922), Arizona whip snake (Ortenburger 1928)

Masticophis bilineatus bilineatus Jan 1863. Fig. 129; Map 36

Other common names: Arizona racer; half-striped racer; Sonoran whip
snake.

Range: S.e. Arizona, s.w. New Mexico to cent. Oaxaca, Mex.—U.S.A.:
Ariz.; N.M. Mex.: Chihuahua; Coahuila; Colima; Jalisco; Nayarit;
Oaxaca; Sonora; Zacatecas. *Elevation*—2,000 to 5,000 feet.

Size: Adults, 30–67.4 inches. Taylor, 1936, recorded from Sinaloa, Mex.,
one 1,685 mm. long.

Distinctive characteristics: A large, elongate, blue-gray, 17-rowed snake
with 2 lateral white or yellow stripes extending normally not as far as the
region of the vent. Venter from white throat (dotted) to light yellow to
pinkish buff in posterior portions. (See Ortenburger and Ortenburger.)

Color: We found this snake on a ride to Madera Canyon with L. P.
Wehrle and family of Tucson, June 24, 1934. The front ¼ of the back is
light celandine green, deep glaucous-gray, or light medici blue. This dorsal
area occupies 9 scale rows. Each scale has on its forward lateral edge a line
of puritan gray, glaucous gray, or pale king's blue, and a black tip. The skin
between them is rood's lavender. This blue back grades into vetiver green,
grayish olive, or buffy olive for ⅓ of the anterior length. The edges of these
scales are primrose yellow with black tips. The posterior ⅓ of the body and
tail are light grayish olive or smoke gray. About ¼ inch back of the angle of
the mouth, the facial black line forks into two which go backward along the
sides of the body enclosing a light stripe. The lower black line is at first on the
edges of the 4th and 5th scales, then on the 2nd and 3rd. The upper line is at
first on the upper edge of the 5th scale row, then on the upper edge of the 4th,
thus placing the light line on the upper half of the 3rd and lower half of
the 4th scale rows. This light lateral stripe starts as white, and the lateral
stripe below the black border is also white, but each soon becomes reed
yellow. The upper black margin stripe extends backward only about ⅕ of
the body length, while the lower one may extend ⅖. The plates on top of
the head, rostral, internasals, prefrontals, frontal, and supraoculars are drab,
buffy brown, or cinnamon drab. The remainder of the top of the head is
light celandine green, deep glaucous-gray, or light medici blue, like the
forward part of the back. Going across the middle of the rostral and along

suture lines between upper labials, nasals, loreal, and preoculars is a black stripe which sends up vertical black sutures between postnasal and loreal, loreal and preocular, passing around the eye to the anterior margin of the postocular and up its posterior margin. From under the eye, it passes along the upper margin of the upper labials to the angle of the mouth, where it is somewhat broken before extending as 2 stripes along the sides of the body. The upper labials and lower portion of the rostral are white except for a few dots on the extreme lower edges. Each nasal, loreal, preocular, and postocular is white centered except for the upper postoculars, which have the drab, buffy brown, or cinnamon drab of the forward part of the head. The eye is black with a chamois ring. The underside of the head is white with the chin shields and front lower labials slightly dotted with black. Beginning on the 4th ventral plate there is a slight indication of a dark stripe on either end of the ventrals, but this ceases after 15 to 20 plates and becomes buff pink or onion-skin pink for 25 or more plates and then ceases. Down mid-belly for 8 to 10 plates is a median row of indistinct dark dots. Toward the head, the belly is reed yellow or primrose yellow, becoming on the posterior ¼ of the body and the underside of the tail pale pinkish buff.

Habitat: Over half of the authors recorded them as arboreal, finding them in bushes or trees, in *Acacia greggi* and *Celtis pallida,* on limbs, in brushy ground, or in sparse brush. Nearly all agreed it was a mountain form, at least in the region of mountains. They have been assigned to the "semi-desert and chaparral woodland zones"; oak regions of canyons; sahuaro-ocotillo association; on hillsides and walls of rock or in deep canyons. Two or three writers placed them in fairly open ground or in the open near a creek.

Period of activity: *First appearance*—May 21 (Stejneger); June 30 (Van Denburgh, Ariz., 1897). *Fall disappearance*—Oct. (Cope). MVZ dates May 9 to Sept. 24.

Breeding: Oviparous. Males to 1,685$^+$ mm., females to 1,127 mm. *Eggs*— "A female captured near Tucson, Arizona, and sent alive to San Francisco, laid, on June 7, seven eggs of which six measured 37x19, 38x19, 39x19, 40x19, 43x19, and 43x18 mm. They were enclosed in leathery cells roughened with granules. Development in them had just begun, as blood vessels could be seen by transmitted light" (Van Denburgh, Gen., 1922). *Young*—"The young of this species are striped, as the adults" (Smith).

Food: Young birds. Van Denburgh (Gen., 1922), Bogert and Oliver.

Authorities:

Bogert, C. M., and J. Oliver (Ariz., 1945)

Ortenburger, A. I. (Gen., 1928)

Ortenburger, A. I. and R. D. (Ariz., 1927)

Smith, H. M. (Gen., 1941h)

Stejneger, L. (Ariz., 1903)

Taylor, E. H. (Gen., 1936, 1936a)

Lineolate Sonoran whip snake Hensley 1950

Masticophis bilineatus lineolatus Hensley 1950. Map 36

Range: "North branch of Alamo Canyon, Ajo Mountains, 12.9 miles south and 5 miles east of the Ajo-Tucson-Sonoyta Junction, . . . in Organ Pipe Cactus National Monument, Pima County, Arizona" (Hensley). *Elevation*—2,800 to 3,000 feet.

Size: Adults, to 55.2 inches in length. Hensley gave measurements of 3 males as 972, 1,367, and 1,380 mm.

Distinctive characteristics: "Similar to *M. bilineatus bilineatus,* but differing as follows: dorsolateral light line originating on or posterior to the neck region, average 7.75 scale rows posterior to the last supralabial; dorsolateral line narrow, about one half width as in *M. b. bilineatus;* chin-spotting conspicuous and well-defined; 2 well-defined sublateral dark stripes fused anteriorly" (Hensley).

The most distinctive characteristics of this new form are the dark back; the narrow light lateral line only ½ scale in width; the cephalic end of light line beginning on 8th instead of 4th scale caudad of the labials; the second dark sublateral stripe on ends of ventrals; and the number of lower labials 9 instead of the usual 10 of *b. bilineatus* (if this proves true when more material is at hand).

Color and description: Snakes collected by M. M. Hensley, G. T. Bean, and C. L. Fouts. "Adult male; supralabials 8-8, unspotted white, upper edges very dark brown, the color extending from rostral posteriorly to ventral edge of eye where it merges with dorsal pattern behind eye; ventral edges of supralabials also marked with a narrow broken line of the same color extending from rostral posteriorly to the middle of 7th supralabial on the right and through the 6th on the left; infralabials 9-9, white and dark brown irregular spots scattered chiefly on lower edges; mental unmarked; chin shields randomly spotted, the posterior pair narrower and slightly longer (maximum diagonal length) than anterior pair; preoculars 2-2, upper enlarged and contacting prefrontal dorsally, lower greatly reduced, about ¼ size of upper and in contact with 3rd and 4th supralabials, each light centered and with dark edges, the light spot of the upper preocular forming the last of a series of 3 (1 each on the nasal and loreal); postoculars 2-2, both with light centers but not so prominent as on the upper preocular; loreals 1-1; internasals 2; prefrontals 2; nasals divided; temporals, left 2-2-3-2, right 2-2-2-2; scale rows 19-17-13; ventrals 208; caudals 145; total length 1,461 mm.; tail length 450 mm.

"Dorsal color of anterior third of body very dark brown, approaching black on neck region, decreasing in intensity posteriorly to chocolate brown on the tail, top of head slightly lighter in color than neck region with prefrontals, internasals, and rostral approaching the same shade as the tail color;

ventrum white with slight suggestion of fleshy pink appearing on chin region; lateral edges of ventrals on the posterior half of body heavily pigmented, the pigmentation becoming more concentrated toward base of tail; caudals heavily pigmented; irregular dark brown spots scattered profusely over chin, and a median row extending posteriorly to ventral 19; occasional small brown dots scattered over ventrum; *dorsolateral white line covering upper quarter of scale row 3 and the lower quarter of scale row 4,* becoming slightly wider before fading out near ventral 80; *dorsolateral line originating anteriorly on 8th scale row directly posterior to 8th supralabial; lateral black line occupying lower ¾ of scale row 3 and upper half of scale row 2;* sublateral white line covering lower half of row 2 and the upper half of row 1; row 1 with upper half white and lower half dark forming a distinct sublateral dark stripe that is as persistent as the lateral dark line; *lateral ends of ventral scutes also with same black color as lateral stripes, thus forming a second sublateral stripe; the 2 sublateral stripes fused on the anterior 30 scutes forming a wide pronounced dark line originating slightly above ventral 3;* sublateral lines fading posteriorly in sharpness a short distance posterior to their point of union, continuing as brown lines to median third of body (the lower sublateral fades more rapidly, approximating the ground at about anterior 6th) where all lateral stripes merge with the ground color and become indistinct" (Hensley; italics by A.A.W.).

Habitat: "This entire series of specimens was taken from the same location in Alamo Canyon on the west slope of the Ajo Mountains. All were entrapped in a steep-sided tinaja in the canyon floor. The hole, approximately 5 feet long, 3½ feet wide and 4½ feet deep, was half filled with very stagnant water and had sides steep enough to prevent the snakes from escaping. When located, May 15, by G. T. Bean and C. L. Fouts, the tank contained 2 live specimens and 8 carcasses which were in an advanced state of decomposition and unsalvageable. When visited again on May 23 by the writer, 2 more specimens were trapped, one of which was dead but in good shape. One other visit was made to the site on June 8 at which time 7 more specimens were removed, 3 dead. One dead one was salvaged. The 4 alive were completely encrusted with heavy green hardened scum and extremely emaciated but active. The water at this time was about 15 inches deep and thick with algae and debris. The live specimens were not collected but examined superficially and were adjudged identical with those taken previously" (Hensley).

Authority: 1950, M. M. Hensley (Ariz.): "*Comparisons. Masticophis bilineatus bilineatus,* in contrast to the present race, has the dorsolateral line covering upper half of row 3 and lower half of row 4, being twice as wide anteriorly and with the origin on the *4th scale row* (average for 12 specimens 3.87) *posterior to the last supralabial.* . . . The 14 specimens of *Masticophis*

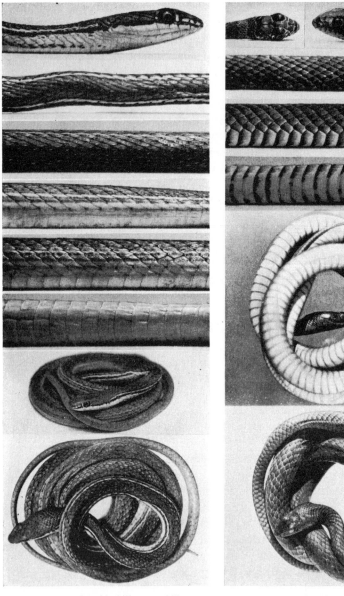

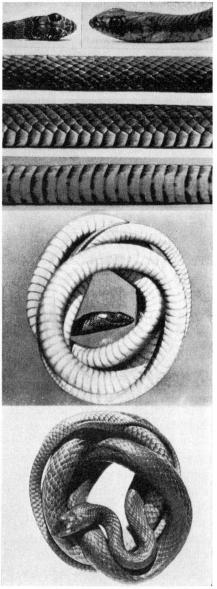

Fig. 129. *Masticophis bilineatus bilineatus,* Madera Canyon, Ariz., L. P. Wehrles and authors.

Fig. 130. *Masticophis flagellum flagellum:* 1, Eustis, Fla., O. C. Van Hyning; 2–5, Silver Springs, Fla., E. R. Allen; 6,7, St. Petersburg, Fla., N. P. Fry and son.

b. bilineatus examined for comparison are from Cochise, Gila, Graham, Pima, and Pinal Cos. in Arizona and from Sonora" (Hensley).

Coachwhip (28—Beyer 1897), **Coachwhip snake** (34—Catesby)

Masticophis flagellum flagellum (Shaw) 1802. Fig. 130; Map 37

Other common names: Black racer; black whip snake; brown thread viper; eastern coachwhip; nasal viper; western coachwhip; whip snake; whiplike nasal viper; whipster.

Range: North Carolina to Florida, w. to e. Texas, n. through e. Oklahoma and s.e. Kansas, e. through s. Missouri to extreme w. cent. Illinois; rare in Kentucky, Tennessee, and n. Mississippi.—Ala.; Ark.; Fla.; Ga.; Kan.; Ky.; La.; Miss.; Mo.; N.C.; Okla.; S.C.; Tenn.; Tex. *Elevation*—Sea level to 2,000 feet.

Size: Adults, 36–102 inches.

Distinctive characteristics: A very large, 17-rowed, lithe snake, very dark brown, drab, or black anteriorly, then rearward becoming lighter to fawn. No prominent longitudinal stripe or cross bands. Under parts mainly white. Ventrals 187–209; caudals 96–119.

Color: A snake from Chesser Is., Okefinokee Swamp, Ga., found July 12, 1922. On the back, toward the head, this snake is drab, in middle portions light drab, and in caudal region, cinnamon-drab. On the neck are 5 blackish bands, with cinnamon-drab or light cinnamon-drab areas between them. A blackish band extends across the rear of the parietal plates and the region posterior to the head. Another one extends from eye to eye across the supraocular and the narrow portion of the frontal. All the head scales in front of the frontal have benzo brown or black edges. The preocular is white, as are also the rostral, lower labials, and gulars. The sutures between the lower labials and gulars bear drab-gray lines. In the eye, the pupil rim is tilleul buff. The upper portion of the iris is fawn color, the front, back, and lower parts bone brown or natal brown. The under parts are white, with 2 lines of vinaceous-fawn for a length of 3 or 4 inches on the neck.

A snake from St. Petersburg, Fla., furnished by N. P. Fry and Son, Apr. 16, 1928. The dorsum on the forward part of the body and also the head are black with beautiful green, blue, or violet reflections. The dorsum of the middle body is army brown, fading rearward to fawn color until, a foot from the vent, the body becomes wood brown and on the tail deep olive-buff with deep olive sutures. In the eye, the pupil rim is light cadmium. The iris is black below, above, in front and behind, with considerable hazel or brussels brown intermixed. Underneath the head and for 8 inches of the forward venter, black, then fawn color or vinaceous-fawn comes in. The next section of the venter is clear tilleul buff with vinaceous-buff ends

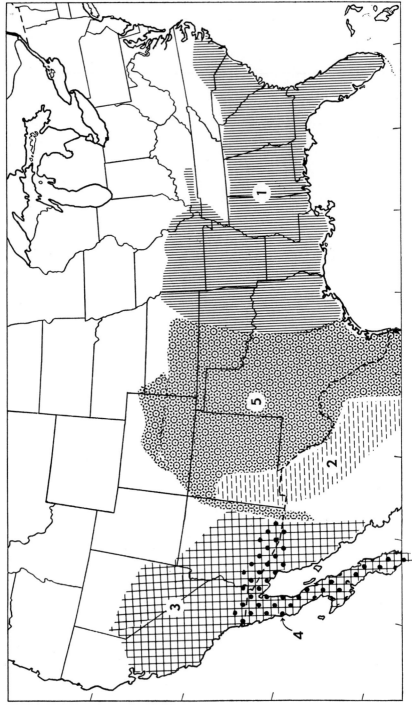

Map 37. *Masticophis*—1, *flagellum*; 2, *f. lineatulus*; 3, *f. piceus (frenatus)*; 4, *f. piceus (piceus)*; 5, *f. testaceus*.

to the ventrals. In the rear half, the ventral plates are olive-buff to tilleul buff with vinaceous-buff reflections.

Habitat: In Louisiana, Fitch (1949) placed it in "all habitats, especially dry uplands, often near cultivated areas." Adjectives frequently applied are dry (6), pine (6), prairie (4), open (3), and high (3). Specimens have been found in high pine forests and cut-over pinelands, in sand hills and on dry oak ridges, in rosemary scrub, broom-sage fields, dry flatwoods, open prairie country, prairie ledges, open fields, grassland, rocky hillsides, and sometimes under rocks or brush or in animal holes. It is one of the frequent DOR snakes of cultivated regions.

Carr wrote about it in 1940: "High pine, rosemary scrub and dry flatwoods. Not rare, but much less common than the racers. Apparently entirely diurnal. Often found in gopher holes, in which they frequently take refuge if pursued. Although alert and very active creatures, coach-whips are frequently killed by ground fires in the flatwoods, more often apparently than any other snake; I once found 7 dead after a fire which burned 10 or 12 acres of flatwoods in Collier County." Bogert and Cowles (Fla., 1947) found the coachwhips of Florida "the most resistant to desiccation of the reptiles maintained in the thermal chamber. . . . Therefore, there is some indication that *Coluber flagellum* is better adapted in this respect for a hot, dry environment than are other serpents."

Period of activity: *First appearance*—Apr. 18 (Perkins and Lentz, Ark., 1934); Apr. 30 (Burt, Kan., 1933). *Fall disappearance*—Aug. 13–15 (Deckert, Fla., 1918).

Breeding: Oviparous. *Mating*—"Apr. 18, 1932, Rattlesnake Mts., Little Rock, Ark. Of 10 *C. atrox* caught on this and succeeding day 8 were found in pairs, . . . 1 in association with a pair and 1 less than 500 yards from the rattlesnake den, and nearby also a pair of *Coluber flagellum flagellum* was seen but only 1 was caught. This seems to indicate that we reached the mountains during the mating periods" (Perkins and Lentz, Ark., 1934).

Eggs—8–24. June 20 (Force, Okla., 1930); July 4 (Brennan, Kan., 1934); August. Our information is indeed scanty for this common species. Brimley (N.C., 1941–42) said: "The eggs resemble those of the Black Snake but are larger." Ortenburger stated: "The eggs of this species are covered with numerous granular excrescences similar to those found on eggs of *Coluber c. constrictor*. They are elongate ellipsoidal; the diameter is about ¼ of the length. A typical egg measures 17 by 63 mm."

Again, as in several other instances, our best notes come from the ardent life-history student, Edith Force. She (Okla., 1930) observed: "Females under observation have deposited complements of 10, 11 and 16 eggs from June 20–July 10. Average number of eggs per brood 12.3. Average size of 37 eggs, 36.5x21.4 mm. Extremes in length and diameter, 31.8 to 49.5 mm.

and 15.5 to 24.4 mm. On Aug. 9, 1928, 11 eggs with embryos measuring 205 mm. in total length with a tail length of 55 mm. were dug from a potato hill." Guidry (Tex., 1953) reported 8 eggs laid July 17, 1952, all hatching Aug. 30.

Young—The most definite statement is usually "spotted like the young of the black snake." Ortenburger and Conant and Bridges (Gen., 1939) defined crossbands (1–3 scales wide; intervals 1–2 scales) more definitely.

Food: Small rodents, lizards, snakes, young birds. Force, Schwardt (Ark., 1938), Löding (Ala., 1922), Ortenburger, Corrington, Ditmars (Gen., 1936).

Authorities:

Bartram, W. (Gen., 1791) Ortenburger, A. I. (Gen., 1928)
Carr, A. F., Jr. (Fla., 1940a) Stejneger, L. (Gen., 1895)
Corrington, J. D. (S.C., 1929)

1928, A. I. Ortenburger: "The lack of published information concerning this form is almost beyond belief. This is particularly astonishing when it is remembered that this snake has been as well known as any on the Atlantic Coast and has been described for over 125 years." (We subscribe to his comments most heartily. This is one of our common forms on which we have scant precise information as to description, life history, food, etc. Possibly most killed specimens are too large for the average collector to save and preserve.)

New Mexican racer

Masticophis flagellum lineatulus H. M. Smith 1941. Map 37

Other common names: Same as names of *M. f. testaceus* below.

Range: S. New Mexico to Guanajuato, Mex.—U.S.A.: N.M. Mex.: Chihuahua; Coahuila; Durango; Guanajuato; San Luis Potosí. *Elevation*—4,000 to 6,000 feet or more. 7,000 feet (Taylor, Gen., 1952).

Size: Adults probably same size as other races. Smith's holotype is 1,481 mm. long. 59 inches (Little and Keller).

Distinctive characteristics: "Scales in 17 rows, . . . posterior portion of the belly, and subcaudal surface red or marked with red (except in juveniles) even in long-preserved specimens (red not fading greatly); each dorsal scale with a longitudinal dark line or a posterior dark spot; head scales not light edged in young, no light loreal stripe (center may be light); young with cross bands 2 or 3 scales long, extending laterally to ends of ventrals, disappearing on middle of body" (Smith). Ventrals 190–198; caudals 99–110.

Color: "Head light yellowish brown, darker toward posterior sutures; sides of head light yellowish brown, with a lighter area in the preocular, loreal, nasal and rostral; a dark, rounded spot in center of nasal; supralabials white (cream) below a line about even with posterolateral border of 7th labial and middle of subocular labials. Dorsal ground color light yellowish brown, becoming more reddish toward middle of body, posteriorly mostly salmon red; all anterior dorsal scales with a central, longitudinal black streak, which becomes more spot-like on scales in middle of body, barely indicated on posterior scales; as the black spots become less distinct, the red areas become more distinct, the posterior scales being mostly red (with a little black near tip), with a white (cream) base; dorsal surface of the tail is even more strongly marked with salmon red.

"Posterior edge of mental and broad areas near the sutures between the infralabials and chin shields, black-marked; a double row of black spots beginning with anterior ventral scales; posteriorly these spots becoming mixed with red and soon mostly red and very little black; anterior ground color of belly yellow, this color extending onto lower dorsal scale rows; toward middle of belly the color is largely replaced by salmon red, and posteriorly the belly is entirely red, with the double row of black spots faintly indicated; ventral surface of tail mostly red, the bases of the scales lighter (cream). . . . The adults of this subspecies are readily distinguishable from *flavigularis* and *piceus* by the striped scales; they also lack the loreal stripe of the latter. Preserved *lineatulus* also retain the red ventral color, while *flavigularis* and *piceus,* although frequently brilliant red in life, lose this color very quickly in preservative" (Smith).

At an elevation close to 4,500 feet, just east of Tolar, N.M., which is not far east of Smith's range of *M. f. lineatulus,* we found a coachwhip dead in the road. The back scales are buffy olive, each one edged on the sides, but not tipped by primrose yellow. On the 2nd and 1st rows this yellow becomes reed yellow or light green yellow, and this color extends for a short distance onto ends of belly plates. Middle of belly is cartridge buff or marguerite yellow. Underside of head and gular scales are light green yellow. The top of the head is buffy olive. The superciliary plate is light brownish olive, as are the rear edges of prefrontals and internasals. Side of head same color as top of head. Lower labials light green yellow. Edges of upper labials mainly light green yellow. The rear edges, but not the middles, of the belly plates are citrine-drab or deep olive. The iris could not be observed.

Breeding: Oviparous. *Young*—"The young of *lineatulus* are strikingly different from those of *flavigularis,* with narrow dark cross bands; *piceus,* with a light loreal stripe and the 2 or 3 anterior dark bands broad and very dark (black), those following conspicuously lighter; and *striolatus,* with light margins on the dorsal head scales" (Smith).

Food: "One 147 cm. long was the longest snake examined. Three had eaten lizards (probably *Uta stansburiana stansburiana*)" (Little and Keller).

Field notes: In 1944 right after Smith's description, we wrote: To someone who has encountered the pink-red racer intergrades for 25 years, any solution is welcome. True, we have not published a paper on our impressions each time we went from Devil's River or Pecos River to Huachuca Mts. and back. Had we, we are sure, we would not be charged with being consistent to the end. Often a ready way is to describe a new form as Smith has done. We hope it is the solution of this perplexing complex. We hold it tentative.

Were one to start from Pecos, he would first go through the very diverse trans-Pecos complex (you have to see it several times to believe it) to El Paso, Tex., then cross the trans-Rio-Grande and New Mexican thumb of Smith's *lineatulus*. Near Rodeo or Chiricahua Mts. one would find a thin sliver of *testaceus* enclosing the N.M. thumb of *lineatulus*. Interspersed with it or immediately adjoining comes *frenatus* and *piceus* phases of *M. f. piceus*. Still far from simple to reconcile to our old categories and their concepts. Nevertheless this new form is established by a good field man, neither a laboratory technician nor a one-technique specialist. One of his criteria seems a good approach, namely the coloration of the young.

Authorities:

Gloyd, H. K. (Ariz., 1937a)
Little, E. L., Jr., and J. G. Keller (N.M., 1937)
Smith, H. M. (Gen., 1941h)
Smith, H. M., and E. H. Taylor (Gen., 1945)

1937, E. L. Little and J. G. Keller: *"Coluber flagellum* subsp.—The Jornada specimens are intergrades between the subspecies *C. flagellum flavigularis* (Hallowell) and *C. flagellum frenatum* (Stejneger). Found on the plain. Cockerell's (1896) specimen cited as *Bascanion testaceum* is now classed as *C. flagellum flavigularis."*

1937: H. K. Gloyd discusses the intergradation of *frenatum* and *flavigularis* at length. An excerpt: "These intermediate specimens furnish definite indications of intergradation between *flavigularis* and *frenatum* in southeastern Arizona. Individuals from southwestern New Mexico should be expected to show a somewhat stronger tendency toward *flavigularis."*

1945, C. M. Bogert and J. Oliver (Ariz., 1945): "The complexity of the situation becomes even more apparent with the recognition of *lineatulus*. According to Smith's interpretation, this form ranges from Guanajuato in Central Mexico, northward to Valencia County, New Mexico, while a few specimens from southeastern Arizona and northeastern Sonora are assigned to *flavigularis* (= *testaceus*). It may be observed that if such a population of *testaceus* exists to the west of the range of *lineatulus,* it would be completely isolated from *testaceus* in Colorado, Oklahoma, and Texas, southward to San Luis Potosí. Such mosaic distributions certainly require more adequate explanation than any that has been offered."

Red racer (36—Van Denburgh 1897), **Western whip snake** (9—Van Denburgh 1897)

Masticophis flagellum piceus (Cope) 1892 (*frenatus* or red phase). Fig. 131; Map 37

Other common names: (Arizona) coachwhip snake; Arizona racer; coppery whip snake (Cronise 1868); (red) whip snake; yellow coachwhip snake.

Range: The whole of Baja California, Mex., n. to San Francisco Bay, Calif., and thence e. across s. Nevada, s.e. Utah, and most of Arizona, s. through Sonora to n. Sinaloa, Mex.—U.S.A.: Ariz.; Calif.; Nev.; N.M.; Ut. Mex.: Baja Calif.; Sinaloa; Sonora. *Elevation*—From the coast to the Colorado River, except the mountains above about 4,000 feet (Klauber, Calif., 1931a); ocean to desert (Perkins); 2,000–5,000 feet (Linsdale); 4,600 feet (Johnson, Bryant, Miller, Calif.; 1948); 4,000–8,000 feet (Bailey, N.M., 1913); 3,500 feet (Little, Ariz., 1940).

Size: Adults, 28–74 inches. Klauber's (Gen., 1943b) measurements are: mean-over-all 790.40 mm. males, 1,009.71 mm. females, maxima 1,481 mm. (tail 395) males, 1,531 mm. (tail 384) females.

Longevity: 12 years 2 months (Perkins, Gen., 1951, 1954).

Distinctive characteristics: "This snake is not always red. Almost any color will do—grayish, light yellow, dark yellow, brownish or reddish. Often the scales are light on the edges with dark tips. There are several whitish bands across the neck and head which are usually dark brown or black. The under parts are usually yellow, with numerous spots of yellow, brown or black on the lighter throat. The young . . . are grayish-blotched or barred across the back with brown" (Perkins).

Color: A snake from La Puerta, San Diego Co., Calif., furnished by L. M. Klauber, May 8, 1929. The cephalic half of the body is marked on the dorsum with transverse spots of russet, verona brown, or walnut brown with edges of warm sepia or vandyke brown and with touches of pompeian red or eugenia red on the scales. The intervals are tawny olive or drab with dorsal and ventral edges of the scales white or pale olive-buff. In the forward part there is some vinaceous-pink in them. On the caudal half of the body, the dorsum is without the transverse spots, each scale being tawny olive or drab in its caudal half and pale olive-buff in the cephalic part. Between the 1st and 2nd light intervals on the neck, there is an irregular black patch on each side and on the dorsum. There is a little black ahead of the 1st light interval. The top of the head is buffy brown or isabella color. The upper labials are white in the lower half. The upper half of the upper labials is light grayish olive. The preoculars are white. Each postocular is marked with a white bar. There is a band of light grayish olive back of the lower white postocular. The pupil rim of the eye is cartridge buff surrounded by another circle of clay color. The iris is black in the lower half and deep olive-buff in the upper portion. The lower side of the head is white, every scale with blotches of black. The neck, for 8 inches, is light coral red or carnelian red, with many large spots or blotches some of which are orange rufous centered. The underside of the body is flesh pink, becoming under the tail geranium pink or jasper pink. On the tail and on the ends of some ventrals are a few black spots.

Habitat and habits: The various habitats assigned to this fast snake are open country, open washes, dry hills, dry washes, cultivated or rough fields, grassy fields or areas, grassy, light, heavy or granitic brush, sandy washes, sand mounds, mountain rocky areas, rocky hills, rocks, level plains, semi-desert, valleys, foothills. These snakes frequently occur among creosote or greasewood, prickly pear, *Celtis, Atriplex,* mesquite tangles, or bushes. They are often found in bushes or trees and very readily betake themselves to such a retreat. In his "Sixteen Year Census" Klauber (Gen., 1939a) had for the coast 112, inland valleys 84, foothills 34, desert foothills 98, desert 23. His ecological conditions were: cultivated fields 59, grass 57, light brush 20, brushy desert 20, sandy desert 12, heavy brush chaparral 9, orchard or vineyard 8, rocks, boulders 7, pond, creek or river bank 5, barren desert 5. They are fast and aggressive and remarkable climbers. They vibrate their tails, try to bite an aggressor, and may or may not become good captives. "In the Colorado and Mohave deserts, *Coluber f. piceus* is the only snake ordinarily seen in daytime during the summer months. Other serpents inhabiting the same region are forced to estivate, adopt a subterranean existence, or become either crepuscular or nocturnal in habits during the warmer months. . . . The subspecies inhabiting the deserts may be even more resistant to dehydration than its Floridian relative" (Bogert, Fla., 1947).

In one of the early accounts Grinnell and Grinnell found it an inhabitant exclusively of the hot, gravelly washes along the bases of mountains. They wrote an appreciative story of its elusive and rapid locomotion.

Period of activity: *First or early appearances*—May 27 (Stejneger, Ariz., 1903); Apr. 29 (Cooper, Calif., 1869); May 21 (Van Denburgh, Calif., 1912a); Jan. 21, Apr. 22, May 1, May 6, May 15 (Stejneger, Calif., 1893); Apr. 4 (Van Denburgh, Baja Calif., 1895a); Apr. 9, 10, 16, 25, June 1 (Linsdale, Baja Calif., 1932); Mar. 13 (Von Bloecker, Calif., 1942). Distribution by months: Feb., 1; Mar., 11; April, 37; May, 132; June, 96; July, 35; Aug., 11; Sept., 21; Oct., 6; Nov., 1 (Klauber, Gen., 1939a). *Fall disappearance*—Aug. 3 (King); Sept. 27 (Stejneger); Sept. 30, Oct. 6 (Van Denburgh, 1895a); Oct. 22 (Baja Calif., Van Denburgh and Slevin, 1913). MVZ dates are Mar. 12 to Sept. 30.

Hibernation—In 1907 Grinnell and Grinnell asserted that they had "never found it anywhere between September and May and [did] not know where it hides away for the winter." "On February 8, 1940, a red racer . . . was found 10 miles northwest of Palmdale, California, at an elevation of approximately 2,500 feet. The snake was in a torpid condition, hibernating under the roots of a dead stump of *Yucca brevifolia,* the Joshua tree, at a depth of between 12 and 18 inches. It was coiled in a resting position. The day was cold and windy although the sun was shining. On being exposed to the direct rays of the sun, the snake became capable of locomotion" (Kinney). "One adult and one juvenile racer were taken on the Bell ranch February 24, 1938. The adult was unquestionably hibernating and was resting stretched out in a vertical position with its head reaching to within approximately a foot of the surface. On attempting to collect the specimen, it was discovered that the body was firmly embedded in the sand. The soil and body temperatures were 17°C. The juvenile racer had been excavated by the passage of the scraper and had warmed up thoroughly before its discovery. The track was followed with the expectation of finding a specimen of *Sonora occipitalis,* but on learning the identity of the animal, the tracks were examined again. It is doubtful if the tracks of an adult *Sonora* and those of a very small slow-moving *Coluber* are distinguishable under any but ideal conditions, thus making the collection of data based on tracks alone a process of dubious value" (Cowles, Gen., 1941a).

Breeding: Oviparous. *Eggs*—"During the afternoon and evening of July 30, 1930, a heavy rain washed out portions of the bank of a highway drainage ditch about 3 miles east of the Huachuca Mountains. The following morning while repairing the damaged road, Mr. Leslie Wilcox of Hereford discovered a snake egg in the ditch. In the edge of the bank above, 11 inches beneath the surface of the ground, were 7 more. They were in a compact mass, not adhering to one another, and all somewhat discolored from contact with the reddish-brown soil. One that was injured contained a young snake about 10 inches long. They appeared spoiled a week later and when opened all young were dead. Dark neck bands typical of *frenatum* could be distinguished in some but the pigmentation was not sufficiently developed to determine whether or not any showed evidence of intergradation with *flavigularis*" (Gloyd).

Young—"In early September 1937, I was traveling down the east side of the Sierras in Nevada and California. In 2 days (the 3rd and 4th of the month) and 542 miles of travel, largely in daylight, we noted 45 snakes alive or dead on the highway, mostly the latter. Of these 22 were juveniles. The racers *Coluber taeniatus taeniatus* in western Nevada and *Coluber flagellum frenatus,* further south in Inyo County, California, comprised a high proportion of these young" (Klauber, Gen., 1939a).

Food: Lizards, mice, young birds. Grinnells, Cowles (1946), Van Denburgh.

Authorities:

Bogert, C. M., and J. A. Oliver (Ariz., 1945)

Brattstrom, B. H., and J. W. Warren (Calif., 1953)

Cowles, R. B. (Gen., 1941a; Calif., 1946)

Cowles, R. B., and C. M. Bogert (Gen., 1944; Fla., 1947)

Gloyd, H. K. (Ariz., 1937a)

Grinnell, J. and H. W. (Calif., 1907)

Kinney, K. (Calif., 1941)

Klauber, L. M. (Gen., 1939a; Calif., 1931a)

Linsdale, J. (Nev., 1938–40)

Mocquard, F. (Baja Calif., 1899)

Mosauer, W. (Calif., 1935a)

Ortenburger, A. I. and R. D. (Ariz., 1927)

Perkins, C. B. (Calif., 1938)

Ruthven, A. G. (Ariz., 1907)

Schmidt, K. (Baja Calif., 1922)

Stejneger, L. (Calif., 1893)

Taylor, E. H. (Gen., 1936)

Van Denburgh, J. (Gen., 1922)

Van Denburgh, J., and J. R. Slevin (Ariz., 1913; Baja Calif., 1921c)

Masticophis flagellum cingulum Lowe and Woodin

C. H. Lowe, Jr., and W. H. Woodin, III (Ariz., 1954) describe a new race occurring in Sonora n. to Amado, Santa Cruz Co., Ariz. It is dark red-brown broken by pink crossbands, which are doubled or paired posteriorly.

San Joaquin racer

Masticophis flagellum ruddocki Brattstrom and Warren

B. H. Brattstrom and J. W. Warren recently suggested (Calif., 1953) that a light yellow racer of the San Joaquin Valley (including the Sacramento Valley) of California constitutes a new subspecies, *M. f. ruddocki*. It is without the dark head and dark neck bands. More information must be at hand before we depart from Klauber's interpretation of the black racers of Arizona.

Black whip snake (9—Ortenburger 1928), Black racer

Masticophis flagellum piceus (Cope) 1892 (*piceus* or black phase). Fig. 132; Map 37

Other common names: Arizona coachwhip snake (Yarrow 1882); pink-bellied racer; red racer.

Range: Baja Calif., Mex., to extreme s. San Diego Co., Calif., e. through s. Arizona and adjacent Sonora, Mex.—U.S.A.: Ariz.; Calif. Mex.: Baja Calif.; Sonora. *Elevation*—Mostly below 2,000 feet, some to 4,000 feet.

Size: Adults, 20–70 inches.

Longevity: 11 years 2 months (Perkins, Gen., 1951, 1954).

Distinctive characteristics: Van Denburgh, who did not consider it a separate species or subspecies, quotes Ruthven's description: "Body and tail above, broadly including the ends of the ventral scutes, blue black without markings. Head dark brown with a few irregular reddish markings above.

Fig. 131. *Masticophis f. piceus* (red), San Diego Co., Calif., L. M. Klauber.

Fig. 132. *Masticophis f. piceus* (black), spotted head, Phoenix, Ariz., V. Householder.

The loreals, preoculars and postoculars, and first 6 supralabials, have bright orange yellow centers. Anterior part of throat marbled with bright yellow and black. Throat black with scattered spots of yellowish orange. About the 20th gastrostege the light color increases in amount and the black becomes restricted to small blotches that become fewer posteriorly, only a few small widely scattered spots being present on the ¾ of the body length and none on the tail. For most of the length the belly is an orange yellow tint, becoming a dark orange tint on the posterior ¼ of the body and on the tail." (In most we have seen the venters are various tints of pink.)

Color: A snake from Phoenix, Ariz., furnished by Vic H. Housholder, Oct. 8, 1936. The dorsal scales are blackish (i.e., dusky purplish gray, plumbeous-black, or blackish mouse gray) with brownish tinges. The dorsum of the tail and somewhat of the dorsum of the extreme rear of the body is a mingling of tawny olive and the dusky purplish gray of the forward back. These scales are often edged with the pinks of the belly so that the tail dorsum may have a verona brown or bister cast. The pinkish of the belly becomes the general interscale color of the whole dorsum and occasionally shows as edges on some of the scales. The dorsal color extends en bloc as a dusky purplish gray, plumbeous-black, or blackish mouse gray area on the ends of all the ventrals and has a very clear-cut margin with the pinkish belly. This color is above the angle of the belly. On top of the head, the parietals and frontal have patches or washes of saccardo's umber or dresden brown. The region caudad of the angle of the mouth has a few shrimp pink scales or spots. The 2 postoculars and the suture of the 5th and 6th upper labials have each an ivory yellow spot, making a vertical series back of the eye. In front of the eye, there is a vertical spot of pale chalcedony yellow on the upper preocular and a horizontal spot of the same on the loreal. The rim is purple narrow, or is white or ivory yellow with a slight indication of shrimp pink at the edge of the iris. The iris is black with touches of dresden brown in the forward part and a tawny spot above the pupil which under the lens is shown as a black or dark network on a warm buff ground. The underside of the head is white, heavily blotched with dorsal color. This is followed on the lower neck and for a length of 2 inches by a solid block of the dark dorsal color which is succeeded by cream buff, warm buff, and pale yellow-orange. This gives place to orange-pink, coral pink, and shrimp pink, and grades posteriorly on the rear of belly and underside of tail to a clear eosine pink.

Snake received from Miss Ruth Hegener, October, 1937. Unlike Housholder's specimen, the whole head of this snake is dark with no white touches. The head is mummy brown above and bister or mummy brown on the underside. For 30 ventrals this black, bister, or mummy brown extends down the venter, which thereafter becomes shrimp pink, grading through la france pink to begonia rose under the tail. On the cephalic half of the venter some spots of dorsal color appear on the middle of the belly.

Habitat and habits: If the reader looks at the zonal and ecological distribution, he will find that this species is in Sargent's Northern Mexican forest, Harshberger's Sonoran desert region (western part), Shreve's Arizona succulent desert and California microphyll desert, or Gloyd's south-central desert area. Klauber in 1931 assigned it to brush and foothills. This speedy red racer when chased seeks an animal hole or burrow of the desert floor. It is of the mesquite or cholla associations, occasionally but not often in bushes, and is abroad in the early hours of the forenoon. One writer held that it was not in the canyons but in the sandy washes of canyon mouths. We have usually seen it on the gravelly level desert floor. There are records of it in foothills in brush clumps. It is seen most often as it is speeding away.

Period of activity: *First appearance*—May 1 (Van Denburgh and Slevin, Nev., 1921a); Mar. 24, June 17 (Linsdale, Baja Calif., 1932). "Sixteen Year Census"—Apr., 1; May, 1; June, 1; Sept., 1 (Klauber, Gen., 1939a). MVZ dates are Mar. 24–June 17.

Breeding: Oviparous. *Mating*—"Two specimens were captured in the bed of the Santa Cruz River near Tucson, May 29, 1912, and one was seen near the steam pump 18 miles north of Tucson, and a fourth specimen was found dead in the central part of Pima County. The specimens caught May 29, 1912, were apparently mating. They were lying on the sand at full length but entwined. When disturbed they immediately separated and instantly mounted to the top of a willow tree some 20 feet high, where they were captured with much difficulty. Both were jet black with the lower surfaces a beautiful coral pink. The fact that these two black snakes were mating is very interesting, since it would seem to indicate that they may really represent a distinct species rather than a melanistic phase of *Bascanion flagellum frenatum*" (Van Denburgh and Slevin). *Eggs and young*—In 1907 Ruthven wrote: "Nothing is known of the habits of this species," and 31 years later Perkins (Calif., 1938) declared: "Nothing is known of the coloration of the young." Neither eggs nor young had been described by 1950.

Food: Lizards, rattlers, young birds, mice. Ortenburgers, Perkins (Calif., 1938), Taylor.

Authorities:

Allen, M. J. (Ariz., 1933)

Klauber, L. M. (Gen., 1942; Calif., 1934a)

Linsdale, J. M. (Baja Calif., 1932; Nev., 1938–40)

Ortenburger, A. I. and R. D. (Ariz., 1927)

Perkins, C. B. (Calif., 1938)

Ruthven, A. G. (Ariz., 1907)

Smith, H. M. (Gen., 1941h)

Taylor, E. H. (Gen., 1936b)

Van Denburgh, J. (Ariz., 1897; Baja Calif., 1896a)

Van Denburgh, J., and J. R. Slevin (Ariz., 1913)

1896, J. Van Denburgh: "That *B. piceum* is based on anything more than melanistic individuals of *B. flagellum frenatum*, I have great doubt."

1922: K. P. Schmidt (Baja Calif., 1922) considered *frenatus* and *piceus* phases of one *Coluber flagellum piceus* (Cope), and remarked, "Two of these (37559 and 37552) are of the dark color phase originally described as *piceus*."

1942: L. M. Klauber in a thorough 10-page discussion, concluded: *"Coluber flagellum frenatus* and *Coluber piceus,* the red and black whip snakes of the southwest, usually considered separate species, are found to be color phases of a single subspecies which should be known as *Coluber flagellum piceus,* for differences hitherto used in separating them are not evident in new material now available."

Prairie coachwhip, Western coachwhip

Masticophis flagellum testaceus (Say) 1823. Fig. 133; Map 37

Other common names: Black racer; blotched coachwhip snake; coachwhip; coachwhip snake (11—Mozley 1878); green racer; pink racer; prairie racer; prairie runner; prairie whip snake; race runner; red racer; Texas coachwhip snake; western coachwhip snake; whip snake (9—Brons 1882); white racer; yellow coachwhip snake.

Range: Cent. Kansas to Matagorda Bay, Tex., and s. to Mexico (Tamaulipas and San Luis Potosí, w. to Nuevo León and Coahuila) through trans-Pecos Texas to n.w. New Mexico and cent. Colorado, with a long spur through e. Arizona into n.e. Sonora, Mex.—U.S.A.: Ariz.; Colo.; Kan.; Neb.; N.M.; Okla.; Tex. Mex.: Coahuila; Nuevo León; San Luis Potosí; Sonora; Tamaulipas. *Elevation*—500 to 5,000 feet. 2,800–5,000 feet (Bailey, N.M., 1913); 4,800 feet (Gloyd and Smith, Gen., 1942); 5,000–5,800 feet (Ruthven, *Geog. Rev.,* **10:** 243).

Size: Adults, 30–74 inches.

Longevity: 11 years 2 months (Perkins, Gen., 1948); 10 years 3 months (Perkins, Gen., 1947); 13 years 5 months (Perkins, Gen., 1951, 1954).

Distinctive characteristics: Structurally like *Masticophis flagellum flagellum,* but differing in coloration, the anterior portion not being distinctly darker. In life much of venter is from coral pink to coral red. Dorsally some specimens may be tawny, others yellowish or clay, and still others may have pinkish tints interspersed in dorsal coloration. No light lines in centers of scales.

Color: We caught this snake under a log above Comstock, Tex., near the second crossing of the Devil's River, July 3, 1925. The back in its mid-portion is tawny olive or clay color, the scales edged with pinkish buff, light pinkish cinnamon, or light vinaceous-cinnamon. The upper parts for 6 or 8 inches back of the head are terra cotta or congo pink. The plates of the top of the head are pompeian red, eugenia red, or brick red. The cephalic edge of the chin is jasper pink or coral pink. The rear edges of the supraocular, frontal, prefrontals, internasals, prenasals, and rostral are black. Pupil rim of the eye is a cream-colored ring. The iris is xanthine orange above, black in front, behind, and below the pupil. The forward portion of the venter is coral red or light coral red, becoming, toward the vent, coral pink and, under the tail, flesh pink with the rear portion pinkish buff.

Another coachwhip, which we caught near the Sisterdale crossing of the Guadalupe River, Apr. 12, 1925, has hardly any specklings on the throat and fewer cinnamon spots on the 1st ventrals.

Another snake came from Brownsville, Tex., Apr. 21, 1925. The body is marked with crossbands of cinnamon brown and lighter areas. One area on the neck bears 2 cinnamon brown bars with intermediate drab areas. Then follows an area of smoke gray for 8 or 9 scales edged with baryta yellow and sulphur yellow, succeeded by 6 cinnamon brown bars with lighter drab intermediate areas. These have less yellow. The neck area is sayal brown, as are the head plates also except for the supraoculars and the rear edges of most of the plates, which are warm sepia.

A snake from Waco, Tex., received from Murray, May 1, 1937. The back is crossed by 6 lighter and 6 darker areas. The darker areas are 15 to 16 scales longitudinally; the lighter ones 8 to 12 scales long. In the dark areas, the scales of the 8 dorsal rows are centered with bister, and those on the sides for 4 rows are uniform light brownish olive. In the light areas the scales are isabella color to citrine-drab, edged forward with primrose yellow or naphthalene yellow.

Habitat: This is a snake of the semiarid regions, frequently recorded in prairie pastures and cultivated fields. Far more records, however, are from the roadsides or roads, where they frequently are killed by the auto. Other habitats are sunny hillsides; open woods; along a river or in a river bottom; semibrushy areas; dry rocky situations; rock ledges. For cover it may use rock piles, brush, logs, fallen signs, grass, or trees. More than one collector has chased this swift aggressive snake to mesquites.

We quote two recent summaries: "*Coluber flagellum testaceus* Say—The coachwhip occurred more commonly in the Plains belt than in the Roughland belt. Of 10 specimens collected, only 2 were from the Roughland belt. One of these was in the streambed association, and the other was in the lechuguilla-beargrass association on top of the mesa. Specimens from the Plains belt were from the following associations: catclaw-tobosa, 4; creosotebush-catclaw-blackbrush, 1; mesquite-huisache-blackbrush, 1; and yucca-tobosa (near the center on the plain on the road from Valentine to Marfa), 1. Several others were seen on the highway, but they escaped into the rocky banks of drainage culverts" (Jameson and Flury). "In Terrell County, [Tex.] 3 specimens were collected in the cedar savannah, 15 in the mesquite-creosote, 3 in the mesquite-sumac-condalia, and 2 in the live-oak association" (Milstead, Mecham, McClintock, Tex., 1950).

Period of activity: *Early appearances*—Apr. (Strecker and Williams, Tex., 1928); May 23 (Ellis and Henderson, Colo., 1913); Apr. 12, 21, 25, 26 (A.H.W.); Apr. 2, 16, 24, 28, May 1 (Marr). *Fall disappearance*—Aug. 30 (A.H.W.); Sept. 23, Oct. 21 (Marr); Aug. 28 (Burt, Kan., 1933). *Hibernation*—"There is good reason to believe that this whipsnake hibernates with *Crotalus atrox atrox* as this was vouched for by the former supervisor of the Wichita National Forest, S. M. Shanklin, and the rangers there, among them Earl Drummond. These whipsnakes were actually seen in 1925 in a rattlesnake 'den'" (Ortenburger and Freeman).

Breeding: Oviparous. Female 1,324 mm. *Eggs*—Number, 4–24. In Kansas, Marr recorded a specimen May 22 with 11 eggs and one June 6 with 4 eggs. In the Wichita Mts., Ortenburger and Freeman took a female with 13 eggs. In Nebraska, Hudson and Davis (1941) gave the complement as "1 to 2 dozen eggs." On Apr. 25, 1934, at Somerset, Tex., we found in Kirn's material several (at least 10) eggs. Their surface roughness was produced by an even sprinkling of round white tubercles. The intervening areas had fine ridges parallel to the long axis of the egg. Four of these eggs were laid in a quart fruit jar, 4 in the tool box of Kirn's car. These eggs measured as follows: 42x25 mm., 41x23, 39x22.5, 42x25, 43x24, 43x25.5, 39x22, 40x24, 42x24, 44x25. Werler (Gen., 1951) describes 8 eggs laid on June 6, 1950, by a female 1,324 mm. as white, granular, 40–57 mm. long by 22–25 mm. wide.

Young—"The pattern of young specimens of *flavigularis* is made up of rather distinct alternating light and dark brown crossbands. The dark crossbands, 1 or 2 scales in width, are separated by light bands 3 or more scales in width. . . . These crossbands usually cover the anterior fourth of the body, gradually fading out posteriorly.

Food: Lizards, insects, young birds, snakes, young turtles.[1] Strecker (Tex., 1902, 1908c, 1909b), Brons (Kan., 1882), Bailey (N.M., 1913), Ortenburger, Marr, Borell and Bryant (Tex., 1942), Milstead, Mecham, McClintock (Tex., 1950).

Field notes: Aug. 1, 1942 about 6 miles east of Sanderson: Anna was walking along a rocky roadside ditch looking under bushes and grass clumps for coiled snakes. She saw what looked like a brown stick in the middle of a small bush. As she paused to look closely, it ran out its tongue. I saw it was a snake in an animal hole with about 4–6 inches of its neck standing up very straight and stiff. She called me to bring the fishpole. How I got a noose over that neck I know not, but imagine my surprise to pull out of the hole with that fishpole and line a long pink or red racer.

---

[1] Fouquette and Lindsay (Tex., 1955) add frogs.

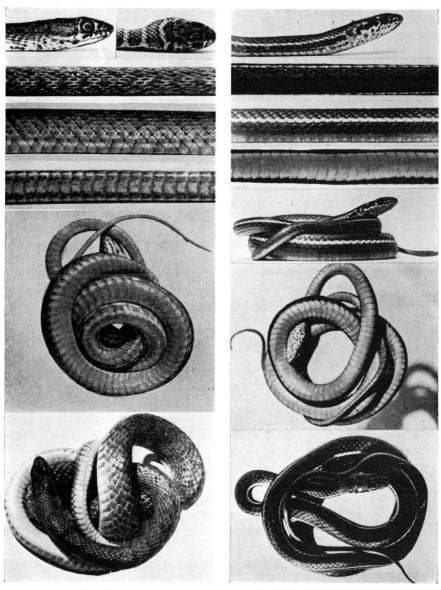

Fig. 133. *Masticophis f. testaceus:* 1,3–6, Brownsville, Tex., H. C. Blanchard; 2, Boerne, Tex.; 7, San Antonio, Tex., Mrs. W. O. Learn.

Fig. 134. *Masticophis lateralis:* 1,3,5–7, San Diego Co., Calif., L. M. Klauber; 2,4, San Diego, Calif., C. B. Perkins.

Authorities:

Brown, A. E. (Tex., 1903)

Jameson, D. L., and A. G. Flury (Tex., 1949)

Marr, J. C. (Gen., 1944)

Maslin, T. P. (Colo., 1953)

Murray, L. T. (Tex., 1939)

Ortenburger, A. I. (Gen., 1928)

Ortenburger, A. I., and B. Freeman (Okla., 1930)

Shannon, F. A., and H. M. Smith (Tex., 1949)

Smith, H. M. (Gen., 1941h; Kan., 1950)

In 1953 T. P. Maslin posed the problem of the pink and brown phases of *M. f. testaceus*. He wondered if it would not be wise to restrict the pink phase to *M. f. testaceus* and the brown eastern phase to *M. f. flavigularis*.

California striped racer (15—Grinnell and Camp 1917), California racer (6—Van Denburgh 1897)

Masticophis lateralis lateralis (Hallowell) 1853. Fig. 134; Map 36

Other common names: Banded racer; few-striped whip snake (Cronise 1868); Hallowell's coachwhip snake; striped racer; striped-side whip snake.

Range: From the Sacramento Valley, Calif., s. through w. California into Baja California to lat. 26°.—U.S.A.: Calif. Mex.: Baja Calif. *Elevation*— Coastline to the desert foothills; it descends only to about 2,700 feet on the east side of the divide (Klauber, Calif., 1931a); 400, 700, 2,300 feet (Grinnell, Dixon, and Linsdale); 2,000–6,000 feet (Grinnell and Camp, Calif., 1917); 1,800, 2,220, 4,500, 4,900, 6,000 feet (Atsatt, Calif., 1913); 7,000 feet (Bogert, Calif., 1930).

Size: Adults, 18–60 inches. Klauber's (Gen., 1943b) measurements of 23 males and 24 females are: mean over-all 858.87 mm. males, 894.38 mm. females; maxima 1,218 mm. (tail 380) males, 1,385 mm. (tail 417) females.

Distinctive characteristics: A large medium (17-rowed) elongate, active snake with black, brown, or purplish dorsum defined on either side on the 3rd and 4th row with a continuous white or buffy stripe. Labials and underside of head cartridge buff spotted with dark followed on venter by yellows. Before and back of vent are various pinks—a handsome serpent.

Color: A snake from L. M. Klauber described May 11, 1928. The dorsum is fuscous black. On the upper half of the 3rd and the lower half of the 4th rows of scales is a pure white or cartridge buff stripe extending from neck to vent. This stripe is black edged above and below. The sides below the stripe are dark grayish olive, which extends onto the ends of the ventrals. In the main, the top of the head is deep olive, the plates ahead of the eye being buffy brown or mikado brown. The postocular, the spot on the temporals, and a broken line from eye to eye forward around the snout are cartridge buff. The upper and lower labials and the underside of the head are the same, but marked with black spots. In the eye, the pupil rim is capucine yellow broken in front where the iris is black. The same yellow is below and back of the iris pupil rim. The rest of the iris is pale orange yellow or maize yellow above, forward the corner of the pupil. The black spots of the underside of the head continue on the venter for 3 or 4 inches as 2 obscure rows. The color of the ventrals of the neck is flesh ocher or onion-skin pink for 2 or 3 inches, then antimony yellow, citron yellow, and light chalcedony yellow. In about the middle, a foot before the vent, hermosa pink and eosine pink come in. The underside of the tail is geranium pink or rose doree.

Habitat: This agile, striped racer has been placed in the neighborhood of ponds, lakes, and banks of rivers, often escaping into the water. It is of the Lower and Upper Sonoran and Transition zones. It is seldom seen in the open but rather in brushy places, grassy slopes, grassy meadows of the foothills and mountains. Klauber (1939a) called *Coluber lateralis* a daytime (diurnal) snake. He placed it in a cultivated habitat 4 times; grass 28; light brush 4; heavy brush-chaparral 52; also coast 165; inland valleys 147; foothills 216; mountains 19; desert foothills 35; undetermined 7.

Fitch in 1949 wrote: "The California racer . . . usually avoided capture by its speed and wariness. Twenty-six were marked and released, mostly in 1938, but none was recaptured. . . . General behavior—This chaparral-hunting species was nearly always seen in the vicinity of manzanita or ceanothus thickets into which it climbed to escape. Sometimes, at an alarm, one would dart through a bush to its farther side, and lie motionless there until closely approached. In such situations they were difficult to see. Another escape reaction consists of darting away with a violent lateral thrashing, causing a commotion that draws attention, then gliding back silently to the point where it had started, where an enemy might be least likely to look for it."

Period of activity: "Sixteen Year Census"—Jan., 2 snakes; Feb., 5; Mar., 26; Apr., 146; May, 187; June, 91; July, 55; Aug., 29; Sept., 29; Oct., 6; Nov., 5; Dec., 3 (Klauber, Gen., 1939a). *First appearance*—May 11; May 29, June 3 (Linsdale, Baja Calif., 1932). *Fall disappearance*—Aug., Sept. 14, Oct. 6 (Cope, Gen., 1900); Sept. 14, Oct. 6 (Stejneger, Calif., 1893). MVZ has Mar. 23–Nov. 10. *Hibernation*—"On November 26, 1947, while digging in Alvarado Canyon, near San Diego State College, I found a California Striped Racer *Masticophis lateralis* hibernating. The specimen was located about half way up the side of a steep slope on the shady side of the canyon in a topography characterized by chaparral type vegetation and large boulders of triassic felsite. The site itself consisted of a cavity about 12 inches below the surface of the ground, which was composed of loosely packed rocks and soil. The earth adjacent to the cavity was still cold and damp from a recent rain; the temperature was approximately 55 degrees Fahrenheit. . . . Apparently it is not imperative that a snake go deep in order to hibernate in this semi-arid climate" (Schwenkmeyer).

Breeding: Oviparous. *Mating*—"A pair of *Coluber lateralis* mated Apr. 1, 1941. No previous courting had been observed. The female dragged the male around the cage, not only on the ground but backward up into a small tree. The tail of the male was not entwined around that of the female. The pumping movements of the male occurred at the rate of 11 to the minute, when first observed at 11:50 A.M. These slowed down to 5 by 12:15 P.M. and to about 1 per minute at 1:02 P.M No more pumping was noticed and they parted between 2:10 and 2:25 P.M. Eight eggs were laid on May 27, 1941" (Perkins, Gen., 1943). *Eggs*—Klauber (1931a) records that on July 29, 1925, "Eight eggs were laid by a captive specimen" and on "July 30, 1927, a batch of eggs were measured having average dimensions of 54 mm. x 15 mm. (2⅛ in. x ²¹⁄₃₂ inch)." *Young*—"The young are striped like the parents, and are hatched from eggs. Last year's young are often found under boards, logs, etc., in likely places early in April" (Perkins, Calif., 1938). "Young of these racers were not often seen, and none was secured for measuring" (Fitch). Klauber's (Gen., 1943b) minimal measurements are: 343 mm. (tail 99) males, 406 mm. (tail 117) females.

Food: Rattlers, small mammals, lizards, snakes, young birds. Van Denburgh (Gen., 1922), Grinnell and Storer, Perkins (Calif., 1938), Fitch.

Field notes: (Most of our live specimens came from friends from Los Angeles to San Diego. Ernest Thompson Seton in one of the first volumes of *Bird Lore* emphasized the importance of journal-keeping. If space were available, we would substitute for this paragraph a set of field notes to direct your attention to the significance of a daily journal. Specimen notes on this species in Klauber's 1931(a) journal [pp. 69–70] emphasize the importance of study of the material at one's own door.)

Authorities:

Cope, E. D. (Gen., 1895)
Fitch, H. S. (Calif., 1949)
Grinnell, J., J. Dixon, and J. M. Linsdale (Calif., 1930)
Grinnell, J., and T. Storer (Calif., 1924)
Hallowell, E. (Calif., 1864)

Klauber, L. M. (Gen., 1939a; Calif., 1931a, 1932, 1934a)
Mocquard, F. (Baja Calif., 1899)
Perkins, C. B. (Gen., 1943; Calif., 1938)
Riemer, W. J. (Calif., 1954)
Schwenkmeyer, R. C. (Calif., 1949)

1938, C. B. Perkins: "This snake is the most common of the San Diego County racers and in my experience the hardest to catch. I do not believe it is as fast as the Red Racer, but it is usually found in the brush, and it's there one moment and gone the next."

San Francisco racer

Masticophis lateralis euryxanthus Riemer

W. J. Riemer discovered that east of San Francisco Bay six snakes constituted a new subspecies (*M. lateralis euryxanthus*). Roughly their characters were: a broad dorsolateral stripe, 1 and 2 half scales wide (not 2 half scales, *M. l. lateralis*). Venter of head and neck unspotted, light continuous stripe from eye to nostril; lateral light stripe and supralabial light stripe continuous; heavy suffusion of orange rufous on anterior light parts. (Not indicated on Map 36.)

Western striped racer (17—Van Denburgh 1922), Striped racer (14—Van Denburgh 1897)

Masticophis taeniatus taeniatus (Hallowell) 1852. Fig. 135; Map 36

Other common names: Great Basin striped racer; many-striped whip snake (Cronise 1868); mountain racer; Nevada striped racer; Pacific coachwhip snake; striped whip snake; western coachwhip snake.

Range: From Chihuahua, Mex., n.w. through w. New Mexico and w. Colorado, Utah, s. Idaho to s.e. Washington, thence s. through e. Oregon, n.e. California, Nevada, and across n. Arizona on the Colorado plateau to the Mexican highlands.—U.S.A.: Ariz.; Calif.; Colo.; Ida.; Nev.; N.M.; Ore.; Tex.; Ut.; Wash.; Wyo. Mex.: Chihuahua. *Elevation*—2,000 to 8,000 feet; 3,500–6,000 feet (Little); 4,000–6,500 feet (Linsdale); 4,000–8,000 feet (Bailey, N.M., 1913); 4,100, 4,700, 5,000 feet (Taylor); 4,100, 5,000, 6,200 feet (Van Denburgh, Gen., 1922); below 5,300 feet (Cary, Colo., 1911); 5,400 feet (Stejneger, Maslin); 5,500–6,500 feet (Eaton, Ariz., 1935b); 6,300 feet (Johnson, Bryant, and Miller).

Size: Adults, 30–61 inches.

Distinctive characteristics: A large medium, slender, 15-rowed, agile snake with white-edged head plates. Mid-dorsum of 5 scales and 2 half scales solid brownish olive or grayish brown flanked on either side by 5 (caudad 4) lateral stripes of white, light yellows, or light buffs. Underside of head is white mottled with dark, changing caudad to buffs and yellows to coral pink.

Color: A snake from 30 miles north of Delta, Ut., received from L. M. Klauber, July 18, 1928. Five rows and 2 half rows of mid-dorsal scales are brownish olive, sepia, olive brown, or grayish olive, becoming drab or drab gray on the tail, and deep olive or buffy olive on the dorsal head plates. For 6–8 inches or more, all the dorsal scales and all the dorsal and lateral head scales from the front of the eyes backward are white edged. Thereafter the white edgings become fainter caudad. The most prominent lateral stripe of cartridge buff, ivory yellow, or even white is on the lower edge of the 1st row of scales and along the ends of ventrals. On the 3rd and 4th rows is another stripe and a similar one also on the upper edge of the 4th and lower edge of the 5th rows of scales. In midlength these 2 latter stripes unite into 1 in the caudal half and are close together on the cephalic half of the body. Thus the sides bear 2 prominent light stripes, the one the combination stripe, the other on 1st scale row and ventrals. These stripes are all equally developed on the neck region. The upper labials are marguerite yellow. The pupil rim of the eye is white or cartridge buff. The iris is salmon orange, orange chrome, or mikado orange. Slightly in front of the pupil there is a dark vertical bar of the same sepia, olive brown, or brownish olive of the outer parts of the eye. The underside of the chin is white, changing on the first 15 or more ventrals to colonial buff, thence to ivory yellow or primrose yellow. For 6 inches or more, the chin and under parts are heavily spotted with pale purple-drab or pale brownish drab. Thereafter the mid-venter is free of it, and these spots are arranged on either end of the ventrals below the light lateral stripe. Finally, they look like a continuous dark pale drab band extending to the vent, slightly broken on each belly plate. Along either end of ventral plate below the dark area, a little pinkish buff appears, which later becomes light vinaceous-cinnamon, buff pink, or salmon. About midway of the body length, this crowds out the ivory or primrose yellow. The underside of the tail is solid coral pink or flesh pink.

Habitat: One author reports that "when chased it climbs into a sage brush and sticks its head out threateningly." The habitats are numerous: sage brush (4), *Artemisia* tangle (1), plains (2), creeks (3), hot mesa (1), brush (1), side of canyon (1), mountain road (1), open desert with bushes (1), foothills (1), beds of prickly pear (1), sandy knoll (1), alfalfa field (1), rocky slope (1), shad-scale flats (1), rocks (2), below piñon belt (1), and several more. Some record it beside or near streams or even in semidesert. Over half of the writers remark its climbing facility. "I have found it mostly among the trees and bushes (mostly oak) of Zion Canyon, where I have often seen it climb through the branches of the trees and brush almost as fast and gracefully as on the ground" (Woodbury, Ut., 1931). "The striped racer apparently is confined to dry hot and rocky chaparral-covered foothills. It is rare, and I have seen only 6 individuals" (Fitch).

In 1950 Lewis (N.M.) gave an excellent account of the Organ Mts. region. He described the different habitats with associated animals and plants of the varying elevations, the highest, 6,000–9,082 feet, being the rough and broken mountain ridge of igneous and sedimentary rocks. "The monolithic granite peaks of the Organ Range protrude from vast bajadas which slope far out into the valley. These alluvial fans, a mixture of huge boulders, smaller water-worn stones and areas of sand, fine gravel, and earth are deeply dissected by interconnecting dry washes." Among the representative flora are several oaks, a juniper, a fir, a willow, cacti, *Dasylirion, Agave, Berberis trifoliata*. The snakes found there in order of frequency are: *Masticophis t. taeniatus, Pituophis, Salvadora, Thamnophis,* and *Crotalus m. molossus.*

The photographs by Lewis of his *M. taeniatus* from the Organ Mts. have much in common with our photographs of *M. t. ornatus* from the vicinity of El Paso, the white lateral lines extending from nape to tail tip, and each separated into 2 white threads by the gray or black centers of scales of the 4th row. Our photographs of *M. t. taeniatus* came from the distant portion of the range of that form in Utah. Future comparisons will be valuable.

Period of activity: *Early appearances*—May 4–8 (Van Denburgh and Slevin, Nev., 1921a); May 4, 5, 11, 18, 19 (Stejneger); May 24 (Slater); May 2, 28 (Hardy, Ut., 1938). MVZ dates are May 7 to Oct. 26. *Fall disappearance*—Aug. 29 (Van Denburgh and Slevin, Ida., 1921b); Sept. (Quaintance, Ariz., 1935); Sept. 2 (Van Denburgh, Ariz., 1913); Aug. 13, Sept. 30 (Cary, Colo., 1911); Oct. (Hardy, Ut., 1939); Oct. 3 (Johnson, Bryant, and Miller).

Hibernation—"The den is located in a mass of cobblestone rocks that lie just below the old shoreline of ancient Lake Bonneville and probably represent the outlet of former springs that washed out the soil between the rocks and left underground channels into which the snakes can descend for hibernation. The den is surrounded by a sea of sagebrush. If they descend the slope more than a mile, they would encounter shadscale, and if they ascend the slope a similar distance, they would find juniper and pinyon forests. Seven species of snakes were found inhabiting the den. These included the following, listed in descreasing numerical order: the Great Basin rattlesnake, *Crotalus viridis lutosus;* western striped racer, *Masticophis taeniatus taeniatus*" (Woodbury and Smart). See also under "Young" below.

Breeding: Oviparous. Males 600–1,150 mm., females 575–1,000 mm. *Eggs*—"A specimen from Stockton (Tooele County) May 30, 1920, contained 9 elongate eggs 6 mm. by 33 mm. An individual from Osceola, White Pine County, Nevada, June 4, 1920, contained 8 large elongate eggs 10 mm. by 35 mm. The egg membranes are apparently without deposits of lime salts" (Pack). "Each of 2 females collected at 6,300 feet altitude in 1939 contained large eggs, measuring 27 mm. in length in a specimen taken May 20, and 40 mm. in one taken May 22" (Johnson, Bryant, Miller). "June 20, 1946. . . . Both specimens were gravid, each carrying 4 large eggs that could be easily recognized by their outlines through the abdominal walls. One of the eggs, when removed and examined, was 63 mm. long and 14 mm. in diameter and covered with a heavy membranous shell irregularly studded with small sharp rugosities about 1 mm. apart. No embryo was found in the egg, which at this stage was made up of an irregular yolk mass and an exceptionally large amount of albumen, constituting about a third of the volume" (Maslin).

Young—In 1928 Ortenburger held that "the young of *taeniatus* may easily be distinguished from the young of the other species of *Masticophis,* since only *taeniatus* and *girardi* have 15 rows of scales and in addition light borders to the head plates. . . . The majority of the juvenile specimens are marked exactly like the adults . . . some few juvenile specimens showing an interesting coloration, which is apparently more like *semilineatus* than like adult *taeniatus."* In 1951 Heyrend and Call, in the symposium of Woodbury et al., wrote that "Hatchlings of striped racers that enter the den in the fall are easily recognized not only by their size, usually between 14 and 17 inches in length, but also by their appearance. After a winter hibernation, they emerge in the spring with negligible change. Most of the yearlings that enter the den at the end of the following summer season, are also easily recognized by size, but thereafter more and more difficulty is encountered in determining age and size from recapture records."

Food: Lizards, rodents, snakes, young birds, insects. Pack, Woodbury (Ut., 1933), Fitch.

Authorities:

Barry, L. T. (Colo., 1933)
Brooking, W. J. (Ore., 1938)
Dodge, N. N. (Ariz., 1938)
Ellis, M. M., and J. Henderson (Colo., 1913)
Fitch, H. S. (Ore., 1936)
Johnson, D. H., M. D. Bryant, and A. H. Miller (Calif., 1948)
Linsdale, J. M. (Nev., 1938–40)
Maslin, T. F. (Colo., 1947)
Mocquard, F. (Baja Calif., 1899)

Ortenburger, A. I. (Gen., 1928)
Pack, H. J. (Ut., 1930)
Stejneger, L. (Calif., 1893)
Taylor, W. P. (Nev., 1912)
Woodbury, A. M. (Ut., 1928, 1931, 1933)
Woodbury, A. M., et al. (Ut., 1951)
Woodbury, A. M., and E. W. Smart (Ut., 1950)
Woodbury, A. M., and R. M. Hansen (Ut., 1950)

Ornate racer (5—Ditmars 1907), Texas coachwhip snake (3—Yarrow 1882)

Masticophis taeniatus ornatus (Baird and Girard) 1853. Fig. 136; Map 36

Other common names: Central Texas racer; Girard's racer; mountain racer; ornate whip snake; striped racer; Texas whip snake.

Range: Edwards plateau, trans-Pecos Texas, and s. into Coahuila, Chihuahua, Durango, and Zacatecas, Mex.—U.S.A.: Tex. Mex.: Chihuahua; Coahuila; Durango; Zacatecas. *Elevation*—1,000 to 5,000 feet.

Size: Adults, 24–72 inches.

Distinctive characteristics: A slim, beautiful, satiny-black, or purplish black 15-rowed snake with a light lateral stripe more or less broken. A light line or a row of light spots is present on ends of ventrals and 1st row. Ventrals gray or slate; underside of tail coral red.

Color: A snake from Helotes, Tex., caught Mar. 17, 1925. The back is a

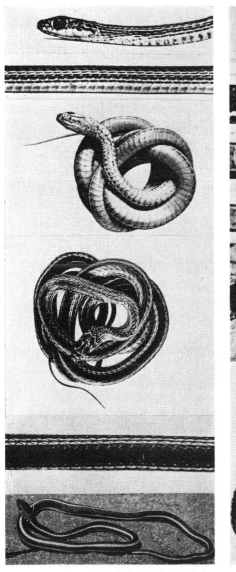

Fig. 135. *Masticophis taeniatus taeniatus:* 1–4, Delta, Utah, L. M. Klauber; 5, Buena Vista, Ore., S. Jewett, Jr.; 6, New Mexico, photo by T. H. Lewis.

Fig. 136. *Masticophis t. ornatus:* 1,6, El Paso, Tex., M. L. Crimmins; 2–4, San Antonio Reptile Garden, Tex.; 5, Helotes, Tex.

satiny black. Sometimes all the blacks of the body look dull purplish black. On the sides of the body ahead of the vent is a broken white longitudinal stripe, located on ½ of the 3rd, on the 4th, and on ½ of the 5th row of scales. This white band, 1 whole and 2 half scales wide, is marked longitudinally in its middle on the 4th scale row with a grayish olive, buffy olive, or hair brown longitudinal center. Or this center marking may be black toward the head and buffy olive behind on each scale. The first 2 cephalic longitudinal white lines are 6 scales long; the 3rd 7 scales, the 4th 9, the 5th 11, and the 6th 17. After the first 5 or 6 of these longitudinal stripes, only the buffy olive scale centers of the 4th scale row show, and these faintly. There are 9 of these bands on each side. The 1st and 2nd scale rows and sometimes the 3rd are vinaceous-rufous or hay's russet. Particularly is this true on the intervals between the white or light longitudinal bands. This same color occurs on the outer and inner edges of each scale when the skin is stretched. The space between the scales is pale medici blue, vinaceous-rufous, or hay's russet. There is a band 1 scale long across the top of the neck about 5 scales back of the parietals. This neck band is buffy olive or drab. This same color appears on the upper half of the rostral, internasals, prefrontals, frontal, and inner edge of the supraocular. The postnasal, loreal, preocular, and first 4 upper labials have white centers and rims of blackish slate. The postocular centers are buffy olive as is also the prenasal. The pupil has a white edge. The iris is marked with a circle of ochraceous-tawny which spreads over the top of the eye. The rest of the iris is blackish slate or dull purplish black. The underside of the head is white with the upper labial edge, the lower labials, the chin shields, and the lower neck spotted with black or blackish slate. The ventrals are mainly covered with dark gull gray, slate color, or blackish slate as the neck is approached. The ends of the ventral plates and also their rear edges are vinaceous-rufous or hay's russet. Beginning with the 10th plate, there is a blackish slate quadrangular center with pure white ends. From the angle of the mouth to the end of the 19th ventral is a beautiful white longitudinal band. For about 19 more the band is broken with square blackish slate centers to the scales. Thereafter the band ceases and goes as a line of buffy olive or grayish olive on the outer edges of ventrals and the edge of the 1st row of scales, extending to the vent. The underside of the tail is clear, unmottled, and light coral red.

In a snake from El Paso, instead of the broken white lateral line centered with gray or black, there appear 2 close-set threads of white extending unbroken from a light lateral neck spot to tip of tail.

Habitat: Habitat notes from the field are few. Doubtless we have seen as many of this form as any other observers, yet our information is meager. They may be along rivers, in canyons, "in the foothills" (Little and Keller, N.M., 1937), "at the spring near Frijole, quite close to water" (Mosauer), "up in the bushes" (Bailey, Tex., 1905), or on the hills, some distance from water. All in all, more have been taken near water than away from it. They like bushes or rocks for cover or places to await prey.

Murray has had as much experience with them as anyone. He wrote: "While not a single *Coluber* of the *flagellum* group was seen in the Chisos Mountains above a level of 4,000 feet, *C. t. girardi* is one of the commonest species. They are usually found lying in low bushes growing from among boulders. At the slightest disturbance they quickly disappeared into cavities among the rocks. Some were recovered after considerable labor in moving stones. Others were shot with a lizard gun and some escaped before they could be taken." (See "Field notes" below.)

"The natives know this snake as the black or mountain racer in contradistinction to the prairie racer as the coach-whip is commonly called. It is very difficult to capture as it readily climbs rocks and trees and is so rapid in its movements that it is almost impossible for one person to follow it close enough to be able to grasp it by hand" (Strecker, Tex., 1909a).

"*Coluber taeniatus ornatus* (Baird and Girard). This form is called *Coluber taeniatus girardi* Stejneger and Barbour by those who suppress secondary homonyms. Seven specimens collected on the Miller ranch are from the following associations of the Roughland belt: catclaw-grama, 1; stream bed, 6. One specimen was found dead on the road 15 miles north of Porvenir in the ocotillo-creosote-bush association of the Rio Grande Basin district" (Jameson and Flury).

"This species does not appear to be as limited to the less rocky associations as . . . [*testaceus*]. The 4 specimens collected were from the following 4 associations: cedar savannah, cedar ocotillo, mesquite-sumac-condalia, and walnut-desert willow. One of the sight records was in the persimmon-shinoak association and the other in the walnut-desert willow association" (Milstead, Mecham, and McClintock, Tex., 1950).

Breeding: Oviparous. Males to 1,780 mm., females to 1,500 mm. Though based on scant material, reams have been written on scalation and variation; we know next to nothing, however, concerning the habits, food, and breeding of this snake. Therefore the "Field notes" and "Authorities" sections will be extended.

Food: Snakes. Quillin and Wright.

Field notes: Mar. 16, 1925, Helotes, Tex.: Started up the Helotes creek bed. Under a flat rock near where we espied a fine *Polemonium* saw a black snake disappear. It was a large rock, but I got it up and caught my snake. We wondered when we looked at the rock the next time, how one pair of hands raised it and at the same time snatched the glistening racer from his sheltered hiding place. In fact, we never thereafter could lift that rock. The snake is a racer. It is a beauty. It is one of the *taeniatus-schotti* group. The boys at the store call it a "whipsnake." When seen on the ground, it is merely a streak of motion.

July 18, 1925, Hueco tanks, El Paso, Tex.: Col. M. L. Crimmins and Mrs. R. B. Alves organized a party to visit Hueco tanks for reptiles and Indian pictographs. Mrs. Alves with Mrs. Wright and others went to one side and Col. Crimmins, Margaret Leary (daughter of the late Col. Leary), and I approached from another side. While Col. Crimmins was showing Miss Leary how to noose a *Cnemidophorus* and while I stood with my back to them she noosed one of these lizards and it flew out of the noose and landed in a bush right beside me. I sensed a movement beside me and grabbed, expecting a lizard. Lo! A beautiful ornate racer seized me. Who was the most surprised, snake, I, Miss Leary, or Col. Crimmins? Later in the day when we came up to the other party, we planned to present proudly our exhibit, but alas, the bag it was in slipped from under my belt, and the snake is still there in Hueco tanks unless it is one of the 3 racer finds later sent us by good friends in that city. That day we saw several ornate racers which escaped us.

June 23, 1930, San Antonio, Tex.: R. Quillen tells me about climbing 25 feet up in a sycamore after a summer tanager's nest. He saw a swift (lizard) start over him. When he recovered from his surprise, on ornate racer was going over him pell-mell to safety. The ornate racer raises its head above ground a considerable distance and also raises its tail showing the pink underside. They are a streak compared to a mountain boomer. Are in ravines. Go under boulders for cover. Once in a while they find them on top of the hills.

Apr. 29, 1934, north of San Antonio, Tex.: On Classen's ranch Quillin and I went up the ridge to look for rock sparrows' nests. He doesn't care for crowds. We were about to turn back for the barbecue and Texas Conservation Commissioner Tucker's speech when I saw what looked to be a black racer. Then I thought it a pair. Then I saw the other in its mouth. This ornate racer had a *Salvadora* half down. It is the biggest ornate racer I ever saw, pink or reddish under the whole under parts except the forward parts. Never could have caught it if it had not been busily occupied. Lots of flat rocks on this ridge. Roy had just remarked that these ridges were where the ornate racer lived. We had a great trip and when we got back for the barbecue for a thousand people, we found our friends were little interested in our finds. I found myself besieged to be the impromptu substitute for the absent Commissioner. Such is the life of a snake hunter.

Authorities:

Brunner, H. L. (Tex., 1898)
Cope, E. D. (Gen., 1900)
Gloyd, H. K., and R. Conant (Tex., 1934a)
Jameson, D. L., and A. G. Flury (Tex., 1949)
Mosauer, W. (N.M., 1932)

Murray, L. T. (Tex., 1939)
Ortenburger, A. I. (Gen., 1928)
Schmidt, K. P., and T. F. Smith (Tex., 1944)
Strecker, J. K., Jr. (Tex., 1909a, 1915, 1930)

1937: E. L. Little and J. G. Keller (N.M.) wrote that their New Mexico specimens were "intermediate between *C. t. taeniatus* (Hallowell) and *C. t. girardi.*"

1939: L. T. Murray, who lived much of his early life in the Big Bend country as guide, student, and teacher, in one of his comments to us queried whether the black or mountain racer in the hilly country to the west of Waco was the same as the one in trans-Pecos Texas. His paper states: "The specimens from the Chisos Mountains are typical in coloration (Ortenburger, 1928, p. 36) but the single specimen from Helotes may be said to have melanistic tendencies. There are no white margins on the cephalic plates. The light areas normally found between the dark lines on scale rows 1, 2, 3, and 4 are completely covered or supplanted with black pigment. The non-pigmented areas found at intervals on scale rows 3, 4, and 5 in typical specimens are not entirely obliterated in this specimen. The typical white nuchal areas and the white on the nasals, loreal, preoculars, labials, and throat are present in striking contrast with the black ground color. The ventral surface is also much more heavily marked with black than in a typical specimen. Similar specimens from the Helotes area have been reported by Gloyd and Conant (1934, p. 3) and attributed to intergrading between *C. schotti* and *C. t. girardi*. While it is true that the absence of light margins on the head plates and the absence of median dorsal portions of white cross bands agrees with the coloration pattern of *C. schotti,* the black pigment that has covered or replaced these lighter areas is darker than the normal colors of either *schotti* or *girardi*. If intergradation is the explanation, complex inheritance of color in these snakes is indicated."

Ruthven's racer (Ditmars 1936), Tamaulipas racer (Perkins 1949)

Masticophis taeniatus ruthveni Ortenburger 1923. Fig. 137; Map 36

Range: From s. tip of Texas into Tamaulipas, Nuevo León, and San Luis Potosí, Mex.—U.S.A.: Tex. Mex.: Nuevo León; San Luis Potosí; Tamaulipas. *Elevation*—Sea level to 500 feet.

Size: Adults, 36–66 inches. Ortenburger (Tex., 1923b) in his description of this form found that 19 adult males measured 131–168 cm. (52–66 inches) and 9 adult females 126–155 cm. (50.4–62 inches).

Distinctive characteristics: "Characters very similar to those of *Masticophis schotti* (B. and G.) from which it differs primarily in possessing no dark lateral stripes" (Ortenburger, Tex., 1923b).

Habitat and habits: "Nothing is recorded concerning the habits or habitat of this form. In captivity, like others of the genus, *ruthveni* is extremely nervous, refusing food and striking whenever an object moves in the vicinity of its cage. Like at least one other member of its group, *semilineatus*, it attacks in a rather peculiar fashion; after the initial stroke, the anterior end of the body is relaxed in a loose loop and before it releases the teeth a strong jerk is given by suddenly straightening the body, which results in the flesh of the victim being torn and lacerated rather than merely punctured" (Ortenburger, Tex., 1923b).

Breeding: Oviparous. Males to 1,680 mm., females to 1,550 mm. *Young—* The smallest that Ortenburger (Tex., 1923b) gave was a young male, 48.5 cm. (less than 20 inches). Smith observed: "That the young of the true *ruthveni* are not striped is shown by EHT-HMS no. 23517 from Ciudad Maiz. This specimen measures 495 mm. in total length, the tail 160 mm. In color and pattern it is precisely like typical adult *ruthveni* save that the dorsal scales are but very faintly light-edged anteriorly. No distinct stripes whatever are evident anteriorly; a faint, threadlike light line is visible on the neck at the lower edge of the 4th scale row, but in no sense is this similar to the lateral light line of *schotti* or *australis*; adult *ruthveni* also show an exactly similar line (see Ortenburger, pl. 9)."

Field notes: June 18, 1930, Brownsville, Tex., at the Snake King's. He has a racer which may be Ruthven's racer. Blanchard also has a Ruthven's racer. He thinks they are different.

May 2, 1934, Brownsville: We went with Mrs. D. Mulaik to see W. A. King, Jr. They have no Schott's or Ruthven's racers. Whenever he does receive any, he sends them to Gloyd. [This was the year of the good paper by Gloyd and Conant on this form and Schott's racer.] Normally and in previous years they seldom received them because these slim racers are too fast and weigh too little. The collectors are paid by the pound.

Authorities:

Gloyd, H. K., and R. Conant (Tex., 1934a)
Ortenburger, A. I. (Gen., 1928; Tex., 1923b)

Shannon, F. A., and H. M. Smith (Tex., 1949)
Smith, H. M. (Gen., 1941h)

1923: A. I. Ortenburger described this racer, naming it after his mentor, Dr. A. G. Ruthven. He had 30–33 specimens (not 3 as Cope had for *schotti*). Of each species, moreover, Ortenburger had live specimens, and what a difference! Ortenburger later (1928) extended his discussion of this form: "There can be no question that *schotti* is the closest relative of *ruthveni* as it is the only geographical possibility. Moreover we have in the young of *ruthveni* a most interesting resemblance to *schotti* which is significant in view of the ranges of the 2 forms. Also *schotti* and *ruthveni* are the only 2 forms of the genus possessing dorsal scales with yellow anterior margins, another fact worthy of note."

1934(a), H. K. Gloyd and R. Conant: "A study of the material now

Fig. 137. *Masticophis t. ruthveni*, Brownsville, Tex., H. C. Blanchard.

Fig. 138. *Masticophis t. schotti:* 1–4,
Brownsville, Tex., H. C. Blanchard; 5,6, Til-
den, Tex., Mrs. W. O. Learn.

available indicates that the forms *girardi* and *schotti* intergrade in at least 2
regions at the southern edge of the Edwards Plateau, and that the forms
schotti and *ruthveni* intergrade in the lower part of the Rio Grande Valley."

Many of these so-called locality labels from Helotes northward are doubtful, as they knew.

1944, A. H. and A. A. Wright: We once had on our porch a dozen or more live *schotti* and *ruthveni* which were later lost. We still distinctly want *ruthveni* to be better defined.

Schott's racer (6—Strecker and Williams 1927),
Green racer (2—Ortenburger 1928)

Masticophis taeniatus schotti (Baird and Girard) 1853. Fig. 138; Map 36

Other common names: Eagle Pass racer; Scott's racer (a misspelling of *Schott's*); striped coachwhip; striped racer; striped whip snake.

Range: From south of e. edge of Edwards plateau in s. Texas into Coahuila, Mex.—i.e., "South Texan portion of West Gulf Coastal Plain" (Fenneman, Ecol., 1931) or Shreve's "Texas semidesert" of 1921.—U.S.A.: Tex. Mex.: Coahuila. *Elevation*—100 to 500 or 1,000 feet.

Size: Adults, 30–66 inches. Few know this species in the field.

Distinctive characteristics: A slim, long, 15-rowed, green-blue-gray snake with a solid mid-dorsum of 8 scale rows outlined by a thin light stripe; and with a broader dark-bordered light line on edge of the ventrals and 1st row of scales. The chin is white, the belly spotted and flecked with gray. Underside of tail different pinks; more or less of reds and pinks on venter.

Color: A snake caught Apr. 22, 1925. The 8 middorsal rows are in the forward part andover green, passing through olive to brownish olive or almost sepia on the tail. The dorsal head plates are saccardo's olive or buffy olive to citrine-drab. The preocular has a sulphur yellow center. The postrictal scales are sulphur yellow with xanthine orange centers. From this area, a xanthine orange band extends forward along upper edge of upper labials to lower edge of eye. The lower edge of upper labials is calamine blue or black, with chin shields washed with the same. The upper and lower labials are ivory yellow or sulphur yellow, the chin white or sulphur yellow. The iris rim is pinkish buff with pinkish cinnamon around it, and below at the rear and partly in front black or sepia. The first 3 scale rows are andover green in the forward part of the body, as are 4 scale rows in the rear of body. Along the suture line of ventrals and 1st scale row is a pale green-yellow longitudinal line which becomes sulphur yellow and is lost in the rear third of the body. Through the middle of the first 21 of the 1st row of scales is a thread of xanthine orange, becoming orange-rufous and then for 20 scales sulphur yellow. The xanthine orange covers the 2nd row for 10 scales, then becomes sulphur yellow for 8 scales, and the same xanthine orange covers the first 4 or 5 scales on the 3rd row. There begins on the neck on the upper edges of scales of 4th row a long longitudinal line of pale green-yellow which is lost in the caudal third of the body. The belly is sky gray or pale mission blue, becoming toward the vent pale salmon and under the tail coral pink, jasper pink, or light jasper red. From the 16th ventral there extends along the sides of these plates to the vent a line of sulphur yellow becoming pale green-yellow, then pale salmon color. Toward the tips of the ventrals, beginning on the 4th plate, is a band of xanthine orange, passing into light niagara green, then andover green.

Another snake caught May 15, 1925. The dorsal scales are glaucous gray or clear green-blue gray, becoming caudally andover green or slate olive.

A snake from Brownsville, Tex., received from H. C. Blanchard and described Sept. 22, 1929. Recently dead. The back between the 2 upper light stripes is deep olive, light olive, or dark grayish olive, becoming on the tail, olive-brown to buffy brown or drab or wood brown. The lateral color between the 2 lateral light stripes may be dusky olive-green, andover green, or slate olive. The under part of the tail is testaceous or terra cotta, becoming vinaceous-cinnamon ahead of vent.

Habitat: Gloyd and Conant assign this form to the mesquite and desert grass savannah area of the Gulf coastal plain of southern Texas. Its range falls in the poplar-oak savannah of Texas, the Texas coastal to Edwards plateau edge, or the Texas succulent desert and grassland deciduous forest transition of Shreve (Ecol., 1921). In our own experience we would not limit it to any one habitat. The area from near the mouth of the Rio Grande to Zapata is different from the desert area between Falfurrias and Edinburg. Each area had this form.

Period of activity: *First appearance*—Apr. 16, May 5, June 30 (Wright); Apr. 2, 10 (Marr). *Fall disappearance*—Sept. 22 (Wright).

Breeding: Oviparous. The only notes on this subject are Gloyd and Conant's on 3 sets of eggs: 3 eggs, June 6, 1930; 10 eggs, June 3, 1931, 38–49 mm. long x 22–35 mm. in diameter; 12 eggs, May, 36.5–47 mm. by 25–27 mm.

Food: Mice, rats, young sparrows, frogs. Gloyd and Conant.

Authorities:

Brown, A.. E. (Gen., 1901)
Gloyd, H. K., and R. Conant (Tex., 1934a)
Marr, J. C. (Gen., 1944)
Ortenburger, A. I. (Gen., 1928)
Schmidt, K. P., and D. W. Owens (Gen., 1944)
Shannon, F. A., and H. M. Smith (Tex., 1949)
Strecker, J. K., Jr. (Tex., 1922, 1928c)

1901, A. E. Brown: In his day no one received more material than Brown did from El Paso to San Antonio. His collectors just were not in the range of this form. Had he seen one alive, he never would have confused *schotti* and *taeniatus*. "It must be admitted that no great reliance can be placed upon color characters in specimens which have been for so many years in spirits" (Brown).

1909(b)–15 J. K. Strecker, Jr. (Tex.): Both in 1909 and 1915 he discussed *t. taeniatus,* not *schotti* nor *girardi.* When he worked over the collection of the Scientific Society of San Antonio in 1922, he had no *schotti* for comparison. We saw some of this society's collections. He did not in 1922 or 1925 know *schotti,* for he wrote, "Mr. Marnock collected several specimens of this rare snake (*Coluber schotti*) in the Helotes neighborhood. Two small examples are in the Baylor University collection." Around Mr. Marnock's home in Helotes in 1925 we saw and collected *ornatus,* the black mountain racer, not *schotti.* But at that time, no herpetologist knew the two in the field. Not until 1925 did we realize its distinctness, when we saw live *schotti* in Mrs. Learn's cages. We had already learned the *ornatus* racers in the field trips with our friend Roy Quillin, who has seen more of them than anyone else.

On a field trip with the versatile naturalist Strecker, he told me he had had little experience with the *taeniatus* group of racers. We are sure he had not then known *schotti,* nor too many *ornatus* specimens. When in his later years he began connecting with the Quillins and R. D. Camp, he surely must have seen *schotti.* In his 1930 catalogue of Travis County he clearly recognized *girardi* (*ornatus*).

1928: A. I. Ortenburger had only 3 specimens, but with his monographic discussion and his 4 photos (the first ever published) from life, workers had a distinct start toward clarification of Texan racers.

1934(a): H. K. Gloyd and R. Conant did a good job. Here is one of the finest problems of southern Texas. Like them we are wary of *schotti* records north and northwest of San Antonio. From years of experience in the regions involved, we believe all records from San Antonio to west of Waco are *ornatus.*

1944: K. P. Schmidt and D. W. Owens posed a problem: "The subspecies in the Chisos area across the river from Carmen Mountains is *Masticophis t. ornatus.* Additional collections are required to trace the area of intergradation between *schotti* and *ornatus* in Coahuila."

1944, J. C. Marr: "From their distributional records, SNHM 9864 [near Del Rio, Val Verde Co., Tex.] might be expected to be a *schotti-girardi* intergrade, but such tendencies were not noted. At least 2 other *schotti* were observed in the vicinity, but their extreme rapidity, terrestrially and arboreally, prevented their capture."

WATER SNAKES

Genus *NATRIX* Laurenti (Figs. 23, 25)

Size, small to large, 15–72 inches; small, *kirtlandi;* small medium, *rigida* and *compressicauda;* medium, *clarki* and several subspecies of *sipedon;* large medium, *cyclopion;* large, *rhombifera* and *taxispilota;* form usually chunky, slender in Regina group and *s. clarki* and *s. compressicauda;* tail short; head usually distinct from neck (small and indistinct in Regina group); anal divided; scales heavily keeled, rarely the 1st row smooth (*rigida* and *grahami*); in 19–33 rows; scale pits double; head plates normal; nasal divided or semi-divided (*septemvittata, rigida, grahami*); oculars 3–5 (6 or 7), preoculars 1 (2), postoculars 2–3, suboculars 2 (3) present in *cyclopion;* upper labials 6–10, the rear 2 or 2½ turned upward except in Regina group; lower labials 6–12; temporals 1 + 2 (3); posterior chin shields well developed, separated completely or incompletely, with 1–2 rows of gulars between their tips and ventrals; ventrals rounded; maxillary teeth smooth, increasing posteriorly with last 3 or 4 abruptly enlarged; mandibular teeth subequal; hemipenis: sulcus undivided; many spicules, a few spines, enlarged basal hook or hooks. Regina group = *grahami, kirtlandi, rigida, septemvittata.* Synonyms: *Clonophis, Coluber, Ischnognathus, Nerodia, Regina, Storeria, Tropidoclonium, Tropidonothus, Tropidonotus, Vipera.*

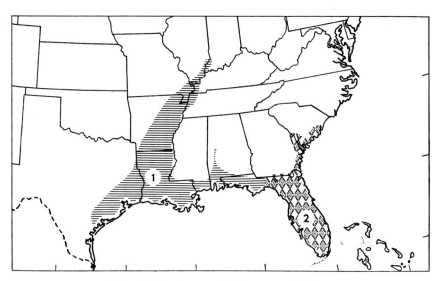

Map 38. *Natrix*—1, *cyclopion;* 2, *c. floridana.*

KEY TO THE GENUS *NATRIX*

a. Scale rows 19; head small, temporal region not greater or slightly greater than neck, really less (.9–1.1); no sharply upturned angle on rear upper labial margin, labials not swollen or bearing ridge nor projecting particularly beyond facial plates; eye over 3rd and 4th upper labials, rarely over 2nd and 3rd; labials 5–7/7–11; temporals 1 + 1, 2 or 3; body slender, medium, less than 40 inches. (**Regina** group)

  b. Preocular 1, postocular 2; upper labials 6 (4–6), lower 7 (6–9); nasal divided; all scale rows keeled, 1st row scales somewhat larger; dorsum spotted, pattern 4 longitudinal rows of small black or dark brown spots, outer rows alternating with inner, 43–65 in 1 row; venter, warm buff to orange-rufous; dark ventral spots separated on neck (2).   *N. kirtlandi*

 bb. Preoculars 2, postoculars 2; nasal semi-divided; upper labials 7; dorsum striped or uniform; ventral spots in 1–4 rows, if in 2 rows uniting as 1 on neck (1); light stripe or area more or less evident on rows 1–3.

    c. All scale rows keeled, 1st row largest and partially keeled; anterior chin shields shorter than posterior; 4 square brown spots on each ventral (2 close-set rows down middle, ends of ventrals brown) 3 light bands of drab or gray on venter; with or without 3 dark dorsal stripes (middorsal and on 5th row).

        N. septemvittata

   cc. First lateral scale row smooth; 1 or 2 rows of semicircular spots on ventrals; thread of black outlines 1st light lateral or hazel row and light ventrals; with or without 2 obscure dark threads bordering an indistinct middorsal band.

      d. Light lateral stripe if present on 1st row of scales (is hazel or sudan brown in life); anterior chin shields equal posterior.

           N. rigida

    dd. Light stripe on 1st 3 scale rows (pale ochraceous-buff); anterior chin shields much shorter than posterior; dorsum practically uniform, venter light buff.   *N. grahami*

aa. Scale rows 19–33; head large, distinct from neck (1.2–1.5 rarely 1.6); rear upper labial margin turned upward in sharp angle, labials swollen, making them wider than top of snout and visible in dorsal view, as are both eyes; a sharp line of demarcation between top of upper labials and facial plates and temporals; some labials with distinct ridge; temporal region swollen; eye over upper labial 4 (*rhombifera, pictiventris*) or 4 and 5 (5th often separated from eye by postocular); upper labials 8 (7–10); lower labials 10 (9–12); temporals 1 + 2 or 3.

  b. Rear of parietals broken into many small scales; upper labials 8; 2–4
anterior temporals; dorsal pattern distinct in young and adults, 21–26
distinct isolated quadrate spots on back to vent, also lateral series,
venter white to olive-buff, pale vinaceous-drab down center, heavily
marked with black; scale rows 27–33; stocky, long.   *N. taxispilota*
bb. Rear of parietals not broken into many small scales; normally 1 anterior
temporal; dorsal spots if present more than 26.
  c. Suboculars present; upper labials 8; dorsum uniform or with indistinct
  lateral bars (41–57) and small indistinct dorsal spots.
    d. Scale rows 27 in ♂s, 29 in ♀s; subcaudals 73 ♂, 64 ♀; tail in
    total length ♂ .249, ♀ .225; dorsal color olive brown with faint
    lateral threads of black in forward portion (lateral bars if present
    41–50 av. 45); venter yellow, heavily spotted with brown; under
    surface of tail black.   *N. cyclopion cyclopion*
    dd. Scale rows 29 in ♂s—31 in ♀s; subcaudals 82 ♂, 73 ♀; tail in
    total length ♂ .269, ♀ .249; dorsal color deep olive (lateral bars
    if present 49–57 av. 52); venter white to pale pinkish buff with
    spots of orange-vinaceous on outer edges of some plates, sub-
    caudals white with smoke gray edges.   *N. c. floridana*
  cc. No suboculars, 4th or 4th and 5th upper labials contact eye.
    d. Scale rows 25–31, usually 27; 4th upper labial contacts eye; back
    brown with 26–33 black rhombs on back connected with alternating
    lateral rhombs by diagonal bars, the lateral rhombs extending
    slightly onto ventrals; venter of body and tail buff with some black.
          N. rhombifera
  dd. Scale rows 19–25 (rarely 27 in *transversa*).
    e. Scale rows 23–25 (rarely 27 in *transversa*).
      f. Belly immaculate, at least in the center, uniform (including
      tail), or with small dark margins, never heavily flecked or
      blocked dark pattern on light ground.
      g. Adults spotted, subcaudal sutures dark.
        h. Dorsal pattern of 4 rows of uniform dark spots 58–65
        in a row; venter pink with center red, a little pigment
        at corners of plates and sutures on tail, where color is
        rose; head narrow, elongate; labials 8/10; anterior
        chin shields slightly longer than posterior; 23 scale
        rows.   *N. harteri*
        hh. Dorsal pattern of 3 rows of dark spots (middorsal
        saddles + smaller laterals), the pattern of the young
        persistent in part in the adult; 2 or less transverse
        bands on neck in young; venter buff or yellow; scale
        rows 23–27.   *N. e. transversa*

gg. Adults not spotted.

    h. Venter buff or yellow, subcaudals with dark sutures; dorsal pattern obsolete or reduced to 35–40 narrow light bars (remnants of youth pattern noted above); scale rows 23–27.   *N. e. transversa*

   hh. Venter red or orange (Atlantic coast) or yellow (Mississippi region); dorsum often uniform brown to fuscous black, but pattern (of youth) may be evident, particularly when wet, of median series of dorsal blotches alternating with lateral spots, 2–5 united to form cross bands on neck; 31–45 middorsal spots (young similar to *N. s. sipedon* and *N. e. transversa*); scale rows 23–25.

      i. "Venter usually salmon, but varying from pale pinkish orange to orange red." Normally no dark pigment on belly, or only a little of pale hue on corners of ventrals. Range: Coastal plain, Maryland to n.w. Florida and e. Alabama.

                                    N. erythrogaster erythrogaster

      ii. Venter yellow or lemon; normally only a little dark pigment and that of pale hue. Range: Extreme s.e. Missouri and w. Tennessee s. to Gulf and across extreme e. Texas.

                                        N. e. flavigaster

     iii. Venter red or scarlet, sometimes orange red; profuse black or dark brown pigment on sides of belly. Range: S. cent. Michigan, n.w. Ohio to mouth of Wabash River.   *N. e. neglecta*"
(Foregoing data from Conant [Gen., 1949])

ff. Belly blocked, flecked, or patterned with black or black and rufous; (adult dorsum often uniform in each subspecies notwithstanding described pattern).

   g. Complete cross bands entire length of body; venter with square or elliptical light spots surrounded or outlined by black or rufous areas.

    h. Dorsal saddles 11–17; ventrals 129–138; venter buff heavily checked or clouded with mahogany red and posteriorly with black; underside of tail almost entirely black.   *N. s. confluens*

   hh. Dorsal saddles on body 20–35; underside of tail usually with 2 rows of light spots outlined with black.

      i. Dorsal saddles on body 24 (19–35); ventrals more than 128 (126–139).

        j. Belly marked with few or many quadrate dark or reddish spots invading from the dorsum; saddles 19–33.   *N. s. fasciata*

       jj. Belly pink, with 1–3 dark triangular areas on each plate (base anterior margin); underside of tail black and white; dorsal blotches smaller, more numerous 34–35.   *N. s. engelsi*

  ii. Dorsal saddles on body commonly 27–29 (24–35); ventrals
  128 or fewer (120–139); ventrals partly or wholly covered
  by transverse elliptical white or yellowish spots surrounded
  by black or chestnut.   *N. s. pictiventris*

gg. Dorsal pattern of 3–16 complete cross bands in anterior portion of
  body; light ventral areas surrounding 2 rows of dark semicircular
  spots, or venter dotted, flecked, or uniform.

  h. 5–16 anterior transverse bands; posterior dorsum of 2 types:
  Cope's type—No dorsal spots, only lateral ones. Clay's type—
  Middorsal spots + alternating lateral spots 23 or 24–30 spots
  and bars on back. Intervals between lateral bars wider than
  bars—often 1 1/2–2x bars; venter apricot buff to vinaceous-
  rufous, marked in the center with 2 irregular rows of semicircular rufous spots, white or yellow in lighter parts; sometimes
  merely flecked or mottled.   *N. s. pleuralis*

  hh. 3–11 anterior transverse bands; posterior dorsum with saddles
  and alternating lateral spots; intervals less or greater than
  lateral bars (.5–1.5 rarely more than 1.5).

    i. Anterior bands 3–10; 28–45 dorsal spots or bars; lateral in-
    terval normally less than bars (.5–.8x); venter heavily
    flecked or commonly marked with 2 irregular rows of large
    russet black-bordered crescents; pattern commonly reduced
    to short dorsal light bars, or dorsum may be uniform dark
    almost black.   *N. sipedon sipedon*

    ii. Anterior bands 8–10; lateral intervals equal or somewhat
    greater than lateral bands (1–1.5); dorsal pattern of adults
    normally obsolete, color gray to greenish black, but if present
    more or less of *N. s. sipedon* type; belly uniform white or
    yellowish white, often heavily flecked in caudal region, and
    lateral bars may extend onto ventral plates.   *N. s. insularum*

ee. Scales 19–23; labials 8/10; temporals 1 + 2 (2 or 3).

  f. Scale rows 21–23; head not as broad as in larger heavier forms; body
  slender, medium (–40 in.); laterally compressed snakes.

  g. Dorsum of body with 4 russet, red, or black longitudinal stripes
  on 3rd to 5th and 8th to 9th rows; venter vinaceous-rufous with
  midventral row of semicircular spots; 1st scale row larger with
  light keel; caudals 57–80.   *N. s. clarki*

  gg. Dorsum more or less spotted (lateral spots, transverse bands)
  rarely uniform, or striped on anterior region, but not whole length;
  caudals 67–89; venter bears median series of light spots 1 to each
  plate distinct anteriorly (except in some *usta* phases).

                                    N. s. compressicauda

Color phases:

[h. Spotted, banded, or uniform (if stripes, then confined to neck); caudals 50–80, av. 60–71.

    i. Spotted or banded. (*obscura*) transverse bands anteriorly, 3 series spots posteriorly; (*walkeri*) numerous transverse bands on body; (*compressicauda*) dorsal vertical and lateral round spots posteriorly, 4 longitudinal neck bands; (*compsolaema*) closely placed cross bands.

    ii. Uniform. (*usta*) uniform or indistinct lateral vertical spots and transverse bands posteriorly.]

hh. Striped. 4 series of longitudinal spots, 2 on dorsum form stripes most of length, laterals from stripes on neck succeeded by spots; caudals 72–88, av. 74–82.   *N. s. taeniata*

ff. Scale rows 19. Caudals 65–82; dorsum uniform gray, sometimes black markings on base of scales 1st, 4th, 5th, and 8th rows; venter grayish yellow, tips of plates tinged with color of back.   *N. valida* (Some young with spotted backs and others with light lateral stripe prominent. Some adults with prominent light stripe on lower 3 scale rows; quite dark on underside of head and venter. Scales heavily keeled except lowest row. A.H.W. and A.A.W.) (Melanistic *celaeno*—ground color above and below grayish black, lighter stripe neck to tail on 2nd, 3rd, part of 1st scale rows). (Baja California and elsewhere in w. Mexico.)

Green water snake (20—Ditmars 1907), Cyclops
water snake (3—Rhoads 1895)

Natrix cyclopion cyclopion (Duméril and Bibron) 1854. Fig. 139; Map 38

Other common names: Cyclope water snake; cyclops; cyclop snake; Florida water snake; water snake (Yarrow 1882); western green water snake.

Range: From Apalachicola River, Fla., w. to Arkansas Bay, Tex., and n.e. through e. Arkansas, s.e. Missouri to the tips of Illinois and Indiana, thence e. of the Mississippi across the tip of Kentucky and n.w. Tennessee, thence w. of the Mississippi River to Louisiana.—Ala.; Ark.; Fla.; Ill.; Ind.; Ky.; La.; Miss.; Mo.; Tenn.; Tex. *Elevation*—Sea level to 500 feet.

Size: Adults, 25–60 inches.

Distinctive characteristics: A large, 27-to-29-rowed snake; olive-brown on mid-dorsum of 5 scales, then faint vertical bars 5 scales deep which send faint diagonal lines to another alternating series of vertical bars which extend to the ventrals. Unlike those of *taxispilota,* the parietals are not broken rearward, and unlike it and *rhombifera,* it has a sclerotic eye ring. The venter is light yellow on throat, then deeper yellows, and rearward heavily spotted with brown or flecked with black. Ventrals 136–148; caudals 57–70.

Color: Two snakes from Grammercy, La., received from G. Meade, May

17, 1943. The smaller snake has slightly more pattern. The 5 middorsal scale rows are uniform olive-brown or saccardo's olive. Below these rows on the side is a series of faint vertical bars crossing about 5 scale rows and spaced 3 scale rows apart. From the lower end of each bar 2 oblique black lines of interscale color extend diagonally backward and forward to an alternating series of bars or areas which are about 5 scales deep and extend to the ends of the ventrals. Practically all the color of these bars is due to black interscale color except in the lower ones where the bases and tips of the scales are very dark. The space between the lower bars is citrine-drab or dull citrine. In the middle of the body the whole dorsal color is olive-brown with only a slight suggestion of the bars. The top of head, face plates, forward upper labials, and upper third of other upper labials are brownish olive with the eye the same. Back of the eye, the lower ⅔ of upper labials is naples yellow, as are the lower labials, the suture lines being natal brown. Of the ventral color, the underside of head is light cadmium or primuline yellow passing through apricot yellow or mustard yellow to buff-yellow or naples yellow on about 30 unspotted ventrals. The succeeding ventrals are baryta yellow or massicot yellow more and more heavily spotted with natal brown flecked with black. These spots are arranged 2 on 1 plate, 3 on the next with 3 semicircular yellow spots on most plates. The underside of the tail is mostly black except for a massicot yellow mid-sutural line.

The larger snake. About 15 middorsal rows are dark olive. The lateral bars, though faint, are fuscous or black with the dark color on the scales more prominent than the black interscale color. The belly is much like that of the other snake. *Note:* These snakes suggest the *N. erythrogaster-rhombifera–transversa* group.

Habitat: Hurter (Mo., 1903, 1911), Viosca (La., 1923), Strecker (Tex., 1926c), Allen (Miss., 1932), and Penn (La., 1943) all agree that this species is a marshland form of small lakes and wooded swamps. It has been taken sunning itself on *Ceratophyllum emersum* and other surface plants and is very common in a prairie or brackish marsh. Both shallow and deep-water habitats have been recorded for this mud- and shore-loving snake.

Period of activity: *First appearance*—Mar. 15 (Corrington, Miss., 1927); May 19, 22 (Hurter). *Fall disappearance*—Oct. 3 (Hurter).

Breeding: Viviparous. Males 626–900 mm., females 660–1,250 mm. *Sexual dimorphism*—"The typical subspecies is distinguished by having the belly brown, scale rows 27 in males and 29 in females and the caudals averaging 73 in males and 64 in females" (Clay, Gen., 1938). *Mating*—"Mating activities were observed among the members of the 3 species *cyclopion, rhombifera,* and *fasciata* during the first 3 weeks of April. The matings invariably occurred on land, that is, in the gravel-covered portion of the cage, and generally started during the morning. . . . The female lay in a rather extended position with the male above in sinuous curves as described by Blanchard (*Bull. Antivenin Inst. Amer.,* IV [4], 1931). The male never grasped the female in his mouth as has been observed in the case of mating king-snakes" (Meade).

Young—"July 3, 1904 I shot a female basking in the sun on water plants. I hit it in the eye, which only stunned it long enough for me to catch it. I kept it in captivity until Sept. 20th, when it bore 19 live snakes, 265 mm. long" (Hurter). "The only specimen of *cyclopion* which was retained gave birth to 7 young on August 11, about 4 months after mating season" (Meade). The smallest specimen we have seen was 254 mm. Guidry (Tex., 1953) reported a brood of 16 born Aug. 10, 1949, and another brood of 9, July 16, 1952.

Food: Fish, frogs, toads. Rhoads (Tenn., 1896), Parker (Tenn., 1937), Strecker (Tex., 1926c), Guidry (Tex., 1953).

Authorities:

Cope, E. D. (Gen., 1900)   Meade, G. (La., 1934)
Goff, C. C. (Fla., 1936)   Viosca, P., Jr. (La., 1924)
Hay, O. P. (Ind., 1892)   Werler, J. E. (Tex., 1948)
Hurter, J. (Mo., 1911)

(1898) 1900 D. D. Cope: "I have seen [suboculars] in a specimen of the *N. taxispilota.*"

Florida green water snake (3—Conant and Bridges 1939),
Green water snake (5—Safford 1919)

Natrix cyclopion floridana Goff 1936. Fig. 140; Map 38

Common name: Congo water snake.
Range: Peninsular Florida with a narrow coastal tongue into South Carolina.—Fla.; Ga.; S.C. *Elevation*—Seacoast to 300 feet.
Size: Adults, 20–60 inches.
Distinctive characteristics: "Similar to *Natrix cyclopion cyclopion* . . . in having the eye separated from the upper labials by subocular scales but with the following distinctive differences: belly dominantly white or yellowish instead of dominantly brown as in *cyclopion;* scale rows usually 29 in males and 31 in females instead of 27 and 29, respectively, in *cyclopion;* subcaudal scutes average 82 in males, and 73 in females, as contrasted to 73 and 64, respectively, in *cyclopion;* tail length divided by total length average .269 in males and .249 in females, as contrasted to .249 and .225, respectively, in *cyclopion;* ventrals for males and females together average 137, as contrasted with 142 in *cyclopion;* lateral bars average 52, compared to 45 in *cyclopion*" (Goff). Ventrals 132–142; caudals 69–84. Lower labials 11–14.
Color: A snake from Eureka, Marion Co., Fla., Apr. 25, 1930, and checked with a snake from Silver Springs, Fla., received from E. R. Allen, Apr. 22, 1936 (this snake just dead). The scales of the back are deep olive or dark

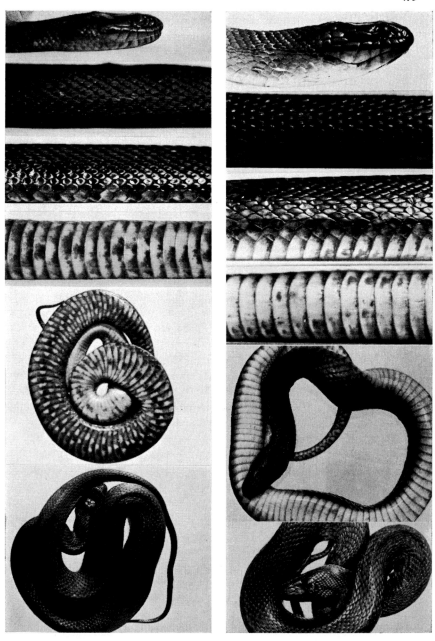

Fig. 139. *Natrix cyclopion cyclopion,* Mississippi, through E. R. Allen.

Fig. 140. *Natrix c. floridana,* Eureka, Marion Co., Fla., through B. C. Marshall.

greenish olive with some whole scales or edges of the scales black. The sides are grayish olive or citrine-drab. Amongst the scales of the first 6 rows are a few which are cartridge buff, ivory yellow, or tilleul buff. The top and sides of the head are dark greenish olive or dark olive. The labials are deep colonial buff, ecru-olive, or dull citrine with vertical sutures of dark greenish olive or dark olive. The iris is grayish olive like the back, drab, or buffy brown with an outer circle of black. The throat and lower neck are deep colonial buff. The belly is white, pale olive-buff, or pale pinkish buff, some of the plates having small spots of orange-vinaceous on their outer edges. On the underside of the tail, each caudal is white with a smoke gray edge or each 2 plates have a smoke gray edge with an intervening plate of white or olive-buff.

Habitat: Various writers have recorded them in the sloughs and pools of the Everglades, in roadside ditches in the Jacksonville areas after heavy rains, in streams, ponds, lakes, and marshes in central Florida, and in open rice fields in South Carolina. Carr found them in maiden cane along the beach of Lake Okeechobee and lying in the sun on rafts of maiden cane in lakes Harris and Griffin.

Period of activity: It may be more or less active throughout the year (see Carr's report Dec. 20, 1932). There are few records, but our own cursory notes include Mar. 17, 18, 24, Apr. 22, 25–30, May 4, 5, and June 21. Neill and Rose (S.C., 1953) give Feb. 23, Mar. 5, 28, Apr. 6, and Dec. 19.

Breeding: Viviparous. Males 675–980 mm., females 720–1,650 mm. *Sexual dimorphism*—"Distinguished from *N. c. cyclopion* by having the belly predominantly yellow or white, scale rows 29 in males and 31 in females, and caudals averaging 82 in males and 73 in females" (Clay).

Young—7–101. "Two female green water snakes, which were in the same cage, both gave birth to young on the same night, July 15, 1928. The next morning there remained but 15 living and 5 dead young. It was evident that both specimens had given birth to young during the night, of which, no doubt, they had eaten a large number before I arrived. This cannibalistic tendency is not unusual among water snakes in captivity" (Van Hyning, Fla., 1931). "Two specimens from Marion County, Florida, bore young in captivity." Fourteen young born on July 27, 1936—222–249 mm. long; 10 young born on Aug. 7, 1936—240–259 mm. (Conant and Downs). The smallest young snake of this species that we have seen was 254 mm. "On July 15, 1948, a 4 foot 2 inch *Natrix cyclopion floridana*, in my collection, gave birth to 101 young. Only 41 of these were alive at birth, but the others were perfectly formed. There were no infertile ova. Ten specimens were selected to be measured: the young snakes measured between 253 and 275 mm., with an average of 261 mm. The female was captured Apr. 11, 1948, about 20 miles SW of Lake Okeechobee, in Hendry Co., Fla. At the time of capture, the snake weighed 6 pounds. While in captivity she refused all food and vigorously resented any handling. Another specimen captured in 1946 was 5 feet 6 inches in length and weighed 9 pounds. This specimen contained 67 well-formed embryos" (Telford, Fla., 1948). On May 4, 1950, E. H. McConkey of Gainesville, Fla., said that he had a record of 91 eggs. Neill and Rose (S.C., 1953) recorded a female which, on Aug. 15, 1940, gave birth to 7 young.

Food: Frogs, fish, salamanders. Van Hyning (Fla., 1932).

Authorities:

Carr, A. F., Jr. (Fla., 1940a)

Clay, W. M. (Gen., 1938)

Conant, R., and A. Downs, Jr. (Gen., 1940)

Goff, C. C. (Fla., 1936)

Loennberg, E. (Fla., 1895)

Safford, W. E. (Fla., 1919)

Van Hyning, O. C. (Fla., 1931, 1932)

Red-bellied water snake (47—Smith 1882)
Copper belly (18—Holbrook 1849)

Natrix erythrogaster erythrogaster (Forster) 1771. Fig. 141; Map 39

Other common names: Agassiz's water snake; copper-bellied moccasin; copper-bellied snake (6—Catesby); copper-bellied water snake; orange-bellied moccasin; red-bellied black snake.

Range: Coastal. From Pocomoke River, Maryland and Delaware, through s.e. Virginia, e. North Carolina, e. and cent. South Carolina and Georgia, e. Alabama and n. Florida.—Ala.; Del.; Fla.; Ga.; Md.; N.C.; S.C.; Tex.; Va. *Elevation*—Mainly below 1,000 feet, possibly some to 2,000 or more feet.

Size: Adults, 24–54 inches.

Longevity: 8 years 10 months (Conant and Hudson, Gen., 1949).

Distinctive characteristics: Adults with no pattern, midback deep browns; chestnut brown to citrine, greenish, or buffy colors on side; venter in front may be buffy, then rufous, and on rear jasper red. Ventrals 137-158; caudals 60-87 (Clay). This probably expresses the *N. e. erythrogaster* condition, although the numbers are from a study which includes *neglecta, flavigaster,* and *erythrogaster*. Conant (Gen., 1949), however, states: "There is remarkably little variation in scutellation among the several races of *erythrogaster*."

Color: A snake from St. Stephens, S.C., received through E. R. Allen, Aug. 31, 1937. The midback for about 8 scale rows is chestnut-brown. Then the sides for 2 to 3 scale rows are dresden brown. The 1st, 2nd, and part of 3rd scale rows tend to become buffy citrine with the keels on the 1st row and other parts touched with ventral color. The interspaces between the scales of the dorsum are prominently black. The top of the head and dorsal scales for 3 or 4 inches are mummy brown. This color extends along the side of the head from the eye backward, not involving the upper labials or face colors except as dark sutures. The upper labials, face plates, and rostral

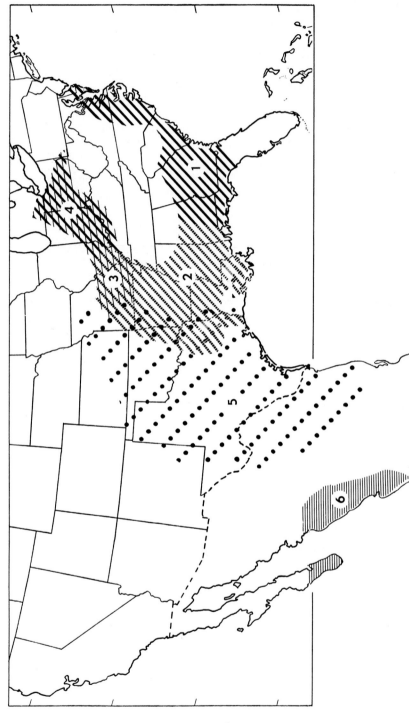

Map 39. *Natrix*—1, *e. erythrogaster*; 2, *e. flavigaster*; 3, *e.* (intergrade); 4, *e. neglecta*; 5, *e. transversa*; 6, *valida*.

are hazel. The rear upper labials to the vertical of the eye and the lower labials are marked with apricot orange, which is prominent on the side of the neck back of the angle of the mouth. The iris is mummy brown with a thin pupil rim of apricot buff or apricot orange. The first 3 ventrals, some of the lower gulars and the chin shields are ivory yellow or white, each centered with apricot orange except the anterior chin shields. The lower neck for 3 or 4 inches is apricot buff with the ends of the ventrals apricot orange. The middle section of the belly is rufous, shading through carnelian red on rear of belly to jasper red or coral red.

Habitat: With this race, as with the other 3 of *N. erythrogaster,* field information in scanty. Deckert (Fla., 1918) found it in a "bayou"; Harper (Ga., 1930) placed it at the "edge of a mill pond." For North Carolina, Brimley (1942), and for South Carolina, Corrington (1929), gave no habitats. Carr (Fla., 1940a) held it a "rarity in northern Florida, apparently a fluvial form." But Brimley (N.C., 1909) wrote: "One a little over 1,200 mm. taken in May, 1906, and two, one 1,200, the other 1,100 mm., in May, 1907. These Copperbellies, as they are called in North Carolina, are uniform rusty red above, and yellowish red below."

Period of activity: *First appearance*—Apr. 5 (Harper, Ga., 1930); May (Brimley, N.C., 1907, 1909). *Fall disappearance*—Aug. 13–15 (Deckert, Fla., 1918). *Hibernation*—"No hibernation records for this rather common species" (Neill).

Breeding: Viviparous. *Sexual dimorphism*—(See *N. s. sipedon.*) *Mating*— "George Van Hyning presented me with 2 live specimens collected May 22, 1938, in the Suwannee River near Fannin Springs, Gilchrist County (D.B.U.F. 1919). This pair, a male and female, were kept alive for a month and fed on frogs and fish; during this time the male kept up a nearly continuous courtship, lying for hours at a time across or entwined with the female. Copulation apparently never took place, however, and no eggs or young were found in the oviduct of the female" (Carr, Fla., 1940a).

Young—"I have no knowledge of the small individuals of *erythrogaster*" (Brown, Gen., 1901). "All I have seen have been large specimens and I have never satisfactorily identified the young" (Brimley, N.C., 1941–42). We have in our notes measurements of small individuals 283, 283, 284, and 295 mm. but we have no locality data for these except that one was from South Carolina.

Ecdysis: "A large red-bellied water snake (*N. e. erythrogaster*) with an inch-long gash on the neck, shed 5 times at intervals of 19 to 26 days, and thereafter shed at the more usual rate of once every 35 to 45 days" (Neill).

Food: Fish, crayfish, frogs, salamanders. Ditmars (Gen., 1907), Schmidt and Davis (Gen., 1941).

Field notes: Once we stopped off at Columbia, S.C., to see Corrington's collection of live snakes, his annual exhibit in the college chapel (horror of horrors!), and we marveled at his easy handling of a beautiful huge copper-bellied specimen which was very well behaved.

May 6, 1950, Panama City, Fla., at Jack Tillman's Snakeatorium: He has 2 *erythrogasters,* salmon on the belly like *N. e. erythrogaster* but light olive-green on back, more like *N. e. flavigaster* of Mississippi valley.

Authorities:

Brimley, C. S. (N.C., 1909, 1941–42)   Holbrook, J. E. (Gen., 1836–42)
Conant, R. (Gen., 1949)   Meanley, B. (Md., 1951)
Corrington, J. D. (S. C., 1929)   Neill, W. T. (Ga., 1950b)
Dunn, E. R., and R. Allen (Pa., 1935)

1901, A. E. Brown (Gen.): "There is not the least doubt in my mind that this form is again the result of darkening with age of the red specimens of *fasciatus.*"

We smile at two notes we made in 1940 and 1950:

1940, A. H. Wright: I was a sophomore when Clark published his 1902 note and wondered at its slow acceptance by Michigan herpetologists, but the red-bellied snake question is not yet completely solved. We have seen specimens collected by our students and we ourselves have collected in the Mississippi valley and on the Atlantic coast. Does the recent school know from sufficient live firsthand experience with each region that the Mississippi Valley yellow belly is the same as the Atlantic coastal copper belly? Are we sure all the specimens identified as *erythrogaster* are *erythrogaster*? (Witness Pennsylvania; Lake Erie islands [see *N. s. insularum*]; Connecticut—Cope, Eckel, Stejneger; Lake Superior—Agassiz.) See the clearance with elucidations of the *transversa* problems from Viosca and Taylor. Are all the red-bellied and yellow-bellied specimens really alike? I have been on the side lines for 40 years and have sometimes smiled at the positive opinions and overcautious acceptances. Nevertheless we have surely had some clarification.

1950: Surely Conant's study is a great help. Here is where museum and university studies of alcoholic material for revisions are supplemented by *zoos with live material.* Living animals collected in the field are the very best clues. For example two of the very best contacts with it come from Corrington and Brimley, but they give us no detailed habitat notes. Corrington writes, "The Red bellied form is less frequent than the typical, (*fasciata*), but runs to larger size and is locally held in decidedly greater fear by most persons, to whom it is known as the Copperbelly or Copper-bellied Moccasin. My own experience has been that in this color phase the Water Snake is much more tractable and will more often permit capture and handling without resentment than will the typical form."

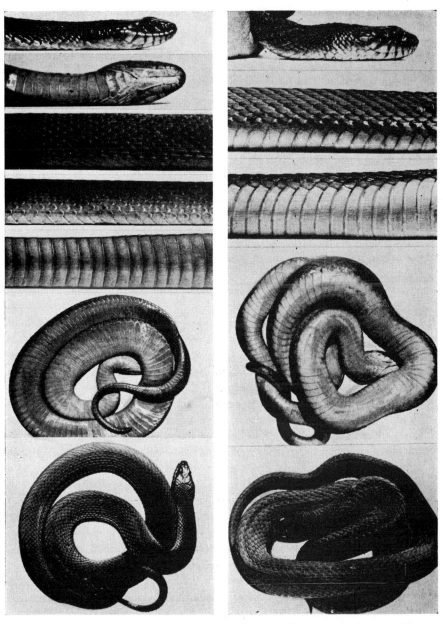

Fig. 141. *Natrix erythrogaster erythrogaster,* St. Stephens, S.C., through E. R. Allen.

Fig. 142. *Natrix e. flavigaster,* Imboden, Ark., B. C. Marshall.

Yellow-bellied copper belly, Mississippi Valley copper belly

Natrix erythrogaster flavigaster Conant 1949. Fig. 142; Map 39

Other common names: Yellow-bellied water snake (Conant); yellow-belly water snake.

Range: From cent. Alabama and Mississippi embayment to s. tip of Illinois; s.w. through s. Missouri and all of Arkansas to e. Oklahoma and n.e. Texas; s.e. to mouth of Mississippi River.—Ala.; Ark.; Ill.; Kan.; Ky.; La.; Miss.; Mo.; Okla.; Tenn.; Tex. *Elevation*—Mainly below 500 feet; records, however, to 1,250 feet.

Size: Adults, 17–48 inches.

Distinctive characteristics: "A large water snake of the genus *Natrix* that is characterized by a more or less uniform grey or greenish grey dorsum and a plain (or nearly plain) yellow or lemon-colored venter. From adults of the subspecies *erythrogaster* and *neglecta,* it may be distinguished by its coloration; it differs from *transversa* in not (normally) retaining strong indications of the juvenile pattern throughout life" (Conant). Ventrals 147–153; caudals 65–81.

Color: A snake from Imboden, Ark., from B. C. Marshall, Apr. 18, 1929. The dorsum of the body and top and sides of the head are fuscous, fuscous-black, drab, or black. The upper and lower labials except for their dark sutures, the posterior chin shields, and the gulars are light salmon-orange or bittersweet pink. The anterior chin shields are ivory yellow or white. The background color of the iris is deep plumbago blue or deep dutch blue clouded or faintly washed with olive-buff, light yellowish olive, or ecru-olive. The ventral surfaces are buff-yellow or maize yellow. The anal plate, the one ahead of it, and 1 or 2 behind it are clear salmon-buff or light pinkish cinnamon. The caudals have a wash of the same, with the sutures marked with dorsal color; hence the tail is darker than the rest of the venter. (For color of young, see under "Breeding" below.)

Habitat: See *Natrix e. erythrogaster.* However, for this marsh, pond, bayou, and river-bottom form, Parker (Tenn., 1948) reported: "Copperbellies are perhaps more likely residents of isolated woodland ponds than even the more abundant *Natrix r. rhombifera.*"

Period of activity: *First appearance*—Apr. 20 (Allen, Miss., 1932); May 13 (Hurter). "Like the other water snakes, the Copperbelly is seldom found before April" (Parker, Tenn., 1948).

Breeding: Viviparous. Females to 1,250 mm. *Mating*—"*Natrix erythrogaster* (Forster).—Two adults were discovered mating among the grass and weeds at the edge of a swampy area adjoining a drainage ditch, a little before noon of a sunny day, June 16" (Blanchard, Ill., 1925).

Young—"A female which I found in Randolph County, Illinois, gave birth to 13 young on September 4th. From one of these the following color description was made. Young born in captivity, showed at the age of 2 days the following color pattern. The first impression is that it is a young *Natrix fasciatus*. Twenty-seven saddle-like blotches of dark brown, nearly black, on the back. These blotches extend over the back from the ventral on one side to the other. These blotches are widest on the back, where they are separated from each other by a light narrow streak. They become greatly reduced in width at the sides, where the space between the blotches is red. On the posterior third of the body the blotches are of the same dark color as those on the back and in a red field. On the anterior ⅔ of the body the ventrals have a dusky bluish edging on the sides, leaving the central part plain yellow. The rest of the body and the tail, all the ventrals and subcaudals, have an edging of the same bluish color across the posterior edge of the plates" (Hurter).

(See "Authorities" below for Viosca's Louisiana brood in September, 1922.) The same year in Henry, Tenn., Blanchard observed: "Surely [it is] not time to synonymize the name with *sipedon*. . . . It appears that young examples of *erythrogaster* show the dorsal pattern of *sipedon* but not the ventral. It is particularly desirable that numerous entire broods of both these forms from the same region be obtained for examination."

Parker (Tenn., 1937) spoke thus: "Young specimens show a pattern of blackish saddles anteriorly and alternating dorsal and lateral blotches posteriorly. These markings practically disappear before the snake reaches maturity. The belly is plain yellow, or reddish, except for dusky mottlings on the ends of the ventral plates." On Sept. 9 and 10, 1952, Guidry (Tex., 1953) reported broods of 18 and 5.

Food: Fish, frogs, toads, sirens. Hurter, Blanchard (Ill., 1925), Parker (1937), Guidry (Tex., 1953).

Authorities:

Blanchard, F. (Ill., 1925; Tenn., 1922)   Shannon, F. A., and H. M. Smith
Conant, R. (Gen., 1949)   (Tex., 1949)
Hurter, J. (Mo., 1911)   Viosca, P. (La., 1924)
Parker, M. V. (Tenn., 1937, 1948)

1924, P. Viosca: "*Natrix erythrogaster*: According to old records there have been found in Louisiana both *erythrogaster* and *transversa* which, when recognized at all, are still considered as phases of *sipedon* or *fasciatus*. Almost all specimens corresponding to *erythrogaster*, which I have taken in this state, had a yellow instead of a copper belly, however, and many were of large size, the largest individuals approaching the size of *rhombifera*. On the other hand, I had a series of small specimens which were typically like *transversa*. As the series grew, it became evident that the transversely banded specimens were the young of the larger unbanded species, and in September, 1922, I was rewarded with a brood of young from a 4-foot individual, which cleared away all doubts. . . . Although some links of evidence are still missing, there is sufficient to indicate that the Louisiana form, which loses its regular and symmetrical transverse bands rather early in life, gradually intergrades with the typical central Texas *transversa* which never completely loses its markings."

Finally R. Conant reported: "Intergradation occurs with all 3 other races of the species—with *erythrogaster* in central Alabama, with *neglecta* near the head of the Mississippi Embayment, and with *transversa* through a broad area extending from northwestern Arkansas and eastern Oklahoma southward through east central Texas." The radius around the mouth of the Ohio River is a very variable center.

Northern copper belly

Natrix erythrogaster neglecta Conant 1949. Map 39

Range: From s.w. Pennsylvania (?) to s. Michigan and s.e. Wisconsin; thence through Illinois to the Wabash River and extreme n. Kentucky.— Ill.; Ind.; Kan.; Ky.; Mo.; O.; Okla.; Pa. (?); Wis.; W. Va (?). *Elevation* —Mainly above 500 feet and up to 1,000 feet.

Size: Adults, 18–55.5 inches.

Distinctive characteristics: "A large water snake of the genus *Natrix* that is characterized by a uniformly black or very dark brown dorsum and by the presence of red, scarlet, or reddish orange upon the abdomen. From other races of *erythrogaster* it may be distinguished by its coloration and by the marked tendency of the dark dorsal pigmentation to descend upon the belly, heavily involving the ends and bases of the ventral plates and often almost crowding out the red pigment on the posterior part of the belly. Among juveniles there is a strong tendency for the dorsal and lateral blotches to be fused irregularly" (Conant, Gen., 1949). Ventrals 144–158; caudals 64–80.

Habitat: Clark (Mich., 1903) made many observations which were long ignored. He wrote: "Both are very aquatic in their habits, but *erythrogaster* (known about Olivet as the 'red-bellied black snake') is more often seen away from the nearest stream, while *sipedon* is rarely seen more than a few feet from water. Both are very active, and when once alarmed are very shy, but *erythrogaster* is decidedly the more wary and somewhat more rapid in its movements. Both swim with speed and grace and can remain under water for some time. Like all of our snakes, these water snakes have a very strong odor, especially during breeding season. . . . Both of these water snakes are accustomed to come out of the water, especially on sunny days, and lie, more or less coiled, upon the bank, on logs in or beside the water, upon the branches of bushes overhanging the water, or upon piles of brush through the open spaces of which they can drop quietly down into the water below. Such piles of brush are their favorite spots, and one often sees three or more snakes coiled up together on the same pile. When so resting they seem rather stupid and may be closely approached and killed with a stick; but I think this is due, not to stupidity, but to reliance upon their protective coloration, for when once convinced that they are observed they will glide into the water without delay."

Blanchard (Ind., 1926) found the form "by a ditch in cypress woods on the Ohio River flood-plain near Smith Mills, Henderson County, Kentucky, June 15," and "by a pool in same cypress woods."

Conant (O., 1938a) declared: "The red-bellied water snake is rare in Ohio but although it has been taken in only two restricted localities, it appears to be well established in each. The conditions in both are similar. There are small woodland ponds, shallow in spring but frequently becoming dry in summer. Second growth woods border at least a portion of them, but open grassy meadows (devoted to grazing) are adjacent to or even surround the smaller ones. Cat tails rise in many and in the majority there is a profuse growth of the button-bush (*Cephalanthus occidentalis* L.). . . . Red-bellies are active and aggressive. They plunge into the water when approached and once alarmed they often remain motionless on the bottom where several were found by probing for them with the hands. They strike and bite viciously and their sharp teeth are capable of producing deep scratches or may be broken off in the captor's hand or glove. Some individuals flatten their bodies perceptibly when they are in striking position. The musk glands are used freely and the fluid, which is of a most unpleasant odor, is copiously discharged."

Breeding: Viviparous. Males 760–1,218 mm., females 685–1,270 mm. *Mating*—"In no case were *sipedon* and *erythrogaster* found on the same pile of brush, and specimens of the 2 forms were never seen together or even near each other, although males of *erythrogaster* were on several occasions found mating with females of the same form and male *sipedons* with females of their own race" (Clark, Mich., 1903). "On May 7, 1932, much activity was noted in the colony of the red-bellied water snakes near Blakesley, Williams County. Many were swimming about in the water and one, evidently oblivious to the collector's presence, swam close enough to be caught easily. Mating activities were evidently in progress, for several pairs were found together; it was impossible to ascertain whether they were actually in coitu for they became alarmed and separated when approached. In the same locality, April 22, 1933, a pair was found mating and another male lay coiled nearby" (Conant, O., 1938a).

Young—"The absence of small specimens of *erythrogaster* is one of the most puzzling facts met with and one for which it is difficult to account. Possibly the young are born later than those of *sipedon* and careful searching in the late summer or early fall may yet reveal some of them" (Clark, Mich., 1903). "Three litters of young were born in captivity. A female 43 inches in length (but with part of the tail missing), collected near Mt. Victory, Hardin County, July 23, 1932, gave birth to 8 young September 30, 1932. Another female 43⅞ inches in length, taken in the Williams County locality, April 22, 1933, bore a litter of 10 young, plus 4 dead, but well-formed embryos, October 10, 1933. On October 14, 1933, a third female 48¾ inches in length, with the same collecting data, gave birth to 8 young plus 19 dead embryos, and also passed 3 infertile ova. Further evidence that the birth was abnormal is seen in the fact that several of the embryos were malformed and showed signs of having been dead for some time. Lengths of the living young from the 3 groups varied from 8⅝ to 10⅜ inches at birth" (Conant, O., 1938a).

Food: Frogs, toads, fish. Clark (Mich., 1903), Conant (O., 1938a).

Authorities: [1]

Clark, H. L. (Mich., 1903, 1903a, 1904a, 1904b, 1904c)
Clay, W. M. (Mich., 1934)

Conant, R. (O., 1934, 1938a)
Dunn, E. R., and R. Allen (Pa., 1935)
Funkhouser, W. D. (Ky., 1925)

1934: W. M. Clay's note on the rediscovery of the red-bellied watersnake, *Natrix erythrogaster* (Forster), in Michigan gives the history of literature on this snake in Michigan and recounts how Dr. Conant with a party from the University of Michigan visited Clark's locality and found the snake.

1935: E. R. Dunn and R. Allen wrote on the red-bellied water snake in Pennsylvania.

1951: Dr. Norman Hartweg wrote us that "six students and myself searched Clark's locality very diligently but found no sign of *N. erythrogaster*. We will try again next spring."

Hallowell's water snake (18—Strecker 1902), Blotched water snake (10)

Natrix erythrogaster transversa (Hallowell) 1852. Fig. 143; Map 39

Other common names: (Couch's) water snake; green-banded water snake; (water) moccasin; Woodhouse's water snake (6—Yarrow 1882); yellow-bellied water snake (5).

Range: From n.w. Missouri, through e. Oklahoma and Texas, eastward in coastal Louisiana to Mississippi River, s. into Coahuila, Nuevo León, and Tamaulipas, Mex., thence n. through s.e. New Mexico and n.e. across the panhandles and s.e. Kansas.—U.S.A.: Ark. (?); Kan.; La.; Mo.; N.M.;

---

[1] 1955: Conant (*Ohio Jour. Sci.,* **55**:61) reported two new stations in Williams Co., O., added much about habitat—bog meadow and marsh swale—and noted the presence of this snake in Union Co.

Okla.; Tex. Mex.: Coahuila; Nuevo León; Tamaulipas. *Elevation*—Seacoast to 5,000 feet, mainly between 1,000 and 4,000 feet. 2,800–5,000 feet (Bailey, N.M.; 1913).

Size: Adults, 18–67½ inches.

Longevity: 4 years 3 months (Conant and Hudson, Gen., 1949).

Distinctive characteristics: A large-medium, olive, grey, or brown snake with a row of darker dorsal saddles plus an alternating series of lateral square spots. Under parts almost immaculate from olive-buff to ochraceous-orange; sometimes there is a dark spot near ends of ventrals, or ends of ventrals have a deeper color than middle of venter. Often a pair of parietal spots. Dorsal scales 23–27; ventrals 141–155; caudals 61–86.

Color: A snake from Helotes, Tex., Mar. 13, 1925 (a young one from last year's brood). This snake is marked with dorsal bands of olive-brown or clove brown separated by cross lines 1 scale wide of pale olive-buff. The dorsum of the tail is buffy brown with no crossbands visible. On the sides alternating with the dorsal saddles are vertical spots of clove brown. The interspaces here are vinaceous-fawn or light vinaceous-fawn, with some touches of peach red or carnelian red. The head is deep olive on top except for the supraoculars and the front part of frontal and facial scales which are deep olive-buff or citrine-drab. The edges of the upper labials are of 3 colors: wood brown behind; clove brown in the middle plates, and fawn color or orange-cinnamon in front. The pupil rim is a thin line of light green-yellow followed by the general color of the iris, clouded fawn or tawny-olive, with the outer part olive-brown. The ends of the ventrals are pale vinaceous-fawn, becoming in the middle olive-buff, and have dark edges formed by elongate dark spots on either end of the cephalic part of each plate.

A young snake received from J. Wottring, Houston, Tex., Apr. 1, 1951. Total length 10½ inches, body 8¼ inches, tail 2¼ inches. Its colors in general are like the above, it has 2 complete transverse neck bands and 2 in which a lateral spot is united with dorsal on one side; 25 dorsal body spots and only 2 visible on base of tail, the rest of tail uniform; the red of the sides is etruscan red, terra cotta, or dragon's blood red; the dark lateral spots are black; underside of tail except for base is dragon's blood red, as is also the anal plate.

Habitat: Much of our knowledge and literature of this form comes from Strecker (Tex., 1902, 1909b, 1910, 1915, 1922, 1926, 1927, 1928e, 1929b, 1933, and others). He began by saying it was "apparently our commonest water snake." In 1909 he found it in rivers and creeks. In 1915 he remarked, "This is the common water snake of Texas and is found in suitable localities throughout the State. Unlike *fasciatus,* this species is partial to open streams." He found it "wherever water is found, in lakes, bayous, ponds, sloughs and along rivers," and "in water tanks."

In 1950 Milstead, Mecham, McClintock wrote that "eleven specimens were collected from three associations," namely salt-cedar, field, and walnut-desert willow.

Period of activity: *Early appearances*—Mar. 24 (Gloyd, Kan., 1932); Apr. 19, 21, May 5, 28 (Marr); Apr. 20, May 6, 12, 13, 17 (Gloyd, Kan., 1928); May 12 (Hurter, Mo., 1893). *Fall disappearance*—Oct. 3 (Gloyd, Kan., 1928); Nov. 26 (Strecker, Tex., 1927).

Breeding: Viviparous. Males 724–1,037 mm., females 865–1,335 mm. *Sexual dimorphism*—(See *N. s. sipedon*.)

Young—Time of birth, last of August–October. Last of August and early September (Force, Okla., 1930); Sept. 5 (Conant and Downs); Sept. 4 (Barton, Tex., 1948). Number, 15–21. Barton reported that an intergrade between *N. e. erythrogaster* and *N. e. transversa,* "caught July 13, 1947, north of Bammel, Harris Co., Tex., produced 17 young on Sept. 4." Milstead, Mecham, and McClintock recorded 15 embryos. The young from the female of Sept. 14 recorded by Gloyd (Kan., 1932) underwent their first ecdysis at the age 3 days. Size, 9–11 inches (223–271 mm.). The smallest young we have seen were 223, 245, 267, and 287 mm. (Garni in Strecker, Tex., 1926d) said, "Came across several in dried out parts of the Cibolo. All the specimens I captured were small, some not even a foot long. The Cibolo is full of water snakes, but I never could get ahold of the bigger fellows."

The most extended account of newly hatched young comes from Conant and Downs: "These small snakes began eating chopped fish almost at once. As they grew they were measured and weighed. On December 9, 1933, they averaged 259.3 mm. and 6.61 g.; on Apr. 5, 1934, 19 of them (one having died) averaged 306.8 mm. and 10.90 g.; on June 13, 1934, 331.6 mm. and 13.33 g. All but 3 had died by May 2, 1935, when the survivors averaged 420 mm. and 26.70 g. These snakes did not hibernate; they were kept warm and active over both winters. Several young of this subspecies were born at the Toledo Zoological Park during September, 1930, to a female from New Braunfels, Texas. They grew rapidly in captivity on a diet of fish, but as a result of cannibalism the group was eventually reduced to one. This large female passed a large, red infertile ovum on September 2, 1933, and 2 others on Sept. 4, 1933. Thus it would appear that the snake was sexually mature at the age of 3 years. At that time it weighed 429.7 g. and measured 960 mm. in length. While it was still light in color, its pattern had become rather indistinct and the contrast between blotches and ground color was considerably lessened. The light crossbands between the dorsal blotches were the most prominent feature of the pattern."

Food: Fish, frogs. Strecker (Tex., 1909b), Gloyd (Kan., 1928), Burt and Burt, Marr, Klein (Tex., 1949), Wrights.

Fig. 143. *Natrix e. transversa:* 1, Helotes, Tex.; 2, San Antonio, Tex.; 3–8, Brownsville, Tex., H. C. Blanchard.

Fig. 144. *Natrix grahami,* Bayou Bouff, La., P. Viosca, Jr.

Authorities:

Anderson, P. (Mo., 1945)
Burt, C. E. (Kan., 1933)
Burt, C. E. and M. D. (Ariz., 1929)
Conant, R. (Gen., 1949)
Conant, R., and A. Downs, Jr. (Gen., 1940)
Garman, S. (Tex., 1892)
Gloyd, H. K. (Kan., 1928, 1932)

Hallowell, E. (Gen., 1852–53)
McLain, R. B. (Ark., 1899)
Marr, J. C. (Gen., 1944)
Milstead, W. W., J. S. Mecham, and H. McClintock (Tex., 1950)
Strecker, J. K., Jr. (15 citations)
Taylor, E. H. (Kan., 1929a)

1929, E. H. Taylor: "The form is unquestionably specifically distinct from *Natrix sipedon* and has practically the same range throughout the state [Kansas]." (*Unquestionably* this simple statement did more to influence the direction of our thinking on this question than any other contribution. In some meeting or conversation we heard Taylor speak at length and with finality on his evidence and reasons.)

Graham's water snake (35—Hay 1892), Graham's queen snake (7—Yarrow 1882)

Natrix grahami (Baird and Girard) 1853. Fig. 144; Map 40

Other common names: Arkansas water snake; Graham's leather snake; Graham's snake (9—Smith 1879); prairie water adder; prairie water snake; striped moccasin.

Range: From n. Illinois, s.w. across Missouri, w. Arkansas, and Louisiana to the mouth of the Mississippi River, w. to Corpus Christi, Tex., n. across the Red River, w. into n.e. corner of Texas panhandle, n.e. across cent. Kansas and s.e. Nebraska and eastward.—Ark.; Ia.; Ill.; Kan.; La.; Mo.; Neb.; Okla.; Tex. *Elevation*—100 to 2,000 feet; most records below 1,500 feet.

Size: Adults, 10–47 inches.

Distinctive characteristics: A medium-sized, olive-brown, 19-rowed snake with a dark-edged, middorsal, buffy brown band. On the 3 lowest rows, a cream-colored or light band. Lower edge of this band and ends of ventrals have a thin line of black; sometimes also down middle of venter a row of black spots. Lower labials 9–11; ventrals 155–178; caudals 51–66; preoculars 2.

Color: A snake from San Antonio, Tex., May 13, 1936. There is an indistinct middorsal band of buffy brown or buffy-olive, the outline faintly indicated by black dots on the bases of the scales of the adjoining row on either side. The ground color of the sides is light brownish olive or olive-brown. On the 1st to 3rd rows of scales is a light stripe of avellaneous, light pinkish cinnamon, or pale ochraceous-buff, which becomes on the side of the neck warm buff. Below the stripe are dull purplish black or black tips on the ventrals which zigzag along the edge of the belly. The interspaces and the cephalic end of each scale of the 4th row are marked with the same black, thereby making the upper border of the light band more distinct. The top of the head is brownish olive or olive. The labials are light buff. The iris is buffy brown with an indistinct pupil rim of isabella color. Outside the buffy brown is a clear circle of chamois or honey yellow, which is in turn outlined on the dorsum with dull purplish black. The underside

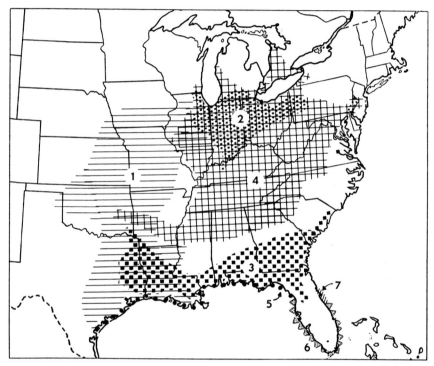

Map 40. *Natrix*—1, *grahami;* 2, *kirtlandi;* 3, *rigida;* 4, *septemvittata;* 5, *sipedon clarki;* 6, *s. compressicauda;* 7, *s. taeniata.*

of the chin and the first 15 or 20 ventrals are cartridge buff or cream-buff. The rest of the belly is pale ochraceous-buff or pale pinkish buff. In the third quarter of the belly is a median row of black or dull purplish black spots on the sutures of the ventrals. This row extends to the vent. The underside of the tail has a dusky area in the middle, pale pinkish buff on the ends of the caudals, and an intermediate area of light grayish olive or grayish-olive. *Abnormal*—Guthrie (Ia., 1930) reports a specimen without the zigzag line between the end of the lowest row and the end of the ventrals.

Habitat: Under logs (rotten or otherwise), boards, rocks, or other cover of edges of small creeks, ponds, sloughs, ricefield ditches. Also in water holes, crayfish holes, or depressions in rotting logs, mud of bottom lands, or even under rocks in a dry creek bed. Sometimes on overhanging shrubs or brush near the water, though not so often as with larger water snake species. A prairie species and lowland form.

Period of activity: *Early appearances*—Early March (Force, Okla., 1930); Apr. 9, 1927, May 14, 1926 (Gloyd, Kan., 1928); Apr. 15, 22, May 24 (Hurter, Mo., 1911); May 3 (Beyer); Apr. 27, 1939 (Anderson); Apr. 14, 1934 (Viosca); May 9 (Curtis). *Fall disappearance*—Middle October (Force); Nov. 13 (Hurter); Aug. 31, 1928 (Gloyd, Kan., 1932); Nov. 26, 1924 (Gloyd, Kan., 1928); late November (Smith, Ill., 1947).

Breeding: Viviparous. Males 525-675 mm., females 550-775 mm. *Sexual dimorphism*—We have long suspected this species of being sexually dimorphic. Sometimes a snake appears with no ventral spots like the *transversa* and *flavigaster* races of *Natrix erythrogaster*. In a pair of snakes from Bayou Bouff near New Orleans given us Apr. 14, 1934, by Viosca the male had a distinct row of large ventral spots while the female had only slight indications of a few spots. (See *N. s. sipedon* for knobby dorsal scales.)

Mating—Records of Apr. 14, 1934 (Viosca), and May 10, 1938 (Anderson), are of mated pairs; Gloyd (Kan., 1928) on Apr. 9 saw "3 tightly rolled up in a ball-like mass although it was not determined whether or not they were mating." Recently, in Texas, Curtis recorded that "on the night of May 9, in a small pond in the southeastern part of the county, I observed 3 mating pairs of Graham's water snake. The individual pairs were entwined about each other with their tails hanging downward while floating in the water of about 2-foot depth. The temperature was 59° F." "A captive pair was observed in coitus on May 10, 1938" (Anderson).

Young—Number, 6-25. 6, 8 (Baker and Woodruff); 10 (Conant and Bridges; Guthrie, Ia., 1930b); 10-15 (Schmidt and Davis; Strecker, Tex., 1926e); 12-15 (Hudson, Neb., 1942); 13 (Branson, Kan., 1904); 14 (Beyer); 14, 25 (Anderson). Time of birth, Aug. to Sept. 10. July 29, 1897 (Baker and Woodruff); Aug. (Branson); mid-August (Strecker, Tex., 1926e); late Aug. (Hudson); Sept. (Beyer); Sept. 3, 5 (Anderson); Sept. 10 (Guthrie, Ia., 1930b). Size, 7-10 inches (175-246 mm.). 7 inches (Hay); 183 mm. (Anderson); 8 inches (Conant and Bridges, Schmidt and Davis); 205-230 mm. (Guthrie, 1930b); 9 inches (Conant and Bridges); 9½ inches (Branson); 246 mm. (Baker and Woodruff). We have seen small Graham water snakes 198, 199, 208, 211, 239, and 271 mm. long and advanced embryos 172, 173, and 176 mm. "Young snakes are found among piles of drift material and under stones and planks along the water's edge even during the extreme hot months. As many as 4 or 5 are often found under the same object" (Strecker, Tex., 1926e).

Food: Crustaceans, fish, frogs, salamanders. Strecker (Tex., 1926e), Klein

(Tex., 1949), Weed (Ill., 1922), Grant, Gloyd (Kan., 1928), Curtis, Boyer and Heinze (Mo., 1934).

Authorities:

Anderson, P. (Mo., 1942)
Baker, F. C., and F. M. Woodruff (Ill., 1897)
Beyer, G. E. (La., 1900)
Curtis, L. (Tex., 1949)
Goodman, J. D. (Mo., 1915)

Grant, C. (Kan., 1937)
Guthrie, J. E. (Ia., 1930a, 1930b)
Ruthven, A. G., and C. Thompson (Gen., 1913)
Strecker, J. K. (Tex., 1926e, 1927c, 1915)

Harter's water snake (3—Trapido), **Brazos water snake**

Natrix harteri Trapido 1941. Fig. 145; Map 42

Another common name: Palo Pinto water snake.

Range: Headwaters of Brazos and Colorado Rivers from Palo Pinto County to Tom Green County, Tex. *Elevation*—800 to 1,800 feet.

Size: Adults, 12–36 inches.

Distinctive characteristics: *"Diagnosis:* This differs from all other North American snakes of the genus *Natrix,* excepting *N. erythrogaster,* in the presence of 23 scale rows and a nearly unmarked venter. From *N. e. erythrogaster* it differs in the persistence of the dorsal pattern to maturity; from both *N. e. erythrogaster* and *N. e. transversa* in the pattern of alternating dorsal spots, 2 scales long, alternating with lateral spots. The number of dorsal or lateral spots is 58 or more, exceeding that of all the races in the related species, *N. erythrogaster* and *N. sipedon.* The dorsal pattern is uniform in intensity throughout life . . . while *N. e. erythrogaster* loses the pattern completely with maturity, and *N. e. transversa* has the pattern prominent with youth and obscure with age. The venter is Pale Vinaceous Pink (color names which are capitalized are from Ridgway, matched with specimens in life) becoming Japan Rose under the tail, while *N. e. transversa* from the same region has the belly Pinard Yellow. The number of dorsal scale rows at mid-body never exceeds 23 in *N. harteri* while it may reach 25 in *N. e. erythrogaster* (Clay, 1936) and 27 in *N. e. transversa* (Clay, 1936). The head is narrow and elongate in form, rather more like *Thamnophis angustirostris* than a *Natrix.* The high number of ventrals (145 to 150) further separates *N. harteri* from the races of *N. sipedon* as presented by Clay (1938). *Holotype:* U.S. National Museum No. 110927 (H.T. No. 1302), adult male, collected in rocky stretches along the Brazos River north of Palo Pinto, Palo Pinto County, Texas, early April, 1940, by Philip Harter" (Trapido)

Color: A snake from Palo Pinto, Tex., received from Philip Harter, Nov. 4, 1938. There are 2 rows of 56 alternating olive-brown spots down the back, 5 or 6 scales wide and 2 scales longitudinally. The skin of the interstices is clove brown or black. The scales between the dorsal spots are drab with interstices of cream-puff or pale pinkish buff. Alternating with the dorsal series is a lateral row of bars 6 scales high and 1½ longitudinally of buffy brown or drab with interstices of clove brown or black. The intervals between the lateral spots are light grayish olive with interstices of light mineral gray or court gray. The top of the tail is uniform buffy brown. The top of the head is saccardo's umber. The iris is cinnamon-brown with a pupil rim of light buff or cream color. The upper and lower labials are edged with tawny or russet. The lower edges of the upper labials and the underside of the head are cream color or massicot yellow. This extends as clear color down about 30 ventrals. It then becomes suffused down the middle of the venter with carrot red or carnelian red. Caudad of the middle of the snake, the ends and rear margins of ventrals are light pinkish buff. The underside of the tail is solid vinaceous-cinnamon with the edges of caudals black.

Habitat: "For information on the habitat of *N. harteri,* I am indebted to Mr. Philip Harter and Miss Catherine D. Hemphill [now Mrs. S. M. Brown, Jr.—A.H.W.]. This snake is captured along the Brazos River either under rocks along the edge, or under rocks in water less than ankle deep. . . . Occasionally a snake is seen in the open water or when surprised, will swim across the river to the opposite shore. One specimen was caught on a log in a large pile of driftwood. *N. harteri* is only found along the Brazos River where the bed is covered with rocks, or on the rocky portions of the banks. It has not been found on sandy stretches of the river. This species has been taken along the river at the mouth of Elm Creek, at a second rocky place along the river about one-half mile west near the bridge between Palo Pinto and Graford, and at a third locality, Chick Bend, about 3 miles upstream from the bridge. (For these localities, see Pickwick Quadrangle, Texas, U.S. Geological Survey.) This habitat is quite different from that of the other two local water snakes, *N. e. transversa* and *N. r. rhombifera.* These are found along the creeks which are tributary to the Brazos, such as Elm Creek and Little Keechi Creek, where *N. harteri* has not been collected. The region of the Brazos River along which Mr. Harter has taken *N. harteri* is 830 to 840 feet in altitude, while the other *Natrix* are at altitudes of 900 to nearly 1,100 feet" (Trapido).

In his noteworthy paper of 1944, Marr wrote: "These specimens SNHM 9896–7 were taken near the South Fork of the Concho River near Christoval. . . . This new locality is some 165 miles to the southwest [of Palo Pinto] and is on the Colorado River watershed. . . . The Concho River specimens agree with those from the Brazos River with slight variations. The dorsal body spots, ventrals, and subcaudals are all somewhat fewer than the minimum given for the types. The dorsal coloration and pattern are the same. The venter is largely the same, but no pink was observed (in alcohol). The dark pigment on the anterior ⅓–½ of the caudals is evidently more pronounced in the Concho River individuals. The ecological distinctions between *N. harteri* and *N. e. transversa* made by Trapido (1941) were observed here. The two *harteri* were coiled under one rock on a small (8 square feet) 'island.' One *transvera* was taken within 50 feet of this island in a small pool left by a bypass from the main stream by receding waters."

Breeding: Viviparous. Males 273 mm. and up, females 467–798 mm. *Young*—Number, 7, 16, 23. Time of birth, Sept.–Oct. Size, 7–9 inches long. Conant (Tex., 1942a) received on Apr. 3, 1941, from Palo Pinto, Tex., a female 678 mm. long and 99.7 grams in weight. On Sept. 24, 1941, it gave birth to 7 young, 205–225 mm. long (av. 213.9 mm.) and 2.5–3.1 grams in weight (av. 2.8 grs.). Most of our material came in October or April, and we had specimens from 9 inches (225 mm.) onwards or close to hatching stage.

In 1944 McCallion (Tex.) added considerable to our knowledge of this form: "Two adult *Natrix harteri* Trapido were received from Mr. Philip Harter on July 20, 1942. They were from the type locality, Palo Pinto, Texas. Both specimens were female, obviously gravid. The larger of the two, 798 mm. long, died on August 2, 1942. Sixteen half-developed embryos were present in the oviducts. The smaller female, measuring 753 mm., gave birth to a young snake, fully-developed, but dead, on September 16, 1942. Two days later the mother snake died of a lung infection. There were 22 well-advanced embryos in her oviducts. They averaged 200 mm. in length; the shortest was a deformed specimen of 174 mm.; the longest measured 216 mm. These embryos were like the mother in color and pattern."

Food: "The following items of food have been accepted: salamanders (*Desmognathus f. fuscus, Eurycea bislineata*), frogs (*Rana s. sylvatica, R. clamitans, R. catesbeiana,* and tadpoles of the latter), and fresh and salt water fish (perch, smelts, and killifish). One specimen ate a small crayfish" (McCallion, Tex., 1944).

Field notes: We have never visited the habitat of this form. Only 2 of our students, Mrs. S. M. Brown and Miss Edith Force, have given us first-hand notes on the region and its collector. For several years from 1936 or 1937 onward our classes enjoyed the live amphibians and reptiles we received from Harter, particularly the "mountain boomers." When this snake first appeared, we were playing with *N. s. pleuralis* (Cope's definition with dorsal spots missing in caudal half), which Allen had sent from Mississippi. The pink of the belly, the size, and several other features led me (A. H. W.) to compare them carefully, but the form was just beyond the range of this subspecies. We then queried, "Could this be an outlier?" We still believed it of the *N. sipedon* group, but whence we knew not. We first labeled the material *Natrix erythrogaster?* or *Natrix erythrogaster transversa?* because it was within the range of *transversa,* and one (A. A. W.) of us for a time suspected that it arose from *transversa.* Possibly this is its source. We must remember that the Palo Pinto country is in the Pennsylvania sandstone-limestone tail of the midcontinent basin, above the Edwards plateau and west of the cretaceous rim.

Authorities:

Conant, R. (Gen., 1943; Tex., 1942a)   Trapido, H. (Tex., 1941)
Marr, J. C. (Gen., 1944)

1942, R. Conant: "Unlike Trapido, I do not believe that 'the almost un-marked belly presumably relates it [*harteri*] most closely to *Natrix erythro-gaster.*'"

1943, R. Conant: "The recent discovery of *Natrix harteri* (Trapido 1941) . . . has supplied a clue which makes it possible to show that *kirtlandi* shares certain characteristics with at least one other species, and indicates that its affinities lie with the largest and most widespread group of American water snakes—*Natrix sipedon,* its subspecies, and related species. *Natrix kirtlandi* and *Natrix harteri* are similar in several respects. Basically their patterns are much alike. Dorsally each is marked with 4 rows of blotches, the blotches being solid and averaging 50 or more in number from the head to a point above the anus. No other North American *Natrix* has so many dorsal markings of this type. Ventrally the ground color of both *harteri* and *kirtlandi* is orange or reddish, and there is a dark spot or clouded area toward the lateral end of each ventral and subcaudal scute. In these characteristics *kirtlandi* shows a greater resemblance to *harteri* than it does to any other species. Recently I have presented evidence (1942) to indicate *harteri* is a member of the *sipedon* group of *Natrix.* It can also be shown that *kirtlandi,* in all probability, is a degenerate member of the same group and allied to it through a common ancestor of both *kirtlandi* and *harteri* which no longer exists."

Kirtland's snake (18—Yarrow 1882), Kirtland's water snake (17—Guthrie 1926)

Natrix kirtlandi (Kennicott) 1856. Fig. 146; Map 40

Other common names: Cora Kennicott's snake; Kirtland('s red) snake; little red snake; Ohio Valley water snake; spread head.

Range: From s.e. Wisconsin and n.e. Illinois to n. cent. Kentucky; thence n.e. into w. Pennsylvania and w. across Ohio and s. Michigan. An isolated record in Trenton, N.J., region.—U.S.A.: Ill.; Ind.; Ky.; Mich.; N.J.; O.;

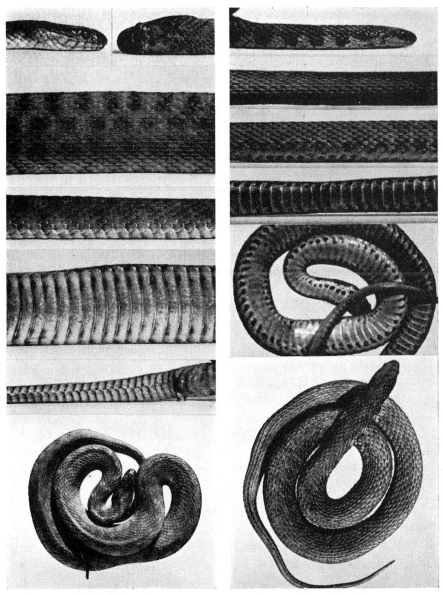

Fig. 145. *Natrix harteri*, Palo Pinto, Tex.,
P. Harter.

Fig. 146. *Natrix kirtlandi*, Toledo, Ohio,
R. Conant.

Pa.; Wis. Can.: Ont. *Elevation*—Mainly below 1,000 feet; 300 to 1,500 feet;
367–460, 394–457, 485, 481–552, 1,192, 1,063–1,129, 1,099, 985–1,085 feet (Conant,
Gen., 1943). In Delaware Valley (?) 9–210 feet, possibly 400 feet; 2,200 feet
(Smith, Pa., 1945).

Size: Adults, 14.5–22 inches.

Distinctive characteristics: A small, 19-rowed, brown snake with 4 rows of quadrangular spots, black or brown and more or less alternating. Below this series to end of ventrals, gray. Near end of each ventral is a black or bluish-violet spot, these being in a row on each side of belly, which is cream color or yellow on chin and throat, succeeded by oranges to reds. The middle of belly may be clear or dotted with gray. Ventrals 121–135; caudals 44–69; infralabials 7 (6–9); supralabials 6 (4–5).

Color: A snake from Toledo, O., loaned by R. Conant from the Zoo, Mar. 15, 1930. The background color of the back is pecan brown, mikado brown, or at times onion-skin pink, vinaceous-cinnamon, or pinkish cinnamon. On either side of the middorsal line, from the 7th scale row to the dorsal ridge, is a row of black, brownish olive, warm sepia, or burnt umber spots. On the 2nd to 5th or 6th scale rows is a lateral line of large spots which are the same color as the dorsal ones and alternate with them. The scales of 1st row are saccardo's umber or snuff brown. The top of the head is olive or brownish olive, as are the temporals, oculars, rostral, and the upper edges of the upper labials from the eye forward. The upper and lower labials are cream-buff or colonial buff slightly punctulate, and ahead of the eye heavily washed with buffy olive. The iris is bluish from the covering scale due to approaching shedding. The throat and chin are almost pure light buff, pale pinkish buff, or cream-buff. By the 10th to 12th ventral, the middle color has become apricot orange, rufous, flesh, ocher, vinaceous-cinnamon, or orange cinnamon. It then soon passes into pale flesh color, flesh pink to alizarine pink, or from pinkish vinaceous to vinaceous. This central band of color is bounded on either side by conspicuous spots of deep dull bluish-violet (2), dark dull bluish-violet (2), or dark dull violet-blue, which is located some distance from the end of the plate.

Habitat: Thanks to E. B. Williamson and later to Conant, we now know this snake to be no longer in the rare category. This least aquatic species of our northern water snakes has been recorded under cover in marshy land and in open prairie and other prairielike situations. They have been found in wooded areas along prairie streams, in ravines, on hillsides, in pastures, in places moist in spring and dry in summer, and even in public parks. Normally, they are found close to small streams, near the margin of a pond or marsh.

Period of activity: *Early appearances*—Jan.–June (Conant, Gen., 1943); Jan. (Morse, O., 1901); Jan. 25, Mar. 21 (Hay); Mar. 3–May 13 (Conant); Apr. 4 (Wood and Duellman); Mar. 5 (Minton). *Fall disappearance*—Aug. 24 (Hankinson, Ill., 1917); Sept. 1, 2, 4, 16, Oct. 22 (Wood and Duellman); mid-October (Hay); November (Conant, Gen., 1943). *Hibernation*—"This snake probably hibernates underground in the same areas which it frequents during the active season. A number of individuals, found in early spring, were coated with mud and were still sluggish from the cold. All were taken in open meadowland where they had apparently spent the winter. Hay states that 'on the 21st of March, one was dug out of the mud on the margin of a pond.' Some evidence is at hand that *kirtlandii* congregates in denning areas during hibernation" (Conant, Gen., 1943).

Breeding: Viviparous. Males 350–449 mm., females 361–533 mm. *Sexual dimorphism*—None recorded in color. "The tail length in males averages about 25% of the total length; in females it averages about 22%. . . . Some scales in the anal region of males bear knobbed keels" (Conant, Gen., 1943).

Young—Time of birth, Aug. 4–Sept. 24. Conant (Gen., 1943) gives August 4, 4, 10, 15, 24, 28, 28, 28, Sept. 7, 8, 18–24, 21. Minton records a brood Aug. 5. Number, 4–22. 6, 8 (Hay, Ind., 1892; Gen., 1893); 6 (Atkinson, Pa., 1901); 6 (Surface, Pa., 1906); 6 (Minton); 5–11 (Schmidt and Davis, Gen., 1941; Yarrow, Gen., 1888). Conant from preserved material records 7, 8, 8, 12. His table of 13 broods gives 4, 5, 7, 7, 7, 7, 8, 9, 11, 11, 22, 22, 22. Size of young, 5–6.75 inches. Minton's brood averaged 5¼ inches. Conant's records for 91 young range from 125 to 168 mm. "New born young averaged 1.39 grams in weight. . . . All shed their skins within 36 hours of birth."

Food: Earthworms, minnows, slugs, frogs, toads, salamanders. Minton, Atkinson (Pa., 1901), Conant (Gen., 1943).

Authorities:

Conant, R. (Gen., 1943; O., 1938a)   Minton, S., Jr. (Ind., 1944)
Hay, O. P. (Ind., 1892)   Wood, J. T., and W. E. Duellman (O.,
Kennicott, R. (Ill., 1857)   1941)

1943, R. Conant: "In many respects, especially in habits and its relationships to other snakes, *Natrix kirtlandii* is comparable to *Thamnophis butleri* and *Tropidoclonion lineatum* (*Thamnophis lineatus* of Dunn, 1932 and other authors). It may be said to occupy a position in relation to *Natrix* which is analogous to that occupied by *butleri* and *lineatum* in relation to the genus *Thamnophis*. These 3 snakes have much in common, and each is the small, degenerate representative of a natural group—*butleri* of the *radix* group of *Thamnophis* as defined by Ruthven (1908); *lineatum* of the *elegans* (*ordinoides*) group of the same genus, as suggested by Dunn, *op. cit.*; and *kirtlandii* of the *sipedon* group of *Natrix*. Each shows its closest affinities with a related form occurring chiefly or entirely to the west of its own range.

Diamond water snake (23—Hay 1892),
Diamond-backed water snake (14)

Natrix rhombifera rhombifera (Hallowell) 1852. Fig. 147; Map 41

Other common names: Diamond-back moccasin; diamond-back water snake; diamond black water snake; diamond moccasin; false moccasin; Holbrook's water snake (14—Jordan 1876); moccasin snake; North American rhomb-marked snake; water adder.

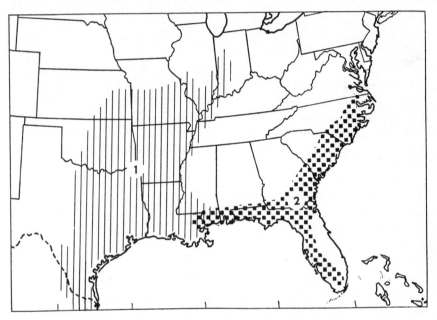

Map 41. *Natrix*—1, *r. rhombifera;* 2, *taxispilota.*

Range: From cent. Indiana along Ohio and Mississippi Rivers to the Gulf, e. to Mobile, Ala., w. and s. to the tip of Texas, into Tamaulipas to s. Veracruz, Mex., n. through e. Texas, Oklahoma, and Kansas, thence e. across s. Missouri and Illinois to Wabash River.—U.S.A.: Ala.; Ark.; Ill.; Ind.; Kan.; Ky.; La.; Miss.; Mo.; Okla.; Tenn.; Tex. Mex.: Coahuila; Nuevo León; Tabasco; Tamaulipas; Veracruz. *Elevation*—Seacoast to 500 feet normally, sometimes up some rivers to 2,000 feet.

Size: Adults, 32–67 inches.

Distinctive characteristics: A large, 25–31-rowed brownish olive or buffy brown snake with 26–66 dark rhombs on the back linked at their corners by oblique black lines to an alternate series of black vertical bars. The venter is from cream-buff through deep olive-buff to olive-buff under tail. Rear edges of ventrals have black spots. Ventrals 133–150; caudals 57–81.

Color: A snake caught at Cotulla, Tex., Apr. 2, 1925. The background of the back to the tail tip is light brownish olive or olive-brown, becoming buffy brown on the sides. The scales outlining the rhombs of the back and also the lateral bars are black. The top of the head and the temporal region are citrine-drab or deep olive. The lower labials and 5 to 7 of the upper labials are straw yellow with black sutures. The pupil rim is cream-buff. The iris is a beautiful ring of ferruginous, cinnamon-rufous, hazel, or apricot orange. The forward portion of the venter is colonial buff, deep colonial buff, or cream-buff; the midportion is deep olive-buff while the under surface of the tail is olive-buff or pale olive-buff. The ventrals caudad of the 50th are marked on the rear edges with black spots which are extensions of the lateral bars.

A snake from San Antonio, Tex., received from Mrs. W. O. Learn, Apr. 11, 1925. This smaller snake differed from the larger one thus: The under parts are vinaceous-fawn becoming deep olive-buff on the edges of the ventrals and toward the throat. The iris is ferruginous or vinaceous-rufous with a pupil rim of light buff.

Habitat: In Alabama, Löding reported it "common in ponds and creeks"; in Mississippi, Allen found it "in thick swamps"; in Louisiana, Beyer observed that "there is scarcely a water hole that is not inhabited by an individual of this species"; Strecker found it over much of Texas except the panhandle and the plains; Cope made it a resident of "the entire low country of Texas"; in Oklahoma, Smith and Acker held it "common along water courses"; in Missouri, Boyer and Heinze recorded it "closely associated with water"; and Hurter had it common in the "so-called American Bottom in Illinois"; while in Kansas, Gloyd found "numerous individuals of this species in the open along the lake shore, in marshland swamp at night, and beneath logs, bark and debris in the vicinity of the lake." Some peculiar spots are given: 3 adults in a floating automobile tire; in a nursery water tank; in a garden. These habitats have been recorded: rivers (2), water courses (1), water holes (2), creeks (4), small streams (3), bottom lands (3), backwaters (1), sloughs (1), bayous (1), ponds (6), lakes (3), swamps, cypress or thick or alluvial (3), marshes (1), ditches (2), tanks (1). At times it is under boards, stones, debris, or other cover. Hurter's picture is: "Middle of April, I found this rather vicious looking snake already mated, lying on the branches of small trees and limbs, overhanging the borders of creeks, ponds, and sloughs, from which at the slightest noise they quickly dropped into the water. When cornered, they bite viciously."

Period of activity: Early appearance—Mar. 24, 25, Apr. 6, 21 (Gloyd); Apr. 9, 16, 24, 29 (Burt and Hoyle, Gen., 1935). *Fall disappearance*—Sept. 5 (Hurter); Sept. 23 (Gloyd).

Breeding: Viviparous. Males 722–1,190 mm., females 820–1,450 mm. *Sexual dimorphism*—Blanchard observed that almost all males 800 mm. or more possess chin tubercles and knobbed anal keels, but the females usually have neither structure. He holds that the males breed in the spring of their fourth season, i.e., when 2½ years old. *Mating*—Already mated by middle of April (Hurter). "Late in the afternoon of May 7, 3 or 4 medium-sized *N. rhombifera,* 2 of which when captured proved to be males, were seen in close contact with a much larger individual which was doubtless a female. . . . It is probable that the males were attempting to copulate with the female. Mr. Clanton saw a pair in coitu May 15" (Gloyd). (See also quotation from Meade under *N. c. cyclopion.*)

Young—Number, 18–62. 8, 13, 17, 18, 30, 42, Cagle; 14, Barton (Tex., 1948), Curtis (Tex., 1949); 16, Ditmars (Gen., 1907); 18, Schmidt and Davis (Gen., 1941); 22, Boulenger (Gen., 1914); 25, 34, Gloyd; 36, Strecker (Tex., 1908b); 43, Force (Okla., 1930); 62, Guidry (Tex., 1953). "Dr. Woodhouse observed one with *many* young on one of the sand banks of the Arkansas River" (Hallowell, Gen., 1852–53). Time of birth, Aug.–Nov. 8. Aug. 27, Sept. 3, 10 (Cagle); Sept. 7 (Force); last of August (Parker, Tenn., 1937); Nov. 7 (Gloyd); Sept. 25 (Barton, Tex., 1948); Oct. 2 (Curtis, Tex., 1949); Sept. 10 (Guidry, Tex., 1953). Size, Cagle's excellent natural history omits measurements of his 3 broods. It is true Cagle measured specimens 72½, 89½, 100, 142, 299, 365 mm., of which the first 4 must be developing young. Mittleman (Ind., 1947) in Gibson Co., Ind., recorded a young specimen 290 mm. long. Blanchard in 1931 recorded young 250 and 300 mm. Strecker (Tex., 1908b) took 5-inch specimens from a female, yet Boulenger (Gen., 1914) recorded them as 11 inches at birth. The smallest we have seen were 283 and 326 mm., which we recorded at the time as "too big for size at birth."

Food: Frogs, toads, fish, crayfish, young turtles. Hurter, Boulenger (Gen., 1914), Gloyd, Allen (Miss., 1932), Minton, Cagle, Klein (Tex., 1949), Guidry (Tex., 1953).

Authorities:

Blanchard, F. N. (Gen., 1931)
Cagle, F. R. (Tenn., 1937)
Gloyd, H. K. (Kan., 1928)
Hurter, J. (Mo., 1911)

Meade, G. F. (La., 1934)
Minton, S., Jr. (Ind., 1944)
Smith, H. M. (Kan., 1950)

For a long period *N. rhombifera* was poorly known, and much confusion resulted.

1897, J. Hurter: "They represent plainly only a variety of the common water snake as Professor Samuel Garman . . . has arranged them."

1931, W. L. Haltom (Ala., 1931): "The author fully agrees with Mr. Löding that this species *taxispilota* is a color variation of *rhombifera."* (We reluctantly concluded that our versatile horticultural friend and frequent host, H. P. Löding, was distinctly wrong and confused.)

1917–1950, A. H. Wright: From Louisiana to Texas and Arkansas we have

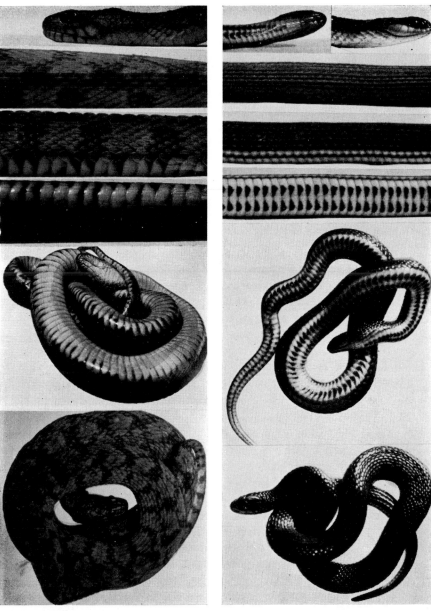

Fig. 147. *Natrix rhombifera rhombifera:* 1–4,6, San Antonio Reptile Garden, Tex.; 5, Cotulla, Tex.

Fig. 148. *Natrix rigida:* 1,2,6,7, Eustis, Fla., O. C. Van Hyning; 3–5, Gainesville, Fla., Museum.

seen *N. rhombifera* in the field. We honestly believe that if we take one look at the rear frayed part of the parietals of *N. taxispilota* we can tell it from other water snakes every time. Nevertheless, in Louisiana one's reactions operate strangely; we can expect anything in Louisianian amphibians and reptiles. Viosca and Meade have assured me that puzzling water snakes appear. We visitors do not always solve the puzzle by describing a new form. We, however, believe *N. rhombifera* and *N. taxispilota* distinct. Still, despite all this confidence, as recently as May 14, 1950, at Doddridge we did not instantly name a 5-foot *N. rhombifera* but queried whether it was *N. taxispilota*.

Striped water snake (10—Ditmars 1907),
Stiff snake (12—Hay 1892)

Natrix rigida (Say) 1825. Fig. 148; Map 40

Other common names: Brown banded leather snake; brown water snake; green queen snake (Yarrow 1882); Holbrook's water snake; rigid queen snake; striped moccasin; (two-lined) water snake.

Range: From n. cent. Florida to a point half way up the coast of South Carolina; thence w. to Arkansas, Louisiana, Oklahoma, and Texas; thence s. to coast.—Ala.; Fla.; Ga.; La.; Miss.; Okla.; S.C.; Tex. *Elevation*—Seacoast to 500 feet.

Size: Adults, 11–29 inches.

Distinctive characteristics: A small medium 19-rowed olive or greenish olive snake with a light band along side on 1st row of scales. This line is defined above and below with a black line. The black zigzag edges on all the dorsal scales form many very narrow longitudinal lines. On the 8th row of scales is an indistinct line or band of violet blue. The belly is light yellow with 2 rows of black spots down its middle, these uniting on the lower neck. A dark line runs between ends of caudals. Ventrals 132–144; caudals 51–71; preoculars 2.

Color: A snake caught on Billy's Island, Okefinokee Swamp, Ga., June 29, 1921. The upper parts are yellowish olive, dark greenish olive, or deep olive. Down the back are 2 narrow rather obscure lines of dark aniline blue, dusky blue-violet, or dusky violet-blue (2). These are located on the 8 rows of scales above the venter. The intermediate band of body color covers 3 scale rows. The upper and lower labials are aniline yellow or ochraceous-tawny, the same color marking the gulars to some extent. The iris has a thin pupil rim of aniline yellow or ochraceous-tawny while over the rest of the iris this color is heavily clouded with black. The belly and lower surface of the tail are reed yellow or lime green marked with black spots, 2 rows on the belly, united into 1 row on the 1st 3 plates of the throat, and becoming on the tail a middorsal line along the inner sutures of the caudals.

Another snake found dead on a railroad line near the east Negro quarters, Billy's Island, Ga., June 5, 1921. The upper labials and side of the neck are sudan brown or hazel. This color continues as a narrow line or band on the 1st scale row above the line formed by the black ends of the ventrals. The belly is naphthalene yellow or pale chalcedony yellow with 2 rows of black spots down the middle, each appearing as a narrow black line from head to vent.

Melanism—Etheridge in Louisiana recorded 2 completely melanistic juveniles, 211 and 216 mm. long, April, 1948.

Habitat: This timid, retiring, very aquatic form has been taken normally at the water's edge or on the shore of lakes, ponds, alluvial swamps, and fresh-water tidal marshes. Strecker's most extended accounts said that they were usually discovered only "after the slabs were turned and after the muck was stirred with a stick," or were taken "in the mud under a rotten stump or log close to the water's edge." They have been taken near streams in upland woods of sand jack oaks. We took them with a fish seine in rice fields and in the open water of marshes.

Until a few years ago this species was one of the rarest eastern water snakes in museum collections, but several floods have much increased the series. Unpublished and generally unknown is the greatest collection of *Natrix rigida,* made by Mr. E. B. Chamberlain of Charleston, S.C., who collected at one time far more than were known in all the other collections combined. After an extensive flood, he found many of them (my memory of 70 or 80 may be exaggerated). Over in the Mississippi Valley similar episodes have happened. We dare say Viosca knows this species alive as well as anyone.

Period of activity: *Early appearances*—Mar. 5, Apr., 1931 (Allen, Miss., 1932); Apr. 8, 1928 (O. C. Van Hyning, Fla.); Apr. 29, 1925 (Viosca); Apr. 6 (Brown); April (Livezey, Tex., 1951). *Fall disappearance*—Oct. 28, 1939 (N. D. Richmond for Virginia).

Breeding: Viviparous. Males 350–546 mm., females, 493–705 mm. *Young*— Few definite data available. Authors have spoken of its breeding habits thus: Unknown (Schmidt and Davis, Gen., 1941); "born alive; about 8 inches" (Conant and Bridges, Gen., 1939); "the number of young in one brood is probably small" (Strecker). Viosca implies that Apr. 29 was the mating date. Baird and Girard in 1853 (Gen.) had one specimen 7¼ inches. The smallest specimen we have seen is 183 mm. (of which the tail is 43 mm.), i.e., the same size as the Baird and Girard specimen. Conant gives 8 inches. Beyer (La., 1898) wrote, "I have noted the entire period of gestation of at least 3 of our venomous snakes from the time of sexual union to the end of the term, and I dare say with comparative certainty that the same length of gestation occurs as well in *Natrix rigida* and *Natrix grahami.*" In 1951 Curtis and Tinkle took one (184 mm.) with an umbilical scar.

Food: Sirens, fish, crayfish. Strecker.

Field notes: May 5, 1950: While I was measuring a specimen of *N. rigida*, 175 mm. long, in the Allen-Neill collection, Neill told me that he found it easy to collect these small snakes in shallow pools in pine flatwoods. They were in the piles of needles at the shore and appeared as these were scooped out by hand.

Authorities:

Brown, B. C. (Tex., 1947)   Say, T. (Pa., 1825)
Curtis, L., and D. Tinkle (Tex., 1951)   Strecker, J. K., Jr. (Tex., 1926c)
Etheridge, R. E. (Fla., 1950)   Viosca, P., Jr. (La., 1926)

1892, O. P. Hay (Ind.): "A specimen with 170 ventrals, from Illinois, on which in Jordan's manual I assigned *rigida* to that State, seems to be rather a specimen of *N. grahami.*"

1853–1936: Doubtful northern records. It is questionable whether any one of these people saw one alive: *Pennsylvania*—1842, De Kay (N.Y.); 1853, Baird and Girard (Gen.); 1873, Higgins (Gen.); 1901, Pennsylvania to Gulf, Brown (Gen.); 1906, Pennsylvania to Georgia, Surface (Pa.). *Ontario* —1881, Garnier (Ont.); 1908, Nash (Ont.). *Illinois*—1892, Hay (Ill.); 1899, McLain (Ill.). *Iowa*—1892, Osborn (Ia.); 1911, Somes (Ia.). *Maryland*— 1936, Kelly, Davis, and Robertson (Md.).

Queen snake (49—Blatchley 1891), Leather snake (31—Jordan 1876)

Natrix septemvittata (Say) 1825. Fig. 149; Map 40

Other common names: Banded water snake; brown queen snake; diamond-back water snake; garter snake; moon snake; (North American) seven-banded snake; olive water snake; pale snake (Shaw 1802); queen water snake; seven-striped water snake; striped water snake (13); three-striped water snake; willow snake; yellow-bellied snake (12—De Kay 1842).

Range: Cent. New Jersey across s. Pennsylvania into w. New York and Lower Ontario, s. Michigan to s.e. corner of Wisconsin; thence s.e. of Mississippi River to n. Mississippi; w. to e. Oklahoma; thence e. to cent. Mississippi, n. Alabama, and n. Georgia; and n.e. through w. South Carolina, North Carolina, and cent. Virginia.—U.S.A.: Ala.; Ark.; D.C.; Del.; Ga.; Ill.; Ind.; Ky.; Md.; Mich.; Miss.; N.C.; N.J.; N.Y.; O.; Okla.; Pa.; S.C.; Tenn.; Va.; W. Va.; Wis.   Can.: Ont. *Elevation*—500 to 1,500 feet. 900–1,600 feet (Smith, Pa., 1945).

Size: Adults, 16 or 18–39 inches.

Distinctive characteristics: "*N. septemvittata* is distinguishable from other forms having 19 scale rows by the presence of 4 dark stripes on the belly, 2 near the mid-line, and 2 lateral, the latter extending on to the lower half of the 1st row of dorsal scales and bordered above by a yellow lateral band covering the upper half of the 1st row and all of the 2nd. The remainder of the back is medium brown with 3 more or less distinct, narrow black stripes. All the dorsal scales are keeled" (Clay, Gen., 1938). A medium brownish olive or olive-brown snake. The venter is various with buffs, vinaceous drab, and grays. Ventrals 133–154; caudals 64–81; preoculars 2.

Color: A snake described May 22, 1928. The upper parts are light brownish olive, olive-brown, or grayish olive. The interspaces between scales in the first 3 or 4 rows are large and black, thus giving a darker band above the light lateral band. The light stripe extends along the labials, neck, and sides and is light pinkish cinnamon or pale cinnamon-pink. There is a faint middorsal stripe of black, faint because the interspaces of black on either side of the middle row of scales are scant. The iris cannot be described because of the unshed scale covering the eye. Below the light lateral stripe, on the lower half of the 1st scale row and on the ends of the ventrals is an area of cameo brown or light vinaceous-drab. Then comes light buff, pale pinkish buff, or cartridge buff. The central portion of the plates, in the cephalic part of the belly, is light vinaceous-drab separated into 2 bands by a narrow line of cartridge buff down the middle. This light vinaceous-drab soon changes to light olive-gray, olive-gray, or light grayish olive. The light midventral line becomes obscure caudad, the buffs disappear, and the grays cover most of the venter. The tail becomes wholly gray.

Habitat: All agree that this best-known member of the Regina group of water snakes is very aquatic, an excellent swimmer. Fifteen or more authors ascribe it to small streams. Swift-flowing branches, brooks, and creeks are preferred. If it is found along ditches, canals, sloughs, bayous, lakes or ponds, it is around the edges. Lowland large rivers and larger streams are not its first choice. Many remark its fondness for resting on overhanging willows, trees, shrubs, brush, logs, or other debris from which it drops when disturbed. It is alert, difficult of capture under normal circumstances, gentle or aggressive, mild- or ill-tempered (authorities disagree). Many hold it is fond of hiding under rocks, though mud or any cover serves its purpose. Ideally we picture this form in hilly, rocky streams, yet these unusual habitats have been recorded: Force (Okla., 1926) says that they "frequent the water holes and small streams and sometimes projecting rocks of dry creek beds." Weed (Ill., 1922) says: "There are some old abandoned quarries a few miles southwest of Chicago, which are well stocked with this snake. They live in crevices, in the piles of rubbish and waste stones, mainly at the water line. When the water is warm, they may be seen in large numbers with only the head out of the water and with rear end firmly anchored around a handy stone."

A typical habitat is described by Raney and Roecker for Erie County, N.Y.: "These creeks are shallow, meandering streams of alternating pools and riffles with gravel and rubble bottoms. The width varied from 30 to 50 feet and the riffles averaged a foot in depth while some pools were 6 feet deep Small willows lined the mud banks and some emergent aquatic plants were along the shallows near shore. Most snakes were captured under flat stones near the edge of the stream both in and out of the water."

Blatchley (Ind., 1891) held that, "unlike the next species, it is seldom if ever found about deep pools or ponds, but frequents shallow running water, gliding gracefully among the stems of the water willow (*Dianthera Americana*) and other aquatic plants, and when pursued takes refuge beneath one of the many stones usually found in such a place."

Period of activity: *Early appearance*—"This is regularly the earliest snake to appear in the spring and the last to disappear in the fall. It was first noted March 22, 1885 and March 20, 1886. Mr. Edward Hughes reports seeing one apparently very recently killed Nov. 7, 1886; at that date the ground was frozen and on the 5th there had been a fall of 2 inches of snow" (Butler, Ind., 1887a). "It appears very early in the spring" (Hay, D.C., 1902a). Mar. 20, 22 (Butler); Apr., Apr. 4, May 6 (Conant); May 10 (Raney and Roecker). *Fall disappearance*—Aug. 31 (Dunn, Va., 1915b); Sept. 19-23 (Raney and Roecker); Oct. (Conant); Nov. 7 (Butler).

Hibernation and aggregations—Wood (O., 1944) reported "an aggregation of *Natrix septemvittata,* prior to hibernation, involving 47 specimens." They were basking in the sun on trees 10-15 feet above the water. "These snakes were collected at a time when individuals of *septemvittata* were becoming quite scarce along the river. A week earlier some cold weather was experienced in this locality. It seems that these snakes had either already gathered for hibernation, and had ventured out because of warm weather, or were gathering for hibernation." In 1949 Wood reported that "a more striking aggregation" had been found by Duellman, Ladd, and Reicken. "In this instance 125 *Natrix septemvittata* were collected in a shallow rocky creek, in a distance of 100 yards, in less than 1 hour. As many as 24 were collected at one time from beneath a single rock. This field work was in fall, on September 22, 1946, and appears to be another instance of aggregation prior to hibernation." Neill (Ga., 1948) "in November 1936, saw dozens upon dozens of snakes of this species, lying in the bushes bordering a short stretch of Spirit Creek, a Coastal Plain tributary of the Savannah River. The weather had been cool, and the snakes were quite lethargic. The species is moderately common in the rocky creeks of the Piedmont portion of the county, is very rarely met with in Spirit Creek and other streams of the Coastal Plain and apparently does not range more than a few miles below the Fall Line in eastern Georgia."

Breeding: Viviparous. Males 375–692 mm., females 375–787 mm. *Young*— Number, 5–18. 5 (Dunn, Va., 1915b); 6, 12 (Atkinson, Pa., 1901); 6 (Hudson, Pa., 1954); 8 (Hay); 8, 13 (Conant and Bridges, Gen., 1939); 8, 11 (Schmidt and Davis, Gen., 1941); 8, 10, 11, 14 (Wood, O., 1949); 9 (Pope); 10

(Ramsey, Weber, Ind., 1901); 10, 11 (Conant); 12 (Reddick, Ind., 1896); 13 (Neill, Ga., 1941b); Brimley, Conant and Downs (Gen., 1940); 18 (Minton). Funkhouser (Ky.) reports that "like the garter snakes, these reptiles . . . bring forth large numbers of living young, a brood of 30 or 40 being not unusual." Do they attain 30 or 40? Time of birth, (July 6) July 30–Sept. 7. July 6, Aug. 4, 7, 10, Sept. 5 (Wood); July 30 (Minton); Aug. 5 (Reddick); Aug. 12 (Ramsey); Aug. 18 (Brooking, Ore., 1934); Aug. 23 (Conant and Downs); Aug. 31 (Dunn); Sept. (Atkinson); Sept. 7 (Neill); Sept. 9 (Hudson). Size, 6.8–9.2 inches (169–230 mm.). 6.8, 7.8 (Wood); 7, 8 (Brimley, N.C., 1895, 1941–42); 7.5, 8, 9 (Conant and Bridges); 7⅝, 7⅞, 8.5 (Conant); 8 (Schmidt and Davis); 8.25, 9.2 (Conant and Downs). We have seen and measured young specimens 179, 188, 192, 193, 203, and 235 mm., all within the above range. In Stanford University Museum are 2 combined broods born to 2 females collected Aug. 26–27 by Anita Daugherty at Huntsburg and near Windsor. They are 13 in number, measuring from 190–231 mm. Raney and Roecker wrote that some queen snakes "all recently born, taken in September 19–23, ranged from 7.7 to 9.1 inches, mean 9.2 inches." They held that the year-old range was probably from 12 to 16.6 inches as in $N. s. sipedon$. "A female 557 mm. in length gave birth to six young on September 9, 1942. . . . Their total lengths varied from 149 to 198 mm." (Hudson, Pa., 1954).

Food: Crayfish (8 authors), minnows, froglets, newts. Raney and Roecker, Wood (O., 1949), Taylor (Nev., 1892a), Bateman (Gen., 1897), Garman (Ill., 1890), Conant and Bridges (Gen., 1939), Weed (Ill., 1922), McCauley, Schmidt and Davis (Gen., 1941), Minton, Conant, Uhler, Cottam, and Clark (Va., 1939).

Authorities:

Conant, R. (O., 1938a)
Dunn, E. R. (N.C., 1917)
Goodman, J. D. (Gen., 1915)
Hay, O. P. (Gen., 1893; Ind., 1892)
McCauley, R. H. (Md., 1945)
Minton, S., Jr. (Ind., 1944)
Pope, C. (Ill., 1944)

Raney, E. D., and R. M. Roecker (N.Y., 1947)
Ruthven, A., and C. Thompson (Gen., 1913)
Triplehorn, C. A. (O., 1949)
Wood, J. T. (O., 1944, 1949)
Wood, J. T., and W. E. Duellman (O., 1950)

1928, W. J. LeRay (Ont.): "Recent examination shows that Dr. Garnier's collection now in the Department of Biology contains 4 specimens referable to $N. septemvittata$." Then LeRay records 2 specimens of his own collection.

Fig. 149. *Natrix septemvittata:* 1,3–7, Miami and Erie Canal, Toledo Zoo, Ohio, R. Conant; 2, D. L. Gamble.

Fig. 150. *Natrix sipedon sipedon,* Ithaca, N.Y.

Water snake (105—Macauley 1829), **Common
water snake** (56—Hurter 1893)

Natrix sipedon sipedon (Linné) 1758. Fig. 150; Map 42

Other common names: Banded water snake (9); black water adder; black
(water) snake; brown water snake; common northern water snake; eastern
water snake; moccasin (snake); "moccasin" water snake; mud moccasin;
North American water snake; northern banded water snake (2); northern
water snake; spotted water adder; spotted water snake; streaked snake;
Washington water snake (*bisectus*); water adder (21); water moccasin
(13); water pilot; water viper.

Range: From s.w. Maine across s. Quebec, s. Ontario, and n. peninsula
of Michigan to w. Wisconsin and s.e. Minnesota; s. into e. and s.w. Iowa;
westward to e. Colorado; s.e. to corner of Oklahoma, Arkansas, Texas, n. in
Arkansas to s. Missouri; e. to s.w. corner of Indiana; s. to cent. Tennessee; e.
and n.e. above the fall line and along the coast to Maine.—U.S.A.: Ala.;
Ark.; Colo.; Conn.; D.C.; Del.; Ia.; Ill.; Ind.; Kan.; Ky.; La.?; Mass.;
Md.; Me.; Mich.; Minn.; Mo.; N.C.; Neb.; N.H.; N.J.; N.Y.; O.; Okla.;
Pa.; R.I.; S.C.; Tenn.; Tex.; Vt.; Va.; W. Va.; Wis. Can.: Ont.; Que.
Elevation—900 to 2,200 feet (Smith, Pa., 1945); 4,000 feet (Rhoads, Tenn.,
1896); 2,450, 3,250 feet (Barbour, Ky., 1950).

Size: Adults, 16–52 inches. Brown holds that "4 feet seems to be very
close to maximum size for females. . . . Among males a 36-inch specimen
would be considered a very large example." W. J. Hamilton, Jr., found a
specimen run over on the highway near Ithaca which was said to measure
55 inches (1,395 mm.).

Longevity: 7 years (Flower, Gen., 1937).

Distinctive characteristics: "Usually 3–10 (rarely more) anterior transverse
bands and a total of more than 30 bands and dorsal spots on the body;
ventrals 135–155, many with 2 dark or red half-moon shaped marks and with
flecking and mottling; dorsal spots and bands generally darker, less distinct
from the ground color and separated by interspaces narrower than those of
pleuralis (lateral interspaces narrower than lateral bars)" (Clay).

Color: A snake taken on a class trip to Duck Lake and Fairhaven, N.Y.,
June 2, 1946. The back is blackish brown, the scales dull; the top of head is
clove brown in sharp contrast because the plates there are very shiny. The
upper labials are dark olive-buff with sutures of clove brown. The transverse
dorsal bars are grayish olive, crossing 12–15 scale rows and less than 1 scale in
longitudinal extent. On the lower side, these light bars fork and border an
area 3–4 scales deep of kaiser brown outlined with black. The first 7 dark
areas are continuous from venter to venter, but thereafter ensue the dorsal
saddles and alternating dark areas as described above. The eye is clove
brown, the pupil rim ivory yellow or olive-buff. On the forward corner of

each ventral plate is a triangle of kaiser brown margined caudad with black; the other corner is clear white or ivory yellow in strong contrast. The underside of head and forward ventrals are ivory yellow, and as this color extends down mid-belly it becomes colonial buff or deep colonial buff and as midbody is approached becomes heavily specked with black. On underside of tail, the caudals are marked in the center with white and kaiser brown surrounded by heavy black margins.

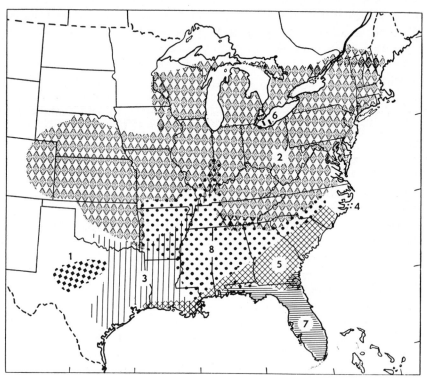

Map 42. *Natrix*—*1, harteri; 2, s. sipedon; 3, s. confluens; 4, s. engelsi; 5, s. fasciata; 6, s. insularum; 7, s. pictiventris; 8, s. pleuralis.*

Abnormal coloration—Clay (Mich., 1935) recorded 6 young albinos in a brood of 23. In 1922 Ortenburger (Mass.) recorded an albino water snake, *Natrix sipedon sipedon* (L.) collected by Dr. D. R. Clark at Mountain Lakes, N.J. Many melanistic and some erythristic specimens have long been known.

Habitat: The characterizations often run somewhat as follows: (a) "Aquatic and semiaquatic habitats." (b) "Abundant along all creeks and streams." (c) "Abundant about the river marshes and along most water courses." One author writes, "Common in *suitable* localities." We fear suitable is almost *universal* in this species. If we say aquatic, we have to qualify it with "semiaquatic" or the like. Here is a list of some habitats and the number of times used: streams (45), ponds (35), creeks (21), lakes (9), rivers (13), brooks (3), branches (2), inlets (1), outlets (2), water courses (5), sloughs (1), bayous (1), bays (1), coves (1), rain pools (1), runs (1), springs (3), open water-ways (1). Of low lands we have marshes (6), swamps (6), wet places (1), meadows (4), salt water marshes (3), reedy marshes (1), boggy areas (1), sphagnum (1), river bottoms (1). If we consider the snakes when sunning or abroad, we have them on overhanging brush, branches, or other vegetation (15), on overhanging logs (6), on floating logs, brush (5), on rocks or rock piles (2). They may be hiding under any cover, e.g., stones (16), boards (5), waste or trash or debris (5), banks (2), crawfish holes (2), logs (3).

Period of activity: *First appearance*—Feb. 3 (Brimley, N.C., 1925); Mar. 1 (King); Mar. 15 (Wright, N.Y., 1919b); Mar. 24 (Gloyd, Kan., 1932); Mar. 28 (Wright and Allen, N.Y., 1913); Mar. (Conant, O., 1938); Apr. 7, May 7 (Brimley, N.C., 1925); Apr. 15 (Burt, Kan., 1931); May 2, 9 (Fowler, N.J., 1909); May 3 (Evermann and Clark); May 16 (Ellis and Henderson, Colo., 1915). *Fall disappearance*—Sept. 1–Nov. 3. Aug. 31 (Gloyd); Sept. 2 (Brimley); Sept. 18 (Evermann and Clark); Oct. 2, Nov. 3 (Brimley); Oct. (Conant); Nov. 1 (Wright). *Hibernation*—In Brown's thesis we find allusions to burrows (rat, crawfish, meadow mouse, and others), old rock dams, rock piles, bridge fills, old or creviced masonry. If they are recorded in springs, he wonders how long they submerge in near-freezing water or whether they are in nearby portions of the ground.

Breeding: Viviparous Males 635–1,148 mm., females 650–1,295 mm. DeWitt Miller had males 770–873 mm. and some adult females 640–975 mm., yet in one instance he recorded a 782-mm. female as subadult.

Sexual dimorphism—"In males above a certain size in the genus *Natrix* the keels of the dorsal scales in the anal region are knobbed. Such structures have been identified in the species *N. sipedon sipedon, N. sipedon transversa, N. sipedon erythrogaster, Natrix fasciata confluens, Natrix fasciata fasciata, Natrix fasciata pictiventris, N. grahami, N. rhombifera, N. taxispilota* and *N. kirtlandi*" (Blanchard, Gen., 1931). "Among adults the female normally attains much greater size, has a heavier body, larger and broader head, relatively shorter and more rapidly tapering tail. The adult male is ordinarily smaller, more slender of head and body and with a longer tail which does not taper rapidly posterior to the anus. . . . Chin tubercles . . . [are] absent in *sipedon*" (Brown, N.Y., 1940–41). Brown considers knobbed anal keels and anal ridges good characters for the male, but not always indicative of sexual maturity. He holds the sex ratio to be 1:1.

Mating—Many herpetologists have seen mating masses of water snakes on overhanging horizontal limbs, branches, rocks over the water, but few have described them in detail. Evermann and Clark and Minton (1944) in Indiana, Perry (1920) in Pennsylvania, King in Tennessee, and several others have published on this topic. In New York, Brown (1940–41) described courting and mating behavior in this species, saw matings lasting 2 to 4 hours, and noted one female courted by as many as 6 males at once. He saw no fighting and no fall mating. He did not find 50 per cent fertility until the female was over 850 mm. in length.

Young—Number, 9–70 or 76, 99. 8 (Atkinson); 9 (1 author); 11 (1); 14 (1); 15 (1); 16 (6); 18 (3); 19 (1); 20 (7); 21 (3); 22 (5); 23 (2); 24 (1); 25 (5); 26 (3); 27 (1); 28 (2); 29 (2); 30 (4); 37 (1); 38 (1); 39 (1); 40 (6); 41 (1); 44 (5); 45 (1); 46 (1); 50 (1); 60 (Lowe, Me., 1928); 70 (Fowler, N.J., 1915); 82,102 (Woodruff, estimate in 1835); 99 (Slevin). Brown had 21 records of birth from literature and 69 of his own. He had 124 broods, 75 his own records. These 75 ranged from 9 to 47.

Time of birth, Aug. 12 to Oct. 12, sometimes to Oct. 30. Some records are: Aug.–Sept.; Aug. and early Oct.; Aug.–early Sept.; Aug. 9; Aug. 12–Oct. 12; Aug. 15–Sept.; Aug. 17–Sept. 30; Aug. 17; Aug. 18; Aug. 19, Aug. 20; Aug. 21, Aug. 22; Aug. 23; Aug. 24; Aug. 26; Aug. 29; Aug. 30, Aug. 31 to early Sept.; Sept. 3; Sept. 6; Sept. 8; Sept. 9; Sept. 11; Sept. 15; Sept. 23; Oct. 10; Oct. 12. From Aug. 15 to Aug. 31, there are records for almost every day. Brown (N.Y., 1940–41) has 3 records for the first three weeks of October, but questions records for November.

Size, 6.5–9.5 inches. The 2 modes of sizes most often recorded are: 7.5 and 8 inches; average 8 inches. Babcock (N.E., 1929a) recorded 7 as one extreme and (Hurter, Mo., 1911) 9.5 inches. It is seldom below 7 inches, though we have Dunn's record of 167 mm. Most of our records average about 184 mm. We have seen and measured young 203, 208, 209, 243, 246, and 278 mm. long. Brown (N.Y., 1940–41) from 962 young gives their sizes as 162–251 mm., mean 220, and 78 per cent of them 209–238 mm. The mass of data now available impresses these septuagenarians with the immense growth of herpetology in the last 50 years—since Cope's volume (Gen., 1900).

Food: Fish, frogs, salamanders, crustaceans, insects, small mammals. Many authors, principally Surface, Brown (N.Y., 1940–41), Lagler and Salyer (Mich., 1945, 1947), Raney and Roecker, Uhler, Cottam, and Clark (Va., 1939).

Authorities:

Atkinson, D. A. (Pa., 1901)
Axtell, H. H. (N.Y., 1947)
Brimley, C. S. (N.C., 1941–42)
Brown, E. E. (N.Y., 1936, 1940–41)
Clay, W. M. (Gen., 1938)
Dunn, E. R. (Va., 1915c)
Evans, H. E., and R. M. Roecker (Ont., 1951)

Evermann, B. W., and H. W. Clark (Ind., 1920)
Gloyd, H. K. (Kan., 1928)
King, W. (Tenn., 1939)
Lagler, K. F., and J. C. Salyer II (Mich., 1947)
Nichols, J. T. (N.Y., 1916)
Raney, E. C., and R. Roecker (N.Y., 1947)
Surface, H. A. (Pa., 1906)

Clark's water snake (14—Beyer 1897),
Salt water moccasin (2—Löding 1922)

Natrix sipedon clarki (Baird and Girard) 1853. Fig. 151; Map 40

Other common names: Bay moccasin; Clark's snake (Yarrow 1882); salt marsh water snake; striped moccasin; striped water snake.

Range: Gulf coastal region from n.w. Florida to s. Texas.—Ala.; Fla.; La.; Miss.; Tex. *Elevation*—Sea level.

Size: Adults, 15–36 inches.

Distinctive characteristics: "The following combination of features will distinguish this snake from similar forms: 21 to 23 scale rows at middle of body; belly with a median row of half-circular, yellowish spots one per scute; back with 4 longitudinal stripes of deep brown, more or less irregular and separated by narrower areas of yellowish brown" (Clay). Ventrals 125–138; caudals 57–80.

Color: An adult and a young snake from Aransas Pass, Tex., caught by R. Quillin, June 8, 1928. The back of the adult is marked with 4 hay's russet or brick red stripes, the lowest lateral one being on the 3rd to 5th rows of scales, the next on the 8th to 9th rows. The intervals between and below these stripes from 5 lines of light grayish olive. On the top of the neck or on the parietal plates the 2 dorsal hay's russet stripes enlarge, forming 2 spots which sometimes unite. The top of the head in general is light grayish olive, but may be black in the center behind the line of the eyes. There is a fine black vitta from the eye backward to the vertical of the angle of the mouth. The upper labials are marked along the upper edges with a bar of hay's russet and black. The rostral is straw yellow with a vertical bar of black on either end. This black is also on the prenasal. Each lower labial has a black suture margin. The iris has a deep olive pupil rim, and an outer edge in the rear part and upper edge in front of bright chalcedony yellow. The underside of the head is straw yellow. The belly is marked with a midventral row of hemispherical spots of straw yellow. There is one spot on each ventral and it is more or less black-edged except on its caudal margin. The rest of the plate except the olive-buff outer edge is vinaceous-rufous or ferruginous. Each ventral is more or less margined with black except back of the hemispherical yellow spot. Each caudal has a light spot, thus making 2 rows of straw yellow spots on the underside of the tail, these spots abutting on the inner ends of the plates. The rest of the under-tail surface is vinaceous-rufous or hay's russet.

The young snake. The 4 dark stripes of the back are black except for the tips of the scales which are apricot yellow or ochraceous-tawny. The lowest light lateral stripe is olive-buff, the next one pale smoke gray, the mid-dorsal one grayish olive. There is a prominent black bar on the margin of each upper labial, except on the 1st and last. The lower labials, mental, and chin shields have prominent black margins. The iris is saccardo's olive with tawny near the pupil rim, which is light ochraceous-buff. The under parts are black where they were vinaceous-rufous in the adult, and the middle series of hemispherical spots is white or cartridge buff.

Abnormal coloration—No water snake can be more puzzling in color variations than Clark's. Viosca (La., 1924), for example, found as follows: "It was interesting to note that in both *fasciatus* and *clarkii* red color on the sides or ventral portions is associated with the lighter phases and is totally obscured by black in the darkest phases. The pure *fasciatus* specimens, however varied in color, were next separated from the typical, longitudinally striped *clarkii* specimens, but there still remained a large group of inter-mediates. Those inclined to the transverse banded effect were placed in one lot and those in which the longitudinal effect predominated were placed in another. About 10 of the intermediates were just about on the border between the 2 species." For other aberrant Clark's water snakes consult Allen (1932a) and Chamberlain.

The following incident relating to *N. s. clarki* happened some years ago: One day C. B. Perkins asked me (A.H.W.) to look at a queer water snake in his tank. While I looked at this aberrant dorsal-striped *N. clarki,* I yelled to him, "Looks like *N. clarki.* Ask Klauber; he will tell you." I had met Klauber but once years before at the U.S. National Museum. Much to my surprise, a man looking down at me from the rails said, "No, he will not tell you. He keeps to the western forms." It was L. M. Klauber himself.

Habitat: We summarize Beyer, Cope, Löding, Viosca, Strecker, Allen, Chamberlain, the Quillins, and Kirn. This coastal-strip species, an inhabitant of brackish marshes, does not like permanently fresh water, though the snakes are sometimes driven to levees in freshets. At times, they are recorded on the banks of small streams running into bays which are slightly backish. The grassy edges of many Gulf coastal islands have them in considerable numbers. All in all, it is a salt water snake.

Breeding: Viviparous. Males up to 637 mm., females 367–926 mm. *Young*—Number, 2–44. Information on this interesting form is scarce. In 1903 Mitchell (Tex.) gave his paper on poisonous snakes of Texas. In his comparison of cottonmouths he said: *"Tropidonotus clarkii,* another harmless cousin of *A. piscivorous* inhabiting the salt marshes along the Texas coast, gestates in the same manner as *A. piscivorus,"* with 2–12 young. Bailey in his "Biological Survey of Texas" (1905) wrote: "The following letter from Mr. Mitchell accompanied the specimen and 8 of the well-developed embryos: 'This snake was captured with 3 others in a salt marsh on Carrancahua Bay, Calhoun County. It took to the salt water freely. One had 4 small mullets in its stomach, another fiddler crabs. The other inclosure is a part of the womb of one of the snakes, showing embryos. She had 4 on one side and 10 on the other, 14 in all.'" (The snake was taken Jan., 1892. We measured one of these embryos. It was 153 mm. long.) In 1937 Chamberlain wrote: "The Chain Islands snake, a female, measured 695 mm. in total length, with a tail measurement of 121 mm. Scale count 20-21-19; ventrals +132; caudals +46. The snake contained 12 eggs, with small embryos. The eggs averaged approximately 15x19 mm." In 1940 Carr mentioned a *pictiventris-clarkii* intergrade with 44 unborn young. In 1952 Guidry (Tex., 1953) gave 6 young, born Aug. 11. In 1955 Smith and List (Miss.) reported that "three . . . gave birth to broods of four, eight and eleven young (plus two undeveloped eggs) in the laboratory. The young varied from 180 mm. to 240 mm. in total length, averaging 211 mm."

Field notes: May, 1928: Quillin had described to me in considerable detail the brackish water snakes he and Albert Kirn used to see each spring when they took their vacation in the Aransas country. He and Mrs. Quillin made a trip to Corpus Christi and secured for us an adult and young of Clark's water snake, the form they used to see.

Apr. 7, 1934, Mobile, Ala.: Went with Mr. Löding and Mr. Van Aller to Bayou le Batre. On the flats as we were walking along the edge with fiddler crabs everywhere, Löding said, "There go *N. clarkii*." There were several swimming out from shore. It is a very striking, brighter snake than *T. saurita*. It has 5 stripes on its dorsum. Stepped on one and picked it up by the tail. Of course it bit me, but only once. It is not aggressive, is a beautiful snake above and below. Anna saw one start out from the shore. Put a broken net in front of it, and, because of turbid water, it went into the net without deviation.

Apr. 8, 1934: Went over Löding's collection. Löding has *N. clarki* in his collection. Even if he merely records, "Bayous and beaches of the Mississippi Sound, Coden and Bayou la Batre," he and his friend Van Aller have probably seen more Clark's water snakes firsthand than any other naturalists unless it is Viosca. They are two of the old naturalist type of which we have so few today—all-around men!

Authorities:

Allen, M. J. (Miss., 1932, 1932a)
Bailey, V. (Tex., 1905)
Carr, A. F., Jr. (Fla., 1940a)
Chamberlain, E. B. (Tex., 1937)
Clay, W. M. (Gen., 1938)

Cope, E. D. (Gen., 1900)
Haltom, W. L. (Ala., 1931)
Löding, H. J. (Ala., 1922)
Strecker, J. K. (Tex., 1928c)
Viosca, P., Jr. (La., 1923, 1924)

1938, W. M. Clay: "Long regarded as a distinct species, this form intergrades with *compressicauda* and occupies an adjacent geographic range. The writer concludes that both *clarkii* and *compressicauda* are geographic races or subspecies of the complex and wide-ranging *Natrix sipedon,* which is to be discussed in detail in a later paper." (We regret that his thesis has not appeared in its completed form.)

1940, A. F. Carr: "The rassenkreise is completed by extensive intergrading between *compressicauda* and *pictiventris* along the southern Gulf Coast; Mr. Clay has examined intermediate specimens, and I have seen 7 from Charlotte and Sarasota Counties which exhibited various stages of intergradation.

1944, A. H. and A. A. Wright: If *clarki* comes from *compressicauda* through *pictiventris,* as current theory implies, then *N. clarki* of Texas, just touching *N. pictiventris* if at all in western Florida, comes from a distant and relatively recent form. Can this be? Why not from *N. s. confluens* or *N. s. fasciata* in the center of its range and a form with which Viosca found intergrades? Nevertheless this distinct habitat form may be separate, though in 1950 we conform and call it *N. s. clarki.*

Flat-tailed water snake (11—Yarrow 1882), Salt-water moccasin (Stejneger and Barbour 1917)

Natrix sipedon compressicauda (Kennicott) 1860. Figs. 152–154; Map 40

Other common names: Florida water snake (*compsolaema*); salt water snake; water snake; yellow water snake (*usta*).

Range: Coast of peninsular Florida from the Gulf hammock around the tip to the Indian River region (in Marine limestone area). *Elevation*—Sea level.

Size: Adults, 15–27 inches.

Distinctive characteristics: "The color pattern of this snake is extremely variable. Its most constant feature is a midventral row of light spots, one on each scute; posteriorly the series may become irregular or indistinct. The back usually has a series of about 30 dark, ill-defined cross-bars, each of which is so expanded or constricted at intervals as to tend to produce longitudinal stripes. The presence of 2 or 4 longitudinal stripes is not unusual, especially in the neck region. Some specimens are almost uniformly melanistic, while others are reddish or straw-colored and entirely without dorsal markings" (Clay, Gen., 1938).

Color: A female snake from Gainesville, Fla., received from O. C. Van Hyning, Oct. 17, 1928. The ground color of the dorsum is grayish olive becoming ecru-olive or water green on the lower rows of scales. On either side are 2 rows of large spots of cinnamon-brown or hazel. Sometimes these spots unite transversely forming an occasional irregular bar, but usually, the dorsum is marked with 4 rows of spots. Back of the eye is a stripe of cinnamon-brown, extending to the angle of the mouth. For 4 inches along the neck, the spots are united into 4 longitudinal bands, the upper 2 meeting on the parietals and making the top of the head dresden brown. The usual citrine-drab or ecru-olive occurs only on the upper labials. The lower labials

Fig. 151. *Natrix s. clarki:* 1,3,5,6, San Antonio, Tex., R. D. Quillin; 2,4, Mobile, Ala., H. P. Loding, T. S. Van Aller.

Fig. 152. *Natrix s. compressicauda* (*walkeri*), Gainesville, Fla., O. C. Van Hyning.

are primrose yellow or mustard yellow with dark fleckings and with the sutures partially black. The gulars are yellow ocher or ochraceous-tawny. The iris is verona brown, rood's brown, or russet with the pupil rim ochraceous-buff. Down the middle of the venter are hemispherical spots of amber yellow, becoming toward the rear ochraceous-orange. In front, these spots are bordered with black, followed by chamois, which soon becomes tawny or russet half way to the vent. In this form the russet does not connect with the dorsal spots as occurs in the *walkerii* form.

A male snake (*walkerii* form) from Gainesville, Fla., received from Van Hyning, Oct. 17, 1928. The back is crossed by 39 dark crossbars of olive-brown. For 7 or 8 dorsal scale rows, the first 10 bars cover 3 scales longitudinally, then become 2 scales wide for 1 or 2 rows and on the lower side are 1 scale wide. The next 10 bars rearward are narrower, and thereafter the bars are made up of isolated or slightly connected spots. Sometimes it looks as if there were 3 rows of spots on the side, or this arrangement may be lost. The 1st transverse bar becomes 2 parallel nuchal spots meeting on the frontal. These spots are also connected with the 1st true transverse bar. The 39 intervals, each 2 scales longitudinally, are slightly darker on the dorsum, where they incline toward grayish olive, citrine-drab, or buffy olive. The spaces on the sides are grayish olive inclining toward ecru-olive or light yellowish olive. The top of the head is citrine-drab or ecru-olive, as are most of the upper labials, which are in addition somewhat dark sutured. The lower edges of the last 3 are seafoam yellow like the lower jaw. The lower labials are dark sutured also. There is an olive-brown spot just above the angle of the mouth, and a smaller one just behind it, the remains possibly of a postocular stripe which is otherwise absent. The iris is clouded with orange-cinnamon; the pupil rim is cream-buff or chamois. The ground color of the forward part of the venter is seafoam yellow, becoming chartreuse yellow halfway to the vent or before. Like *Natrix clarki,* the center of each of the first 40 or 50 ventrals is marked with an elliptical area of seafoam yellow. This is surrounded by light grayish olive, which is in turn bordered by dark olive-buff, which is divided by the background color of seafoam yellow. In other words, on the neck and near it, there is a row of elliptical centers of seafoam yellow, then longitudinal stripes of light grayish olive, deep olive-buff, seafoam yellow, deep olive-buff succeeded by a clear area of seafoam yellow on the ends of the ventrals. A short distance back of the neck, the deep olive-buff longitudinal stripe meets the encroaching transverse bars of the dorsum, becoming tawny-olive, buckthorn brown, or ochraceous-tawny. These surround the centers of seafoam yellow or chartreuse yellow with irregular marbling.

A snake (*usta* form) from Englewood, Fla., received from Stewart Springer, June 15, 1937. The upper parts of the body, head, and tail are uniform dresden brown, medal bronze, isabella color, or buffy olive. The iris is colored like the upper parts with the pupil ring faintly marked above with pinkish cinnamon or vinaceous-cinnamon. The sutures of the labials are slightly dark-edged. The labials and the ends of the belly plates are pinkish cinnamon, flesh ocher, or vinaceous-cinnamon. The underside of the tail is honey yellow, reed yellow, or citron yellow. The front of each ventral is tinged with these yellows while the rear is pinkish cinnamon. The centers of the first 25 or more ventrals are white or have a slight wash of the above cinnamons.

Cope's key (Gen., 1900) summarizes the color types which formerly were called subspecies:

compsolaema: above blackish brown, with numerous closely placed crossbands.

taeniata: 4 series of longitudinal spots above, those of the median pair forming 2 longitudinal stripes on greater part of length, the laterals forming stripes on the neck only.

compressicauda: numerous dark crossbands which are resolved into 3 rows of spots just anterior to the tail, and 4 longitudinal stripes on the neck.

obscura: sooty above, with transverse bands anteriorly.

walkerii: yellowish, with narrow brown crossbands; no postocular band. Add to these his—

usta: brownish yellow; immaculate.

bivittata: Cope (Fla., 1889).

In 1940 in "Notes concerning two broods of young of *Natrix compressicauda*" Bishop wrote: "Color phases of adults observed in this locality indicate that there are more individuals of the uniformly henna-red color than there are of the banded form which are usually described as typical. Of a total of 51 specimens examined, 29 were henna-red, 20 banded, and two a black phase. The writer also collected 18 *compressicauda* at Lower Matecumbe Key, Florida, in February 1938; all these 15 were banded and 3 were henna-red."

Habitat: The literature is scanty. From Loennberg, Reynolds and Barbour (Fla., 1916), Barbour (Gen., 1935), Allen and Slatten, and Swanson, one could well conclude that the name salt water snake is appropriate. Carr's summary will suffice: "Salt marsh and mangrove swamp; bays, estuaries, salt and brackish water canals and ditches; sea-beaches. Chiefly nocturnal, concealing themselves under rocks and logs during the day; they are most active, and may be found most readily on spring tides at night."

Breeding: Viviparous. *Mating*—One of the mated pair that Van Hyning sent us was of the *walkeri* type (♂) and one of the *compsolaema* type (♀). "Probably mating takes place in the vicinity of Key West between the dates of January 24 and February 22" (Swanson). Swanson then remarks on the male's exploratory approaches.

Young—5–22. Barbour and Noble report one brood of 15 which were dichromatic, 10 like the *compressicauda*-colored mother and 5 with a *walkeri* pattern. Of the 24 young born July 28, 1940, from a *N. compressicauda* (*usta* type), 10 were uniform brown and 14 dark gray or black. Two pertinent broods were recorded by Bishop: "Fortunately one of the breeding females to be discussed is henna-red and the other typically banded. On July 23, slightly over 3 months after capture, the henna-red female produced 14 young, 10 resembling the parent and 4 banded. Measurements of these young range from 140 mm. to 185 mm. Of the lot, one prematurely born measured 95 mm. It is impossible to draw many conclusions regarding relative size at birth of the banded and the henna-red because only 2 broods have been studied. However it is interesting to note that the banded of the first brood measured 183 mm. to 185 mm., whereas one of the henna-red measured 140 mm., another 166 mm., and the remaining 8 measured from 179 mm. to 183 mm. . . . On August 11, 1939, the banded female was preserved. Upon dissection, she was found to be carrying 5 young. Judging by their appearance they were within a few hours of birth. Four were banded, and 1 showed a strong tendency toward the henna-red phase. Measurements of the banded are 200 mm., 210 mm., 215 mm., and 218 mm. The henna-red individual measured 187 mm."

Food: Fish. Carr, Swanson.

Authorities:

Allen, E. R., and R. Slatten (Fla., 1945)

Barbour, T., and G. K. Noble (Fla., 1916)

Bishop, M. B. (Fla., 1940)

Carr, A. F., Jr. (Fla., 1940a)

Cope, E. D. (Gen., 1900; Fla., 1889)

Etheridge, R. E. (Fla., 1950)

Goodman, J. D. (Gen., 1915)

Loennberg, E. (Fla., 1895)

Swanson, P. L. (Fla., 1948)

Blanchard's water snake (7—Strecker 1928), Mississippi River water snake

Natrix sipedon confluens Blanchard 1923. Fig. 155; Map 42

Other common names: Banded water snake (Strecker and Frierson 1926); black water snake; broadbanded water snake; copper belly (2—Strecker and Frierson 1926); copper-belly moccasin; widebanded water snake; yellow water snake.

Range: From Wabash valley down the Ohio and Mississippi Rivers to s. Arkansas; w. in s. Oklahoma, then s.w. through e. Texas to the Gulf; thence e. along Louisiana coast.—Ark.; Ill.; Ind.; Ky.; La.; Miss.; Mo.; Okla.; Tenn.; Tex. *Elevation*—seacoast to 500 feet.

Size: Adults, 15–40 inches.

Distinctive characteristics: "Similar in scutellation and proportions to *Natrix sipedon fasciata* (Linnaeus), but with the dorsal saddles very much larger and only about half as numerous. . . . Dorsal saddles on body about 11 to 17 (not 20 to 33). . . . Furthermore the postocular light band is very prominent" (Blanchard). Ventrals 127–143; caudals 56–80.

Fig. 153. *Natrix s. compressicauda* (*compsolaema*), Key West, Fla., through E. R. Allen.

Fig. 154. *Natrix s. compressicauda* (*usta*): 1–4,15, Englewood, Fla., S. Springer; 5–14 young born in Ithaca from female of pictures 1–4.

Color: A snake from New Orleans, La., received from P. Viosca, Mar. 14, 1930. The background of the back is black or olive, becoming on the sides buffy olive. From head to vent, the body is crossed by 15 to 18 frequently broken and indistinct bars of deep colonial buff or isabella color. These bars are narrow, often covering less than 1 scale in width. On the lower sides are areas of bay or claret brown feebly outlined behind with deep colonial buff or isabella color, which are extensions from the mahogany and buff areas of the belly. The top of the head and the parietal plates are dark olive or black. The upper labials have a tendency toward buffy olive or grayish olive on the upper portions and cartridge buff on the lower. The lower labials are largely white. All the labials have sutures of burnt sienna. From the eye backward is a band of isabella color or snuff brown. The iris is olive-buff or has an avellaneous or chamois tinge, the rim being one of these 3 colors. The chin is white or slightly gray. The throat is light salmon-orange or capucine orange. Of the ventrals, groups of 2 or 3 are brazil red or mahogany red, the color extending entirely across the plates. Interspersed between these groups are light buff or warm buff areas which may be a full plate or ½ plate wide. In the latter case, the same color appears on the opposite end of the adjoining ventral. On the forward part of the body, the arrangements are less regular, the surface being almost entirely brazil red and light buff. On the caudal half of the body, there is usually some black associated with the edges of the light buff or cream-buff areas. On the tail, the cream-buff is entirely absent, and black tends to obscure the red, making it morocco red or garnet brown.

Habitat: In some 10 or more papers Strecker speaks of this form. He has it in "sloughs," "moister parts of the river valley," "river bottoms," "lakes with *N. rhombifera*," "water courses," "lagoons and bayous with heavily wooded banks. Never in open lakes or streams." He says, "This is the Copper-belly Moccasin of eastern and northeastern Texas."

Blanchard, its describer, found "one small female at the edge of an area of bushy overflowed land at the edge of the Mississippi levee in Pemiscot County, 10 miles southeast of Portageville, Missouri, June 17." Fitch (La., 1949) in 1949 in n.w. Louisiana found "one near river in wooded bottom-land, and 2 in dry upland woods," while Trowbridge (Okla.) in 1937 placed it "beneath debris of drift piles, under logs or along margins of the sloughs." A recent comment comes from Parker: "The habitat is primarily water courses and sloughs of the wooded bottom lands. It is found about ponds and streams of uplands and hills but not so often as the 2 water snakes (*erythrogaster* and *rhombifera*) listed before this one." The latest note is by Curtis, who found it in "the lowlands of the Trinity River . . . where it is found in ponds, swamps, or streams."

Breeding: Viviparous. Males 410–658 mm., females 500–910 mm. *Mating*— "Mating activities were observed among the members of 3 species, *cyclopion,* *rhombifera,* and *fasciata,* during the first 3 weeks of April. The matings invariably occurred on land" (Meade). In 1940 he placed *N. s. confluens* in the Grammercy area, and doubtless the 1934 observation applies to *confluens* also. *Sexual dimorphism*—Knobby dorsal scales in anal region of males above a certain size (see Blanchard, Gen., 1931).

Young—"Word has been recently received that a female *fasciata* which I sent to a private collection in Minneapolis produced 17 young which would indicate that the period of gestation for both *cyclopion* and *fasciata* are the same" (Meade). "One of these gave birth to 13 young on August 13" (Curtis). Mitchell (Tex., 1903) wrote that the number of cottonmouths is "small compared to the productiveness of their harmless cousin, the *Natrix fasciatus,* which is often mistaken for *A. piscivorus* and which brings forth from 25 to 50 young at a birth." In 1951 Werler (Gen., 1951) recorded a female 715 mm. long giving birth, July 25, 1950, to 10 young 179–239 mm. long.

Food: Frogs. Strecker and Williams (Tex., 1928).

Authorities:

Blanchard, F. N. (Gen., 1923a)
Curtis, L. (Tex., 1949)
Meade, G. (La., 1934)
Parker, M. V. (Tenn., 1948)

Strecker, J. K. (Tex., 1928; ten or more papers)
Viosca, P., Jr. (La., 1924)

(Although *N. s. confluens* was not discussed by Viosca, he knew it as Blanchard conceived of it. Being in the very midst of this intergradation, he had to be satisfied that a new description by a nonresident helped to solve the question. After the description of *confluens* he remarked to me that he jokingly enjoyed showing Blanchard in the field a pair of water snakes mating, one *confluens,* one *fasciata.*)

1925–. Later Blanchard visited us and asked if we had any of his new form, *confluens.* When he asked for them, we could pick them out at once because of the light postocular band. He remarked, "You have more *confluens* than all the material I had when I described it." Where did they come from? Prof. G. D. Harris, our palaeontologist, was also State Geologist of Louisiana for many years. Each spring term he would take a group of graduate students and exceptional seniors to camp in Louisiana. Then J. D. Whitney (now Professor of Geology, University of Texas), A. G. Hammar (Brazil, U.S. Department of Entomology), K. P. Schmidt (Field Museum), and others collected Louisianian cold bloods. A wonderful training school!

Banded water snake (27—Goode 1873), Southern water snake (12—Hurter 1897)

Natrix sipedon fasciata (Linné) 1766. Fig. 156; Map 42

Other common names: Banded snake; black water snake; blue snake;

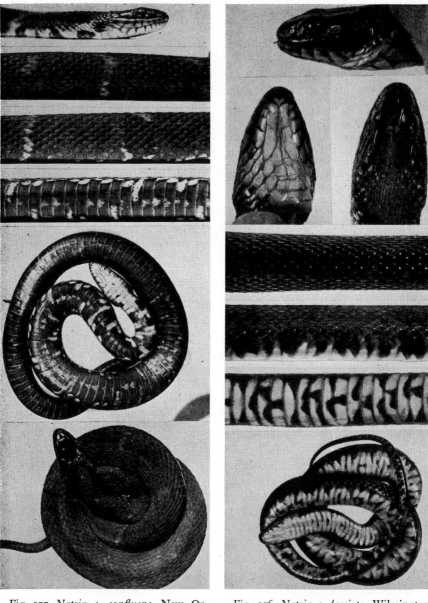

Fig. 155. *Natrix s. confluens,* New Orleans, La., P. Viosca, Jr.

Fig. 156. *Natrix s. fasciata,* Wilmington, N.C., H. Trapido.

brown snake; common water snake; fasciated (water) snake; moccasin; (North American) moccasin snake; red-bellied water snake; (southeastern banded) water snake; southern banded water snake (4); wampum snake (Catesby, Gen., 1731–43); water adder; water moccasin; water viper.

Range: From s.e. North Carolina to the n. rim of Florida; w. to Sabine River, Texas; thence e. as a thin border across Louisiana, Mississippi, and s.e. Alabama; n.e. across cent. Georgia and e. and cent. South Carolina.— Ala.; Fla.; Ga.; La.; Miss.; N.C.; S.C.; Tex. *Elevation*—Seacoast to 500 feet.

Size: Adults, 15–50 inches. Many references to *N. s. fasciata* from Shaw in 1802 to Clay in 1938 mention other subspecies. Clay's longest male was 850 mm. and female 1,115 mm. We have seen them at least 4 feet long.

Distinctive characteristics: After the abstraction of *pictiventris, confluens, pleuralis,* and *insularum,* Clay defines the remains as follows: "This snake may be distinguished from the peninsular *N. s. pictiventris,* which it resembles rather closely, by the shape of the ventral markings, squarish spots in *fasciata,* elongate dark areas near the anterior margins of the ventrals in *pictiventris*—and by the presence generally of more than 128 ventrals in *fasciata* and fewer than this number in *pictiventris.* The dorsal pattern of transverse bands through the length of the body will usually distinguish *fasciata* from *pleuralis* in which most often the posterior portion of the dorsal pattern is composed of alternating dorsal and lateral spots. Furthermore, the belly of *pleuralis* is marked with half-circular lateral spots. *N. s. confluens* and *fasciata* may be separated on the basis of the number of dorsal saddles, the former having 11 to 17, the latter about 19 to 30." Ventrals 126–143; caudals 56–83.

Color: Three snakes from the center of its distribution, Statesboro, Ga., received Apr. 30, 1951, from W. J. Hauck. The back of one is marked with rhombs, which now being moist appear fuscous. When the snakes arrived, the general appearance of the dorsum was snuff brown. It was then dry. These rhombs unite with the lateral bars to make complete transverse bands the full length of the snake. The lateral bars are hay's russet partially bordered with black flecks, the russet extending onto the end of a ventral as a block of coral red or brazil red. Between the rhombs are 29 narraw intervals of snuff, sayal brown, or buckthorn brown, which become toward the venter an enlarged area of dresden brown about 7 scales deep and 3 scales long. The top of the head is black or fuscous; the face around the eye and a bar from supraocular to a point caudad of the angle of mouth are clay color or tawny olive; the rostral and upper portion of upper labials are clouded with clay color; the sutures of upper and lower labials are strongly marked with mingled black and russet. The eye is dull violet black with a light iris rim. The general ventral color is sulphur yellow to baryta yellow which appears up the sides for 1 or 2 scales beside the hay's russet lateral bars. The conspicuous red blocks of the belly are carnelian red or coral red; chin and throat plates are almost white, but some gulars are like venter. Many of the ventrals have at their ends black borders which are more intense on the caudals. The underside of tail in general background is chalcedony yellow with caudals outlined with black. Caudals of opposite sides are in alternating groups of 1–3 separated by black or rufous bars from the dorsum.

The second snake has 30 fuscous to black dorsal transverse bars separated by hair brown to drab intervals.

The largest snake is a female 52 inches in total length. It is marked with 27 transverse bars entirely black on dorsum and sides, and the black of each lateral band extends well onto the ends of 2 or 3 ventrals. The intervals are saccardo's umber or snuff brown, becoming on end of belly plate sayal brown. The belly is cinnamon buff with red areas. The caudals are heavily stippled with black, yellow, and some of the light jasper red of the belly.

A snake at Billy's Lake, May 10, 1921. Belly plates ivory white or cream white with wash of cream or straw yellow or amber yellow. At intervals small black encircled spots appear on posterior lateral edge of ventrals. These spots are burnt sienna, kaiser brown, or hazel. This color extends rarely up on side from 6–7 rows of scales and 1½ scales in width. Some of the side gulars are light orange yellow.

The water snake that Hack and Harper killed on Floyd's Island prairie has ventrals edged with deep carnelian red or Pompeian red or vernonia purple. At end of ventrals this reddish edge enlarges. Every 6th or 7th plate the color goes up side 8 or 9 scales. This reddish color looks strange on the caudals where all the edges are thus outlined.

Habitat: Much was written under *N. s. fasciata* when it was a Mother Hubbard for almost all water snakes east of the Mississippi. We use it in the restricted sense as Clay proposes it. In its present narrowed range, this species like the other fluviatile water snakes is found in rivers, ditches, ponds, creeks, wooded alluvial swamp lands—almost any spot with some fresh water.

Period of activity: *First appearance*—Feb. 21 (Corrington, S.C., 1929). *Fall disappearance*—Sept. (Brimley, N.C., 1925). *Hibernation*—"Occasionally found beneath logs or rocks in swampy areas; young examples are sometimes found nearly frozen, in such places. I believe the bulk of the population seeks safer retreats" (Neill, Ga., 1948).

Breeding: Viviparous. Males 600–1,090 mm., females 660–1,300 mm. *Sexual dimorphism*—(See *N. s. sipedon.*) *Mating*—(See quotation from Meade [La., 1934] under *N. n. cyclopion.*)

Young—Number, 9–50. "Several specimens of the snake have been born from time to time in the Zoological Gardens, London, and were reared upon small frogs. The Moccasin Snake has sometimes produced live young ones and eggs at the same time" (Bateman). "The mother of brood 1 (Sept. 3, 1926, 22 young) had 11 complete crossbars, about the same as the average of her offspring; the mother of brood 2 had about the anterior ⅔ of the crossbands in front of the vent complete, while the posterior third had the bands complete on one side but alternating with spots on the other. The appearance in both broods of one or more specimens with all crossbars complete shows that this one character alone will not necessarily identify a water snake (at least in this region) as *fasciata* rather than *sipedon*" (Brimley). "The body cavity of a large female was opened on Aug. 11, 1932, and found to contain 23 well-developed young measuring 225 to 230 mm. in length" (Allen, Miss., 1932a). We have seen young from 200–240 mm. long. We need more definite records on this race. At first we gave the number of young as 20–40, then 15–50, 17–50, and 30–40, but revised it to 9–50, and that is none too certain a limit because of the paucity of definite data.

"Extra-uterine embryos in snakes. While dissecting a large female *Natrix sipedon fasciata* from Augusta, Georgia, I noticed a chalky ovoid mass lying in the body cavity of the reptile. When tapped with the butt end of the scalpel, the mass flaked off to reveal a well-developed embryo, coiled in the characteristic prenatal fashion" (Neill, Ga., 1948c).

Ecdysis—"A similar circumstance was noted in a specimen of *Natrix s. fasciata* [i.e., several sheddings after 19–26 days, then 35–45 days]. However, another example . . . with cuts on the posterior part of the body, displayed no increase in the rate of ecdysis" (Neill, Gen., 1949c).

Food: Frogs, smaller reptiles, newts, fish, toads, worms, tree frogs. Holbrook, Bateman, Wright and Bishop.

Field note: May 7, 1950, Panama City: Jack Tillman had many *Natrix sipedon fasciata,* at least 3 types, many with dark green bands and whitish intervals. He was puzzled by one he had apart. It had reddish spots on the belly not outlined with black. All 3 types seemingly are *N. s. fasciata.*

Authorities:

Bateman, G. C. (Gen., 1897)
Brimley, C. S. (N.C., 1927)
Clay, W. M. (Gen., 1938)
Holbrook, J. E. (Gen., 1836–42)

Viosca, P. (La., 1924)
Wright, A. H., and S. C. Bishop (Ga., 1916)

Lake Erie water snake (2—Schmidt 1941), **Island water snake** (Conant and Bridges 1939)

Natrix sipedon insularum Conant and Clay 1937. Figs. 157, 158; Map 42

Another common name: Lake water snake.

Range: Point Pelee and Put in Bay archipelago in w. end of Lake Erie—U.S.A.: O. Can.: Ont. *Elevation*—572 to 1,000 feet.

Size: Adults, 30–50 inches.

Distinctive characteristics: "This snake is similar in scutellation and size to *Natrix sipedon sipedon* (Linné), but differs in the complete, or almost complete absence of a dorsal and ventral color pattern. The coloration tends

Fig. 157. *Natrix s. insularum*, Toledo, Ohio, R. Mattlin.

Fig. 158. *Natrix s. insularum*, young, Toledo, Ohio, R. Mattlin.

to be uniformly gray above and cream white below. The pattern is present from time of birth and is not lost during ontogenesis as in *Natrix erythrogaster erythrogaster* (Forster)" (Conant and Clay). "*N. s. insularum* may be distinguished from *N. e. erythrogaster* by the duskiness of the subcaudals of the former (those of *erythrogaster* being immaculate, especially near the tip of the tail), and by the grey dorsal coloration (that of *erythrogaster* being reddish-brown to black)" (Clay, Gen., 1938). Ventrals 137–153; caudals 58–81.

Color: Ten snakes from Toledo, O., received from Robert Mattlin, Aug. 21 and described Aug. 29, 1937. These snakes show considerable variation in color pattern. Six are uniform on the back. In photographing the snakes we used the words *The, New, York,* and *Times* to indicate four of the individuals.

"Times," a female, is the second largest of the group. The back is buffy olive to buffy brown. Caudad of the first 6 inches (32 ventrals) a row of tawny-olive or clay color spots occurs on the 1st, 2nd, and sometimes on the 3rd scale row. For the first half of the snake's length, these spots hardly extend on to the ventrals, but in the caudal half, they become prominent, sometimes as triangles on the cephalic angle of the ends of the ventral plates. The intervals between these spots are light grayish olive or smoke gray. The skin between the scales is black. The top of the head is olive or citrine-drab, as are the face and upper labials. Between the 5th and 6th upper labials, the suture is apricot orange, and the next 2 sutures caudad are ochraceous-orange. The lower labials are cartridge buff. The sutures and patches of color on the 1st lower labial and symphyseal are grayish olive. There is a touch of ochraceous-orange on the last 3 lower labials. The iris is grayish olive or like the face or top of head and has a broken pupil rim of cartridge buff or colonial buff with little touches of apricot orange. The underside of the head is cartridge buff or colonial buff, and a few gulars caudad of the angle of the mouth are touched with ochraceous-orange. The colonial buff of the underside of the head slowly changes into primrose yellow and is immaculate for about 50 ventrals. On about the 50th plate, the middle of the belly has a touch of honey yellow or chamois which becomes increasingly prominent to the anal plate. At the sides of the ventral plates, the primrose yellow is increasingly specked with black and smoke gray. The underside of the tail is heavily specked with black, and each caudal in its cephalic half or two-thirds has a prominent tawny-olive or clay color spot. The rest of the caudal and mesal sutures are primrose yellow.

"York." The back is marked with a series of indistinct squarish chaetura drab spots, 10 scales wide and 3 scales longitudinally. The space between, about 1½ scales longitudinally, is light grayish olive. The resulting pattern is somewhat like Plate 2, Fig. 2, Type B of Conant and Clay. The first 5 or 6 rows of scales are deep grayish olive with an occasional indistinct black area on the 1st scale row in the rear half of the body. These areas are about an inch apart. The forward venter is a clear ivory yellow or white toward the ends of the ventrals, and has a very meager mid-band of chamois. The caudals have black in place of the tawny-olive of "Times," and the general effect is one of heavy specking of black and gray on the rear half of the snake.

"The." This snake has the same general color as the larger snake "Times," but in "The" the spots of the typical *sipedon* pattern are evident on the back. The dorsal spots are buffy brown or olive-brown, the lateral ones buffy olive. The first 6 or 7 series of dorsal and lateral spots form transverse bands across the dorsum, but thereafter dorsal and lateral alternate. The lateral ones are 7 scales deep, the dorsal ones about 9 scales transversely and 3 to 3½ longitudinally. The interspace is sayal brown. The underside of the head and throat is cartridge buff, with the general venter colonial buff in the center.

"New." The interspaces of the sides are smoke gray, those of the back between the buffy brown dorsal spots, deep olive-buff. The dorsal spots are prominent, and the first 10 merge with the lateral ones to form complete saddles. The rear half of the venter is marked with 2 series of crescents of buffy brown or deep olive-brown which is a typical *sipedon* pattern.

Abnormal coloration—"In order to indicate the relative proportions of typical *insularum,* typical *sipedon,* and the intergrades, 4 pattern types were defined into which were assorted the specimens whose patterns we studied. These pattern types may be described as follows: A. Typical *insularum.* Dorsal pattern entirely absent or represented by a slight indication of dorsal blotches along the middorsal surface, or a slight indication of lateral blotches on the first 1 to 3 rows of scales. Belly uniformly light-colored, the ventrals often with dark bases. B. Pattern of *sipedon* somewhat in evidence, but with the blotches imperfect, contorted, narrow or obscure. Along each side a gray, patternless area covering approximately the 4th to 10th scale rows and imparting to the specimen a light gray lateral stripe. Belly uniformly white anteriorly, darker and sometimes well marked posteriorly. C. Rather similar to that of *sipedon,* but with the blotches not sharply defined and often narrow. A slight indication of a light lateral stripe usually present. Belly fairly well marked with half-circles as in *sipedon.* D. Typical *sipedon.* Well patterned above and below" (Conant and Clay).

Habitat: "Islands of Lake Erie" (Morse). "Edges of limestone islands; among rocks strewn upon the shores, where low cliffs are close to the water's edge or where docks extend into the water. The islands are all limestone, which is often of a porous nature, and ponds and bogs are rare upon them. The water snakes, for the most part, appear to be restricted to the edges of the islands. They are not numerous on sand and gravel beaches but where the rocks are strewn upon the shores, where low cliffs are close to the water's edge or where docks extend into the water they are abundant. On June 1, 1935, three collectors on Put-in-Bay Island caught 234 specimens in exactly 4 hours, or an average of almost a snake a minute! In some instances as many as 12 or 14 large individuals were found hiding under a single rock" (Conant and Clay).

Period of activity: Few observations have been made before May 1, though the snakes must come out earlier. There are fall records from Sept. 5 to October.

Breeding: Viviparous. Males 685–900 mm., females 562–1,151 mm. *Mating*—A female collected at Put in Bay, June 1, 1935, was bred in captivity Feb. 22, 1936. On May 20, 1936, it gave birth to 10 young, which varied from 8¼ to 9⅞ inches in length. The female measured 37⅛ inches in length.

Young—Among the 10 snakes sent us by Robert Mattlin was a large pregnant female, which, owing to the hot weather at the time of its arrival, was a uniform tea green on the back with a row of irregularly shaped and spaced black spots on the lowest scale rows and belly of straw yellow. With captivity and cold weather, the snake assumed a uniform dull greenish black (1) back. At 8 o'clock on Monday morning, Sept. 27, we found in the cage 27 young born Sept. 26.

Of these I separated 7 as the most spotted and most nearly approaching the *N. sipedon sipedon* pattern. In 4 of these the background of the cephalic dorsum is light grayish olive, with lower sides of pale smoke gray. The dorsal spots are olivaceous black (1) and the lateral spots black. In these 4 snakes, 3–11 cephalic bars extend to the ventrals, these bars being widest in middorsum and tapering on the sides, and several other dorsal spots extend down between the black lateral vertical bars. Caudad of this point, the dorsal spots become quadrate and less distinctly marked, the lateral spots remaining narrow black vertical bars. In the other 3, the olivaceous black (1) dorsal spots are less regular in shape, though extending well across 10 middorsal scale rows, and the black lateral spots are less barlike. In one the dorsal spots terminate on the sides before the black lateral spots begin, thus leaving a narrow gray lateral stripe.

Another 8 young have the irregular dorsal spots, small lateral ones which nonetheless are very black, and a conspicuous gray stripe along the side between dorsal and lateral spots. In these 8 young the underside of the head is uniformly light as are also the first 2 inches of the venter, but the caudal half is usually flecked with black.

In the other 12, the pattern is faded in varying degrees—the top of the head is olivaceous black (1 or 2), the back and sides are light neutral gray or smoke gray with space between the lateral spots pale smoke gray. The lateral spots may be lacking on the first 2 inches and often are reduced to small dashes or small irregular in shape. In these the underside of head and the forward half of venter are clear white, the caudal portion increasingly marked until the underside of tail is quite dark.

Conant reported: "A large female collected on Kelly's Island September 5, 1930, gave birth to 19 young which averaged 8⅞ inches in length."

The most concise account comes from our associate, W. J. Hamilton, Jr.: "An April female showed no visible embryos. Four May females are all visibly gravid. Two specimens with a body length of 652 mm. and 770 mm. respectively, each contained 22 small embryos. Another female (body length 562 mm.) carried 8 embryos, averaging 35 mm. in total length. The yolks were 17 by 13 mm. A fourth (body length 571 mm.) held 11 embryos; the average total length of these embryos was 84 mm. A large female (body length 913 mm.) collected Aug. 4, 1947, contained 26 embryos. Five of these had an average total length of 176 mm. Mr. Robert H. Mattlin collected a female at Put-in-Bay, Lake Erie. This snake had a body length of 921 mm. It was received in Ithaca, Aug. 21, 1937. Twenty-seven young were born September 25, a rather late date for birth of northern water snakes. The young, of undetermined sex, averaged in total lengths 227.1 mm., tail 53.2 mm. A young specimen, at least 3 times the bulk of the young described above, was collected in May 1948. Total length 251 mm., tail 56 mm. This individual is presumed to be the young of the past year. . . . Those considered sexually mature ranged from 793 mm. to 1,151 mm. Perfect specimens give the following ratio of tail to total length: 12 males, 23.4; 6 females 21.1. Twenty-seven males and 8 females are represented in the collection."

Food: Fish, amphibia. Hamilton, Conant.

Authorities:

Conant, R. (O., 1938a)
Conant, R., and W. M. Clay (O., 1937)
Hamilton, W. J., Jr. (Ont., 1951)
Logier, E. B. S. (Ont., 1930)

Morse, M. (O., 1904)
Smith, W. H. (O., 1882)
Thomas, E. S. (Ont., 1949)

1778, J. Carver (*Travels*): "There are several islands near the west end of [Lake Erie] so infested with rattle-snakes that it is very dangerous to land on them. It is impossible that any place can produce a greater number of all kinds of these reptiles than this does, particularly of the water-snake. The lake is covered near the banks of the islands with the large pond-lily; the leaves of which lie on the surface of the water so thick, as to cover it entirely for many acres together; and on each of these lay, when I passed over it, wreaths of watersnakes basking in the sun, which amounted to myriads."

(See Conant and Clay under "Habitat" above. Their experience tends to substantiate Carver's account of 170 years before).

1944, A. H. and A. A. Wright: We accept this race, but we have felt there are populations mainly of *sipedon* which might show as much variation as these of the Lake Erie Islands. Do the Lake Huron islands, the North Carolina bars, or other types of areas have similar aberrant patterns? In our region and in many other areas we are sure that we have seen as wide a range of variation of *sipedon* as here revealed, but never such a preponderance of the uniform belly and almost absent dorsal pattern (uniform gray) in adults.

1949: E. S. Thomas in "A population of Lake Erie Island water snakes" recorded 25 and 57 embryos.

1954: J. H. Camin, C. A. Triplehorn, and H. J. Walter (O., 1954) collected several hundred of this subspecies on Middle Island. "There is no evidence that the pattern ever changes from one type to another during the life time of an individual snake." Conant and Clay's "A" pattern is predominant. Predation may possibly be the selective factor.

Florida water snake (4—Conant 1930),
Florida banded water snake

Natrix sipedon pictiventris (Cope) 1895. Fig. 159; Map 42

Other common names: Banded snake (Wachtel); Cope's water snake (2—Ditmars 1936); "moccasin"; painted water snake (2); spotted belly (Safford 1919).

Range: Florida except for the northern rim. *Elevation*—Seacost to 500 feet.

Size: Adults, 18–54 inches.

Longevity: More than 2 years 6 months (Kauffeld, Gen., 1951).

Distinctive characteristics: "Brown transverse bands numerous, separated by short intervals, and extending to the belly throughout the length. Gastrosteges narrowly margined at the base with brown, the margins turning at or before reaching the ends of the gastrosteges and uniting so as to inclose transverse yellow spots, which are wider than those seen in *N. compressicaudus*. Sides of head light brown, generally with a black postocular band; top of head black. Scales in 25 rows; in one specimen . . . in 27 rows" (Cope, Gen., 1900). A large, medium, black- or deep-brown-saddled snake with yellow or white ellipses on the belly. The black saddles may have brown centers. Ventrals 121–131; caudals 65–89. Scale rows 23–27 on mid-body.

Color: A snake from Royal Palm Park, Fla., caught March 17, 1934. The dorsal saddles, covering 3 or 4 scales longitudinally on the middorsum, are black and have united with the lateral spots and the black ends of the ventrals, making transverse bands from end of belly plate to end of belly plate. The interspaces of the back and sides forming transverse light bands are buffy olive or grayish olive. These are 1 scale wide between the dorsal saddles and 2 scales wide between their lateral extensions. On the sides the interspaces have a few white scales, or scales with white tips. The first dorsal saddle extends far down on the neck and forward over the top of the head to the rostral. The side of the head including the upper labials is buffy olive or grayish olive. Both upper and lower labials have black sutures. There are 2 parietal spots and a spot on top of the head extending backward from the parietal of the same color. The iris is like the labials, grayish olive, with hair brown cloudings. The iris rim is deep olive-buff. The background of the belly is glistening white. In the forward part of the body, the black squares on the ends of the ventrals may be separated by intervals of about 2 plates with an occasional smaller black intervening spot. These black ends do not meet across the ventrals in the forward portion, but in the rear half they begin to meet, leaving conspicuous elliptical central spots of white. On the tail the black becomes so prominent that there are 2 irregular rows of light spots.

A smaller specimen has the intermediate ground color obscure, buckthorn brown on the back and straw yellow on the sides. The ventral color is straw yellow, and the black spots have chestnut centers.

Habitat: This very abundant snake of peninsular Florida is to be found in or near all fresh water, in sloughs, pools, and lowland and cypress swamps. Carr expected them in "nearly any aquatic situation; more numerous in small marshes and bodies of water than in larger lakes and waters." They may be in the water hyacinths, seen with heads through the vegetation mats, or they may be resting on floating boards, stumps, emergent vegetation, or vegetation rafts. They frequent the borders of ditches, canals, and water courses.

Breeding: Viviparous. Males 425–818 mm., females 700–1,195 mm. *Sexual dimorphism*—(See *N. s. sipedon* for knobby dorsal anal scales.) *Mating*—"Mating takes place from March 11 to May 14" (Carr).

Young—Number, 25–57. U.S. Nat. Mus. has 31 specimens of juveniles from J. Bell, Gainesville (No. 12528) 181, 185+, 190, 191, 194, 194, 196, 197, 199, 200, 201, 201, 202, 203, 204, 204, 205, 206, 206, 207 mm. and 11 more of which 3 are 130, 140, 144 mm., possibly embryonic. "A female banded water-snake gave birth to 31 young while being brought home in a bag, July 16, 1928. Four of these were dead, probably smothered" (Van Hyning, Fla., 1931). *"Natrix sipedon pictiventris* (Cope). July 17, 1928, a large female of this species gave birth to 57 young, 3 of which were born dead. A litter of 33 was produced by a medium-sized female on July 10, 1928, all of which were living; and on July 13, 1928, another snake had 29 young, one of which was dead. The young of both *Natrix sipedon fasciata* and *Natrix sipedon pictiventris* show a great variation of color pattern. A female of either form may produce in the same litter typical young of both forms, as well as intermediates between the two. As all degrees of variation and intergradation may be found in the same locality, it is questionable if *Natrix sipedon fasciata* and *N. s. pictiventris* are distinct, at least in central Florida" (Van Hyning, 1931). "The young are born from May to August and often remain with the mother for some time after birth" (Carr). "Young were born on August 2, 1936, to a specimen from near Palmetto, Florida, collected by the late C. C. Goff. The female weighed 368.9 gr. and measured 771 mm. in length. Most of its tail was missing. (25 young from 180–223 mm. in length, average 207.36, from 2.9–4.4 grams in weight, average 3.73 grams)" (Conant and Downs).

Food: Frogs, treefrogs. Carr.

Authorities:

Carr, A. F., Jr. (Fla., 1940a)
Conant, R., and A. Downs (Gen., 1940)
Cope, E. D. (Gen., 1895)
Fowler, H. W. (Fla., 1906)
Loennberg, E. (Fla., 1895)
Safford, W. E. (Fla., 1919)
Van Hyning, O. C. (Fla., 1931, 1933)
Wright, A. H., and S. C. Bishop (Ga., 1916)

1894, E. Loennberg: "Another variety, still more distinct, is the one I found in February, 1893, at St. John's River, not far from Lake Jessup; if more specimens of the same kind should be found it may be regarded as a subspecies, for which I would propose the name *Natrix fasciata atra.*"

Cope's water snake (Conant and Bridges 1939)

Natrix sipedon pleuralis Cope 1892. Fig. 160; Map 42

Other common names: Banded water snake; common water snake; midwest water snake; Mississippi water snake.

Range: From cent. North Carolina, s.w. to s. Mississippi, n.w. to w. Arkansas; n. and e. through s. Missouri and Illinois to the Wabash River; s. across w. Kentucky and w. Tennessee; e. through s. Tennessee and n. Georgia—Ala.; Ark.; Fla.; Ga.; Ill.; Ind.; Ky.; La.; Miss.; Mo.; N.C.; S.C.; Tenn. *Elevation*—Seacoast to 1,000, sometimes 1,500 feet.

Size: Adults, 14–41 inches.

Distinctive characteristics: Cope's description is: "The color characters are quite peculiar. On the anterior part of the body the brown bands cross the ground color reaching the gastrosteges, the lateral parts having parallel sides, and being separated by spaces wider than themselves. The dorsal parts of these crossbands gradually disappear and posterior to the middle or last third of the length are wanting so that the coloration consists of lateral erect parallelogrammic spots separated by spaces of a yellow or gray ground color,

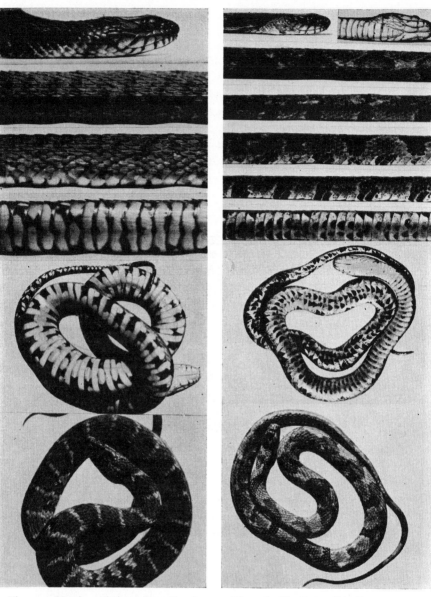

Fig. 159. *Natrix s. pictiventris:* 1, Eureka, Marion Co., Fla., through B. Marshall; 2,3,4, Silver Springs, Fla., E. R. Allen; 5,6, Royal Palm Park, Fla.

Fig. 160. *Natrix s. pleuralis,* Greenwood, Miss., through E. R. Allen.

equal to or a little wider than themselves. Belly yellow, with brown, rounded spots on the anterior parts of the gastrosteges; spots few on the anterior third of the type. Head brown without markings; labials lighter."

Clay's revised description is: "*N. s. pleuralis* is likely to be confused only with *N. s. sipedon* or *N. s. fasciata*. It is more readily distinguished from the latter than from the former. Although typical *pleuralis* and typical *sipedon* are decidedly different and may be differentiated at a glance, the transition is very gradual in the region of the Mississippi Valley, where many intermediate specimens occur. The most striking feature of *pleuralis* is its more widely spaced dorsal and lateral bars upon a relatively lighter ground color. The belly bears crescent-shaped marks similar to those of *sipedon,* but these tend to be more definitely in 2 rows, usually are redder, and remain more distinct in old individuals, whereas those of *sipedon* frequently break down into flecks and mottling. *N. s. pleuralis* usually has fewer than 30 dorsal spots and crossbands, *sipedon* usually more. The areas between the lateral bars of *pleuralis* are generally wider than the bars; the converse usually holds for *sipedon* . . . markings, and a line from the eye to the angle of the mouth is more pronounced in *fasciata* than in *pleuralis*. Remarks—It is not surprising that this common snake escaped recognition for nearly half a century, when one considers that Cope did not describe it well, make clear its difference from *sipedon,* determine its geographic range, nor ascertain whether his specimens represented a geographic race or a 'variety.' Furthermore, the identity and locality of the type specimen is a matter of some doubt. The specimen (U.S.N.M. No. 1092, from "Mississippi") designated by Cope as the type does not fit the description and is a *fasciata* recorded in the accession catalog as from Ft. Morgan, Ala. (a locality definitely beyond the range of *pleuralis*). In the same bottle is another specimen which very likely is the one described by Cope, and an old and faded label which seems to bear the inscription '1080 *Nerodia fasciata* B. & G. Summerville, S.C.' "

Color: The larger of 2 snakes from Greenwood, Miss., sent by E. R. Allen, Sept. 25, 1937, for correct identification. The background of the back is sayal brown or mikado brown, covering longitudinally on the sides intervals 4 to 4½ scales, and on the dorsum 2 to 2½ scales. The anterior half of the body is crossed by 10 perfect bars formed by the union of dorsal and lateral spots. The dorsal spots are diamond shaped, covering 4½ scales longitudinally. The lateral spots are vertical rectangles covering 2 scales longitudinally and 6 vertically. These transverse bars are bordered with black or mummy brown and have centers of russet. On the sides, the black borders encroach on the russet centers. The 11th transverse band is oblique. The succeeding 3 lateral spots are united with their fellows across the dorsum in zigzag bands. Thereafter, the dorsal spots are very indistinct or lacking, and the lateral spots conspicuous and either opposite or alternate, continuing so almost to the tip of the tail. The posterior lateral spots which are divorced from dorsal spots have black borders heavily encroaching on the russet centers. On the tail, the spots are almost wholly black. The posterior part of the tail is crossed by 5 or 6 black bars. The dorsal transverse bars and the lateral bars to the vent have their black borders outlined in turn with ochraceous-salmon or ochraceous-buff. The top of the head is dresden brown, as are also the temporals, the face, and the rostral. The upper labials are heavily washed with ochraceous-salmon or zinc orange with sutures of russet, as are the sutures of the lower labials. The underside of the head is white. The outer portion of the iris is dresden brown with a pupil rim of warm buff. The ends of the ventrals are white or marguerite yellow. The anterior edges are marked with 2 irregular crescents of vinaceous-rufous in the forward stretches or hay's russet caudad. These are black-bordered, and the 2 rows of spots are much reduced on the first 50 to 60 ventrals, being practically absent on the first 10 or 12. On the tail, these 2 rows of spots are black. Down the middle of the belly and more or less between the rows of ventral spots is a wash of apricot buff to vinaceous-rufous. There is a touch of this on the tail between the black spots. On the ends of the ventrals and the 1st row of scales is a prominent series of vinaceous-rufous spots outlined with black. These alternate with the ends of the lateral bars. When the lateral spots have no corresponding dorsal spots for transverse bar formation, then this row of alternating spots on ventrals and 1st scale row ceases, and the lateral bars extend on to the ends of the ventrals, as they do not do in the cephalic ten.

Habitat: This is an upland form of streams, creeks, ponds. Parker held that in the gravel-bottomed tributaries of the Tennessee River it was the abundant form. He found it less frequent in mud- and sand-bottomed water courses adjoining the Mississippi River where the 3 forms—*confluens, erythrogaster,* and *rhombifera*—reigned.

Period of activity: *First appearance*—"Their season of activity is long, and some individuals will come out of hibernation in the midst of winter if a few consecutive warm days occur" (Schwardt). May 6 (Schwardt). *Fall disappearance*—Sept. 25, 1937 (Greenwood, Miss.); Oct. 6, 1932 (Schwardt).

Hibernation—"Probably overwinters in cavities beneath the banks of ponds and streams, where they would not be encountered by collectors. The lack of hibernation records of *N. sipedon* is astonishing considering the abundance and widespread distribution of the species" (Neill). He questions Summerville, S.C., as the type locality.

Breeding: Viviparous. Males 441–747 mm., females 475–1,003 mm. *Mating*—"Mating was observed on May 6, 1932, and May 6, 1936" (Schwardt). *Young*—Number, 23–40(?). Time, August. "There are estimates from 17 to 40 or 50 but few definite records. A female 3 feet long brought into the laboratory in the summer of 1932 gave birth to a litter of 23 young early in August" (Schwardt). "A female I had in captivity gave birth to 23 young ones on the 26th of August" (Hurter).

Food: Fish, crayfish, frogs (Schwardt).

Authorities:

Clay, W. M. (Gen., 1938)

Cope, E. D. (Gen., 1900)

Hurter, J. (Mo., 1911)

McLain, R. B. (Ark., 1899)

Neill, W. (Ga., 1948)

Parker, M. V. (Tenn., 1948)

Rhoads, S. N. (Tenn., 1896)

Schwardt, H. H. (Ark., 1938)

1935 and later, A. H. and A. A. Wright: From 1917 onward, as we went from South Carolina to Louisiana across Piedmont areas, we wondered about Cope's *pleuralis,* but not until about 1935 did we have the conviction that it could not be ignored. Not until Sept. 25, 1937, did we truly awake to its distinctness. E. R. Allen sent us two specimens for identification. They came from Greenwood, Miss., and were provisionally labeled *Natrix s. confluens.* The larger one strictly conformed to Cope's original *pleuralis* description. They were delicate vinaceous-rufous-bellied water snakes, not like the customary solid stocky water snakes. Clay did a good service in re-establishing Cope's *pleuralis* as did Blanchard in his establishment of *confluens,* but neither form is yet fully understood, nor is the now narrowly restricted *fasciatus* very well known. All three seemingly overlap in their described ranges, and we are not fully satisfied that Clay's expanded and independent characterization of *pleuralis* entirely clears the atmosphere. We would like to have someone start from Greenwood, Miss., or thereabouts with much live material and young broods to see if Cope's described *pleuralis* is a more restricted form or not. Unfortunately for workers, Clay's thesis is not published. We have only his synopsis. But Clay's expanded notes and subsequent work would be much welcomed.

Salt water snake, Eastern Florida water snake

Natrix sipedon taeniata (Cope) 1895. Fig. 161; Map 40

Range: N.e. coast of Florida, from "Volusia" (now National Gardens) to the lower end of Mosquito Lagoon. *Elevation*—Sea level.

Size: Adults, 12–24 inches.

Distinctive characteristics: "A small, slender, laterally compressed water snake, distinctly *Thamnophis*-like in superficial appearance, and evidently a representative of the *compressicauda-clarkii* complex. It may be distinguished from *clarkii* by the breaking of the lateral stripe to form a series of roughly diamond-shaped blotches, and from *compressicauda* by the presence of longitudinal stripes, the smaller size, and the greater number of subcaudals" (Carr and Goin).

Color and description: "Head small and slender, olive with inner edges of parietals dusky and with a small interparietal light spot. Dorsum with olive ground color and a nearly continuous dorsal light stripe broken occasionally by bars connecting pairs of dorsolateral dark stripes; separated

Fig. 161. *Natrix s. taeniata* and tidal flats at Mosquito Inlet, Fla., photos by Isabelle Hunt Conant.

from the dorsolateral dark stripe by a light stripe there is anteriorly a lateral dark stripe which, at the point of enlargement of the body, breaks to continue posteriorly as a series of blotches; the light interspaces separating these blotches connect the dorsolateral light stripe with a ventrolateral light stripe formed by confluent blotches on the outer ends of the ventrals and on part of each scale of the lower row. Belly black with median row of cream-colored, broadly lanceolate spots that have their bases flush with the posterior margins of the ventral scutes; ventral surface of tail black, the inner end of each subcaudal light. Each scale in dorsolateral dark stripe black anteriorly; each scale in lateral blotches black with olive posterior margin. Scales strongly keeled; loreal present; supralabials 7–9, usually 8; infralabials 9–11, usually 10; preoculars 1; postoculars 2 or 3, usually 2; temporals 1–2 or 1–3; abdominals 127–131 (males), 128–131 (females); subcaudals 76–88 (males), 72–76 (females); scale rows 21-21-17; anal divided. Measurements in millimeters, (largest male) head-body 406, tail 166; (largest female) head-body 437, tail 127 (broken?)" (Carr and Goin).

Habitat: "All of the specimens for which we have exact data were taken in tidal flats overgrown with glassworts (*Salicornia perennis*). They were collected at night with the aid of a head-light just as the tide was beginning to overflow the flats. Several drainage ditches had been cut through the flats, and along these ditches the snake could be seen lying on the mud under the glassworts. Although we hunted diligently at different tidal stages, the snakes were never seen except when the water was just beginning to flow over the mud-bottomed flats. Repeated searches were made during the daylight hours, but only once did we see a snake, one of which started to emerge from a crab hole but quickly withdrew its head when we appeared. All individuals taken were extremely gentle for *Natrix*, and made no attempt to bite, even when picked up roughly. They were, however, shy and extremely agile; and if not caught with the first grab, they usually dived into the water and disappeared, or escaped through the *Salicornia*. One large individual tried to escape by crawling off across the tops of the glassworts" (Carr and Goin).

Authorities:

Carr, A. F., and C. J. Goin (Fla., 1942)   Cope, E. D. (Gen., 1895)

1895, E. D. Cope: "*Natrix compressicauda taeniata* subsp. nov. Scales in 21 rows; 4 series of longitudinal spots above, those of the median pair forming 2 longitudinal stripes on the greater part of the length; the laterals forming stripes on the neck only. Labials 8/10, oculars 1–3; temporals 1–3. Frontal narrow, not widened anteriorly; parietals rather wide. First row of scales keeled. Gastrosteges 131; anal 1-1; urosteges 82. The lateral black spots extend as far as the tail. The dorsal stripes are connected by a transverse lighter brown shade for a short distance in advance of the vent. Belly black with a median series of semidiscoid yellow spots; gastrosteges with yellow extremities for the anterior ⅔ of the length of the body. The median neck stripes touch on the nape, and after enclosing a pale space unite on the parietal plates. Muzzle brown, the labials with blackish shades. Lower labials, genials, and gulars with yellow spots. Indistinct parietal paired spots. Total length 378 mm.; of tail 98 mm. Two specimens in my private collection from Volusia, Florida. In this form the striping which appears on the neck of the form *compressicauda* is extended the entire length. It bears thus a partial resemblance to the *Natrix clarki* which is not far removed in affinity from the *N. compressicauda*. The form next described (*N. fasciata pictiventris*) connects the latter with the *N. fasciata*."

1916, T. Barbour and G. K. Noble (Fla.): "Although the museum has a series from Tampa Bay and Key West, no topotype of *N. c. taeniata* is at hand. Nevertheless, some of these specimens before us from Tampa Bay and Key West show most of the characters of this supposed race."

1942, A. F. Carr and C. J. Goin: This fast and similar-patterned *taeniata,* like *clarki* and unlike sluggish *compressicauda,* is of the Melbourne-Coronado-Florida strip. *Taeniata* and *clarki,* now separated by 100 miles of intermediate land, Carr and Goin interpret as having come from a population of striped water snakes continuous from the Gulf to the East Coast. They use C. Wythe Cook (*Scenery of Florida,* Fla. Geol. Surv. Bull., 17, 1939) to support their conclusions.

1944, A. H. and A. A. Wright: We now wonder if the strange specimen we saw in the San Diego tank was this form or some other *clarki* aberrant. Notes on the M.C.Z. specimens: 46498—22⅛ inches, of which the tail is 6¼ inches; 46499—11⁹⁄₁₆ inches; 46500—11⁵⁄₁₆ inches, of which the tail is 3¹⁄₁₆ inches. Row of white or light areas on middle of belly, then a dark band *either* side of mid-belly, then light on ends of ventrals and first row of scales. First quarter of snake with dark longitudinal band either side of a light median stripe. Very strikingly *clarki*.

1950, A. H. and A. A. Wright: We now know the region of this form quite well, have conversed with Goin about it, and have some of Mrs. Isabella Hunt Conant's prints of it.

Brown water snake (15—Yarrow 1882), **Water pilot**

Natrix taxispilota (Holbrook) 1842. Fig. 162; Map 41

Other common names: Aspic; false moccasin; great water snake; pied water snake; southern water snake; water rattle (5); water rattler.

Range: Lower coastal region from s.e. Virginia to n. and w. Florida and w. to Louisiana.—Ala.; Fla.; Ga.; La.; N.C.; S.C.; Va. *Elevation*—Normally below 500 feet to sea level.

Size: Adults, 30–72 inches.

Distinctive characteristics: A large, very stout 27–33-rowed, strongly keeled, brown water snake having a middorsal row of rectangular black-bordered, dark brown-centered spots with a distinct alternating series of similar spots. Venter white or buff, with purplish drab strongly marked with black. Rear of parietals broken into several small scales. Ventrals 136–152; caudals 70–99.

Color: A snake from Billy's Island, Okefinokee Swamp, Ga., June 21, 1921. The back is marked with transverse spots that have black borders and centers which are sometimes slightly lighter or darker than, and sometimes about the same color as the intervening spaces. These spaces between the dorsal spots are clove brown, seal brown, or warm sepia. There is a lateral row of spots, also black-bordered, which may have centers of mikado brown, snuff brown, or cinnamon brown. The interspace color here is ecru-drab or pale ecru-drab. The skin between the scales on the forward part of the body is pale vinaceous-drab or pallid vinaceous-drab. The interspace back of the angle of the mouth and also the first 8 or more interspaces are warm buff. The head is a uniform brownish drab or benzo brown. The upper and lower labials are heavily dotted with very fine spots. The iris has a cinnamon-drab or wood brown ring, and also much of the same color over its surface except in the front part, which is dusky. The underside of the head and a short distance on the venter are cream color finely dotted with black. Each ventral bears a fuscous or black spot near either end. Down the middle of the belly is an area of pale vinaceous-drab or ecru-drab heavily clouded with fine black spots. The rest of the belly is white or pale olive-buff.

A young snake from Cedar Landing, near Folkston, Ga., July 26, 1922. The back is marked with transverse bars, and the side with a row of alternating spots. These bars and spots are clove brown or blackish brown (1), (2), or (3). Sometimes the scales are edged with ground color or interspace color of mouse gray, hair brown, drab, or light brownish olive. The iris is buffy brown. The chin and lower neck are olive-buff or deep olive-buff. The belly is white with clove brown or blackish brown spots, and down its middle an area of pale ecru-drab and pallid purple-drab.

Habitat: This, one of the largest water snakes, may also be one of the most arboreal. Our experience with it in Okefinokee Swamp will reveal some facets of its life. "This snake is par excellence the snake of the open water courses in the swamp or narrow runs just wide enough for a boat. Either along Log River [Ga.] or Minne Lake Run one can hear a succession of pied water snakes as they drop off into the water. They may climb upon the dead branches or live shrubs which line the water courses or rest on the little islets or verdant hummocks where many an individual is hidden. Particularly does one find them in the latter situations on the hottest days, and not infrequently we have approached close enough on such days to club them. As they shoot into the water sometimes the pied belly reveals that it is *T. taxispilota* and not *T. fasciatus* or any of its subspecies. . . . The natives call them 'water moccasins' and consider them as poisonous as rattlesnakes or true moccasins. Once when one of us was bitten by a medium-sized specimen, the Lees awaited the result with considerable solicitude for the supposed unfortunate. After two weeks of attempts, we were growing impatient because we had taken none of the largest individuals, and Alligator Joe, one of the visitors, when fishing stunned a 'water moccasin' and considerately put it in the prow of his boat. We almost reached him when the snake revived, and in the twinkling of an eye he had thrown his present into the lake with his oar. Man and live 'water moccasin' in the same boat was not conceivable" (Wright and Bishop).

In 1951 Neill (Gen.) reported it in salt water areas in the lower course of the Combahee River, South Carolina.

Period of activity: *Hibernation*—"I believe that this snake overwinters in cavities or burrows near the water's edge, since a rise of water level will bring out numbers of them regardless of the temperature. The reptiles thus forced from the retreats hang in bushes in the sunlight for several hours, and then disappear, probably having been 'thawed out' sufficiently to search for another shelter" (Neill).

Breeding: Viviparous. Males 670-1,100 mm., females 710-1,350 mm. *Sexual dimorphism*—(See *N. s. sipedon* for knobby dorsal scales.) *Mating*—"Frank Young and I discovered a pair in copula on a willow limb 15 feet above the water on the Santa Fe River (Alachua County), Mar. 20, 1937; lying on top of the mated pair intimately intertwined with them, and apparently sound asleep with a large *N. s. pictiventris*" (Carr). Franklin holds the breeding season to be the latter part of May.

Young—Until our studies in 1914-1915, few notes were at hand. Franklin has since made significant observations. Time of birth, June 15-Nov. 1, mainly August. June-Nov. 1 (Wright and Bishop); June 15-October (Franklin). Number of young, 14-58; the range in 30 broods was 30-40 (Franklin). Size of young, 7-10.75 inches (178-268 mm.). The smallest we have measured were 295 mm. long. Thanks to Franklin's study we learn that "the young are born out of the water and usually molt within 18 to 48 hours after birth. . . . The young were inactive until after molting, when they became very active and capable of drawing blood when they bit. . . . On September 13, 1941 a female 1,245 mm. in length gave birth to 34 young, 5 of which were stillborn. One of the living young had a deformed spine and the tail was twisted and kinked. The specimen died 3 days later. The 21 females ranged in length from 178 to 246 mm., average 238.5 mm. In 13 males the range is 238 to 259 mm., the average 251.8 mm. On Aug. 5, 1942, a female 1,285 mm. in length gave birth to 37 young, of which 2 were stillborn. There were 21 females, ranging from 236 to 252 mm., average 242.5 mm. The 16 males measured 246-258 mm., average 251.7. On August 5,

1942, a third female gave birth to 40 young, of which 22 were females and 18 males. The female specimens measured 190–251 mm., average 241.1 mm., and the males 200–268, average 250.6. The sex ratio altogether for the 3 broods is ♂ ♂ 47; ♀ ♀ 64. The juvenile males average larger than the females, while the reverse is the case in adults."

We append a note by Wright and Bishop: "This species is ovoviviparous. The specimens taken in the middle of June showed the developmental stages little advanced. One specimen (No. 6113), 2 feet 10 inches long, had only 14 embryos, while another 4½ feet long and about 8 inches in circumference had 40 embryos. It is rather a significant fact that all the larger individuals taken are females. Either the large males were too fast for us or the females are larger or occupy more exposed positions and may prove more sluggish or braver. The individuals taken from July 15–Nov. 1, 1912, showed the embryos much farther advanced and some had unborn embryos 26 or more cm. long. One specimen (No. 6256) had 58 embryos, 32 on the left side and 26 on the right side. The normal number seems to be 35–40 embryos."

Food: Fish, frogs. Wright and Bishop, Carr, Richmond.

Authorities:

Carr, A. F., Jr. (Fla., 1940a)

Franklin, M. A. (Fla., 1944)

Heilprin, A. (Fla., 1887)

Loennberg, E. (Fla., 1895)

Neill, W. T. (Ga., 1948)

Richmond, N. D. (Va., 1944)

Schwartz, A. (Fla., 1950)

Wright, A. H., and S. C. Bishop (Ga., 1916)

1952, F. R. Cagle, *A Key to the Amphibians and Reptiles of La.*

1955, W. T. Neill, *Ross Allen's Reptile Inst., Publ. Res. Div.*—No. 7.

These authors hold *Natrix rhombifera* to be a subspecies of *Natrix taxispilota*.

PROBLEMATICAL FORM

Banks water snake

Natrix sipedon engelsi Barbour 1943. Fig. 163; Map 42

Range: Shackleford Banks, Carteret County, N.C. *Elevation*—Sea level.

Size: Adults. The type is 520 mm. or 20.8 inches long.

Color: A snake from Mullet Pond, Shackleford Banks, 3 miles south of Beaufort Inlet, Carteret Co., N.C., loaned by H. A. Dundee and R. B. Loomis, July 29, 1950. The dorsum is fuscous marked with 34 bands on the body, the cephalic 13 bands being complete to venter, but thereafter the alternation of lateral band and dorsal spot begins. The interval on meson is 1 scale long, but expands for several rows above the venter to 2½ scale rows. These intervals are pompeian red and extend onto the belly on the ends of 2 plates. The dark dorsal bands extend onto the belly a short distance as solid black bars. In the forward half of the body this black bar on ends

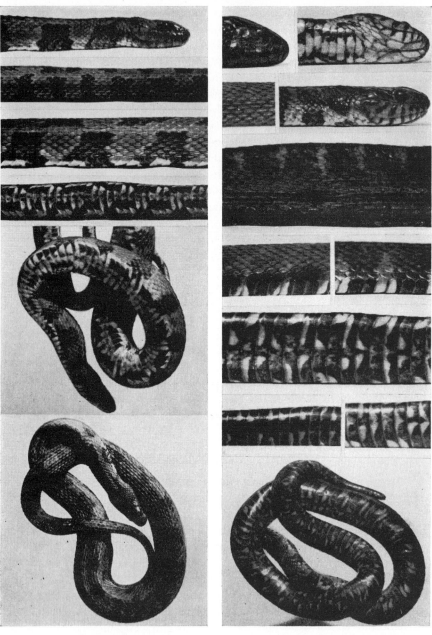

Fig. 162. *Natrix taxispilota:* 1,3, Marion Co., Fla., through E. R. Allen and W. Boden-stein; 2,4–6, Royal Palm Park, Dade Co., Fla.

Fig. 163. *Natrix sipedon engelsi,* Pea Is., N.C., J. A. Gustafson.

of ventrals bears on each plate a pompeian red center. The top of the head is black, but back of the eye are several spots of amber brown, chestnut, or russet. The eye is fuscous or black with chalcedony yellow pupil rim. The pattern of the belly in the rear half is more black than pink or red, in the forward half more pink than black. The underside of the head is white or pale chalcedony yellow. The labial sutures are black with pompeian red edgings, and some of the plates of underside of head, chin shields, and gulars bear little spots of the same red. The first 10–12 ventrals extend across the venter as clear areas of chalcedony yellow thinly outlined with black, reminding one somewhat of the pattern of *N. pictiventris*. This black increases rearward till it becomes the dominant background color of the belly. For a distance of 10–12 more ventrals the pale chalcedony yellow is flecked with coral pink and instead of extending all the way across the venter becomes crescents of light color with bases on the rear margins of the plates. Caudad of the first 6 inches, the pattern becomes more or less immediately a series of coral red to dragon's-blood red crescents, with the reddish dorsolateral intervals encroaching on the ends of 2 belly plates as coral red areas. In the rear of the body, the black becomes more extensive and the red crescents increasingly smaller, until the under tail is almost black. In the forward half of the body, the black of the belly frequently has small central patches of pompeian red.

A snake from Hatteras Island, Outer Banks, N.C., on the Pea Island National Wildlife Refuge, approximately 40 miles north of Cape Hatteras, found in a salt marsh on the Pamlico Sound side of the island by John A. Gustafson, March 30, 1949. The general color of the back is bone brown to fuscous. In the cephalic region, transverse dorsal saddles are distinctly separated by bands of buffy brown a scale or less in length. Thereafter the dorsal spots are obscure and intervals inconspicuous and poorly indicated. The 39 dark lateral bars of the body are outlined with black and centered in the lower portion with scales margined and flecked with ocher red to vinaceous-russet. These bars are 2–2½ scales longitudinally, about 6 scales deep and usually extend onto the ventrals as solid bars. When the snake is wet, these vertical bars appear black and shiny. The light intervals on the sides, distinctly triangular in the cephalic region, are buffy brown. They are 5 scales high, 1 scale and 2 half scales longitudinally at the base and 1 scale or less at the top. At its base this light interval may extend onto 1, 2, or rarely 3 ventral plates, where it becomes (like the midventral spots) colonial buff in the forward half to marguerite-yellow in the caudal portion. The top of the head is black with an area ahead of and below eye of buffy brown, and the parietals are partly margined with buffy brown. The eye is dark mouse gray. The upper labials are buffy brown with broad margins of vinaceous-russet to burnt umber. The lower labials are narrowly margined with the same color. The gulars and underside of head are cream to colonial buff. This color becomes confined to a median triangle on each ventral plate, naples yellow in the neck region and fading a bit caudad through straw and massicot yellow. In the cephalic region this yellow triangle is outlined on either side by a black-margined triangle of ocher red to vinaceous-russet or terra cotta (of the quality of the vinaceous-pink venter of Barber's *Natrix s. engelsi*). On the rear half, the median yellowish triangle is lost and the pattern becomes 2 irregular rows of pale cartridge buff spots on an otherwise black venter, with more black and less light spots on the tail. The cephalic half of venter back of the first 4–6 inches reminds us very much of the coloration of Barber's figure. In general it impresses us as being close to *Natrix sipedon sipedon*. *Structure*—The 4th and 5th labials enter the eye.

Authorities:
Barbour, T. (N.C., 1942)

Barbour, T., and W. L. Engels (N.C., 1942)
Engels, W. L. (N.C., 1942)

It will be observed that this *Natrix* occurs on Ocracoke Island—a barrier beach or offshore bar "probably now the most nearly inaccessible to invading species."

1942, W. L. Engels: "The relative accessibility of offshore bars [in N.C.] varies with their age. The young bars, formed at some distance from the mainland, are accessible only to such forms as can cross the intervening salt water barrier. These species would be of 3 types: those that fly, those that swim, and such others as could withstand the rigors of transport on drift over salt water. The first group includes birds and bats; the second, turtles, some snakes and especially *Natrix*, and probably some mammals, such as mink, otter, muskrat, and perhaps rice rats. The third group would include any form which because of its habits might sometimes be caught up by flood waters or otherwise find itself accidentally adrift in a current." We have talked with Dr. Engels about the "Vertebrate fauna of North Carolina coastal islands" and now hope other publications will follow this excellent paper. (On Ocracoke, Engels recorded Fowler's toad, glass snake, *Cnemidophorus, Opheodrys aestivus, Coluber constrictor, Lampropeltis getulus,* and *Natrix sipedon*.)

T. Barbour and W. L. Engels: (See discussion of *Elaphe quadrivittata parallela* and *Lampropeltis getulus sticticeps*.)

1942 on, A. H. and A. A. Wright. We have examined this specimen on two different trips. We made many notes on the first trip, but now find only the following jottings from the second trip: "The underside of the tail is not entirely black but has some light spots. For the first (cephalic) 3 inches the venter is light with dark edges, then comes a pattern more like Dr. Barbour's figure. The light vertical intervals on rear are about 5 scales high." It is truly an interesting specimen. Is it an aberrant *N. s. sipedon*?

1949, A. H. and A. A. Wright: Mr. John A. Gustafson tried for water snakes in the spring vacation of 1949, and our color description of his snake approaches Barbour's belly pattern of this form.

1950, R. B. Loomis and H. A. Dundee: We interviewed Dr. Engels, and as a consequence, we believe, Loomis and Dundee loaned us a living specimen from the bars. Their data read, "Mullet Pond, Shackleford Banks, Carteret Co., N.C. Mullet Pond is a fresh water pond near the western tip of the island, and is the exact type locality of the subspecies."

GREEN SNAKES

Genus *OPHEODRYS* Fitzinger (Fig. 21)

U.S. forms: Size, medium small to medium, 5–47 inches; slender; head distinct, scuta normal; tail long; anal divided; back and head light green (bluish gray in alcohol); belly yellow or greenish yellow (sometimes white); scale rows 15, smooth (*Liopeltis*), or 17, keeled (*Cyclophis*); nasal plate not divided; frontal shield angulate in front, sides straight and evenly tapering; posterior chin shields long and widely spreading for half their length; loreal present; temporals 1 + 2; preocular 1; postoculars 2; upper labials 7; teeth equal; hemipenis, "calyces numerous, fringed" (Cope, Gen., 1900). Synonyms: *Anguis, Chlorosoma, Coluber, Contia, Cyclophis, Entechinus, Euripholis, Herpetodryas, Leptophis, Liopeltis, Natrix, Phyllophilophis.*

KEY TO THE GENUS *OPHEODRYS*

a. Scale rows 17; scales keeled; newborn young grayish green; size to 47 inches; ventrals 148–166; caudals 110–148 (*Cyclophis*).

O. aestivus aestivus

aa. Scale rows 15; scale smooth; size to 24 or 26 inches; ventrals 116–154; caudals 60–95 (*Liopeltis*).

  b. Males normally with less than 131 ventrals, females less than 140; young dark olive-gray above, pale grayish blue below.

O. vernalis vernalis

  bb. Males normally with 131 or more ventrals, females with 140 or more.

O. v. blanchardi

Rough green snake (62—Hay 1892), **Keeled green snake** (27)

Opheodrys aestivus aestivus (Linné) 1766. Fig. 164; Map 43

Other common names: (Green) bush snake; (green) grass snake; green (summer) snake; green tree snake; green whip snake; huckleberry snake; keel-scaled green snake; little green snake; magnolia snake; pine snake; rough-coated green snake; rough-keeled snake; rough-scaled green snake; southern green snake; summer (green) snake; true snake; vine snake.

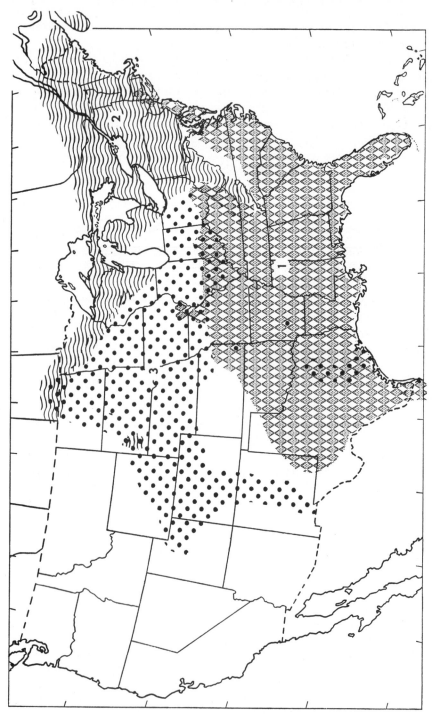

Map 43. *Opheodrys*—1, *a. aestivus*; 2, *v. vernalis*; 3, *v. blanchardi*.

Range: From s.w. Connecticut s. in coastal plain and Piedmont to Florida; w. to Mexico (Tamaulipas and Nuevo León); n.w. to s.e. New Mexico; and n.e. across Texas and Oklahoma to s.e. Kansas; across Missouri, s.e. Iowa, s. Illinois, Indiana, and Ohio to the Alleghany Mts.—U.S.A.: Ala.; Ark.; Conn.; D.C.; Del.; Fla.; Ga.; Ia.; Ill.; Ind.; Kan.; Ky.; La.; Md.; Miss.; Mo.; N.C.; N.J.; N.M.; N.Y.; O.; Okla.; Pa.; S.C.; Tenn.; Tex.; Va.; W. Va. Mex.: Nuevo León; Tamaulipas. *Elevation*—Sea level to 2,000 feet. 1,000–2,500 feet (King, Tenn., 1939); 2,800–5,000 feet (Bailey, N.M., 1913); 1,400 feet (Barbour, Ky., 1950).

Size: Adults, 15–47 inches.

Distinctive characteristics: A medium, keeled, 17-rowed green snake with sulphur yellow or green-yellow venter. Tail very long. Ventrals 148–166; caudals 111–148.

Color: A snake from Okefinokee Swamp, Ga., caught June 5, 1921. The back is cerro green or calla green. The upper labials and the lower part of the head are light greenish yellow. The rest of the venter is sulphur yellow.

A snake from Boerne, Tex., caught Apr. 12, 1925. The upper parts are yellowish oil green. The upper labials are lemon yellow or lemon chrome. The iris is olivaceous black below, in front, and behind, with pale yellow-green above, and a pupil rim of sulphur yellow. The under parts except under head and neck are light green-yellow.

A snake from San Antonio, Tex., Apr. 13, 1925. The back is cerro green. The upper labials and rostral are light greenish yellow to light yellow-green. The lower labials and mental are sulphur yellow. The iris is back or olivaceous black with a pupil rim of sulphur yellow and with the upper part of the iris pale yellow-green. The underside of the head is white, the first 10 or 15 ventrals light green-yellow, the belly pale yellow-green, and the underside of the tail light yellow-green.

Abnormal coloration—"In all the living specimens which I have seen from tropical Florida and the Keys, the ventral surface was entirely unpigmented, while in North and Central Florida examples it is invariably light cream yellow" (Carr).

Habitat: There are 45 records of climbing, making it decidedly an arboreal form. The most frequent habitats are: bushes 29, small or growing trees 16, vines 10, hedges 5. Individual trees mentioned are: oaks 5, scrub pines 3, magnolia, sassafras, alder, orange, sumac, dogwood, cedar, cherry, elm, sycamore, and pecan. The forests may be called: wooded meadow, hammocks 2, scrubs, wooded rocky hillside, flatwood, wooded pasture, wooded river bottom 2, forest glades, tree savannah, prairie trees, second growth, palmetto ridge, wooded district or area 5, wooded canyon 2, forest upland. A miscellaneous list is: foot of plains, shaded locations, margins of creeks, streams, lakes, or marshes, cypress swamps, creek bottom, fence row, grass, low grass, low ground, branch (both senses), bayous, stones, road or roadside 2, leaves 2, open grassland, bed of packed leaves, blackberries, pasture land. In all, at least 60–75 different habitats were given, mostly arboreal. Some authors believe *O. vernalis* more terrestrial than *O. aestivus,* but as time goes on, authors will find *O. vernalis* more of a "bush" snake than once supposed. Because of the behavior of one captive, Cope in 1872 suspected *O. aestivus* of being nonarboreal.

We choose three exceptional habitat accounts: "From a range over the whole eastern or humid division of Lower Sonoran zone the species apparently reaches in Texas its western limit. It does not enter the plains region nor the arid region except where brushy gulches enable it to cross the rough country south of the lower arm of the Staked Plains. The specimens from near Kerrville and Rock Springs were taken in gulches with such vegetation as pecan, sycamore, elm, black cherry, oak, and abundant underbrush" (Bailey).

In describing the vegetation of southern Florida hammocks, Dr. J. K. Small, a botanist, referred to this species as follows: "There is everywhere present a beautiful green snake. It inhabits the hammocks and is especially abundant in those of the Everglades. It lies outstretched on the branches of shrubs and trees and glides along the branches from one tree to another with surprising ease. One has usually to be careful to look before laying hold of the limb of a tree for support, or he may grasp something of quite different consistency from that of wood" (in Safford, Fla., 1919).

"Green snakes are common not only on Hog Island [Va.], the only wooded island visited, but on all the neighboring bars and spits where coarse grass and myrtle bushes can afford the animals some cover. One specimen was found on Pig Island crawling leisurely through a colony of black skimmers (*Rhynchops nigra*)" (Brady).

Period of activity: *First appearance*—Apr. 6 (Allen, Miss., 1932); Apr. 26, 27, 28 (Gloyd). *Fall disappearance*—Aug. 9, Sept. 13, Oct. 30 (Gloyd); Sept. 13 (Anderson, Tenn., 1942); Oct. 1 (Peterson, Tex., 1950). *Seasonal catch*—Jan., 2; Mar., 1; June, 4; July, 3; Aug., 3; Sept., 1; Oct., 7; Nov., 3; Dec., 1 (Brimley, N.C., 1925). *Hibernation*—"One was found September 13, 1936, under a stump that had been pulled from the ground. Seven red-barred garter snakes *Thamnophis sirtalis parietalis* were also under the stump" (Anderson, Tenn., 1942).

Breeding: Oviparous. Males 345–797 mm., females 335–805 mm. *Eggs*—Number, 4–11. There are records of 3 complements of 4, 1 of 5, 1 of 6, 1 of 7, 1 of 8, 2 of 9, 1 of 10, and 1 of 11 eggs. Time of birth, July 1–Aug. 31. Most records are in mid-July. There are definite records of July 8, July 13, July 20, July 22, Aug. 1, Aug. 28 and Aug. 31. Several authors merely give July. Size, .8–1.5x.4–.5 inches. Walker gave in 1931 31x11 mm., 30x11 mm., 30x10 mm., 29x10 mm. for 4 eggs. In 1911 Hurter (Mo.) gave them as 38 mm. long. Brimley's oviducal eggs July 5 were 20–22 mm. long, but in

1941 he called the eggs "not quite one inch long." Force (Okla., 1930) had diverse results—eggs 15 mm. x 8 mm. in one complement and 25x10 mm. in another. Conant (O., 1938a) gave egg lengths of 23–29 mm., widths 10–11 mm. The eggs are elongate, smooth, shiny, white, and rather hard shelled. The most recent observation is that of Laurence Curtis (Tex., 1950a): "On the morning of the following June 19, 6 eggs were found deposited in a clutch near the center of the cage. The eggs were adhesive, smooth and cream colored, with length and width measurements as follows in millimeters: 22x8.5, 25x10, 25x10, 26x9.5, 27x11, and 29x10."

Young—Hatching time, late August or September. There are records of July 22, Aug. 25, Aug. 31, late August or September, Sept. 9. Curtis (Tex., 1950a) has hatching July 23 and 24 from his June 19 eggs. From 5 eggs he had 6 snakes, as one egg produced twins. Each of these was monocular, the left eye lacking. Size, 5–8 inches. One wonders if the Hurter 5-inch or Force 5.5-inch specimens were *O. aestivus*. Curtis (Tex., 1950a), in his brood of 4 females and 2 males, has total length and tail length as follows: males, 190.5/71 mm.; 190.5/68.5; females, 210/67.5, 200/67.5, 140/49, 151/51, the last two the twins.

Food: Insects, spiders, snails, frogs. Boulenger (Gen., 1914), Parker (Tenn., 1937), Wright and Bishop, Van Hyning, Metcalf (Gen., 1930).

Authorities:

Bailey, V. (Tex., 1905)
Blatchley, W. S. (Ind., 1891)
Brady, M. K. (Va., 1925)
Burger, L. W. (Gen., 1947)
Carr, A. F., Jr. (Fla., 1940a)
Duellman, W. E. (Va., 1949)
Garman, S. (Tex., 1892)
Gloyd, H. K. (Kan., 1928)
Holbrook, J. E. (Gen., 1836–42)

Shufeldt, R. W. (Gen., 1897)
Stejneger, L., and T. Barbour (Gen., 1940)
Swanson, F. L. (Ind., 1939)
Van Hyning, O. C. (Fla., 1932)
Walker, C. F. (O., 1931)
Wright, A. H., and S. C. Bishop (Ga., 1916)

Green snake (79—Bartram 1791), **Smooth green snake** (55—Hay 1887)

Opheodrys vernalis vernalis (Harlan) 1827. Fig. 165; Map 43

Other common names: American smooth green snake; common green snake; grass snake (25—DeKay 1842); green grass snake; green whip snake; northern green snake; northern grass snake; smooth-coated green snake; smooth grass snake; smooth-scaled green snake; spring snake; summer snake.

Range: From Nova Scotia, New Brunswick, s. Quebec, and Ontario across the upper peninsula of Michigan to s.e. Saskatchewan; e. through n. North Dakota, extreme n. Minnesota, n. Wisconsin, n. half of s. peninsula of

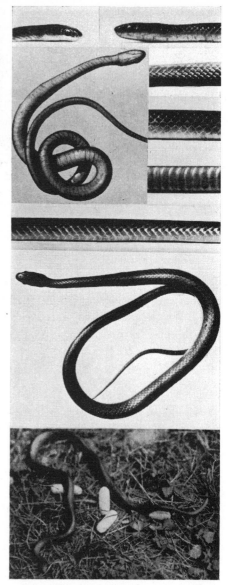

Fig. 164. *Opheodrys aestivus aestivus:* 1,4,7, Auburn, Ala., H. Good; 2,3,5, Silver Springs, Fla., E. R. Allen; 6, Brownsville, Tex., H. C. Blanchard.

Fig. 165. *Opheodrys vernalis vernalis:* 1,4,7, Putnam, Conn., A. B. Klots; 2,3,5,6,8, Ithaca, N.Y.; 9, Palisades Park, N.Y., photo by A. B. Klots.

Michigan to e. Ohio; down the Appalachians to e. Tennessee; thence n.e. to New England.—U.S.A.: Conn.; D.C.; Mass.; Md.; Me.; Mich.; Minn.; N.C.; N.D.; N.H.; N.J.; N.Y.; O.; Pa.; R.I.; Tenn.; Va.; Vt.; W. Va.; Wis. Can.: Man.; N.B.; N.S.; Ont.; Que.; Sask. *Elevation*—Sea level to 5,000 feet. Most records below 2,000 feet; sea level to 1,050 feet (Manville, Me., 1939); 2,300 feet (Smith, Pa., 1945); 840 feet (Wilson and Friddle, W. Va., 1950).

Size: Adults, 11–26 inches.

Distinctive characteristics: A small, smooth, lithe, 15-rowed green snake, with a long tail. Grobman described this subspecies as "males with less than 131 ventrals, females with less than 140 ventrals." Ventrals 116–144; caudals 60–95.

Color: A snake from Ithaca, N.Y., received from Mrs. W. J. Hamilton, July 24, 1936. Just killed in the road. The scales of the back except for the lower 1½ rows are light hellebore green or parrot green. The lower 1½ rows are dull green-yellow or yellow-green. The top of the head is like the back. The upper labials are bright chalcedony yellow. The iris is warm sepia or natal brown with the portion just above the pupil rim olive-buff, pale dull green-yellow, or pale chalcedony yellow. The underside of the head is between pale chalcedony yellow and white, with some of the gulars back of the angle of the mouth marked with bright chalcedony yellow. The ventrals are light chalcedony yellow or pale chalcedony yellow.

Habitat: The most common habitats by count of authors are grassy fields or places 12, meadows 8, sides or tops of mountains 4, low bushes 7, boggy areas 3, fields 3. Those mentioned twice are: grass-covered fields, under rocks or stones, small trees, cultivated spots, marshes, dry open woods, under boards. Other habitats are: sandy ridges, margins of quiet pond, open aspen country, sand, edge of intervale, underneath a pile of tent poles, grassy face of an escarpment, in logs, moist meadowlands, clearings, berry bushes, undergrowth brambles, smilax vine, hardwoods, old uncultivated fields, damp places, and poplar-bordered field. Loveridge in his one-season study of it found it beneath boards, stones, a tarpaulin, drums, linoleum, and asbestos buried in grass, and one he found in a bush.

Our orchid-hunting friends were some of the first to insist that this form was a bush snake of sphagnum bogs, and we as teachers *in the summer* always sought a sphagnum bog to produce a green snake. We write this because of such comments as, "It seldom if ever climbs above the ground," and "It does no climbing." Whenever we went with the Eameses (joint authors of *Our Wild Orchids*), we found this form.

In 1950 Seibert (Ill.) in a study of an area of 3.2 acres near Chicago, arrived by the Lincoln index at 44 of these snakes per acre, and by the Hayne method at 74 per acre.

Period of activity: *First appearance*—May 6 (Jones, N.S., 1865); May 24,

26 (Evermann, N.H., 1918c); Apr. 10 (Wright, N.Y., 1919b); Apr. 16 (Pope, Wis., 1928); Apr. 26 (Loveridge). "Of the 44 live individuals seen, 25 (57%) were observed at dens in April and early May. All but 2 of the 25 were beneath stones. Later, however, after the green snakes had presumably left their dens for the summer, of 19 live ones seen, only 8 were under stones, and 11 in the open, not beneath anything" (Axtell). He found "23.7 per cent (14) of all the specimens that we recorded were dead on the road." This snake wanders in the open more than most species. *Fall disappearance* —Aug. 11, 12, 15, 21 (Bishop and Alexander, N.Y., 1927); Oct. 10, 20 (Wright); Oct. 24 (Loveridge).

Breeding: Oviparous. Males 300–650 mm., females 280–575 mm. *Mating*— "On August 18, 1931, the senior author discovered 2 snakes of this species copulating. The male was 43 cm. and the female 36 cm. in length. . . . A few days later, on August 22, Dr. G. H. W. Lucas and Mr. Fry discovered another copulating pair. . . . Both in 1930 and 1931 it was noticed that green snakes were seen much more frequently in August than earlier in the summer" (Dymond and Fry).

Eggs—Number, 3–12. 3 (5 authors); 4 (1); 5 (2); 6 (4); 7 (5); 8 (1); 9 (2); 11 (3); 12 (4)—average 7.4 eggs. Time of deposition, June 24 to July 30 (Smith); July (Wright and Allen); July 22 (Duellman); July 24–Aug. 29 (Blanchard); Aug. 8 (Conant); Aug. 9 (Zarrow and Pomerat); Aug. 11, 12, 21, Sept. 2 (Bishop and Alexander); Aug. 12, mid-August, Sept. 15 (Surface); Aug. 14 (Langlois); Aug. 18 (Ellis); Aug. 19 (Conant); Aug. 23 (Fisher); Aug. 30 (Putnam). Size, "The eggs vary in length from 19.5 to 34.0 mm. and in diameter from 8 to nearly 18 mm. Most common, however, they vary within the limits of 20 to 30 and 10 to 15 millimeters" (Blanchard). Conant's (Pa., 1942) clutch of 5 eggs were 33.3x11.2 mm., 34.9x11.4, 36.0x11.5, 36.9x10.4, 33.8x10.0 mm. Putnam (Gen., 1868) gave 1x½ inches, Langlois 1x⅓ inch, Babcock (N.E. 1929) 1 inch. Dexter (O., 1948) had eggs 1¹⁄₁₆x¼ inch. They were cylindrical, thin, parchmentlike, blunt-ended.

One of our former students, H. E. Evans (1948), while in a Boy Scout camp at Crystal Lake, N.Y., took 31 specimens in June–August. He wrote: "Many of the captive individuals laid fertile eggs which were easily incubated in sawdust."

In 1954 W. T. Stille (Ill.) made the most comprehensive study to date. Among his results we choose these details: Measurements of 97 eggs, mean length of 21.9 ± .39 mm. and a mean diameter of 10.4 ± .13 mm.; eggs hatched one month after deposition. Here we introduce, with our italics, a note of levity. In 1875–76 J. B. Gilpin (N.S.) wrote: "It produces eggs *very like the garter snake and receives its young in its mouth when in danger.* I have identified its eggs."

Young—Hatching period, Aug. 2–Sept. 18 or Oct. 5. Aug. 2 (Weber, N.Y., 1928); Aug. 5 (Blanchard); Aug. 12 (Surface, Pa., 1906); Aug. 20 (Ellis,

Mich., 1917); Aug. 23, Aug. 28 (Langlois); Aug. 30 (Fisher, Me., 1921); Aug. (Ditmars, N.E., 1929); Sept. 2 (Surface); Sept. 4 (Blanchard); Sept. 11 (Conant, Pa., 1942); Sept. 18 (Hollibaugh and Wright); Oct. 5 (Surface, Pa., 1906). Size, 4–6.6 inches. Blanchard's smallest was 101 mm., and his largest 166 mm. Conant's 5 young were 123, 123, 124, 125, 128 mm. or about 5 inches. Other records range from 4⅜, 4½, 4⅝, to 5¹³⁄₁₀₀ inches. Eggs laid Aug. 5 hatched for Le Buff (Mass., 1951) on Aug. 30 into snakes 6 inches long, which by October grew to 8 inches.

Two good life histories of the green snake are those of Langlois and Blanchard. Langlois: "Three gravid female green snakes were taken and kept for their breeding records, 2 from Douglas Lake, Cheboygan County, and 1 from Cecil Bay, Emmet County. Two of them laid their eggs on Aug. 14, one laying 3 eggs, the other 4. The third and largest was collected on August 15, and, although her abdomen was quite as distended as the others' had been, she retained her eggs and must have absorbed them, as her abdomen was of normal girth about October 1. The eggs were cylindrical, with rounded ends and were encased in a white leathery covering. They ranged in length from 27 to 38 mm. and averaged about 12 mm. in diameter at the middle, 10 mm. at one end, and 11 mm. at the other. The 6 good eggs were kept on moist sand, and covered with sphagnum. All 6 hatched on August 28.

Blanchard: "Eggs are usually laid during the first 3 weeks of August, although they may be deposited a week earlier or later than this. Extreme dates on record are July 24 and August 29. The hatching period in northern Michigan varies from August 5 to September 4, and these dates include all the records from other localities. In any one year the longest hatching period has proved to be only 17 days. The interval from laying to hatching varied in the cases under observation from 4 to 23 days."

Food: Insects, salamanders, spiders, slugs, snails, centipedes, millipedes. Surface (Pa., 1906); Uhler, Cottam, and Clarke (Va., 1939).

Field notes: Some outcoming dates at Ithaca are Apr. 9, 1910, Apr. 20, 1912, Apr. 21, 1915, May 8, 1904, and May 9, 1909, and fall disappearance Oct. 11, 12, 1912.

On Aug. 11, 1935, Mr. and Mrs. G. O. Hollibaugh brought us a female green snake which was taken on Connecticut Hill July 26. The snake laid eggs Aug. 10. These were put in leaf mold in a glass jar covered with a cloth. On Sept. 18 four eggs hatched. The little snakes are slaty gray in color, not green. The weather at this period was cool. On Sept. 23 we dampened the leaf mold for the first time since the jar was brought to us. We have had 3 warm days. On Sept. 27: The little snakes are a deep olive green above and white below. They measure 4¾, 4⅞, 5, 5¹⁄₁₆ inches. We forgot to mention that 2 shells had each a longitudinal opening on the side of the shell, one slit ³⁄₁₆ inch, another ¼ inch in length. The other 2 eggs are irregularly split—a short split near one end.

Authorities:

Allen, G. M. (N.H., 1899)
Axtell, H. H. (N.Y., 1947)
Blanchard, F. N. (Mich., 1933)
De Kay, J. E. (N.Y., 1842)
Dymond, J. R., and F. E. J. Fry (Ont., 1932)

Grobman, A. B. (Gen., 1941)
Langlois, T. H. (Mich., 1925)
Loveridge, A. (Mass., 1927)
Stille, W. T. (Ill., 1954)
Williams, J. B. (Ont., 1902)

All of us who have planted many Chinese and Japanese shrubs and perennials on our home background, and all of us who have noted spoonbills, alligators, catfishes (*Ameiurus*), *Ancistrodons,* skinks, hellbenders, and many more animals more or less common to China and e. United States were not surprised to have Dr. Pope, on Chinese evidence, upset our longestablished *Liopeltis vernalis* with *Eurypholis vernalis* 1935. One year later Schmidt and Necker held two generic names tenable—*Opheodrys* and *Entechinus*—and chose Stejneger's suggestion of the former name. Thus we have *Opheodrys vernalis* a smooth snake and *Opheodrys aestivus* a rough-keeled snake.

1927: A. Loveridge in one area, in one season, collected garter, De Kay's, and green snakes. His observations on the green snake extended from Apr. 26 to Oct. 24 and are a noteworthy addition to our knowledge of this form.

1941, A. B. Grobman: "During the initial stages of this variational study it became apparent that there are at least 2 well-differentiated races (one of which is herein described) of *O. vernalis* with, perhaps an incipient (incipient either in actual development or in our knowledge) race in the Black Hills."

Western smooth green snake (5—Schmidt 1941), Green snake (19)

Opheodrys vernalis blanchardi Grobman 1941. Fig. 166; Map 43

Other common names: Common green snake; (green) grass snake; little green snake; northern green snake; smooth grass snake; smooth green snake; spring snake; summer snake.

Range: From w. Ohio n.w. through Wisconsin and Minnesota to Manitoba; then s.w. to cent. Colorado with a spur n.w. to Great Salt Lake and another down the Rio Grande to s. New Mexico; thence n.e. to Nebraska and n.e. Kansas; eastward to s. Indiana.—U.S.A.: Ark.; Colo.; Ia.; Ill.; Ind.; Ia.; Kan.; Minn.; Mo.; Neb.; N.M.; N.D.; O.; Okla.; S.D.; Ut.; Wis.; Wyo. Can.: Man. *Elevation*—500 to 8,000 feet. 4,000–8,000 feet (Bailey, N.M., 1913); Mt. Timpanogos, Ut., to 7,500 feet (Ruthven, Ut., 1932); above 9,500 feet (Ellis and Henderson).

Size: Adults, 12–24 inches.

Distinctive characteristics: Similar to *O. v. vernalis.* Grobman described it as a subspecies having "males with 131 or more ventrals, females with 140 or more ventrals." Ventrals 125–154; caudals 68–95.

Color: A snake from the north fork of the Provo River at 6,000 feet, about 15 miles from Provo, Ut., captured on a trip with W. W. Tanner, May 31, 1942. The top of the head to the lower level of the eye and touching the first 3 upper labials, also 5th, 6th, and 7th, are oil green, as are the 7 or 8 rows of middorsal scales. The eye rests on the 4th upper labial, which is free of oil green. The upper labials and lower portion of rostral are pale greenish yellow with white lower edges. The color of the sides is cosse green. The iris is clove brown with a patch of avellaneous or olive-buff above the pupil. The underside of head and neck, the lower labials, mental, and chin shields are white. The ends of ventrals are lemon yellow, becoming in the middle baryta yellow to martius yellow, and under the tail sulphur yellow.

Abnormal coloration—"Buff Green-Snakes." Within 10 years Necker took 6 light buff snakes. Four of these 6 aberrant snakes were young of the year.

Habitat: "In the east, this snake lives among the grass and underbrush, where it can conceal itself by its color of green. . . . It appears to be restricted here to medium or high altitudes, and does not appear to be found in the low valleys or desert areas" (Woodbury). At least two more authors place it in mountains. The most common habitats are low bushes 6, meadows 4. Other habitats are upland prairies, high grass, the ground, bark of a stump, and pastures.

"This brilliant little creature is abundant along the Assiniboine River, south of Carberry [Man.]. During August, Green-snakes can be seen in numbers where the hot, sunny banks of the river valley rise near any grassy thickets, affording basking places near coverts of safety. . . . An individual that I caught on the banks of the Assiniboine, July 14, 1884, and kept captive at Carberry, produced 6 eggs on July 27th; it refused all food and died July 31st" (Seton).

The very puzzling records from Texas have been generally discredited. Strecker (Tex., 1915) summarized thus: "The smooth-scaled green snake has been reported from only two widely separated localities, i.e., Washburn, Armstrong County (Bailey), and Deming's Bridge, Matagorda County (Garman)." Recently Davis has given a different aspect to this question: "The status of *Opheodrys vernalis* in Texas is again brought to attention by the capture of a male specimen 2½ miles west of Sealy, Austin County, on Apr. 23, 1949. . . . Because of this recent capture of *vernalis*, I am inclined to accept the records from Basque, Ellis and Matagorda counties as authentic."

Period of activity: *First appearance*—Apr. 16 (Pope, Wis., 1928); May 22 (Gloyd, Kan., 1928); June 6 (Cary, Wyo., 1917). *Fall disappearance*—Sept. 5, 14 (Ellis and Henderson); Sept. 25 (Criddle).

Hibernation—One of the most startling snake stories is a true one published by Stuart Criddle of Treesbank, Man., in "Snakes from an ant hill": "On September 25, 1934, two smooth green snakes (*Opheodrys vernalis*) were killed on an ant hill located on the farm of the author. The ant hill, a flat mount about 6 inches high and 3 feet in diameter, was occupied by black ants, probably of the genus *Formica*. It was located among hazel and haw-thorne scrub at the edge of a small opening, which is surrounded by oak and aspen woods. Not far away are some willow swamps and muskegs, such as are commonly found along the Assiniboine River, which is about a mile distant. The hill was provided with the normal entrances, some of which seemed to be slightly larger than usual. It had a rather abandoned appearance, although a few ants were still crawling about. Later digging showed that very few ants were present, but it is impossible to say whether they had abandoned it voluntarily or had been eaten by the snakes. After the hill had been carefully examined, 6 red-bellied snakes (*Storeria occipito-maculata*), discovered by digging into the hill by hand, were removed. The next day 4 more snakes were dug out, and it became evident that a great many more remained in the deeper parts of the hill.

"The spot was again visited on October 6. Careful digging with a spade revealed that the lower galleries were almost alive with snakes. In 40 minutes of digging 75 snakes were removed. On October 10 the hill was completely dug out. The diameter of the hill increased with the depth, so that the excavation took on the form of an inverted funnel. Some of the galleries were closely packed with snakes, so that 5 or 6 were often exposed with one shovelful of sand. Water was found at a depth of 4 feet 9 inches. While no snakes were found below the water level, some had the lower parts of their bodies submerged in it. All the snakes that were in contact with the water or close to its level had their heads up, pointed toward the surface, and were in a semi-dormant condition. In the higher galleries they were found in all positions, usually singly, although occasionally 2, 3 or more were closely coiled together. A total of 181 snakes was added to those previously taken out; so that 257 snakes in all were removed from this single hill. Eight of these were *Thamnophis radix,* 101 were *Storeria occipito-maculata,* and 148 *Opheodrys vernalis.*

"The garter snakes, which were not adult, were found between 1 foot and 3 feet down, and were all quite active. Individuals of the other 2 species were scattered from close to the surface down to water level, some of the green snakes being partly submerged. Most of the large adults were lowest down, while the majority of the smaller individuals were nearest the surface. This suggests that the adults may have arrived first and were followed later by the younger ones."

Breeding: Oviparous. Males 344–488 mm., females 444–522 mm. *Eggs*— Reproduction in this race is not so well known as with the eastern form, *O. v. vernalis.* Number, 6–12. The modal number is 6. Three authors mention 12, one 8, one 10. Time of deposition, July 11–early August. Most records indicate the last of July as the usual period of deposition. Size: The only definite record we can find is Pope's (Ill., 1944) short note. "Six eggs . . .

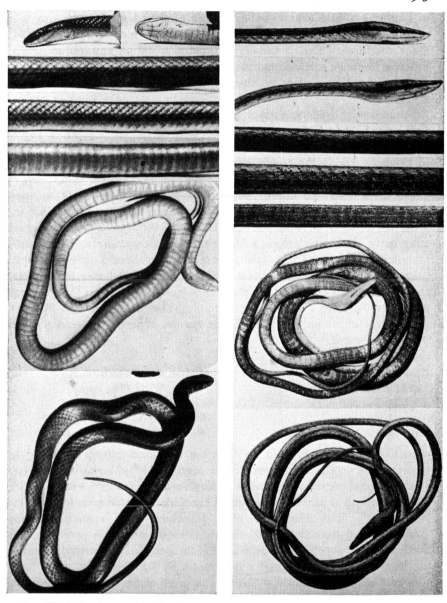

Fig. 166. *Opheodrys v. blanchardi,* north fork of Provo River, 6,000 foot elevation, Provo, Utah, W. W. Tanner and authors.

Fig. 167. *Oxybelis aeneus auratus,* Pajaritos Mt. section of southern Arizona, west of Nogales, C. T. Vorhies.

were discovered under a tie of a deserted railroad in northern Cook County on July 10. They were white and from ¾ to ¹⁵⁄₁₆ inch long."

Young—We know no records of newborn young. The smallest we have noticed in literature is 4⅝ inches. We have several indefinite statements such

For Reference

Not to be taken from this room